Lecture Notes in Computer Science 4662

Commenced Publication in 1973
Founding and Former Series Editors:
Gerhard Goos, Juris Hartmanis, and Jan van Leeuwen

Cécilia Baranauskas
Philippe Palanque   Julio Abascal
Simone Diniz Junqueira Barbosa (Eds.)

Human-Computer Interaction – INTERACT 2007

11th IFIP TC 13 International Conference
Rio de Janeiro, Brazil, September 2007
Proceedings, Part I

 Springer

Volume Editors

Cécilia Baranauskas
UNICAMP, State University of Campinas, SP, Brazil
E-mail: cecilia@ic.unicamp.br

Philippe Palanque
LIIHS – IRIT, Université Paul Sabatier
31062 Toulouse, France
E-mail: palanque@irit.fr

Julio Abascal
University of the Basque Country
Laboratory of Human-Computer
20018 Donostia, Spain
E-mail: julio@si.ehu.es

Simone Diniz Junqueira Barbosa
PUC-Rio, Departamento de Informática
22453-900 Rio de Janeiro, RJ, Brazil
E-mail: simone@inf.puc-rio.br

Library of Congress Control Number: 2007934538

CR Subject Classification (1998): H.5.2, H.5.3, H.3-5, I.2.10, D.2, K.3, K.4, K.8

LNCS Sublibrary: SL 3 – Information Systems and Application, incl. Internet/Web
and HCI

ISSN   0302-9743
ISBN-10   3-540-74794-X Springer Berlin Heidelberg New York
ISBN-13   978-3-540-74794-9 Springer Berlin Heidelberg New York

Springer is a part of Springer Science+Business Media

springer.com

© IFIP International Federation for Information Processing 2007
Printed in Germany

Typesetting: Camera-ready by author, data conversion by Scientific Publishing Services, Chennai, India
Printed on acid-free paper   SPIN: 12119158   06/3180   5 4 3 2 1 0

importance so to facilitate the access to technology by all kinds of users. We hope that INTERACT 2007 will be remembered as a milestone in the progress towards a world able to share and balance the benefits of computer technologies.

September 2007   Simone D.J. Barbosa
                                                        Julio Abascal

Foreword

INTERACT 2007 was the 11th of a series of INTERACT international conferences supported by the IFIP Technical Committee 13 on Huma – Computer Interaction. This year, INTERACT was held in Rio de Janeiro (Brazil), organized by the Informatics Department at the Pontifcia Universidade Catlica do Rio de Janeiro, with the support of PETROBRAS, CGI.BR (Comit Gestor da Internet no Brasil), and Microsoft.

Like its predecessors, INTERACT 2007 highlighted, to both the academic and industrial world, the importance of the human – computer interaction (HCI) area and its most recent breakthroughs on current applications. Both experienced HCI researchers and professionals, as well as newcomers to the HCI field, interested in designing or evaluating interactive software, developing new interaction technologies, or investigating overarching theories of HCI, found in INTERACT 2007 a great forum to communicate with people with similar interests, to encourage collaboration, and to learn.

INTERACT 2007 had "socially responsible interaction as its special theme. Human beings have evolved for many millennia; during most of that time, our major social contacts were within small, tightly knit groups who shared a common language culture and physical context. In the last historical eyeblink, we rather suddenly find ourselves part of a global community. We have very different cultures, languages, perspectives, and physical contexts. Moreover, as a species, we face the possibility of bringing about our own extinction if we cannot solve some exceedingly challenging problems. Our individual brainpower has not increased significantly in the last 100,000 years. Computing and communication technologies offer some potential, however, to increase greatly our collective intelligence and creativity. With the proper attention to both the human and technological aspects of HCI, we have the possibility to make a crucial difference in a variety of issues. For example, it is now possible as never before to design technology to support universal usability and accessibility. We desperately need new thinking for our political, social, economic, and ecological problems. We can now build tools to support creativity, discovery, and innovation. Recently, we have begun to understand more about how to use technology to help integrate how we work as a team or in groups and communities. Medical informatics and personal medical devices offer new opportunities to reduce skyrocketing health care costs in the developed world and offer new hope to eradicate disease in developing countries.

Being the first edition in Latin America, INTERACT 2007 served as a window to new purposes, focuses, and cultural approaches. If one of the main aims of the International Federation for Information Processing is to balance the development of computer technology internationally and to assist in the sharing of the knowledge in this area among all the countries, then the HCI field is of vital

IFIP TC13

Established in 1989, the International Federation for Information Processing Technical Committee on Human – Computer Interaction (IFIP TC13) is an international committee of 29-member national societies and 5 working groups, representing specialists in human factors, ergonomics, cognitive science, computer science, design and related disciplines. INTERACT is its flagship conference, staged biennially in different countries.

IFIP TC13 aims to develop the science and technology of human – computer interaction (HCI) by encouraging empirical research, promoting the use of knowledge and methods from the human sciences in design and evaluation of computer systems; promoting better understanding of the relation between formal design methods and system usability and acceptability; developing guidelines, models and methods by which designers may provide better human-oriented computer systems; and, cooperating with other groups, inside and outside IFIP, to promote user-orientation and humanization in system design. Thus, TC13 seeks to improve interactions between people and computers, encourage the growth of HCI research and disseminate these benefits world-wide.

The main orientation is towards users, especially non-computer professional users, and how to improve human – computer relations. Areas of study include: the problems people have with computers; the impact on people in individual and organizational contexts; the determinants of utility, usability and acceptability; the appropriate allocation of tasks between computers and users; modeling the user to aid better system design; and harmonizing the computer to user characteristics and needs.

While the scope is thus set wide, with a tendency towards general principles rather than particular systems, it is recognized that progress will only be achieved through both general studies to advance theoretical understanding and specific studies on practical issues (e.g., interface design standards, software system consistency, documentation, appropriateness of alternative communication media, human factor guidelines for dialogue design, the problems of integrating multimedia systems to match system needs and organizational practices, etc.).

IFIP TC13 stimulates working events and activities through its working groups (WGs). WGs consist of HCI experts from many countries, who seek to expand knowledge and find solutions to HCI issues and concerns within their domains, as outlined below.

In 1999, TC13 initiated a special IFIP Award, the Brian Shackel Award, for the most outstanding contribution in the form of a refereed paper submitted to and delivered at each INTERACT event. The award draws attention to the need for a comprehensive human-centred approach in the design and use of information technology in which the human and social implications have been taken into account. Since the process to decide the award takes place after papers are submitted for publication, the award is not identified in the proceedings.

WG13.1 (Education in HCI and HCI Curricula) aims to improve HCI education at all levels of higher education, coordinate and unite efforts to develop HCI curricula and promote HCI teaching.

WG13.2 (Methodology for User-Centred System Design) aims to foster research, dissemination of information and good practice in the methodical application of HCI to software engineering.

WG13.3 (HCI and Disability) aims to make HCI designers aware of the needs of people with disabilities and encourage development of information systems and tools permitting adaptation of interfaces to specific users.

WG13.4 (also WG2.7) (User Interface Engineering) investigates the nature, concepts and construction of user interfaces for software systems, using a framework for reasoning about interactive systems and an engineering model for developing user interfaces.

WG13.5 (Human Error, Safety and System Development) seeks a framework for studying human factors relating to systems failure, develops leading-edge techniques in hazard analysis and safety engineering of computer-based systems, and guides international accreditation activities for safety-critical systems.

WG13.6 (Human-Work Interaction Design) aims at establishing relationships between extensive empirical work-domain studies and HCI design. It will promote the use of knowledge, concepts, methods and techniques that enables user studies to procure a better apprehension of the complex interplay between individual, social and organizational contexts and thereby a better understanding of how and why people work in the ways that they do.

New Working Groups are formed as areas of significance to HCI arise. Further information is available at the IFIP TC13 Web site: http://www.ifip-hci.org/

IFIP TC13 Members

Australia
Judy Hammond
Australian Computer Society

Austria
Horst Hörtner
Austrian Computer Society

Belgium
Monique Noirhomme-Fraiture
*Federation des Associations
Informatiques de Belgique*

Brazil
Cecilia Baranauskas
Brazilian Computer Society (SBC)

Canada
Gitte Lindgaard (Secretary)
*Canadian Information Processing
Society*

China
Zhenquing Zong
Chinese Computer Society

Czech Republic
Vaclav Matousek
*Czech Society for Cybernetics and
Informatics*

Denmark
Annelise Mark Pejtersen (Chair)
*Danish Federation for Information
Processing*

Finland
Kari-Jouko Räihä
*Finnish Information Processing
Association*

France
Philippe Palanque
*Association Francaise des Sciences et
Technologies de l'Information et des
Systemes (AFCET)*

Germany
Horst Oberquelle
Gesellschaft fur Informatik

Greece
John Darzentas
Greek Computer Society

India
Anirudha Joshi
Computer Society of India

Ireland
Liam J. Bannon
Irish Computer Society

Italy
Fabio Paternò
*Associazione Italiana per l'Informatica
ed il Calcolo Automatico*

Japan
Masaaki Kurosu
*Information Processing Society of
Japan*

Netherlands
Gerrit C. van der Veer
*Nederlands Genootschap voor
Informatica*

New Zealand
Mark Apperley
New Zealand Computer Society
(NZCS)

Nigeria
Chris C. Nwannenna
Nigeria Computer Society

Norway
Svein A. Arnesen
Norwegian Computer Society

Poland
J.L. Kulikowski
Poland Academy of Sciences

Portugal
Joaquim A. Jorge
Associacao Portuguesa de Informatica

Singapore
Kee Yong Lim
Singabore Computer Society

South Africa
Janet L. Wesson (Vice chair)
The Computer Society of South Africa

Spain
Julio Abascal
Federacion Espanola de Sociedades de Informatica

Sweden
Lars Oestreicher
Swedish Federation for Information Processing

Switzerland
Ute Klotz
Swiss Federation for Information Processing

UK
Phil Gray
British Computer Society

USA
John Karat
Federation on Computing US (FoCUS)
Nahum Gershon
IEEE

Working Group Chairpersons

WG13.1 (Education in HCI and HCI Curricula)
    Paula Kotzé, *South Africa*
WG13.2 (Methodology for User-Centered System Design)
    Peter Forbrig, *Germany*
WG13.3 (HCI and Disability)
    Monique Noirhomme-Fraiture, *Belgium*
WG13.4 (also 2.7) (User Interface Engineering)
    Nick Graham - *Queens University, Canada*
WG13.5 (Human Error, Safety, and System Development)
    Philippe Palanque, *France*
WG13.6 (Human-Work Interaction Design)
    Annelise Mark Pejtersen, *Denmark*

INTERACT 2007 Technical Committee

Conference Committee

General Co-chairs

Julio Abascal - *Universidad del País Vasco, Spain*
Simone Diniz Junqueira Barbosa - *PUC-Rio, Brazil*

Technical Program Co-chairs

Cecília Baranauskas, *Unicamp, Brazil*
Philippe Palanque, *University Paul Sabatier, Toulouse III, France*

Socially Responsible Interaction

Special Theme Co-chairs

John C. Thomas, *IBM, USA*
Zhengjie Liu, *School of Computer Science & Technology of Dalian Maritime University, China*

Technical Program

Doctoral Consortium Co-chairs

Mary Czerwinski - *Microsoft Research, USA*
Marcelo Pimenta - *UFRGS, Brazil*

Full-Paper Co-chairs

Cecília Baranauskas, *Unicamp, Brazil*
Philippe Palanque, *University Paul Sabatier, Toulouse III, France*

HCI Societies Worldwide Co-chairs

Carla Freitas - *UFRGS, Brazil*
Fabio Paternò - *ISTI/CNR Pisa, Italy*

Interactive Experience Co-chairs

Tom Gross - *Bauhaus University Weimar, Germany*
Carlos Scolari - *Universitat de Vic, Spain*

Interactive Poster Co-chairs

Júnia Coutinho Anacleto - *UFSCar, Brazil*
Monique Noirhomme-Fraiture - *Facultés Universitaires Notre-Dame de la Paix, Belgium*

Keynote Speaker Co-chairs

Nahum Gershon - *MITRE, USA*
Matthias Rauterberg - *Technical University Eindhoven, The Netherlands*

Organization Overview Co-chairs

Lucia Filgueiras - *Poli-USP, Brazil*
Laurence Nigay - *University Joseph Fourier Grenoble 1, France*

Panel Co-chairs

Stefano Levialdi - *La Sapienza, Università degli Studi di Roma, Italy*
Clarisse Sieckenius de Souza - *PUC-Rio, Brazil*

Short-Paper Co-chairs

Andy Cockburn - *University of Canterbury, New Zealand*
Manuel A. Pérez-Quiñones - *Virginia Tech, USA*

Special Interest Groups (SIGs) Co-chairs

Paula Kotzé - *University of South Africa, South Africa*
Jonathan Lazar - *Towson University, USA*

Student Poster Co-chairs

Regina Bernhaupt - *University of Salzburg, Austria*
Juliana Salles - *Microsoft Corporation, USA*

Tutorial Co-chairs

Jan Gulliksen - *Uppsala University, Sweden*
Raquel Prates - *UFMG, Brazil*

Video Paper Co-chairs

Nick Graham - *Queens University, Canada*
John Zimmerman - *Carnegie Mellon University, USA*

Workshop Co-chairs

Oscar Mayora Ibarra - *CREATE-NET, Italy*
Jean Vanderdonckt - *Université Catholique de Louvain, Belgium*

Organization

Proceedings Publication Co-chairs

Vaclav Matousek - *University of West Bohemia, Czech Republic*
Marco Winckler - *University Toulouse 3, France*

Sponsoring Co-chairs

Ana Cristina Bicharra Garcia - *UFF, Brazil*
Gerrit van der Veer - *Open Universiteit, The Netherlands*

Student Volunteer Co-chairs

Effie Law - *ETH Zurich, Switzerland*
Kristijan Mihalic - *ICT-S, University of Salzburg, Austria*
Luciana Nedel - *UFRGS, Brazil*

Program Committee Members

Abascal, Julio - *Spain*
Abowd, Gregory - *USA*
Apperley, Mark - *New Zealand*
Avouris, Nikolaos - *Greece*
Bannon, Liam - *Ireland*
Baranauskas, Cecilia - *Brazil*
Barbosa, Simone - *Brazil*
Bass, Len - *USA*
Baudisch, Patrick - *USA*
Baudouin-Lafon, Michel - *France*
Bernhaupt, Regina - *Austria*
Blandford, Ann - *UK*
Blignaut, Pieter - *South Africa*
Bonacin, Rodrigo - *Brazil*
Bottoni, Paolo - *Italy*
Braendle, Alexander - *UK*
Brewster, Stephen - *UK*
Buono, Paolo - *Italy*
Campos, José C. - *Portugal*
Catarci, Tiziana - *Italy*
Celentano, Augusto - *Italy*
Chittaro, Luca - *Italy*
Cockton, Gilbert - *UK*
Coninx, Karin - *Belgium*
Correia, Nuno - *Portugal*
Costabile, Maria Francesca - *Italy*

Coutaz, Joëlle - *France*
Crowley, James - *France*
Cunha, João - *Portugal*
da Silva, Sergio Roberto - *Brazil*
Davies, Nigel - *UK*
De Angeli, Antonella - *UK*
De Carolis, Berardina - *Italy*
de Ruyter, Boris - *The Netherlands*
de Souza, Clarisse - *Brazil*
Del bimbo, Alberto - *Italy*
Dewan, Prasun - *USA*
Di Nocera, Francesco - *Italy*
Doherty, Gavin - *Ireland*
Faconti, Giorgio - *Italy*
Felix, Daniel - *Switzerland*
Ferre, Xavier - *Spain*
Filgueiras, Lucia - *Brazil*
Forbrig, Peter - *Germany*
Francisco Borges, Marcos Augusto - *Brazil*
Furtado, Elizabeth - *Brazil*
Garcia, Laura Sanchez - *Brazil*
Gea, Miguel - *Spain*
Glavinic, Vlado - *Croatia*
Graham, Nicholas - *Canada*
Granollers, Toni - *Spain*

Gray, Phil - *UK*
Gross, Tom - *Germany*
Grudin, Jonathan - *USA*
Grundy, John - *New Zealand*
Gulliksen, Jan - *Sweden*
Hammond, Judy - *Australia*
Harning, Morten Borup - *Denmark*
Harrison, Michael - *UK*
Hayes, Gillian - *USA*
Herczeg, Michael - *Germany*
Holzinger, Andreas - *Austria*
Hosking, John - *New Zealand*
Hvannberg, Ebba - *Iceland*
Jacko, Julie - *USA*
Johnson, Chris - *UK*
Jones, Matt - *UK*
Jorge, Joaquim - *Portugal*
Karat, John - *USA*
Kazman, Rick - *USA*
Kotzé, Paula - *South Africa*
Kulikowski, Juiliusz *Poland*
Law, Effie Lai-Chong - *Switzerland*
Leclercq, Pierre - *Belgium*
Lecolinet, Eric - *France*
Leporini, Barbara - *Italy*
Levialdi, Stefano - *Italy*
Lieberman, Henry - *USA*
Lindgaard, Gitte - *Canada*
Liu, Zhengjie - *China*
Mäntyjärvi, Jani - *Filand*
Martens, Jean-Bernard -
    The Netherlands
Matousek, Vaclav - *Czech Republic*
McCrickard, Scott - *Czech Republic*
Mihalic, Kristijan - *Austria*
Moher, Tom - *USA*
Moriyon, Roberto - *Spain*
Navarre, David - *France*
Nicolle, Colette - *UK*
Nigay, Laurence - *France*
Noirhomme, Monique - *Belgium*
Noldus, Lucas - *The Netherlands*
Nunes, Nuno - *Portugal*

Oberquelle, Horst - *Germany*
Oestreicher, Lars - *Sweden*
Oppermann, Reinhard - *Germany*
Palanque, Philippe - *France*
Paris, Cecile - *Australia*
Paternò, Fabio - *Italy*
Pederson, Thomas - *Sweden*
Pejtersen, Annelise - *Denmark*
Piccinno, Antonio - *Italy*
Pleuss, Andreas - *Germany*
Pribeanu, Costin - *Romania*
Puerta, Angel - *USA*
Räihä, Kari-Jouko - *Finland*
Rauterberg, Matthias -
    The Netherlands
Rist, Thomas - *Germany*
Rosa, Lanzilotti - *Italy*
Salles, Juliana - *USA*
Santoro, Carmen - *Italy*
Sauer, Stefan - *Germany*
Savidis, Anthony - *Greece*
Scapin, Dominique - *France*
Schmidt, Albrecht - *Germany*
Schwabe, Gerhard - *Switzerland*
Shneiderman, Ben - *USA*
Springett, Mark - *UK*
Stolze, Markus - *Switzerland*
Stuerzlinger, Wolfgang - *Canada*
Sukaviriya, Noi - *USA*
Sutcliffe, Alistair - *UK*
Thalmann, Nadia - *Switzerland*
Thapliyal, Mathura - *India*
Truong, Khai - *Canada*
Tscheligi, Manfred - *Autria*
van der Veer, Gerrit -
    The Netherlands
Vanderdonckt, Jean - *Belgium*
Vertegaal, Roel - *Canada*
Wesson, Janet - *South Africa*
Winckler, Marco - *France*
Wulf, Volker - *USA*
Ziegler, Jürgen - *Germany*

Additional Reviewers

Al Mahmud, Abdullah -
The Netherlands
Alexander, Jason - New Zealand
Almas, Almir - Brazil
Almeida, Rodrigo - France
Aquino Junior, Plinio Thomaz - Brazil
Ardito, Carmelo - Italy
Bellucci, Andrea - Italy
Bhamidipaty, Anuradha - India
Block, Florian - UK
Bowman Doug - USA
Braz, Christina - Canada
Buchmann, Volkert - New Zealand
Camelo Pinto, Vladimir - Brazil
Capra, R. - USA
Cassens, Jörg - Norway
Coutinho Anacleto, Júnia - Brazil
Champion, Erik - Singapore
Clemmensen,Torkil - Denmark
Cockburn, Andy - New Zealand
Coyle, Cheryl - USA
de Oliveira Neto, João Soares - Brazil
de Oliveira, Rodrigo - Brazil
Deepak P - IBM Research, India
Diniz, Nancy - UK
Eng, Kynan - Switzerland
Farooq Ali, Mir - USA
Farrell, Stephen - USA
Foglia, Efrain - Spain
Freeman, Isaac - New Zealand
Freitas, Carla M.D.S. - Brazil
Fujisawa, Kumiko - Japan
Gonçalves, Daniel - Portugal
Gonzalez,Victor - UK
Graniæ, Andrina - Croatia
Grasset, Raphael - New Zealand
Gundelsweiler, Fredrik - Germany
Hauber, Joerg - New Zealand
Hazlewood, William - USA
Hoggan, Eve - UK
Howarth, Jonathan - USA
Hüsken, Peter - Germany

Ibanez Martinez, Jesus - Spain
Kanis, Marije - UK
Khalil, Ashraf - USA
Lazar, Jonathan - USA
Light, Ann - UK
Lima, Fernanda - Brazil
Looser, Julian - New Zealand
Maciel, Cristiano - Brazil
Makri, Stephann - UK
Mayora-Ibarra, Oscar - Italy
Melo, Cassio - Brazil
Melo, Paulo - Brazil
Morris, Meredith - USA
Mueller, Hendrik - USA
Nacenta, Miguel - Canada
Nadine, Vigouroux - France
Nagamatsu, Takashi - Japan
Nagasaki, Hitoshi - Japan
Neris, Vania - Brazil
Otjacques, Benoit - Luxembourg
Paterman,Ilana - UERJ - Brazil
Pérez-Quiñones, Manuel - USA
Pimenta, Marcelo - Brazil
Ponsa, Pere - Spain
Prates, Raquel - Brazil
Riche, Yann - France
Salminen, Mikko - Finland
Scolari, Carlos - Spain
Shi, Qingxin - Denmark
Silva, Elton - Brazil
Singh, Shawren - South Africa
Stach, Tadeusz - Canada
Sugimoto, Masanori - Japan
Suh, Sunah - USA
Takeda, Tatsuya - Japan
Taneva, Svetlena - Switzerland
Tripathi, Sanjay - India
Tungare, Manas - USA
Turner, Scott - USA
Yin, Jibin - Japan
Zimmerman, Thomas - USA

Sponsors and Supporters

Platinum

Gold

Bronze

Promotion

Organization

 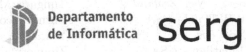 

Table of Contents – Part I

Part One: Keynote Speakers

Human Values for Shaping the Made World 1
  Ben Shneiderman

Getting Your Message Across to Your Users 2
  Clarisse Sieckenius de Souza

Perspectives on Social Computing................................. 4
  Wendy Kellogg

Part Two: Long and Short Papers

Social Computing 1

Face-to-Face Sociability Signs Made Explicit in CMC 5
  *Carla Faria Leitão, Clarisse Sieckenius de Souza, and
  Clarissa Maria de A. Barbosa*

Exploring Temporal Communication Through Social Networks 19
  *Liaquat Hossain, Kon Shing Kenneth Chung, and
  Shahriar Tanvir Hasan Murshed*

Identifying Potential Social Impact of Collaborative Systems at Design
Time 31
  *Clarissa Maria de A. Barbosa, Raquel Oliveira Prates, and
  Clarisse Sieckenius de Souza*

Social Computing 2

Group Efficacy in Asynchronous vs. Multi-synchronous Virtual Teams:
An Empirical Study 45
  Yingxin Pan and Chen Zhao

Mutual Awareness in Collocated and Distant Collaborative Tasks
Using Shared Interfaces 59
  *A. Pauchet, F. Coldefy, L. Lefebvre, S. Louis Dit Picard,
  A. Bouguet, L. Perron, J. Guerin, D. Corvaisier, and M. Collobert*

Web

A Proxy-Based Infrastructure for Web Application Sharing and Remote
Collaboration on Web Pages..................................... 74
    Richard Atterer, Albrecht Schmidt, and Monika Wnuk

Investigating User Attention and Interest in Websites................. 88
    Alistair Sutcliffe and Abdallah Namoune

FaericWorld: Browsing Multimedia Events Through Static Documents
and Links.. 102
    Maurizio Rigamonti, Denis Lalanne, and Rolf Ingold

Degree-of-Interest Visualization for Ontology Exploration 116
    Peter Hüsken and Jürgen Ziegler

S^3: Storable, Shareable Search 120
    Meredith Ringel Morris and Eric Horvitz

UI Prototyping

Trainable Sketch Recognizer for Graphical User Interface Design 124
    *Adrien Coyette, Sascha Schimke, Jean Vanderdonckt, and
    Claus Vielhauer*

UI Prototyping for Multiple Devices Through Specifying Interaction
Design... 136
    *Jürgen Falb, Roman Popp, Thomas Röck, Helmut Jelinek,
    Edin Arnautovic, and Hermann Kaindl*

Multi-fidelity Prototyping of User Interfaces 150
    Adrien Coyette, Suzanne Kieffer, and Jean Vanderdonckt

User-Centered Design and Business Process Modeling: Cross Road in
Rapid Prototyping Tools 165
    *Noi Sukaviriya, Vibha Sinha, Thejaswini Ramachandra,
    Senthil Mani, and Markus Stolze*

User Centred Design Methods and Techniques 1

Ubiquitous Substitution 179
    *Christina Brodersen, Susanne Bødker, and
    Clemens Nylandsted Klokmose*

Meta-design: Expanding Boundaries and Redistributing Control in
Design... 193
    Gerhard Fischer

User Centred Design Methods and Techniques 2

Improving Users' Comprehension of Changes with Animation and
Sound: An Empirical Assessment 207
*Céline Schlienger, Stéphane Conversy, Stéphane Chatty,
Magali Anquetil, and Christophe Mertz*

Designing a Free Style, Indirect, and Interactive Storytelling
Application for People with Aphasia.............................. 221
*Elke Daemen, Pavan Dadlani, Jia Du, Ying Li, Pinar Erik-Paker,
Jean-Bernard Martens, and Boris de Ruyter*

Supporting the Planning and Organization of Multiple Activities in the
Workplace 235
Victor M. González, Leonardo Galicia, and Jesús Favela

Creators, Composers and Consumers: Experiences of Designing a
Digital Library 239
*Ann Blandford, Jeremy Gow, George Buchanan,
Clare Warwick, and Jon Rimmer*

Intelligent User Interfaces

A Common Sense-Based On-Line Assistant for Training Employees..... 243
*Junia Coutinho Anacleto, Muriel de Souza Godoi,
Aparecido Fabiano Pinatti de Carvalho, and Henry Lieberman*

Proactive Assistive Technology: An Empirical Study.................. 255
*Amedeo Cesta, Gabriella Cortellessa, Vittoria Giuliani,
Federico Pecora, Riccardo Rasconi, Massimiliano Scopelliti, and
Lorenza Tiberio*

Use and Implications of a Shared, Forecasting Calendar 269
Joe Tullio and Elizabeth D. Mynatt

Interaction on the Move 1

Utilizing Sound Effects in Mobile User Interface Design 283
Hannu Korhonen, Jukka Holm, and Mikko Heikkinen

Multimodal PDA Interfaces to Assist Drivers in Monitoring Their
Vehicles 297
Giuseppe Ghiani and Fabio Paternò

Interaction on the Move 2

The Adaptive Hybrid Cursor: A Pressure-Based Target Selection
Technique for Pen-Based User Interfaces 310
Xiangshi Ren, Jibin Yin, Shengdong Zhao, and Yang Li

ThumbSpace: Generalized One-Handed Input for Touchscreen-Based
Mobile Devices 324
   Amy K. Karlson and Benjamin B. Bederson

Optimizing on Mobile Usage Cost for the Lower Income Group: Insights
and Recommendations 339
   Deepak P. and Anuradha Bhamidipaty

Button Keyboard: A Very Small Keyboard with Universal Usability for
Wearable Computing 343
   *Hyunjung Kim, Minjung Sohn, Seoktae Kim, Jinhee Pak, and
   Woohun Lee*

Accessibility

Electronic Communication: Themes from a Case Study of the Deaf
Community 347
   *Valerie Henderson-Summet, Rebecca E. Grinter,
   Jennie Carroll, and Thad Starner*

Accessibility and Interactive TV: Design Recommendations for the
Brazilian Scenario 361
   *Lara Schibelsky G. Piccolo, Amanda Meincke Melo, and
   Maria Cecília Calani Baranauskas*

Guidelines for Designing Mobility and Orientation Software for Blind
Children 375
   Jaime Sánchez and Miguel Elías

SymAB: Symbol-Based Address Book for the Semi-literate Mobile
User 389
   Anuradha Bhamidipaty and Deepak P.

Accessibility of Assistive Software Installation Interfaces 393
   *Lucia Filgueiras, Edson Sales, Lucy Gruenwald,
   Ana Maria Barbosa, and Renato Facis*

Designing for Multiples Devices

Model-Driven Adaptation for Plastic User Interfaces.................. 397
   *Jean-Sébastien Sottet, Vincent Ganneau, Gaëlle Calvary,
   Joëlle Coutaz, Alexandre Demeure, Jean-Marie Favre, and
   Rachel Demumieux*

The Beautification Process in Model-Driven Engineering of User
Interfaces 411
   *Inés Pederiva, Jean Vanderdonckt, Sergio España,
   Ignacio Panach, and Oscar Pastor*

Consistency Priorities for Multi-device Design 426
  Rodrigo de Oliveira and Heloísa Vieira da Rocha

A Flexible Presentation Tool for Diverse Multi-display Environments ... 430
  Kazutaka Kurihara and Takeo Igarashi

Interaction Techniques 1

A Pressure-Sensing Mouse Button for Multilevel Click and Drag 434
  Masaki Omata, Kenji Matsumura, and Atsumi Imamiya

DeskJockey: Exploiting Passive Surfaces to Display Peripheral
Information 447
  Ryder Ziola, Melanie Kellar, and Kori Inkpen

Interaction Techniques 2

Drag-and-Guess: Drag-and-Drop with Prediction.................... 461
  Takeshi Nishida and Takeo Igarashi

Wave Menus: Improving the Novice Mode of Hierarchical Marking
Menus... 475
  Gilles Bailly, Eric Lecolinet, and Laurence Nigay

Nearly-Integral Manipulation of Rotary Widgets 489
  Rodrigo Almeida and Pierre Cubaud

CATKey: Customizable and Adaptable Touchscreen Keyboard with
Bubble Cursor-Like Visual Feedback 493
  Kentaro Go and Yuki Endo

Affective Computing 1

A Conceptual Framework for the Design and Evaluation of Affective
Usability in Educational Geosimulation Systems 497
  Elizabeth Furtado, Vasco Furtado, and Eurico Vasconcelos

TEMo-Chine: Tangible Emotion Machine 511
  Omar Mubin, Abdullah Al Mahmud, and Christoph Bartneck

Characterizing the Diversity in Users' Perceptions.................... 515
  Evangelos Karapanos and Jean-Bernard Martens

Affective Computing 2

Stay on the Ball! An Interaction Pattern Approach to the Engineering
of Motivation... 519
  Kirstin Kohler, Sabine Niebuhr, and Marc Hassenzahl

Motivational Needs-Driven Mobile Phone Design 523
  Judy van Biljon, Paula Kotzé, and Gary Marsden

Mobile Application for Increasing Contextual and Emotional Work
Group Awareness 527
  Mikko Salminen, Kari Kallinen, Kliment Yanev,
  Niklas Ravaja, and Timo Saari

3D Interaction and 3D Interfaces

Employing Dynamic Transparency for 3D Occlusion Management:
Design Issues and Evaluation 532
  Niklas Elmqvist, Ulf Assarsson, and Philippas Tsigas

Towards Applicable 3D User Interfaces for Everyday Working
Environments 546
  Frank Steinicke, Timo Ropinski, Gerd Bruder, and Klaus Hinrichs

Dwell-Based Pointing in Applications of Human Computer
Interaction 560
  Christian Müller-Tomfelde

A Miniature, One-Handed 3D Motion Controller 574
  Kynan Eng

Evaluation Methods 1

Use Case Evaluation (UCE): A Method for Early Usability Evaluation
in Software Development 578
  Kasper Hornbæk, Rune Thaarup Høegh,
  Michael Bach Pedersen, and Jan Stage

Evaluating Reduced-Functionality Interfaces According to Feature
Findability and Awareness 592
  Leah Findlater and Joanna McGrenere

Evaluation Methods 2

Playful Probing: Making Probing More Fun 606
  Regina Bernhaupt, Astrid Weiss, Marianna Obrist, and
  Manfred Tscheligi

Do I Do What I Say?: Observed Versus Stated Privacy Preferences 620
  Kay Connelly, Ashraf Khalil, and Yong Liu

In and Out of the Hospital: The Hidden Interface of High Fidelity
Research Via RFID 624
    Svetlena Taneva and Effie Law

Exploring Multiple Usability Perspectives 628
    Tobias Uldall-Espersen

Author Index 633

Human Values for Shaping the Made World

Ben Shneiderman

Department of Computer Science, University of Maryland
A. V. Williams Building, College Park, MD 20742, UV
ben@cs.umd.edu
http://www.cs.umd.edu/~ben

Abstract. Interface design principles have been effective in shaping new desktop applications, web-based resources, and mobile devices. Usability and sociability promote successful online communities and social network services. The contributions of human-computer interaction researchers have been effective in raising the quality of design of many products and services. As our influence grows, we can play an even more profound role in guaranteeing that enduring human values are embedded in the next generation of technology. This talk identifies which goals are realistic, such as universality, responsibility, trust, empathy, and privacy, and how we might ensure that they become part of future services and systems.

Short Bio. Ben Shneiderman is a Professor in the Department of Computer Science, Founding Director (1983-2000) of the Human-Computer Interaction Laboratory (http://www.cs.umd.edu/hcil/), and Member of the Institute for Advanced Computer Studies at the University of Maryland at College Park. He was elected as a Fellow of the Association for Computing (ACM) in 1997 and a Fellow of the American Association for the Advancement of Science (AAAS) in 2001. He received the ACM SIGCHI Lifetime Achievement Award in 2001.

Ben is the author of Software Psychology: Human Factors in Computer and Information Systems (1980) and Designing the User Interface: Strategies for Effective Human-Computer Interaction (4th ed. 2005) http://www.awl.com/DTUI/. He pioneered the highlighted textual link in 1983, and it became part of Hyperties, a precursor to the web. His move into information visualization helped spawn the successful company Spotfire http://www.spotfire.com/ . He is a technical advisor for the HiveGroup, Groxis, and EasyUse. With S Card and J. Mackinlay, he co-authored Readings in Information Visualization: Using Vision to Think (1999). His books include Leonardo's Laptop: Human Needs and the New Computing Technologies (MIT Press), which won the IEEE Distinguished Literary Contribution award in 2004.

C. Baranauskas et al. (Eds.): INTERACT 2007, LNCS 4662, Part I, pp. 1, 2007.
© IFIP International Federation for Information Processing 2007

Getting Your Message Across to Your Users

Clarisse Sieckenius de Souza

Departamento de Informática, PUC-Rio
Rua Marquês de São Vicente 225, RDC sala 501
22451-900 - Rio de Janeiro, RJ
clarisse@inf.puc-rio.br
http://www-di.inf.puc-rio.br/~clarisse/

Abstract. Most models, theories and perspectives in human-computer interaction focus on users communicating with systems. The very name of our discipline illustrates how pervasive is the idea that users and systems are the only relevant parties involved in the process we want to design or investigate. For over a decade, the Semiotic Engineering Research Group (SERG) has elaborated an alternative account of HCI. In it, what we traditionally call human-computer interaction is characterized as a particular instance of a more general process of computer-mediated human communication.

Semiotic Engineering views HCI as a case of designer-to-user metacommunication, or communication about how to communicate (with/through the system), when and what for. The designer's metacommunication message conveyed by means of a wide range of communicative exchanges between the users and the system. The system represents designers at interaction time, and each turn of communicative exchange adds a significant piece of knowledge and experience to what eventually becomes the user's interpretation of the designer's message. Thus the metacommunication process is achieved.

In this talk I will provide various examples of designer-to-user metacommunication, and discuss some of the main implications of bringing designers onto the stage where human-computer interaction takes place. I will place a special emphasis on how this alternative perspective encourages designers to express certain values, beliefs and expectations regarding the interactive artifacts they produce, compared with what is enabled and encouraged by more traditional views of HCI. Given the theme of INTERACT 2007, I will illustrate the differences with systems that clearly demand, and encode, an attitude of social responsibility from their designers and developers.

I will wrap up the talk with some final considerations about the cultural roots of Semiotic Engineering, and a conjecture that HCI theories developed outside North America and Europe will reflect their proponents' concern and engagement with remarkably different social and cultural backgrounds. Perhaps, our international community's investment in encouraging the development of such theories will foster progress of our discipline in some innovative directions.

Short Bio. Clarisse Sieckenius de Souza graduated as a Translator and Conference Interpreter from PUC-Rio, where she also obtained an M.A. in Portuguese and a Ph.D. in Computational Linguistics. In 1988 she joined the Informatics Department at PUC-Rio, where she started the Human-Computer Interaction (HCI) area.

C. Baranauskas et al. (Eds.): INTERACT 2007, LNCS 4662, Part I, pp. 2–3, 2007.
© IFIP International Federation for Information Processing 2007

Clarisse was the first Brazilian Representative in IFIP's TC13 (the Technical Committee for Human-Computer Interaction). She created the Brazilian Computing Society's Special Interest Group in HCI and coordinated the first of a now successful series of Brazilian Conferences on Human Factors in Computing (the IHC series). In 1996 she founded SERG (the Semiotic Engineering Research Group), which she headed till 2003. Among the 13 M.Sc. and 16 Ph.D. students that she has (co-)supervised, more than a half are faculty in various Brazilian universities, and nearly one third work in the industry.

Along with Alfredo Sánchez (UDLA - Mexico), Clarisse was General Co-Chair of CLIHC2003 - the first Latin American Conference on HCI (Rio de Janeiro, August 17 to 20, 2003). She is also the author of The semiotic engineering of human-computer interaction, published by The MIT Press in 2005. The book presents a full-blown semiotic theory of HCI that was completely and independently developed by SERG, in Brazil.

Perspectives on Social Computing

Wendy Kellogg

IBM T.J. Watson Research Center,
P.O. Box 704, Yorktown Heights, NY 10598 USA
wkellogg@us.ibm.com
http://www.research.ibm.com/people/w/wkellogg/index.html

Abstract. Social computing has emerged as a broad area of research in HCI and CSCW, encompassing systems that mediate social information across collectivities such as teams, communities, organizations, cohorts, populations, and markets. Such systems are likely to support and make visible social attributes such as identity, reputation, trust, accountability, presence, social roles, expertise, knowledge, and ownership. Social computing is transforming organizations and societies by creating a pervasive technical infrastructure that includes people, organizations, their relationships and activities as fundamental system components, enabling identity, behavior, social relationships, and experience to be used as resources. In this talk, I argue for a broad definition of social computing, selectively review emerging applications, and discuss current research within and beyond IBM that is driving and is driven by the emerging vision of social computing.

Short Bio. Wendy A. Kellogg is one of the founders of the field of social computing, forming the first research group focusing on Social Computing in 1998: the Social Computing Group at IBM's T. J. Watson Research Center. Topics addressed by the group have included social translucence (a conceptual framework pioneered by Erickson and Kellogg), computer-mediated communication, social proxies, the design of social software, knowledge management, awareness systems, enhanced audio conferencing, collaboration and human productivity in high performance computing, social and task visualizations, and most recently, serious games, virtual worlds for business use, and "Enterprise 2.0."

Kellogg's work in human-computer interaction (HCI) over more than two decades has spanned areas including theory, evaluation methods, design, and development. She holds a Ph.D. in Cognitive Psychology from the University of Oregon. She is author and editor of publications in the fields of HCI and CSCW, and currently serves on the editorial board of ACM's Transactions on Computer-Human Interaction. Wendy chaired CHI 2005 Technical Papers, DIS 2000's Technical Program, and the CSCW 2000 and CHI'94 conferences. She chaired Workshops for CHI 2004 and has served numerous times as an associate chair for CHI, CSCW, ECSCW, and DIS. She served on the National Academy of Science's Computer Science and Telecommunications Board and in 2002 was elected ACM Fellow "for contributions to social computing and human-computer interaction."

C. Baranauskas et al. (Eds.): INTERACT 2007, LNCS 4662, Part I, p. 4, 2007.
© IFIP International Federation for Information Processing 2007

Face-to-Face Sociability Signs Made Explicit in CMC

Carla Faria Leitão, Clarisse Sieckenius de Souza, and Clarissa Maria de A. Barbosa

SERG – The Semiotic Engineering Research Group, Informática, PUC-Rio
Rua Marquês de São Vicente, 225, Gávea, 22453-900, Rio de Janeiro, RJ, Brazil
{cfaria, clarisse, cbarbosa}@inf.puc-rio.br

Abstract. This paper discusses how semiotic engineering can support the formulation of problems and solutions involved in handling face-to-face (F2F) sociability models in computer-mediated communication (CMC). Based on a case study where a group of users migrated through different types of CMC systems, we show that the designer's model of F2F sociability is extensively signified and encoded into technology, whether they know it or not. Users are deeply affected by the designers' F2F sociability models. Two qualitative methods of analysis are used to reveal the richness of interpretive and communicative processes in which online communities are involved, and the interplay of designers' and users' signs at interaction time.

Keywords: Semiotic engineering; CMC; Sociability models.

1 Introduction

Nearly two decades past the dissemination of Information and Communication Technology, the fears about the dissolution of social ties [1] are not as threatening as they used to be. Computer-mediated communication (CMC) has allowed users to complement their face-to-face sociability. Nowadays, far from being extinguished by technology, F2F relationships constitute the reference model for online relationships. Both designers[1] and users leave the imprint of their social values on the technology that they produce and adopt [3]. The integration of the values related to F2F forms of interaction constitutes a *face-to-face sociability model* (F2F model).

This paper sets out to present the contribution of semiotic engineering [6], a semiotically-inspired theory of human-computer interaction (HCI), to the study of some of the problems involved in migrating F2F communication practices into CMC environments. Most current research into this migration concentrates on users, their expectations and experience. Although a user-centered perspective is fundamental to HCI, of no less importance is a perspective that centers on designers, and on how they project their values and vision onto the technology they build.

In semiotic engineering, the main function of computer systems interfaces is to bring designers and users together at interaction time, and to communicate the designers' vision to users through computer-human interaction. This vision carries not

---

[1] In this paper, the word designer(s) will be used to refer not only to those that specifically 'design' technology, but also to those that develop and produce it.

C. Baranauskas et al. (Eds.): INTERACT 2007, LNCS 4662, Part I, pp. 5–18, 2007.

only the design rationale (*i.e.* the 'why', 'what for', and 'how to' of technology), but also the subjective and cultural values that guide design choices. Therefore, interface signs always communicate elements of the designers' F2F model to CMC users. Nonetheless, the sense users will make of such signs is largely unpredictable.

In order to illustrate how F2F model communication is achieved, and how it can affect users and their own sociability models, we present a case study. The specific context of the study is especially significant. Firstly, this is primarily a group of multiple sclerosis (MS) sufferers, with the occasional participation of family members and care-takers. MS is a seriously debilitating disease, and sufferers often have considerable difficulty to move about and socialize in diversified physical settings. As a result, for some, CMC may be the only opportunity to socialize with a group, representing a radical movement from F2F sociability to online interactions. Secondly, this group (or "SPEM" – *Sociedade dos Portadores de Esclerose Múltipla*[2]) is a successful one. The duration of the group (approximately 5 years by now), the volume of messages (over 14000), the number of members (200 to 500 members, approximately, at different points in time), and messages exchanged by members explicitly alluding to the fact that they are a successful online group are all good evidence of their success. Thirdly, the study covered a period of technological migration. SPEM had been using a particular kind of technology till January 2004, but then they were forced to move to another kind of technology because of problems experienced with their Internet Service Provider. Together, these contextual factors allowed us to take a deep perspective into some of the hard challenges brought about by technology designed to support CMC.

The SPEM case study led us to the following conclusions:

1. Groupware designers, whether they know it or not, imprint in the systems they design cultural and personal values that emerge from their F2F models of groups.
2. The force of cultural values shared by community members constantly (re)introduces signs of such values, in practice. When they are contradictory with those imposed by design, signs of conflict or ambiguity can be found.

The remainder of this paper is organized in four additional sections. In section 2, we present the gist of semiotic engineering, providing the necessary concepts for the reader to appreciate our discussions. Then, in section 3 we briefly present two models of F2F sociability, originating in classical sociology. Based on these two models and on the ontology of semiotic engineering, we present our case study in section 4. Section 5 wraps up the case with our discussions and conclusions.

2   A Semiotic Theory of HCI

Semiotic engineering [6] is a theory of HCI, whose ontology is rooted in such fundamental semiotic concepts as: sign, signification, communication, and interpretation. The first and last concepts stem from Peirce's semiotics [14]; the other two are inspired by Eco's theory of semiotics [9]. The aim of semiotic engineering is not the same as any of these two theories – we do not seek to investigate signs,

---

[2] Multiple Sclerosis Sufferers Society.

signification, communication or interpretation processes *per se*. We seek to investigate human-computer interaction, a well-defined object of study, where human and technological components are brought together to form an indivisible whole.

The foundational concepts that support the semiotic engineering ontology are:

1. A *sign* is *anything* that is taken to *mean* something, by some mind (human or not), in one respect or another [14]. This very broad definition bears some interesting implications. For example, it implies that signs don't have to be consensual. Of course there are many kinds of signs: some are cultural conventions, some are produced and processed by humans alone, and others may be produced and processed by machines. According to Peirce, the human species is biologically equipped to constantly produce and exchange an unlimited range of signs.
2. *Signification* is the process by which certain expressions are systematically associated with certain contents based on culturally established conventions [9]. This process establishes a variety of sign systems in every culture – verbal and non-verbal, limited or unlimited, and so on. The units of signification systems are *signs*.
3. *Communication* is the process by which people use signs and explore the possibilities of signification systems to achieve an unlimited range of purposes [9]. Inasmuch as communication is structured in terms of well established and contextualized signs, recipients and interpreters are likely to get the communicator's message with relatively little effort. However, for communicators, the available signification systems are a resource, and not a limitation. They can easily twist the system (as in jokes), use it creatively (as in metaphors), and even expand it (as in neologisms). Because receivers and interpreters are equally apt to twisting, adapting and expanding culturally-determined signification systems, such steps outside their limits are most frequently successful, and often go unnoticed.
4. *Interpretation*, in semiotic engineering, is aligned to the notion of semiosis [14]. The sign is structured by the mutual relations of three components: the representation of the sign, the object to which the representation refers, and the particular interpretation by virtue of which representation and object are bounded. The relation between a sign representation and its object, or referent, is mediated. Moreover, the mediating interpretation that relates representation to referent is not a value, but a process – called semiosis. Semiosis unfolds over unlimited time and space – it is not a finite calculation producing one definitive value.

The implications of the concepts above reach far, and shed new light on HCI. The very possibility of taking *anything* as a potential sign (from 1), and the unlimited nature of semiosis (from 4), explains why communication (from 3) can be successful. Interlocutors 'make up' signs of their own, or use known signs in completely novel ways, but since their interpreters have exactly the same abilities, communication *is based on* but *not limited to* the systematic associations of expression and content, conventionalized by culture. Therefore, in this perspective, it is not possible to capture or predict *the* meaning of any sign – whatever correspondence is made between expression (a sign) and content (a meaning, or range of meanings) involves a *selection* of some interpretations to the detriment of others.

As a result, humans often communicate without sharing the same meanings. It is only when counter factual evidence of their mutual understanding arises that they revise their meanings. A key resource for revising meanings in communication is 'metacommunication' – communication about communication. This pervasive resource encourages us to precipitate our conclusions about what this or that sign means – we reckon that if we are wrong, some other signs will give the evidence of our misunderstanding, and our interlocutors will correct us. For as long as they do not correct us, we assume that mutual understanding is in place. Mutual understanding depends on the ability and disposition of interlocutors to engage in learning and discovery. In conversation, speakers and listeners control semiosis by halting and resuming the ongoing interpretive process when they have evidence of successful and unsuccessful hypotheses, respectively. In some cases, this kind of control can be costly in emotional and social terms.

In the HCI scenario, systematic research about the social [8] or the emotional [13] [15] aspects of computing has been gaining momentum in recent years. In all these cases, however, theories and approaches have resorted to different ontologies when they talk about design time and interaction time. Such is not the case of semiotic engineering, and some important consequences of integrating design and interaction under the same ontology naturally follow.

Semiotic engineering views HCI as a particular case of CMC. In it, computer systems are defined as a one-shot designer-to-user message communicating the design intent, the designer's understanding of users' needs and aspirations, the vision of how the designed artifact will affect the users' lives, and how the artifact should be used to achieve its ultimate purpose. The message can be paraphrased as follows [6]:

"Here is my understanding of who you are, what I've learned you want or need to do, in which preferred ways, and why. And this is the system that I have therefore designed for you, and the way you can or should use it to fulfill a range of purposes that fall within this vision"

The metacommunication message gradually unfolds as users interact with the artifact and, in the process of semiosis, build their own interpretation of what the artifact means. The various meanings exchanged in successive turns of interaction contribute to the global sense-making process by which users appropriate the artifact as an achieved sign. Through metacommunication, the designer is present at interaction time. However, not physically present – the designer's communication about what he or she meant to communicate, and about how users can or should, themselves, communicate with the artifact, is delivered through the user interface. In semiotic engineering, the user interface is the designer's deputy at interaction time. The communication codes for user-system interaction do not need to be verbal. Direct manipulation interfaces, for example, privilege visual codes. However, explicit metacommunication messages (such as explanations, instructions) take verbal form.

The main difference introduced by semiotic engineering compared to existing theories of HCI is thus to frame the whole process of software production and software use as a homogeneous case of relayed communication. A similar idea was discussed by Winograd and Flores [18] two decades ago. Although the authors were proposing new foundations for software design, their work did not cover the details of how and why all layers of linguistic representation in computing are built, related, and eventually interpreted and used in all sorts of applications. They concentrated on computer-supported collaborative work contexts, and used speech act theory [17] to inform design decisions. Semiotics, however, provides a much broader and more general range of concepts than speech act theory. Humans and their computer counterparts are engaged in semiosis. The same ontological status of 'interlocutor' is conferred to users, designers and systems. As a result, an unbroken thread of concepts can be used to trace meanings in software production and software use.

The kinds of tools semiotic engineering provides for scientific research and professional practice in HCI are inspired by Schön's reflection-in-action perspective [16]. They are *epistemic tools*. They are meant to guide the naming and framing stages of design problems. In agreement with semiotic processes, Schön's perspective on design is that every design activity is unique. Thus the most important knowledge it requires is an epistemology of practice. Instead of knowledge about solutions for known categories of problems, an epistemology of practice is knowledge about methods and interpretive frameworks to be used in understanding, categorizing, and solving an unlimited range of HCI problems. Hence, the epistemic tools proposed by semiotic engineering aim at improving and expanding the researchers' and designers' knowledge about problems and solutions in design.

One such epistemic tool is the interpretive schema embedded in the metacommuni cation message from designer-to-user. For the specific category of multi-user applications, the message is extended in order to include crucial meaning elements related to how computer-mediated communication among users is designed to take place. The message content can be paraphrased as follows [6]

> *"Here is my understanding of who you are, what I've learned you want or need to do, in which preferred ways, and why. And this is the system that I have therefore designed for you, and the way you can or should use it to fulfill a range of purposes that fall within this vision. You can communicate and interact with other users through the system. During communication, the system will help you check:*
> *Who is speaking? To whom?*
> *What is the speaker saying? Using which code and medium? Are code and medium appropriate for the situation? Are there alternatives?*
> *Is(are) the listener(s) receiving the message? What if not?*
> *How can the listener(s) respond to the speaker?*
> *Is there recourse if the speaker realizes the listener(s) misunderstood the message? What is it?"*

Notice that by trying to elaborate the instantiation of this message for any CMC application, a designer is naturally led to reflect on expressive, semantic, pragmatic, and intentional aspects of communication.

Designers and researchers can use other semiotic engineering models and methods to gain deeper insight into the signs and signification systems that are used to support the users' interaction. One such method has been used in our case study – the semiotic inspection method [5][7]. The aim of the study was to find out how two classical F2F models were encoded in CMC technology used by SPEM members, and how users reacted to them.

3   From Face-to-Face to Online Sociability Models

A community is a key sociological concept, classically defined in opposition to society. In spite of much variety in perspective, there are some recurring ideas in the traditional studies of communities. Communities have been characterized as a group of people who experience a high degree of personal intimacy and emotional depth. They are self-sufficient, in that members can satisfy all their needs within the space defined by their mutual relations and collective values. Each member's identity is constructed in terms of the community itself. Social relations clearly define boundaries, unify the group, and provide protection against the threats of dissolution brought about by diverse and open-ended relations in a society [2] [12].

By opposition, society is defined by the multiple social roles played by each member, and the varying degrees of intimacy and emotional depth that they achieve in their relationships. To live in society is to have multiple sources for building one's identity, and to experience different kinds of belonging. It also implies the ability to live in and with various open groups, with multiple intersections with each other [12].

There is commonality between the notions of society and community: in classical sociology, they are both reference models for F2F relationships. However, early CMC environments were clearly inspired by the F2F community model [3]. Later, the original spirit was left way behind. Side by side with community models, other models sprang up, with very different sociability references, this time closer to the traditional concept of *society* than to that of *community*. A full-blown cultural and social technology-enabled phenomenon, the Internet welcomed developers and users who no longer sought unity, homogeneity, and group cohesion. They sought ego-centered and multiple forms of interaction, based on both strong and weak ties, and motivated by individual needs [3]. Inspired by an F2F society model, online interactions became open, flexible, heterogeneous and diverse. Now both community and society models coexist and dictate the development of the Internet [3].

In order to further the discussion about the role of F2F models in the development and deployment of CMC, we now describe our case study, where different types of technologies were used, and their sociability models affected users in different ways.

4 The Semiotic Engineering Account of SPEM

The object of this study is a long-standing online group, the Multiple Sclerosis Sufferers Society, whose members are mainly MS sufferers and their families. The community was closely observed from October 2003 to March 2004, during which period the community migrated from one setting to another. This migration was a prime opportunity for us to detect some of the impacts of technology on groups. Then, in order to update our initial analysis of such impacts and verify its medium-term effects, we revisited and analyzed the community in March 2006 and in January 2007.

A combination of two qualitative methods was used in these analyses: the semiotic inspection method [5] [7] and the Underlying Discourse Unveiling Method (UDUM) [11]. Just like other qualitative methods, semiotic inspection and UDUM are non-predictive, exploratory, and interpretive procedures that seek to expand the researcher's understanding of the study domain, based on the recurrence of meanings [4]. Semiotic inspection seeks implicit signification of design signs. UDUM, however, seeks to make the latent meanings present in the users' discourse explicit. By comparing results achieved by both methods, we set out to identify breakdowns and inconsistencies among design intent and the users' experience.

Semiotic inspection should help the analyst reconstruct the designer-to-user message, and detect opportunities for breakdowns in communication. The inspection proceeds in five steps. In the first step, the analyst examines online and offline documentation and help content. In the second, the analyst examines static signs in the system. Static signs are those that appear on individual system screens, and are typically part of what designers refer to as *interface layout*. In the third, the analyst examines dynamic signs. These are signs that result from interaction, and include important meanings such as the causal effects of activating the various controls on the interface. In the fourth step, the analyst makes a contrastive comparison of designer-to-user metacommunications identified in previous steps. Finally, in the fifth step, the analyst is able to produce a conclusive appreciation of the quality of the overall designer-to-user meta-communication.

UDUM complements the semiotic inspection by providing an analysis of natural language discourse produced by system users during interaction. The analysis is carried out in an iterated two-step procedure [11]. The *inter-participant* step examines the discourse of all users participating in the community's discussions. Identified recurring categories in what they say show the main trends in the group's thoughts. The *intra-participant* step examines the discourse of each single user, highlighting occasional inconsistencies and identifying the elaboration of meanings across all his or her interventions. The iteration of inter- and intra-participant analyses contributes to a very detailed characterization of what is actually being said.

The major findings of the combined analysis are grouped in four categories: the history of SPEM in cyberspace; the designers F2F sociability models; the users F2F sociability models; and designers and users together at interaction time.

4.1 The History of SPEM in Cyberspace

By January 2007, with approximately five years of existence, SPEM had 208 members and a repository of over 14.000 messages. By March 2004, however, SPEM had nearly 500 members, who had exchanged messages in three different discussion forums: InForum, MSN Groups and *Yahoo!Groups*. The role of each of these is made explicit in each one of the three environments, as well as on the group's homepage[3]. In addition to pointing to the other forums, the group owner introduces himself, and provides some information about multiple sclerosis. He also reveals the main purpose of SPEM: the exchange of experiences.

The history of SPEM shows three distinct eras, determined by the technology that the group was using. **Period 1** (10/2003-01/2004) corresponds to the use of two different forums: InForum, used only for exchanging textual messages, and MSN Groups, for both textual communication and photo exchanges. MSN also provided support for chatting online, which a number of members used to do. **Period 2** (02/2004-03/2004) corresponds to the use of three different forums. By this time, due to technical problems with InForum, the group owner decided to abandon the main forum and migrate to *Yahoo!Groups*. For one month, SPEM members we confused by using all three technologies. Finally, in **Period 3** (04/2004 onwards) the group migrates to *Yahoo!Groups*, and chooses this environment to be the locale for all group activities. Figure 1 presents the distribution of the group over time and space.

---

[3] http://marcelomorita.net/em

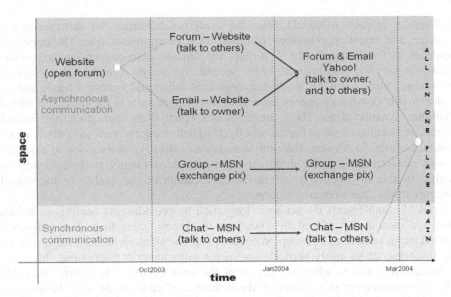

Fig. 1. SPEM community history – transitioning communicative locales

4.2 The Designers' Face-to-Face Sociability Models

The goal of semiotic inspection is to recover the overall metacommunication message of the designers of online forums used by SPEM. Designers signs allowed us to focus on one particular aspect of the metacommunication message, namely the one that says: *"Here is my understanding of who you are, what I've learned you want or need to do, in which preferred ways, and why. And this is the system that I have therefore designed for you, and the way you can or should use it to fulfill a range of purposes that fall within this vision."* Through the recovery of signs and meanings involved in this portion of the message, we have made explicit the F2F model of each technology.

InForum is a non-structured bulletin board, where messages appear in sequence, one after the other, with no threading. This is an online space with shallow verbal communication facilities, available to anyone interested in reading messages and posting material for users from all over the Internet to see. Messages are all presented in the same format, one after the other, in reverse chronological order. There are no signs indicating the number of participants, neither an indication of privacy policies. There is no way to register members (anyone is a member who wants to read/search/post messages), and there can be no role differentiation among members. Members' *presence* can only be traced through message-posting, because it is only when composing a message that a member's identity is captured for other forum members to see. InForum does not support posting of pictures and other media files; neither does it support synchronous communication. The designers' meta-communication message in this case shows that the design vision was based on a *society* F2F model. This part of the metacommunication message can be paraphrased as this: "Here is an open space for socialization. Anyone can participate, by reading messages posted by others, only, or by posting messages, too. These messages are public in the Internet. Just like in offline society, you can choose different spaces to socialize. This is one such space, where all you can do is to read and exchange asynchronous text messages. If you wish other kinds of resources, I encourage you to find them on the Net, and to publish the appropriate links in here."

MSN Groups and *Yahoo!Groups* metacommunication is much more sophisticated than InForum's. They look very much alike, and their designers' signs communicate the same F2F model: that of a ***community***. In both systems, group members must register and obtain a group ID. Thus, when they log in, they appear in the members list on the group's homepage, where the designers also tell users about how many members there are in this particular group, and what are the group configuration features. One such configuration (chosen by the group owner) is that, after registering and getting an ID, group members must wait for the moderator to accept their registration. Both systems allow group owners to choose whether they wish the group messages to be public on the Internet or not, as well as other privacy protection alternatives. MSN Groups and *Yahoo!Groups* both offer sophisticated chat tools. Messages can be viewed in different ways, and members can attach smileys to messages in order to express their mood. Texts and photos posted by members are stored in specifically structured spaces. Finally, other tools to coordinate activities, like a database, search mechanisms and alternative visualization forms, enable members to engage into complex goal-oriented activities. MSN Groups and *Yahoo!Groups* metacommunication message can be paraphrased as this: "Here is a place for you to create an online community. In these communities all members are identified, even if they keep silent and don't take initiative in socializing activities. You can choose who you want to have in this community, and who you don't. I offer you useful communication and coordination resources. All you need to keep your community going is here, and you are protected against the outside world."

Having identified the designers' F2F models, let us see how these models were interpreted and appropriated by SPEM users them.

4.3 The Users' Face-to-Face Sociability Models

The UDUM-based analysis of members' discourse allows us to identify their underlying sociability models over the three periods of SPEM's existence.

In **Period 1**, when InForum and MSN Groups were both used, the content of messages exchanged in InForum was predominantly related to, in the group owner's own words, "making friends and talking to MS sufferers". Members would almost never talk about the technology they were using, and – notice this – they would always talk about themselves as a society, as their very name said: the Multiple Sclerosis Sufferers Society. The 'community' sign was never used to characterize SPEM. When using MSN Groups for chatting and posting pictures, all they needed to do was to get an MSN ID and log into the group's page (the group had declined the possibility offered by designers of having every registration request be authorized by the moderator). Occasionally, members would post text messages in the forum, but InForum was always referred to as the preferred place for this sort of communication. See what the message below expresses[4].

---

[4] Transcribed messages were posted originally in Portuguese and translated by the authors, keeping up with the original writing style.

"I am a bit late in welcoming you. (...) I'd like to ask you to go to www.inforum.insite.com.br. There you will find the same people who are here, and I also believe that things move much faster there."

MSN Groups was defined by a member as "a branch of SPEM". Introduced some time after Inforum, MSN Groups was easily incorporated by SPEM members. Resistance to use the new technology was not observed, since there were no messages about difficulties generated by the introduction of a more complex tool. Thus, there were no signs that social experiences were not negatively affected by the introduction of a new technology. MSN Groups users seemed to ignore the MSN designers' metacommunication message, tacitly declining most of the designers' incentive to get the group organized, and protected against outsiders. They refused to adopt the community model that was signified in the interface. They creatively used MSN Groups as a complementary tool, supporting the activities of a group defining itself as a "society". Throughout this initial period, then, SPEM clearly adopted the society F2F model, and there was no significant interference of the technologies they adopted on the activities they were engaged in.

However, **Period 2** is marked by an extensive interference of technology in SPEM's social life. Because of technical problems with InForum, the group owner decided to create a forum in *Yahoo!Groups*. This dispersion turned into a major issue for the group. During this period, SPEM was using InForum, MSN Groups and *Yahoo!Groups* concomitantly. There was still uncertainty about the possibility of a complete migration to *Yahoo!Groups*, although there was a tendency to gradually concentrate SPEM activities in this space. As can be seen in the message below, members had doubts about how they would function as a group in the future.

"I can ask some questions, can't I? Are we all going to move there [Yahoo!Groups], and this space here [InForum] will be closed down? Will we be allowed to be in both places? (...) Have we solved our issues or created problems?"

During this period, the number of messages exchanged by SPEM members increased significantly, and their content was mainly about how members related to technology. Messages conveyed essentially two sub-categories of meanings: nostalgic feelings about their former space and feelings of loss and confusion in the new space. Here is a message from the group owner himself, posted at InForum:

"Subject: WHERE IS EVERYBODY??? Hi, I just came here to tell you how things are going in Yahoo. I see that all have moved there or given up. If you are still here, waiting, I have to say that:(...) it's all a matter of time to adapt and learn. If you haven't moved yet, we're waiting for you."

He calls the group's attention to the fact that a little learning effort is required to use *Yahoo!Groups* and that with time the technology will become familiar to everybody ("it's all a matter of time do adapt and learn"). Expressions of nostalgic feelings at this stage could perhaps be explained by the users' resistance to change. However, further evidence shows that there is yet another reason behind nostalgic feelings. Namely, members *were used to interacting with MSN groups*, and MSN groups and *Yahoo!Groups* look very much alike. For those who knew how to use MSN groups, *Yahoo!Groups* should have seemed easy (and familiar). So, unless we consider SPEM's sociability models in both systems aspects of the users' nostalgig feelings remain unexplained.

As previously mentioned, in MSN groups SPEM members seemed to ignore the designer's metacommunication. They were a society whose members used MSN as a complementary tool. At *Yahoo!Groups*, however, they started to work as a community, in consistence with the designer's metacommunication. Various messages express the fear to loose happiness and friendship. Even members who were used to post many messages at MSN groups (and therefore had skills to use the system) clearly express the melancholy caused by the migration: *"Hi everyone, I hope we will be happy here ... as happy as we were there."* Ambiguity and resistance seem to hide more than the need of learning more sophisticated features of a new system. It seems to be a matter of choice: should SPEM be a society (according to user's sociability model) or a community (in consistence with the designer's sociablity model)?

After this period of ambiguity, in March 2004, when **Period 3** started, the creator of SPEM decided for a complete migration to *Yahoo!Groups*. The moderator wrote:

"About the forums: Inforum – is paid for till mar/04 (...) When this date expires, the forum will depend exclusively on Insite, who provides InForum services. I know that if they don't discontinue [the forum] there will always be someone there, other than me. Yahoo Brasil – was the best free forum option I found in the Internet because here: 1) They don't have as many problems in peak hours;2) It is possible to send almost instantly, via e-mail, everything that is in the forum, as long as one requests this at registration time; 3) There are many services available, like: polls, databases, chat, and others. And, best of all, its all 'gratis'! As for me, I am also trying to adapt to Yahoo, but I prefer the InForum/SPEM design. But I find Yahoo's services better than all other free Internet options that I have been trying."

Thus, technological issues, allied to the personal choices made by the moderator, seemed to have altered the sociability of SPEM. They turned from a society model into a community model. Nevertheless, the transition caused some loss. Various SPEM members dropped out, as message below shows:

"Subject: Jade says good bye and thanks to the Gang
My beloved friends! (this is my good bye). I want to thank you all for your kindness (...) through all this time we've been together (...) However, because I haven't been able to adapt to the new place I have asked to un-register. (...) I will keep with MSN and my email addresses for those who want to keep in touch online. (...) If you have something to tell me, do so... but I will only reply to your individual addresses, and no longer here or in Yahoo. I'm leaving taking my memories in my bag!"

In March 2006, two years after the migration, we saw that whereas in 2004 SPEM had some 500 members, now they were down to approximately 300, an important indication that various members did not adapt to the community model encoded in the technology, embraced by those who stayed. Another prime indication of the change is that the community *sign* made its way into the discourse of SPEM members: on their homepage, SPEM define themselves as a "virtual community". In January 2007, we saw that the community model has been consolidated. In line with this kind of model, the number of group members decreased to about 2/3 (208 members), policies were clearly defined and stated, and group membership required approval from the moderator. The number of posted messages is still good (about 100 per month), and the content indicates a high level of intimacy among members.

4.4 Designers and Users Together at Interaction Time

Further analysis of the results above led us to conclude that there were three kinds of signs affecting SPEM's life online. First, there were signs referring to their own lives and experience with MS, and to their feelings and opinions about other things, including their attitude toward technology. We called these *user signs*. Second, there were signs referring to design decisions and the features and behavior of each one of the three technologies. These were typically *interface signs*. They were encoded by technology designers, and users have sometimes learned them, sometimes ignored them, sometimes they didn't notice them, and sometimes they rejected or misinterpreted them. These signs carry the designers' values, their intent, the mark of their cultural background, and similarly subjective content. Lastly, there were signs imposed by computation itself, like the fact that every computable entity must have a unique symbolic identification (hence the need for names and ID's). This kind of sign may be in striking contrast with the semiosis of a non-institutionalized group. In previous work [5] we have discussed some social consequences of the limits imposed by *computation signs*. For the purposes of this paper, however, the most important finding with respect to this case study was the clear contrast between the designers' and users' signs that made their respective F2F sociability models explicit. From a semiotic engineering perspective designers communicate their vision to users at interaction time, and this vision includes their F2F model. Users, in their turn, have their own sociability models. At interaction time designers and users negotiate meanings related to these models, and the success of such negotiation will dictate the history of groups online.

5 Discussion and Conclusion

We believe that semiotic engineering has a relevant contribution to make for the study of CMC with respect to the migration of F2F to online communication. It calls the attention of researchers to the importance of *consciously* and *systematically* reflecting upon the underlying sociability models that are encoded in CMC technology. As seen with SPEM, these models are signified consciously or unconsciously by designers, in the systems interface. And users give strong evidence that such signs get into their semiosis, thus affecting their own sociability models and practices.

At interaction time, each group of users: (i) carries their own F2F sociability models to the online environment; (ii) interprets and reacts to the designers' communication about the F2F sociability model(s) they have encoded into the technology; and (iii) negotiates different sociability models, making conscious and/or unconscious judgments and decisions about the possibilities of using the technology.

Regarding (i), semiotic engineering suggests that there cannot be an ideal and universal sociability model for CMC. Users always bring with them different models and, therefore, personal reactions to different kinds of CMC environments will always vary. Some users will adapt quickly, others will never adapt, but there will always be a negotiation between technologically-encoded sociability models, on the one hand, and diverse culturally-inherited sociability models, on the other. Negotiation can be initiated because both are based on human (designers' and users') F2F social relations. But the success of negotiation will largely depend on the designers' awareness of what can be negotiated, why, and how. So, it we should beware of predictive models and universal solutions for online sociability. At best, we should seek for widely-applicable knowledge-generating methods to support CMC design. This alternative has the advantage to circumvent the embarrassing singularity of design cases where received heuristics and guidelines are not followed, but the design product is nevertheless evaluated as satisfactory by its users. In the SPEM case, we saw that the community loved the old discussion forum, which compared to MSN or *Yahoo!Groups* was precarious, according to established HCI design practices. The same situation was reported by Maloney-Krichmar and Preece [10], in their study of an online health community.

Regarding (ii), semiotic engineering explains that systems interfaces can signify things that designers are not even aware of having consciously expressed. In group settings, group semiosis can considerably amplify the semiotic effect of interface signs, as we have seen in our case study. Semiotic engineering calls the designers attention to the fact that users will interpret not only the signs that they have intentionally designed and encoded in the interface, but also those signs that they (designers) have unconsciously signified in the technology. The greater the designers' awareness of their own social values about F2F sociability models, and of how these relate to the users' sociability models, the greater the chances of successful negotiations at interaction time. The necessary mechanisms to support the users' choices will more likely be in place, and ready to be used.

Regarding (iii), through a comprehensive characterization of metacommunication, semiotic engineering encourages designers to spell out their metacommunication message at design time. They are stimulated to think of all static and dynamic signs, along with explicit explanatory signs directly expressing design rationale, which users should have access to in order to resolve potential disparities between their vision of sociability online, and the designers'. Careful and intentional selection of signs to communicate design intent will instigate a rich variety of computer-mediated communication between designers and users.

This is an interesting possibility because it allows us to examine CMC in greater detail, framing technological and natural signs, delivered by machines and humans alike, under a uniform set of concepts that constitute the semiotic engineering ontology. The theory amplifies the explicit knowledge of technology producers and researchers about what communication is, and the infinite variety of signification alternatives that users and designers may choose to communicate what they mean to and about each other. Thus the design process itself becomes a rich and sophisticated intellectual activity, very distant from a mere selection and application of existing solutions that will predictably work in previously known use situations.

In this paper we have presented a case study to illustrate how F2F sociability models are communicated and interpreted over CMC. However, the semiotic engineering ontology and the epistemic resources that we have used in an analytic process may perfectly be used for reflection at design time. The introduction of the designer's discourse as a specific stance of sign types in CMC allows us to detect subjective and cultural values incorporated to design patterns. Thus the message to CMC developers is that they may improve the quality of their products by: reflecting carefully about their context(s) of use, and the F2F sociability models that future users embrace; thinking critically about their own sociability models, rationalizing as many aspects of them as possible before they start encoding sociability models into the technology; and designing powerful negotiation mechanisms for users to understand the technology, adapt it to their purposes, and eventually use it to compose wider social spaces with technologies that suit their needs better in some particular respect.

Acknowledgments. Clarisse de Souza thanks CNPq for continuing support to her research. Clarissa Barbosa thanks CNPq and CAPES for her Ph.D. scholarships. All authors thank Marcelo Morita for facilitating this study, for his cooperation.

References

[1] Baudrillard, J.: The Vital Illusion. Columbia University Press, New York (2000)
[2] Bauman, Z.: Community: seeking safety in an insecure World. Blackwell Publishers, Malden, MA (2001)
[3] Castells, M.: The Internet galaxy: reflections on the Internet, business, and society. Oxford University Press, Oxford, New York (2001)
[4] Denzin, N.K., Lincoln, Y.S.(org.): Handbook of Qualitative Research, 2nd edn. Sage Publications, Thousand Oaks, CA (2000)
[5] de Souza, C.S., et al.: Compulsory institutionalization: investigating the paradox of computer-supported informal social processes. Interacting With Computers 16(4), 635–656 (2004)
[6] de Souza, C.S.: The semiotic engineering of human-computer interaction. The MIT Press, Cambridge, MA (2005)
[7] de Souza, C.S., et al.: The Semiotic Inspection Method. In: VII Simpósio sobre Fatores Humanos em Sistemas Computacionais, IHC'2006, Natal, RN (2006). Anais do VII Simpósio sobre Fatores Humanos em Sistemas Computacionais. Porto Alegre, RS: SBC, vol. 1, pp. 148–157
[8] Dourish, P.: Where the action is. The MIT Press, Cambridge, MA (2001)
[9] Eco, U.: A theory of semiotics. Indiana University Press, Bloomington, IN (1976)
[10] Maloney-Krichmar, D., Preece, J.: A multilevel analysis of sociability, usability, and community dynamics in an online health community. ACM Transactions on Computer-Human Interact 12(2), 201–232 (2005)
[11] Nicolaci-da-Costa, A.M., et al.: Como conhecer usuários através do Método de Explicitação do Discurso Subjacente (MEDS). In: Anais do VI Simpósio sobre Fatores Humanos em Sistemas Computacionais, pp. 47–56. SBC, Porto Alegre (2004)
[12] Nisbet, R.A.: The Sociological Tradition. Basic Books, New York (1966)
[13] Norman, D.A.: Emotional Design: why we Love (or hate) everyday things. Basic Books, N.Y. (2004)
[14] Peirce, C.S.: The Essential Peirce: Selected Philosophical Writings. In: Houser, N., Kloesel, C. (eds.), vol. 1, 2, Indiana University Press, Bloomington, IN (1992-1998)
[15] Picard, R.: Affective computing. The MIT Press, Cambridge, MA (1998)
[16] Schön, D.A.: The reflective practitioner. Basic Books,Inc., N.Y. (1983)
[17] Searle, J.R.: Expression and meaning. Cambridge University Press, Cambridge (1979)
[18] Winograd, T., Flores, F.: Understanding computers and cognition. Addison-Wesley, New York, NY (1986)

Exploring Temporal Communication Through Social Networks

Liaquat Hossain, Kon Shing Kenneth Chung, and Shahriar Tanvir Hasan Murshed

School of Information Technologies, University of Sydney,
Sydney, Australia
{lhossain, ken, tanvir}@it.usyd.edu.au

Abstract. The dissemination of information in social networks and the relative effect of ICT (Information and Communications Technology) use has long been an interesting area of study in the field of sociology, human computer interaction and computer supported cooperative work. To date, a lot of research has been conducted regarding an actor's mobile phone usage behavior while disseminating information within a mobile social network. In this study, we explore the structured network position of individuals using mobile phone and their ability to disseminate information within their social network. Our proposition is that an actor's ability to disseminate information within a social group is affected by their structural network position. In this paper, we determine an actor's structural network position by four different measures of centrality—(i) degree, (ii) closeness, (iii) betweenness, and (iv) eigenvector centrality. We analyse the Reality Mining dataset, which contains mobile phone usage data over a 9 month period for exploring the association between the structural positions of different actors in a temporal communication. We extract relational data to construct a social network of the mobile phone users in order to determine the association between their position in the network and their ability to disseminate information. The following questions form the basis for this study: Does information dissemination capability of an actor reflect their structural position within a social network? How do different measures of centrality associate with the information dissemination capability of an actor? Are highly central actors able to disseminate information more effectively than those who have a lower central position within a social network?

Keywords: Social Networks, Mobile Usage Behaviour, Centrality, Information Dissemination, Temporal Communication.

1 Introduction

Mobile telephone use has proliferated in recent years. They have become embedded in society culture and are no longer unusual to view people using mobile phones in various different contexts. Recent studies regarding mobile phones have primarily focused on the usage behaviour of individuals over a set period of time. Studies have also been conducted into the usability of the mobile communication devices for

C. Baranauskas et al. (Eds.): INTERACT 2007, LNCS 4662, Part I, pp. 19–30, 2007.
© IFIP International Federation for Information Processing 2007

understanding dissemination behaviour and innovation patterns [3, 15]. Concrete research into the relationship between a user's position in the mobile social network and their ability to disseminate information in that particular network are relatively few. The objective of this study is to explore this relationship to discover the effect of different network structure and positions on an actor's ability to effective disseminate information within the network. In particular, the study explores how different types of centrality measures give an actor the best ability to disseminate information within a social network. We suggest that the positioning of an actor within a network is closely associated with their ability to disseminate information. An actor's structural position is determined by various measures of centrality: in-degree, out-degree, closeness, betweenness and eigenvector centrality [10]. These measures allow for calculation of an actor's position in the network whilst determining their relationship with surrounding actors in the network. We analysed the reality mining dataset, which contains information collected on 100 mobile users over a nine month period, to elicit the mobile social network for the study. We then conducted preliminary analysis of the mobile usage behavior of the individual subjects contained within the dataset to form the basis for argument. A model representing different network structures affecting information dissemination is constructed using the software application to illustrate the differences between the different measures of centrality. This study may have a profound impact on the way organisations select individuals for projects due to their capability to co-ordinate resources, which directly come from their ability to disseminate information. Furthermore, insights on the association between an individual's social structure and capacity to disseminate information provide us with an awareness of human-interactions in mobile and temporal contexts. This is useful for building contextualized awareness HCI tools.

2 Background

The Reality Mining project represents one of the largest mobile phone experiment attempted in academia to date [8]. The study consists of 100 Nokia 6600 smart phones pre-installed with several pieces of software developed by the Massachusetts Institute of Technology (MIT), as well as a version of Context application from the University of Helsinki. The dataset, which is a MySQL relational database, was collected for the purpose of monitoring mobile phone usage behavior in order to model complex social systems. The information collected includes call logs, Bluetooth devices in proximity, cell tower IDs, application usage and phone status (such as charging and idle). The Reality Mining dataset contains data collected by one hundred human subjects over the course of nine months and represents approximately 350,000 hours of data on users location, communication and device usage behavior over the course of the 2004-2005 academic year. The project is still ongoing and upon completion of the study the dataset will contain 500,000 hours (~60 years) of continuous data on daily human behavior. The subjects contained in the dataset are 75 users who are either students or faculty in the MIT Media Lab, while the remaining 25 users are incoming students at MIT Sloan business school. Of the 75 users at the Media Lab, 20 are incoming masters students and 5 are incoming MIT freshmen.

3 Information Dissemination Through Social Network

Disseminating information in social networks is a complex and nuanced process that is the sum of many individual actions. It is difficult to overestimate the importance of social networks in the processes of disseminating and receiving information [13]. Based on the information itself and on contextual factors, a person may choose to share the information as it to selected people in his social network or may modify the information (e.g. remove details) before disseminating it. Goecks and Mynatt [11] state that contact and availability information is often closely guarded and shared only with the people in one's personal social network. Friends talk about books that they've recently read and share photos of their children. Colleagues share ideas, data, and references when collaborating. These are some examples of the types of information disseminated in a social network. Fisher and Dourish [9] argue that the information disseminated can be traced and that there is structure in dissemination. Furthermore, such network structures can be used to build contextualized awareness tools that successfully present an appropriate selection of information.

Borgatti [5] documented how different measures of centrality can be matched to the kinds of information flows that they are appropriate for. Specific simulations were conducted to examine the relationship between type of information flow and the differential importance of nodes with respect to measurements such as speed of reception of traffic and frequency of receiving traffic. It was discovered that traditional centrality measures were fully applicable only for specific flow processes they are designed for, can be regarded as generating expected values for certain kinds of node outcomes (such as speed and frequency of reception) given implicit models of how information disseminates. There are five well known measures of centrality which are commonly used in social network analysis. These are in-degree, out-degree, closeness, betweenness and eigenvector centrality.

Closeness centrality of a node (or actor) as defined by Freeman [10], is the sum of the graph-theoretic distances from all other nodes, where the distance from a node to another is defined as the length (in links) of the shortest path from one to the other. Borgatti [5] argues that in a flow context, ordinarily you would interpret closeness as an index of the expected time until arrival of something flowing through the network. Borgatti also noted that nodes with lower raw closeness scores have short distances from others so will tend to receive flows sooner, assuming that what flows originates from all other nodes with equal probability, and also assuming that whatever is flowing manages to travel along shortest paths.

Betweenness centrality is defined as the 'share' of times that a node i needs a node k (whose centrality is being measured) in order to reach a node j via the shortest path (Freeman 1979). Betweenness is conventionally thought to measure the volume of traffic moving from each node to every other node that would pass through a given node [16]. Thus, it measures the amount of network flow that a given node 'controls' in the sense of being able to shut it down if necessary.

Eigenvector centrality is defined as the principal eigenvector of the adjacency matrix defining the network [4]. The idea proposed by Bonacich is that even if a node influences just one other node, who subsequently influences many other nodes (who themselves influence still more others), then the first node in that chain is highly influential. At the same time it can be seen that eigenvector centrality is providing a model of nodal risk such as a node's long term equilibrium risk of receiving information traffic is a function of the risk level of its contacts [5].

Finally, degree centrality can be defined as the number of ties incident upon a node [10]. That is, it is the sum of each row in the adjacency matrix representing the network. Degree centrality can also be defined as the number of paths of length one that emanate from a node [14]. As a result, one way to interpret the measure would be in terms of an implicit process that involves no indirect links. For information flow this means that a highly central actor will be more active in disseminating information in that they have more ties to other actors in the network. In light of the social network concepts and measures discussed for making information dissemination structure visible, we ask the research questions: (i) does information dissemination capability of an actor reflect their structural position within a social network? (ii) How do different measures of centrality associate with the information dissemination capability of an actor? (iii) Are highly central actors able to disseminate information more effectively than those who have a lower central position within a social network?

4 Method

The initial dataset contained voice and text message data regarding interactions made by the 100 participants in the study to members, both internal (eg. other subjects) and external (eg. friends, family) to the study. As a first step in data analysis, we concentrated on the interactions made by the participants (in the study) to other members who were also involved in the study. Such interactions were considered to be internal interactions. Interactions between members of the study and outsiders were deemed as external interactions.

There are a total of 897,921 interactions contained in the Reality Mining Dataset. We decided the best way of separating the data was to create a new table containing only the voice records which contained internal interactions. We then used certain thresholds to gather only the data we thought would be suitable to determining valid relationships between members of the study. We applied the bootstrapping mechanism by applying a threshold limit of a minimum of 5 interactions to take place before a valid relationship could be deemed to have substantial information disseminated. This approach is similar to the email study conducted by Adamic and Adar [1]. Calls of duration 0, which surprising there were many of, were also deemed as invalid data for our study. It could only be assumed that such calls were made to retrieve voice messages as the number called by the sender was the same as the number of the sender.

From this threshold we were able to gain a table of internal interactions for our data of 30,620 voice call records. The respective strengths, which were the number of interactions between each participant, were then calculated and exported into a text file, later which was read into the UCINET program [7] for social network analysis. We were then able to alter the view of the network diagram according to different variables based on the strengths of the relationships, for example only displaying relationships with tie strength greater than 10.

In order to calculate the information spread, we used an information dissemination index adapted from Bae [3]. According to Bae, the information dissemination index was a numerical value based on data collected that determined which members of a network had been more involved in communicating with other members. Our own information dissemination index to determine which participants contributed more to the information flow in the network was as follows:

Information Dissemination Index:

$$\frac{\#voice\ calls\ sent - \#voice\ calls\ received}{\#voice\ calls\ sent + \#voice\ calls\ received}$$

Regardless of range, the information dissemination index is +1 if somebody only makes calls and doesn't receive any calls. The index is -1, if somebody only receives calls and does not make any calls. The index is 0, if somebody has totally balanced communication behaviour, sending and receiving the same number of calls.

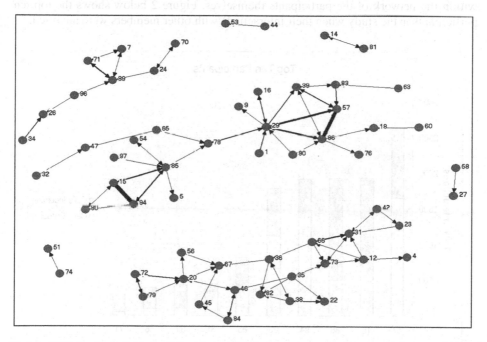

Fig. 1. Visualisation of the mobile phone interaction pattern between participants with tie strength

Results and analysis were gathered by mining the modified dataset using PHP scripts with embedded SQL commands. Using these commands we were able to discover call activity information which could then be combined with centrality information from UCINET to report the findings seen in the next section.

5 Results and Analyses

From the preliminary analysis that was conducted, it was revealed that an actor who was centrally based in the mobile communication network was more likely to have a greater ability to disseminate information throughout the network. Figure 1 depicts a visual analysis (sociogram) of the communication of the participant network - that is, calls made to and from the participants with the threshold applied are represented in the sociogram. Clearly, there are three major components in the sociogram which represents a clique group or cluster. It is possible that such cliques arise as a result of participants belonging to the same school or group within MIT (eg. Sloan School of Management). There are also a couple of periphery actors who do not belong to any of the clusters. Their communication frequency is low. The number of interactions made is visually represented as strength of the tie, as indicated by thickness of the lines. Hence, actors 57, 86, 15, and 94 are interesting nodes to take interest of as communication pertaining to these actors is particularly high. Further analysis shows that these actors represent the top four participants who communicated the most within the network of the participants themselves. Figure 2 below shows the top ten participants in the study when their interactions with other members were analysed.

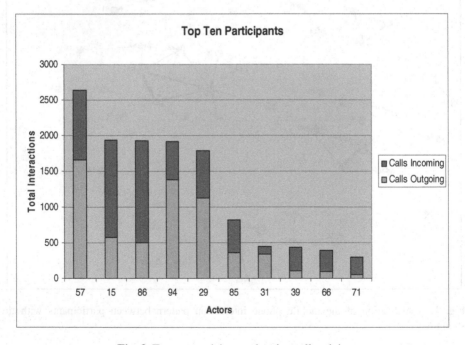

Fig. 2. Top ten participants showing call activity

Table 1 below highlights particular actor's in and out degree statistics as well as their information dissemination index calculations.

Table 1. Information dissemination index and degree values of the top ten participants of the study

Actor	OutDegree	InDegree	Total Interactions	Information Dissemination Index
57	1660	974	2634	0.26
15	578	1362	1940	-0.404
86	503	1425	1928	-0.478
94	1381	537	1918	0.44
29	1126	663	1789	0.258
85	367	448	815	0.042
31	339	111	450	0.504
39	108	325	433	-0.501
66	99	297	396	-0.5
71	56	237	293	-0.618

Hanneman [12] states that degree centrality is actually the greatest measure of actors in positions to disseminate information. He suggests that actors who have more ties to other actors may be advantaged to an extent because they have many ties, they may access to, and be able to call on more resources of the network as a whole. The evidence and the results from our study seem to agree with this notion, that an actor with a high degree of centrality is in a better position than others to disseminate information to other members of the network.

Table 2. Betweeness compared to degree centrality – scores and rankings

Actor	Betweeness	Ranking	InDegree	Ranking	OutDegree	Ranking
29	9.585	1	663	4	1126	3
15	8.914	2	1362	2	578	4
86	8.741	3	1425	1	503	5
85	7.663	4	448	6	367	6
94	7.614	5	537	5	1381	2
57	6.987	6	974	3	1660	1
35	5.195	7	10	71	65	20
20	5.309	8	109	21	191	10
66	4.24	9	297	8	99	17
71	3.713	10	237	9	56	23

It can be seen from table 2 that the actors with high betweenness centrality scores generally agree with their high scores for degree centrality. Actors 29, 15, 86, 85, 94 and 57 have high betweenness centrality scores which are well above average for the network. There is also a low level of variance in the network relative to the mean when betweenness is concerned (table 3); this could mean that the actors with high

Table 3. Summary statistics for all measures

	Degree	Closeness	Betweeness	Eigenvector
Mean	4.068	2.332	1.034	7.814
Std Dev	2.593	0.347	1.952	16.501
Sum	244.068	139.939	62.069	468.868
Variance	6.722	0.120	3.809	272.267
Min	1.695	1.695	0.000	-0.000
Max	13.559	2.670	9.585	72.480

betweenness scores can be deemed as quite centralised. The top six actors in betweenness scores also feature prominently in the rankings for out and in degree. These members are considered to have a lot of influence in the network as a lot of other participants depend on them to make connections with other people. In other words, as they are "between" a lot of other interactions, their level of call activity is relatively high. Interesting though are some of the participants that scored highly with regards to betweenness but have a quite a low ranking with in degree or out degree compared. A prime example of this is actor 35 who has the 7th highest betweenness centrality score but fares quite lowly when in degree is concerned. This can be seen as an indication that actor 35 may have a structural network position of a peripheral facilitator to separated sub networks within the entire network. This position may not be apparent when just viewing the network using in and out degree measurements. This is also the case for actor 20, whose betweenness centrality score ranking is much higher than their degree calculations. In both cases they have a higher out degree score than in degree, which agree with a position of passing on information to other groups in the network. It can thus be proposed that different types of centrality measures affect a participant's network position. Clearly, some members of the network have a higher position when a different centrality measure is used and this can distinguish their position in the network for different purposes, where it may become apparent of different positions a member may hold.

Closeness centrality and eigenvector centrality measures were also calculated to discover if it has any impact on the findings about actors who have demonstrated to have a better position to disseminate information. Table 4 shows the top ten eigenvector centrality scores achieved by participants in the study and is compared to their ranking in the closeness centrality calculations.

The eigenvector approach is an important measurement as it is an effort to discover the most central actors (i.e. those with the smallest farness from others) in terms of "global" or "overall" structure of the network, and to pay lesser attention to patterns that are more "local". In other words, we want to find nodes that have an influence on the way other nodes may disseminate information. Again it can be seen from table 4 that actors 29, 86, 57, 39 and 94 have high eigenvector centrality scores and this indicates they are more central to the main pattern of distances among all of the actors. There is high variance in the eigenvector calculation relative to the mean (table 3). This may add to the fact that these actors have a lot of influence in the network which aids the results already seen that they are able to disseminate more information due to their structural position in the social network.

Table 4. Eigenvector versus closeness centrality

Actor	Eigenvector	Ranking	Closeness	Ranking
29	72.48	1	2.67	1
86	63.661	2	2.656	3
57	56.145	3	2.654	4
39	56.145	4	2.654	4
94	50.76	5	2.633	12
90	34.347	6	2.648	7
85	30.256	7	2.655	6
78	22.13	8	2.667	2
16	18.286	9	2.643	8
1	18.286	10	1.881	31

Closeness centrality approach emphasises the distance of an actor to all others in the network by focusing on the distance from each actor to all others. Again, even though the numbers of results of the closeness calculations vary very little, the same highly central actors which were mentioned previously are again ranked very quite highly but with a very low standard deviation. It seems the actors are quite close to one another which facilitates dissemination of information for the central actors.

Finally, we conducted a multi-mode analysis taking into account all forms of centrality measurements and actors call activity, which can be deemed as their information dissemination ability. The basis of the multi-mode analysis is based on evidence that out-degree centrality is the most important determinant of an actor's position in a social network because it indicates the level to which an actor is able to communicate [12]. With this in mind we have taken the top 25 actors as per their out degree centrality score and compared these ranks with their ranking in all other measurements of centrality to determine each actor's position in the network and how this compares to their call activity.

Each actor is given a rank for each respective centrality measure out of 25, if an actor scored 0 for that particular centrality measure then they are given a rank of 25 for that measure. Once all the ranks have been determined then are then added up across each row to determine an actor's total score. The lower the score the more centrally positioned an actor is deemed.

Once again, familiar actors which have been previously reported to have the highest call activity are deemed to be the most centrally positioned and are therefore proposed to be in a better position to disseminate information. Below is a diagram which depicts these results in graphical form with the more central actor's closer to the centre of the circle.

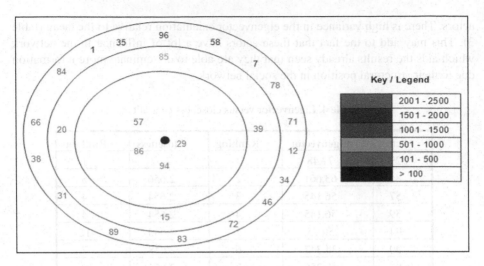

Fig. 3. Actors' central position with call interactions colour-coded

From figure 3, the closer the actor is to the centre the better their overall centrality score is, which leaves them in a better position to disseminate more information than members who are less centrally located. This correlates to the particular actor's call activity, which is also the amount of information disseminated. As seen from figure 3, actor 29 is most centrally positioned in the network and also has the 5th highest call activity with a total of 1789 interactions. Actor 57 who has the highest number of interactions in the group is the 4th best centrally positioned member of the network. Overall, it can clearly be seen that all of the actor's with high call activity (> 1500) are in the two inner most circles which gives them the ability to disseminate more information because they are more central in the network than the other members of the study. In general, the results and findings from this study seem to converge to the argument that an actor's structural position in a social network affects their ability to disseminate information. The pattern indicates that actors who have high centrality scores figure prominently in outgoing and incoming calls which corresponds to their increased ability to disseminate more information. The findings bear implications for researchers and scholars in the human computer interaction field and those involved in computer-supported and cooperative work. First, structure and position of individuals dictate information dissemination and flow. Second, traces from the network structure generate insights which are invaluable for the design and development of communication tools in mobile and dispersed personalised contexts.

6 Conclusion

Drawing on the results and findings from this study, it can be seen that an actor in a more centrally favored position does have an increased ability to disseminate more information to other members of a network than someone with a more peripheral position. That said, it can also be seen from the results that the importance of a particular actor may not become apparent until different centrality measures are taken into account. This can dramatically change the structural position of a particular actor and increase their prominence in a social network, without the actor necessarily being a central figure.

The results seem to agree with Hanneman's [12] view, in suggesting out-degree as an influential centrality measure when determining a central figure in an information flow. Although this does not mean they automatically are in the best information disseminating position in the network, eigenvector and betweenness measures also play a critical part in discovering which actors have the most influence and connections to distribute information to key divisions of the network. These measures become just as an important as out and in degree centrality measures for understanding an actors' communication structure [2, 6]. Further study needs to be carried out to explore centrality and information dissemination abilities in terms of correlation within different and similar group scenarios (eg. groups with high information dissemination indices as compared to low ones) rather than a large network to discover if these patterns stay consistent. A multiplex relational analysis (such as short message sent and received, and video calls sent and received) also needs to be conducted within the group and outside the group of the participants' network to gain a further understanding of the complexities and dynamics of information dissemination behaviour, in relation to the actor's network. Such understanding helps us to model social exchange behaviour from a social networks perspective. Furthermore, the interactions of these same actors at different time-periods (quarterly) can be studied to understand changes in individual and group communication structures longitudinally.

References

[1] Adamic, L., Adar, E.: How to Search a Social Network. Social Networks 27, 185–203 (2005)
[2] Ahuja, M.K., Galletta, D.F., Carley, K.M.: Individual Centrality and Performance in R&D Groups: An Empirical Study. Management Science 49(1), 21–38 (2003)
[3] Bae, S.J., Gloor, P., Schnorf, S.: Detection of Power User Patterns among High School Students in a Mobile Communication Network. In: Applications in Social Network Analysis 2005 (University of Zurich, Switzerland 2005)
[4] Bonacich, O.: Power and Centrality: A Family of Measures. American Journal of Scoiology 92, 1170–1182 (1987)
[5] Borgatti, S.: Centrality and Network Flow. Social Networks 27, 55–71 (2005)
[6] Borgatti, S.P., Everett, M.G.: Notions of Position in Social Network Analysis. Sociological Methodology 22, 1–35 (1992)
[7] Borgatti, S.P., Everett, M.G., Freeman, L.C.: Ucinet for Windows: Software for Social Network Analysis, Analytic Technologies, Harvard, MA (2002)
[8] Eagle, N., Pentland, A.: Reality Mining: Sensing Complex Social Systems. Pervasive Ubiquious Computing 10, 255–268 (2006)
[9] Fisher, D., Dourish, P.: Social and Temporal Structures in Everyday Collaboration. In: CHI 2004 Conference. Vienna, Austria, pp. 551–558 (2004)
[10] Freeman, L.C.: Centrality in Social Networks: Conceptual Clarification. Social Networks 1(3), 215–239 (1978)
[11] Goecks, J., Mynatt, E.D.: Leveraging Social Networks for Information Sharing. In: Proceedings of the 2004 ACM Conference on Computer Supported Cooperative Work, Chicago, Illinois, pp. 328–331. ACM Press, New York (2004)

[12] Hanneman, R.A.: Introduction to Social Network Methods. 2004 (August 8, 2001), http://faculty.ucr.edu/~hanneman/SOC157/NETTEXT.PDF

[13] Matsuo, Y., Mori, J., Sugiyama, T.: Real-world Oriented Information Sharing using Social Networks. In: Proceedings of the ACM-SIG GROUP 2005, pp. 81–84. ACM Press, New York (2005)

[14] Scott, J.: Social Network Analysis: A Handbook. SAGE Publications, London (2000)

[15] Song, X., Lin, C.-Y., Tseng, B.L., Sun, M.-T.: Modeling and Predicting Personal Information Dissemination Behavior. In: Knowledge Discover from Data 05, Chicago, Illinois, USA (2005)

[16] Wasserman, S., Faust, K.: Social Network Analysis: Methods and Applications. Cambridge University Press, New York (1994)

Identifying Potential Social Impact of Collaborative Systems at Design Time

Clarissa Maria de A. Barbosa[1], Raquel Oliveira Prates[2],
and Clarisse Sieckenius de Souza[1]

[1] SERG – Departamento de Informática – PUC-Rio,
R. Marquês de São Vicente, 225, Gávea, Rio de Janeiro – RJ
[2] Departamento de Ciência da Computação – UFMG,
Av. Antônio Carlos, 6627, Prédio do ICEx, sala 4010, Belo Horizonte - MG
{cbarbosa, clarisse}@inf.puc-rio.br, rprates@dcc.ufmg.br

Abstract. This paper presents Manas, a Semiotic Engineering epistemic tool for the design of collaborative systems (CoSys) whose aim is to expand the designers' knowledge and awareness of their influence on groups and group dynamics. Manas has been developed to help designers represent their conception of computer-mediated communication and reflect upon some of its potential social effects, springing from user-system interaction, as well from user-user interaction (through the system). The paper illustrates how Manas can lead designers to reflect upon both the design problem and its proposed solution(s), which allows them to make more conscious decisions. Increased knowledge and awareness should then enhance the quality of CoSys design.

Keywords: Semiotic Engineering, Collaborative Systems, Online Communities, Design Models, Computer-Mediated Communication, Social Aspects of HCI.

1 Introduction

Collaborative systems (CoSys) support and enable human interaction online. CoSys allows users to communicate not only with the system, but also, and mainly, with each other, through the system. The purpose of interaction varies widely, from working together, to exchanging personal and professional experiences, or just having fun. According to this broad definition, computer-supported cooperative work (CSCW), communities of practice, health support communities and games are all examples of CoSys.

For the last 20 years, researchers have pointed out the complexity involved in designing collaborative systems [1], [12]. One of the main aspects involved in the use of CoSys, which should be carefully considered during the design process, is the social effect caused by the system on groups or communities of users [8],[19]. A number of tools, models and frameworks have been proposed to support CoSys designers. They are usually task-based, allowing designers to analyze or describe, at different levels of abstraction, which tasks can be performed by all group members and how tasks relate to each other. Such is the case with Groupware Task Analysis

C. Baranauskas et al. (Eds.): INTERACT 2007, LNCS 4662, Part I, pp. 31–44, 2007.

(GTA) [22], ConcurTaskTrees (CTT) [14], Collaboration Usability Analysis (CUA) [16], and 3C Collaboration Model (3C) [10]. In all of these, communication among group members is represented implicitly or in necessary association with tasks.

In this paper, we present Manas [3], a Semiotic Engineering [6] epistemic tool to support designers in representing and reflecting upon how users can or should communicate with each other (USU communication) through CoSys. Manas separates communicative from task-related dimensions, and provides a design language in which to describe the envisaged USU communication. It also provides qualitative feedback on some of the potential social effects that USU design decisions may have on the group of users. By doing so, Manas can lead designers to reflect upon both the problems being handled and their proposed solution(s). Thus designers are prompted at design time to take potential social impacts of the designed system into more careful consideration.

As a by-product of language description and model-based reasoning for providing feedback on design decisions, Manas traces the USU communication design rationale, a valuable asset for ulterior steps in the design process, as well as for system documentation, maintenance and online help design.

In spite of their widely recognized relevance, social aspects of CoSys design have not received as much support as needed, especially in the form of design tools. Although useful general recommendations (e.g. sociability guidelines [19]) are available, they do not necessarily help designers understand or perceive how they should be applied when conflicting indications are met, or what implications are brought about by choosing one guideline to the detriment of others. Previous approaches such as Action Workflow [13], DEMO [7], Milan Conversation Model [5], and the BAT model [11], for instance, had already brought communication among group members to the center of designers' attention. However, they focused almost exclusively on the communicative actions and patterns made available at interaction time. The potential social consequences of choosing one or another were not explored. A paradigmatic example of a communication-centered perspective on CoSys design, The Coordinator [24] implemented a mapping of speech acts onto a workflow model, having the USU communication model subsume (or virtually stand for) other models involved in group interaction (task models, social models, coordination models, etc.).

Manas' main contribution is then to: (i) provide the representational means to describe the social dimensions of CoSys design decisions, isolating communication issues from tasks issues (but not having one subsume the other); and (ii) to provide qualitative feedback for such decisions, based on various theories about (or related to) interpersonal communication (*e.g.* semiotics [9][15], conversation and discourse analysis [4] and speech act theory [20][21][23]).

In section 2 we illustrate some of the social issues associated to design choices in an online discussion forum, so that the reader can see concrete examples of the range of problems Manas can deal with. Then in section 3 we present a brief overview of Manas' structural and functional profile, with a more detailed description of its design language. In section 4 we show how Manas can help designers deal with some of the issues raised in section 2. And finally, in section 5, we conclude the paper by discussing Manas' perceived value and by presenting our next steps in this research.

2 Social Effects of an Online Forum

Online forums provide very popular examples of the kinds of activities and interaction supported by CoSys. In order to illustrate the purpose of Manas and the benefits that designers can gain from using it as a design tool, we will use an online forum especially developed to support long-term scientific discussions of our research group – OriOn V1[1]. Compared to standard online forums (*e.g.* MSN Groups), the most salient difference introduced by OriOn is that when users post messages they qualify it by a rhetorical marker that binds it to the superordinate message it is supposed to respond to. In MSN Groups, for example, you find messages structured in a recursive subordination chain that we can represent like this[2]:

```
User 1: hi...
when i start fidller, i can't debug or use view in browser in visual
studio 2005, i get error 404 in ie, do you know why?
thank you...
        User 2: What happens if you try to use IE while Fiddler is
        running?  What URLs are you hitting in VS?
            User 1: hi...
            I can use the internet and any internet service when the
            fiddler is runing.
            he      url      that      hit      from      vs:
            htttp://localhost/projectName/default.aspx
            so, do you know why its happening?
                User 1: hi...
                I forgot to attach the error message:
                >> Server Error in '/' Application.

                >> The resource cannot be found.
```

In OriOn the above conversation would be structured in a rhetorical chain (i.e. a chain of messages whose relations with each other are rhetorical, such as question-answer, statement-elaboration, statement-concession, etc.) built by users themselves. So, for example, users might choose to prefix their messages with question-answer and conjunction markers like this:

```
User 1 ASKS: hi...
when i start fidller, i can't debug or use view in browser in visual
studio 2005, i get error 404 in ie, do you know why?
thank you...
        User 2 ASKS: What happens if you try to use IE while Fiddler is
        running?  What URLs are you hitting in VS?
            User 1 ANSWERS:  hi...
            I can use the internet and any internet service when the
            fiddler is runing.
            the      url      that      hit      from      vs:
            htttp://localhost/projectName/default.aspx
            so, do you know why its happening?
            User 1 AND: hi...
            I forgot to attach the error message:
            >> Server Error in '/' Application.
```

---

[1] OriOn V1 is the 1st version of the forum (now in its 2nd). In the remainder of the paper "OriOn" always refers to OriOn V1.

[2] The anonymized conversation in this example has been extracted from a public MSN Group in January 2007.

```
>> The resource cannot be found.
```

The value of OriOn's rhetorical structuring is that it readily characterizes the above dialogue as an open conversation: a question has been asked, and another question was asked in response (requesting further information); the requested information has been given, in two subsequent messages (ANSWER + ADDENDUM). Especially in long-term scientific discussions, where the structure of arguments is elaborate – typically including concessions, illustrations, elaborations, etc. – these markers can support text summarization or visual (abstract) representations of the state of discussions, helping discussants address open questions, identify lively debates, spot the discussants who are leading conversations here and there, and so on. This can make discussions more agile, efficient and productive.

However, after five years of regular use, and a number of redesigns (all keeping with the rhetorical markers, but none including the expected summarization and visualization facilities yet), two related phenomena were observed. First, non-directed questions like the ones above (i.e. questions that were not directed to one particular discussant of the group, but to all) often took longer to be answered, because everybody passed the baton to everybody else. Locks of this type were usually resolved outside OriOn, in face-to-face conversations or emails. Second, questions could be explicitly directed to one or more discussants (e.g. "Hi, Albert and/or Amelia – when I start a fiddler I get this error message [etc.]. Do you know why?"). This second alternative could be more successful than the first, the answer being given more quickly. However, regarding the top-level issue that OriOn's designers were trying to address – a more accurate representation of the state of discussions in order to make them more agile, efficient and productive – this was a "work around", rather than a solution. Why? Because when summarizing or visualizing texts based on structural elements, there would be no representation for the fact that "Albert" and "Amelia" were the expected respondents of that particular request.

At closer examination, we saw that the problem with OriOn's structuring in this case is that, although it is perspicuous enough to represent rhetorical relations and help users distinguish between pending vs. complete argumentations, for example, an important item was missing: the identification of addressed listeners. OriOn's design, like that of most discussion forums, conceives that messages posted in a forum are for all to see and for anyone to answer. Although this is true, there is an important distinction in the semantics of *for all to see* that designers missed: that, just like in any face-to-face group discussion, some parts of the conversation may take place between "Albert" and "Amelia", but they are not private – they are public. And because they are public, everybody is welcome to contribute, but it would be impolite not to recognize that the conversation is going on between the two. For example, it would be in principle impolite to suggest changing subject right after Amelia asks Albert a question, not giving him the opportunity to answer. This suggestion, in face-to-face situations, would very probably be interpreted as an equivalent of one of the following: "This conversation has lasted long enough.", or "Amelia, you should not have asked this question.", or "Let's help Albert not lose face by having to answer this question."

The cost of missing this sort of scenario at design time can be charged later in the currency of social relations among users, group discussion dynamics, or software redesign and upgrades. For instance, if no one had answered User 1's question, he could have perceived it as "No one knows the answer to my question.", or "I was expected to know how to solve this.", or he could even have taken it to a more personal side "No one cares about me or my problems.". The social effects of perceived impoliteness can be very undesirable: users may be discouraged to reengage in discussions, users may inadvertently be caught up in social *quid pro quos*, etc. In some kinds of groups, more than others – for instance in health support online communities – these effects can be disastrous. The point for CoSys design is that the system (Orion, in this case) does not support users in "managing" their level of politeness, to the extent that they can often be inadvertedly impolite with others. Manas thus sets out to help designers oversee this kind of issue at design time, rather than only facing it in longitudinal evaluation studies after the system is implemented.

3 Manas – An Epistemic Tool

Manas is an epistemic tool based on Semiotic Engineering [6]. In this semiotic theory of HCI, user-system interaction is viewed as a particular kind of computer-mediated metacommunication (communication about communication). In it, the designer (or the spokesperson of the design team) sends users a message about how they can or should interact with the system in order to achieve a certain range of goals and experiences which it has been designed to support. This message tells users the designer's vision, including her understanding of who the users are, what they need or wish to do, how they prefer to do it, and why. In the context of CoSys, it also tells them the designer's understanding of their communicative needs, namely: who the interlocutors of the group communication processes are; who they can communicate and interact with; about what; for what purposes; and how.

   In order to support designers in conceiving better metacommunication messages the theory offers them a variety of epistemic tools. These are tools that allow them to leverage their knowledge about the situation at hand, the problems involved in it, their solution, as well as their expected impacts on users. They are not tools that present ready-made solutions (*e.g.* patterns) for designers to choose and apply. Rather, they assist designers in carefully elaborating the essence of their metacommunication message with respect to the users' communicative needs. Manas [3], which is the result of research started by Prates [17], [18] and extended by Barbosa [2], is one such tool. It helps designers to describe their vision for the communication among users, and gives them feedback on the social effects of design descriptions.

   Manas embodies a conceptual architecture model for CoSys design-support tools comprising the following components: (a) a design language, L ComUSU, in which to describe USU communication; (b) an interpreter of L-ComUSU, whose output (or interpretation) is a model of USU communication, m-ComUSU, plus feedback assertions (the analog of *warnings* issued by programming language interpreters); and (c) an annotated derivative of m-ComUSU, which is the equivalent of the design rationale. Next we present Manas and each of its components. Manas' architecture model is depicted in Figure 1.

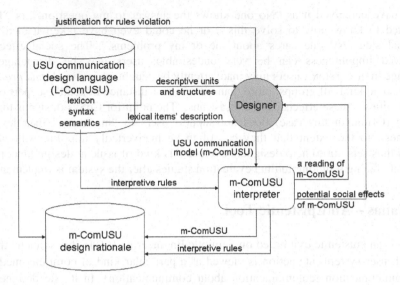

Fig. 1. Manas' conceptual architecture

The underlying interpretive rules that give consistency to Manas, binding L-ComUSU semantics, m-ComUSU configurations, the detection of potentially problematic design decisions, and the structure of annotations on L-ComUSU representing the design rationale, are mostly drawn from theory. Conversation and discourse analysis [4], speech act theory [20][21][23], and Semiotic Engineering [6] are the main sources [3].

L-ComUSU defines lexical items and syntactic rules. Lexical items typically represent communication elements, whereas syntactic rules define how such elements relate to each other. Elements and relations are qualified by attributes. The possible values that attributes may take are also defined by L-ComUSU. The semantics of the language constitutes a cohesive abstract model of CoSys communication and associated social effects, and is encoded in Manas' interpreter. Thus, a full L-ComUSU description of the designer's vision is interpreted as an instance of the abstract model that constitutes the semantics of the design language. Figure 2 depicts the lexical and syntactic components of the underlying L-ComUSU model.

Users' communication must be defined in terms of communicative structures which are composed by communicative acts and involve interlocutors. A communicative act may be a speech (a speaker's utterance to one or more listeners) or a conversation (speakers and listeners alternate roles, producing various utterances). Commmunicative acts achieve a goal or purpose. In speeches these are associated with individual utterances, whereas in conversations a goal or purpose should be shared by all interlocutors. All the components in Figure 2 are *types*, not *tokens*, that is, they describe what can be represented by L-ComUSU, but do not depict any specific communicative situation. There are many possibilities for instantiating m-ComUSU models, depending on which components are chosen by designers, and which values are assigned to them. Hence the type-level representations.

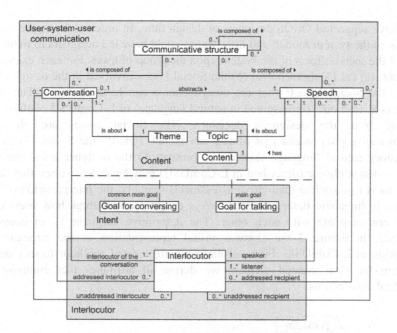

Fig. 2. Lexical and syntactic components of the L-ComUSU model

When describing `interlocutors` the designer must inform whether they are ratified or not, addressed or not. A `ratified` interlocutor is one that is perceived by others as authorized to participate in the communication. Ratified interlocutors may be `addressed` or `not-addressed`. `Addressed interlocutors` are those to whom the communicative act is being directed, whereas `not-addressed interlocutors` are the others participating in that same communication process. For instance, in a chat room all users are ratified interlocutors. If in that chat room User 1 says: "`User 2, do you want to play a game now?`", then User 2 is the addressed interlocutor of User 1's communicative act, whereas all the other participants of the chat room are not-addressed interlocutors.

For each of these elements, the designer must also define a series of attributes. Among other things, attributes indicate the following: whether the element will be explicitly represented in the system or not; the possible values it may assume; who is responsible for determining its value (user, system or both); if it is a mandatory value or not; if it has a default value, and which value this is (if there is one).

The interpretive rules that comprise the semantics of L-ComUSU embody specialized knowledge about the social implications of specific model configurations. In the next section we will illustrate how Manas as a whole support design decisions relative to social aspects of communication.

4   How Manas Supports Designers

In section 2 we illustrated some of the social impacts that design decisions underlying an online forum could have on its users. In this section, we illustrate how Manas could have supported OriOn designers at design time. In order to do so, we describe portions of the system model, and how Manas could have led designers to think about some of the social effects of the system upon the group of users. For each example we represent: (a) the Design Choice; (b) the Social Issues involved in the design choice; and (c) the Social Effects that the design choice can have on users. The Design Choice is a "read out" (represented in natural language) of L-ComUSU configurations resulting from the designer's decisions. The Social Issues are classes of communicative phenomena that Manas can model. Finally, the Social Effect is an explanatory natural language text Manas presents to the designer about the social impact a design choice (described in L-ComUSU) may have. So, we see that the gist of Manas is to associate qualitative assessments (namely, the interpretation of social impacts) to linguistic descriptions of CoSys design choices about how users can or should communicate with each other. The descriptive language is, of course, L-ComUSU. In Figure 3 we show a visual representation of the structure of a description in L-ComUSU. First, all elements are created (without further details), and then for each created element we define all attributes that compose their individual descriptions.

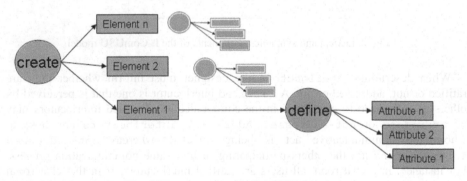

Fig. 3. The structure of L-ComUSU descriptions

The passage below is a partial description of OriOn defining aspects of how users communicate through the system. The description is in the form of natural language sentences paraphrasing constructs of L-ComUSU[3].

> *In this system, any group member is an interlocutor, and there is only one communicative act - a discussion. All interlocutors (speakers and listeners) are explicitly represented in the design model. The system sets them as addressed interlocutors. Not-addressed listeners are not explicitly represented in the system. Interlocutors may engage in conversations about any theme they like. Both the theme and purpose of conversations are explicitly represented in the system, and their value is defined by the user at interaction time.*

---

[3] An extract of the description written on Manas' design language would require an explanation of its syntax which is beside the point of this paper.

Based on this partial description Manas is then apt to provide feedback on its potential social effects. These may affect the group's privacy, codes of politeness and communication efficiency.

Design Choice [4]: *Explicitly represent the conversation's purpose.*
Social Issues pointed by Manas: *politeness and communication efficiency*

`Social effect:` On one hand, explicitly representing the communication's purpose may make it clearer and more perspicuous. On the other hand, some purposes may not be pleasant to the listener and may put the speaker in an awkward or embarrassing position.

Based on this potential social effect, the designer may come to the conclusion that although explicitly representing the purpose of the communication may contribute to having more precise or focused discussions, this could also cause problems. For instance, one member of the group could sound impolite to another if among the possible purposes of communication were the equivalent of this: "Dissuade interlocutor from a bad decision". Prompted by the comment on the "social effects" of her decision, the designer may explore different alternatives. For example, one would be to give users the option of not informing the purpose of communication. Another would be to allow them to introduce their own phrasing of such purpose. In both cases, users would be trading communication efficiency for politeness and good social relations with others.

Design Choice: *Explicitly represent the addressed listeners of the conversation, but not the not-addressed listeners.*
Social Issues pointed by Manas: *communication efficiency*

`Social effect:` Every communication is addressed to a set of listeners, but in a specific context there may also be ratified not-addressed listeners. In that case, in order to successfully achieve the communication's purpose it is important to explicitly identify these listeners. When they are not explicitly represented, users may use alternate system resources to distinguish between addressed and not-addressed listeners. For instance, the speaker may identify addressed listeners as part of the topic or content of the communication (if they are available). In some cases, the distinction between addressed and not-addressed listeners may be clear in the context in which the system is being used.

Although all users are always addressed listeners of every discussion in OriOn, that is not how our research group actually interacts. While some discussions involve all members, others involve only specific subgroups. "Involving" should not be taken as a matter of *authorization* (because there are no secret scientific discussions going on), but rather as a matter of *interest* or *competence*. So, for example, a discussion about mobile devices is not likely to be of interest or competence for group members specializing in semiotic theories. Thus, OriOn users have chosen to represent addressed (interested and competent) users as part of the title of the discussion (as shown in Figure 4[5]).

---

[4] L-ComUSU equivalent.
[5] Figure has been translated to English and anonymized.

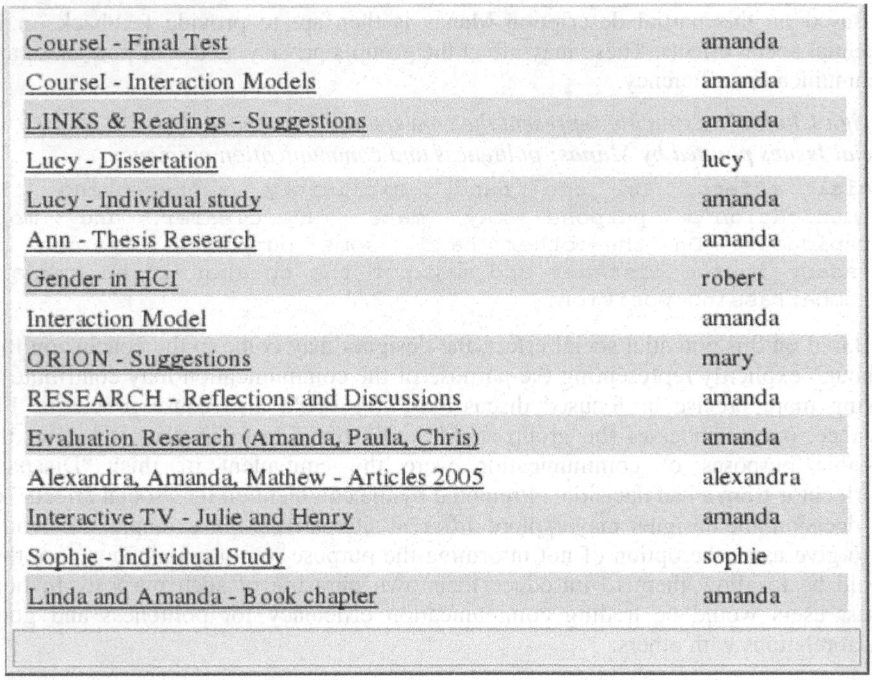

Coursel - Final Test	amanda
Coursel - Interaction Models	amanda
LINKS & Readings - Suggestions	amanda
Lucy - Dissertation	lucy
Lucy - Individual study	amanda
Ann - Thesis Research	amanda
Gender in HCI	robert
Interaction Model	amanda
ORION - Suggestions	mary
RESEARCH - Reflections and Discussions	amanda
Evaluation Research (Amanda, Paula, Chris)	amanda
Alexandra, Amanda, Mathew - Articles 2005	alexandra
Interactive TV - Julie and Henry	amanda
Sophie - Individual Study	sophie
Linda and Amanda - Book chapter	amanda

Fig. 4. OriOn with members listed on discussion topics

If the designer had been warned about this situation at design time, she might have been able to perceive that even though the group was a cooperative and cohesive one, it could be better not to describe all group members as addressed, but rather let users say who is directly involved (addressed) in a particular discussion, and thus expected to make contributions. One of the implications of not allowing users to distinguish between addressed and not-addressed listeners becomes even clearer when we take into consideration the next potential social effect, which Manas would also indicate.

Design Choice: *Addressed listeners are determined by system.*
Social Issues pointed by Manas: *privacy*
Social effect: The system is not being designed to (fully) support private conversations. If the listeners are determined by the system, a user can only succeed in having private conversations with other users, if the intended listeners coincide with the ones that have been determined by the system. If the designer intends to allow users to communicate privately with each other, then users should be the ones to determine who the listeners of their communicative act are.

As the designer thinks about these social effects, she may realize that by explicitly representing addressed and not-addressed listeners, she may also provide the group with more ability to express the privacy of subgroups. She could then consider if it would be interesting to make a distinction between public discussions (all could listen and speak), private discussions taking place at a public space (all could listen, but not all would be expected or allowed to speak), and private discussion (only a subgroup would be able to listen and speak).

Design Choice: No explicit representation for not-addressed listeners.
Social Issues pointed by Manas: *communication efficiency*

```
Social  effect:  Explicit  representations  of  communicative
elements  give  users  the  opportunity  to  highlight  relevant
elements  to  the  success  of  the  communication.  Also,  it  allows
the  system  to  process  the  information  associated  to  it,  e.g.
offering  users  information  retrieval  functionalities.  Also  the
explicit  representation  of  an  element  may  favor  clarity  and
efficiency.
```

This effect pointed by the system could provide designers with more information regarding costs *vs* benefits of explicitly distinguishing between addressed and not-addressed users. It points out that by making this distinction the system could use it to provide new visualizations and information to the users. For instance, they might be able to see, quickly, who is working on what. This new possibility could support some of the group's characteristics valued by its members, such as cohesiveness and interaction.

The explanations provided by Manas do not intend to tell designers what the appropriate decision is, its goal is to call their attention about the potential social effects caused by their decisions regarding users´ communication through the system. By leading designers to reflect upon these situations and issues Manas may encourage them to make clearer decisions about what would be relevant for the group and/or feasible for the development team. For instance, at one point the designers might realize that they did not have enough information about the group's intent or needs (*e.g* Is it important to be able to have public and private communications?). In that case, the need to talk more to users would have been made clear. Designers could even discuss with them the pros and cons of the issue, based on Manas' feedbacks about design alternatives.

It is important to point out that the situations and social effects identified by Manas are not prescriptive, that is, they are not intended to dictate the best solution, but rather to lead designers to consider the issues raised in their own context. In the OriOn examples, we have discussed social aspects of communicative situations faced by a cohesive and cooperative research group. In other contexts, such as when the idea is to foster competition among group members, or design a generic system that could work for any group, the effects pointed out by Manas could (and probably would) entail different considerations and decisions.

5 Discussion and Conclusion

In this paper we have presented Manas an epistemic tool that supports designers in defining the USU communication of a CoSys, and provides them with feedback on the social effects their decisions may have on the users' group. Manas can be defined as context separable, in the sense that it takes into account the combination of values of the communicative elements, their relations and attributes in identifying the potential social impacts of the system, but not the domain or context in which the system will be used. Thus, Manas does not aim at indicating a solution to the designers, but rather at pointing out how their design choices may impact users' experience, in respect to social aspects, such as privacy, politeness and communication efficiency. By informing the designer on possible effects, Manas prompts them to consider these effects in the context at hand, reflecting upon their proposed solution, and thus, making a more conscious decision on the USU communication of the system being conceived.

Manas is not the first proposal to support designers during the design of collaborative systems. Guidelines and models have been proposed and used by CoSys designers. However, Manas presents an innovative and original approach that differs from the existing proposals in relevant aspects. First of all, like the existing models it offers a representation in which to describe relevant aspects of the CoSys being conceived. However, different from them it provides designers with feedback based on their design choices pointing to social impacts they may have on users' experience.

In comparison to task models [10][14][16][22], it has a significant difference as it decouples communication from tasks. By doing so, it extends the contexts in which it can be used by designers to CoSys in which tasks are not the focus, such as health support online communities. Other models have focused on communication [5][7][11][13][24]. In relation to them, Manas brings a new level of abstraction in which to consider communication, since it does not define communicative patterns that constrain users' communicative acts, but rather the types of communicative acts that may be available to users. This higher level approach allows the designer to characterize communication and reflect upon it, not only as an exchange of content between users, but as a socio-cultural activity.

Finally, Manas is different from the other models described since it is based on an HCI theory, Semiotic Engineering [6]. The advantage of being grounded on this theory is that the proposal takes into account not only the step of the design process it is aimed at, but also its characterization of the human-computer interaction phenomenon as a designer to user metacommunication. Manas makes it clear to designers that their decisions are conveyed to users through the system and influences the users experiences. Therefore, Manas can also help designers understand better their own design activity.

Since Manas is grounded on an HCI theory, it has a scientific contribution to HCI, and particularly to Semiotic Engineering theory. In a scientific research, theory and practice must complement each other and provide input to each other. Hence, as Manas is used, empirical data on its use and how it influences the design process can be collected. This data can then be analyzed and used to support (or not) the Semiotic Engineering premises in which Manas was grounded.

Manas proposed support to designers has been initially evaluated through a prototype system developed and in two case studies [3]. The prototype was developed in Prolog, and its use required knowledge of L-ComUSU lexical elements, their attributes and syntax. The first case study was an analytical evaluation which involved describing an existing CoSys using L-ComUSU to verify whether all communicative acts encoded in the system could be described by the language. The second case study aimed at assessing whether other designers not involved in the Manas research would be able to understand it and use it. In this case study, the participants were graduate students who knew Semiotic Engineering, and they were asked to describe portions of

OriOn using L-ComUSU. Both case studies provided positive indicators on the L-ComUSU expressive power, on how it may be used and its usefulness to designers. The next step in this research involves the development of a usable system based on Manas that can be used by designers in conceiving their systems. As the system is used data on how it supports the designer, their perception of its usefulness and how it is integrated to existing design processes can be collected and used to evaluate Manas and define the next steps in this research.

One relevant point to notice is that Manas' feedback is on the social impact of the CoSys being designed. However, social aspects are culturally dependent. Thus, rules and social effects that are currently defined in Manas may not be applicable to other cultures different from the Brazilian culture, or maybe western culture. Thus, how to adapt Manas to CoSys being developed for other cultures or for an international audience must be investigated.

Acknowledgments. The authors thank participants of the initial evaluation of Manas for their contribuition. Clarisse de Souza thanks CNPq for a supporting her research and Clarissa Barbosa thanks CAPES and CNPq for scholarships received during her PhD.

References

1. Ackerman, M.: The Intellectual Challenge of CSCW: the gap between social requirements and technical feasibility. Human-Computer Interaction 15(2), 181–203 (2000)
2. Barbosa, C.M.A.: MetaCom-G*: especificação da comunicação entre membros de um grupo. MSc Dissertation. Computer Science Department, PUC-Rio, Brazil (2002)
3. Barbosa, C.M.A.: Manas: uma ferramenta epistêmica de apoio ao projeto da comunicação em sistemas colaborativos. PhD Thesis. Computer Science Department, PUC-Rio, Brazil (2006)
4. Brown, P., Levinson, S.C.: Politeness: some universals in language use. Cambridge University Press, Cambridge (1987) (first published in 1978)
5. De Michelis, G., Grasso, M.A.: Situating conversations within the Language/Action Perspective: the Milan Conversation Model. In: CSCW'94. Proceedings of the 1994 ACM conference on Computer supported cooperative work, Chapel Hill, North Carolina, USA, October 22-26, 1994, pp. 89–100. ACM Press, New York, NY (1994)
6. de Souza, C.S.: The Semiotic Engineering of Human-Computer Interaction. The MIT Press, Cambridge, MA (2005)
7. Dietz, J.L.G.: DEMO: towards a discipline of organisation engineering. European Journal of Operational Research 128(2), 351–363 (2001)
8. Dourish, P.: Where the Action Is. The MIT Press, Cambridge, MA (2001)
9. Eco, U.: A Theory of Semiotics. Indiana University Press, Bloomington (1976)
10. Fuks, H., Raposo, A.B., Gerosa, M.A., Lucena, C.J.P.: Applying the 3C Model to Groupware Engineering. Monografias em Ciência da Computação. PUC-Rio Inf.MCC01/04. Computer Science Department, PUC-Rio, Brazil (2004)
11. Goldkuhl, G., Lind, M.: The Generics of Business Interaction - emphasizing dynamic features through the BAT model. In: LAP 2004. Proceedings of the 9th International Working Conference on the Language-Action Perspective on Communication Modeling, New Brunswick, NJ, June 2-3, 2004, pp. 15–40. Rutgers University, New Jersey, USA (2004)

12. Grudin, J.: Groupware and Social Dynamics: eight challenges for developer. Communications of the ACM 37(1), 92–105 (1994)
13. Medina-Mora, R., Winograd, T., Flores, R., Flores, F.: The Action Workflow Approach to Workflow Management Technology. In: CSCW'92. Proceedings of the 1992 ACM Conference on Computer-supported Cooperative Work, Toronto, Ontario, Canada, October 31 - November 4, 1992, pp. 281–288. ACM Press, New York, NY (1992)
14. Paternò, F.: The ConcurTaskTrees Notation. In: Paternò, F. (ed.) Model-based Design and Evaluation of Interactive Applications, Springer, London, UK (1999)
15. Peirce, C.S.: Collected Papers of Charles Sanders Peirce. In: Hartshorne, C., Weiss, P. (eds.) Collected Papers of Charles Sanders Peirce, vol. 1-8, pp. 1–8. Harvard University Press, Cambridge, MA (1958)
16. Pinelle, D., Gutwin, C., Greenberg, S.: Task Analysis for Groupware Usability Evaluation: Modeling Shared-Workspace Tasks with the Mechanics of Collaboration. ACM Transactions on Computer-Human Interaction 10(4), 281–311 (2004)
17. Prates, R.O.: A Engenharia Semiótica de Linguagens de Interfaces Multi-usuário. PhD Thesis. Computer Science Department, PUC-Rio, Brazil (1998)
18. Prates, R.O, de Souza, C.S.: Towards a Semiotic Environment for Supporting the Development of Multi-user Interfaces. In: CRIWG '98. Proceedings of the Fourth CYTED-RITOS International Workshop on Groupware, Búzios, RJ, Brazil, September 9-11, 1998, pp. 53–67 (1998)
19. Preece, J.: Online Communities: Designing Usability, Supporting Sociability. John Wiley & Sons, Chichester, UK (2000)
20. Searle, J.R., Vanderveken, D.: Foundations of illocutionary logic. Cambridge University Press, Cambridge (1985)
21. Searle, J.R.: Conversation reconsidered. In: Parret, H., Verschueren, J. (eds.) (on) Searle on conversation, pp. 137–148. John Benjamins, Amsterdam (1992)
22. van der Veer, G.C., van Welie, M.: Groupware Task Analysis. In: Tutorial Notes for the CHI'99 workshop Task Analysis Meets Prototyping: towards seamless UI Development, Pittsburgh, PA, USA, May 16, 1999 (1999)
23. Vanderveken, D.: Illocutionary logic and discourse typology. Revue Internationale de Philosophie 55(216), 243–255 (2001) (special issue: Searle, with his replies)
24. Winograd, T., Flores, F.: Understanding computers and cognition: a new foundation for design. Ablex Publishing, Norwood, NJ (1986)

Group Efficacy in Asynchronous vs. Multi-synchronous Virtual Teams: An Empirical Study

Yingxin Pan and Chen Zhao

IBM China Research Lab, Bldg. 19, Zhongguancun Software Park,
Beijing, P.R. China, 100094
{panyingx, zhaochen}@cn.ibm.com

Abstract. Group efficacy has begun to receive more attention in HCI. The paper describes a mixed-design experiment aimed to explore the effect of time on group efficacy development in two computer-mediated virtual conditions: asynchronous vs. multi-synchronous teams. The relationships of group efficacy measures at different times and tool evaluation, team satisfaction and performance are also explored. Forty university students who participate in the study are administered questionnaires over the course of the assigned ten-day task. Results show group efficacy changes as a function of time in the asynchronous environment. In addition, the positive relations between group efficacy and tool evaluation and adoption and team satisfaction were demonstrated for asynchronous groups. The findings indicate group efficacy is dynamic with team development and useful in signaling how technology and collaboration modes impact user experience and interaction in the asynchronous environment.

Keywords: Group Efficacy, Asynchronous & Multi-synchronous communication, groupware, virtual team, CSCW.

1 Introduction

Efficacy beliefs are constructed as future-oriented judgments about capabilities to pursue a course of action to meet given situational demands. Since Bandura introduced the concept of self-efficacy perceptions, research in many arenas has demonstrated the power of efficacy judgments in human learning, performance and motivation [7]. An extension of Bandura's self-efficacy is collective or group efficacy which captures a member's beliefs about the capacity of a group or organization. Although both self- and group efficacy are widely recognized in many fields, in human-computer interaction community, efficacy theories have been largely unnoticed [11]. Ramalingam et al. reported that self-efficacy in computing could be used as a predictor of technology learning and achievement [17]. Recent work has begun to make explorations into group efficacy. Carroll et al.'s work provided evidence that community collective efficacy is a valid construct in community computing domain. Still, the collective efficacy of workgroups in computer-mediated interaction has not been well studied yet. Of particular interest is the development and

C. Baranauskas et al. (Eds.): INTERACT 2007, LNCS 4662, Part I, pp. 45–58, 2007.
© IFIP International Federation for Information Processing 2007

role of group efficacy over time in today's virtual groups which are more relying on technologies, as the beliefs of group members evolve with the group development [1] and have been proved effective in predicting future group achievement in traditional teams.

During the course of a project or a task, group members adjust their judgments on how well their group can achieve, while in previous studies group efficacy is often measured at a separate point of time during a task and then used as a general indicator of the collective expectation of future performance. Baker's study found that group efficacy changes over time as group receives feedback in traditional small task groups [1]. However, for virtual teams the topic of group efficacy development is left open. To better understand group efficacy in virtual teams, two typical virtual collaborative modes are identified in the study: asynchronous vs. multi-synchronous. Asynchronous communication has many advantages to enable dispersed collaboration, whereas prolonged response and weak awareness of people and events make the newly-formed groups hard to build swift trust which is closely related to group efficacy [5]. Multi-synchronous collaboration seemed to have benefits to overcome the difficulties, but it is often made up of scattered working environments or tools. This sometimes may lead to such a problem as information chaos [16]. Therefore, it is worth the research effort on how group efficacy differs and develops in the two virtual environments supported by technologies.

Another relatively untouched topic is the effect of group efficacy for understanding human-computer interaction. It is known that an individual's interaction with or through a computer is directly influenced by how well the technology facilitates their abilities [11]. In virtual group contexts, people interact with each other by means of different sophisticated technologies. Group efficacy is expected to be a valuable measure for assessing the consequences that computer-mediated tools have on the starting capabilities of a group [4].

In this paper, therefore, group efficacy was investigated in two comparative conditions - asynchronous and multi-synchronous environments of virtual teams. The study explored two questions: 1) does group efficacy perception change as a virtual team develops and how; and 2) how well group efficacy measures at different times indicate technology impact on virtual team results and interaction?

2 Group Efficacy

2.1 Group Efficacy Development and Measurement

Group efficacy has been defined as the group members' collective estimate of the group's ability to perform a specific task. Like self-efficacy, group efficacy differs from general confidence because confidence is a general affective state, whereas efficacy is extremely task specific [15]. When a task starts that requires much team interdependence, team members have the opportunity to develop shared mental models and to use this shared knowledge to guide their behavior.

So when team members set out to do a specific task, how is group efficacy initially developed? Bandura [2] proposed four sources of information that lead to the development of self efficacy. They are past performance accomplishment, vicarious experience, verbal persuasion and physiological and emotional arousal respectively. Other than these aforementioned sources of information on self-efficacy, its effect on team results can also be moderated by other variables, for example, complexity of the task and clarity of goals [18]. Along the same train of thoughts, researchers began to explore antecedents of group efficacy, although Bandura addressed this issue by stating that self- and collective efficacy shared the similar sources [2]. For example, Pescosolido [15] found a strong link between the informal leaders' perceptions of efficacy and group-level measurements of efficacy. In Watson et al.'s study [21], collective efficacy was found to be influenced by both individual-level variables such as self-efficacy, optimism and group-level variables of group size, past team performance and confident leadership.

However, actually many real tasks or projects do take some time to complete and teams go through development cycles. Apart from external variables, time itself has an effect on how group efficacy develops as team develops. Some studies have explored whether certain variables have an effect on collective beliefs over time. Middup et al.'s [11] empirical work showed how group exercises and group memories of activities affect self- and group efficacy as a function of time. As Baker [1] claimed, the beliefs of group members have a dynamic quality and evolve with the development of the group. Especially when a group is confronted with a new situation to perform a task, group efficacy could reasonably be assumed dynamic as time goes and at the same time based on how members react to the situation. Therefore, how group efficacy develops in virtual teams with different collaboration modes deserves research.

With respect to efficacy measurement, there has been generated much literature in clarifying and testing different methods of measurements. Generally, there exist three major types of methods. The first method is group-level aggregation of individual self-efficacy beliefs. The second is group-level aggregation of individual group efficacy beliefs and the third way is conducted by achieving group consensus. All these methods have their own pros and cons. Researchers have attempted to see which one is more predictive in specific contexts. Whiteoak et al. [22] compared the three methods of assessing group efficacy in a laboratory study. The conclusion is the three methods didn't differ - neither in terms of their capacity of discriminating high and moderate task-difficulty conditions, nor in their consistency, magnitude of their relationship with goals and the extent to which they are influenced by performance. In Hardin et al.'s study [8] of measuring group efficacy in virtual teams, these methods differed: the aggregated method had greater predictability than a group consensus method.

Nevertheless, no matter which method is chosen, there is another issue that needs to be taken into consideration. As stated in the aforementioned part, group efficacy as a collective belief is of the dynamic quality. When a team is first formed, team members can hardly form a common understanding or belief simultaneously. They know little about what each other are like, how competent they are, etc. Their roles in the team and the procedures for interaction may be unclear as well. Hence the expectations of members of newly formed teams are somewhat blurry or even inaccurate. Their perceptions of group efficacy for performance may be primarily dependent on perceptions of individual self-efficacy. Baker [1] held the same argument on this. If members don't share expectations about team outcomes, group efficacy is not likely to exist. So the measurement of group efficacy at the very beginning of team forming or a task might be not that appropriate or valid in predicting team outcomes, particularly when there is much uncertainty either in terms of the task or the interaction environment. Therefore, at what time the assessment of group efficacy would be most effective is worth exploring. In virtual teams who are rarely meet face-to-face, various technologies or tools are employed to facilitate communication. Shared understanding of the group's capabilities couldn't be generated at the very outset. Technologies may enhance or impede the communication or even team building. As a result, the question is to be answered: when group efficacy is formed and effectively predicts group outcomes in computer-mediated collaborative virtual teams?

Based on this logic, this paper tried to explore how group efficacy develops during the cycle of team development and see how it may change as a function of time in two different collaborative HCI virtual environments.

2.2 Group Efficacy with Group Outcomes

Numerous studies have proved the strong linkage between performance and self-efficacy. Researchers also found the positive relationship of group efficacy with a variety of group and organizational outcomes. With a plenty of research done in traditional teams and its consistent ability to predict performance, many researchers began to make extension into virtual team environment [20] and community computing domain [11]. How technology enhances or hinders people in working or collaborating through human interaction with computer is one of the fundamental issues in HCI. In Carroll et al.'s work [4], community collective efficacy is proposed to be useful for understanding the experiences of people using a community network. Hardin et al.'s study [8] called for more efforts to investigate the relationship between group efficacy and virtual team performance which is actually lacking in current research. Nevertheless, how group efficacy can work to indicate group outcomes, particularly technology impact, is still deficient.

In this paper, the relationship of group efficacy with such group outcome variables as group satisfaction, technology evaluation and adoption were investigated.

3   Asynchronous vs. Multi-synchronous Virtual Teams

Virtual or distributed teams are formed for any number of reasons, from educational purposes, to business process redesign or resources reallocation. They perform projects or tasks with a host of constantly emerging technologies. Broadly speaking, there are two fundamentally different approaches to network-based collaboration for virtual teams [19]. Team workspace or *asynchronous* applications provide an electronic space where members of distributed task groups can share and edit documents and other data, chart the progress of tasks, and communicate in threaded discussions. *Synchronous* is all about communicating in the present. Examples of this synchronous communication include a telephone conversation, video conferencing and instant messaging. However, practical work often involves more complex situations, as work is a cycle of divergence and convergence [12]. *Multi-synchronous* environment is consequently becoming desirable where direct communication and asynchronous means are combined to satisfy varying needs of people.

There are two major important distinctions between virtual teams and traditional teams [8]. One is lack of collocation and the other is the need to use sophisticated information technology [10]. These two factors add complexity to team interactions. It is not surprising how a rich array of cues normally experienced in co-located teams is absent during distributed work. In a face-to-face environment, the cues such as body language and vocal inflection are easily accessed that even the most high-fidelity video conferencing systems cannot fully reproduce. In a virtual environment, participants have no such access, where diminished trust could be caused. Closely related to trust is group efficacy within teams [3]. Some researchers have suggested that important aspects of group efficacy include shared beliefs in the team's abilities at communication and perceived competence for coordinated group activities [14]. Distributed interaction may hinder the development of this efficacy within teams [3]. This issue seemed more obvious for asynchronous communication in that normal interaction with human cues gets more difficult. Multi-synchronous collaboration makes up for what asynchronous may miss, but scattered working environments or tools can engender other problems, such as information chaos [16] which can increase task load. In terms of the impact of information technology in virtual teams, group efficacy construct as a simple method is promising to be useful to investigate the issue of how technology really works in HCI.

Group efficacy in computer-mediated virtual groups has begun to receive more attention [13, 17] but is not well studied yet. It is worthwhile to make further exploration to see how group efficacy develops over time and how it indicate technology impact and group outcomes in different collaborative modes of virtual working.

4 Method

4.1 Participants and Design

In total, forty Chinese university students participated in the study as members of 5 experimental and 5 control workgroups performing the same assigned task. Each group was made up of 4 students who are all senior undergraduates and master students. The 5 experimental groups consisted of 11 males and 9 females and control groups of 12 males and 8 females. All groups were of mixed sex. The participation was voluntary. The students didn't know each other before. They were encouraged to make efforts and would be given gifts of different prices – better final performance will be acknowledged by higher-value gifts as recognition to their team.

In experimental groups, participants were required only to use a web-based *asynchronous* communication platform - Lotus Notes TeamRoom. Besides TeamRoom, The 5 control groups could use other real-time and asynchronous communication tools including ICQ, MSN, emails and phone calls, except face-to-face, which created a *multi-synchronous* environment. This design ensures the two types of groups both simulate virtual working environments.

The task is to explore eastern-western cultural differences and thus to provide suggestions to people in dealing with cultural affairs. The task was chosen for a few reasons: firstly, it is a task involving both brainstorming and problem-solving; secondly, there is no universal description of eastern-western cultural differences and how they could be categorized. Participants can contribute whatever they think makes sense from any perspective, no matter what academic background they are of. Third, the task also involves document sharing and management which made it closer to real working scenarios. In the task, participants were asked to: (1) discover possible cultural differences and categorize them in a way they prove reasonable, (2) compose a report based on the work (Deliverable 1) and (3) make course slides to present the findings and provide implications and tips in cross-cultural affairs (Deliverable 2).

The task duration is ten-day for each group. It's not very long, nor short. But there is no literature that specifies the minimum or maximum duration of a short duration team. Of the 50 teams studied by Tuckman [20] investigating team development, teaming durations ranged from 1 hour to a few years. Considering the task load and complexity and according to team results, ten days were appropriate.

4.2 Procedure and Technology

Participants of each group met face to face on the first day for about 1.5 hours to get to know their team members. Also, the kick-off meeting served other purposes of: (1) signing agreements by participants, promising they would commit themselves to their team performance; (2) providing training on basic functions of Notes TeamRoom for about 30 minutes; each group had one private TeamRoom which only the four team members and the experimenter could access. They were randomly assigned a user id and password for logging on; (3) providing participants with the instructions about the task, procedures and experiment requirements; (4) filling in the group efficacy questionnaire for the first time at the end of the meeting and (5) sending the first thank-you gifts to all of them for their interest in joining the study. Participants were strongly encouraged by the instructor to work on the task collaboratively.

During the ten days, participants were requested to deliver two results as mentioned above which the 2nd deliverable would have a heavier weight for their final performance. Participants were encouraged to reach their agreement on the categories cultural differences fell into before they worked out the 1st report. Participants only needed to submit deliverable 1 (by the 6th day) and 2 (by the 10th day). By manipulating the task, participants had a better sense of time and deadline so that they wouldn't rush just in the last few days to meet the deadline. The work was delivered to the experimenter via any electronic means.

To approximately match the four team development phases, group efficacy was assessed for four times over the ten-day span. Participants were required to finish the group efficacy questionnaire for another three times in addition to the first measurement at the kick-off meeting: at day 4, day 7 and day 10. The exact time on these days to complete it was not the same, slightly moderated according to their progress. All questionnaires were administered and collected by email except the first completion. Participants would finish two more questionnaires about team satisfaction and TeamRoom evaluation when the task is completed. In addition, TeamRoom data, chatting logs, exchanged emails and other task-relevant communication information, together with their individual self-reports, should be kept and submitted.

TeamRoom 7.0 used in the study is a Lotus Domino application, accessible via a web browser. It allows for the creation of threaded, yet asynchronous, discussion. Information and documents could also be easily shared. Each group owned a new and independent TeamRoom which was inaccessible to other groups.

4.3 Measures

Group Efficacy: In this study, group efficacy was measured by individual-level assessment of group efficacy beliefs [23]. As group efficacy is specific to a domain or a group task, a task-specific eleven-item scale was developed. The sample items are: "I believe that our group has the ability to find the key cultural differences" and "I believe that our group has the ability to conduct effective discussion to reach good results". All items were completed on an 11-point scale (0= not at all confident, 5 = moderately confident to 10 = totally confident). Nevertheless, to determine if it is appropriate to aggregate the individual beliefs when investigating the relationships between group efficacy and group-level outcomes, the within-group interrater reliability should be calculated to assess the level of agreement within groups on the group efficacy measure [22]. In this study, the Kendall's concordance coefficients were for group efficacy .91, .92, .96 and .96 at time1, time2, time 3 and time4 respectively. The values demonstrated that the group-level analysis of efficacy was meaningful.

Group Satisfaction: Three items were developed to measure group satisfaction on 5-point scale after task is finished. The sample item is: "In all, how satisfied are you with your group?" (1 = completely dissatisfied to 5 = completely satisfied). Cronbach's alpha is .8085.[1]

TeamRoom Evaluation: Three items were used to assess the users' ratings of TeamRoom on 5-point scale after task is finished. The sample items are: "Based on this experience, how do you like TeamRoom?" (1= completely dislike to 5 = completely like) and "How much possibility will you choose to use TeamRoom in other situations?" (1= never to 5 = always). Cronbach's alpha is .8028.

Group Performance: Two independent evaluators who were expert at cross-cultural issues assessed the final report and course slide from each group. Both the report and the slides were rated (full score is 10) and their weights were .3 and .7 respectively. The final performance was calculated by averaging the two scores given by two evaluators.

5 Results

All groups completed the task on time and each delivered one report and course presentation slides. TeamRoom data showed members of experimental groups had asynchronous group discussion, sharing documents, made team announcements, wrote the team report and edited TeamRoom settings. Of the five control groups,

---

[1] As a measure of the reliability of psychometric instrument, Cronbach's alpha indicates the extent to which a set of test items can be treated as measuring a single latent variable.

three groups chose to use TeamRoom mostly to share documents. Of the two groups who didn't use TeamRoom, one registered a public mailbox where they could share documents and post chat logs and the other just used individual emails to share documents. Other than TeamRoom, self-reports and experiment-related data submitted by control groups revealed that they communicated by means of ICQ, MSN, email and text messaging over cell phone. They relied more on real-time communication tools, mostly ICQ which is the most popular synchronous communication software in China and occasionally MSN to perform the task. Four control groups built a team-shared ICQ discussion room. Members would discuss at the same time in the room. One control group just communicate one-to-one by ICQ and sent out the discussion results and pushed the progress via emails. A few participants from control groups used text messaging of cell phones to make notifications for discussion. Although control groups were given much freedom, they still chose to use what they are used to: they use emails and real-time communication tools all the time. Overall, the two conditions were both as designed: asynchronous vs. multi-synchronous virtual teams.

To test the effects of time on group efficacy development in experimental and control groups, a repeated measurement MANOVA was carried out with one between-group variable - condition (asynchronous vs. multi-synchronous condition) and one within-group variable (time). Group efficacy belief was used as dependent variable. Results showed that the interaction effect of time * condition was significant (F=6.062, $p<.05$, see figure 1). Subsequent univariate tests showed that the differences of group efficacy between time1 and time2, time 2 and time 4 were significant ($p<.05$) and the difference between time 1 and time 3 ($p = .055$) was marginally significant in experimental groups. Group efficacy didn't differ significantly over time in control groups (see table 1).

Results also showed that both time (F=3.373, $p<.05$) and condition (F= 6.062, $p<.05$) had a significant main effect on group efficacy. Subsequent univariate tests revealed that at time 2 and time 3, experimental and control group in the two comparative conditions revealed significant differences in their collective efficacy beliefs ($p < .05$). Control groups showed a significantly higher level of group efficacy than experimental group. That is to say, when the team members started working in two different conditions, group efficacy as a collective estimate in group's ability to perform the task differed. At time 1, the two conditions showed no significant difference in group efficacy beliefs. This indicated that the sampling was valid and the two groups had no pre-study bias in group efficacy. At time 4 when the task was approaching the end, their group efficacy estimations didn't differ significantly either.

Prior to relating group efficacy with group-level outcomes, a t-test was conducted to see if these variables in two conditions differed: TeamRoom evaluation, team satisfaction, performance and *TeamRoom Adoption* for which the following two indicators were used. Function Usage is calculated by the number of TeamRoom functions used; Content Contribution is assessed by the number of postings posted in TeamRoom. The results were presented in table 2 (N=5 for experimental groups; N = 5 for control groups for team satisfaction and performance and N=3 for TR Evaluation & using patterns). Except for the TeamRoom Adoption, all the other three variables didn't show significant differences. As expected, experimental groups made a much more frequent use of TeamRoom in terms of content contribution and function usage.

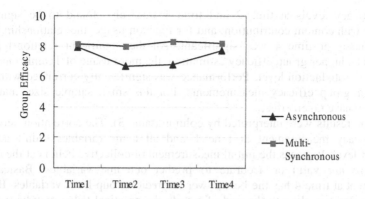

Fig. 1. Group Efficacy Development with Time in two Conditions (N = 40)

Table 1. Between-group comparison of Group Efficacy scores (N = 20 for each condition)

	Experiment Group		Control Group	
	M	SD	M	SD
Time 1	7.95	0.75	8.13	1.31
Time 2	6.69	1.09	7.98	1.08
Time 3	6.75	1.26	8.32	0.51
Time 4	7.70	1.21	8.18	0.97

Finally, to test how group efficacy correlates with team outcomes and to explore how the measurements of group efficacy at different times would better correlate with team outcomes, two correlation analyses were made respectively for the two conditions. All the correlations were based on aggregated data at the group level. Table 3 presented the results of experimental groups.

Table 2. Between-group tests of group outcomes

	Experimental Group		Control Group	
	M	SD	M	SD
TR Evaluation	10.15	1.58	9.55	1.31
Team Satisfaction	11.80	1.41	11.90	1.17
Content Contribution*	80.80	34.82	19.20	0.51
Function Usage*	7.80	2.17	2.40	1.51
Team Performance	7.67	0.96	7.73	0.85

$*p < .01$

First the table for experimental groups was interpreted row by row (table 3). Overall, group efficacy measurement was quite effective in indicating how participants think of the tool they used in performing the task, as the correlations with TeamRoom evaluation were all significant at time 2, 3 and 4. Team satisfaction was significantly correlated with the measurements of group efficacy at time 2 and 4.

Group efficacy levels at time 2 and time 4 were also found to be significantly correlated with content contribution; and for function usage, the relationship with the group efficacy at time 4 was significant. All the significant relationships were positive. The higher group efficacy estimation, the more usage of TeamRoom and the higher team satisfaction level. Performance was significantly correlated with no one of the four group efficacy measurements. For this small sample size, many other factors may have taken effect.

Then the results were interpreted by column (table 3). The correlation between the group efficacy measurement at time 1 and all team variables didn't achieve a significant level. It means the initial measurement of collective beliefs at the outset of a task was *not* valid or accurate to predict outcome variables. Basically, the measurement at time 4 has the best power to predict group-level variables. But since time 4 is often too close to the end of a task, the practical value may be weakened. Group efficacy measurement at time 2 turned out to be an alternative as it was significantly correlated with 3 of the group variables including team satisfaction and TeamRoom evaluation. For the measurement at time 3, the result was not very strong. The *GE_Avg.* was a simple average calculation of the four-time measurements. Its power was not distinctively stronger than that of other separate assessments. Thus it can be concluded that group efficacy was effective in reflecting some group-level outcomes in the asynchronous condition.

However, the correlation results in control groups were totally different. The relationships of all pairs of the variables were not significant. It showed group efficacy measurement were invalid in indicating group outcomes in the multi-synchronous environment.

Table 3. Correlations between group efficacy and team outcomes for experimental groups (N = 5)

	GE_t1	GE_t2	GE_t3	GE_t4	GE_Avg.
TR Evaluation	.374	**.976***	**.876***	**.911**	**.922***
Team Satisfaction	-.082	**.823**	.584	**.839**	.703
Content Contribution	.444	**.838***	.633	**.856***	**.906**
Function Adoption	.455	.785	.586	**.840***	**.894**
Team Performance	-.742	-.383	-.657	-.208	-.504

Note: Given a sample size of 5, it was necessary to set the significance level at .10 and even using the level of .10, power was only sufficient for detecting large effects (r>=.8) [8].
* $p < .01$. ** $p < .05$. *** $p < .10$.

6 Discussion

It has been part of life for people to use different information technologies such as email, groupware and real-time communication software to interact with copartners doing their daily work or perform tasks. Virtual teams have taken advantages of technology advancements and become popular in current organizations. This paper has presented an empirical study to explore how group efficacy developed over time and related with group outcomes in two kinds of typical virtual team computer-mediated environments. Results indicated that group efficacy changed over time in asynchronous condition and that group efficacy assessments differed across two comparative conditions. Group efficacy was found to be significantly correlated with TeamRoom rating and adoption and team satisfaction in asynchronous condition as well.

In the experimental condition where participants were constrained to work completely in a new groupware-supported environment, very interesting results were discovered. Group members experienced an abrupt drop at time 2 shortly after they formed a new team to start the task. According to team development theory, time2 during the task should be closest to the storming status [20]. In the storing phase, members began to realize the task is different or more difficult than they previously imagined. Anxious about progress, members might argue about what actions the group should take. And this situation was exacerbated especially when they were required to communicate and perform by a strange groupware system. It demanded extra efforts for them to get used to the system, and change their familiar ways to interact with other members. Experimental group members have tried to make most use of the shared space: having asynchronous threaded discussions, uploading and downloading documents, publishing team announcements and setting milestones. In addition, lack of immediacy prevented the group from clarifying status quo quickly; lack of personal interactions made it difficult for team building. Trust was weak. As members knew TeamRoom for the first time, it took time for them to know how to use it to push things forward. Collective beliefs in their group capability and future performance at that time turned weak. That's the probable reason why the groupware-supported groups experienced such a steep drop at time 2, 3 days later from time 1 when they met each other on the first day. The situation continued to time 3. After that, experimental groups recovered their efficacy beliefs gradually and had almost the same group efficacy estimation with control groups.

As opposed to that, control groups didn't share this pattern, although three out of the five groups used TeamRoom as well. As data indicated, control group members took TeamRoom largely as supplementary. The volume of TeamRoom content contribution and number of functions used by control groups were significantly smaller than those of experimental groups. They used TeamRoom more for document sharing than for discussion and further task management. So the new tool could be reasonably considered to have not much impact on the overall progress. Control group members did the task mostly in a way they usually did: scheduling on-line discussion with familiar real-time communication tools, sharing documents by email and notifying occurrences by cell phone message, etc. Despite no face-to-face meeting, the multiple ways of communication and frequent on-line interaction decreased the spatial and psychological distance among members. Across the ten days, group efficacy didn't show significant change within control groups.

However, the two groups did show significant differences in their group efficacy ratings at time 2 and time3: control groups exhibited a higher level of group efficacy than experimental groups. This result can be explained somewhat from the above description. What's more, as Bandura stated, one of the four sources of group efficacy is physiological and emotional arousal [2]. In the asynchronous environment where are solely supported by a new technology, the prolonged response and unfamiliarity with the working environment were likely to strengthen members' perception of task difficulty. This also would lead to negative emotions that decreased efficacy estimation.

Group efficacy was found to be significantly correlated with several group-level outcomes in experimental condition. TeamRoom evaluation ratings and adoption degree (content contribution and function usage) were significantly correlated with group efficacy. The higher level of group efficacy indicated a better evaluation of the tool and a stronger using inclination for the tool. Also, the higher group efficacy estimation means better group satisfaction. It validated the usefulness of group efficacy construct in possible longitudinal studies of technology adoption and impact [4]. From the study, it can be concluded that group efficacy is effective to indicate if users like the technology or if it works well when the technology really comes into play for interaction, at least in an asynchronous condition. Another interesting result is that the first measurement of group efficacy seemed invalid to signal team outcomes. It implies using group efficacy as a predictor, too early measurement would be of little use. Group efficacy measurement at time 2 was proved to be a good indicator as time 4 is often too late to make sense. In contrast again, control groups didn't get any significant correlation.

There is no significant relationship found between group efficacy and performance. Actually the paper is an initial exploration to examine the relationship between group efficacy and virtual team performance according to Hardin et al. [8]. Although strong links between group efficacy and performance among collocated teams has been established, the same relationship has not been established in virtual teams. The two important group outcomes - team satisfaction and performance, didn't demonstrate any significant difference between experimental and control groups either. A few possible explanations could be presented here. First, the small sample made the result not very strong. Second, task performance could be easily affected by other factors. For example, experimental group members had less personal interaction, which might make group communication more task-focused. Or some group might more depend on one or two members' exceptional capabilities instead of collective efforts. Third, as it was actually a "lab" study, participants joined the study voluntarily and had no steadfast obligation to perform the task to the utmost. These factors also pointed out the limitations that should be noted for the paper.

To sum up, group efficacy changes over time in asynchronous virtual teams, and is proved to be effective in investigating how technology impacts human-computer interaction and indicating technology adoption, especially when technology remarkably alters the way people usually work rather than just plays a minor role. In similar working contexts, group efficacy can be used as a signal to show if the environment serves collaboration well by avoiding the drop at the storming phase. Future research is needed to do deeper explorations with field data, e.g., practical virtual project teams, and to analyze the specific technology impacts on collaborative activities. The relationship of group efficacy and performance in virtual teams with the effect of technology should be investigated in more details.

References

1. Baker, D.F.: The Development of Collective Efficacy in Small Task Groups. Small Group Research 32(4), 451–474 (2001)
2. Bandura, A.A.: Self-efficacy: The Exercise of Control. Freeman, New York (1997)
3. Berry, G.R.: Can Computer-mediated Asynchronous Communication Improve Team Processes and Decision Making? Journal of Business Communication 43(4), 344–366 (2006)
4. Carroll, J.M., Rosson, M.B., Zhou, J.Y.: Collective Efficacy as a Measure of Community. In: CHI 2005, Portland, Oregon, USA, April 2-7, pp. 1–10 (2005)
5. Fiore, S.M., McDaniel, R.: Building Bridges: Connecting Virtual Teams Using Narrative and Technology. THEN 3 (2006)
6. Gibson, C.B.: Do They Do What They Believe They Can? Group Efficacy and Group Performance across Tasks and Cultures. Academy of Management Journal 42, 138–152 (1999)
7. Goddard, R.D., Hoy, W.K., Hoy, A.W.: Collective Efficacy Beliefs: Theoretical Developments, Empirical Evidence, and Future Directions. Educational Researcher 33(3), 3–13 (2004)
8. Hardin, A.M., Fuller, M.A., Valacich, J.S.: Measuring Group Efficacy in Virtual Teams: New Questions in an Old Debate. Small Group Research 37(1), 65–85 (2006)
9. Hardin, A.M.: Testing the Influence of Collective Efficacy Beliefs on Group Level Performance Metrics: An Investigation of the Virtual Team Efficacy-Performance Relationship in Global Information Systems Project Management Teams. Washington State University MIS Brown Bag Series, Pullman, Washington (2005)
10. Lipnack, J., Stamps, J.: Virtual Teams: People Working Across Boundaries with Technology. John Wiley and Sons, New York (2000)
11. Middup, C.P., Johnson, P.: Towards Using Technological Support of Group Memory in Problem-Solving Situations to Improve Self and Collective Efficacy. In: Proceedings of the 39th Hawaii International Conference on System Science, pp. 1–10 (2006)
12. Molli, P., Skaf-Molli, H., Oster, S., Jourdain, S.: Sams: Synchronous, asynchronous, multi-synchronous environments. In: The Seventh International Conference on CSCW in Design, Rio de Janeiro, Brazil (2002)
13. Neale, D.C., Carroll, J.M., Rosson, M.B.: Evaluation Computer-supported Cooperative Work: Models and Frameworks. In: Proceedings of CSCW, Chicago, November 8-10, pp. 368–377. ACM, New York (2004)
14. Paskevich, D.M., Brawley, L.R., Dorsch, K.D., Widmeyer, W.N.: Relationship between Collective Efficacy and Team Cohesion: Conceptual and Measurement Issues. Group Dynamics 3, 210–222 (1999)
15. Pescosolido, A.T.: Informal Leaders and the Development of Group Efficacy. Small Group Research 32(1), 74–93 (2001)
16. Qu, C.T., Nejdl, W.: Constructing a Web-based Asynchronous and Synchronous Collaboration Environment using WebDAV and Lotus Sametime. In: SIGUCCS '01, Portland, Oregon, USA (2001)
17. Ramalingam, V., Wiedenbeck, S.: Development and Validation of Scores on a Computer Programming Self-efficacy Scale and Group Analysis of Novice Programmer Self-efficacy. Journal of Educational Computing Research 19(4), 365–379 (1998)
18. Stajkovic, A.D., Luthans, F.: Self-efficacy and Work-related Performance: A Meta-analysis. Pschological Bulletin 124(2), 240–261 (1998)

19. Stevenson, T.: Synchronous and Asynchronous Collaboration...Collaborate (2005), VoIP Planet Webcast: www.voipplanet.com
20. Tuckman, B.W.: Developmental Sequence in Small Groups. Psychological Bulletin 63, 384–389 (1965)
21. Watson, C.B., Chemers, M.M., Preiser, N.: Collective Efficacy: A Multilevel Analysis. Personality and Social Psychology Bulletin 27(8), 1057–1068 (2001)
22. Whiteoak, J.W., Chalip, L., Hort, L.K.: Assessing Group Efficacy: Comparing Three Methods of Measurement. Small Group Research 35(2), 158–173 (2004)
23. Zellars, K.L., Hochwarter, W.A., Perrewe, P.L., Miles, A.K., Kiewitz, C.: Beyond self-efficacy: Interactive effects of role conflict and perceived collective efficacy. Journal of Managerial 13, 483–499 (2001)

Mutual Awareness in Collocated and Distant Collaborative Tasks Using Shared Interfaces

A. Pauchet, F. Coldefy, L. Lefebvre, S. Louis Dit Picard, A. Bouguet,
L. Perron, J. Guerin, D. Corvaisier, and M. Collobert

France Télécom R&D, 2 Av. Pierre Marzin, 22307 Lannion
{alexandre.pauchet, francois.coldefy}@orange-ftgroup.com

Abstract. Shared interface allowing several users in co-presence to interact simultaneously on digital data on a single display is an uprising challenge in Human Computer Interaction (HCI). Its development is motivated by the advent of large displays such as wall-screens and tabletops. It affords fluid and natural digital interaction without hindering human communication and collaboration. It enables mutual awareness, making participant conscious of each other activities.

In this paper, we are interested in Mixed Presence Groupware (MPG), when two or more remote shared interfaces are connected for a distant collaborative session. Our contribution strives to answer to the question: Can the actual technology provide sufficient presence feeling of the remote site to enable efficient collaboration between two distant groups?

We propose DIGITABLE, an experimental platform we hope lessen the gap between collocated and distant interaction. DIGITABLE is combining a multiuser tactile interactive tabletop, a video-communication system enabling eye-contact with real size distant user visualization and a spatialized sound system for speech transmission. A robust computer vision module for distant users' gesture visualization completes the platform.

We discuss first experiments using DIGITABLE for a collaborative task (mosaic completion) in term of distant mutual awareness. Although DIGITABLE does not provide the same presence feeling in distant and or collocated situation, a first and important finding emerges: distance does not hinder efficient collaboration anymore.

1 Introduction

Shared interfaces allowing multiuser interaction in co-presence on a single device is a challenging Human Computer Interaction (HCI) research field. Though, from the Xerox Parc Colab project in 1986 dedicated to informal group meetings [1] [2], the domain produces relatively few literature in comparison to collaborative systems based on distant personal workstation.

The relevance of shared interfaces has been yet precisely identified. Shared interfaces are complementary to common personal digital devices, such as Personal Computers (PC), Personal Digital Assistants (PDA) and personal phones. It does not hinder interaction between people when accessing to the digital world. It conveys more conviviality and does not draw the attention of the participants

C. Baranauskas et al. (Eds.): INTERACT 2007, LNCS 4662, Part I, pp. 59–73, 2007.

from their interaction. In contrast, the one-person/one-computer paradigm of personal interfaces *de facto* tends to impede direct human communication whenever interaction with data is needed: a user has to focus his/her attention on his/her personal device to find data, while his/her partners are waiting to see the sought information. With shared interfaces which use large displays such as wall-screens or tabletops, data are reachable by every participant at anytime. No disruptive turn-taking occurs anymore. Interactions are explicit, visible (hand gesture, pen pointing) and thus understandable by everyone: shared interfaces are in line with day-to-day people interaction. They help bridging the gap between physical world (human to human interaction) and digital world (human to computer and human to computer to human interaction).

We are especially interested in distant collaboration between groups, and the so called Mixed Presence Groupware (MPG) [3], connecting two (or more) distant shared interfaces. Creative domain, such as co-design, architecture, urbanism, etc., is particularly concerned by MPG: it often involves remote teams manipulating graphical objects (images, drawings, plans, etc.) for which shared interfaces propose adapted natural interactions (pen based, tactile or gesture interactions). However, distant collaboration has to preserve as far as possible the fluidity of interaction and the mutual awareness provided by co-presence. Following Tang *et al.* [3], we focus on remote gesture visualization of distant users, as it conveys major information facilitating distant communication such as intentionality (who is intending to do what), action identity (who is doing what) and pointing [4] [5].

We propose DIGITABLE, a platform combining a multiuser tactile tabletop, a video-communication system enabling eye-contact with real size distant user visualization and a spatialized sound system. A robust computer vision module for distant users' gesture visualization completes the set-up. The main question this paper strives to answer is: may the collaboration between two distant groups be as efficient as the collocated collaboration, providing technical tools to convey elements of the distant context (real size distant user video, remote gesture visualization)? We present a collaborative application designed to investigate collaboration efficiency and presence feeling in distant and collocated situation.

Many parameters are involved to evaluate the efficiency of conveyed context elements: it depends on the type of the task which induces more or less importance to the person or to the task-space [6], on the spatial configuration of participants around the table (face-to-face, side-by-side in collocated or remote situations), the type of the manipulated documents (abstract, figurative or textual) and the technology provided by the remote platform (remote gesture visualization). In this paper, we focus on a digital puzzle completion task as first experiment. We investigate how document type may influence implicit creation of private and shared spaces and the way participants tightly or loosely collaborate whether they are in a remote or collocated configuration.

The remain of this paper is organized as follows: Section 2 presents a state of the art on shared interfaces, distant collaboration and mutual awareness. In Section 3 we specify our objectives. Section 4 describes the DIGITABLE platform whereas Section 5 details the experiment. Findings are resumed in Section 6. Conclusion and future work are in section 7.

2 Related Work

The development of shared interfaces relies on the advent of new display devices, such as large wall-screens or tabletops, and on the development of platforms assuming multiple independent inputs. Thus, in a first attempt to address multiuser application on a single display in co-presence, the Xerox Parc Colab Project (1987-1992) [1] proposed a PC network allowing private work as well as control of a shared digital white-board. In 1993, Pederson et al. [2] extended the Xerox Liveboard concept and proposed Tivoli, an electronic white-board application for supporting informal workgroup meetings, using a large screen pen-based interactive display allowing up to three simultaneous pen interactions. Tivoli strove to provide its users with simplicity of use, easily understood functionalities, and access to computational power to augment informal meeting practices. However, multiuser interaction was not the main focus of [1] [2].

In 1991, also at Xerox Parc, Bier et al. [7] developed MMM, a multiuser editor managing up to three mice simultaneously on the same computer. In 1998, Greenberg et al.[8] proposed a Shared Notes system investigating how people move from individual to workgroup through the use of both PDA and a shared public display. Later in 1999, Stewart et al. [9] defined the Single Display Groupware concept (SDG), which stemmed from their work on children groups. Their experiments on a shared drawing application on PC showed that multi-mouse implementation was largely preferred by children to single mouse version because it provides more fun and more activity. Hourcade et al. [10] proposed a Multiple Input Devices (MID) offering a Java toolkit for simultaneous use of multiple independent devices for Windows 98. Tse et al. [11] proposed a toolkit for fast SDG prototyping on Microsoft.Net. Microsoft Research India renews the challenge on multi-mouse interaction for computers to respond to educational needs in rural primary schools in developing countries where very few computers are available per student (one PC for ten students) [12].

The Calgary University GroupLab has investigated groupware interaction for long time. Gutwin [13] analyzed workspace awareness for distributed groupware. In line with Gutwin, Tang et al. [14] extended the SDG concept to MPG, by connecting two or more SDG at distant places for remote and collocated collaboration. The authors focused on presence disparity, describing that people do not interact similarly with their collocated and distant partners. They proposed and analyzed distant groupware embodiments, such as telepointers or remote gesture visualization in distant communication and collaboration [3].

We focus on tabletop displays as a horizontal surface which encourages group members to work in a socially cohesive and conducive way. It affords seamless role-changing and more equitable decision-making and information access [15]. TableTop, as a shared input/output device, is an emerging interdisciplinary domain involving augmented reality, user interface technologies, multi-modal and multi-user interaction, CSCW, and information visualization. Scott *et al.* [16] proposed first guidelines for collocated collaborative work design on Tabletop based on human factor analysis.

In 2001, Dietz *et al.*[17] presented MERL Diamond Touch, a multi-user touch table for which each tactile interaction is associated to one user. Enabling up to 8 simultaneous user interactions, bi-manual or multi-touch interaction per user is however hindered by the hardware, which does not provide the loci of the contacts, but the bounding box encompassing these user's contacts. In contrast, Rekimoto's Smartskin [18] is a real multi-touch device, but without user identification. Note that several multi-touch devices have emerged: Bérard's Magic Table [19], Wilson's TouchLight [20], the low-cost Multi-touch sensing surface of Han [21] and Philips 's Entertaible [22] among numerous examples. By now, the Diamond Touch is the only commercially available multitouch tabletop.

3   Motivations

We aim at designing a collaborative platform for distant groupware collaboration which preserves the characteristics of a real face-to-face interaction. Our approach is based on Gutwin's workspace awareness analysis [13], who organized previous works of Endsley on situation awareness [23], Segal on consequential communication [24] and Clark *et al.* on conversational grounding [25].

Situational awareness is knowledge of a dynamic environment, it is maintained through perceptual information gathered from the environment and others' activities. It is peripheral to the primary group activity [13]. It depends on perception, comprehension and prediction of the environment and of others' actions [23]. It relies on non intentional informational sources such as *consequential communication, artifacts manipulation*, and on *intentional communication. Consequential communication* is information that emerges from a person's activity [24]. It is non intentional and most of it is conveyed by the visual channel: position, posture, head, arms, hands' movement, *etc. Artifacts* are a second source of information about the current actions in progress because their characteristic sound depending on the action (moving, stacking, dividing, and so on) gives salient feedbacks of their use. Finally, *intentional communication*, through conversation and gestures (deictic, manifesting or visual evidence actions), completes the perceptual information gathered about the environment. Situational awareness is the way people maintain up-to-date mental models of complex and dynamic environments. It helps to be aware of the state of task objects and of one another's activities. It facilitates to plan what to say or to do and to coordinate speech and actions.

Visual information helps also people to communicate about the task to be done by ensuring that their message is properly understood. It enables the expansion of their common ground during the session and facilitates mutual understanding between participants. There is significantly less talk about the talk, or about the task to be done [25].

We aim at conceiving a platform which preserves at most situational awareness for remote groupware collaboration. We choose tabletops first because it is a now available shared interface, and above all because it is probably the most common tool used for group meetings and human interaction. Interaction and communication around a table are observed to be more equally distributed between participants in contrast to white-boards which often induce role disparity as the person at the board is given to be the leader's meeting [15].

To facilitate intentional communication and presence feeling, we choose to use a video-communication system providing real size visualization of the distant users and eye-contact by means of a spy camera (see section 4 for details). As Tang et al. [3] [14], we add a computer vision module allowing to capture the local gesture of the participant on or above the table and to transmit it to the distant site for overlay on the distant desktop image. This remote gesture visualization module, similar but probably more robust than Video-Arms [14], combined with the video-communication system, participates in conveying most of the visual information needed to feed situational awareness.

Thus DIGITABLE, the designed platform, should provide people with coordination, as participants can see each other through video-communication and others' actions through remote gesture visualization on the tabletop. It should support action identity as participants are able to perceive who is doing what. They also can anticipate which action the distant participants intend to do, and which digital object they are about to grasp as they see arms and hands above the table at the distant site. Most of the common social rules are therefore preserved, as involuntary conflicts about availability of objects are avoided. Finally, intentional communication is partially enhanced as participant also can point to digital object to show something or explain an action or an idea.

We aim at investigating how distance affects collaborative interaction when most of visual information needed for mutual awareness is provided. Many parameters are involved: the type of the task which induces more or less importance to the person or to the task space [6], the spatial configuration of participants around the table (face-to-face, side-by-side in collocated or remote situations), the type of the manipulated documents (abstract, figurative or textual) and the technology provided by the remote platform (remote gesture visualization).

We focus on a digital mosaic completion task for a first experiment application. In contrast to puzzles, mosaics are composed of squared pieces. Task domain prevails in such an application as participants feel implicitly challenged to complete the mosaic as fast as possible although this is not required.

On-table textual puzzle completions has been investigated by Kruger et al. [26] who observed three roles of the piece orientation: understanding (ex: reading), coordination (an implicit private space is created when a piece is oriented toward a particular user) and communication (voluntary orientation of a piece toward a user is used to raise his/her attention). Their main finding was that users significantly touch more often pieces oriented toward themselves than those oriented toward another user. Pieces perpendicularly oriented are considered as public. The authors focused mainly on document orientation but not on the document localization. We are interested in extending Kruger *et al.*'s results to mosaic completion in collocated and distant digital situation. We think that the localization of the pieces on the table may also contribute to design implicit private areas, as Kruger *et al.* showed for piece orientation. We will also focus on the influence of the image type of the mosaic on the completion processes. Finally, we will experiment in both remote an collocated configuration involving two participants.

4   DigiTable Platform

DIGITABLE is a platform combining a multiuser tactile interactive tabletop, a video-communication system enabling eye-contact with real size distant user visualization, a computer vision module for remote gesture visualization of the distant users and a spatialized sound system. (see Fig. 1 and Fig. 2).

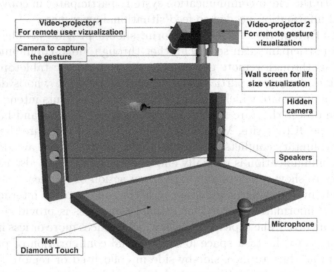

Fig. 1. DIGITABLE is a platform combining a Diamond Touch, a video-communication system, a spatialized audio system and a computer vision module

We use Merl Diamond Touch [17], which is hitherto the only available shared tabletop for simultaneous multiuser interaction. This device is a passive tactile surface on which the desktop image is projected from a ceiling mounted video-projector (video-projector 2 of Fig. 1).

The video-communication system uses a spy camera hidden behind a rigid wood-screen and peeping through an almost unnoticeable 3mm wide hole. A second video-projector (video-projector 1 of Fig. 1) beams on the wall-screen the video of the distant site captured by the symmetric remote spy camera (see Fig. 2). Eye-contact is guaranteed by approximately placing the camera peephole at the estimated eyes'height of a seated person and beaming the distant video on the screen such that the peephole and the distant user's eyes coincide.

Fine tuning of hole's design and video-projector beam's orientation is performed to avoid camera's dazzle.

The computer vision module uses a camera placed at the ceiling and pointing at the tabletop. The module consists of a segmentation process detecting any object above the table by comparing, at almost the frame rate, between the captured camera image and the actual known desktop image projected on the tabletop, up to a geometric and color distortion. In output, it produces an image mask of the detected objects (hands, arms, or any object) extracted from the camera image. The mask is compressed using RLE (Run Length Encoding) and is sent through the network to the distant site. There, the image mask is decompressed and then overlaid with the current desktop image before projection on the tabletop. We use semi-transparency to let the user see the desktop "under" the arms of his/her distant partner.

DIGITABLE manages a network-based video-conference system (see Fig. 2). If necessary, to avoid lag problems due to network, the video system can also be separated from the rest of the architecture and runs with direct cable connexion.

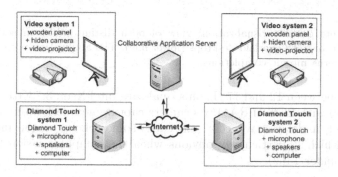

Fig. 2. DIGITABLE Architecture: shared application and remote gesture analysis is implemented at each distant site on a single work station

Fig. 3 shows users' gesture and their visualization on the remote site. The left bottom image shows the overlay of the detected hand of site 2 (upper right image); the right bottom image shows the overlay of the detected arms of the site 1 (upper left image).

The computer vision module improves four technical weaknesses of VideoArms [3]. 1) it detects any object on or over the table without needing any learning stage or *a priori* knowledge about the object to detect; 2) no restriction on the projected images is imposed (Video-Arms needs dark tones images); 3) it is robust to external lightning changes (variation in the daylight or in the artificial lightning); 4) calibration is automatic. The computer vision algorithm provides 32 image masks per second when running alone for a SXGA (1280x1024) image desktop and a medium camera resolution (384x288) (we use a Sony EVI-D70 whose pan, tilt and zoom functions facilitates the camera view control). When combined with the shared Java application, the image masks are refreshed on

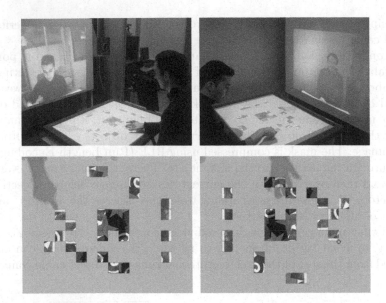

Fig. 3. Remote gesture visualization: view of both distant tables in action (upper line) and view of both overlaid desktops (lower line). The application presented in the pictures concerns mosaic completions.

each site at between 12 and 17 Hz on a dual-core Intel Xeon 3.73GHz (Netburst architecture) with 2GB of RAM. As camera capture and desktop image are not synchronized, a delay may occur and cause some echoes on the image mask detection, which is particularly obvious when the computer vision frame rate drops low (under 14hz).

5   User Study

We aim at investigating how distance affects interaction and collaboration when most of visual information needed for mutual awareness is provided. As said earlier, many parameters are involved: the type of the task, the spatial configuration of participants around the table, the type of the manipulated documents and the technology provided by the remote platform (remote gesture visualization).

We focus on a digital mosaic completion task as first experiment application. Collaborative mosaic completion will be performed by two users in both collocated or distant situations in order to evaluate the role of distance in term of task efficiency. Furthermore, mosaic completion will be analyzed according to the role of the piece orientation.

In the collocated situation, the users are sitting side-by-side in front of the table as this configuration seems the most natural. In remote configuration, the users are virtually sitting face-to-face, on both sides of the table, using

the DIGITABLE platform. We thought that this arrangement was more convenient to distant communication as it was compatible to video-communication.
This follows Tang recommendation [27], as face-to-face collaboration is more
comfortable for verbal and non-verbal interaction. Furthermore, it was compliant with the situated-literal approach suggested by Gutwin's [13] for shared
workspace conception: the situated-literal configuration consists of displaying
distant visual awareness information *literally* (not symbolic) at the workspace
place where it is originated from. It is in line with the way people use their
existing skills with mechanism of feedthrough[1], consequential and gestural communication [13].

The experiment is designed to be series of 6 mosaic completions, 3 in collocated situation and 3 in distant situation. The mosaics are composed of 5x5
squared pieces. For each situation, 3 different mosaic types (abstract, figurative
and textual) are completed by the pairs of participants. A textual mosaic represents a text (here a poem): the "right" orientation of each piece can be easily
inferred as it contains words and typos. A figurative mosaic represents a scene
or a portrait: the "right" orientation of each piece is more ambiguous and can
necessitate to assembly many pieces before being deduced. An abstract mosaic
represents an abstract painting or a fractal: the only orientation constraint is
that all the pieces have the same final orientation.

To solve the mosaics, a Java application has been designed to run locally
on a Diamond Touch and on the DIGITABLE platform. Because of the Diamond Touch technical limitations, the application supports multiuser manipulation of pieces but only one-finger interaction per user. Only two action types
on the mosaic pieces are allowed: moving or rotating a piece. A mosaic piece
can be moved by the users along an invisible grid by touching it near its center and dragging it from one place to another. It can also be rotated but in
90 degrees steps as its edges have to remain parallel to the table sides. The
user has to touch around one of the 4 piece corners, and to perform a rotational motion. A visual feedback is given to let the user identify the current selected action (a cross pointer for dragging, and a round arrow for
rotation).

During the mosaic completions, the pairs of subjects were filmed and all their
actions were recorded (piece number, situation and orientation on the table of
the touched piece, action type - rotation or moving).

A total of 24 participants took part in the study, randomly put in pairs. There
were one female pair, six male pairs and five mixed pairs. All participants were
postgraduates, had normal or corrected to normal vision. During the experiments, the order of the mosaic completions were counterbalanced in situations
(collocated and distant) and in mosaic types (abstract, figurative and textual).
The pairs of participants completed an individual training period before the 6
collaborative mosaic completions.

---

[1] As Dix *et al.* remarks [28], when artifacts are manipulated, they give off information
which is *feedback* for the person performing the action and *feedthrough* for the persons
who are watching.

6   Findings

6.1   Objective Evaluation

Comparison of Mosaic Types: Figurative mosaics are completed more quickly (M=362s, SD=182s) than textual mosaics (M=435s, SD=394s). Abstract mosaic completions are the most time consuming (M=565s, SD=394s). The completion times of the three mosaic types are compared using a Friedman Anova and a significant difference is observed (F(2)=30.3, p<0.001). Post-hoc comparisons are performed which reveal significant differences between the completion time of each pair of mosaic types. The same observations are made when considering the two conditions (collocated vs distant) separately.

Textual mosaics are completed with less rotations (M=29, SD=5) than figurative mosaics (M=59, SD=31). Abstract mosaic completions require more rotations (M=86, SD=52). The three mosaic types are compared using a Friedman Anova and a significant difference is observed (F(2)=33.1, p<0.001). Post-hoc comparisons are performed which reveal significant differences between each pair of mosaic types. The same observations are made when considering the two conditions (collocated vs distant). These differences reflect the difficulty to find the right orientation of each piece of abstract mosaic pieces.

Comparison Between Collocated and Distant Situations: For all the kind of mosaic (Text, figurative or abstract), a Wilcoxon test reveals no significant differences between mosaic completions times in co-presence (M=397s, SD=221s) and in remote configuration (M=441s, SD=237s).

Concerning the particular class of textual mosaics, no significant difference exists between resolution times in remote configuration (M=456s, SD=210s) and in co-presence (M=368s, SD=149s). No significant differences are observed between number of rotations in co-presence (M=53, SD=23) and in remote configuration (M=56, SD=26) as well as between number of movings in co-presence (M=132, SD=43) and in remote configuration (M=146, SD=56).

Mosaic Completion Processes in Collocated and Distant Situations: In the side-by-side/collocated situation, the subjects exploit a larger surface on the table than in the face-to-face/distant situation (see Fig. 4). Moreover, the strategies used to complete the mosaics are different. In the side-by-side/collocated situation, each user tends to work independently before merging their assemblage: two distinct areas are visible on the right image of Fig. 4. In distant/face-to-face situation the users tends to work together on the same zone of the table (only one main area on the left image of Fig. 4).

The dominant orientation of the pieces for textual mosaics is also different in side-by-side/collocated and face-to-face/distant configuration since in the first case, the orientation of the pieces is not conflicting whereas in the second case the subjects have to negotiate to find the more comfortable orientation. With no surprise, in the side-by-side situation, the pieces are oriented toward the two subjects. In the face-to-face situation, two strategies were equally used by

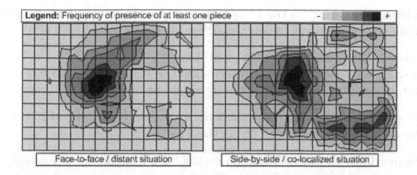

Fig. 4. Dominant localizations of the pieces on the table during the mosaic completions

the subjects: orientate the pieces toward one of the subject or perpendicularly. Pieces oriented toward a particular subject are mostly situated around his/her right hand (*i.e.* on the right of the table for pieces oriented toward the downside of the table and on the left of the table for pieces oriented toward the upside of the table).

Discussion: From these first results from objective criteria, no significant difference can be observed between distant and collocated situations when considering completion time, type of mosaic and piece manipulation (number of rotations and moves). Consequently, the actual technology conveys sufficient context's elements of the remote sites to enable efficient collaboration between two distant groups without hindering the completion of the task.

However, distant and collocated configurations differ in term of coupling. Coupling [29] qualifies the degree people are working together. It can evolve to loose coupling when each person can work without needing information from another person, to tight coupling when they collaborate. This observed difference may be due more to the spatial configuration (side-by-side *vs* face-to-face) than to the co-localization or distant parameter. Indeed, in side-by-side configuration, people tend to impede each other's interaction on piece access and manipulation. This probably favors a first independent phase during which each user tries to complete an independent part of the puzzle. Furthermore, such coupling may be biased by the fact that our mosaic application does not facilitate independent work merging. One can not move and rotate a group of pieces. This interaction is actually boredom as it has to be done one piece at a time. Thus, loose coupling may be hindered in the face-to-face configuration in favor of an early collaboration.

6.2   User Experience

Subjects were asked to comment the mosaic completions by focusing on the application and on the differences between the distant and collocated situations.

Mosaic Application: To the 1st question ("What do you think of the mosaic application?"), the most common remarks made by the 24 subjects are:

- It is difficult to rotate the pieces (19 subjects).
- Moving many pieces simultaneously should be managed (14 subjects).
- Rotating many pieces simultaneously should be managed (9 subjects).

These remarks confirm that some users have completed sub-parts of the mosaic and would have needed tools to merge these parts.

Configuration: To the 2nd question ("Could you compare mosaic completion in collocated and in remote situations?"), the most common remarks made are:

- When concentrated on the mosaic completion, the video-communication system is not useful, but the sound system is (14 subjects).
- The major trouble is reading the textual mosaic in face-to-face (distant) situation (13 users).
- The distant gesture representation is interesting since it brings communicational and intentional information (7 users).
- The same users also remark that the other user's hands are not always easy to see (7 users).
- 6 users find the mosaic completions more pleasant in collocated situation, 3 in distant situation and 2 found the two situations identical. The other users did not compare the two situation in that way.

As our experiments were focused on a mosaic completion task, people do not need to look at each other during interaction. The participants feel useless the video-communication system.

Only 6 over 24 users openly prefer the collocated situation, the others are indifferent at worst case. Thanks to remote gesture visualization, collocated and distant collaboration are both worthwhile experience. Distant collaboration is not seen as a poor ersatz of co-present interaction.

The reading problems due to orientation of textual pieces in the face-to-face situation are more critical. It is not explicitly due to the distant configuration.

Subjective Opinions: We have selected a few comments from the subjects which are particularly representative of how the experiment was felt:

- "It is better in the remote configuration, more efficient, arms do not cross: we do not bother each other"
- "There is no presence feeling with the video system. I felt as if I played alone and the robot sometimes helps me."
- "In the distant situation, we are forced to speak, other's actions are more difficult to perceive."
- "We are more efficient in the side-by-side configuration, it is easier to read."

The users sometimes mix remarks about distance factor and spatial configurations (face-to-face *vs.* side-by-side configurations) since distant and collocated situations are not symmetric. Although experiments have shown that collocated and distant collaboration are comparable in terms of efficiency, presence feeling may be radically different (see the second comment about the robot). This can be seen as the fact that we respect almost all the Gutwin's recommendations about workspace awareness (we provide tools for intentional and consequential communication) but not the artifacts and feedthrough. Remote gesture visualization lacks of incarnation. The presence feeling of the distant participant may be enhanced with sound effects of piece manipulation.

Further experiments are necessary to conclude on the influence of each parameter on the collaboration strategy.

7   Conclusion and Future Work

In this paper, we propose DIGITABLE, a collaborative platform which combines a multiuser tactile interactive tabletop, a video-communication system enabling eye-contact with real size distant user visualization, a spatialized sound system and a computer vision module for distant users' gesture visualization.

Preliminary evaluation of DIGITABLE highlights important issues for the design of collaborative tabletop interfaces. Distance does not hinder efficient collaboration anymore. No significant difference has been observed between collocated or distant situations in term of task efficiency or object manipulations whatever the document type was (here abstract, figurative or textual mosaics). Participants find the distant gesture visualization useful. Thus, distant or collocated tabletop collaboration are now both worthwhile experiences. However, our mosaic application compelled participants to focus on the tasks space. Therefore, communication and negotiation are reduced to a very tiny part, so that users consider useless the real size visualization of their partner. Furthermore, DIGITABLE does not provide the same presence feeling in distant or collocated situations: remote people need to be more incarnated as their presence is still abstractly felt.

It is currently too early to pronounce a definite evaluation on such a platform. A lot has to be experimented as many parameters are involved: the type of the task which induces more or less importance to the person or to the task space, the spatial placement of the participants (face-to-face, side-by-side for a collocated or remote configuration), and the type of the manipulated documents (abstract, figurative or textual). In a further work, we will conduct two different experiments : the first one will focus on the spatial placement of the users in remote and collocated situations, the second will address an application for which the negotiation between participants will take precedent on the completion. This last experiment will complete our observation on the role of video-communication channel.

Finally, DIGITABLE needs also a few technical improvements to enhance the presence feeling: improve of the quality of video and sound, increase the opacity of hand representation and take into account more feedthrough such as rubbing noises. Concerning the mosaic application, the rotation problems encountered by the users could be easily solved by increasing the surface dedicated to the rotations on the pieces. To avoid asymmetric behaviors from the users on each distant sites, the fact that users can be right or left handed has to be thoroughly considered. Finally, the application should support containers to move and/or rotate set of pieces at the same time, to enable fitting of mosaic parts independently completed. This last point should induce more loose coupling in the collaborative task. A new series of experiments will be launched when these technical improvements will be integrated.

Acknowledgments. This work is supported by the French government within the RNTL Project DIGITABLE and the Media and Networks Cluster.

References

1. Stefik, M., Bobrow, D., Foster, G., Lanning, S., Tatar, D.: Wysiwis revised: Early experiences with multi-user interfaces. ACM Transactions on Office Information Systems 5(2), 147–167 (1987)
2. Pederson, E., McCall, K., Moran, T., Halasz, F.: Tivoli: an electronic whiteborad for informal workgroup meeting. In: interCHI'93, pp. 391–398 (1993)
3. Tang, A., Neustaedter, C., Greenberg, S.: Videoarms: embodiments in mixed presence groupware. In: the BCS-HCI British HCI Group Conference (2006)
4. Kraut, R., Fussel, S., Siegel, J.: Visual information as a conversational resource in collaborative physical tasks. HCI journal 18, 13–49 (2003)
5. Kirk, D., Stanton, D., Rodden, T.: The effect of remote gesturing on distance instruction. In: CSCL'05 (2005)
6. Buxton, W.: Telepresence: integrating shared task and person spaces. In: Graphics Interface '92, pp. 123–129 (1992)
7. Bier, E., Freeman, S.: Mmm: A user interface architecture for shared editors on a single screen. In: UIST'91, pp. 79–86 (1991)
8. Greenberg, S., Boyle, M.: Moving between personal devices and public displays. In: Workshop on Handheld CSCW (November 1998)
9. Stewart, J., Bederson, B.B., Druin, A.: Single display groupware: a model for co-present collaboration. In: CHI'99, pp. 286–293 (1999)
10. Hourcade, J.P., Bederson, B.B.: Architecture and implementation of a java package for multiple input devices (mid). Tech Report HCIL-99-08 (1999)
11. Tse, E., Greenberg, S.: Sdgtoolkit: A toolkit for rapidly prototyping single display groupware. In: CSCW'02 (November 2002)
12. Pawar, U., Pal, J., Toyoma, K.: Multiple mice for computers in education in developing countries. In: ICTD (2006)
13. Gutwin, C., Greenberg, S.: A descriptive framework of workspace awareness for real-time groupware. Awareness in CSCW 11, 411–446 (2002)
14. Tang, A., Boyle, M., Greenberg, S.: Understanding and mitigating display and presence disparity in mixed presence groupware. Journal of Research and Practice in Information Technology 37(2) (2005)
15. Rogers, Y., Lindley, S.E.: Collaborating around vertical and horizontal large interactive displays: which way is best? Interacting with Computers 6, 1133–1152 (2004)
16. Scott, S.D., Grant, K.D., Mandryk, R.L.: System guidelines for co-located, collaborative work on a tabletop display (2003)

17. Dietz, P.H., Leigh, D.: DiamondTouch: A Multi-User Touch Technology. In: UIST'01, pp. 229–226 (November 2001)
18. Rekimoto, J.: Smartskin: An infrastructure for freehand manipulation on interactive surfaces (2002)
19. Bérard, F.: The Magic Table: Computer-Vision Based Augmentation of a Whiteboard for Creative Meetings. In: PROCAM'03, Nice, France (June 2003)
20. Wilson, A.: Touchlight: an imaging touch screen and display for gesture based interaction. In: ICMI'04 (2004)
21. Han, J.: Low-cost multi-touch sensing through frustrated total internal reflection. In: UIST, pp. 115–118 (2005)
22. Hollemans, G., Bergman, T., Buil, V., van Gelder, K., Groten, M., Hoonhout, J., Lashina, T., van Loenen, E., van de Wijdeven, S.: Entertaible: multi user multi-object concurrent input. In: UIST'06 (2006)
23. Endsley, M.: Toward a theory of situation awareness in dynamic systems. Human Factors 37(1), 32–64 (1998)
24. Segal, L.: Designing team workstations: The choreography of teamwork, in local applications. Local Applications of the Ecological Approach to Human-Machine Systems (1995)
25. Clark, H., Brennan, S.: Grounding in communication. In: Readings in Groupware and Computer Supported Cooperative Work: Assisting Human- Human Collaboration (M.-K. Publishers, ed.), pp. 222–233 (1991)
26. Kruger, R., Carpendale, S., Scott, S., Greenberg, S.: How people use orientation on tables: comprehension, coordination and communication. In: GROUP'03, Sanibel Island, USA, pp. 369–378. ACM Press, New York (2003)
27. Tang, J.: Findings from observational studies of collaborative work. International Journal of Man-Machine Studies 34(2), 143–160 (1991)
28. Dix, A., Finlay, J., Abowd, G., Beale, R.: Human-Computer Interaction (1993)
29. Salvador, T., Scholtz, J., Larson, J.: The denver model for groupware design. ACM SIGCHI Bulletin archive 28, 52–58 (1996)

A Proxy-Based Infrastructure for Web Application Sharing and Remote Collaboration on Web Pages

Richard Atterer[1], Albrecht Schmidt[2], and Monika Wnuk[1]

[1] Media Informatics Group
Ludwig-Maximilians-University Munich, Germany
richard.atterer@ifi.lmu.de, monius@fnuked.de
[2] Fraunhofer IAIS; BIT, University of Bonn
Schloss Birlinghoven, St. Augustin, Germany
albrecht.schmidt@acm.org

Abstract. When people collaborate remotely, the WWW is part of the shared resources they use together. However, web pages do not offer support for collaborative interaction such as viewing or influencing another user's browsing session – additional software needs to be installed for these features. In this paper, we present UsaProxy 2, an HTTP proxy that allows the same web page or application to be viewed and used in two browsers at the same time, without client-side software installation. This includes a visualisation of the remote user's mouse pointer, scrolling, keyboard input, following links to other pages and more. Our open-source proxy modifies HTML pages before delivering them to the browsers. The added JavaScript code provides session monitoring and shared browsing facilities. We conducted an experimental evaluation which shows that our approach works for different scenarios, such as shopping online and exchanging ideas on what to buy. The user study showed that our approach is accepted and liked by users. Combined with audio or text chat communication, it provides a very useful tool for informal, ad-hoc collaboration.

1   Introduction

Informal collaborative use of the WWW is nowadays very common, but not supported well by current technologies. Typically, users have a chat or audio connection and use their web browsers independently of each other, exchanging URLs via text messages or by spelling them. As a result, much of the conversation is about the current context and the content the users look at, and not about the task at hand that needs to be solved. Often, problems arise – for example, a web page may not be viewable by the remote user because of the use of session cookies. In our paper, we investigate how shared browsing sessions can be supported with lightweight technologies, i.e. in such a way that neither client-side software installation nor server-side changes are necessary. We have designed and built a system which uses an HTTP proxy and AJAX technology to enable users to collaborate on web pages. The WWW is increasingly used as a platform for web applications. With our work, we present a general approach for application sharing in this domain. In the following, we present version 2 of UsaProxy, our system for remote collaboration while using the WWW. We consider two different modes of collaboration:

C. Baranauskas et al. (Eds.): INTERACT 2007, LNCS 4662, Part I, pp. 74–87, 2007.

Monitoring. In this mode, all actions performed by a user on a web page are monitored and immediately communicated to the second user's browser. There, the captured interaction is visualised and the browser follows the actions taken by the first user, such as scrolling, text selection or following a link to another page. The second user is not able to influence the browser session. A typical scenario of use is to provide support and guidance to a user while being aware of the state and actions of their browser.

Shared Browsing. Here, two browsers' sessions are locked together. Actions in one browser result in identical changes in the other browser. Both users can see the other user's mouse pointer and both users have full control over the web page. This also means that the users can perform conflicting actions, e.g. by clicking on different URLs at the same time. For resolution of these conflicts, the presence of social protocols is assumed, and no token passing is required. In this paper, we explore two scenarios of shared browsing: Two people looking for a present in an online shop, and a teacher-learner experience.

The central contribution of this paper is a web-based technical infrastructure for monitoring and shared browsing. It was essential for us to create a solution that does not take over the complete desktop of a remote user, require software installation or changes to the web-based applications. The technology is based on UsaProxy which was introduced in [2]. Whereas our earlier work on UsaProxy concentrated on supporting remote usability tests of websites, this paper highlights a different use of the technology: Providing support for collaborative work processes. A significant number of technical problems had to be solved for this, such as how to "replay" users' actions in the second browser, distinguishing UsaProxy sessions from private browsing sessions, finding adequate visualisations for the actions, and dealing with varying formatting of pages due to differing window sizes and font sizes. A further contribution is a study that explored how people use such a web-based collaboration technology and what the potential application scenarios are.

This paper first discusses related work in section 2. In section 3.1, we introduce the concept of web-based collaboration using lightweight web technologies and describe the implementation in section 3.2. To evaluate the feasibility (with regard to the technical solution) as well as the usability of the approach, we conducted an experimental evaluation with 12 users exploring different scenarios in section 4. Finally, section 5 discusses our findings and highlights potential improvements to the technology.

2   Related Work

Client-side Software Installation. One of the earliest efforts in the direction of a shared browser application was GroupWeb [6] from 1996. The GroupWeb prototype was a custom-built browser application which could display the pages viewed by other GroupWeb users. W4 [5] is similar to GroupWeb, but also allowed bookmarks that are shared between users. Furthermore, it supported the creation of "sticky notes" on visited web pages and included a number of other tools, e.g. a drawing editor. Kobayashi et al. [9] propose a system that is comparable to our approach. However, they use a plug-in to control a standard web browser, so the plug-in has to be installed on each client machine.

In comparison to the systems above, our own efforts have resulted in a more lightweight shared browsing solution. Whereas these projects demand that all participants first install special software on their computers, our solution better supports spontaneous shared browsing sessions, and it supports situations in which users are unable or unwilling to install software. Furthermore, unlike with GroupWeb and W4, the users are not forced to abandon the web browser they normally use, with all its custom settings, personal bookmarks etc. Thus, the remainder of this section concentrates on technologies which do not require client-side software installation.

CGI-based Filter. The CoBrow project [11] used a CGI-based web interface to share pages: In this case, the browser tells a CGI program to serve it a certain page on the WWW. Before returning the page, this program rewrites all URLs on the page to make them refer back to the CGI. Only a prototype version of the tool was ever implemented. This technique is more likely to fail with complicated web pages than our own technology, which is based on an HTTP proxy. In particular, problems can be expected if pages create URLs dynamically using JavaScript.

HTTP Server, Java Applets. CoWeb [8] used a different strategy to share the content of web pages between users: Similar to CoBrow's CGI program, the CoWeb HTTP server acts as a filter for pages. It replaces some parts of the HTML content (e.g. form fields, images) with Java applets which perform the same function as the original HTML element, but provide additional functionality, such as painting inside an image and discussing its contents in a text chat. As the page is modified heavily by the CoWeb server before being passed on to the browsers, the page layout will often be significantly altered, and problems will arise if the page includes JavaScript code which accesses and changes the DOM tree.

HTTP proxy, Java Applets. With the approach of Cabri et al. [3], users reconfigure their browsers to access the web via an HTTP proxy. This proxy adds a single applet to all pages. The applet contains a list of all users taking part in a shared browsing session and a list of pages visited by them. Due to technical restrictions, the system can only visualise other users' mouse pointer positions inside selected images on the page. Additionally, users can paint in these images, and a text chat is available.

WebSplitter [7] is another proxy-based system. A Java applet causes the browser to load new pages. The system concentrates on providing different partial content to different users depending on their devices or role. Special XML pages and policy files need to be created manually, it is not possible to collaboratively browse arbitrary web pages. Furthermore, mouse movements, key presses etc. are not shared between the participating users.

Java Servlet, JavaScript. The Collaborative Web Browsing system introduced in [4] takes advantage of JavaScript to track user actions. It is designed as a lightweight system which can be used immediately by visitors of a site. The system only supports collaborative browsing on a single website which must have been prepared in advance by making a Java servlet available on the server. Collaboration is restricted to one particular page at a time – it is not possible to move the shared session to another page by following a link.

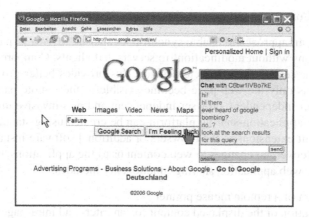

Fig. 1. During a shared browsing session, both users can interact with the page or watch the other user's actions, including his mouse movements. They do not need to install software.

Our technology combines the advantages of [3] and [4]: By using an HTTP proxy, the necessity to rewrite URLs is avoided, as all page requests and responses automatically pass through the proxy. UsaProxy 2 causes its own JavaScript code to execute on all pages when they are displayed by browsers.

Different architectures are possible when building a system for shared use of applications. In [1], this is discussed for desktop application sharing, but some of the results are applicable to the area of web application sharing. Our solution uses the "replicated execution" approach, but a "single-site execution" approach is preferable and an area for future work.

A scenario for which a shared browsing architecture may be useful is presented in [10]: During online shopping, users can leave a shared session temporarily and look at "nearby" items in the same shop. The technical solution relies on the implementation of certain APIs by the owners of web shops.

3   Using the Web Browser for Interaction and Collaboration

As many developers and companies move classical desktop applications to the WWW, new technical opportunities for creating collaborative applications arise. Inspired by tools for application sharing that are available for different operating systems, we investigated how a comparable tool can be created for web-based applications. We looked at how current browsers can support sharing and collaborative use of web pages and applications. Figure 1 depicts a simple example showing the basic functionality: In their browsers, two users see the same web page. In addition to their own mouse pointer, they are provided with a visualisation of the collaborator's mouse pointer (which was doubled in size in the figure to make it better visible) and a chat application. In this section, we first describe the concept and requirements and then explain our implementation, which is based on client-side JavaScript code and a special HTTP proxy.

3.1 General Concept

Our focus is on an approach to enable synchronous sharing of WWW pages and web-based applications without modifications to servers and clients. Compared to solutions which provide access to the complete desktop, this provides better protection of the user's privacy, as only the web page becomes visible to the remote partner. Furthermore, a platform-independent, browser-independent and non-invasive implementation is possible – an application-sharing platform can be created using standard web technologies, without extensions to the browsers or additional software installation on the client side. Moreover, no changes to web content or to the applications are required to share them. The web application sharing functionality includes:

- Visualisation of a remote mouse pointer
- Synchronisation of the displayed content (on an inter- and intra-page level)
- Visualisation of remote interaction (e.g. selection of text)
- Synchronisation of interaction with the content (e.g. text entry in a form)
- Provision of synchronous communication (e.g. chat)
- Means for shared drawing and annotation (e.g. shared blackboard)

Technically, our approach uses a proxy that adds JavaScript code to existing applications and pages before delivery. The added code tracks user actions in one browser, transmits information about it back to the proxy and replays it in the remote browser.

With regard to the mode of operation and the control in sharing we discriminate two cases, remote monitoring (one user watches the other's actions) and shared working (both users have full control and can interact with the page). Furthermore, the proxy can be inserted in various ways between the client and the server:

- Manual reconfiguration in the browser
- Transparent proxy for all machines in a local network
- Transparent insertion of the proxy in front of a server

Due to the fact that users have different browsers, different window sizes and use different font sizes, there is no true WYSIWIS ("what you see is what I see"), so that e.g. a submit button may appear in different positions. Our approach to synchronisation is not to use screen coordinates, but rather to identify the object a user interacted with by its position in the browser's DOM tree.

3.2 Implementation

UsaProxy is an open-source Java program which implements an HTTP proxy. UsaProxy 2 always forwards browser requests to the web server, except in one case: It implements caching of the server's response and uses the cache to serve identical content to the two browsers of a shared browsing session. Furthermore, a small modification is made to returned HTML pages in order to run custom JavaScript code in the context of all pages. This JavaScript code records information on user actions, such as mouse movements, and transmits it back to the proxy. Through a polling mechanism, the second browser gets notified of this. It then downloads and visualises the information, e.g. by moving a layer which symbolises the remote user's mouse pointer. See figure 2 for an overview

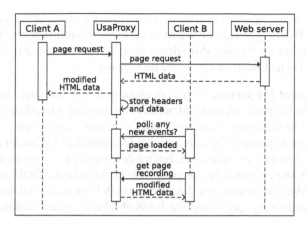

Fig. 2. When a page is requested, identical content is served to both participants of a shared session. By modifying the HTML content, UsaProxy 2 executes its JavaScript code on all pages.

of the communication between the involved entities. The following requirements were identified for the system:

- Real-time tracking of user actions, such as navigation between pages, actions on a page (mouse movements, scrolling), and any input provided to the browser (clicks, key strokes, text input, drop-down selection)
- Platform independence both from the server technology and the client operating system/browser
- As few client-side and server-side changes as possible
- Easy, flexible deployment in order to support a variety of usage scenarios
- Intuitive visualisation of remote user activity
- System should work even if the two browsers have different browser window sizes, different font settings, or render a page in slightly different ways
- Integrated chat functionality as one means of interpersonal communication

Tracking User Activity on Web Pages. When UsaProxy forwards server responses to the browser, it adds a <script src='...'/> tag to HTML pages on the fly before returning them to the browsers. This minimal change is very unlikely to interfere with the correct operation even of complex web pages. The exact URL used in the script tag depends on the proxy mode. However, in all cases the URL contains a special path starting with /usaproxylolo/, which the proxy recognizes: If it is present, the request is not forwarded to any server. Instead, UsaProxy itself acts as an HTTP server, performing one out of a number of different actions depending on the exact URL. In the case of the script tag's URL, the client-side JavaScript part of UsaProxy 2 is served.

The JavaScript code is loaded in the context of the web page, so the browser's security model does not prevent its execution. It is carefully written so as not to interfere with any JavaScript code used by the page. It records all interesting data and periodically sends it back to the proxy using another, different /usaproxylolo/ URL. On the proxy, the data is logged to a file together with the headers of any requests that were sent to servers, and with the headers and response bodies of all replies sent back by servers.

Compared to earlier versions of UsaProxy (see [2]), the range of captured events has been extended: The logged data now also includes onmouseover events, changes to form field values (radio buttons, drop-down menus, checkboxes, text fields), and the selection of text (in text fields or elsewhere on the page).

Additional Element Properties. When an event (e.g. a mouse click) has taken place for an element on the page, the element needs to be uniquely identified in the log message that is sent to the proxy. However, many elements, such as anchors or images, are not assigned an id property by page authors. Utilizing the href and/or src properties helps to identify elements in some cases, but we developed a more robust technique: We uniquely identify the elements by mapping their position in the DOM tree to a string representation. More accurately, we describe the path from the root document element to the node by recursively specifying which nth child is an ancestor of the node.

Session Cookies. We use session cookies in order to uniquely differentiate between users on all sites they visit. For security reasons, browsers do not support "global" cookies which are sent to all visited sites, so if UsaProxy 2 simply added its own cookie to response headers before forwarding the web server's response to the browser, then identifying the different users would only work as long as they did not leave the current website. For this reason, the cookie is not set for the domain that the user visits, but always for the same fixed domain name: The site the UsaProxy JavaScript code is fetched from.

Mouse Movements and Scrolling. When capturing the mouse cursor position with each corresponding event, the transmission of absolute x/y page coordinates is less valuable than the identification of the object the mouse pointer currently moves over, due to differences in output when pages are rendered. Therefore, UsaProxy 2 records the offsets of the mouse pointer position relative to the hovered-over DOM element. Apart from an offset property (e.g. offset=25,10), the DOM path and any i.e. id value are also specified in a mousemove event log. Scrolling is handled similarly: The rendered height of a page will differ, so the page offset is recorded as a percentage which gives the position of the viewport relative to the entire page height.

Clock Synchronisation. UsaProxy 2 records a variety of events which are timestamped both by the client-side JavaScript (e.g. mouse movement) and the proxy server (e.g. page requests). As the system time of the client and proxy machines may differ, the proxy transmits a timestamp to the client when it serves an HTML page. The JavaScript code then only calculates its timestamps relative to the proxy's timestamp, avoiding problems related to clock skew.

Steering a Browser Using Tracking Data. In order to reconstruct what has occurred in the partner's browser, each client constantly polls UsaProxy 2 for remote events. This is achieved using an XMLHttpRequest object. A request is composed of the special path component /usaproxylolo/getevents followed by the user's session ID and an ID specifying the last fetched event, for instance /usaproxylolo/getevents?sid=GH6zD4k233nw&lastid=37. UsaProxy 2 captures the request, queries its event index structure which holds all clients' event logs, and returns a list of new events encoded in an XML document. Figure 3 shows the

```
<?xml version="1.0"?>
<event>
 <sid>8hK8283u23Hh</sid>
 <type>mouseover</type>
 <coord>247,152</coord>
 <id>f</id>
 <dom>abae</dom>
</event>
```

Fig. 3. After polling the proxy for new remote events, each client receives the other user's actions in the form of XML-encoded data. Elements are identified using their position in the DOM tree.

XML representation for a mouseover event. Having received the XML response, the JavaScript code can parse it and replay the event in the user's browser.

Remote Event Representation. A second green mouse pointer is displayed to represent the remote user's pointer. It is implemented by inserting a layer containing the pointer image into the document. Remote mouse movements are directly applied to the mouse layer by assigning it the coordinates specified in the XML event description. As the coordinates are always relative to the hovered-over element, the remote pointer appears in the right spot even if the page is formatted differently in the local browser. In the case of a mouseover event, a hand-shaped cursor image appears instead of the pointer. Additionally, the hovered-over element is underlined in green. Remote scroll bar movements are repeated locally by calculating the local offset of the viewport in the HTML page using the transmitted percentage offset value. The result is assigned to the page offset, which causes the user's page to automatically scroll to the new position.

Value changes in text fields, drop-down menus, radio buttons or check boxes are directly applied to the corresponding field. Furthermore, we provide basic support for AJAX applications by re-executing locally all those event handlers which were also executed in the remote browser as a result of an event like mousedown, mouseup, mouseover or change. As testing of our prototype has shown, this system for re-executing event handler code on all browsers is not reliable for advanced AJAX applications in all cases. A future version of UsaProxy could be extended to support copying the DOM tree of one "primary" browser to the other participants of a shared session.

Putting it All Together: A Web-based Shared Browsing Application. As pointed out in section 3.1, UsaProxy 2 may be launched in several different modes, which are specified using command line arguments. By default, it starts in HTTP proxy mode. In this mode, the proxy settings of clients must be modified to make them send requests to UsaProxy. Additionally, in this mode the software also automatically recognizes whether it is being used as a transparent proxy. Thus, instead of reconfiguring the browsers, the local network gateway can be set up to forward all outgoing HTTP requests to the proxy, and no client reconfiguration is necessary.

Finally, the software can also be deployed in server mode. In this mode, it is installed in front of a particular website. It behaves like a regular web server to clients, but forwards all requests to the actual web server. The browsers of site visitors do not need to be reconfigured. On the server side, only a simple reconfiguration is necessary: Either the original server needs to listen on a different port to allow UsaProxy 2 to

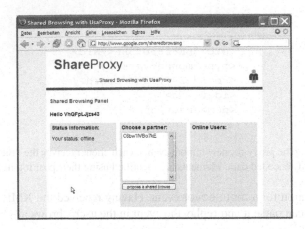

Fig. 4. Overview page for the management of shared browsing sessions. Users can select a partner and send him a proposal to start a shared session.

filter incoming requests on port 80, or the website's DNS entry needs to be pointed to a separate server on which a copy of UsaProxy 2 is running.

Independently of the above modes, UsaProxy 2 may also be configured for a specific shared session mode. With the simple variant – the asymmetrical remote monitoring – users may only view another browser's actions, e.g. any pages that are visited. The browser whose actions are monitored does not poll the proxy for remote events. The more advanced symmetrical shared browsing mode allows two browsers to participate in the same browsing session, where each user can e.g. click on links to visit new pages. In this mode, both browsers poll for new events. The mode of operation is selected on the command line when UsaProxy 2 is started.

In order to start a shared session, one party needs to send a "proposal" which must be accepted by the other party. This process is realized by a session initiation handshake during which both parties verify their mutual acceptance. If UsaProxy 2 is deployed for live support usage, only a simple "Live Support" button needs to be added to the web-site. In that case, the support staff is provided with an overview web page displaying a list of proposals, each of which was initiated by a click on the support button. For symmetrical usage, both parties can access a similar page with a list of potential session partners – see figure 4 for a screenshot. When a partner is selected and the button "pro-pose a shared browse" is pressed, a pop-up immediately appears in the other browser, asking for the remote user's consent to start a session. Once this consent has been given, either user can simply enter a new URL in the address bar or use other means to visit a new page, and his actions will be replayed in the other user's browser.

After a shared session has begun, each participant's browser window is augmented with the remote user's pointer, and an integrated chat panel may be dragged around and positioned where the users like – see figure 1 for a screenshot. This permits users to directly communicate without resorting to external tools. The chat window is UsaProxy's metaphor for the fact that the shared browsing session is active; if either user closes it (with a click on the "×" in the upper right corner), the shared session is terminated. This way, users can easily distinguish between shared web pages and privately visited pages.

For the purpose of steering another user's browser correctly, it is required that the same content is delivered to it as to the local browser. As identical requests to a server may lead to different server responses, the approach taken by UsaProxy 2 is to record each server response (headers and data) together with a unique page ID. Later, the recorded version of the page is fetched by the second browser via a special request which contains the ID (see figure 2).

In order to permit users to have other browser sessions which are independent of the shared session, the shared session window is assigned the name "sharedsession_UsaProxy" the first time our JavaScript executes. When the Java-Script code executes on later occasions (new page visited, URL entered manually in address line), it can read the name and decide whether it is the shared session window, i.e. whether tracking and logging should be performed.

4 Experimental Evaluation

In order to analyse whether our technology is suitable for the envisioned areas of use, we have performed a number of tests with users who had no prior experience with application sharing over the web, and no relation to the project. The 12 test persons were students of Computer Science (8) and members of staff. Teams of two people had to complete the same three tasks, which were designed both to test whether UsaProxy 2 worked at a technical level and whether it worked for the different application areas. Before the tasks, the participants were given a short five-minute overview of UsaProxy's features and of how to use it to create a shared or monitored browsing session. The tests took place in a lab where several machines had already been prepared for use – a copy of UsaProxy 2 had been started and the browsers had been reconfigured to access the web via the proxy. After the tasks, the users were asked to fill out a questionnaire.

4.1 Looking for a Present Online (Shared Browsing)

The two members of each team could not see or hear each other directly for this scenario, whose objective it was to test UsaProxy's "shared browsing" mode. They were given the following instructions:

After you have started a shared browsing session, visit amazon.de. *Try to find an item to give to a common friend of yours as a present. Do this by proposing items to each other and looking at them.*

This task causes a fairly large amount of communication between to the test users. It was considered complete as soon as one of the users put the product into the website's shopping basket.

For most participants, the same observations could be made with regard to their first reactions: Upon discovering their counterpart's mouse pointer and the ability to perform actions on the same web page, they were impressed by the system, expressed that they liked the idea and played around a little, e.g. by chasing their team member's mouse pointer. However, after exchanging a few chat messages and starting to use the website for the given task, this was often replaced by a certain amount of confusion: They had

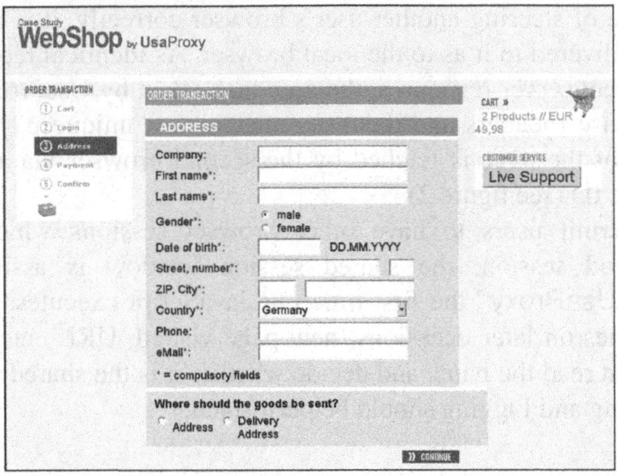

Fig. 5. On the example website, visitors can request immediate help using the "Live Support" button. From that moment, their mouse movements and other actions on the page become visible to the website's live support staff.

not been given any rules as to who should do which things in the browser window. This could lead to conflicts, such as situations where one user was still typing in a search query, but the other user clicked on a link, discarding the semi-complete query. While some teams continued to interrupt each other in a rather chaotic way, others began to develop a "social protocol" – typically, one user would stop performing actions after a while, watch his partner's actions and give comments via the text chat. On at least one occasion, the roles were switched once more, after the active user had written in a chat message that he had run out of ideas.

It is imaginable that with more experience in using the system, and with more complicated tasks, the participants would have developed more elaborate usage patterns. For example, they might have started taking turns for the main interaction and pass control to their counterpart via a chat message. Another alternative would have been to start a separate, non-shared browser session in another window or tab and only to use the shared session when something interesting is actually found.

Despite the problems they had, at the end of the three experiments 11 of the 12 test participants said that they liked the general idea, or that they liked it very much, and only one person said he did not like it. (For all such questions, five options were available in the questionnaire, ranging from "I like it very much" to "I do not like it at all".) However, only about half of the participants said they would actually use this mode of the proxy in practice (6 would tend to use it, 5 would not tend to use it, 1 undecided).

4.2   User Support in a Web Shop (Remote Monitoring)

With this scenario, UsaProxy's "remote monitoring" mode was tested. Again, the two test users were not able to communicate directly. A web page was set up for this task (figure 5), it showed a delivery address form, as found on many shopping websites. The first user was given the following task:

Complete the form on the website. As the delivery address, enter "Kingsgard Dry-Cleaning, Munich main station, 80335 Munich". In case of problems, use the "Live Support" facility of the website.

The second user was told to play the role of a support hotline of the web shop. He was shown how to log into the system and wait for a request for live support. Furthermore, he was given information on how to assist the first user with the form, e.g. to let the user enter "0" in the house number field if the address does not have a house number. During the test, the user filling out the form had to describe his problem to the support hotline: The fields "first name", "last name" and "number" were required by the form, it was not possible to leave them empty. The hotline then gave give hints via the chat only, using text messages to guide the user towards completing the form.

The setup and behaviour of the monitoring feature did not present a problem to the users. In contrast to the first test above, the support hotline could not directly influence the page displayed by the browser, so much time was spent communicating via chat. Using the hints given by the online support, all users were able to complete the form. Unlike with the first scenario, users did not get confused – the text-based chat was a familiar form of communication for them, and they were fine with waiting for instructions on how to solve their problem. Later, eight of the 12 users mentioned in the questionnaire that they would use (or probably use) this kind of live support in practice, three were undecided and one would probably not use it.

This scenario is tailored towards the "server-side" mode of operation of UsaProxy 2: The proxy could be installed on a company's server and visitors of the company website could request help without any changes to their setup, not even a reconfiguration of their browser settings.

4.3   Teaching the Use of a Web Application (Shared Browsing)

The final task used the "shared browsing" mode of UsaProxy 2. Only one test user took part in the test, the second user's part was always played by an operator. The presence of a voice connection (e.g. via VoIP) between the two users was now assumed. The task was as follows:

Your friend has mentioned to you that he found a certain interesting publication with the topic of "why do people blog" or "blog communication". During a shared browsing session, search for it on the web. If you are unable to locate it, let your friend assist you in your search.

The test user first attempted to perform the task, but was unable to do so using the provided information. He then informed the other user (our operator) about this by talking to him. The operator demonstrated the correct solution in the shared browser session by visiting Google Advanced Search, and making the correct settings in the search form. Thus, the "teacher" (operator) was able to observe the mistakes of the "learner" (test user), react to them and guide him towards the right solution. On the other hand, the learner was able to see how the solution was reached. This scenario was well received by the participants, and several persons noted that they liked how they had been able to see all the actions that led to the desired search results.

5   Discussion and Conclusion

In this paper, a detailed concept for the shared use of web applications was introduced, together with a prototype implementation which allows two users to collaborate in web applications. We have successfully conducted an evaluation of the prototype, demonstrating that it is feasable at the technical level and that the browser session sharing features are appreciated by users. Compared to previous work, our approach is minimally invasive, as it does not require software installation on the client or server side, works with most existing web pages, allows shared browsing sessions to span across multiple domains, and does not change the behaviour of web pages beyond the addition of the collaboration features. With our work, we hope to provide the technical infrastructure for further work in the area of web-based collaboration.

The scenarios used in the experiment are only some examples for the potential of application sharing and monitoring. Many others can be imagined, such as annotation of pages (e.g. with virtual Post-Its) or special concepts for online learning and online gaming. The topic of using the monitoring data for usability testing, semi-automated improvements to websites, visualisation of their usage, marketing etc. has already been discussed in detail in previous work [2]. Finally, sessions could be recorded and played back at a later time, and the number of participants in a session could be raised beyond the current limit of two.

As monitoring can be made invisible to the user of a web page (e.g. by running the proxy transparently in front of the server), privacy issues arise. Our current implementation is not capable of hiding the fact that a monitoring session is active (the presence of the chat window makes this apparent at all times), but the technology can obviously be abused to monitor people's behaviour on web pages without their consent. It is the responsibility of anyone using the tracking code to inform users that it is being employed.

While we believe that we have addressed all security issues in our implementation, it should be noted that with the current state of the technology, using a shared browsing session will always make the participants of the session more vulnerable than if they were using the web alone. The most obvious attack vector is that a malicious user directs the shared session to a page which exploits known browser security vulnerabilities. Furthermore, session cookies are shared between the browsers, so "stealing" them is trivial. Thus, we recommend that shared browsing sessions should only be performed by users who trust each other.

In our experience, adding JavaScript on the fly to existing web pages is a very useful technique which has applications beyond those shown in this paper. Current systems and browsers offer enough performance and the needed capabilities for this approach.

The linking of interaction events like clicks to the DOM objects proved to be a very important design decision. Many problems related to different layouts on different browsers and systems are solved by this approach. However, many challenges are still ahead – in particular, fully supporting the sharing of complex AJAX applications, while conceptually feasible, is not easy to implement.

So far, we have decided not to include support for explicit protocols which support passing control over the shared browsing session from one user to another. This is due to the fact that we believe that audio connections are likely to be present in most collaborative settings, so social protocols will be the most efficient means for coordination. Thus, the system is not suitable for scenarios where users compete.

Acknowledgement. This work was funded by the BMBF (intermedia project) and by the DFG (Embedded Interaction Research Group).

References

1. Ahuja, S.R., Ensor, J.R., Lucco, S.E.: A comparison of application sharing mechanisms in real-time desktop conferencing systems. ACM SIGOIS Bulletin 11(2-3), 238–248 (1990)
2. Atterer, R., Wnuk, M., Schmidt, A.: Knowing the User's Every Move – User Activity Tracking for Website Usability Evaluation and Implicit Interaction. In: WWW2006. Proceedings of the 15th International World Wide Web Conference, Edinburgh, Scotland (May 2006)
3. Cabri, G., Leonardi, L., Zambonelli, F.: Supporting Cooperative WWW Browsing: a Proxy-based Approach. In: Proceedings of the 7th Euromicro Workshop on Parallel and Distributed Processing, Madeira (P), pp. 138–145 (February 1999)
4. Esenther, A.W.: Instant Co-Browsing: Lightweight Real-time Collaborative Web Browsing. In: WWW2002. Proceedings of the 11th World Wide Web Conference, Honolulu, Hawaii, USA (May 7-11, 2002)
5. Gianoutsos, S., Grundy, J.: Collaborative work with the World Wide Web: Adding CSCW support to a Web Browser. In: Proceedings of the Oz-CSCW'96. DSTC Technical Workshop Series, pp. 14–21. University of Queensland, Brisbane, Australia (1996)
6. Greenberg, S., Roseman, M.: GroupWeb: A WWW Browser as Real Time Groupware. In: CHI 1996 Short Papers: Proceedings of the Conference on Human Factors in Computing Systems, Vancouver, British Columbia, Canada (April 13–18, 1996)
7. Han, R., Perret, V., Naghshineh, M.: WebSplitter: A Unified XML Framework for Multi-Device Collaborative Web Browsing. In: Proceedings of the 2000 ACM conference on Computer supported cooperative work, Philadelphia, Pennsylvania, United States (2000)
8. Jacobs, S., Gebhardt, M., Kethers, S., Rzasa, W.: Filling HTML forms simultaneously: CoWeb – architecture and functionality. In: WWW1996. Proceedings of the 5th World Wide Web Conference, Paris, France (May 6–10, 1996)
9. Kobayashi, M., Shinozaki, M., Sakairi, T., Touma, M., Daijavad, S., Wolf, C.: Collaborative customer services using synchronous Web browser sharing. In: Proceedings of the 1998 ACM conference on Computer supported cooperative work, Seattle, Washington, United States, pp. 99–109. ACM Press, New York (1998)
10. Puglia, S., Carter, R., Jain, R.: MultECommerce: a distributed architecture for collaborative shopping on the WWW. In: Proceedings of the 2nd ACM conference on Electronic commerce, Minneapolis, Minnesota, United States, pp. 215–224. ACM Press, New York (2000)
11. Sidler, G., Scott, A., Wolf, H.: Collaborative Browsing in the World Wide Web. In: Proceedings of the 8th Joint European Networking Conference, Edinburgh, Scotland (May 1997)

Investigating User Attention and Interest in Websites

Alistair Sutcliffe[1] and Abdallah Namoune[2]

Centre for HCI Design, School of Informatics, University of Manchester, UK
alistair.g.sutcliffe@manchester.ac.uk,
abdellah.namoune@postgrad.manchester.ac.uk

Abstract. Users' attention was investigated by eye tracking, combined with reported rating of areas of interest, and free recall memory of six operational websites. The sites differed in the pattern of fixations recorded depending on their layout structure. Fixation durations and areas of interest were generally correlated but exceptions were present in both directions. The sites which were rated more attractive overall had an open layout and high density fixations on animations. The sites which were preferred overall had column layout, and content with brand seemed to be the more important determinants for preference. Fixation densities were closely related to reported user interest for 4/6 sites but not for two e-commerce sites. Reported attention, positive memory and overall preference were weakly related.

Keywords: Eye tracking, visual attention, website evaluation.

1 Introduction

Eye tracking studies of websites have been popular as a means of diagnosing the effectiveness of designs, for instance in comparing optimal navigation pathways and user attention patterns as revealed by eye tracking pathways [9]. Eye tracking, either using sequence analysis or overall fixation durations and densities, is being used as a diagnostic tool to evaluate designs by comparing patterns of fixation with areas of interest on websites; for example, an F-shaped pattern has been proposed as evidence of good design [13]. Eye tracking studies have indicated influences on users' attention, such as animation having a dominant influence on directing fixations [4] and the influence of the cursor's locus on users' attention [17]. In a website study, users' reported attention from concurrent protocols was compared with eye tracked fixations showing that 70% of the reported areas of interest were also fixated [12]. However, what users attend to and what they look at may not be so closely correlated; for instance, Burke et al. [3] have demonstrated that saccades and limited fixations in the proximity of objects may be sufficient for cognitive processing, and that banner adverts are not always fixated and can be ignored.

Fixations as revealed by eye tracking studies could be determined by image salience and goal-directed attention [10,11]; however, objects that are actively processed by users may not be the same as those that are fixated. Therefore we investigate the link between fixations, users' perceived attention to objects of interest, their overall preference and memory. The paper is organised as follows. A review of

C. Baranauskas et al. (Eds.): INTERACT 2007, LNCS 4662, Part I, pp. 88–101, 2007.

related work is followed by a description of the selected websites and the experimental methods. Then the results of eye tracking analysis, users' perceived attention, and overall preference ratings are described. Finally the discussion reviews the contributions of the study and implications for future use of eye tracking as an evaluation tool.

2   Related Work

Eye tracking studies have investigated how people read news web pages [14], suggesting that the first entry point for most web pages is located in the upper left corner and is usually a headline. Animation has been considered to have a dominant effect on user attentions and directing fixations [4,5]; however, in studies on banner adverts in web pages, no significant effect was found on the ability to recall and recognise banner ads [1]. Burke et al. [3] found that banner ads distracted the users' visual search and significantly increased their search time; furthermore, memory recall for animated banners was worse than for static banners.

Zhang instructed participants to identify and count text strings on a web page that contained an animated distractor [18]. She found that animations decreased user performance while searching for information and the effect of animation on performance was determined by the complexity of the task. The more similar an animation was to the task, the worse user performance became; brightly coloured animations interfered more than dull coloured animations. Eyetracking sequences are influenced by the layout and density of displays [7,8]; however, the relationship between fixation sequences and densities and users' attention is less clear.

Eye tracking studies [15] on 11 websites in four categories – shopping, business, search and news – showed that the nature of the task (browse/search) did not significantly influence the fixation patterns, although gender, the viewing order of web pages, and the interaction between page order and site type influenced user eye movements. Guan et al. [6] investigated the association between eye tracked fixations and user attention reported in a retrospective protocol for problem solving tasks using graphical displays. Agreement between the reported and fixated areas was modest (53%); in contrast, better agreement (70%) was found by Johansen and Hansen [12] who used concurrent protocols.

3   Materials and Methods

Six websites (see Figure 1) were chosen to represent a diverse set of applications and types of design. The sites were selected to investigate exploratory hypotheses associated with two or more of the sites.

1.   Fixation patterns will be influenced by the structure and layout of the site.
2.   Animations and images of people will receive high fixation frequencies, as suggested by the computer as a social actor paradigm [16].
3.   Areas of high fixation durations/frequencies will be correlated with users' reported areas of interest.
4.   Sites with more frequent fixations and reported interest will invoke more detailed memory.

Fig. 1. BBCNews (upper left), Nylon (upper right), PCWorld (middle left), TigerDirect (middle right), IntelliPage (lower left) and Nike (lower right)

The hypotheses were posed to explore associations between users' attention, their perception of interesting design features and content, memory for features and content, and their overall rating for the site. The following sites were selected:

BBCNews: an information provider site with a strong brand image. The BBCNews site follows a traditional columnar block structure. This site had small animations in the centre above the top stories section.

Nylon: an information provider. Nylon magazine has similar goals to BBCNews, portraying interesting content to the user with good navigation to facilitate exploration of content. Animation was used on the central image.

PCWorld: an e-commerce site retailing computers and related technology. This site had a traditional block-structured column layout. Animated banner adverts were used in the central column.

TigerDirect: an e-commerce site retailing computers as a direct competitor to PCWorld, although with a less well known brand. One banner advert was present at the top of the page.

IntelliPage: an information provider that also sells design services. It has an open design format. Animation was used on the main central image with two concurrently running effects.

Nike: an e-commerce site with a strong brand image and design emphasis. It made extensive use of animation and graphics and had a more open design format.

Thirty subjects (15 males, 15 females, mean age 24, range 18-46 years) who were students and researchers at the University of Manchester took part in the investigation. Most subjects (26/30) had 3 years or more Internet experience, and all used the Internet daily or at least once a week. The subjects were familiar with the BBCNews website (68% had visited it > 5 times) and some were aware of the PC World site (33% had visited it 2-5 times); while only 3 had visited Nike 2-5 times. None of the other sites were known to the subjects. The experimental procedure consisted of the following steps.

(a)   The participants completed a pre-test questionnaire recording their Internet experience, whether they had viewed any of the sites, and their interest in the subject matter of the sites.

(b)   The participants were asked to view six different web pages for 60 seconds on a 17" monitor with screen resolution set to 1024*768 pixels. User eye movements were recorded with a Tobii 1750 eye tracker. The number of fixations, duration of fixations, and dwell time by screen area (heat map) were analysed. The participants were instructed to browse the page for any items that might interest them.

(c)   They completed a free recall memory test by listing any objects or areas on each site that they could remember, and rating each item as either positive (liked), neutral or negative (disliked).

(d)   They then recorded their perceived attention to different areas on each site by marking the areas on a screen dump image. They ranked the areas of the screen by order of interest.

(e)   The participants rated each site on a questionnaire capturing their preference for the sites, taking their purpose into account, and overall rating of the website's attractiveness in terms of design quality.

The order in which the home pages were presented was counter-balanced. Every user was first asked to freely browse the home page of each site for 60 seconds. Participants were explicitly instructed not to click on links within the pages; however, they could freely scroll down to view all the area of the page. After viewing all web pages, the subjects re-viewed the home pages and reported their sequence of attention by pointing to and verbally describing areas on-screen. They then specified and ranked areas of interest by pointing to areas on a print-out of the home page. Web pages were divided into areas of interest according to their structure and media, e.g. menus, text boxes, images, animations, link panels and logo, to enable the subjects' reports to be classified. Subjects were paid £10 for the experiment, which concluded with a debriefing interview to elicit their opinions about the designs, features that interested them, reasons for preferring any particular design, and criticism of design quality.

4 Results

4.1 Eye Tracking Analysis

There were no differences in the overall fixation duration between the sites, which received between 46.5 and 47.1 secs fixation out of the total measured period of 55 seconds. However, the total number of fixations (defined as foveal focus held in a constant location >200ms) did differ between the sites (F = 7.05, df 5, p<0.001) with means ranging from 163 (BBCNews, Nylon and TigerDirect) to 162 (PCWorld), 155 (Nike) and 146 (IntelliPage). Sites with column block structures (BBCNews, PCWorld, TigerDirect, and Nylon - see Figure 2) had heat map patterns that followed the columns, with more attention being paid to the top of the page. For BBCNews users, viewed the lead stories in the middle and right hand columns with associated images and text in the adjacent columns. In PCWorld, users fixated on the products following each of the four columns, and a similar pattern occurred in TigerDirect with a more diffuse pattern of fixations. Nylon showed an intermediate pattern since it had a large prominent centrally located image which attracted users' attention with the text located beneath it. The subjects also fixated on areas following the column layout.

Nike and IntelliPage had a different pattern, which reflected their non-columnar layout. Users' fixations were focused on animations and salient images without any evidence of a layout order; furthermore, the number of distinct fixated objects/areas was lower. In these sites users' attention seemed to be located on one prime area with 3-4 sub-areas.

The areas fixated showed a strong influence for animation in three sites: Nike, IntelliPage and Nylon; the remaining sites showed less effect, even though they did have animations and banner adverts. This appears to confirm previous findings of users selectively ignoring banner adverts, while interesting animations receive considerable attention.

The sequence of fixations was analysed by dividing each screen into 0.5 cm cells to plot the locus of fixations. A common fixation path for all subjects was calculated by starting with the cell with the highest first fixation count, then taking the cell with the highest frequency of second fixations, and so on. The first 15 fixations in the most frequent surviving pathway were analysed, which accounted for approximately 10-15 secs duration. Most pathways started with >50% of the users, but branching reduced the commonality for nodes later in the sequence. Fixation sequences are shown in figure 3a-c with the square box outline, circled numbers and solo numbers refer to

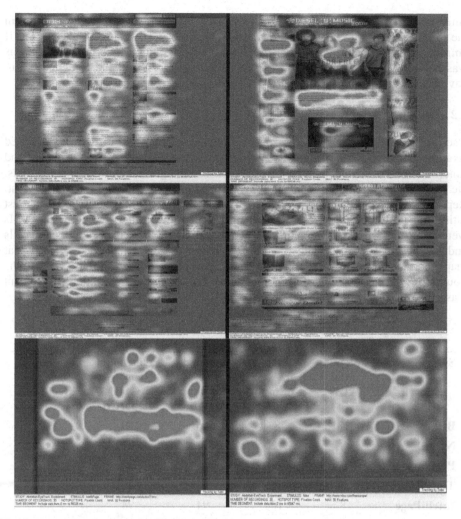

Fig. 2. Heat maps showing distribution of fixation densities for BBCNews (upper left), Nylon Magazine (upper right), PCWorld (middle left), TigerDirect (middle right), IntelliPage (lower left) and Nike (lower right)

high ranked reported areas of interest and areas with high total fixations (explained in section 4.2). In the BBC site (see Figure 3a) initial fixations follow the main news stories, with some attention (13-15) to an animation. Early fixations in the Nylon site were on the central image which was animated, with later ones on the news stories. For PCWorld and Tiger Direct the sequence suggests the users scan the content of the sites in the top menu bars and left hand menu in PC World, and the products on the top part of the screen. In contrast to other sites, animations and banner adverts did not attract fixations in the early sequence. The sequence observed in the Nike site did follow the appearance of animations, while the Intellipage sequence was also located by animated areas on the screen, although the sequence was more erratic since the animations started concurrently. Generally many of the areas which were fixated in the initial sequence do not appear in the top interest or total fixation ranked order. If animations are present they appear to determine the fixation sequence, although this was not true for PCWorld and TigerDirect where products and site content seem to have been more dominant.

4.2 Perceived Attention

Users' reported attention to areas on each site was compared to their eye tracked fixation durations. Each site was divided into areas based on its structure and functionality, i.e. segmented display areas, menus, images, animated areas, link lists, etc. The subjects' reported interests were mapped to these potential areas of interest. Reported areas of interest (AOIs) were ranked by calculating the average interest rating for each area multiplied by the % of users who rated that area. Reported AOIs were compared with higher fixation densities by dividing the screens into 0.5 cm cells and then comparing cells with fixation densities > 1% total fixations with the heat maps, and the users' retrospectively reported areas of interest; see Table 1. Where the boundaries of fixation cells and reported areas showed partial overlapping, agreement was scored as 0.5.

Table 1. Agreement between reported areas of interest and high density fixation areas

Site	Potential total AOIs	Reported areas % of total	Fixated areas % of total	Fixated and Reported % of Reported	Animations Fixed and Reported
BBC	18	83	66	80	yes
Nylon	8	100	77	77	yes
PCWorld	19	84	26	31	no
TigerDirect	23	87	35	40	no
IntelliPage	8	100	94	94	yes
Nike	7	100	76	76	yes

In all sites most potential AOIs were attended to from the users' reported evidence, and, apart from PCWorld and TigerDirect, there was close agreement between reported and fixated areas. The animations in close agreement sites were also fixated and reported. No areas were fixated but not subsequently reported as interesting. And all areas containing images of people were reported as interesting and fixated. However, from debriefing interviews only the images of people on IntelliPage (man sitting), in the central Nylon image, and the woman in the TigerDirect advert were commented upon, so small images may have been attended to for their associated text. The lower % of fixations in TigerDirect and PCWorld may be an artefact of the retrospective reporting. These sites had more complex structures and hence higher potential AOIs. The subjects cited interest in most areas, whereas their fixations were concentrated on a few areas where products were displayed. We conjecture that subjects' reported interest was 'reconstructed memory' based on their expectations of e-commerce sites; in contrast, the BBC site, which also had a complex structure, showed better agreement between reported interest and fixations. Debriefing comments suggest this may be due to subjects' interest in the variety of news stories.

The top five areas measured by fixation densities for each site (indicated by numbers) and the user-reported top five interest areas (numbers in circles) are shown in Figures 3a-c. Overall there was considerable agreement between the fixation densities and subjective ratings of areas of interest, apart from PCWorld and TigerDirect. However, when the top five fixation densities and reported AOIs are used as a measure of salience, in all sites there were 1-2 areas which were reported but not fixated, or fixated but not in the reported top five. The rank ordering for fixation densities and reported AOIs in each site were also different. In the BBCNews site, for example, several users reported the left area story and BBCNews video and newsround stories as interesting, even though they did not fixate on them frequently. Conversely, users fixated on other stories and the around the world section, which were not subsequently rated as interesting. This may reflect a scanning strategy to sample items which are later discarded.

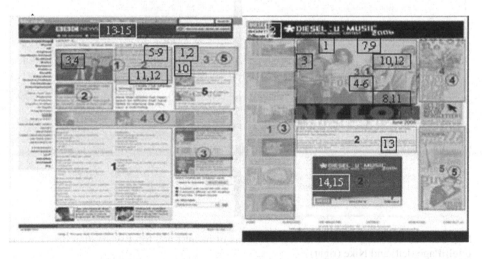

Fig. 3a. User-reported attention to top five areas of interest (number + circle) and top five fixation densities for BBCNews (left) and Nylon (right)

Animations in the centre of the page attracted user attention in the Nylon page and were rated as interesting. One item in the interest list (bottom animation) was not fixated, while the centre text was fixated but not rated as interesting. In this case, it appears that users may read the text from fixation evidence but then relegate it to lower down their interest list.

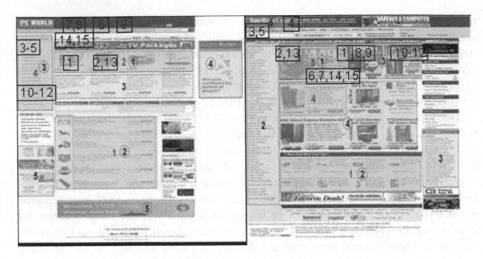

Fig. 3b. User-reported top five areas of interest and top five fixation densities for PCWorld (left) and TigerDirect (right)

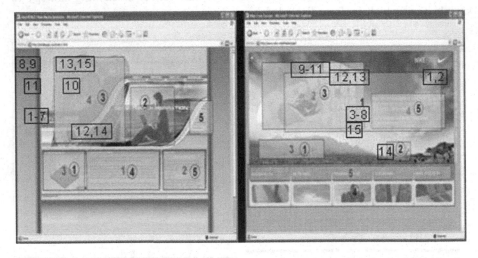

Fig. 3c. User-reported attention to top five areas of interest and top five fixation densities for IntelliPage (left) and Nike (right)

PCWorld and TigerDirect showed a weaker correspondence between the subjective and objective measures, which may reflect a user strategy of scanning these sites, since the heat maps also showed a less dense, more distributed pattern. Images of products in the centre of the page attracted attention in PCWorld and TigerDirect, followed by product images lower down the page. However, banner adverts in both sites were only partially effective. In these block-structured sites, users fixated on the products but tended to ignore the adverts. In their subjective record they reported interest in only a sub-set of the areas they fixated on, so it appears that they were selectively ignoring some areas.

Subjective and objective attention was in close agreement for Nike apart from the second area of interest (giraffe animation) which was reported as interesting but not fixated. In Nike the order of fixation and interest were linked to the unfolding sequence of animations (text, man, giraffe) which led the user towards the menu for product choice and purchasing. Some parts of the IntelliPage animation were fixated but ranked as less interesting. The sequence of animations in Nike followed in a smooth order, whereas the IntelliPage animations ran concurrently and competed with each other. For IntelliPage, both subjective attention and objective measures agreed, apart from area 2 in the interest ranking (man on beach image) which was not highly ranked in fixation density. The heat map shows this area was fixated but not intensely, so it appears that users may register areas of interest from less frequent fixations. Open structure sites (Nike, IntelliPage) showed a stronger correspondence between fixations and reported areas of interest. Nylon appeared to follow an intermediate pattern, probably reflecting its columnar plus large central image hybrid design.

4.3 Memory

The sites differed significantly in the total number of items remembered ($F = 2.74$, df 5, p<0.05) and rating valency (F 9.93, df 5, p<0.001); see Table 2.

Table 2. Memory for each site, total items and likeability weighted by valency. Scoring: positive items $+ 1$, negative items $- 1$.

	Total	% Content	Likeability weighted	% liked/total
BBCNews	166	56	91	55
IntelliPage	159	53	35	22
Nike	188	28	116	62
Nylon	150	33	48	32
PC World	177	37	58	33
Tiger Direct	174	63	19	11

Subjects remembered more items overall and more positively rated items for the Nike site. The differences were significant with all sites except BBCNews (T-tests, p<0.05). However, Nike's content was not so well remembered; instead, users remembered the animations (52% of all items). TigerDirect was remembered well in overall volume, but rated much lower in likeability. A higher proportion of content items were remembered for TigerDirect than for PCWorld, which might be explained by the more diffuse heat map pattern indicating that users scanned this site more completely. Also, the larger images used by TigerDirect may have stimulated users' interest more effectively. The BBCNews site had the second highest volume and liked memorised items, and most of these were content related, so it appears that while BBCNews was remembered for its content and brand, Nike was remembered for its design. Nylon produced more animation-related memory (39%) whereas, unexpectedly, IntelliPage which had an animation-intensive design produced more content memory, but had low likeability ratings. Debriefing comments indicated that users didn't like the animations although they remembered their content (e.g. the pin ball animation) adversely. When the top five reported-interest areas were compared with memorised items, the animations in Nike, IntelliPage and Nylon were in close agreement; BBC content memory and reported areas also agreed, while agreement was poor for PCWorld and TigerDirect apart from general memory for products.

4.4 Overall Preference

The sites were significantly different in overall preference (F = 25.28, df 5, p<0.001) with BBCNews and Nike being the most favoured sites. For attractiveness the difference between sites was also significant (F = 48.72, df 5, p<0.001). For overall preference, BBCNews and Nike were the most favoured websites, followed by Nylon, IntelliPage and PCWorld close together, with TigerDirect in last place. The preference ratings of BBCNews and Nike were significantly higher than in the remaining websites (p<0.01). Nike was perceived to be the most attractive website (p<0.001 on overall measure), followed by Nylon and IntelliPage, with BBCNews in fourth place. TigerDirect scored significantly lower than all other websites in terms of preference and attractiveness (p<0.01). Table 3 summarises the overall preference and attractiveness weighted scores for each website.

Table 3. Mean weighted ratings for overall preference and attractiveness (ranks 1-5 weighted by 0.5, 0.25, 0.12, 0.05, 0.03,0.02)

	Preference		Attractiveness	
	N 1st choice	Overall	N 1st choice	Overall
BBCNews	15	9.85	1	3.86
IntelliPage	2	3.04	2	4.73
Nike	10	8.98	20	12.30
Nylon Mag	1	3.43	6	6.11
PCWorld	1	3.16	1	2.19
TigerDirect	1	1.54	0	0.81

There were no significant correlations between measures of attention (total fixations, fixation duration) and overall preference and attractiveness. Valenced memory (likeability) was correlated with attractiveness (p=<0.001 Spearman r), but not preference. Total memory was not correlated with preference or attractiveness.

In debriefing interview comments, BBCNews was preferred overall for its content, but was deemed to be less attractive; in contrast, Nike was the most attractive site and this corresponded with the attention measures and memory. The Nylon site also received a good attractiveness rating which is consistent with the users' memory. The anomaly is IntelliPage which ostensibly had good graphical design and creative use of animation; however, its attractiveness and preference ratings were poor and this was consistent with the users' memory, giving it fourth place overall. Finally, of the e-commerce sites, PCWorld seems to be the more effective design in terms of preference and attractiveness, although TigerDirect produced more items in the memory test. More volume, however, did not appear to be linked to a positive user attitude.

Nike was second on overall preference, while Nylon ranked third, as well as holding second place for attractiveness. PCWorld and TigerDirect occupied the fifth or sixth positions on most measures, apart from total memory where they both scored well. Nike and IntelliPage both attracted users with an interesting design. However, although IntelliPage attracted attention and evoked high content memory, it was not well rated on overall attractiveness. Users appear to have found the design interesting but ultimately unsatisfying. We speculate that the differences in use of animation between IntelliPage and Nike may account for the users' reaction. Nike was a well crafted sequential story, whereas IntelliPage suffered from concurrent overload of multiple animations. We attribute the attractiveness of the Nylon site to its more adventurous use of animation and images.

5 Discussion

To revisit our hypotheses: we found strong evidence to confirm that the structure of a website does influence user attention in terms of visual fixation. Reported attention to areas of interest and higher density areas of fixations agreed overall but the order of interest ranking and fixation densities were not related, in agreement with previous studies [12,15]. Structure influences the distribution of fixations and the overall number, with columnar sites receiving more fixations than more open designs. Column structured sites had a more evenly distributed pattern of fixation densities in the heat map analysis, whereas the graphical open structure sites had fewer denser fixations areas. This distribution, and the intermediate pattern in the Nylon site, suggests that image and animation may drive fixation attention when layout structure is not dominant; in contrast, strong layout structure may suppress attention to animations, as we found in the PCWorld and TigerDirect sites. Initial fixation sequences were also driven by animations in most sites, part from PCWorld and TigerDirect were site structure or users' conscious suppression of attention to animated banner adverts may provide the explanation. Initial fixation sequences showed poor agreement over fixation densities and reported interests, so eyetracking pathway analysis may not be useful for evaluating how well site features determine user attention and subsequent interest. We confirmed our second hypothesis that animations and images of people attract attention, both from subjective reports of areas of interest and fixation durations. However, we also found some evidence for banner advert blindness, confirming previous studies [1,2], so while animations might attract, users can override endogenous attention for disliked items. There was little evidence to support our last hypothesis that sites attended to more will be remembered in more detail. There were no differences in reported attention, while the differences in total fixations were associated with site layout structure.

Although most of the frequently fixated areas were also highly rated as interesting by the users, there were exceptions in both directions. We found that reported areas of interest did not always agree with high duration fixations and vice versa, so eye tracking may not be reliable for evaluating which key design/content features are attended to. We conjecture that users may discover areas of interest by short fixations or proximal fixations, which agrees with the findings of Halverson and Hornof [3,8]. Conversely, high density fixation areas may not be automatically equated with high interest, since users may subsequently downgrade their interest in an area. The interest report measure we used was essentially a cued recall retrospective protocol, so we believe we were capturing users' activated memory for areas of interest. If these areas are positively valenced then such report might be a good predictor of site acceptability and return visits, as demonstrated by our results on memory and attractiveness ranking. Guan et al. [6] also found that retrospective reports of interest reliably agreed with eye tracking fixations; however, our study found a better agreement (circa 70% v 50% agreement). This may reflect our use of pointing to AOIs compared to Guan et al.'s indirect mapping of verbally reported objects to image areas. However, the poor agreement we found for the two e-commerce sites shows that retrospective protocols may be prone to reconstructed memory bias; alternatively, low density fixations may be sufficient for the registering the users' interest.

Measures of attention generally were not strongly related to users' memory and overall preference. The lead of BBCNews for preference we attribute partly to the influence of brand and our subjects' prior knowledge, combined with stimulating content. Since we had no task/scenario in this experiment we can tentatively suggest that content and information were dominant in user judgment of information and e-commerce sites (i.e. BBCNews, Nylon, PCWorld and TigerDirect), whereas aesthetics dominated for Nike and IntelliPage. Since content could have had a significant effect, particularly for the BBC site which was familiar to our users, the conclusions on the influences on attractiveness and preferences have to be tentative. In our future work we will refine the methodological approach we have proposed and test sites with a stronger scenario and content assessment to investigate how attention, preference and memory are influenced by users' tasks. Based on the modest association between fixations, reported attention, and memory we found in this study, we expect the value of eye tracking as a diagnostic evaluation instrument may be limited to analysing areas which designers wish to be attended to but which received neither high fixations nor reported attention, or were not remembered.

References

1. Bayles, M.E.: Designing Online Banner Advertisements: Should We Animate? In: Proceedings of the SIGCHI Conference on Human Factors in Computing Systems: Changing Our World, Changing Ourselves, pp. 363–366. ACM Press, New York (2002)
2. Burke, M., Gorman, N., Nilsen, E., Hornof, A.: Banner Ads Hinder Visual Search and Are Forgotten. In: Extended abstracts of the 2004 Conference on Human Factors and Computing Systems, pp. 1139–1142. ACM Press, New York (2004)
3. Burke, M., Hornof, A., Nilsen, E., Gorman, N.: High-Cost Banner Blindness: Ads Increase Perceived Workload, Hinder Visual Search, and Are Forgotten. In: TOCHI, vol. 12(4), pp. 423–445 (2005)

4. Faraday, P., Sutcliffe, A.G.: An Empirical Study of Attending and Comprehending Multimedia Presentations. In: Proceedings of 4th Multimedia Conference, pp. 265–275. ACM Press, New York (1996)

5. Faraday, P., Sutcliffe, A.G.: Providing Advice for Multimedia Designers. In: Proceedings of the Conference on Human Factors in Computing Systems, pp. 124–131. ACM Press, New York (1998)

6. Guan, Z., Lee, S., Cuddihy, E., Ramey, J.: The Validity of the Stimulated Retrospective Think-Aloud Method As Measured by Eye Tracking. In: CHI 2006. Proceedings of 2006 Conference on Human Factors in Computing Systems, pp. 1253–1262. ACM Press, New York (2006)

7. Halverson, T., Hornof, A.J.: Strategy Shifts in Mixed Density Search. In: Proceedings of the 48th Annual Meeting of the Human Factors and Ergonomics Society, pp. 1860–1864 (2004)

8. Halverson, T., Hornof, A.J.: Explaining Eye Movements in the Visual Search of Varying Density Layouts. In: Proceedings of the Sixth International Conference on Cognitive Modeling, pp. 124–129 (2004)

9. Heer, J., Chi, C.H.: Separating the Swarm: Categorization Methods for User Sessions on the Web. In: Proceedings of the Conference on Human Factors in Computing Systems, pp. 243–250. ACM Press, New York (2002)

10. Hornof, A.J.: Cognitive Strategies for the Visual Search of Hierarchical Computer Displays. Journal of Human Computer Interaction 19(3), 183–223 (2003)

11. Itti, L., Koch, C.: Computational Modelling of Visual Attention. Nature 2(3), 194–203 (2001)

12. Johansen, S.A., Hansen, J.P.: Do We Need Eye Trackers to Tell Where People Look? In: CHI 2006. Proceedings of Conference on Human Factors in Computing Systems, pp. 923–928. ACM Press, New York (2006)

13. Nielsen, J.: F-Shaped Pattern for Reading Web Content, http://www.useit.com/alertbox/reading_pattern.html

14. Outing, S., Ruel, L.: The Best of Eye track III: What We Saw When We Looked Through Their Eyes (2004), http://www.poynterextra.org/eye track, /main.htm

15. Pan, B., Hembrooke, H.A., Gay, G.K., Granka, L.A., Feusner, M.K., Newman, J.K.: The Determinants of Web Page Viewing Behavior: An Eye-Tracking Study. In: Proceedings of the 2004 Symposium on Eye Tracking Research & Applications, pp. 147–154. ACM Press, New York (2004)

16. Reeves, B., Nass, C.: The Media Equation: How People Treat Computers, Television, and New Media Like Real People and Places. Cambridge University Press, Stanford, California (1996)

17. Rauterberg, M., Cachin, C.: Locating the primary attention focus of the user. In: Grechenig, T., Tscheligi, M. (eds.) VCHCI 1993. LNCS, vol. 733, pp. 129–140. Springer, Heidelberg (1993)

18. Zhang, P.: The Effects of Animation on Information Seeking Performance on the World Wide Web: Securing Attention or Interfering with Primary Tasks? Journal of the Association for Information Systems 1(1), 1–28 (2000)

FaericWorld: Browsing Multimedia Events Through Static Documents and Links

Maurizio Rigamonti, Denis Lalanne, and Rolf Ingold

DIVA Group, Department of Informatics of University of Fribourg
CH-1700 Fribourg, Switzerland
`first name.last name@unifr.ch`

Abstract. This paper describes a novel browsing paradigm, taking benefit of the various types of links (e.g. thematic, temporal, references, etc.) that can be automatically built between multimedia documents. This browsing paradigm can help eliciting multimedia archives' hidden structures or expanding search results to related media. The paper intend to present a novel model for browsing any kind of multimedia archives and further focuses on an archive of meetings recordings, in order to illustrate the advantage of our method to perform cross-meetings and in general cross-documents browsing. First of all, the structure of meeting datasets is presented, describing in particular the media implied, the annotations used for cross-document linking and the major mining techniques integrated in this work. Then, the paper presents at a glance the visual browser we developed that combines searching and browsing by links. Further, the performances of the actual system are discussed, i.e. the automatic indexing and linking processes for the two different meeting corpora, as well as the access and browsing performances. Finally, the paper presents the major unsolved issues and our perspectives for future works.

Keywords: Multimedia browsing, multimedia indexing, multimodal alignments, information visualization, information retrieval, multimedia meetings archives.

1 Introduction

With the new trend in recording events such as meetings and conferences, a huge amount of multimedia data, connected in various ways, is becoming available within large digital libraries. Although those new types of data are rich in content, they often miss high-level abstractions to allow robust indexing and retrieval. For this reason, multimedia data is often hard to retrieve using a standard google-like interface. In the last few years, different works have tackled this issue, aiming at creating new techniques for indexing meeting recordings and for browsing in annotated corpora [18].

Our main idea is based on two observations: 1) static documents such as newspapers and scientific publications are easily indexed using their textual content and 2) multimedia data can be linked to static documents through document alignment methods [14,18]. Thus, it becomes possible to access multimedia content by first searching textual documents and then browsing into the archive through links. The challenge is then to combine

C. Baranauskas et al. (Eds.): INTERACT 2007, LNCS 4662, Part I, pp. 102–115, 2007.

both searching and browsing process in interactive visualizations that does not separate the two processes. Furthermore, still using this link paradigm, this article explains how our system can help replaying a meeting and observe over time its relationships with other documents or meetings, highlighting recurrent topics and themes. In other words, our novel browsing paradigm tackles the issue recently presented by Tucker and Whittaker: *meetings are not isolated events; ideas and decisions can occur over a series of meetings and thus future meeting browsers should attempt to move away from the current perspective of just examining single meetings* [26].

Firstly, this paper presents the context of our work. Then, the section 3 describes the concepts on which is based our engine for indexing corpora of meetings and for representing relationships between documents through links. In section 4, we describe our browser and, in particular, the three steps for accessing multimedia information: searching, browsing and playing. The section 5 is dedicated to our system performances and gives detailed information on the corpora characteristics and links. Finally, the conclusion wraps up the paper and presents perspective works.

2 Indexing and Browsing in Multimedia Archive

Although several works and researches have been proposed in order to index and browse in multimedia archive and existing search engine are rather powerful, retrieving multimedia information is still difficult and related user interfaces are still in early phase of development [21]. Our assumption is that it is necessary to tackle two main challenges for improving search engines: 1) indexing of multimedia documents must take into account the implicit and explicit relationships between different media and 2) browsing techniques need to evolve thanks to these relationships. The following subsections present related works for respectively indexing and further browsing in multimedia archives.

2.1 Indexing Multimedia Documents

Nowadays, search engine are performing well for indexing and retrieving textual content, but their capability for managing multimedia data is still primitive. This lack derives from the difficulty of annotating and indexing media that are poor in semantic content, i.e. images, videos and audio files. Currently, we distinguish four methodologies for creating useful annotations for indexing multimedia documents: manual, automatic, both manual and automatic and, finally, alignment-based.

Browsers like YouTube [28] use manual annotations for indexing videos. Producing such high-level annotations presents two big drawbacks: 1) users personal perception of the document does not guarantee that the labels are entirely satisfying and 2) professional labeling is too expensive.

Various works tried to overcome this inconvenience and tried to integrate automatic methods for indexing images, audio and video streams, but habitually they do not take into account multiple media. For instance, Swain recapitulates different techniques for indexing media in [23]. Moreover, indexing of multimedia data is often based on low-level features that lack of semantic information. Smith et al. proposed to use model vectors for indexing multimedia documents [22], where each vector is correlated with a semantic concept detector. This method produces interesting results, but it is restraint to a limited set of concepts.

Other works combine analysis techniques with manual annotations, in order to reduce and simplify interventions of users. M4Note is a multimodal system for video recording that automatically computes low-level features and that allows users to easily add manual annotations thanks to electronic ink and speech recognition [11]. In the same way, Campanella et al. described a system that visualizes features automatically extracted from videos, in order to support users in defining clusters of shots [5].

A recent trend consists in aligning different media, with the purpose of indexing multimedia data. Alignment techniques enable the transfer of semantic information from richer to poorer medium. MUMIS [10] indexes videos of football matches aligning different textual and multilingual sources, such as news, commentaries, etc. The results of different documents analysis' techniques are combined in respect of specific rules, in order to improve the indexing of all these sources. Behera extracts from videos the slideshows presented in a meeting and aligns them with the original documents [2]. His method augments both media: documents are augmented with temporal dimension and videos gain semantic indexes. Likewise, Mekhaldi and Lalanne proposed an alignment technique based on similarity, which links the textual documents presented in a meeting with the transcript of spoken dialogs [18].

In our work, we integrate the last technique in order to align corpora of meetings and to create the new annotations necessary for indexing multimedia documents poor in semantic information.

2.2 Browsing Multimedia Archives

Today, in Google-like search engines a lot of work is dedicated to the improvement of indexing techniques. In fact, these engines do not completely explore the browsing mechanism, because users generally retrieve the interesting information already after the submission of the first correct query. At opposite, browsing means exploring an archive without having an exact knowledge of the documents it contains. Consequently, relatively recent projects tried to create relationships between documents, in order to structure information and to overcome searching lacks. Citeseer [3] and Scholar [20] interconnect scientific publications with different methods: users are able to read one paper and then to access similar articles. Moreover, the linking mechanism allows proposing the most linked paper in a specific domain as entry point. Similarly, LinkedIn [16] creates a network of interconnected persons, where links are social relations. Kartoo [9] calculates thematic clusters with the documents resulting from a query, whereas Alice in Wonderland [1] uses links for representing the relationships among words in a book. However, none of these systems have explored the use of relationships between multimedia documents, which is the most important aspect of our system.

Browsing mechanism has also been explored in recent multimedia browsers, where users explore one or more meetings [15, 25]. The JFerret-based family browsers [12, 27] have been developed in order to navigate between the synchronized documents of one meeting, using in particular transcript and audio streams. Archivus [17] is another browser that proposes a searching mechanism under constraint for exploring a collection of meetings. Finally, FriDoc [15] allows to navigate in one synchronized meeting using static document as main artifact. However, all these systems considers browsing at the intra-meeting level and thus do not consider browsing of the whole meeting corpus, which is critical when meetings are linked in time, thematically or by people, places, etc. The system we present in this article proposes to tackle this issue.

3   Cross-Linking Multimedia Data

FaericWorld is the system presented in this paper, which deals with corpora of multimedia data. In particular, cross-linked multimedia data is called a *world* and consists of meetings recordings, which are composed of heterogeneous categories of documents. Each document in the archive is a triple of raw data, annotations and links. Raw data are media sources (videos and audio files, PDF documents, etc.), multimedia documents (websites and slideshows) and persons (personal information, photos, etc.). The raw data is enriched with annotations, either manually added by users or automatically calculated thanks to analysis techniques. The use of annotations for indexing documents allows to access data in a structured manner and, consequently, to create more precise indexes [4]. For instance, two words are thematically more significant when belonging to one article's title in a PDF file rather than to an entire document. Moreover, annotations allow augmenting media that are poor in textual content, such as videos and audio files. Finally, links elicit the similarity in terms of content, properties or time of one document with the rest of the documents in the world.

The particularity of this implicitly linked dataset and the novelty of the browsing task prefixed in our work have implied the creation of a new relational engine for indexing and retrieving information. Above all, browsing by links involves that FaericWorld pre-calculates and stores a huge amount of information that describes relationships and similarities between documents.

The following subsections present firstly the different annotations used in our system, and secondly, how to create links between the different media.

3.1   Extracting Annotation from Media

This subsection presents the different annotations that are extracted from the media composing a multimedia meeting corpus and their properties.

- *Static documents* are analyzed thanks to XED tool [19], in order to automatically extract their physical structures (the layout with textual blocs and line). Moreover, some documents have been manually annotated with logical structures, which describe the hierarchy and the logical functions of physical structures. Both annotations allow to access fragments [4] of the static document, which become the main vector of thematic information.
- *Audio* recordings are transcribed either manually or with automatic tools. The transcript is composed of utterances, which are characterized by start and end timestamps, the full name or the id of the speaker, and the textual content. Actually, annotations on audio are rich of temporal and thematic information.
- *Videos* are poorly annotated with only information about the related audio track and a label containing speaker name or id.

Persons are a special kind of objects, entirely defined from its annotations, which are personal and thematic information such as first and last name, email and telephone number.

Meetings are annotated with a descriptor containing the location, the day and the hour of the recording. This information automatically provided is then manually completed with meeting name, content, type (i.e. belonging or not to a scenario) and participants. Last but not least, the descriptors contain a list of all media presented or recorded during the meeting.

Multimedia documents are enriched with all the annotations that could be extracted from individual media.

3.2   Creating Links Between Documents

Annotating documents is a preprocessing step that not only interests indexing, but also the creation of links: in fact, each type of annotation is useful for creating specific categories of links. Table 1 summarizes the links considered by FaericWorld and the type of document that produces these relationships.

Table 1. Each category of document is generating different types of link

type	cross-document links			
	thematic		strict (un-weighted)	
	(weighted)	temporal	Reference	hyperlink
Document	Static document, audio, person, event, multimedia	Audio, video, meeting, multimedia	Static document, multimedia	Static document, multimedia

Thematic links are calculated using alignment techniques [18]: each document of the corpus is compared with other ones in the world, accessing the structured content through annotations. For instance, each physical bloc of a static document is aligned with each speech transcript's utterance computed from an audio recording of the meeting dialogs. This technique allows calculating a similarity score between the content of both documents. Higher is the number of similar and discriminating words in the text, higher will be the score.

Temporal links are generated for time-based documents. For instance, a meeting contains several documents discussed, viewed or created at the same time by participants [13]: the whole documents coexist at the same moment within a particular meeting and, consequently, possess temporal relationships. In this manner, non time-based documents such as static documents and persons acquire a temporal dimension thanks to previous thematic links. Moreover, temporal links can be combined with thematic links to achieve a finer granularity: for instance, when a paragraph in a static document is thematically linked with an utterance, the first one is also synchronized with the timestamp of the second.

References are implicit links to other documents (bibliographies, citations, etc.), whereas *hyperlinks* are explicit links, extracted from textual document and web pages by syntactic analysis.

FaericWorld creates all the links presented in this subsection automatically, at the time the documents are imported in the world. At the importation stage, a new document is aligned with the whole world and the resulting links are computed and stored. Several links of the same type can exist between two documents, because the alignment process takes into account documents' parts.

4 A Combined Searching, Browsing and Playing

The navigation in FaericWorld corpora takes full benefit of the links computed between its different documents. In fact, the task of retrieving information does not require users to have any exact knowledge neither about searched documents nor about indexes allowing for accessing the data. Instead, links allows grouping documents by themes and after the selection of a specific topic allow consulting all the related documents. For instance, Bruno wants to replay what Florian said about the evaluation part of his article during a precedent meeting. So, he first retrieves the article using the keywords of its title. He then opens the document and clicks on the evaluation part, in order to access to the related parts of meetings, further selects the ones in which Florian is speaking and finally plays the corresponding audio/video streams to hear his opinion.

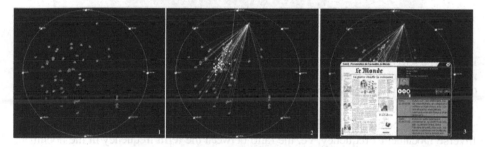

Fig. 1. (1) Searching documents of interest, (2) browsing results through connected documents and (3) playing results are the three main functionalities offered by our system that we propose to combine in a single interactive visualization

This section describes the interactive visualizations proposed by FaericWorld for representing the multimedia corpora, the connection and similarities between meetings and documents, and their relationships through time while playing. Figure 1 illustrates the three main functionalities of FaericWorld, i.e. searching (1), browsing (2) and playing (3), which are discussed in the following sub-sections.

4.1 Searching Through the Archive

The entry point in the archive uses a radial visualization [8], a classical view already used in different works for visualizing large archives of documents (for instance, in

[6]). A query composed of several keywords can be submitted to the system and the set of resulting documents is displayed in the RadViz as illustrated in the center of figure 2. A default query is proposed in order to display from the beginning a preliminary access to the meetings world and to represent an overview of its thematic structure. The default query is composed of the most recurrent terms that belong to disjoint sets of documents.

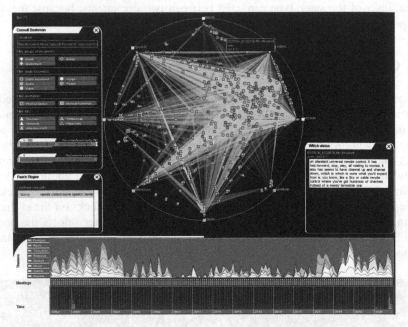

Fig. 2. The screenshot presents an overview of FaericWorld browser, with its two main visualizations and the dialog boxes. The first dialog on the left allows submitting queries, filtering document types, etc. The right dialog is specialized for document previews.

Documents position in the RadViz is defined using their *tf.idf* value (Term Frequency-Inverse Document Frequency, i.e. the ratio between the term frequency in the document over its frequency in the whole archive) for each term of the query. Documents in the center of the RadViz will thus contain all the terms of the query. If the term frequency of a word in a document is very high comparatively to its frequency in the whole corpus, the document will be strongly attracted by the related anchor.

Likewise, the parts of documents (e.g. utterances of speech transcripts or physical blocks of PDF documents) matching the query are displayed in the RadViz and linked to their father document (fig. 3). A mouse over a document of interest for the user, or over a part of document, allows to preview its content and to visualize additional information such as name, number of links, recurrent terms, etc.

A drawback of the radial visualization is the representation of queries with an even number of terms. For instance, sometimes a document is drawn in the visualization's center even if it contains only part of the searched terms, because these terms have the same weight and they are situated exactly at opposite poles on the RadViz. In order to resolve this ambiguity, we used *shapeVis* [24], similar to star coordinates, for repre

Fig. 3. Document parts are visualized as squares in RadViz and linked to the document they belong to, which is represented as a circle. Their colors depend on the document type.

senting the tf.idf value of the document. Figure 4 shows the double interest of this visualization: it represents 1) the terms of the query contained in the document as well as 2) their frequency relatively to the whole corpus of documents (the pie is very accentuated when the frequency of the term in the world is very low).

Fig. 4. The whole images are extracted from the same screenshot. (1, 2) The figures show fragments of document with small pies because the terms frequency in the corpus is high. (3) At opposite, the fragment of this image contains the totality of the terms in the archive and, consequently, the pie is accentuated.

Overlapping of documents provokes the second problem in this radial visualization. In some case and especially for atomic queries, several documents could occupy the same location. Currently, FaericWorld does not provide a valid solution to overcome this lack.

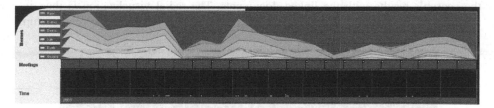

Fig. 5. The second visualization shows themes evolution during time for the whole corpus

The second main visualization in FaericWorld is based on *ThemeRiver* [7] and shows the evolution of themes in the whole archive throughout time (Fig. 5). The bottom part is a representation of the calendar, which indicates when meetings have been recorded. In the middle, the meetings are chronologically sorted one after the other and choosing a meeting highlights its documents in the RadViz (brush and link mechanism). Finally, the top plot represents the evolution of themes defined in the query. Each term is represented in the ordinates axe, whereas meetings occupy the abscissas one. The width of each river depends on the occurrence of each term in the documents linked to the meeting (e.g. speech transcript, attached PDF documents, etc.), weighted by their *tf.idf* values. The meeting having the largest rivers is potentially the most interesting one relatively to the submitted query (for instance, the second meeting in fig. 5). In a recent implementation, we also offered users the possibility to zoom within the ThemeRiver at a meeting level, displaying the evolution of themes within a single meeting, minute after minute.

4.2 Browsing the Results Using Thematic and Temporal Links

The major contribution of this paper is the use of links to discover new documents. The entry point presented in the previous subsection contains a set of results depending on the query. Sometimes, users have already found the documents of interest, but often the query mechanism is not enough to satisfy their needs. Moreover, when media such as audio or video are poorly indexed, searching is not useful. For these reasons, we propose to use links between documents as a new way to browse in a multimedia archive.

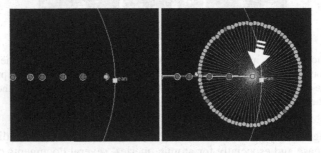

Fig. 6. The user finds an interesting document (1) and she discovers all related documents (2)

When users are interested in a document returned by the query, they can expand the search's results with the linked documents. The radial visualization is thus enriched with these similar documents. Their distribution depends on the relationships

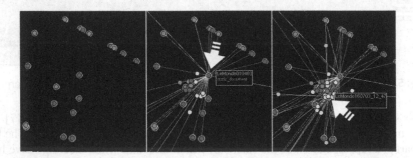

Fig. 7. Some of the new documents are similar or connected to already visualized ones

they have with already visualized documents. On Figure 6, the new documents only share relationships with the selected document and thus, are simply organized around it (the white arrow indicates the clicked document of interest).

The figure 7 illustrates a different case: when a new document is linked with several documents already in the RadViz, its location is defined at the center of mass of all these other documents' locations.

Moreover, users are able to decide that one document displayed in the RadViz is not interesting: hiding this document implies that the most similar documents can be eliminated too from the visualization. Similarity is pre-calculated for each category of links (see section 3.2) and the desired threshold can be changed, thanks to sliders that filter accordingly the search space. In the near future, we will integrate a functionality allowing users to select two or more documents: FaericWorld will then display the documents that optimize the distance between the selected ones.

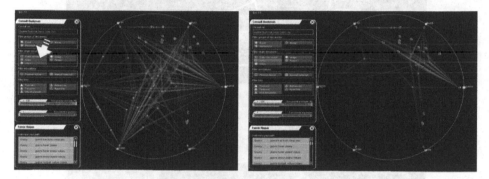

Fig. 8. The image shows all the documents corresponding to the submitted query (1). After filtering, all audio files are hidden (2).

Finally, filtering capabilities have been included in order to facilitate browsing in the world and to configure the RadViz when a large amount of document is displayed (fig. 8). In particular, filters allow selecting the categories of documents or links to visualize. Similarly, two scrollbars control the similarity thresholds: when they are activated, the links with a too low value are hidden and vice versa. Furthermore, when a document discovered while browsing not any more possessed visible links, it is removed from the set of displayed documents.

4.3 Viewing and Playing: Browsing in Time

Finding and consulting a document is only a part of the browsing task. In fact, users are frequently stimulated to extend the browsing experience while consulting a document. Consequently, another contribution of our system consists in using links in order to propose users new related documents while viewing the content of a document. Meetings have a particular property: all the media they contain are strictly synchronized to the meeting time. At opposite of non time-based documents, which are always connected to the same set of related documents, the themes constantly evolve during a meeting throughout time and, consequently, the set of linked documents changes.

Figure 9 is a mockup that illustrates a meeting player. All the media of the meetings are synchronized and when a user for instance clicks a paragraph of a PDF document discussed during the meeting, the transcript of the dialogs moves to the instant when this document was in the verbal focus. This is done through the document/speech alignment that directly benefits from the thematic links. At contemporary, the audio file and the videos are synchronized thanks to temporal links. The meeting view is a screenshot of JFriDoc, a document-centric meeting browser we developed to navigate through meetings.

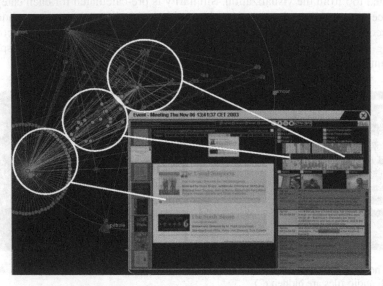

Fig. 9. In the integrated meeting browser, media can be synchronously played, thanks to the temporal alignments. Further, since topics evolve during a meeting, links and relations to the documents in the whole meetings archive dynamically change over time.

Finally, figure 9 illustrates cross-meetings and cross-documents links outside the current meeting. The thematic space of a meeting evolves during time, and thus also the thematic links with non-focused documents. For instance, during the meeting different static documents are projected or discussed and thus different links are activated when the corresponding theme changes.

5   Performances

The performance of FaericWorld has been tested. Currently, two corpora have been integrated in the system: IM2.DI corpus and AMI corpus. The first one consists in 22 meetings recorded in French. The data taken into account by FaericWorld are newspapers that have been manually annotated with logical structures, videos of participants with manual labels declaring speaker identity, audio files enriched with manual transcript, and, finally, meeting descriptors. This corpus has been used for developing the whole system.

FaericWorld system has further been validated with the second corpus, which contains 171 meetings in English. The most part of them belongs to groups of 4 meeting, sharing an identical scenario. The corpus is rich of manual annotations but only part of them has been selected. In particular, FaericWorld uses utterances of audio transcripts (performed manually), tags on videos (id codes for participants) and meetings' descriptors. Each meeting contains PowerPoint presentations, technical reports and summaries, which have been automatically analyzed and annotated with physical structures.

Both corpora of meeting have been automatically imported, creating simultaneously specific annotations for some category of media such as static documents. At import stage, multiple copies of the same document were eliminated. The retained documents were fragmented into their parts thanks to structural annotations (for instance, the physical structure for static document and the utterances composing speech transcript of meeting dialogs). Links were created thanks to thematic alignment of parts, lexical analysis and media synchronization. FaericWorld automatically indexed and structured IM2.DI and AMI corpora. Table 2 summarizes the major characteristics of the loaded corpora.

Table 2. FaericWorld automatically indexed and structured IM2.DI and AMI corpora. The table summarizes corpora and worlds characteristics.

	Corpora	
	IM2.DI	AMI
Meetings	22	171
Imported documents	245	3.644
Unique documents	176	1.697
Fragments (indexed parts of document)	4.278	113.905
Links between documents (similarity threshold: 10%)	38.747	133.139.945

The PC used for importing the corpora and for accessing indexed data has a Pentium 4 CPU at 2.40 GHz, with 512 MB of RAM. Importing time for IM2 and AMI corpora correspond respectively to 50 minutes and 26 hours. Calculation time augments with the amount of imported documents: the alignment is the bottleneck that, however, could be resolved thanks to parallel calculations. With AMI corpus, submitting a query of 8 words and preparing the visualization takes in mean less than half a second. Retrieving and visualizing the documents linked to a document of interest requires in general less than 1 second. At the time of writing, no formal user evaluation of the browser has been performed, but a discount usability evaluation has shown that the RadViz visualization is sometimes hard to interpret. At opposite, the ThemeRiver has been well accepted by users.

6 Conclusion

This paper presents a novel approach, based on cross-media links for browsing through an archive of multimedia documents. Automatically computed links open new thematically and temporally related spaces. Instead of refining search queries step by step, users can select an entry point in the archive and then follow links to jump from one thematic space to another one. Moreover, they are able to discover interesting multimedia documents, such as video and audio, generally hard to index and retrieve because of the difficulty to extract high semantic abstractions. With our approach, multimedia documents become more visible, thanks to their relationships with other documents.

Moreover, browsing is an incremental experience - a discovery process - that requires a shallow consultation of documents, playing parts of meetings, etc. in order to crystallize knowledge. In our system, browsing through links updates continuously the visualization of the archive, in order to expand user's navigation.

Future works will consist in extending user visual and interactive experience. Currently, FaericWorld uses a RadViz in order to visualize the entire world, using an automatic query as entry point. In fact, it is difficult to distinguish thematic groups of documents, because of theirs' high fragmentation. To overcome this problem, we will develop a new entry view that aims at highlighting clusters of documents using their similarity. Another work in progress is related to the diversity of media and annotations involved in our worlds, which implies the development of specific views for visualizing and interacting with each category of document. Up to now, only meetings and static documents profit of interactive views. Moreover, we shall introduce in the system edition capabilities in order to modify, create and destroy annotations and links. Edition capabilities are as well necessary for creating new documents, which can be shared among users as access views to the archive. Finally, a user evaluation shall be performed, in order to measure the usability of links for visually representing multimedia archives and for guiding the user during a browsing task.

Acknowledgments. We thank the Swiss National Competence Center of Research on Interactive Multimodal Information Management IM2 for founding this project and Enrico Bertini for his useful comments.

References

1. Alice in Wonderland, TextArc, http://www.textarc.org
2. Behera, A.: A Visual Signature-based Identification Method of Low-resolution Document Images and its Exploitation to Automate Indexing of Multimodal Recordings. University of Fribourg, Switzerland, thesis Nr. 1529
3. Bollacker, K.D., Lawrence, S., Lee Giles, C.: CiteSeer: an autonomous web agent for automatic retrieval and identification of interesting publications. In: Proc. Of 2nd International Conference on Autonomous Agents, pp. 116–123. ACM Press, New York (1998)
4. Callan, J.P.: Passage-level evidence in document retrieval. In: Proc. of the 17th annual international ACM SIGIR conference on Research and development in information retrieval, pp. 302–310. Springer, Heidelberg (1994)
5. Campanella, M., Leonardi, R., Migliorati, P.: An intuitive graphic environment for navigation and classification of multimedia documents. In: ICME 2005. Proc. Of Multimedia and Expo, pp. 743–746. IEEE Press, Los Alamitos (2005)
6. Carey, M., Heesch, D.C., Rüger, S.M.: Info Navigator: A Visualization Tool for Document Searching and Browsing. In: Proc. DMS'03, pp. 23–38 (2003)
7. Havre, S., Hetzler, E., Whitney, P., Nowell, L.: ThemeRiver: visualizing thematic changes in large document collections. In: IEEE Transactions on Visualization and Computer Graphics, pp. 9–20. IEEE Press, Los Alamitos (2002)
8. Hoffman, P., Grinstein, G., Marx, K., Grosse, I., Stanley, E.: DNA visual and analytic data mining. In: Proc. Of Visualisation'97, pp. 437–441. IEEE Press, Los Alamitos (1997)

9. Kartoo, http://www.kartoo.com
10. Kuper, J., Saggion, H., Cunningham, H., Declerck, T., de Jong, F., Reidsma, D., Wilks, Y., Wittenburgh, P.: Intelligent Multimedia Indexing And Retrieval through Multi-source Information Extraction and Merging. In: Proc of IJCAI, pp. 409–414 (2003)
11. Goularte, R., Camacho-Guerrero, J.A., Inácio Jr, V.R., Cattelan, R.G., Pimentel, M.d.G.C.: M4Note: a Multimodal Tool for Multimedia Annotations. In: Proc. of WebMedia and LA-Web, pp. 142–149. IEEE Press, Los Alamitos (2004)
12. Integrated JFerret Browser and Overlapped Speech Browser, In: Demonstration Session Guide, MLMI'06, http://groups.inf.ed.ac.uk/mlmi06/MLMI-2006-DemoSessionFinal.pdf
13. Lalanne, D., Sire, S., Ingold, R., Behera, A., Mekhaldi, D., Von Rotz, D.: A research agenda for assessing the utility of document annotations in multimedia databases of meeting recordings. In: Proc. of 3rd International Workshop on Multimedia Data and Document Engineering, in conjunction with VLDB-2003, pp. 47–55 (2003)
14. Lalanne, D., Ingold, R., Von Rotz, D., Behera, A., Mekhaldi, D., Popescu-Belis, A.: Using Static Documents as Structured and Thematic Interfaces to Multimedia Meeting Archives. In: Renals, S., Bengio, S. (eds.) MLMI 2005. LNCS, vol. 3869, Springer, Heidelberg (2006)
15. Lalanne, D., Lisowska, A., Bruno, E., Flynn, M., Georgescul, M., Guillemot, M., Janvier, B., Marchand-Maillet, S., Melichar, M., Moenne-Loccoz, N., Popescu-Belis, A., Rajman, M., Rigamonti, M., von Rotz, D., Wellner, P.: The IM2 Multimodal Meeting Browser Family. IM2 technical report (2005)
16. LinkedIn, https://www.linkedin.com
17. Lisowska, A., Rajman, M., Bui, T.H.: ARCHIVUS: A System for Accessing the Content of Recorded Multimodal Meetings. In: Proc. of the Joint AMI/PASCAL/IM2/M4 Workshop on Multimodal Interaction and Related Machine Learning Algorithms, pp. 291–304 (2004)
18. Mekhaldi, D.: A Study on multimodal document alignment: bridging the gap between textual documents and spoken language. University of Fribourg, Switzerland, thesis Nr. 1521
19. Rigamonti, M., Bloechle, J.L., Hadjar, K., Lalanne, D., Ingold, R.: Towards a canonical and structured representation of PDF documents through reverse engineering. In: Proc. of ICDAR'05, pp. 1050–1054 (2005)
20. Scholar, http://scholar.google.com
21. Shneiderman, B., Plaisant, C.: Designing the User Interface: Strategies for Effective Human-Computer Interaction, 4th edn, p. 652. Addison-Wesley, Reading (2004)
22. Smith, J.R., Naphade, M., Natsev, A.(P.): Multimedia Semantic Indexing Using Model Vectors. In: ICME 2003. Proc. Of Multimedia and Expo, vol. II, pp. 445–448. IEEE Press, Los Alamitos (2003)
23. Swain, M.J.: Searching for Multimedia on the World Wide Web. In: Proc. of Multimedia Computing and Systems, vol. I, pp. 32–37. IEEE Press, Los Alamitos (1999)
24. Theisel, H., Kreuseler, M.: An enhanced spring model for information visualization. In: Proc. of Eurographics 98, vol. 17(3), pp. 335–344. Blackwell Publishing, Malden (1998)
25. Tucker, S., Whittaker, S.: Accessing Multimodal Meeting Data: Systems, Problems and Possibilities. In: Bengio, S., Bourlard, H. (eds.) MLMI 2004. LNCS, vol. 3361, pp. 1–11. Springer, Heidelberg (2005)
26. Tucker, S., Whittaker, S.: Reviewing Multimedia Meeting Records: Current Approaches. In: Multimodal multiparty meeting processing workshop, ICMI 2005, International Conference on Multimodal Interfaces (2005)
27. Wellner, P., Flynn, M., Guillemot, M.: Browsing recorded meetings with Ferret. In: Bengio, S., Bourlard, H. (eds.) MLMI 2004. LNCS, vol. 3361, pp. 12–21. Springer, Heidelberg (2005)
28. YouTube, http://www.youtube.com

Degree-of-Interest Visualization for Ontology Exploration

Peter Hüsken and Jürgen Ziegler

Department of Computer Science, Faculty of Engineering, University Duisburg-Essen,
47048 Duisburg, Germany
{huesken, ziegler}@interactivesystems.info
http://live.interactivesystems.info

Abstract. In recent years, improvements in semantic web technologies have given us new expressive description languages for modeling knowledge domains — the so called ontologies. Nevertheless, ontology editors lack of easy and intuitive user interfaces, so that the exploration and creation of ontologies is often too difficult to be efficient. In this short paper, we introduce a new tree widget which utilizes sophisticated visualization and interaction features for ontology exploration and editing as a work in progress study. Due to space limitations we concentrate here on the aspect of ontology browsing.

1 Visualization and Interaction Issues for Ontologies

Collaborative development of ontologies is becoming an important activity in various scientific and professional communities. In the context of the Ontoverse project[1] we are trying to develop more intuitive user interfaces as well as collaboration support for this task. In this paper, we present a novel visualization technique for ontology development.

Existing ontology tools, such as Protege [1] concentrate on visualizing the basic class hierarchy, which can be seen as the structural backbone of any ontology by presenting different kinds of tree views. Graph or network visualizations tend to be less informative when showing ontologies with several thousand nodes [2]. Our efforts are inspired by the family of *Focus+Context* techniques, applying fisheye perspectives that have been introduced by Furnas [3]. Nodes are automatically displayed or elided according to the user's computed degree-of-interest (DOI) as explained in section 2. In this regard, Card et al. [2] describe the application of the DOI concept for tree layouts as *logical filtering* of nodes. Their implementation of the Focus+Context tree is completely visible without the need to scroll. Showing the whole information structure, leads to distorted visualizations where many nodes are typically too small to read their labels.

In our approach, we also use a distortion-based rendering of the tree while keeping the node size at a readable level. As a consequence, scrolling is needed.

---

[1] The Ontoverse project is funded by the Federal Ministry of Education and Research. Project no. 01C5975.

C. Baranauskas et al. (Eds.): INTERACT 2007, LNCS 4662, Part I, pp. 116–119, 2007.

We aim at minimizing the need to scroll however, by providing smart ways to hide parts of the tree that are not relevant in the current context. To provide Focus+Context, the currently selected concept is rendered with a larger size. Further we apply a multifocal approach to highlight also other concepts that the user is probably interested in — those could be all concepts that are directly related to the selected concept by OWL object properties [5]. Object properties are represented as directed lines beside the concept hierarchy, which connect the selected concept with other concepts in the ranges of the selected concept's object properties. These so-called *PropertyLines* are shown on the right side of fig. 1. Here *BioinformaticsTask* is connected to the concepts *ComputationalMethod* and *Program* with additional straight lines beside the tree illustration. In this way, the user gets an impression about the semantic interrelations as being part of the ontology.

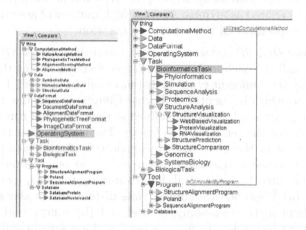

Fig. 1. SmartTree with Focus+Context (left) and Property-Lines (right)

As an additional means to reduce the complexity of the visualization, we have implemented an interactive function called *Condense & Explode*: After selecting the line, connecting subtrees with a common parent node, every subtree outside the focus is faded out (condensed), representing all hidden subtrees by an elision symbol. Clicking on the line once more will show the full tree again. In this way we can better utilize vertical space to provide the user with a more suitable overview of the current relevant parts of an ontology. Future versions of implementation will apply those interaction functions automatically by making use of the DOI concept (see section 2).

2   User Adaptation

For estimating the degree of user interest in a node, we can monitor the observable user behaviour and parameters such as the history of concept selection. In order to estimate the *Degree of Interest* value (DOI) of every concept representation, we have to distinguish two basic factors:

1. *A Priori Importance (API).* Independent of any application context the API value of a concept representation depends on the ontology structure and is constant as long as the given ontology remains unchanged. API values have to be updated after a new ontology version has been released. We identified two simple rules for estimating the API value of concept respresentations:

   – The importance of a concept is the higher the more instances of the concept exist, because the frequency of assertions is a strong indication for an importance independent of any user.
   – The importance of a concept is the higher the more object properties use the concept as part of their domain or range, because we suppose that a concept with many object properties will be used frequently in the concept's related assertions. Again, a high number of assertions probably denote importance of the concept in question.

2. The *Distance D(x, SP)* between concept x and the concept SP that has the focus (also called *Selection Point*). A larger distance means that concept x is less important. Different types of distances can be applied. To produce the fisheye effect, which is essential to Focus+Context techniques, the geometric distance D_{vis} is used. It is usally defined as the number of concepts between SP and x inside the rendered tree layout. The effect is that the user gets a better overview of those concepts being close to the selected concept. It is also possible to use a taxonomic distance D_{tax} as one instance of semantic distance presented by Rada et al. [6]. To sum up the idea, two assumptions are made: (a) Concepts are similar (less distant) when the shortest path between them in the taxonomy is brief and (b) concepts at upper levels of the concept hierarchy are more general and are semantically less similar than concepts at lower levels. A combined type of distance is used by Card et al. [2]. They assume that a node's importance decreases intrinsically with its path distance to the hierarchy root together with the geometric distance to the focus node(s).

The DOI value for concept x with respect to the concept in focus can be calculated by function F:

$$DOI(x, SP) = F(API(x), D(x, SP)) \tag{1}$$

Equation 2 shows an example of F. The additional factor β relatively weights the distance D ($\beta = 0$: only $API(x)$ is considered, $\beta = \infty$: only $D(x, SP)$ is relevant, $\beta = 1$: both arguments are equally weighted). The arguments API and D range from zero to one. As a consequence, the function F_β has the same range.

$$F_\beta(x, y) = \frac{(\beta^2 + 1) \cdot x \cdot y}{\beta^2 \cdot x + y} \tag{2}$$

The explorations of interactive visualizations can be seen as an iterative process, because the user plans the next steps based on attained information. As a consequence the sequence of concept selections has to be followed:

$$DOI_i(x, SP_i) = \begin{cases} API(x) & : i = 0 \\ F(DOI_{i-1}(x, SP_{i-1}), D(x, SP_i)) & : i > 0 \end{cases} \quad (3)$$

Applying user adaption in this way, fast distant calculations are required, otherwise the SmartTree's performance is affected adversely.

3   Summary and Outlook

In this paper we have introduced a customized tree widget for ontology exploration with new interactive functions. User adaptation can be realized by monitoring the sequence of user interactions, so that those concepts get a higher DOI value that have been selected recently.

We are currently working on the implementation of *Semantic Zooming* [2]: As the display is zoomed in and nodes are expanded past a certain threshold their content changes. The larger the concept representations are scaled the more information items will be shown inside them. This information might contain the date, the concept has been added and by whom that has been done.

References

1. Grosso, W.E., Eriksson, H., Fergerson, R.W., Gennari, J., Tu, S.W., Musen, M.A.: Knowledge modeling at the millenium (the design and evoulution of protege 2000). In: KAW'99. Proceedings of the 12th Knowledge Acquisition Workshop (1999)
2. Card, S.K., Nation, D.: Degree-of-Interest Trees — A Component of an Attention-Reactive User Interface International Conference on Advanced Visual Interfaces (2002)
3. Furnas, G.W.: The FISHEYE view — a new look at structured files. Readings in Information Visualization: Using Vision to Think, 312–330 (1981)
4. Munzner, T., Guimbretiere, F., Tasiran, S., Zhang, L., Zhou, Y.: TreeJuxtaposer: Scalable Tree Comparision using Focus+Context with Guaranteed Visibility. In: Proc. SIGGRAPH, ACM Transactions on Graphics, vol. 22(3), pp. 453–462 (2003)
5. Smith, M.K., Welty, C., McGuiness, D.L.: OWL Web Ontology Language Guide. W3C Recommendation (2004), http://www.w3.org/TR/owl-guide/
6. Rada, R., Mili, H., Bicknell, E., Blettner, M.: Development and application of a metric on semantic nets. IEEE Transactions on Systems, Man and Cybernetics, 17–30 (1989)

S^3: Storable, Shareable Search

Meredith Ringel Morris and Eric Horvitz

Microsoft Research
Redmond, WA, USA
{merrie, horvitz}@microsoft.com

Abstract. We present S^3, a system that implicitly captures the process and products of Web *investigations* (exploratory searches involving multiple queries). This automatically-created, persistent representation of an investigation enables future review and continuation of suspended search activities. This persistent representation can reduce unnecessary re-execution of queries and enable users to quickly regain the context of a resumed activity. Stored investigations can also be shared with, and augmented by, collaborators. Furthermore, a stored investigation can act as a *standing query*, proactively updating itself when a user revisits it.

Keywords: Web search, exploratory search, investigation, persistent search.

1 Introduction

Web searches are often exploratory or informational [3] in nature. Such *investigations* can involve issuing multiple queries to a search engine and reviewing a large number of resulting web pages. Browsers and search engines, however, typically model search as a transient activity, treating each query independently from prior queries even though, from the user's point of view, multiple queries are frequently part of a single investigation.

This transient model of Web search can result in extra work for users. For example, research on interruptions [4, 5] has found that users frequently switch tasks, and often experience long delays before task resumption. Intervening tasks may also result in closing or changing the state of the user's Web browser. A user returning to a Web investigation after a delay must remember the state of his task, such as what queries he has already issued and what useful sources of information he has already discovered.

The challenges of recalling the state of a resumed task can result in unnecessary duplication of effort. For example, surveys and Web log analyses [1, 8] reveal that users frequently re-enter previously issued queries in order to re-find information. Another study found that over half of Web page visits are re-visits [7].

To address the limitations of the transient nature of current Web search, we introduce the S^3 system (Figures 1 and 2). S^3 implicitly stores information about the *process* (queries issued) and *products* (useful pages found) of Web investigations. This persistent representation can facilitate resumption of an interrupted or suspended investigation, proactively update itself, and enable collaboration.

C. Baranauskas et al. (Eds.): INTERACT 2007, LNCS 4662, Part I, pp. 120–123, 2007.
IFIP International Federation for InformationProcessing 2007

Prior approaches to managing complex search tasks include bookmarking, histories, or systems that allow users to flag pages or parts of pages for inclusion in a workspace [2, 6]. Our approach differs from this prior work, since we implicitly store several types of metadata associated with an investigation (queries issued, pages visited, contributor identity, and annotations) and use this stored data to facilitate task resumption, proactive information fetching, and collaboration.

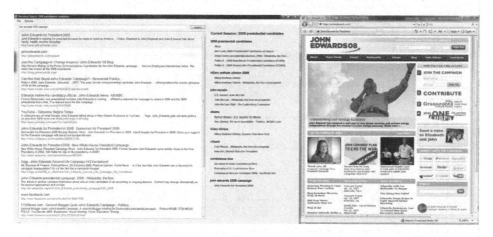

Fig. 1. *Conducting an investigation with S³.* The search box and current search results are shown in the leftmost portion of the interface. The central pane provides an overview of the queries issued and sites visited so far during the investigation. The rightmost portion displays the currently selected result in a browser.

2   The S³ System

When a user opens S³, he can either begin a new investigation by entering a query in the search box (Figure 1), or he can load a saved investigation via the file menu (Figure 2). When a user begins a new investigation, the first query issued is used to provide a default name for the investigation. The user can issue queries via the search box; searches are sent to a Web search engine and the results are shown below the search box (our implementation uses Windows Live Search, but S³'s architecture allows for the substitution of other search sources). Clicking on any result displays it in a browser window.

For each investigation, S³ automatically records all queries entered, results retrieved, and subsequent webpages visited. Additionally, users can associate comments with a search result by right-clicking and choosing the "Comment" option from a context menu.

While searching, a user can see a summary of his current investigation history, including queries issued and pages visited, which is displayed next to the current list of search results (Figure 1). At any time, a user can click on this history panel to see a more detailed representation of his investigation (Figure 2) – this representation is also what a user sees if he opens a previously stored investigation.

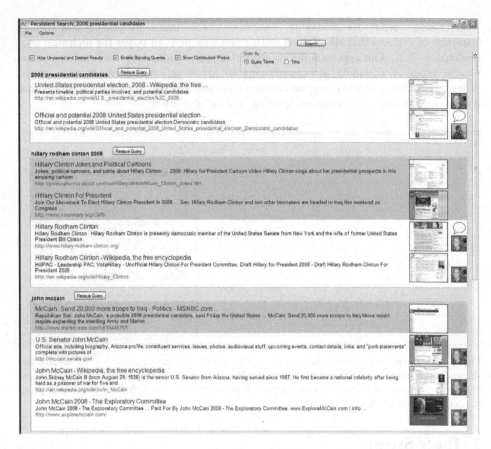

Fig. 2. *Viewing a stored investigation.* The title, url, and thumbnail for each page visited during the investigation is presented beneath the query terms that lead to its discovery. Items highlighted in green represent newly available content that has been proactively fetched via a standing query. Clicking any item opens the corresponding page in the browser window. The user who contributed each page to the investigation is depicted via a thumbnail, and the presence of comments is indicated by a speech bubble icon; hovering over the icon reveals the full comment.

The detailed view of the investigation shows each query issued during the investigation, in chronological order. Below each query, S^3 shows the title, URL, and thumbnail images of the "useful" pages found as a consequence of that query. The current implementation of S^3 counts any page the user viewed in the browser window as "useful" (and provides the ability to delete a page from the "useful" list via a right-click context menu); however, a variety of heuristics, such as the length of time spent viewing a page or whether links within the page were clicked, could also be used.

A "speech bubble" icon is shown next to pages that have comments associated with them; hovering over this icon with the mouse reveals the full text of the comment. Asynchronous collaboration among multiple users is enabled by S^3's document model – a stored investigation is saved as an XML file, which can be sent to others (*i.e.*, by email or other file-transfer protocols) and loaded into their own S³ clients. If more than one user has contributed to the investigation, the users' photos are shown next to the pages that they discovered.

If the user selects the "enable standing queries" menu option, then whenever he loads an investigation S³ will invisibly re-issue each of the investigation's queries, and check whether each has any highly-ranked results (rank ten or higher) that were not among the top ten results when the user initially executed the query. If such new results exist, then S³ displays them along with the previously-visited "useful" pages associated with each query; the proactively-fetched results are visually distinguished by green highlighting.

Clicking on any of the pages listed in the detailed view opens that page in a browser, and clicking any of the query terms listed re-executes that query and returns the user to the "searching" view (Figure 1). The search box is also available in the detailed view, enabling the user to add to a stored investigation – entering a query in the search box also returns the user to the "searching" view.

3 Conclusion

The S³ system can assist users in performing multi-query Web investigations by automatically saving the process and products of a series of related searches. This persistent representation of search aims to help users resume an investigation after an interruption and reduce the need to re-issue queries or re-find sites. The abilities to share investigations with others and to create standing queries are further benefits of our persistent search model. We are currently pursuing studies to evaluate the utility of our persistent search representations in assisting users with multi-session and multi-user searches.

References

1. Aula, A., Jhaveri, N., Kaki, M.: Information Search and Re-access Strategies of Experienced Web Users. In: Proceedings of WWW 2005, pp. 583–592 (2005)
2. Bharat, K.: SearchPad: Explicit Capture of Search Context to Support Web Search. In: Proceedings of WWW 2000, pp. 493–501 (2000)
3. Broder, A.A: Taxonomy of Web Search. ACM SIGIR Forum 36(2), 3–10 (2002)
4. Czerwinski, M., Horvitz, E., Wilhite, S.A: Diary Study of Task Switching and Interruptions. In: Proceedings of CHI 2004, pp. 175–182 (2004)
5. Iqbal, S., Horvitz, E.: Disruption and Recovery of Computing Tasks: Field Study, Analysis, and Directions. In: Proceedings of CHI 2007, pp. 677–686 (2007)
6. Schraefel, M.C., Zhu, Y., Modjeska, D., Wigdor, D., Zhao, S.: Hunter Gatherer: Interaction Support for the Creation and Management of Within-Web-Page Collections. In: Proceedings of WWW 2002 (2002)
7. Tauscher, L., Greenberg, S.: Revisitation Patterns in World Wide Web Navigation. In: Proceedings of CHI 1997, pp. 399–406 (1997)
8. Teevan, J., Adar, E., Jones, R., Potts, M.: History Repeats Itself: Repeat Queries in Yahoo's Query Logs. In: Proceedings of SIGIR 2006, pp. 703–704 (2006)

Trainable Sketch Recognizer for Graphical User Interface Design

Adrien Coyette[1], Sascha Schimke[2], Jean Vanderdonckt[1], and Claus Vielhauer[2]

[1] Belgian Lab. of Computer-Human Interaction (BCHI), Information Systems Unit (ISYS)
Louvain School of Management, Université catholique de Louvain,
Place des Doyens 1, B–1348 Louvain-la-Neuve (Belgium)
{coyette,vanderdonckt}@isys.ucl.ac.be
http://www.isys.ucl.ac.be/bchi
[2] Department of Computer Science/ITI,University Otto von Guericke,
Universitätsplatz 2, – D-39106 Magdeburg (Germany)
sascha.schimke@iti.cs.uni-magdeburg.de

Abstract. In this paper we present a new algorithm for automatic recognition of hand drawn sketches based on the Levenshtein distance. The purpose for drawing sketches in our application is to create graphical user interfaces in a similar manner as the well established paper sketching. The new algorithm is trainable by every user and improves the recognition performance of the techniques which were used before for widget recognition. In addition, this algorithm ay serve for recognizing other types of sketches, such as letters, figures, and commands. In this way, there is no modality disruption at sketching time.

1 Introduction

Designing the right User Interface (UI) the first time is very unlikely to occur. Instead, UI design is recognized as a process that is [19] intrinsically *open* (new considerations may appear at any time), *iterative* (several cycles are needed to reach an acceptable stage), and *incomplete* (not all required considerations are available at design time). Consequently, means to support early UI design has been extensively researched [20] to identify appropriate techniques such as paper sketching, prototypes, mock-ups, diagrams, etc. Most designers consider hand sketches on paper as one of the most effective ways to represent the first drafts of a future UI [1,10,13,14]. Indeed, this approach presents many advantages over other techniques like editing in an interface builder: sketches can be drawn during any design stage [14], it is fast to learn and quick to produce [20], it lets the sketcher focus on basic structural issues instead of unimportant details (e.g., exact alignment, typography and colors) [10], it is very appropriate to convey ongoing, unfinished designs [12,16], it encourages creativity [10], sketches can be performed collaboratively between designers and end-users [15], and last but not least, it is largely unconstrained [4]. This unconstraint character turns to be a fundamental aspect to preserve in sketching tools: if for any reason, this character is disrupted, the end user may be confused or disappointed. Van Duyne *et al.* [20] reported that creating a low-fidelity UI prototype (such as UI sketches) is at least 10 to 20 times easier and faster than its equivalent with a high-fidelity prototype

C. Baranauskas et al. (Eds.): INTERACT 2007, LNCS 4662, Part I, pp. 124–135, 2007.
© IFIP International Federation for Information Processing 2007

(such as produced in UI builders). What is also important is that lowering the design fidelity to sketches does not reduce the design capabilities to discover usability problems. Furthermore, the end user may herself sketch to initiate the development process and when the sketch is close enough to the expected UI, an agreement can be signed between the designer and the end user, thus facilitating the contract and validation.

The idea of developing a computer-based tool for sketching UIs naturally emerged from these observations [8,15]. Such tools would extend the advantages provided by sketching techniques by: easily creating, deleting, updating or moving UI elements, thus encouraging typical activities in the design process [19] such as checking and revision. Some research was carried out in order to propose an approach combining the best of the hand-sketching and computer-assisted interface design, thus providing mixed initiative support. Among these hybrid approaches we can identify two major streams of research: *sketching only* (only a support of sketching activities is provided without interpreting them) and *sketching+interpreting* (other tools do not want to loose the effort and attempt to produce as reusable output some code). The first tools category does not endanger the unconstraint character, but the second may introduce some unexpected problems.

In order to produce the output, the system has to proceed to an analysis of the information provided; storing the input provided by the designer is then insufficient. To this end, these tools proceed to an online recognition of the input and proceed to the construction of the corresponding UI. Through the following section we will mainly focus on this second category. We consider that current restriction on the technique used in the existing tools are too strong and could be improved to unleash the power of this approach, as the actual sketching tools do not take into account the sketcher's preferences: they impose the *same* sketching scheme, the *same* gestures for all types of sketchers and a learning curve may prevent these users from learning the tool and efficiently using it. This can appear a little bit in contradiction with the main statement that would like this approach to be as easy as paper. This is also underlined in two main goals of gesture-based tools [12]: "gestures should be reliably recognized by the computer, gestures should be easy for people to learn and remember".

In order to maximize the power of informal UI design based on sketches, the aforementioned shortcomings should be addressed. It is therefore expected that UI sketching will lead to its full potential, so as to offer the as much freedom as possible to the designer. In this paper, we consider a new kind of approach applied to SketchiXML [4] for the online processing based a combination of a multi-stroke gesture recognizer which has been developed for this purpose and the *CALI* library [6]. Indeed, most sketching tools, including *SketchiXML*, are based on a single recognition algorithm (typically, Rubine's algorithm [17]), using either a trainable gesture recognizer for gesture and shape primitive recognition or fuzzy logic for shape primitives only.

2 State of the Art

Drafting tools are used to capture the general information needed to obtain global comprehension of what is desired, keeping all the unnecessary details out of the process. The most standard approaches for such prototyping are the "paper and pencil technique", the "whiteboard/blackboard and post-its approach" [20]. Such approaches provide access to all the components, and prevent the designer from being distracted from the primary task of design. Research shows that designers who work out conceptual ideas on paper tend to iterate more and explore the design space more broadly, whereas designers using computer-based tools tend to take only one idea and work it out in detail [8,15,19]. Many designers have reported that the quality of the discussion when people are presented with a high-fidelity (Hi-Fi) prototype was different than when they are presented with a low-fidelity (Lo-Fi) mock up. In Lo-Fi prototyping, users tend to focus on the interaction or on the overall site structure rather than details irrelevant at this level [20].

Lo-Fi prototyping offers a clear set of advantages compared to the Hi-Fi perspective [4], but at the same time suffers from a lack of assistance. For instance, if several screens have a lot in common, it could be profitable to use copy and paste instead of rewriting the whole screen each time. A combination of these approaches appears to make sense, as long as the Lo-Fi advantages are maintained. This consideration results two families of software tools which support UI sketching and representing the scenarios between them, one with and one without code generation.

DENIM [13,14] helps web site designers during early design by sketching information at different refinement levels, such as site map, story board and individual page, and unifies the levels through zooming views. DEMAIS [2] is similar in principle, but aimed at prototyping interactive multimedia applications. It is made up of an interactive multimedia storyboard tool that uses a designer's ink strokes and textual annotations as an input design vocabulary. Both DENIM and DEMAIS use pen input as a natural way to sketch on screen, but do not produce any final code or other kind of reusable output.

In contrast, SILK [10], JavaSketchIt [3], FreeForm [15,16], and SketchiXML [4] are major applications for pen-input based interface design supporting code generation. SILK uses pen input to draw GUIs and produce code for the OpenLook operating system. JavaSketchIt proceeds in a slightly different way than Freeform, as it displays the shapes recognized in real time, and generates Java UI code. JavaSketchIt uses the *CALI* library [6] for the shape recognition, and widgets are formed on basis of a combination of vectorial shapes. The recognition rate of the *CALI* library is very high and thus makes JavaSketchIt easy to use, even for a novice user. This library is able to identify shapes of different sizes, rotated at arbitrary angles, drawn with dashed, continuous strokes or overlapping lines, and use fuzzy logic to associate degrees of certainty to recognized shapes to overcome uncertainty and imprecision in shape sketches. FreeForm [15] only displays the shapes recognized once the design of the whole interface is completed, and produces Visual Basic 6 code. The technique used to build the user interface is based uses a trainable single stroke recognizer based on Rubine's algorithm [17] and dictionary for combining simple strokes into Visual Basic widgets and words. SketchiXML is another sketching tool based on the CALI library. It allows the designer to build the widgets in the same manner as JavaSketchIt, but provide coverage for a large set of widgets, and provide UI specifications instead of java. These specifications are written in UsiXML (User Interface eXtensible Markup Language – http://www.usixml.org) which are platform independent. This application is flexible and its behavior can be parameterized according to designer's preferences.

The aim of this work is thus to produce an improved version of SketchiXML so as to enable the construction of more complex widgets. Indeed the actual version based on the CALI library restraints the type of shape to be considered to a small set of shape primitive such as circle, rectangle, etc... Even if the number of widgets recognized is quite high due the possibility to build widget using a combination of more than 2 shape primitives, some widgets are still hardly "sketchable" in a natural manner. To this end we intend to develop a second type of recognition processing providing custom representations for the different kind of widget or part of widgets.

3 New Sketch Recognition Algorithm

As explained, additional to the shape recognizer based on the CALI library, we build a new, trainable recognizer to solve some of the problems of the existing recognizer, that were mentioned above. The main idea of the new sketch recognizer is to divide a hand drawn input into a sequence of line segments with a particular direction and to compare two of these sequences using the so called *string edit distance*. A similar approach has been successfully suggested in biometric user authentication, e.g. in [18].

3.1 Raw Data

The drawing input from a TabletPC, i.e. the information about the pen movement, is available as a sequence of 3-tuples (x_i, y_i, p_i), where x_i and y_i are the coordinates and p_i is the binary pen pressure. In our environment, the coordinates are available in units of screen pixels; the binary pressure is set to 1, if the pen tip is touching the drawing surface and set to 0, if the pen is lifted. While using the mouse instead of pen as drawing input device, the pen-down is simulated by pressing the left button.

3.2 Feature Extraction

The features to be extracted from the raw data are based on the idea, described in [7]. The drawing plane is superimposed with a grid and the freehand drawing input is quantized with respect to the grid nodes (Fig. 1). Each grid node has eight adjacent grid nodes and for each pair of adjacent nodes one out of eight directions can be given. So, from the sequence of successive grid nodes, a sequence of directions can be derived. This sequence can be coded using an alphabet {0-7}, each value representing one direction. This approach was first presented by Freeman in 1974 [7], where it was used for a compressed storage of line drawings. We utilize the sequence-like representation as our basis for sketch recognition, because it is a short description and location invariant description of complex drawing inputs. For each raw sampling point (x_i, y_i) $(i \in [1,...,n]$ for a sequence of n raw sampling points) that closest grid node (qx_i, qy_i) is selected by the following equations:

$qx_i = round(x_i / w_g)$ and
$qy_i = round(y_i / w_g)$, where w_g is the grid width (Fig. 1).

From the sequence of successive grid nodes (qx_j, qy_j) resulting from sketch input, a string of directions (coded as words out of $\{0...7\}^*$) of adjacent grid nodes is build. If two or more successive raw sampling points are quantized as the same grid node point, then this grid node appears only once in the sequence. Depending on the grid width w_g and on the distance of the successive raw sampling points, it is possible for the respective grid nodes not to be direct adjacent to each other. In this case the gap can be filled by using the line algorithm of Bresenham [2].

The gap between two drawing partitions, i.e. the delay between a pen-up and the subsequent pen-down event can be coded with respect to the relative position of the last grid node (qx_j, qy_j) before the pen-up and the first grid node (qx_{j+1}, qy_{j+1}) after the pen-down. Dependent of the distance and the angle between (qx_j, qy_j) and (qx_{j+1}, qy_{j+1}), a different coding can be used to indicate the kind of gap. Using this method, it is possible to extract features from hand drawn inputs, which are represented as strings, consisting of codes, which describe the local direction of line segments in chronological order and the characteristic of gaps between drawing partitions.

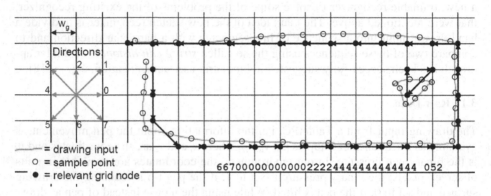

Fig. 1. Square grid quantization of freehand shapes

3.3 String Edit Distance

To compare two strings, a common technique is the so called string edit distance, as a measure of their dissimilarity. The idea behind this distance is, to transform one string into another string using the basic character wise operations *delete*, *insert* and *replace*. The minimal number of these operations for the transformation of one string into another one is called the edit distance or *Levenshtein distance* [Lev65]. The smaller the minimal number of needed edit operations for a transformation from string A to string B, the smaller is the distance between these strings. Instead of only using the number of operations, in some cases it is advantageous to use weights for the different operations. One possibility to determine the edit distance between two strings s and t, with m and n being the respective lengths, is to fill a matrix D of the size $m+1 \times n+1$ as follows [11]:

$D_{0,0} = 0,$

$D_{i,0} = D_{i-1,0} + w_D(s_i),$

$D_{0,j} = D_{0,j-1} + w_I(t_j)$ and

$D_{i,j} = min \{D_{i-1,j} + w_D(s_i), D_{i,j-1} + w_I(t_j), D_{i-1,j-1} + w_R(s_i, t_j) \},$

where s_i and t_j are the ith and j^{th} elements of the strings s and t. $w_D(s_i)$ is the weight for removing operation of a code s_i, $w_I(t_j)$ is the weight for inserting a code t_j and $w_R(s_i, t_j)$

is the weight for replacing a code s_i by t_j. If s_i and t_j are equal, then $w_R(s_i, t_j)$ is zero. The value $D_{m, n}$ is the weighted edit distance of the strings s and t. For a better understanding of the procedure of this computation, we illustrate the resulting matrix in Fig. 2. It is obvious, that the complexity of the straight forward computation of the edit distance is $O(m \cdot n)$. For each matrix element $D_{i, j}$, the three adjacent elements at the left side and on top (marked in Fig. 2 by bold border) are required. In practice it can be shown, that the most relevant elements of the matrix D are those around the main diagonal, so the complexity can be reduced, if the grey fields are pre-initialized with an infinite value, so the min-clause of the calculation procedure considers stronger the more relevant elements around the main diagonal. Therefore, the computational complexity can be reduced to $O(b \cdot max\{m, n\})$, where b is a constant factor.

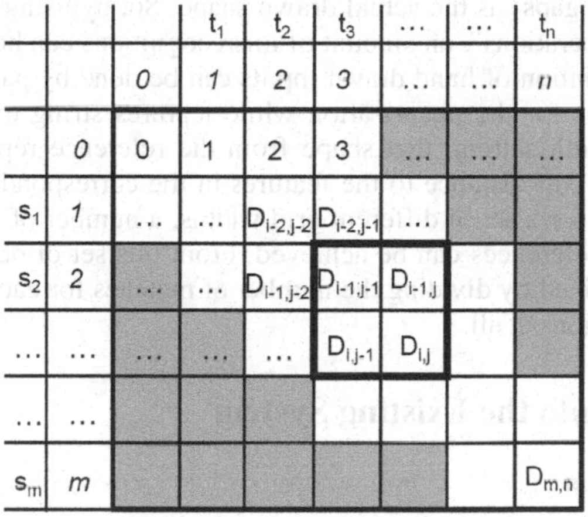

			t_1	t_2	t_3	...	...	t_n
		0	1	2	3	...	...	n
	0	0	1	2	3	...	...	...
s_1	1	...	...	$D_{i-2,j-2}$	$D_{i-2,j-1}$	...		
s_2	2	...	...	$D_{i-1,j-2}$	$D_{i-1,j-1}$	$D_{i-1,j}$		
...	...	...	...	...	$D_{i,j-1}$	$D_{i,j}$		
...	...							
s_m	m							$D_{m,n}$

Fig. 2. Matrix D for computation of edit distance

3.4 Sketch Recognition Using String Edit Distance

As outlined above, the string edit distance can be utilized for the purpose of shape recognition using direction-based feature strings, extracted from hand drawn inputs. The idea is to have a repository, containing a set of reference shapes. For recognition, the unknown shape is compared with all shapes in the repository, i.e. the edit distance between the feature strings of the unknown shape and all reference shapes are calculated. The type of that reference shape, having the smallest edit distance to the unknown shape, is assumed to be the type of the unknown shape. Further, to avoid erroneous recognition of unknown shapes without a representation in the reference repository, a threshold for the maximal allowed edit distance has to be defined.

Due to the nature of string edit distance, the distance value at an average is dependant on the lengths of the strings s and t – the longer the strings, the higher is the average distance value. Therefore a kind of normalization is required. The best solution for considering the lengths m and n in the calculation of edit distance $D_{m, n}$ of two strings s and t is the following:

$dist(s, t) = D_{m, n} / max \{m, n\}$

A second method to normalize the string length impact is to "penalize" large differences in lengths of the two feature strings. It can be assumed, that only if a shape S is different from another shape T, the lengths m and n of the respective feature strings s and t are different. (The inversion is not true – equal lengths of m and n do not imply the equality of the shape types!) By introduction of the string length difference compensation factor the adapted distance could be calculated as follows:

$$dist(s,\ t) = d(m,\ n) \cdot D_{m,\ n} / max\ \{m,\ n\}\ \ with\ \ d(m,\ n) = max\{m,\ n\} / min\{m,\ n\}$$

The effect of $d(m,\ n)$ is to increase the edit distance by the degree of relative difference of string lengths. Finally, as a third improvement, it is possible to "penalize" the operations *replace, insert* and *delete* for the *gap* symbol. The idea is that normally the trained sketches in the repository have the same number of strokes (and consequently the same number of gaps) as the actual drawn shape. So, by using a large weight factor for these "gap operations", an amount of misrecognitions can be avoided.

The actual recognition of hand drawn inputs can be done by parallel using a set of different grid widths for the quantization while features string extraction. Here, for each single grid width setting, that shape from the reference repository is obtained having the smallest edit distance to the features in the corresponding grid size of the unknown input. So, for a set of different grid widths, a number of decisions for possible types of shape references can be achieved. From this set of decisions a degree of certainty can be derived by dividing the number of matches for each reference type by the number of decisions at all.

4   Integration into the Existing System

4.1 Implementation

As presented in [4], the SketchiXML's architecture is based on a set of collaborative agents where each agent is in charge of a specific part of the recognition/interpretation process. In order to meet previously elicited requirements, we have thus developed a new set of agents for the shape recognition process. Indeed, this role was held by a single agent in the first version. The new version is more sophisticated as several agents are participating in the process. A minimum of four agents are now participating in this process, two agents are providing the shape recognition for the shapes primitives and the gestures, a third agent is dedicated to coordination and the integration of the result of these two agents, and the last agent is responsible for dispatching this information to the system. The role of such agents is defined in [5] with the virtual mediator pattern definition. The *virtual mediator* defined in [5] is responsible for the following action:

- Decomposing the client request into sub requests, and then…
- Sending each of these sub requests to the relevant Service Providers.

  When receiving the answer coming from each service provider, the mediator is responsible for:

- Integrating answers from the Service Providers to formulate final result, and then…
- Sending this result back to the Client.

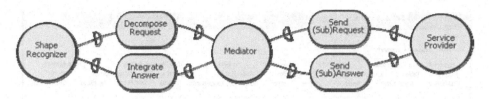

Fig. 3. i* representation of Virtual Mediator

In SketchiXML, the mediator would then be responsible to handle the data provided by the shape recognizer (agent collecting the raw data online) and to decide which agent to invoke. Even if both agents can be called simultaneously, the mediator can decide that only one of the agents is likely to provide the answer. As an example, if the designer is using a tablet pc and draws a sketch with the pen button pressed, then this sketch must be considered as command, and commands are only associated with gesture, it's thus useless to recognize it with the vectorial shape recognizer.

Another possible situation is the reception of a sketch to recognize by the mediator, but as a part of the current user interface. In this situation the mediator does not know the type in advance, as the sketch can be a vectorial shape or a widget. Then, the mediator sends a request to both agent and wait for their answers. If the answer provided by the first agent to reply has a very high degree a certainty then the mediator does not wait for the reply of the other agent and provide the result directly to the interpreter agent, otherwise the mediator wait for all the answers and select be most appropriate answer.

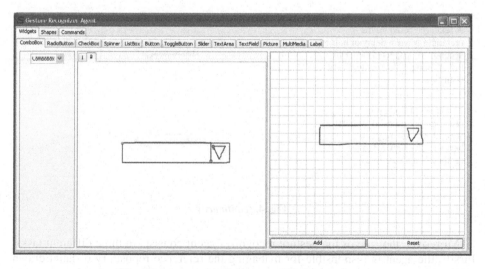

Fig. 4. Management of user trainable shape references

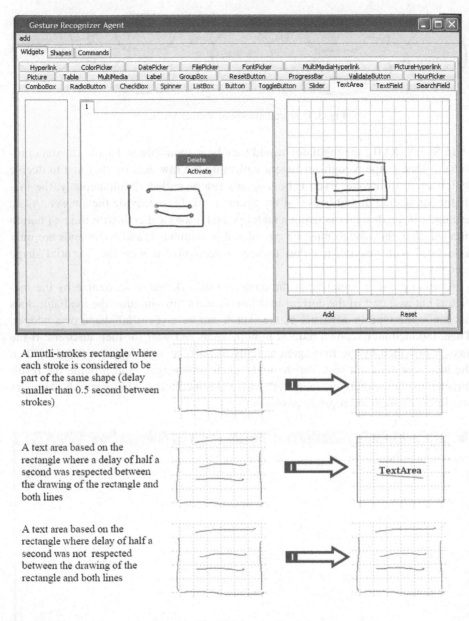

A mutli-strokes rectangle where each stroke is considered to be part of the same shape (delay smaller than 0.5 second between strokes)

A text area based on the rectangle where a delay of half a second was respected between the drawing of the rectangle and both lines

A text area based on the rectangle where delay of half a second was not respected between the drawing of the rectangle and both lines

Fig. 4. (*continued*)

Moreover, the role of the gesture recognizer agent consists in three different tasks. Firstly the agent is responsible for managing the reference repository of hand drawn GUI widgets, geometric primitives and command gestures. To this aim the agent displays a training module (Fig. 4) allowing the designer to add, remove and visualize the current repository. The second task consists in processing the gesture recognition.

So the agent is responsible for feature string extraction of hand drawn inputs from users, comparison of the feature strings with those in the reference repository. The last task of the agent consists listing all the widgets and shapes candidate, annotated with a degree of confidence. This list is then send to the mediator agent presented previously in order to compare the results with the results of the shape recognizer agent, based on geometric primitives. This mediator implements a fusion strategy for the outputs of these two different recognizer modules.

4.2 Interpretation

Previously, when a new shape was recognized, the sketch was replaced by its corresponding vectorial shape if the recognition was enabled. But the extension to cover gesture is not straightforward. Indeed, with the previous version of SketchiXML it was quite natural to replace the sketch by its corresponding vectorial shape, as the sketch was supposed to be similar to its corresponding shape. But, using the gesture recognizer, such an approach does not hold. Even if there is no reason to provide a gesture for the triangle, that is completely different from a triangle, it is possible and the decision belongs to the designer. Another example that is more likely to happen, is a situation where the designer provides a gesture representation for a widget, then it is not possible to replace the sketch by its equivalent in term of vectorial shapes since this sketch may not contain any vectorial shape. The solution would be then to replace, the sketch by its corresponding widget or an informal representation of the widget. But on the other hand we want to keep the informal and unfinished aspect of the user interface, so as to encourage checking and revision. We have thus opted for an alternate solution that just consists in using the sketch provided without any transformation.

The leftmost part of Fig. 5 gives an illustration of a checkbox representation, where we can see that the shape recognized as vectorial shape look very sharp (the last widget) while the representation provided for the three first widgets look imprecise since they are based on the sketch provided by the designer. It is important to maintain this level of uncertainty in order not to give the impression to the end user that it is already a final UI. In contrast, the unconstraint character should be maintained throughout the recognition process without giving the impression that the level of fidelity suddenly changed. Fig. 5 shows other levels of fidelity for the same example.

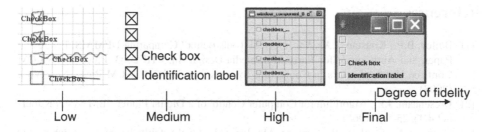

Fig. 5. Sketched widget and related textual label

Another problem faced with the interpretation of such gesture lies in their geometrical properties. When a new shape is handled the interpreter agent extract all the possible candidates from its knowledge set, in order to evaluate if a new widget can be built using this new shape. But, since the gestures do not have the same properties, the constraints set had to be extended so as to cover the entire possible situations. Obviously, the solution adopted is less precise than the situation where only vectorial shapes are used. As an example, if a text area is recognized as a gesture and is displayed on the screen, then if the designer draws a horizontal line inside this widget, then the system should consider the line as a part of the text area rather than a new label. But, as long as the designer is free to define a custom representation of this component, we cannot predict the geometric properties of the widget, we have thus no other choice than to consider an approximation using bounding boxes coupled with Monte Carlo simulations.

5 Conclusion

Through this paper, we have presented an innovative contribution to the domain of sketch based design tools. Most of the existing tools only allow using mono-stroke gestures, and introducing, as a matter of fact, a strong constraint on the number of possible representations. We have proposed in this paper an alternative allowing to recognize multi-stroke gesture combined with the CALI library. Even, if a larger scale study would be appropriate to evaluate the benefit, the results observed shows better results, in any cases, than the previous version of SketchiXML based on the CALI library. Indeed, if the CALI library fails to recognize a scribble, the gesture recognizer may be able to recognize it since its processing is completely different.

Acknowledgements

We gratefully acknowledge the support of the SIMILAR network of excellence (http://www. similar.cc), the European research task force creating human-machine interfaces similar to human-human communication of the European Sixth Framework Programme (FP6-2002-IST1-507609) and the ReQuest project, funded by the Walloon Region (WIST 1).

References

[1] Bailey, B.P., Konstan, J.A.: Are Informal Tools Better? Comparing DEMAIS, Pencil and Paper, and Authorware for Early Multimedia Design. In: CHI'2003. Proc. of the ACM Conf. on Human Factors in Computing Systems, pp. 313–320. ACM Press, New York (2003)

[2] Bresenham, J.E.: Algorithm for Computer Control of a Digital Plotter. IBM Systems Journal 4(1), 25–30 (1965)

[3] Caetano, A., Goulart, N., Fonseca, M., Jorge, J.: JavaSketchIt: Issues in Sketching the Look of User Interfaces. In: Proc. of the 2002 AAAI Spring Symposium - Sketch Understanding, Palo Alto, March 2002, pp. 9–14. AAAI Press, California, USA (2002)

[4] Coyette, A., Vanderdonckt, J.: A Sketching Tool for Designing Anyuser, Anyplatform, Anywhere User Interfaces. In: Costabile, M.F., Paternó, F. (eds.) INTERACT 2005. LNCS, vol. 3585, pp. 550–564. Springer, Heidelberg (2005)

[5] Do, T.T.: A Social Patterns Framework for Designing Multiagent Architectures, Ph.D. thesis, Université catholique de Louvain, IAG, Louvain-la-Neuve (June 2005)

[6] Fonseca, M.J., Jorge, J.A.: Using Fuzzy Logic to Recognize Geometric Shapes Interactively. In: Proc. of the 9th Int. Conf. on Fuzzy Systems FUZZ-IEEE'00, San Antonio, pp. 191–196. IEEE Computer Society Press, Los Alamitos (2000)

[7] Freeman, H.: Computer Processing of Line-Drawing Images. ACM Computing Surveys 6(1), 57–97 (1974)

[8] Hong, J.I., Li, F.C., Lin, J., Landay, J.A.: End-User Perceptions of Formal and Informal Representations of Web Sites. In: CHI'2001. Proc. of ACM Conf. on Human Aspects in Computing Systems, Extended Abstracts, pp. 385–386. ACM Press, New York (2001)

[9] Kolp, M., Giorgini, P., Mylopoulos, J.: An Organizational Perspective on Multi-agent Architectures. In: Meyer, J.-J.C., Tambe, M. (eds.) ATAL 2001. LNCS (LNAI), vol. 2333, Springer, Heidelberg (2002)

[10] Landay, J.A., Myers, B.A.: Sketching Interfaces: Toward More Human Interface Design. IEEE Computer 34(3), 56–64 (2001)

[11] Levenshtein, V.I.: Binary codes capable of correcting deletions, insertions, and reversals. Doklady Akademii Nauk SSSR 163(4), 845–848 (1965) [in Russian]. English translation in Soviet Physics Doklady 10(8), 707–710 (1966)

[12] Long, A.C., Landay, J.A., Rowe, L.A.: Implications For a Gesture Design Tool. In: CHI'2001. Proc. of ACM Conf. on Human Factors in Computing Systems, Seattle, pp. 40–47. ACM Press, New York (2001)

[13] Lin, J., Newman, M.W., Hong, J.I., Landay, J.A.: Denim: Finding a Tighter Fit Between Tools and Practice for Web Site Design. In: CHI'2000. Proc. of ACM Conf. on Human Factors in Computing Systems, The Hague, April 2000, pp. 510–517. ACM Press, New York (2000)

[14] Newman, M.W., Lin, J., Hong, J.I., Landay, J.A.: Denim: An Informal Web Site Design Tool Inspired by Observations of Practice. Human-Computer Interaction 18, 259–324 (2003)

[15] Plimmer, B.E., Apperley, M.: Software for Students to Sketch Interface Designs. In: Proc. of Interact'2003, pp. 73–80. IOS Press, Amsterdam (2003)

[16] Plimmer, B.E., Apperley, M.: Interacting with Sketched Interface Designs: An Evaluation Study. In: Proc. of CHI'2004, pp. 1337–1340. ACM Press, New York (2004)

[17] Rubine, D.: Specifying Gestures by Example. Computer Graphics 25(3), 329–337 (1991)

[18] Schimke, S., Vielhauer, C., Dittmann, J.: Using Adapted Levenshtein Distance for On-Line Signature Authentication. In: Proc. of ICPR'04 (2004)

[19] Sumner, T., Bonnardel, N., Kallag-Harstad, B.: The Cognitive Ergonomics of Knowledge-based Design Support Systems. In: CHI'97. Proc. of ACM Conf. on Human Aspects in Computing Systems, Atlanta, April 1997, pp. 83–90. ACM Press, New York (1997)

[20] van Duyne, D.K., Landay, J.A., Hong, J.I.: The Design of Sites: Patterns, Principles, and Processes for Crafting a Customer-Centered Web Experience. Addison-Wesley, New York (2002)

UI Prototyping for Multiple Devices Through Specifying Interaction Design

Jürgen Falb[1], Roman Popp[1], Thomas Röck[2], Helmut Jelinek[2],
Edin Arnautovic[1], and Hermann Kaindl[1]

[1] Vienna University of Technology, ICT
A-1040 Vienna, Austria
{falb, popp, arnautovic, kaindl}@ict.tuwien.ac.at
[2] Siemens Austria, PSE
A-1210 Vienna, Austria
{thomas.roeck, helmut.jelinek}@siemens.com

Abstract. While user interface (UI) prototyping is generally considered useful, it may often be too expensive and time-consuming. This problem becomes even more severe through the ubiquitous use of a variety of devices such as PCs, mobile phones and PDAs, since each of these devices has its own specifics that require a special user interface.

Instead of developing UI prototypes directly, we propose specifying one interaction design from which UIs can be automatically generated for multiple devices. Our implemented approach uses communicative acts, which derive from speech act theory and carry desired intentions in interactions. Models of communicative acts, UI domain objects and interaction sequences comprise interaction design specifications in our approach and are based on a metamodel that we have defined. We support the development of such models through an IDE, which is coupled with the UI generator. This allows a new form of UI prototyping, where the effects of each model change can be seen immediately in the automatically generated UIs for every device at once.

1 Introduction

User interface (UI) prototypes are generally considered useful, but the effort and time required for building one are often prohibitive. In order to address this issue, "low fidelity" prototyping offers a reasonable compromise.

We propose a novel approach to UI prototyping with "perfect fidelity", where the user interface is automatically generated. The result would be identical to the real UI due to this generation process, assuming that the same interaction design according to our approach is taken as input.

In addition, our approach allows UI prototyping for multiple diverse devices at once (PCs, mobile phones and PDAs), from a single interaction design specification. We are not aware of any previous approach like that.

Of course, this approach to UI prototyping requires certain prerequisites. We build upon our previous work on automatic UI generation for multiple devices.

C. Baranauskas et al. (Eds.): INTERACT 2007, LNCS 4662, Part I, pp. 136–149, 2007.

The underlying approach based on the use of *communicative acts*, and the rendering techniques used for generating user interfaces for multiple devices are published elsewhere. In [1] we sketched the underlying approach, and in [2] we presented the rendering techniques used for generating user interfaces for multiple devices. In essence, they allow automatic generation of UIs for information systems using given widgets as building blocks.

In the current paper, we focus on the support for the designer to specify an interaction design according to our approach and, in particular, the support for UI prototyping. In order to make this paper self-contained, we also describe our metamodel. It defines how models should look that represent interaction design specifications.

We have fully implemented this approach in a tool, which is already in industrial use for real-world applications supporting several diverse devices. As a running example, let us use a small excerpt from a unique and new hypermedia guide that has been put into operation by the Kunsthistorisches Museum (KHM) in Vienna. It had been created with our approach and tools.

The remainder of this paper is organized in the following manner. First, we sketch what communicative acts are and where they come from. Then we present and explain our metamodel of interaction design specifications. After that, we show how the modeling task is supported by an IDE, with a focus on UI prototyping. We also show examples of automatically generated UIs for multiple devices and summarize anecdotic evidence for the usefulness of our approach. Finally, we discuss our approach and compare it with related work.

2   Communicative Acts

By investigating human language communication, philosophers observed that language is not only used to describe something or to give some statement but also to do something with intention — to act. Most significant examples are so-called performatives, expressions such as "I nominate John to be President.", "I sentence you to ten years imprisonment." or "I promise to pay you back.". In these expressions, the action that the sentence describes (nominating, sentencing, promising) is performed by the sentence itself; the speech is the act it effects.

Early and seminal work on speech acts was done by Searle [3]. In this essay Searle claims that "the speaking a language is performing speech acts, act such as making statements, giving commands, asking questions, making promises and so on". Such speech acts are basic units of language communication in this work, and not tokens, words or sentences as previously believed. Each speech act can be represented in the form $F(P)$ where F is the *illocutionary force* (intention) and P its *propositional content*. For example, the speech acts

Sam smokes habitually.
Does Sam smoke habitually?
Sam, smoke habitually!

have the same proposition P (Sam smoking habitually) but different illocutionary forces F: making an assertion, asking a question and giving an order. Speech acts can be further characterized through:

- **Degree of strength**, which describes the intensity and importance of the speech act (e.g., a command and a polite request have more or less the same illocutionary force but different strength);
- **Propositional content conditions**, which describe conditions on the content (e.g., the content has to be about the future);
- **Preparatory condition** (e.g., the receiver must be able to perform the action).

Such speech acts are basic units of language communication. Since speech act theory provides a formal and clean view of communication, computer scientists have found speech acts very useful for describing communication also apart from speech or natural language, e.g., in the area of agent communication languages [4]. To emphasize their general applicability, the notion communicative act is used in this context. The communicative acts simply abstract from the corresponding speech acts in not relying on speech or natural language.

3   Metamodel of Interaction Design Specifications

The metamodel defines what the models of an interaction design specification should look like in our approach. It captures three main concepts used for modeling as well as their relations:

- the intention captured by a communicative act,
- the propositional content modeled by use of an ontology language, and
- the set of interaction sequences modeled with a finite state machine.

Figure 1 illustrates the metamodel for interaction design specification in the form of a UML class diagram containing metaclasses and their relations. The central concept here is the *communicative act*. As stated above, it carries an intention of the interaction: question, assertion, etc. For the purpose of this paper, we show only a selection of the classification of communicative acts.

According to the form of speech acts, the interaction intention as specified by the type of the communicative act, and the propositional content are separated. In the metamodel, the content is represented by UI domain classes and UI domain properties. We prefixed the content entities with "UI" to indicate that the classes and properties model the domain according to the structure presented to the user which should correspond to the user's point of view and need not to be identical to the internal system representation of the domain.

Since we are using the ontology language OWL (Web Ontology Language) [5] for domain modeling, properties are also "first class citizens" and therefore shown separately in the metamodel. Treating classes and properties equally allows us to refer to both independently from a communicative act. This has also practical advantages such as allowing a question about some property per se. For example,

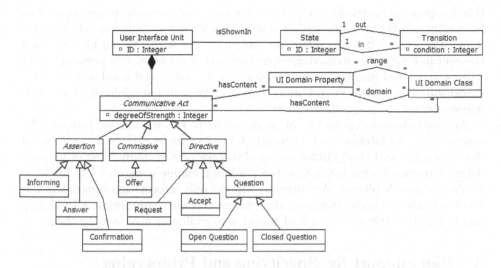

Fig. 1. The metamodel of interaction design specifications in UML

for the UI domain class property *maritalState* related to a UI domain class *Person*, a question about the percentage of married persons can be asked. This is clearly different from a question about a person's marital status. Furthermore, the content of a communicative act can be the class or property itself instead of an instance of a class or property.[1] This results in a discourse about the class or property itself, e.g., talking about what makes up a person in the particular domain/context. Regarding the transformation into user interfaces, a typical application of such a meta-discourse is the generation of help documents.

The UI domain classes and properties also relate to the actual application logic. Thus, they have to be connected technically to the application interface (e.g., Enterprise Java Beans or CORBA). This is done by implementation technology-specific templates describing how UI domain classes and properties get associated with application classes and data. This mapping is not necessary for UI prototyping, it is only required if the prototype should operate on real data or should evolve into a product.

One or more communicative acts are contained in one *User Interface Unit* (UIU). The UIU is a basic unit presented to the user providing choices of different interaction sequences based on the contained communicative acts. However, it is still an abstract entity — it can be mapped to one or several concrete user interface screens according to concrete device profiles.

The set of interaction sequences is modeled with a finite state machine where each state can have multiple ingoing and outgoing transitions representing segments of the interaction sequences. Each state also implicitly defines and fulfills an associated communicative act's preparatory condition. After each state transition, the UIU connected to this state is presented to the user. More precisely,

---

[1] Instances of properties are usually equivalent to statements in ontology languages.

this happens while entering this state. In fact, the machine performs actions as specified in the communicative acts: e.g., it presents a question about some domain object — it asks. When the user interacts with the machine through the user interface, e.g. answering a question, a corresponding communicative act will be generated leading to the execution of its action and a subsequent state transition. The transition conditions between the states are defined in a simple expression language specified by us.

An interaction design specification according to this metamodel provides the essence of a user interface to be generated. For its concrete rendering, additional device profiles and style guides are used to take device characteristics into account. Combined with heuristics, the rendering engine generates UIs for PCs, PDAs and mobile phones. We currently support only information system UIs and no direct manipulation interfaces, since we have neither appropriate UI building blocks for the latter nor rules that would map communicative acts to them.

4   Tool Support for Specifying and Prototyping

Specifying such models directly in OWL or XML syntax is technically on a low level, takes a lot of effort, and does not support rapid prototyping. Therefore, we have also built an IDE for tool support of this modeling task through a graphical interface. This IDE compiles the OWL and XML representations of the models and displays at the same time the generated user interface in a separate window. If designers change parts of the models, the effects of the changes are shown immediately in the generated interface. These results and changes can be seen immediately for all supported diverse devices. In our running example, we present the output generated for PCs and PDAs.

The IDE provides support for modeling the three distinct metamodel parts and their relationships:

- the UI domain model,
- the state machine, and
- the communicative acts.

By using the tool, designers can create the UI domain model and communicative acts from scratch or from predefined templates and change their properties and references to the content. Then they can group the communicative acts into user interface units and assign them to states of the finite state machine. For actually generating a UI, some additional information is required, like style guides and rendering settings for each supported device. They can and should be provided by UI experts even before modeling the interaction design and may be assumed to be given. So, they are not integrated in the IDE and would have to be edited externally. Future experience will show whether their integration into the IDE may be necessary. In the following, we leave these aspects aside and describe the different modeling steps in detail.

The IDE enables designers to construct UI domain models directly or to import ontologies designed with an external ontology editor and stored in OWL format. The designed classes, properties and instances are candidates for the propositional content of communicative acts and for state transition conditions in the subsequent design steps. UI domain models specified within the IDE are stored separately within an OWL file to allow easy reuse for other purposes.

State machines can be either built using graphical UML tools, which generate an XMI representation, or directly within this IDE. The advantage of using our IDE is an immediate check of the transition conditions during design in the following sense. The tool deduces possible occurring communicative acts and their associated content from the model and warns designers if they use information not available in the specified state. This feature relies on a designer having already associated a user interface unit with the state and assigned one or more communicative acts to the UIU.

Upon specifying the user interface units, designers can specify the communicative acts and assign them to a user interface unit. After executing this step, designers can have a first look at the resulting user interface and refine it afterwards. This allows incremental development of the UI prototype.

Figure 2 shows a screenshot of the IDE, that presents a dialogue for editing communicative acts. The left part of the screenshot displays all states, their outgoing transitions, and their associated user interface units (UIU), represented by the user interface description child node of each state. Each UIU contains a list of its aggregated communicative acts that should be presented together. In the example shown in this screenshot, the communicative act named *SearchQuestion* is selected and its properties can be edited in the right part of the IDE.

The right part in the screenshot displays the type and the associated content of the currently selected communicative act. The most important element on the screenshot is the type selection of the communicative act. For asking the search question in our running example, the *Open Question* type is selected that will result in a certain kind of input widgets. Finally, designers can specify the propositional content the communicative act refers to, by graphically specifying instance selectors via predefined queries (like selecting all instances, the current one or instances referred to by another instance). These queries allow designers to specify paths along the properties of classes and to select instances. All queries within the specification are replaced with the actual instances at runtime. In Figure 2, a predefined lookup instance is selected as content for the communicative act, acting as placeholder for the not yet known instances of exhibits. In addition, designers can group multiple communicative acts — not shown in the screenshot — to declare stronger relationships between particular communicative acts. The grouping gives additional hints for rendering regarding the placement of the parts generated from communicative acts, and the splitting into multiple pages on more constraining devices like PDAs or mobile phones.

The generated user interfaces corresponding to the UIU selected in Figure 2 are shown in Figures 4 and 6, for the PC and the PDA, respectively. These are generated immediately after each modification and allow rapid prototyping for multiple diverse devices. In our example, the screenshots display a form for searching exhibits. The communicative act named *SearchQuestion* of type

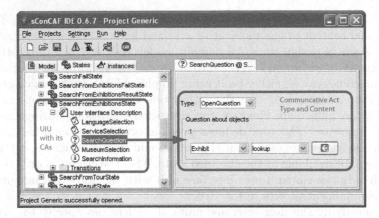

Fig. 2. IDE dialogue for editing communicative acts: specifying an Open Question

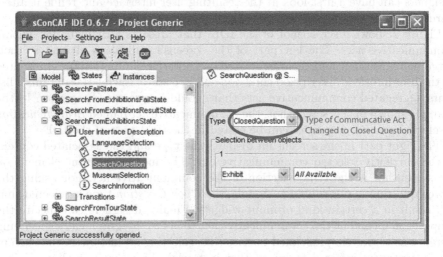

Fig. 3. IDE dialogue for editing communicative acts: specifying a Closed Question

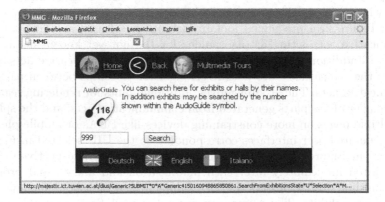

Fig. 4. UI resulting from use of Open Question for search on a desktop PC

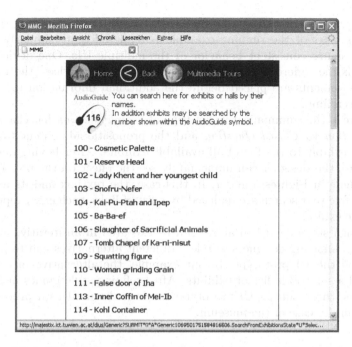

Fig. 5. UI resulting from use of Closed Question for search on a desktop PC

Fig. 6. UI resulting from use of Open Question for search on a PDA

Fig. 7. UI resulting from use of Closed Question for search on a PDA

Open Question is rendered as a textbox with a button for submitting the search string. This part of the running example is rendered quite similarly on both devices to assure consistent behavior of the multiple UIs. One device-specific difference is the different order. On more constraining devices, the important interactive elements are placed before the additional information to avoid unnecessary scrolling.

In Figure 3, the communicative act type of *SearchQuestion* has changed from *Open Question* to *Closed Question* and the propositional content from a not yet known exhibit to the list of all available exhibits. After having made these two changes, the designer can immediately see the effect on the user interfaces as shown here in Figures 5 and 7. In this case, the textbox and its associated button for free text search are replaced by a list of links, each entry representing a selectable exhibit.

The design steps described above can be executed in an iterative and incremental way, allowing designers to select different alternatives and to incrementally extend the UI prototype. In our example, the alternatives are free text search and a selectable list of exhibits. After refining style guides and rendering settings, the resulting UI prototype can even be used as a product, as it happened in the case of the museum.

5   Anecdotic Evidence

We have interviewed four designers, who provided us with subjective evaluations of the approach and the tools implementing it. They do not have very strong formal education or experience in building user interfaces. After a short training period, all designers grasped the modeling concepts and were able to design a user interface for an application using our approach and tools. They state that the design process is intuitive and enables a fast and convenient design of a user interface for diverse devices. The designers also stated, that they need little technical knowledge to model the user interface.

For UI prototyping, the immediate feedback on look and feel of the concrete user interface through its automatic generation is appreciated. We observed a designer exploring the space of design alternatives in terms of various communicative acts and UI domain objects (as well as their attributes to be shown or not). Instead of envisioning how the resulting user interfaces might look on a PC and a PDA, our approach allows immediately seeing and even comparing them. Therefore, it was possible for the designer to select from the design alternatives those resulting in the user interfaces with the highest appeal to him.

An important question for the usefulness of our approach to UI prototyping is, of course, whether the space of user interfaces that can be automatically generated even contains usable ones to select from. After all, usability is said to be a major problem for generated UIs. Based on data gained from the real-world application in the museum, we tend to give an affirmative answer (at least for such kinds of user interfaces).

Let us sketch the essential results here. The evaluation through the museum users is restricted to the UI for the PDA only, since there is still a copyright issue about selling CDs with the PC version pending. For a certain period after the installation of the museum guide running on the PDA, a sample of subjective evaluations by 363 subjects was collected (all of them having used the same version). These users provided answers to a few standardized closed questions and free comments in a subjective questionnaire. We used a multi-point rating scale, more precisely a *Likert scale*. The scale for all closed questions was (*very good, good, medium, less good, not good*).

The answers to our key questions can be summarized as follows:

1. "How did you like the MMG?"[2]
   A clear majority of the subjects replied to this question with *very good* or *good*. Although a portion of visitors did not find the MMG so good, there is some empirical evidence that it has some appeal to museum visitors.
2. "Was the MMG easy to handle?"
   A majority of the subjects replied to this question with *very good* or *good*, and a clear majority with *very good*, *good* or *medium*. While the handling was rated less good than the appeal, there is still some empirical evidence that the handling is at least acceptable to many visitors.

In general, these aspects of usability of the UIs generated was assessed informally as good. It is clear, however, that expert UI designers and implementers can still provide better user interfaces, especially from an artistic perspective or in the details. This situation is reminiscent of code generated by compilers, which can often be "beaten" by experienced humans programming directly on the level of machine code.

6   Discussion

A major advantage for designers is that they can immediately see the resulting UIs, even for multiple devices and in "perfect fidelity", since these UIs are fully automatically generated from the same interaction design specification. There is no separation between UI prototyping and the development of a final UI. Both are served by specifying an interaction design. So, they become essentially the same activity.

Still, such a UI may not be "good enough". Our prototyping approach allows the interaction designer to perform a kind of optimization search for a better UI due to the possibility of quickly trying out alternatives. This is reminiscent of a hill-climbing approach that does not guarantee to find a global optimum, but the resulting UI can be expected to be better than the one from specifying a design without seeing the resulting UI. Whether it is really "good enough" can only be decided by tests with users, of course.

---

[2] MMG is the acronym used there for "multimedia guide", the not very accurate name of this application as used officially, which is rather a hypermedia guide.

Our UI prototyping approach is also usable by non-technicians to create user interfaces, since our interaction design model is based on communicative acts derived from a theory about human communication. Trying out alternatives also supports exploring different UIs by non-technicians, thus making this approach usable by a wide range of designers with different background. Finally, rendering the interaction design to diverse devices supports a variety of user groups.

7   Related Work

Rosenberg states in his review on 20 years of UI prototyping [6] that in order to achieve the best possible UI design it is still most important to enable the designer to iterate through design variations as fast as possible, particularly of the more complex interfaces nowadays. Our approach supports this fast iteration even for multiple devices by easy modification of models based on communicative acts.

So-called low-level prototyping techniques (e.g., [7]) provide great freedom but are used mostly for exploration. In contrast, our approach is more "high-level" and evolutionary. Our prototypes matches the final UIs in layout, colors, sizes, etc. One disadvantage of "high-level" prototyping mentioned by Sefelin in [8] is that designers show less willingness to realize their suggestions. On the other hand, with low-level prototyping the designer can overlook limitations and constraints of the real product.

Earlier approaches had their focus on the data view of the application and have thus prototyped mostly database UIs (e.g., [9]).

Elkoutbi et al. [10] present an approach for requirements engineering that generates a user interface prototype from scenarios. Scenarios are enriched with user interface (UI) information and are automatically transformed into UML statecharts. These statecharts are then used for UI prototype generation. We believe that our approach is more intuitive, since it enables the designer to specify the interaction semantics "naturally" as question, answer, informing, offer, etc. The design process also seems to be more efficient since the designer can see the implications of the interaction specification change in the change of the UIs of multiple devices immediately.

Puerta et al. recently presented a model-based tool to guide early user interface design [11]. Their tool guides the initial specification of user interfaces, so called *wireframes* — a set of elements to be present in, e.g., a Web page or a screen of a desktop application. The elements in wireframes are related to domain objects and user tasks. For the representation of wireframe elements, XIML [3] is used. Our approach differs in taking a more abstract view and concentrating on the intentions of interaction, whereas they try to hide the models. In addition, our UIs are generated immediately to support rapid prototyping, whereas their tool is used to support manual design of UIs.

In [12], they support "low-fidelity" prototyping like with common GUI builders but keep higher-level models consistent with the concrete user

---

[3] http://www.ximl.org/

interface. As a result, they can instantly derive other types of user interfaces (e.g., using HTML or Java GUI) from the high-level model. For the purpose of prototyping, we believe that our approach is more straight-forward since it has only two levels of abstraction and the designer specifies the common basis of the different generated user interfaces.

Furthermore, our approach to specifying interaction design and generating the UI for "high-fidelity" prototyping is related to common model-based UI approaches. Van Setten et al. [13] provide a comparison of classical interaction design techniques (Goals, Operators, Methods and Selection rules (GOMS), Task-Action Grammar (TAG), Command Language Grammar (CLG), and External-Internal Task Mapping (ETIT)) and propose a metamodel for the conceptual basis of interaction design techniques. According to their metamodel, our approach covers almost all concepts like task and object mapping between external (e.g., user view of objects) and internal entities (e.g., system view of objects) and action design (e.g., designing the different communicative acts and their reference to actions in the system). In contrast to their metamodel, we do not include system functionality design and task analysis. Since our approach allows the generation of user interfaces, however, it takes implicitly into account the feedback from the system to the user (e.g., errors) which is not covered by any of the approaches in van Setten's comparison.

Another model-based approach is the User Interface Markup Language (UIML) [14] is a XML-based language used for device-independent descriptions of user interfaces. Abstractly defined user interface structures in UIML are mapped to the individual widgets by the render engine. This work is very important but on a much lower level of detail than ours, which has its focus on specifications of intent for UI prototyping.

Seffah et al. state in [15] that there is a need for new integrative frameworks for modeling, designing and evaluating multi-device user interfaces. They further conclude that model-based and pattern-based approaches are most suitable for designing "multiple user interfaces" once that also obey the different device characteristics. Our approach integrates both design approaches by specifying an interaction design model through the IDE and allowing the designer to select appropriate styles for the different devices. Since we automatically generate UIs for prototyping, the designer can immediately evaluate the consistency and the usability of the selected styles.

An advanced approach to specifying multi-device user interfaces based on task models is presented in [16]. It is widget-oriented employing abstract descriptions of the UI elements as the basic abstraction. Several of the transformations between models have to be done manually. When used for UI prototyping it only provides an abstract structure of the UI as immediate feedback while editing the task model.

Gajos and Weld [17] treat interface generation for different devices as an optimization problem, taking into account interface elements, device properties and usage patterns. The interface elements represent abstract UI widgets and are specified in terms of data exchanged between the user and the application.

The abstraction level is relatively low, since the "raw" data to be shown on the screen are specified. This tool concentrates on the definition of single screens and does not provide any possibility to model communication paths like in our approach.

The work of Eisenstein et al. [18] is in line with ours concerning the importance of high-level UI models for multi-device user interfaces but relies more on designer assistance than our approach to automatically generating the UI prototype.

Generating UIs based on an abstract definition of the user interface and in combination with knowledge of the capabilities of the target display was listed as a system challenge for ubiquitous and pervasive computing recently [19]. In this context, "high-fidelity" prototyping can be a valuable contribution, since it allows incorporating the capabilities and limitations of the various devices without requiring the designer to obey them during prototyping. We think that our implemented approach is a major step in this direction.

8   Conclusion

In this paper, we present a new approach to UI prototyping with "perfect fidelity", where the user interface is automatically generated using our rendering approach described elsewhere. Especially UI prototyping for multiple diverse devices at once, from a single interaction design specification, is new according to our best knowledge.

We also present tool support for specifying such models in the form of an IDE. Through the coupling of this IDE with the generator tool, our new approach to UI prototyping for multiple devices becomes feasible.

Our approach is fully implemented and already in industrial use. A unique and new hypermedia guide has been put into operation by a major museum, which had been created with our approach and tools. Since important aspects of usability of this application have been judged favorably by a sample of random museum users, we think that the usability of our generated UIs is "good enough" for our approach to UI prototyping.

References

1. Falb, J., Popp, R., Röck, T., Jelinek, H., Arnautovic, E., Kaindl, H.: Using communicative acts in interaction design specifications for automated synthesis of user interfaces. In: ASE'06. Proceedings of the 21th IEEE/ACM International Conference on Automated Software Engineering, Piscataway, NJ, USA, pp. 261–264. IEEE Computer Society Press, Los Alamitos (2006)
2. Falb, J., Popp, R., Röck, T., Jelinek, H., Arnautovic, E., Kaindl, H.: Fully-automatic generation of user interfaces for multiple devices from a high-level model based on communicative acts. In: HICSS-40. Proceedings of the 40th Annual Hawaii International Conference on System Sciences, Piscataway, NJ, USA, Jan 2007, IEEE Computer Society Press, Los Alamitos (2007)

3. Searle, J.R.: Speech Acts: An Essay in the Philosophy of Language. Cambridge University Press, Cambridge, England (1969)
4. Foundation for Intelligent Physical Agents: FIPA communicative act library specification. Technical report, Foundation for Intelligent Physical Agents (2002), http://www.fipa.org
5. W3C: OWL Web Ontology Language Reference (2004), http://www.w3.org/2004/OWL/
6. Rosenberg, D.: Revisiting tangible speculation: 20 years of UI prototyping. interactions 13(1), 31–32 (2006)
7. Snyder, C.: Paper Prototyping: The Fast and Easy Way to Design and Refine User Interfaces (The Morgan Kaufmann Series in Interactive Technologies). Morgan Kaufmann, San Francisco (2003)
8. Sefelin, R., Tscheligi, M., Giller, V.: Paper prototyping — What is it good for?: A comparison of paper- and computer-based low-fidelity prototyping. In: CHI '03. Extended Abstracts on Human Factors in Computing Systems, pp. 778–779. ACM Press, New York, NY, USA (2003)
9. Janssen, C., Weisbecker, A., Ziegler, J.: Generating user interfaces from data models and dialogue net specifications. In: CHI '93. Proceedings of the SIGCHI Conference on Human Factors in Computing Systems, pp. 418–423. ACM Press, New York, NY, USA (1993)
10. Elkoutbi, M., Khriss, I., Keller, R.K.: Automated prototyping of user interfaces based on UML scenarios. Automated Software Engg. 13(1), 5–40 (2006)
11. Puerta, A., Micheletti, M., Mak, A.: The UI pilot: A model-based tool to guide early interface design. In: IUI'05. Proceedings of the 10th International Conference on Intelligent User Interfaces, pp. 215–222. ACM Press, New York, NY, USA (2005)
12. Limbourg, Q., Vanderdonckt, J., Michotte, B., Bouillon, L., López-Jaquero, V.: USIXML: A language supporting multi-path development of user interfaces. In: EHCI/DS-VIS, pp. 200–220 (2004)
13. van Setten, M., van der Veer, G.C., Brinkkemper, S.: Comparing interaction design techniques: A method for objective comparison to find the conceptual basis for interaction design. In: DIS'97. Proceedings of the Conference on Designing Interactive Systems, Amsterdam, The Netherlands, pp. 349–357. ACM Press, New York, NY, USA (1997)
14. Abrams, M., Phanouriou, C.: UIML: An XML language for building device-independent user interfaces. In: Proceedings of the XML 99 (1999)
15. Seffah, A., Forbrig, P., Javahery, H.: Multi-devices "Multiple" user interfaces: development models and research opportunities. J. Syst. Softw. 73(2), 287–300 (2004)
16. Mori, G., Paterno, F., Santoro, C.: Design and development of multidevice user interfaces through multiple logical descriptions. IEEE Transactions on Software Engineering 30(8), 507–520 (2004)
17. Gajos, K., Weld, D.S.: SUPPLE: Automatically generating user interfaces. In: IUI '04. Proceedings of the 9th International Conference on Intelligent User Interfaces, pp. 93–100. ACM Press, New York, NY, USA (2004)
18. Eisenstein, J., Vanderdonckt, J., Puerta, A.: Applying model-based techniques to the development of UIs for mobile computers. In: IUI'01. Proceedings of the 6th International Conference on Intelligent User Interfaces, pp. 69–76. ACM Press, New York, NY, USA (2001)
19. Want, R., Pering, T.: System challenges for ubiquitous & pervasive computing. In: ICSE'05.Proceedings of the 27th International Conference on Software Engineering, pp. 9–14. ACM Press, New York, NY, USA (2005)

Multi-fidelity Prototyping of User Interfaces

Adrien Coyette, Suzanne Kieffer, and Jean Vanderdonckt

Belgian Lab. of Computer-Human Interaction (BCHI), Information Systems Unit (ISYS)
Louvain School of Management (LSM), Université catholique de Louvain (UCL),
Place des Doyens 1, B–1348 Louvain-la-Neuve (Belgium)

Abstract. Multi-fidelity prototyping combines within a single user interface prototype several elements whose representations are reproduced with different levels of fidelity with respect to the final user interface: no fidelity at all, low fidelity, medium fidelity, and high fidelity. In order to effectively and efficiently support multi-fidelity, an original set of techniques is defined and discussed: multiple representation manipulation by sketching and gesture recognition, smooth transition between any representation at any time, prototype reusability, multi-platform support, and multiple user interface prototyping facilities. The full implementation of these techniques in prototyping software provides designers and developers with a unique environment for exploring multiple designs with unprecedented support for quickly designing interfaces from scratch or from previously existing design templates. An experimental study reveals that the multiple representation manipulation together with smooth transition represents a valuable advantage for naturally designing user interfaces. The prototyping software supports several aspects involved in the user interface development life cycle and is convenient for non-WIMP user interfaces.

1 Introduction

User-Centered Design (UCD) explicitly recommends in the User Interface (UI) development life cycle a specific stage where the UI could be prototyped based on the input of the future system's stakeholders: designers, developers, usability specialists, graphic experts, and end users. When the time comes to express and gather the user requirements, these stakeholders usually come to a design meeting with many ideas expressed in very different ways. Some prefer to convey their ideas through drawings, sketching, pictures, some others take screenshots of previously used interfaces to communicate representative examples, some others come without anything else than their past interaction experience and history, their own preferences. This therefore means that the prototyping stage should accommodate all these input types and integrate them into one single design. Since the stakeholders' inputs do not all come in the same format and with the same level of details, it is difficult to merge them in a straightforward way. With paper and pencil techniques [18], it is of course possible to manipulate all inputs on paper and to glue them so as to reach a unique UI, but its format remains largely inconsistent and almost not reusable for further design. When this preliminary design will be turned into more precise UI specifications, the quality

C. Baranauskas et al. (Eds.): INTERACT 2007, LNCS 4662, Part I, pp. 150–164, 2007.
© IFIP International Federation for Information Processing 2007

of this representation does matter. Several tools have been invented to support UI design by sketching [1-4, 6, 8, 10, 13-16] since sketching probably represents the most natural way to convey ideas for the human being [1,2,18], but their predominant functioning imposes some dedicated sketching activities that are then recognized (or not) and give rise to a working prototype (or not). None of them truly manipulate UI design artifacts with the aforementioned levels of details with the ability to easily switch from one representation to another.

In the remainder of this paper, Section 2 will define our understanding of the fidelity and how we generalize it into the concept of multi-fidelity. It will then compare state-of-the-art UI sketching tools against a series of seven criteria that will be further addressed throughout the paper. Section 3 will describe a series of techniques which, taken together, will allow our new sketching tool to satisfy the seven criteria. Section 4 will report on an experimental study where end users and UI designers evaluated the different levels of fidelity involved in the multi-fidelity paradigm. Section 5 argues that multi-fidelity could be equally used for other models (i.e., task, domain, abstract user interface) for a same UI or for other families of UI, such as physical UIs.

2 Related Work

Designing the right UI the first time is very unlikely to occur. Instead, UI design is recognized as a process that is intrinsically open (new considerations may appear at any time), iterative (several cycles are needed to reach an acceptable result), and incomplete (not all required considerations are available at design time) [8]. Consequently, means to support early UI design has been extensively researched to identify appropriate techniques such as paper sketching, prototypes, mock-ups, diagrams [18].

Since the needs of rapid UI prototyping vary depending on the project and allocated resources, it makes sense to rely on the notion of prototype fidelity. The *prototype fidelity* expresses the similarity between the final user interface (running in a particular technological space) and the prototyped UI. The UI prototype fidelity is said to be *high* if the prototype representation is the closest possible to the final UI, or almost in the same representation type. This means that the prototype should be high-fidelity in terms of presentation (what layout, what are the UI elements used), of global navigation and dialog (how to navigate between information spaces), of local navigation (how to navigate within an information space). The fidelity is said to be *low* if the prototype representation only partially evokes the final UI without representing it in full details. Between high-fidelity (hi-fi) and low-fidelity (low-fi) [17] exists medium-fidelity (me-fi) [9]. We usually observe that a UI prototype only involves one representation type, i.e. one fidelity level. But due to the variety of stakeholders' input, several fidelities could be imagined together, thus leading to the concept of *mixed-fidelity*, where several different fidelities are mixed in the same UI design [15]. As opposed to mixed-fidelity, we introduce the notion of *multi-fidelity* when a prototype may involve elements of different fidelities (like in mixed fidelity), but only one fidelity is acted upon at a time, thus assuming that a transition is always possible for an element from one fidelity to another for any element.

Prototyping software consequently falls into three categories depending on their fidelity level: *high-fidelity* tools support building a complete UI so that it can be directly executed and tested and as if the UI is a real one ; *medium-fidelity* tools support designing UI mock-ups giving more importance to the contents than the style with which these contents are presented ; *low-fidelity* tools focus more on the UI basic functionalities than on precise details through which these functionalities can be executed. Typical approaches found in lo-fi prototyping tools are the "paper and pencil technique", the "whiteboard/blackboard and post-it approach" [19]. Such approaches provide access to most UI elements and prevent designers from being distracted from the primary UI design task. For instance, Berger [3] provides a predefined paper widget set for drawing a Microsoft Excel form which can then be turned into a true form.

UI designers who work out conceptual ideas on paper tend to iterate more and explore the design space more broadly, whereas designers using computer-based tools tend to take only one idea and work it out in detail [22]. The quality of the discussion among stakeholders is considered more fruitful with a hi-fi prototype than with a lo-fi mock up [18]. Lo-Fi prototyping, however, encourage the stakeholders to focus on the UI interaction rather than on details irrelevant at this level which do not influence the usability. Consequently, lo-fi prototyping offers clear advantages with respect to the hi-fi counterpart, but suffers from a lack of assistance and a lack of transition from lo-fi to hi-fi. On the one hand, maintaining an informal representation in lo-fi is observed to be important [13] so that stakeholders do not believe that the UI being designed is a final one, thus encouraging them to focus on design issues. On the other hand, once a lo-fi is finished, it is unclear how to proceed to a high fidelity level [23]. Me-fi comes in the game to "beautify" a lo-fi prototype without changing its functionality [9] and represents a possible evolution towards a final UI, but this transition is never supported in any software.

A recognized virtue of UI prototyping is its ability to extract usability problems so as to improve the UI design while prototyping [7]. The amount of usability problems extracted in a lo-fi prototype is not inferior to the amount of usability problems for a hi-fi prototype [22]. In addition, paper and computer media have been estimated equally valid for testing lo-fi, me-fi, and hi-fi prototypes [23]. In particular, computer media was considered more advantageous for automatic recording of user actions, for its ability to distribute and document the results of the UI prototype as opposed to paper [19,23]. Table 1 delivers the results of a comparative analysis where major prototyping tools are compared against seven criteria:

1. *Amount of fidelity*: most tools involve one or two fidelity levels (lo-fi and hi-fi), only one of them does support me-fi. When lo-fi is the single fidelity supported, it often means that this representation is converted into UI code afterwards (e.g., Visual Basic code for FreeForms, Java code for JavaSketchiIt, C code for Silk).
2. *Fidelity transition*: even less support a smooth transition between the fidelity levels at design time, even if we include easy transition to code for a final UI.
3. *Shape recognition*: a shape recognition algorithm is implemented in most tools in order to turn a sketched UI element into its real counterpart or to "beautify" it.
4. *Gesture recognition*: very few tools incorporate a gesture recognition algorithm to convert gestures into sketching commands or UI elements.
5. *Output reusability*: converting the sketched UI into a file which could be reused for the rest of the development life cycle is fundamental, but the output expressiveness and exploitability depend on the format (image vs. UI specifications).

6. *Multi-platform support*: still few tools do support UI prototyping for multiple computing platforms ranging from a desktop to a mobile platform.
7. *UI types*: all tools are tied up with a specific UI type (Graphical UI) and cannot be reused for other types of sketching activities or other UI types (e.g., non-WIMP).

The last line of Table 1 shows that our sketching tool is more advanced than the other tools with respect to all criteria, which will be demonstrated in the next section.

Table 1. Comparative analysis of prototyping tools by sketching

	Amount of fidelities	Fidelity transition	Shape recognition	Gesture recognition	Output reusability	Multi-platform	UI types
Berger [3]	1 (hi-fi)				✓ (Excel VB code)		Excel form
Demais [2]	2 (lo-fi, hi-fi)		✓	✓	✗ (animation)		multimedia application
Denim [14]	1 (lo-fi)				✗ (image only)		Web UI
FreeForms [16]	1 (lo-fi)			✓	✓ (Basic code)		GUI
Ink-kit [6]	2 (lo-fi, hi-fi)	✓	✓		✓ (ASCII file)	✓	GUI
JavaSketch-It [4]	1 (lo-fi)		✓	✓	✓ (Java code)	✓	GUI
Meyer [13]	1 (me-fi)				✗ (image only)		GUI
Prototyper [15]	2 (lo-fi, hi-fi)				✓ (XML file)		GUI
Silk [10]	1 (lo-fi)			✓	✓ (C++ file)		GUI
SketchiXML [8]	2 (lo-fi, hi-fi)	✓	✓		✓ (UI specifications)	✓	GUI, PDA, mobile phone
Sketch-Read [1]	1 (lo-fi)			✓	✗ (image only)		GUI
Our tool	4 (no-fi, lo-fi, me-fi, hi-fi)	✓	✓	✓	✓ (UI specifications)	✓	Web UI, GUI, any type

3   Tool Support for Multi-fidelity

The first step in our sketching tool consists of specifying parameters that will drive the prototyping process: the project name, the input device type (e.g., stylus, pen, mouse), the computing platform for which the UI is prototyped (a predefined profile exist for mobile phone, PDA, TabletPC, kiosk, ScreenPhone, laptop and a custom one could added). The user then enters into a UI design mode where any shape can be freely drawn and any text could be written. The tool is equipped with a series of facilities which taken together do support the multi-fidelity process as outlined before.

Shape recognition. A shape recognition engine is able to recognize and interpret 27 different types of widgets with the standard configuration (ranging from check boxes and spin button to search buttons, progress bar, calendar, video input), 8 basic shapes (i.e., triangle, rectangle, cross, line, wavy line, arrow, ellipse, and circle), and 6 basic commands (i.e., undo, redo, copy, paste, cut, new window). Each UI element can be sketched and be recognized or not depending on its shape and the wish for the user to see it recognized or not. The primary mode is lo-fi so as to create a context where the user feels free and unconstrained to draw any kind of shape, whether it can be recognized or not.

Those shapes which are not recognized are simply added and maintained throughout the process. Fig. 2 reproduces a typical session where a wide bunch of UI elements have been sketched in lo-fi mode. In this mode, elements which have been correctly recognized are beautified (the drawing is improved) and the name of the UI element has been added. Fig. 1 reproduces the lo-fi mode where the raw sketching was performed.

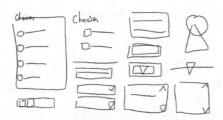

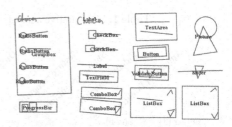

Fig. 1. No-fi mode without labels

Fig. 2. Lo-fi mode for sketchingUI elements (with labels)

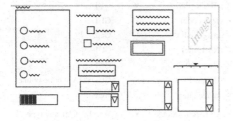

Fig. 3. Me-fi mode without labels

Fig. 4. Hi-fi mode without labels

Fig. 5. Our software toolbar with fidelity level set on lo-fi

Fidelity transition. A slider (Fig. 5) allows the user to easily switch between any fidelity level to another. Fig. 3 shows the representation after the user moved to me-fi, a mode in which only a rough, yet identifiable, element representation is produced. This representation is platform agnostic: it does not produce a representation which would suggest that a particular window manager, toolkit or environment has been selected. If the user really wants to obtain a hi-fi representation, then she may want to switch to the last position of the slider, which is demonstrated in Fig. 4: hi-fi mode without the labels indicating the elements types. In this case, the representation is made up of genuine widgets belonging to the widget set of the currently being used platform (different widget sets and look&feel could be used alternatively). A toggle button "Label" allows the user to display/undisplay the names of the recognized UI elements. If a UI element has not been recognized, it is simply kept as it is. For instance, if a histogram would have been sketched, it would not be altered so as to respect the naturalness of the design process as recommended in [14,17].

Amount of fidelities. Thanks to this process, the user can input any UI element in any fidelity level and see the result in any other level as the interpretation is immediate. In this way, a custom element could be drawn in lo-fi and a predefined widget could be added in me-fi or hi-fi. Therefore, four fidelity levels are supported: none (only the drawing is displayed), lo-fi (the drawing is displayed with recognized portions), me-fi (the drawing is beautified where portions are recognized, including for basic shapes), and hi-fi (a genuine UI is produced with true widgets for those portions corresponding to predefined widgets).

Gesture recognition. Sketching tool users may complain that they are forced to learn a graphical representation for every widget, shape or command. In order to support user flexibility, each such element is encoded in a graphical grammar of objects defined with logical relationships with variable degree of freedom. Fig. 5a shows how a multi-line edit field is graphically represented by a rectangle and two horizontal lines in it. In this way, the tool accommodates a larger variety of alternate representations for a same element. For this purpose, we based our implementation on an experimental study which reported the three most preferred representations for such UI elements [8]. Beyond this study, a gesture recognition system has been implemented based on hand gesture decomposition in order to customize the representation of all widgets, shapes, and commands according to each user's preferences (Fig. 6b).

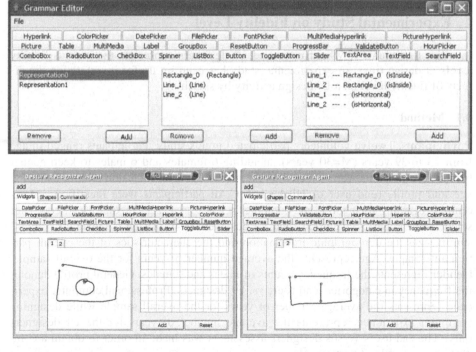

Fig. 6. A grammar editor for a new representation (a) and a gesture recognition system (b) where new gestures replace UI elements (here, a gesture is drawn, added, and activated to represent a toggle button in a custom way)

Output reusability. At any time, our tool produces UI specifications in terms of a User Interface Description Language (UIDL). As opposed to many tools where little or no portions of the sketch could be reused, our tool always maintains up-to-date UI specifications, including the description of custom widgets. It is also possible to define the navigation between these elements in the same way.

Multi-platform. The tool also exports UI specifications in UIML (www.uiml.org, which is able to automatically generate code for HTML, Java, VoiceXML, and WML) and UsiXML (www.usixml.org) [12,20]. As opposed to some tools which are dedicated to a particular environment (e.g., Visual Basic for FreeForms [17] or Java for JavaSketchIt [4]), our tool is shipped with predefined profiles covering a wide range of different computing platforms. Each profile not only expresses constraints imposed by a particular platform (e.g., the screen resolution, a restricted widget set), but could also have a particular gesture data base for sketching those UI elements which are peculiar to this platform (e.g., a gesture associated to a histogram).

The above discussion shows that our tool satisfies the six first criteria highlighted in Table 1. The next section will investigate to what extent this tool supporting multi-fidelity is appreciated by end users and designers. Section 5 will then address the last criteria: it will exemplify how the tool could be used for other types of UI than merely web pages (like in DENIM [14]), GUIs (like in Prototyper [16] or in SketchiXML[8]).

4   Experimental Study on Fidelity Level

In order to evaluate how end users and UI designers appreciate the various fidelity levels at design time, an experimental study has been set up for investigating the effects of fidelity level on a UI design activity by sketching.

4.1   Method

Participants. Twelve volunteers participated in this study. Participants ranged in age from 23 to 39 years (M=30 years), including 6 females and 6 males to keep gender balance. Participants were selected on the basis of general inclusion criteria including age and profile (end user or UI designer). All participants were identified and recruited regarding their job in the computer science area (e.g., regular users, computer science researchers, developers, and UI designers from private companies). Table 2 summarizes the demographic information and the characteristics of the overall participant sample. Age represents the average number of years for the overall sample. Gender represents the frequency counts of males and females. General profile denotes the frequency in categories: end users vs. UI designers. Professional computer experience represents the average number of years for the overall sample while designing computer experience represents the average number of years for the UI designers only. The end users versus designers assessment was made in order to obtain a comprehensive profile of participants.

Table 2. Summary of participants' demographics and characteristics

N	Age	Gender		Handedness	General profile		Computer experience	
		Male	Female		End users	User interface designers	Professional exp.	Designing exp.
12	30	6	6	Right	6	6	5.25	4

Table 3 summarizes the demographic and the characteristics of the participants based on the grouping. Age represents the average number of years for each participant group. Gender represents the frequency counts of males (M) and females (F) within each group. Professional computer experience represents the average number of years for each participant group. Designing computer experience represents the average number of years for the designers only.

Table 3. Summary of group profiles

Group	N	Age	Gender	Professional exp/	Designing exp.
Designer	6	31	M=4, F=2	6.8	4
User	6	29	M=2, F=4	3.7	N/A

Apparatus and experimental task environment. The computer system used in this study was a PC Dell Latitude D820 equipped with an Intel Core 2 Duo T7200 (2.0 GHz, 4 Mo cache level 2 memory) processor and 2 Gb of RAM memory. Participants were seated approximately 30 cm from a 21-inch Wacom Cintiq 21UX touch screen flat panel connected to this computer. Screen resolution was set to 1,600 x 1,200 pixels, with a 32-bit color palette. The keyboard was not required to complete the task since the participants were supposed to use a stylus. The sketching tool used in this experiment is the one whose implementation has been described in Section 3. The experimental task to be carried out by participants consists of designing two UIs (combined in a pair) in each of the following fidelity levels: Lo-Fi, Me-Fi, Hi-Fi, or Nu-Fi. Each UI contains eight widgets amongst the following alternatives: push button, check box, combo box, list box, progression bar, radio button, spinner, text area, and text field. A UI pair is considered to be complete once the eight widgets of both UIs have been entirely designed with the imposed fidelity level.

4.2 Protocol

Prior to experiment, participants were given an explanation of the research study and their role in the study. Following completion of the demographic questionnaire, the participants were briefed on how to use the setup and how to carry out the task. A short training period has been allocated for each participant to sketch a given UI pair until they feel confident in using the setup. They were also allowed switching between the four fidelity levels. The main part of the experiment consisted of designing four pairs of windows by sketching them in a pre-assigned fidelity level. The order of the four pairs of windows was randomly assigned. After these sketching tasks, participants were asked to complete a Computer System

Usability Questionnaire (CSUQ) [11] and were interviewed according to a semi-structured scheme. The interview focused on their subjective satisfaction and perception about the study, the system and their preferences in term of fidelity level. The dependent variable used to assess participant task performance was Window Development Time (WDT), which represents the task duration (in seconds) required by a participant to design a window.

4.3 Results

Statistical analysis. One participant has not followed the instruction related to the order of the conditions. Consequently, the sample includes only 88 entries instead of 96. Due to the sample size, an analysis of variance (ANOVA) was used to examine the presence of significant differences in task performance, as measured by WDT. Table 3 reproduces the results of two analyses: influence of the fidelity level and influence of the user profile. The statistical significance is underlined.

Table 4. Tests for significant differences in performance

ANOVA	Tests of Sig. Diff. Between groups
1) Fidelity (No/Lo/Me/Hi-Fi)-	F=1.8888; p=0.1377
2) User profile (User/Designer)	F=7.2719; p=0.0084

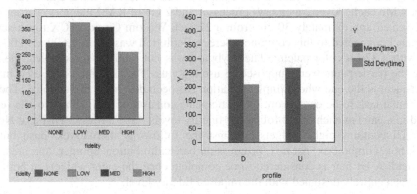

Fig. 7. Mean WDT (seconds) for each fidelity condition, Mean WDT (seconds) for each participant group

Although results from Table 4 show that the fidelity level had no influence on WDT, Hi-Fi demonstrated the fastest WDT (M= 261 seconds), respectively followed by No-Fi (M= 297 seconds), Me-Fi (M= 359 seconds) and Lo-Fi (M= 376 seconds) (Figure 6). In addition, the results from Table 3 show that user profile had a significant influence on WDT (F=7.2719; p=0.0084). Surprisingly, participants from the end users group demonstrated the fastest WDT compared to those from the designers group (respectively, M=267 seconds versus M=369 seconds – Fig. 7).

Table 5. Summary of overall sample CSUQ. Statistical indices are mean, median and standard deviation.

Subscale	Statistical Indices		
	Mean	Median	Std deviation
SYSUSE	4.04	4	1.52
INTERQUAL	5.39	6	1.14
OVERALL	4.83	5	1.17
INFOQUAL	4.45	4.5	1.37

Computer System Usability Questionnaire. The IBM CSUQ [11] is a public domain instrument to measure user satisfaction with computer system usability in the context of scenario based usability studies. The CSUQ is made up of four parts, each consisting of items ranked on a 7-point Likert scale: the overall satisfaction score (OVERALL: all 18 Items), the system usefulness score (SYSUSE: Items 1-8), the information quality score (INFOQUAL: Items 9-15), and the interface quality score (INTERQUAL: Items 16-18). This questionnaire has been chosen because of its acceptable reliability: a coefficient alpha exceeding .89 for all parts has been proved. Seven-point rating scales (1=totally disagree, 7=totally agree) were used because they allow three levels of either positive or negative ratings. Table 5 suggests that the system usefulness is moderately appreciated as well as the information quality (reasonably good mean, but large deviation). However, the interface quality and the overall user satisfaction are both assessed positively.

Subjective general comments and users preferences. Four of 12 participants judged the stylus uncomfortable because of a physical button located too close to their index finger. Four of 12 participants reported that some system functionality was not usable: the copy-paste was estimated too slow and required too many pointing gestures; the lack of drag-and-drop of sketched items was regretted since it is at the present time replaced by the cut-paste functionality. Four on 12 participants considered that the speed of the recognition should be improved in the next version of the tool. In return, nine on 12 participants judged the tool as user-friendly and intuitive. This result is consistent with the INTERQUAL result reported above (Table 4). Moreover, eight on 12 participants considered the tool as fast and accurate in term of drawings/sketchings recognition. Finally, most of the participants reported a pronounced preference for Hi-Fi (5 participants on 12, including 2 designers and 3 users) and Me-Fi (5 participants on 12, including 3 designers and 2 users). They argued they felt "more comfortable" in those two levels because of the real-time interpretation of their drawings and the resulting UI aesthetics. Furthermore, 75% of the participants dislike the No-Fi (9 participants on 12, including 4 designers and 5 users). They claimed that this level "looks like a draft", which is consistent with [13].

Interpretation and discussion. The experimental task used in this study was a simplified version of a UI development life cycle. Time required by participants to develop UIs (WDTs) was used as an indicator on the usability of the fidelity levels. This metric revealed its shortcoming: WDT is not exact enough to be considered as representative of participant performance. Further usability studies need to include other metrics like the number of recognized/unrecognized shapes/texts/gestures, as well as the number of effective "widgets" that are added to the interface.

The statistical analysis revealed no significant impact of the "fidelity level" parameter on the user performances (speed). This result may be due to the fact that the level of fidelity has no influence on the sketching strategies adopted by the users, that is to say they perform the tasks in the same way, no matter what the level of fidelity is. In addition, the statistical analysis revealed a significant impact of the user profile (end user vs. designer) on the performances. Surprisingly, end users –with no experiment in interface design– are faster in performing the sketching tasks than the designers. This result may be due to the fact that designers do care a lot about the quality and aesthetics of the resulting interfaces (e.g., they systematically preserved alignment, symmetry, and semantic grouping of UI elements) compared to end users. Consequently, more time is required for designers to sketch valuable interfaces, regarding their own personal criteria. These results are consistent with some earlier findings [8].

Finally, the qualitative analysis revealed a pronounced user preference for both Hi-Fi and Me-Fi. This result suggests that participants, including both end users and designers, may prefer in terms of visual comfort, visual feedback, and widget recognition the fidelity levels that show a resemblance to the final UI. Differences observed between end users and designers are consistent with some other findings [2,8,22].

5   Multi-fidelity for Other User Interface Artifacts

In the previous experiment, multi-fidelity has been applied to the Concrete User Interface (CUI) level as defined in the Cameleon framework for a UI [5]. We show that our sketching tool can accommodate any UI type for any platform by choosing the right profile containing the constraints imposed by a particular platform. This profile influences the sketch recognition process as well as the trainable gesture recognition system. In this section, we show that the paradigm of multi-fidelity could be equally used for other models involved in the UI development life cycle [3]: the task model [15], the domain model [6], and the abstract UI [20]. Each model consists of basic graphical elements which could be encoded in additional elements both in the graphical grammar and in the gesture recognition system.

For instance, natural development of systems is fostered if a task model is drawn, e.g., on a drawing surface [15]. In our tool, a lo-fi approach could be adopted to sketch such a task model (Fig. 8) which could be straightforwardly recognized, interpreted and converted into a true task model (Fig. 8). In this way, it is possible to sketch all models involved in a particular UI development life cycle and link them together, which supports the principle of "sketching it all together". As long as a sketch could be decomposed into basic shapes such as rectangles, text (there is a ink-based recognition system for this purpose), lines, compound shapes, it is possible to sketch the representation in lo-fi and associate it to a beautification and a complete representation in hi-fi.

Then, we show that we could even sketch other families of UI provided we could imagine different representations belonging to different levels of fidelity. To go

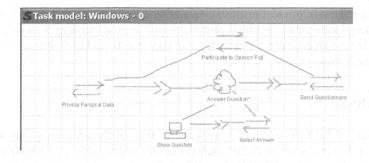

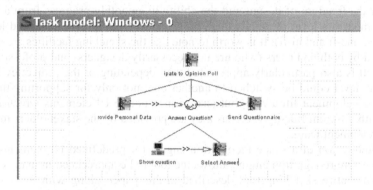

Fig. 8. A task model sketched in lo-fi mode

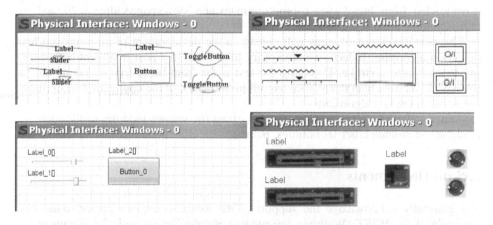

Fig. 9. A simple task model recognized in hi-fi mode from its sketch in lo-fi mode

beyond the traditional paradigm of Graphical UIs, an example of a physical UI consisting of analogic and digital elements could be sketched similarly with the three fidelity levels. The output in this case consists of a description of a physical interface to be imported in the Pin&Play toolkit [21]. This toolkit allows developing physical interfaces by integrating software widgets and physical devices such as slider, toggle button, and potentiometer. Since the toggle button is not a standard element, is has been defined through a new custom gesture (Fig. 6), which could then be associated with the description of the genuine physical toggle button (such as a switch). Fig. 9 respectively reproduces such a physical UI in lo-fi, me-fi, and hi-fi with smooth transition between these modes.

6 Conclusion

As indicated in Table 1, our tool is superior to state-of-the-art prototyping tools by sketching in that it combines multi-fidelity with all criteria addressed simultaneously. The conducted experimental study revealed to what extent end users and designers do appreciate the freedom of design and the ability to smoothly progress from a UI design with moderate level of details (e.g., no-fi and lo-fi) to a more advanced level of details (e.g., me-fi and hi-fi). It is worth to note that the sketching facilities are equally appreciated by both end users (who are not necessarily designers) and professional UI designers. It is also particularly appreciated that, depending of the project evolution, any fidelity level could be switched to another one: not only for supporting the back and forth development life cycle, but also to incorporate UI elements which are expressed with different fidelity levels as they are provided by the stakeholders involved in the development team.

The combination of a shape recognition engine for predefined UI elements and a trainable gesture recognition engine allows the tool to be appreciated in many circumstances. The entire sketching tool described in this paper, along with its shape and gesture recognition systems for supporting multi-fidelity has been implemented in Java 1.5 and today consists of 45.000 lines of code. Our sketching tool can be freely downloaded from http://www.usixml.org/index.php?view=page&idpage=29 and its corresponding open source project.

The next development steps will consist in the development of an improved text detection algorithm. Indeed, we always try to proceed to a post treatment before trying to recognize a stroke. Detecting the text is far from being trivial and should be improved. We also plan to enhance overall performance of the application by optimizing some of the key algorithms.

And, finally, we will investigate to what extent the various modules of the software could accommodate other UI families, perhaps with other notations.

Acknowledgements

We gratefully acknowledge the support of the Request research project under the umbrella of the WIST (Wallonie Information Société Technologies) program under convention n°031/5592 RW REQUEST). We warmly thank J.A. Jorge, F.M.G. Pereira and A. Caetano for allowing us to use JavaSketchIt and the CALI library in our research. We gratefully acknowledge the support of the SIMILAR network of excellence (http://www. similar.cc), the European research task force creating human-machine interfaces similar to human-human communication of the European Sixth Framework Programme (FP6-2002-IST1-507609).

References

1. Alvarado, Ch., Randall, D.: SketchREAD: A Multi-domain Sketch Recognition Engine. In: UIST'2004. Proc. of 17th Annual ACM Symposium on User Interface Software and Technology, Santa Fe, October 24-27, 2004, pp. 23–32. ACM Press, New York (2004)
2. Bailey, B.P., Konstan, J.A.: Are Informal Tools Better? Comparing DEMAIS, Pencil and Paper, and Authorware for Early Multimedia Design. In: CHI'2003. Proc. of the ACM Conf. on Human Factors in Computing Systems, Ft. Lauderdale, April 5-10, 2003, pp. 313–320. ACM Press, New York (2003)
3. Berger, N.: The Excel Story. Interactions 13(1), 14–17 (2006)
4. Caetano, A., Goulart, N., Fonseca, M., Jorge, J.: JavaSketchIt: Issues in Sketching the Look of User Interfaces. In: Proc. of the 2002 AAAI Spring Symposium - Sketch Understanding, Palo Alto, March 2002, pp. 9–14. AAAI Press, Menlo Park (2002)
5. Calvary, G., Coutaz, J., Thevenin, D., Limbourg, Q., Bouillon, L., Vanderdonckt, J.: A Unifying Reference Framework for Multi-Target User Interfaces. Interacting with Computers 15(3), 289–308 (2003)
6. Chung, R., Mirica, P., Plimmer, B.: InkKit: A Generic Design Tool for the Tablet PC. In: CHINZ'2005. Proc. of 6th ACM SIGCHI New Zealand chapter's International Conference on Computer-Human Interaction. ACM International Conference Proceeding Series, vol. 94, pp. 29–30. ACM Press, New York (2005)
7. Cockton, G., Lavery, D.: A Framework for Usability Problem Extraction. In: INTERACT'99. Proc. of 7th IFIP TC 13 Int. Conf. on Human-Computer Interaction INTERACT'99, Edinburgh, August 30-September 3, 1999, pp. 347–355. IOS Press, Amsterdam (1999)
8. Coyette, A., Vanderdonckt, J.: A Sketching Tool for Designing Anyuser, Anyplatform, Anywhere User Interfaces. In: Costabile, M.F., Paternó, F. (eds.) INTERACT 2005. LNCS, vol. 3585, pp. 550–564. Springer, Heidelberg (2005)
9. Engelberg, D., Seffah, A.: A Framework for Rapid Mid-Fidelity Prototyping of Web Sites. In: Proc. of the IFIP 17th World Computer Congress - TC13 Stream on Usability: Gaining a Competitive Edge WC'2002, Montreal, August 25-29, 2002, pp. 203–215. Kluwer Academic Press, Dordrecht (2002)
10. Landay, J., Myers, B.A.: Sketching Interfaces: Toward More Human Interface Design. IEEE Computer 34(3), 56–64 (2001)
11. Lewis, J.R.: IBM Computer Usability Satisfaction Questionnaires: Psychometric Evalution and Instructions for use. Int. Journal of Human-Computer Interaction 7(1), 57–78 (1995)
12. Limbourg, Q., Vanderdonckt, J., Michotte, B., Bouillon, L., Lopez, V.: UsiXML: a Language Supporting Multi-Path Development of User Interfaces. In: Bastide, R., Palanque, P., Roth, J. (eds.) Engineering Human Computer Interaction and Interactive Systems. LNCS, vol. 3425, pp. 200–220. Springer, Heidelberg (2005)
13. Meyer, J.: Creating Informal Looking Interfaces (2005), accessible at http://www.cybergrain.com/tech/pubs/lines_technote.html
14. Newman, M.W., Lin, J., Hong, J.I., Landay, J.A.: Denim: An Informal Web Site Design Tool Inspired by Observations of Practice. Human-Comp. Interaction 18, 259–324 (2003)
15. Paternó, F., Volpe, N.: Natural Modelling of Interactive Applications. In: Gilroy, S.W., Harrison, M.D. (eds.) Interactive Systems. LNCS, vol. 3941, pp. 66–77. Springer, Heidelberg (2006)
16. Petrie, J.N., Schneider, K.A.: Mixed-Fidelity Prototyping of User Interfaces. In: Doherty, G., Blandford, A. (eds.) DSVIS 2006. LNCS, vol. 4323, pp. 26–28. Springer, Heidelberg (2007)

17. Plimmer, B.E., Apperley, M.: Interacting with Sketched Interface Designs: An Evaluation Study. In: CHI'04. Proc. of ACM Conf. on Human Aspects in Computing Systems, Vienna, April 24-29, 2004, pp. 1337–1340. ACM Press, New York (2004)
18. Rudd, J., Stern, K., Isensee, S.: Low vs. high-fidelity prototyping debate. Interactions 3(1), 76–85 (1996)
19. Snyder, C.: Paper Prototyping: The Fast and Easy Way to Design and Refine User Interfaces. Series in Interactive Technologies. Morgan Kaufmann, San Francisco (2002)
20. Vanderdonckt, J.: A MDA-Compliant Environment for Developing User Interfaces of Information Systems. In: Pastor, Ó., Falcão e Cunha, J. (eds.) CAiSE 2005. LNCS, vol. 3520, pp. 16–31. Springer, Heidelberg (2005)
21. Van Laerhoven, K., Schmidt, A., Gellersen, H.-W.: Pin&Play: Networking Objects through Pins. In: Borriello, G., Holmquist, L.E. (eds.) UbiComp 2002. LNCS, vol. 2498, pp. 219–228. Springer, Heidelberg (2002)
22. Virzi, R.A., Sokolov, J.L., Karis, D.: Usability problem identification using both Low- and High-Fidelity Prototypes. In: CHI'96. Proc. of ACM Conf. on Human Aspects in Computing Systems, Vancouver, pp. 236–243. ACM Press, New York (1996)
23. Walker, M., Takayama, L., Landay, J.: High-fidelity or low-fidelity, paper or computer medium? In: HFES'2002. Proceedings of the 46th Annual Meeting of the Human Factors and Ergonomics Society, Baltimore, September 30-October 4, 2002, pp. 661–665. Human Factors and Ergonomics Society, Santa Monica (2002)

User-Centered Design and Business Process Modeling: Cross Road in Rapid Prototyping Tools

Noi Sukaviriya[1], Vibha Sinha[2],
Thejaswini Ramachandra[3], Senthil Mani[2], and Markus Stolze[1]

[1] IBM TJ Watson Research Center, Hawthorne, NY
[2] IBM India Research lab, Delhi, India
[3] IBM Software Group, Bangalore, India
{noi, mgstolze}@us.ibm.com,
{vibha.sinha, thejaswini, sentmani}@in.ibm.com

Abstract. Fast production of a solution is a necessity in the world of competitive IT consulting business today. In engagements where early user interface design mock-ups are needed to visualize proposed business processes, the need to quickly create UI becomes prominent very early in the process. Our work aims to speed up the UI design process, enabling rapid creation of low-fidelity UI design with traditional user-centered design thinking but different tooling concepts. This paper explains the approach and the rationale behind our model and tools. One key focal point is in leveraging business process models as a starting point of the UI design process. The other focal point is on using a model-driven approach with designer-centered tools to eliminate some design overheads, to help manage a large design space, and to cope with changes in requirements. We used examples from a real business engagement to derive and strengthen this work.

Keywords: User-centered Design Process, UI Design, Model-driven User Interface, Low-fidelity UI Tools.

1 Problem Statements and Context

In the world where competition for business is severe, we are in need for better tooling to support the solution design process. One such design activity is the user-centered design process. Whilst user observations and interviews are essential part of the process, these activities are undoubtedly irreplaceable by IT tools. However, some other parts of the user-centered design process – in particular coming up with low-fidelity UI mock-ups in the early design phase – is still lacking by way of appropriate tools. Many popular tools designers use today such as Adobe Illustrator, Adobe Photoshop, or Microsoft PowerPoint, were developed for other purposes such as drawings and presentations. They support high-fidelity drawings in nature and require high-fidelity efforts to produce low-fidelity mock-ups. This class of tools also lacks support for information structure and design management, hence dealing with requirement changes throughout a project is rather painstaking. Another class of tools such as Macromedia Dreamweaver popular for creating web-based interfaces has

C. Baranauskas et al. (Eds.): INTERACT 2007, LNCS 4662, Part I, pp. 165–178, 2007.

more support on data connections and back end services, but the tooling itself is yet another high-fidelity tool. Some research tools were explored such as SILK [1] and DENIM [2] for capturing hand sketches low-fidelity UI and navigation structure. However, the outputs of these tools are not sufficiently organized visually, hence are not practical for business practices.   None of these tools mentioned allow a quick way to come up with low-fidelity mock-ups with support for proper alignment and visual organization.

Many people often associate low-fidelity mock-ups with low-cost, hand-drawn interfaces. While paper and pencil are the most used tools, designers use other tools in conjunction [3]. Our preliminary interviews with several user-centered designers revealed that hand-drawn sketches were not used when they presented their UI mock-ups. They always start out with hand sketching but that typically lasted shortly. Some mentioned that their hand-drawn sketches did not look organized enough. But most agreed that it would take an even larger effort to use hand-drawn sketches including re-drawing repeatedly and scanning paper sketches. Needless to say that maintaining hand-drawn sketch changes even in the early design phase for a large project is far from viable. There's a level of visual organization and alignments, implicitly required in presenting UI design ideas in the early design phase, especially in information intensive applications. Without sufficient visual organization, the review process will suffer. All of the designers we interviewed commonly use high-fidelity tools mentioned above to create mock-ups that look low in fidelity.

In IT consulting practices, many business engagements nowadays often start with business process modeling – be it for an entirely new business process or transforming an old process to a new and improved one. Within our company, while Microsoft Visio is still the most popular tool for business process modeling, many consultants now have switched to use an IBM software product called Websphere Business Modeler (WBM.) In this kind of engagements, business analysts use WBM to draw business process diagrams, which are then used as a way to propose and have the customers approve the work. Prompt demand for low-fidelity UI mock-ups is three-fold in such engagements. First is an earlier need even before the UCD process begins. Low-fidelity UI designs and storyboards are commonly used as a means to visualize how a business process might work. Visualization of connected boxes as usually diagrammed in a business model has limitations; they do not give people a good grasp of a more tangible understanding of the process. Secondly, once the work is approved, low-fidelity user interface mock-ups are needed as an instrument for discussing detailed system design and requirements. Throughout the early design phase, business analysts, subject matter experts, architects, and UCD designers gradually and repeatedly discuss over different parts of the UI design to comb out detailed requirements, conflicts of understanding, and realization of the need for further investigations. The UI design repeatedly changes over the course of this activity. The essence of using low-fidelity mock-ups as a way to share the understanding of a solution is monumental in our experience. Lastly, once the design starts to firm up, user-centered designers review low-fidelity UI mock-ups with the users for early design feedback. This has to be done as quickly as possible before turning the design into high-fidelity as the development team is often ready and waiting for inputs at this stage.

The needs for UI mock-ups early in the design phase do not require high fidelity really. That is, not all buttons have to be in the right place, not all UI components have to be in their final locations. The mock-ups do not need finished styles and look. The mock-ups are used for the purpose of understanding the process. For business executives who view the UI with a business process, the low-fidelity mock-ups merely gives them another, yet very powerful, perspective to the process flow and interactions between people in the process. For business analysts and subject matter experts (SMEs), low-fidelity UIs are just a matter of making sure the required business functions are supported and information is presented with the proper semantics. For the end users, designers use low-fidelity UI mock-ups to solicit their feedback. Designers focus on whether the users can understand the information presented, whether they can perceive what needs to be done, whether some information is missing, and whether certain information is not necessary. We do not want to present high-fidelity UI design to these various reviewers as they may be caught in unnecessary cosmetic discussions [4].

We hope to have convinced the readers at this point of the increasing demand for quick low-fidelity UI mock-ups and their business contributions early in the design process. Lack of proper tooling support for quick UI sketches that can change frequently and rapidly would enhance the requirement gathering process. Our focus is on a fast UI mock up tool that leverages business process models that helps maintain the UCD perspectives. We also focus on helping designers manage a large design space. Our other goal not emphasized in this paper is to support the end-to-end UI design process from low fidelity to high fidelity design to UI code generation. This latter endeavor requires a clean separation of concerns from people with different skill sets, i.e. UCD designers and developers, as moving from design to development increasingly adds technical complexity. Our ultimate goal is to encompass within our model and tools sufficient support for low fidelity design thinking and management, as well as the high fidelity UI production process while maintaining the overall usability of the tools.

2 Related Work

Recent related research with a similar goal to our work of providing UCD support is in by Campos and Nunes in [5]. In this work, they built a user-centered tool for rapid prototyping using the notations for abstract prototypes developed by Constantine [6]. Their focus is on using interaction patterns to fill in design blocks while our work fills in design blocks with connections to business data elements, users' read/write access to information as restricted by the business process, and UI related semantics called upon by the designer.

Automatic generation of user interfaces dated back to the early 90's. In [7], a comprehensive notation for expressing the quality of data attributes was used. The automatic generation effort in this work attempted to lay out page detail as well as a page's grouping and semantic structure; the latter task is proved to be quite easy for an expert designer to do but harder for a machine. While the work in [7] eliminated the tediousness of repeatedly laying out component in detail, the entangled complexity of trying to solve semantic layout problem outweighed the benefits. A smaller piece of work in [8] is much more practical and use a similar technique as deployed by our work here of laying out a small number of components piecemeal.

There has been related research on generating user interfaces from task-based models. The work by Paterno in a series of publications [9, 10, 11] focused on a tool for modeling tasks and automatically generating user interfaces from high-level specification and from analyzing task structures. The task model is device independent therefore can automatically generate to multiple platforms [10]. Venderdonkt in [12] does semi-automatic generations through Automatic Interaction Objects structure. Our work uses the business task model as the input into the design process. We are using business task as requirements but currently are not using it to the full extent in helping generating the UI. We find that large enterprises have rather complex workflow and work context, and only small portion of this complexity is captured in business process model. User-centered designers still depend a great deal on closing the knowledge gap through business requirements and user observations to be able to properly complete their work.

Last but not least, a company called iRise [13] of which products center around simulating UI design and visualizing IT solutions early in the design phase. Their products are capable of generating rather attractive UI. Our work shared a common goal of the ability to visualize IT solution early. However, our work aims also at transporting the low-fidelity mock-ups into high-fidelity as well. Our low-fidelity mock-ups are executable user interface and can be beyond presentation materials.

3 Our Approach

In this section, we will walk the readers through our end-to-end approach. We start from a business model (Section 2.1) then transform it into various views in our user-centered the Human Interactions (HI) perspective (Section 2.2). These views are designed to provide different aspects of user-centric information harvested from a business process. The views are also designed as places upon which a design such as pages and grouping of information are built. Section 2.3 describes how design pages are roughly laid out and filled with some automation help. Section 2.4 describes the user interface generation and illustrates the outputs.

3.1 Business Model as a Starting Point

Our starting point is, but not necessarily always, a business process model. Though there are several process notations used in the industry [14, 15], we find the basic information in business processes having to do with "who" will do which "task" "when" in the business process, the sequence of business tasks, and what are the inputs and outputs of a task, to be the most useful set of information for starting a user interface design. This set of information interestingly shared some characteristics with the user task model commonly used as a starting point for user-centered design process [16]. Let's put aside for later, if it occurs in your mind, whether business modeling and user task modeling, if done in the same tools, would yield the same "task model." In our approach, we gladly take the business process as is and turn it into perspectives that are more in tune with the user-centered design thinking. Before we embark into further detail, let's look at an example of an invoice-to-cash business process in Figure 1.   Please note here that the complete invoice-to-cash process is rather large consisting of several process diagrams. We only reveal a snippet of the process to illustrate the examples in this paper. For confidentiality reasons, we will not reveal much further information on the entire model.

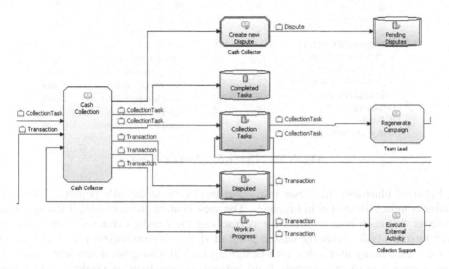

Fig. 1. A snippet of the Invoice to Cash business process shown in the Process Editor in IBM Websphere Business Modeler 6.0

From Figure 1, we want to point out information that is essential for understanding the following steps in our approach. Notice the "Cash Collection" task at the leftmost of the diagram. A user role "Cash Collector" is identified below the task. The cash collection task, as we learned from SMEs and user observations, typically involves the user calling customers based on "transactions," which is one type of input to the task. Another type of input is "collection task" – a group of transactions recommended to Cash Collector for collection. Documents that flow between tasks are referred to in this paper as "information artifacts." Attributes of each artifact in this model and their data types can be defined through other editors in WBM. The directions of arrows indicate the directions of the process flow. Cylinders denote repositories in which information artifacts in various stages are stored.

3.2 Transformation into Human Interaction Perspective

The next step in our approach is converting the business process model into the HI perspective to give designers a schematic summary of the process. There are 4 views in the HI perspective:

- "User role – Artifacts" – shows all information artifacts needed per user role
- "Artifacts – User role" – shows per each artifact user roles with access to it
- "User role – Task" – shows business tasks required for each user role
- "User role – Design"– shows UI design pages that have been defined for each user role. This view has empty content initially.

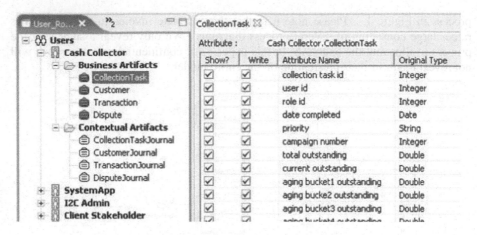

Fig. 2. The "User role – Artifact" View

Figure 2 illustrates the "User role – Artifact" view as initially populated from the business model illustrated in Figure 1. The view centers on user roles; it shows all the artifacts that each role requires for performing their tasks extracted from inputs to each business task. From the design point of view, this summarizes part of the design scope – how many user roles am I designing for? It also gives a sub-scope for each user – what type of information, from business perspectives, is needed by each user role. Since our tool is implemented on an Eclipse-based platform, we use a tree-like structure to present the hierarchical relationships of user roles and artifacts in the Eclipse style. The underlying information model that supports the 4 views is not quite so hierarchical but rather with many interconnections. We made efforts to conceal the UML2 model behind the scene and at the same time conform to standard views in the Eclipse environment.

In Figure 2, notice the two types of artifacts. The "Business Artifact" denotes information artifacts that flow from one task to another. The "Contextual Artifact" denotes artifacts that are inputs or outputs to but do not flow across business tasks. We use this information to guesstimate the importance of an artifact. By assuming that if an artifact flows from one task to the next, and often from one user role to another, it must be significant. This is shared information and is often designed with consistency among user roles. Any artifact that does not flow must be contextual and is used only in a particular task context. The model for the two categories of artifacts are actually similar, the separation is purely to provide designers with a cue on which artifacts might need more careful treatment across user roles. When selecting an artifact from the tree on the left, the attributes of the artifact is shown in an attribute editor shown on the right in Figure 2. We will discuss the use of the attribute editor with the next view.

Complimentary to the "User role – Artifact" view is the "Artifact – User Role" view illustrated in Figure 3. In this view, each artifact is shown with a list of user roles that require access to it. The view is designed to help designers with a concrete understanding of shared artifacts. Knowing that an artifact is used by multiple user roles, designers may and often opt to design similar interfaces to the same artifact, unless dictated otherwise by requirements or by their knowledge of the user tasks.

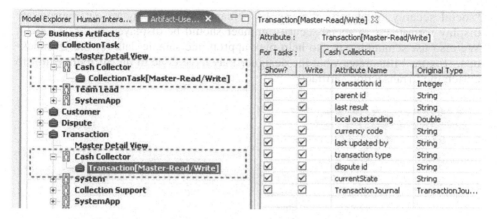

Fig. 3. The "Artifact – User Role" view

The "Artifact – User Role" view is designed to expose business requirements on read/write access to artifacts. This is derived from the business model; if an artifact flows in and out of a business task, we assume the user must update it in the task. Notice in Figure 3 that the Cash Collector has "read/write" access to the "Transaction" and "Collection Tasks" artifacts. For example, the "Cash Collector" user role has a read/write "master" copy of the "Transaction" artifact. Any information refined for the UI in this master copy will govern all partitions of this artifact when they apply to UI designs. This statement will be made clearer in Section 2.3 with examples of "data groups," subsets of this master copy organized to feed into various pages of the UI design.

A user role may have "read/write" and/or "read only" master copies of an artifact. Read/write means the user can modify the information while "read only" means the user can only view it. When a user role has both "read/write" and "read only" access, it means the user cannot always update the information. A common use case is, for example, a contract may not be modified after it is signed. Being explicit about read/write access brings attention to the designer on how the UI may show information artifacts in various stages of the process.

When a master copy is viewed in the attribute editor, the tasks that are applicable to the access rights are shown in the "For Tasks:" attribute illustrated in Figure 4. Since read/write access is derived at the artifact level from the business process, through the attribute editor, the designer can enrich the information by being more specific – whether a user role needs to see all or part of data elements of an artifact, and whether the user can update all or part of data elements of the artifact. This indication of access rights plays an important part of our tool's automation. We have an automatic generation capability that uses data elements and their read/write access to initially call out appropriate UI elements.

The attribute editor also provides the designer with an opportunity to put UI related information with data elements of an artifact to be used throughout her design. She can place a user-friendly label for each data element. In this editor, we introduce a notion of "UI semantic type" which better describes the UI semantics of data elements. For example, a basic type string may in deed be a "social security number." We use UI semantic types to figure out appropriate display format, i.e., a social security number should be displayed as 222-33-4444. We also use semantic types to help pick appropriate sample data for the UI mock-ups. Figure 4 illustrates what the designer may have done in the attribute editor to enrich the "Transaction" artifact.

Transaction[Master-Read/Write] ✕					
Attribute :		Transaction[Master-Read/Write]			
For Tasks :		Cash Collection			
Show?	Write	Attribute Name	Original Type	Semantic Type	User-Friendly Label
☑	☐	transaction id	Integer	ID	Inv #
☐	☐	parent id	String		
☑	☐	last result	String	Paragraph	Last Summary
☑	☐	local outstanding	Double	Monetary Value	Base Currency Total
☑	☐	currency code	String	Word	Currency
☑	☑	last updated by	String	First & Last Name	Last Updated By
☑	☐	transaction type	String	Word	Type
☑	☑	dispute id	String	ID	Dispute ID
☐	☐	currentState	String		
☑	☑	TransactionJou...	Transactio...	List of Complex Rec...	Result History

Fig. 4. Attributes of the Transaction artifact shown in the Attribute Editor after modifications

Fig. 5. The "User role – Task" view

The "User role – Task" view, illustrated in Figure 5, summarizes all business tasks for each user role. Each business task shows inputs, information needed for the task, and outputs, the outcomes of the task. Using this view, the designers are informed of the governing business tasks for each user and should be able to design appropriately.

We will defer the description of the "User role – Design" view to the next section.

3.3 Building Up the Design with Pages and Data Groups

The designer can now start building up the UI design. Imagine this is when a designer would start sketching out design ideas. Let's assume after some initial thoughts, the designer tries out a couple of pages. Figure 6 shows the skeletons of the 2 pages for the Cash Collector user role. While our visual skeletal sketching tool has not been implemented, here is what the designer might visualize in mind and what they might do had the tool existed.

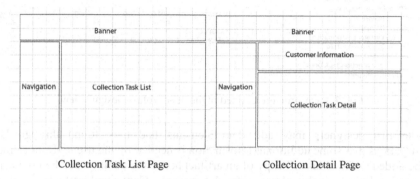

Collection Task List Page   Collection Detail Page

Fig. 6. Visual sketches of Cash Collector interface

The design creates the 2 pages by associating them to the user role Cash Collector and to the "Cash Collection" task. Figure 7 illustrates the page structure above in the "User role – Design" view. In this view, pages associated to a particular user role are specific to that user role. Pages associated with "users" at the top of the user tree are designed to be reused among multiple user roles. A page consists of "UI fragments," which represent visual blocks as shown in Figure 6. A UI fragment is a portion of a page that displays related UI elements, etc. Partitioning a page into UI fragments is purely the designer's discretion.

Next the designer focuses on the information to be placed in various UI fragments on the pages. Here we introduce a "data group" notion denoting a group of selected attributes from an artifact's master copy. A data group singles out data elements chosen to be displayed in a UI fragment. For example, the collection task list in the first page will show a list of tasks, each is shown with 5 elements; the list will contain 5 columns, each column corresponds to a data element in the Collection Task artifact. Figure 8 illustrated the data group for such a list. Notice that in a data group, the designer has another opportunity to localize UI information, for example, the user-friendly label may change to fit a small design space. (In this example, the customer "Location" is re-labeled "Loc" so it occupies a narrower column in the table.) The resulting UI is shown in Figure 9. Read-write access can be reduced to read-only as it is more appropriate for a tabular display in this example. Notice that changing from read only to read/write is not allowed as doing so would violate the restrictions from the business model. For the data group in Figure 8, the sequence of the selected data elements is also shuffled to control the column sequence; this is the way the designer can control the design output.

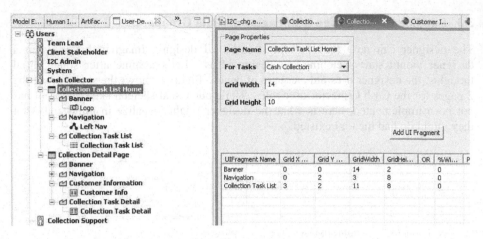

Fig. 7. Page structure defined in the "User role – Design" view

Note that designers may add data elements had they found through UCD investigations that some additional information is needed by the users. Data elements can be added to the "Master" copy of an artifact hence the addition can be used across the board and can be included in various data groups. Contextual artifacts can also be added had the designer found artifacts undocumented in the business model that the user needs to support a task. When data elements or artifacts are added, discussions need to happen with business analysts and architects of how appropriate and plausible to support such information. The result is often a compromise.

We do not allow business artifacts to be added for obvious reasons.

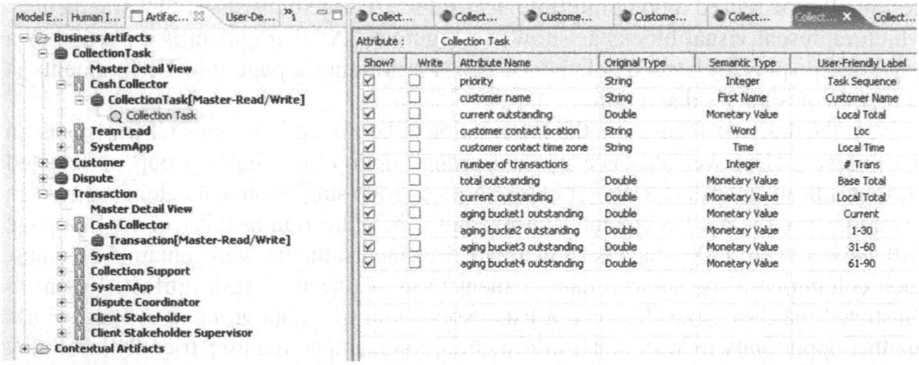

Fig. 8. A data group showing selected attributes for listing Collection Task artifacts

A page is not completed unless the content is filled. In our tool, the designer may choose to use high-level components such as a tabular list or a data layout component and associate data groups to them. The data layout component is one of the most useful components and can be specified to layout matching UI elements in 1 or multiple columns. Additional UI components such as a button, a label, etc., can also be manually added to a UI fragment. Due to space limitation, we will omit detail on this aspect of the tool.

3.4   Generating the User Interface from the Model

Once pages are sketched out with data groups associated to the appropriate UI components, designers can generate a user interface to see the results. In addition to the page layout, the design can also define how pages are linked (not discussed in this paper.) To generate a UI, the design model is transformed to the execution-oriented XML model, which is used to further generate the UI pages and connections to a simulated backend system. Figures 9 and 10 illustrate the resulting interfaces of the 2 pages mentioned in the previous section.

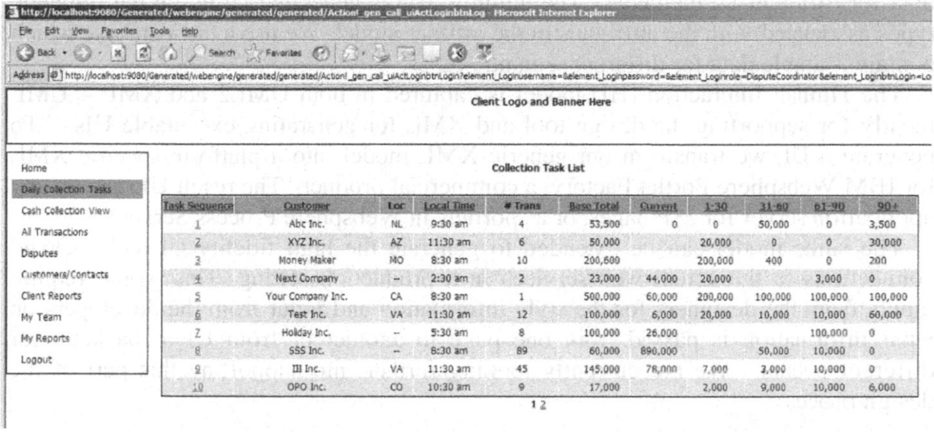

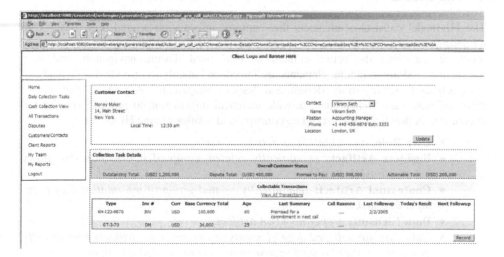

Fig. 9. The generated UI for the collection task list page

Fig. 10. The generated UI for the collection detail page

For each page, the XML model contains 4 main types of information:

- Page content: describes the page layout and placements of UI elements.
- Page bindings: lists the bindings from UI elements to the data elements
- Page interactions: defines actions and page transitions
- Styles: low fidelity design assumes default styles. More elaborate styles can be used when extending the model to generate high fidelity UI

We follow the consumer-provider pattern to link the UI to the backend system that provides data. The page content is used to generate the consumer code and page bindings and interactions define the provider. The generated provider mainly consists of stubs to connect to the backend which can provide actual data and other functions through any of the following: web services, simple java classes, RMI etc. In the absence of connections to actual backend systems, the default provider gives dummy data for different UI elements. The dummy data is generated based on the semantic types associated with the attributes in the artifact model. We use a test database which contains sample data for different semantic types.

The Human Interaction (HI) model is captured in both UML2 and XML – UML mostly for supporting the design tool and XML for generating executable UIs. To generate a UI, we transform our generic XML model into a platform-specific XML for IBM Websphere Portlet Factory, a commercial product. The result UI runs on any application server for JSP pages, or as portlets in Websphere Process Server.

The same model can be extended to generate the high fidelity UI and backend connections to the actual web services in a production setting. This would require inputs from the designers for the style information and input from the developers on what information is passed from one page to another or from UI to backend for different events. We are currently looking further into supporting this part of the design process.

4 The Model

The HI model consists of elements that captures information around user roles. Our modeling concerns cover both the support for the UI design thinking for designers as much as capturing the actual content of the visual design, navigation, and user interactions. Many modeling elements are introduced mainly to provide design analysis perspectives, flexibility in the design, and design management. A number of elements, many of which are well hidden, provide technical information to produce support for execution. Following is the list of key concepts and relations in the HI model:

- **User Role:** *a category of targeted end users*
- **Business Artifact:** *semantically related group of information that flows between business tasks*
- **Contextual Artifact:** *semantically related group of information that is an input of a task*
- **Data Element:** *properties of an artifact*
- **Data Group:** *selected data elements of one or more artifacts semantically grouped together for the purpose of displaying related information*
- **Page:** *a set of design equivalent to a full screen*

- **UI Fragment:** *a portion of a page that is used for displaying related information and functions*
- **UI Element:** *type of UI components rendered on the screen. Basic types include text, text input, text area, link, drop down list, radio group, check box group, two way select list, calendar, etc. Complex types include tabs, list table, data layout component, navigation component, etc.*
- **User role – Artifact:** *a relationship showing user roles that need access to an artifact, an artifact that is used by a user role*
- **Artifact – Attribute:** *a relationship between an artifact and its properties*
- **Data Group – Attribute:** *a relationship collecting selected data elements*
- **User Role – Page:** *A relationship between a user role and pages that are designed for the role*
- **Page – UI Fragment:** *A relationship between a page and its UI fragments. Each UI fragment in turn contains information on its height, width, and position on the page.*
- **UI Element – Data Group:** *A relationship between data group and a (composite) UI element. The type of UI element determines how the data group may dictate the automatic selection of detailed UI elements that fill out the fragment.*

5 Experience and Analysis

Using business models as a starting point for the UI design process is an interesting endeavor. One observation we had was that some business processes provide a rather concrete set of business tasks, to the point that designers can almost visualize what happens on the screen just from viewing a business process model. Some business processes are rather abstract. In this case, designers need to do a great deal of research to understand the nature of these abstract business tasks. The example given in this paper is an example of the latter. As business processes are not and will most likely never be user task models, we take business models merely as requirements. Composing user tasks for these business tasks are upon the discretion of the designers.

Our HI perspective and tool are designed such that designers can start the UI design process with or without a business process. They are also designed such that information can be added, specifically user roles, artifacts, and attributes. There are many reasons why this is a viable design. One, business models may not be available at the time designers need to start. Two, there may be yet ambiguous knowledge at the start of the design but user-centered designer may have higher confidence in the accuracy of information they have collected through user observations and could indeed start mocking up design ideas. Third, we observed that there are often additional user roles not called upon in the business model. These roles are often in managerial positions and are not contributing to the operations of the model; they function as overseers and often require reporting and monitoring capabilities in the UI design. Currently we allow adding user roles but supporting monitoring types of interaction designs has not been addressed in the current tooling.

Our approach currently appears very top down. The UI design process is all – bottom up, top down, and sometimes middle out. We are looking to further support the design process by allowing designers to flexibly approach a design.

Our work is still on-going. One obvious extension is the visual skeletal sketching tool and an ability to drag and drop data groups into UI fragments. There are many other features that we have not addressed in the current tool, for example, shared templates in the design hierarchy; appropriate style sheets for low fidelity mock up, to name a few. We plan to take better advantage of business models even deeper such as using the business flow to help start a UI flow, and using the business task tree as a place to create user subtasks, etc. We have not validated the tool with the general user target at this point. Our near future work also includes user validation and more business cases to refine the tool and research concepts.

References

1. Landay, J., Myers, B.: Sketching Interfaces: Toward More Human Interface Design. IEEE Computer, 55–64 (March 2001)
2. Lin, J., Thomsen, M., Landay, J.A: Interactive Design: A Visual Language for Sketching Large and Complex Interactive Designs. In: Proceedings CHI 2002: ACM Conference on Human Factors in Computing Systems, ACM Press, New York (2002)
3. Campos, P., Nunes, N.J: Practitioner Tools and Workstyles for User-Interface Design. IEEE Software 24(1), 73–80 (2007)
4. Wong, Y.Y.: Rough and Ready Prototypes: Lesson from Graphic Design. In: Proceedings of CHI 92: ACM Conference on Human Factors in Computing Systems, pp. 83–84. ACM Press, New York (1992)
5. Campos, P.F., Nunes, N.J.: CanonSketch: a User-Centered Tool for Canonical Abstract Prototyping. In: Bastide, R., Palanque, P., Roth, J. (eds.) EHCI-DSVIS 2004. LNCS, vol. 3425, Springer, Heidelberg (2005)
6. Constantine, L.: Canonical Abstract Prototypes for Abstract Visual and Interaction Design. In: Jorge, J.A., Jardim Nunes, N., Falcão e Cunha, J. (eds.) DSV-IS 2003. LNCS, vol. 2844, Springer, Heidelberg (2003)
7. Kim, W.C., Foley, J.D.: Providing High-level Control and Expert Assistance in the User Interface Presentation Design. In: Proceedings of CHI 93: ACM Conference on Human Factors in Computing Systems, pp. 430–437. ACM Press, New York (1993)
8. de Baar, D., Foley, J.D., Mullet, K.E.: Coupling Application Design and User Interface Design. In: Proceedings of CHI 92: ACM Conference on Human Factors in Computing Systems, pp. 259–266. ACM Press, New York (1992)
9. Paterno, F., Mancini, C.: Model-based Design of Interactive Applications. ACM Intelligence Magazine Winter, 26–37 (2000)
10. Paterno, F., Santoro, C.: One Model, many Interfaces. In: CADUI 2002. Proceedings of 4th International Conference on Computer-Aided Design of user Interfaces, pp. 143–154 (2002)
11. Paterno, F.: Tools for Task Modeling: Where We are, Where We are Headed. In: Proceedings of International Workshop on TAsk MOdels and DIAgrams for user interface design, pp. 10–17 (2002)
12. Bouillon, L., Vanderdonckt, J., Chow, K.C.: Flexible Re-engineering of Web Sties. In: Proceedings of ACM Conference on Intelligent Interfaces, pp. 132–139. ACM Press, New York (2004)
13. http://www.irise.com/
14. Business Process Modeling Notation, http://en.wikipedia.org/wiki/BPMN
15. Aalst, W.V.D., Hee, K.V.: Workflow Management: Models, Methods, and Systems, 2nd edn. MIT Press, Cambridge (2004)
16. Mayhew, D.: The Usability Engineering Lifecycle: A Practitioner's Handbook for User Interface Design, 1st edn. Morgan Kauffmann, San Francisco (1999)

Ubiquitous Substitution

Christina Brodersen, Susanne Bødker, and Clemens Nylandsted Klokmose

Department of Computer Science, University of Aarhus, Denmark
{sorsha, bodker, clemens}@daimi.au.dk

Abstract. Ubiquitous interaction places the user in the centre of dynamic configurations of technology, where work not necessarily is performed through a single personal computer, but supported by a multiplicity of technologies and physical devices. This paper presents an activity-theoretically based framework for analyzing *ubiquitous substitution*, i.e. a set of mediators that are or can be continuously substituted with the purpose of highlighting expected and indented uses, and the conflicts encountered when attempting substitution between them. The paper develops a four-leveled analysis of such mediators, and point towards a minimalist approach to design of ubiquitous interaction.

1 Introduction

The recent development of computing–whether it is called pervasive, ubiquitous, tangible, or ambient–changes the relationship between the human being and the computer from "one-to-one" to "many-to-many". This development challenges our understanding of human-computer interaction; where previously the focus of HCI has been on one technology-one application-one user, all packaged into one monolithic unit, ubiquitous interaction is about changing configurations of input and output devices, applications and users.

In classical HCI, there has until now been two ways of understanding and designing to suit users: Either to ignore user competence and design for novices only, as was often done in the first generation of HCI; or to do in-depth analyses of user needs as in the second (Bannon & Bødker, 1991). In both ways of thinking, however, the idea has been to design a new mediator as a *permanent* substitution of the old.

In first generation HCI, very minimal assumptions about the users were made explicitly. Yet, Buxton (1986) derives the underlying model of the human user from an analysis of existing mediators at the motor-operational level. Bannon (1986) notes how all mediators contain a theory of the user and the task domain, with reference to "idiot-proof" design philosophies that were implicit in some first generation HCI. With a few exceptions, such as key-stroke level analysis (Card et al, 1990), this quite reductionist approach did not provide any methods to help compare mediators and forms of interaction.

In the second generation, the focus has been on context and on understanding current and future use situations to understand the needs of the users. Learning has been important and hence, it was OK for users to spend time learning, and accordingly developing a new repertoire of actions and operations. Bardram & Bertelsen (1995) and Bødker & Graves Petersen (2001) took early steps towards focusing on learning

C. Baranauskas et al. (Eds.): INTERACT 2007, LNCS 4662, Part I, pp. 179–192, 2007.
© IFIP International Federation for Information Processing 2007

from one mediator to another, yet the challenges for ubiquitous interaction design are a bit different: The *ubiquitous substitution* that we design for is not a permanent substitution of a full mediator with another (for example a typewriter with a word processor). It is a sort of design that focuses on how to substitute one mediator with another in a way that enriches the human repertoire of actions possibilities, hence, making possible continuous substitutions in terms of switching between mediators. Ubiquitous substitution is not a matter of breaking down and replacing one kind of mediation with another, but providing a larger "toolbox" and a better understanding of which mediator to apply when.

This paper focuses on such ubiquitous substitution. The theoretical account is based on activity theoretical HCI as it has been developed by Bødker (1991), Bertelsen (2001), Kaptelinin (1995a), with more recent inspiration from Gibson as developed by Bærentsen & Trettvik (2002), and from Bedny et al. (2000). We use the term *mediator* to cover a configuration of physical devices, logical interaction possibilities, functionality, etc., that serves a particular purpose to users (Kaptelinin, 1995b). We will return to these theoretical concepts in the following.

To illustrate our theoretical elaborations, we use examples from a recent empirical study (Bouvin et al., 2006), where geographical maps were used on three different technologies: A paper map in a telephone book, a web based digital map on a tablet-PC, and a digital map on a GPS enabled Nokia smart phone. The mediators are different but share some similarities: All three devices are relatively small and can be carried around, shared between users, and handed from one person to another while in use. In the study, we asked groups of two users to solve simple assignments looking at the map and out the window. Each group was given eight assignments that they had to solve, e.g., locate north, identify a local school and find the distance and direction to it. All assignments were created to relate to buildings and objects that were visible through a large window. The sessions were recorded with two videocameras covering different angles; still-shots were taken with high frequency, and all sessions were transcribed and analyzed in activity theoretical terms (Bertelsen & Bødker 2002).

The paper is structured as follows: First, we develop the theoretical framework with emphasis on functional organs. Through an analyis of the use of different map technologies, we demonstrate elements of the framework and discuss how the results can be used to understand substitution between mediators. We conclude by describing the challenges they pose for ubiquitous substitution, and the formation of functional organs in ubiquitous interaction.

2   Human Activity and Functional Organs

Human activity can be analyzed according to three layers: Activity, action, and operation (Bertelsen & Bødker, 2002). Activity is directed towards satisfying a need through a material or ideal object and the activity layer focuses on motivation and analytically addresses the question of *why* something takes place. Human activity is carried out through actions. These actions are governed by the conscious goals of the subject, and accordingly the analytical layer focuses of *what* takes place. Goals are different from the motive. They belong to the level where we immediately meet human activity in an analysis, because they are conscious. Goals reflect the objective results of action. Actions are realized through series of operations; each "triggered" by the conditions and structure of the action. They are performed without conscious thinking, but are oriented in the world by what Kaptelinin (1995a) calls an unconscious orienting basis. According to Bærentsen & Trettvik (2002), operations may be cultural-historically developed or naturally evolved, ecologically determined. Accordingly, they may realize internalized cultural-historical patterns of conduct or inborn species-specific patterns of behavior. Thus they result from appropriated use of tools, educated manners towards other human beings or movements in the physical world according to concrete physical conditions. Actions are dynamic structures where only the goal can be assumed to be conscious. Operations are never fixed, but adapted dynamically to the conditions of the environment. Actions are thought as a recursive structure, consisting of both conscious and non-conscious sub-actions and operations.

Bedny et al. (2000) introduce the concept of strategies described as plans for goal achievements that are responsive to external and internal conditions. We distinguish between strategies and routines; strategies have to be consciously developed when human beings are to perform an action. Strategies turn into routines when the predisposition to perform a certain action becomes partly automated, or into non-conscious–meaning we become familiar with while performing the action and similar actions. Figure 1 is adopted from Bertelsen & Bødker (2002), Bærentsen (1989) and Bærentsen & Trettvik (2002) and shows the relation between the three analytic layers.

Analytic layers	Mental representation	Realizes	Level of description	Analytical question
Activity	Motive (need)–not necessarily conscious, but may become conscious	Personality	The social and personal meaning of activity, its relation to motives and needs	Why?
Action	Goal–conscious	Activities (systems of actions organized to achieve goals)	Possible goals, critical goals, particularly relevant sub-goals Strategies	What?
Operation	Condition of actions (structure of activity)–normally not conscious, only limited possibilities of consciousness	Actions (chains of operations organized by goals and concrete conditions)	The concrete way of executing an action in accordance with the specific conditions surrounding the goal. Routines	How?

Fig. 1. Human activity and its analytic layers

Activity theory understands human beings as dialectically recreating their own environment (Bertelsen & Bødker 2002). Subjects are not merely choosing from possibilities in the environment, but actively creating the environment through activity; *"new tools shape new goals"*, as Kaptelinin (1995a) puts it. Whereas any specific human activity can be understood as activity, action or operation, none of these are fixed; an action can become an operation through internalization, and an operation becomes an action through conceptualization in breakdown situations (Bødker 1991).

The historical development of activity implies a development of artifacts and environments. Modes of acting within an activity system are historically crystallized into artifacts. In this sense, the historical development of activity can be read from the development of artifacts mediating the practice (Bærentsen 1989, Bannon and Bødker 1991). Activity is crystallized into artifacts in two ways. Firstly, they are externalizations of operations with earlier artifacts, and secondly, they are representations of modes of acting in the given activity. Kaptelinin (1995b) captures the functionally integrated, goal-oriented configurations of internalized operations and procedures (routines and strategies), and external mediation in the term *functional organ*. When a mediator is well integrated into the functional organ, it augments the human capacity, whereas if not, the mediator is outside the human user.

This means that when we study mediators, tools and devices, it is important to understand the extent to which they can be integrated into a functional organ. What efforts are needed to provide such integration? How may exploration of the intended use be supported, and how may some of the possible, yet less desirable uses be blocked (Bærentsen & Trettvik, 2002)?

2.1 Mediation and Functional Organs

Bødker (1991) proposes to analyze mediation through three aspects of the mediator: *The physical aspects* are the support for human operations towards the computer application as a physical object; *the handling aspects* support operations towards the computer application. The handling aspects are the conditions that allow the user to focus on the objects of the activity. *The subject/object* directed aspects constitute the conditions for operations directed towards objects or subjects dealt with in or through the artifact.

Bærentsen & Trettvik (2002) combine and extend the use of Gibson's (1979) affordances with activity theory. They talk about the *"network of technologies and praxis that are the basis of (..) affordances"*, and identify three types of affordances to match activity, action and operation in activity theory: Need-related, instrumental, and operational affordances. The need-related affordances relate to what motivates people, the instrumental to the socio-culturally shaped action possibilities in instruments and objects surrounding us. The operational affordances, Gibson's original type of affordances for movement in the four-dimensional physical world, describe action possibilities relating to our *"naturally evolved, ecologically determined patterns of behavior and conditions."* By distinguishing between the adaptive operations that are our low-level response to natural conditions, and conscious operations that are our repertoires of cultural-historical "training", we are able to identify the lowest level in the operation hierarchy, where we are confronted with the operational affordances. Affordance is a concept focusing on the relationship between the human being and the environment. In order to grasp how devices or artifacts are and become part of such relationships, we need concepts that help us focus on the device as well as on human action. Bødker's (1991) three kinds of aspects match these three types of affordances in a manner that makes it possible to understand how current mediators are integrates in the functional organ of the human users; which possible and desirable uses they afford and how, and which they do not. The relationship between affordances, aspects and activity can be seen in figure 2. This mapping requires a re-interpretation of Bødker's aspects and integration with the concept of functional organs. Physical aspects encompass adaptive operational affordances, and we will choose to use this term, since "physical" is slightly misleading. In Bødker's three aspects, the need-related or activity-related aspect is missing, and since Bærentsen & Trettvik's convincingly argue that it needs to be there, we include it. We prefer to use the term 'instrumental' to subject/object directed aspects, whereas we use handling rather than conscious operational, as it indicates to us a focus on how mediators become transparent in use, rather than on how they have once been conscious. The resulting four analytical layers of a functional organ can be seen in figure 3.

Affordance	Aspects	Activity
Need-related		Activity–why
Instrumental	Subject/object directed aspects	Action/strategy–what
Operational - Conscious - Adaptive	 Handling aspects Physical aspects	Operation/procedure–how

Fig. 2. Mapping between affordance levels, Bødker's aspects and activity

Analytic layer	Functional organ	
	Mediator/external	Routines/internal
Need-related–why?	Need-related aspects	Motivational routines
Instrumental–what?	Instrumental aspects	Actions and strategies
Operational–how? Handling Adaptive operational	Operational aspects - Handling aspects - Adaptive aspects	Operation and routines - learned handling - adaptation

Fig. 3. A functional organ mapped to the (revised) aspects of the mediator coupled with the internalized routines on the three layers of activity

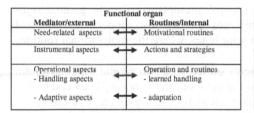
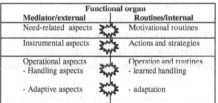

Fig. 4. Well-integrated and non-integrated functional organ

By mapping the way the mediator supports *intended* action possibilities and blocks other uses on the one hand, and the routines that the user is equipped with when exploring the mediator on the other (the *expected* action possibilities) on the four analytic layers of the functional organ, we explore and compare mediators in connection with the repertoires of actions and operations connected to them. Hence, we provide a better understanding of how one mediator may substitute another, and how well the substituting device may be integrated into the functional organs of the users (e.g. which effort it takes to do so)(figure 4).

A well-integrated functional organ is one where there is a fit as regards all four layers, whereas understanding problems of the integration focus on discrepancies at either layer (figure 4), or, as we shall see later, across layers. We talk about *breakdowns* whenever the integration stops working, and non-conscious routines become conscious actions (Bødker (1991). In the following, we will use our map examples to illustrate each layer of analysis of a functional organ.

3 Analyzing Functional Organs

Integration of a mediator into a functional organ clearly played an important role in the success or failure of solving a task on multiple levels of interaction: Groups who were familiar with a particular device had achieved a type of transparency in the interaction which allowed them to focus on the task/map specific issues, rather than on how to make the device perform in a certain way. Similarly, groups who were familiar with maps could focus on e.g. identifying different relevant waypoints rather than on interpreting the map; groups who were familiar with the local area visible through the window, could focus on verifying distance and direction by contrasting multiple visible waypoints and/or information on the map.

In the following, we will discuss the four analytical layers with examples from the map study, and for each level we will give examples of principal conflicts in the integration of mediators in functional organs. Such conflicts illustrate the fits and misfits of the functional organs on and between layers, and point to where misfits may occur when aiming to make ubiquitous substitution happen.

3.1 Need-Related Fits and Misfits

Given a specific task or work domain, the need-related layer defines and sets the stage for the analysis. The need-related aspects refer to the question of *why* is there use for a given mediator. Our examples reflect the groups' attempts to solve the given assignments. We note that the need-related possibilities of a map also support e.g. being lost in a new city, looking for the way back to your hotel, where the motivational routines lie outside a very specific assignment.

In the map study examples, all assignments started with two people who had a joint assignment, access to a map-device and to the view out the window. They resulted in the two people agreeing on a target, common orientation, distance, etc. (the answer as it was defined by the assignment). The size of the map, and the way it was shareable affected how the two users would orient each other to the direction outside the window, on the map and in their common orientation.

Need-related misfits can be trivial; does the device match the needs of the user at all? But they can also be subtler; does the given implementation of the functionality needed match the actual needs? In our study, the tablet-pc provides tools for fine-grained distance measuring, but this does not match the need of the users, who were quite satisfied with a more coarse measure.

3.2 Instrumental Fits and Misfits

The instrumental layer relates to the question of what *is*, what *seems* or what *should* be possible to do with a mediator. Understanding these aspects of a mediator is fundamental for appropriating it as a functional organ. When analyzing ubiquitous substitution, this appropriation gets more complex, as there may be more mediators in play as background experience–mediators more or less appropriated as functional organs. It is necessary to know these individual mediators and understand what is normally possible, or assumed to be possible with them. To ascertain such assumptions, we require the mediator to clearly indicate the extent of its capabilities at the instrumental level.

We exemplify how the combination of functional organs can create instrumental conflicts by focusing on one group using the cell-phone map. During one task, the group members used routines for interaction with the phone developed in everyday use of cell phones (e.g. using menus, joystick). They focused on the task (in this case finding a specific street name) and the response they got from the phone map. The interaction with the cell-phone was fluid and unencumbered, and the understanding of the menu structures, and general information hierarchies associated with cell-phones was clear. However, the group experienced a breakdown despite a high degree of familiarity with the technical device and knowledge of maps in general: The group members expected to find a measuring tool for the map on the phone, and started looking for it by browsing through the menus before the researchers stopped them by telling them that feature did not exist.

Drawing upon the description of a functional organ in figure 4, we focus on the relevant layer of analysis (in this case the instrumental) to be able compare the different mediators and highlight any misfits found. The result is seen in figure 5.

Mediator:		Instrumental layer
Phone	E	Computational power
	I	
Map	E	Computational distance measuring
	I	No distance measuring available

Fig. 5. Misfit at the instrumental layer: a breakdown is caused by the expectations of a functionality (*expected action possibilities* E) that is blocked or not supported in the actual, implemented functionality (*intended action possibilities* I)

So, even though both the cell-phone and the map had become functional organs for the group members, the combination of the two had not. This was caused by their expectations of the functionality exceeded what was actually offered by the cell-phone map, given their current need for providing a distance measure (figure 5).

To avoid instrumental conflicts, it is necessary to understand the needs catalyzing the interaction: The need-related level frames what we do with the mediators on the instrumental level, and consequently plays an active part in deciding what to support and what to block. If the users had focused on the phone as a communicative device, the computational power might not have been the centre of the users' expectations as was the case in this example.

3.3 Handling Fits and Misfits

The handling and adaptive operational layers both refer to *how* an action is performed through a mediator. The handling layer covers acquired, once-conscious operations. Our examples show a variety of device-type dependent action-possibilities: E.g. leafing over the paper map using the number grid for orientation is an alternative to zooming and panning. None of those are natural. They have to be taught and trained; yet, they both lead to the same set of overall strategies. We have identified a high-level landmark-based identification strategy that is supported on all three devices, while the repertoires of operations used to carry the strategy through are clearly different. On the paper map, landmark-based identification is achieved through homing by placing hands and fingers on the map, indication of direction with hands on or over the map, adjusting the map either north-up or towards the target, and moving between map views by means of the number grid and leafing through the pages. In addition, several visual landmarks, e.g. churches and schools are marked on the map. On the tablet, landmark-based identification is achieved through homing, which in turn is achieved by panning/zooming (albeit not as precise as on the paper map or on the mobile phone), and indication of direction with pen or fingers over the screen. On the cell-phone, landmark-based identification is achieved through homing by means of the GPS-unit, panning/zooming for a wider or more detailed view, adjusting the map by moving the phone and one's own physical orientation, and handing over the device to support sharing. The well-integrated functional organ is, handling-wise, a matter of supporting routines for moving around on the map, panning, zooming, scaling, and for connecting the map to visible landmarks and streets as they appear in the view. With the existing map-devices, there is very little overlap between the necessary routines at the handling layer.

Our example of a handling misfit arised from the unfamiliarity of the paper map, experienced by particularly one group who did not recognize the grid-system for moving through maps, and consequently had a difficult time finding the right section of the map. This is in contrast to most other groups, who identified the relevant map section almost without verbalizing it, and flipped through the map pages while keeping focus on the identification task.

Mediator:		Handling layer	Adaptive operational layer
Paper	E		Leafing pages
	I		
Map	E	No perceived structure	
	I	Grid structure	

Fig. 6. Misfit with the grid structure: While the group can leaf pages they do not expect a support structure for this, and they do not recognize the grid structure even though it is visible

In this example (figure 6), the group members had no experience in recognizing the grid structure, and consequently no routines to rely on for getting to the part of the map they needed. There is no adaptive operational conflict; the group members were well aware of how one leafs through a book. However, the mere leafing of pages did not support the group members in recognizing the grid structure on the handling level. Thus, the group members experienced a handling breakdown that was overcome by getting clues from bystanders about how to decipher the encoding of the grid. On closer scrutiny, the grid structure provided its own clues on how to proceed, and, as such, the grid structure was not difficult to appropriate.

Handling conflicts originate from a lack of recognizability on an instrumental level; in this case, the inability to understand the grid structure of the map. Taken to the extreme, the lack of recognizability at the handling layer will make users unable even to create a new strategy to help them proceed, because strategies are constructed through fragments of routines based on recognizable elements on the instrumental level (Bedny et al, 2000).

The grid-structure misfit is an example of the importance of making the handling of a mediator explicit, in order to support the conscious appropriation of it, if the structure is unfamiliar to the users. This, however, must be done without compromising or blocking the automated use by those who recognize it.

3.4 Adaptive Operational Fits and Misfits

In contrast to the handling layer, the adaptive operational layer describes our low-level responses to the physical conditions of and surrounding a mediator.

At this layer, an important issue is how maps are used when indicating direction, hence co-orienting the two participants. On the paper map it is sufficient to place one finger on home (their current location which is commonly known to the participants), and another in the relative direction on the map (figure 7). This pointing is supplemented with the movement of the finger back and forth.

 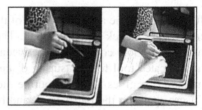

Fig. 7. North is in this direction–fingers give direction from "home" on the paper-map

Fig. 8. Giving directions on tablet-map

This kind of dynamic pointing is also used on the tablet (figure 8), where also a strategy unique for the tablet-PC is shown–holding the pen flat over the surface of the tablet in the direction of choice. As with the tablet, hand-waving is the most common way of indicating direction on the phone. This is supplemented with people holding their hand steady, upright pointing the fingertips in the direction of choice (figure 9). One group turns the cell-phone to align the map with the view in order to indicate direction. At this layer, the well-integrated map-device is a matter of turning, holding hands on, and handing over.

To illustrate the type of adaptive operational conflict, we use an example of how the groups measured distance on the tablet-map (figure 10). The tablet-map used a pen-like device that actually functions as a mouse. Even though all users knew how a mouse worked, and were told that the pen worked like a mouse, they ended up in situations where they tried to use the pen as a pen: They drew a line from point to point when wanting to measure distance, rather than what was supported by the map: To click on the end-points.

In this example, the pen suggested action possibilities that were blocked, because the tablet-map only supported measuring distance by clicking at end-points, and not through "drawing" by dragging a line from end-point to end-point.

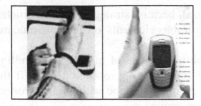

		Adaptive operational layer
Tablet	E	Drawing with pen
	I	Drawing and clicking with pen
Map	E	Drawing with pen
	I	Clicking with pen

Fig. 9. Using hand to indicate direction on the cell-phone map

Fig. 10. Conflict with the pen device

The pen example clearly shows how using the pen as a mouse cannot be taught by instruction, but must be appropriated through use (by changing routines) because these belong to the adaptive operational aspects of the mediator.

Adaptive operational conflicts force the user to change routines, possibly with the consequence of causing a ripple effect, shaking the basic foundations of other functional organs involving the same or similar mediators.

3.5 All Together Now!

To fully spell out the analytic power of the functional organ, it is essential to bring the layered analysis back together again. The example of distance measuring on the tablet-map shows how connections between layers need to be addressed: The tablet map has a dedicated tool for measuring distances between two points or along a series of segments. This gives a very accurate measure of distance in contrast to the routines that users apply on the paper map, and helps compensate for the dynamic map scale. As the scale changed with zooming, the distance-measuring tool provides an immediate and accurate mapping of scale to the map segment in focus. The measuring distance tool supports what the users are trying to accomplish in terms of needs; it is an externalization of a whole range of routines developed through other mediators and collapsing routines from several different levels, and, as such, it is a quite complex mediator in it self. However, the tablet map fails to support several groups in distance measuring because of the ambiguity of the pen-like input. One of the underlying assumptions of the tablet map is that the pen-shaped device is recognized as a mouse rather than a pen (which, for other tasks are unproblematic). This is a problematic assumption because it forces the users to disassociate the physical shape of the input device from the act of using it.

To target what mechanisms in the mediator that help and prevent development of the functional organs, we turn to Bærentsen & Trettvik's (2002) question of how exploration of the intended use may be supported, and how some of the possible, yet less desirable uses may be blocked? Evidently, the possible uses are numerous, which is a methodological problem. The best indicator to us in our map study of possible and desirable uses, is what uses the groups make of the other map devices. Obviously, there are many more, some of which are outside our limited setup. But even within this framing, the possibilities are virtually limitless. In figure 11 we summarize examples of the supporting and blocking mechanisms we have seen in the three map-devices.

	Paper-map	Tablet-map	Cell-phone map
Support of intended uses	Homing with fingers Coarse-grained distance measure Exploration by leafing Grid-based navigation	Fine-grained distance measuring Exploration of map through zooming and panning by pointing and clicking	Homing on home by GPS
Blocking of possible uses	Distance measure over large distances	Homing–no fingers on	Homing on target–no fingers on Distance measure

Fig. 11. Example mechanisms for supporting and blocking

4 Ubiquitous Substitution

We now address the challenge of ubiquitous substitution–substitution that does not abandon the old mediator, but supports the ongoing re-substitution of the mediators. There are two motivations for doing so: a desire to perform direct comparison of mediators vis-à-vis a certain purposeful activity, and an analysis of a design space of existing mediators with the focus of building a new one. In terms of our examples, we are interested both in what it take to become fluent users of several existing maps (creating more complex functional organs), and in approaching the design of a new map-device (to be appropriated as a functional organ).

As we have shown, many elements must be in place for creating a well-integrated functional organ: There must be a match between the mediator and the routines at all four layers. It takes little to disturb this harmony–we have seen that a paper map is a well-integrated functional organ to most groups, but that it only takes a breakdown at one layer, e.g. the lack of experience with the grid structure, to disturb this. Even worse, the cell-phone map is neither map, nor PC, which causes a lot of misfits. When functional organs become integrated into a new one that supports ubiquitous substitution, and e.g. lets the user apply both a paper-map and a tablet-map fluently for a task, the case becomes even more complex. Here, it is important that the use of one mediator does not disturb the understanding and routines connected to another. Again, we see this at all layers - learning to use the pen as a mouse - may not only be difficult, it may actually also prevent the future use of the mouse; getting used to scrolling in one manner may be disturbed by the introduction of an application that scrolls differently. In Bødker & Bøgh Andersen (2004), we see an example where historical generations of machine telegraphs are used on a ship bridge, as supplements to one another. Thus, it becomes essential to study the current repertoires of actions, operations and handling aspects as the starting point for new design. This is not to directly aim to replicate these in the new mediator, but rather to understand what minimal sets of action possibilities are necessary, which to be supported, and which to be blocked.

In a direct evaluation of how the tablet-map as new mediator may substitute the paper-map which is part of an existing functional organ, we found that such substitution becomes a matter of

- fitting into the needs of the user (though not as a direct substitution of one set of motivational elements with another).

- being understandable in terms of what it does or does not offers to the user; a minimal set includes visible scale, visible direction, and means for navigation.
- supporting (minimal) sets of routines at the handling level, so that e.g. the necessary strategies can be planned and carried out; at the same time, it may block other action possibilities.
- supporting adaptability (e.g. that all map-devices need to be turn-able to face north-up).

When looking at how navigation is supported on paper versus on tablet–a direct comparison on the handling level–we compare the grid-structure with panning and zooming through pointing and clicking. Those who have been taught the grid structure handle this well, and those, who were not, encounter problems. Panning through pointing and clicking instantly became routine (through instant feedback from the tablet). Thus, as an example of the minimal sets of routines to support, we would go for panning and zooming without making use of the grid structure known from paper maps. Yet, a new map-device would benefit from offering itself more to putting and holding hands on the map, and borrowing visible building-landmarks as they are marked out on the paper map.

In our design-oriented analyses, we see a move of focus away from the handling, which previously in HCI has been the predominant focus (e.g. in GOMS and key-stroke level analyses (Card et al. 1980)), and towards the instrumental one on the one hand, and the adaptive operational one on the other. This obviously does not mean that the handling will or should disappear from consideration. If that happened, every user would be faced with a device where every step, except the basic holding and turning, would need to be planned and consciously carried out, i.e. the total break-down. At the other extreme, handling could be highly standardized, just like car manufactures apply strictly standardized support for handling, which means that anybody can basically jump into–and securely drive–any car. We do not argue for any of those solutions. Instead, we argue that it is essential to identify and support minimal sets of routines at the handling level (e.g. the ones needed for using a map, together with the ones of using a cell-phone), so that the necessary strategies can be planned and carried out; at the same time other action possibilities may be blocked. It is equally essential that the action possibilities are recognizable as action possibilities in order to be included in strategies that get transformed into new routines through use.

This way of thinking gives indicators as to how to design a new functional organ, e.g. a map-device, yet the actual implementation of e.g. pan and zoom on a new technology depends on the capabilities of the technology in question, and must ultimately be evaluated in use like any other interaction design.

With this paper, we have taken the first step in confronting the challenges of ubiquitous interaction; we have provided a theoretically based foundation for describing and understanding *ubiquitous substitution* by analyzing interaction across different technologies in terms of mediators and functional organs intended and expected use. Breaking mediators down into four analytical levels has provided us with a strong analytical tool that, through examples from a recent case study, enabled us to analyze interaction, and pinpoint exactly from where trouble stem. This points towards development of new mediators from the perspective of minimalist handling.

5 Discussion

We have chosen to focus entirely on the topic of substitution of mediators, while in many ways ignoring the many kinds of complexity surrounding the use of the particular mediators. We have for instance largely ignored the juxtaposition of mediators (Bertelsen & Bødker, 2002), i.e. the combination of address register with the paper map, and even the view out the window, or the binoculars that one might use to enhance the view. We have ignored the web of activities and mediators (Brodersen & Kristensen, 2004) that surrounds the substituting mediators in general, and the wayfinding situations in particular. Nevertheless, with the proposed framework, we provide a concrete basis for designing within "webs of technology" (Nielsen, 2002). We have not ignored these elements because they are irrelevant, or because the theoretical framework does not deal with them. On the contrary, the framework reflects those exact ideas, and our only reason is to reduce the complexity of the analyses.

The mediator and the functional organ are the centrepieces of our analyses. The mediator is everything, from a simple cursor shape applied for a particular purpose in a design, a scrollbar, the Windows desktop, to other complex arrangements. The framework helps us spot misfits, breakdown in any of these. This is indeed a strength and a weakness. A strength because we escape the separation of hardware from software, which to the best of our belief matters little to the user, while maintaining a comparison across designs. Also, because we have seen that a tiny problem in one element may jeopardize the entire functional organ. The weakness is obviously that we inherit the problem from activity theoretical HCI of limiting the analysis (Bødker 1991). By taking up the challenge of ubiquitous interaction, we have, however, gone a long way towards analysis and designs that cross interaction styles.

Acknowledgements

Allan Hansen and Niels Olof Bouvin are kindly acknowledged for their contribution to the map study, Olav Bertelsen, Steven Harris and Johan Trettvik for many fruitful theoretical discussions, and Dorthe Haagen Nielsen for language improvements.

References

Bannon, L.: From Human Factors to Human Actors. In: Greenbaum, J., Kyng, M. (eds.) Design at Work. Cooperative Design of Computer Systems, pp. 25–44. Lawrence Erlbaum Associates, Mahwah, MA, USA (1991)

Bannon, L., Bødker, S.: Beyond the interface: Encountering artifacts in use. In: Carroll, J. (ed.) Designing interaction: Psychological theory at the human-computer interface, pp. 227–253. Cambridge University Press, New York, NY (1991)

Bardram, J.E., Bertelsen, O.W.: Supporting the Development of Transparent Interaction. In: Blumenthal, B., Gornostaev, J., Unger, C. (eds.) EWHCI 1995. LNCS, vol. 1015, pp. 79–90. Springer, Heidelberg (1995)

Bedny, G.Z., Seglin, M.H., Meister, D.: Activity theory: history, research and application. Theoretical Issues in Ergonomics Science 1(2), 168–206 (2000)

Bertelsen, O. W.: Elements to a theory of design artefacts: a contribution to critical systems development research, ph.d.-thesis, Aarhus University. DAIMI PB-531 (1998)

Bertelsen, O.W.: Design artefacts: towards a design-oriented epistemology. Scandinavian Journal of Information Systems 12(1-2), 15–27 (2001)

Bertelsen, O.W., Bødker, S.: Activity Theory. In: HCI Models, Theories, and Frameworks: Toward an Interdisciplinary Science, ch.11, pp. 291–324. Morgan Kaufman Publishers, Francisco, CA, USA (2003)

Bouvin, N.O., Brodersen, C., Bødker, S., Hansen, A., Klokmose, C.N.: A comparative study of map use. In: CHI '06. CHI '06 extended abstracts on Human factors in computing systems, pp. 592–597. ACM Press, New York, NY, USA (2006)

Brodersen, C., Kristensen, J.F.: Interaction through negotiation. In: NordiCHI'04. Proceedings of the third Nordic conference on Human-computer interaction, pp. 259–268. ACM Press, New York, NY, USA (2004)

Buxton, W.: There is more to interaction than meets the eye: some issues in manual input. In: Norman, D.A, Draper, S.W. (eds.) User Centered System Design, pp. 319–337. Lawrence Erlbaum Associates, Mahwah, NJ, USA (1986)

Bærentsen, K.B.: Mennesker og maskiner. In: Hedegaard, M.V.R., Hansen, V.R., Thyssen, S. (eds.) Et virksomt liv. Udforskning af virksomhedsteoriens praksis, pp. 142–187. Aarhus Universitetsforlag, Århus (1989)

Bærentsen, K.B., Trettvik, J.: An activity theory approach to affordance. In: Bertelsen, O., Susanne Bødker, K.K. (eds.) Proceedings of the Second Nordic ConferenceonHuman-Computer Interaction-Nordichi2002, pp. 51–60 (2002)

Bødker, S.: Through the Interface. In: A Human Activity Approach to User Interface Design, Lawrence Erlbaum Associates, Inc., Mahwah, NJ, USA (1991)

Bødker, S., Andersen, P.B.: Complex mediation. Human Computer Interaction 20(2), 353–402 (2005)

Bødker, S., Petersen, M.G.: Design for learning in use. Scand. J. Inf. Syst. 12(1-2), 61–80 (2001)

Card, S.K., Moran, T.P., Newell, A.: The keystroke-level model for user performance time with interactive systems. Communications of the ACM 23(7), 396–410 (1980)

Gibson, J.J.: The Ecological Approach to Visual Perception. Lawrence Erlbaum Associates, Mahwah, NJ, USA (1979)

Kaptelinin, V.: Activity theory: implications for human-computer interaction. In: Context and consciousness: activity theory and human-computer interaction, ch. 5, pp. 103–116. MIT Press, Cambridge, MA, USA (1995a)

Kaptelinin, V.: Computer-Mediated Activity: Functional Organs in Social and Developmental Contexts. In: Context and consciousness: activity theory and human-computer interaction, ch. 3, pp. 103–116. MIT Press, Cambridge, MA, USA (1995b)

Nielsen, C.: Designing to support Mobile Work with Mobile Devices. PhD dissertation, University of Aarhus (2002)

Meta-design: Expanding Boundaries and Redistributing Control in Design

Gerhard Fischer

Center for Lifelong Learning and Design
University of Colorado, Boulder
http://l3d.cs.colorado.edu/~gerhard/

Abstract. *Meta-design* is an emerging conceptual framework aimed at defining and creating socio-technical environments as living entities. It extends existing design methodologies focused on the development of a system at design time by allowing users to become co-designers at use time. Meta-design is grounded in the basic assumption that future uses and problems cannot be completely anticipated at design time, when a system is developed. Users, at use time, will discover mismatches between their needs and the support that an existing system can provide for them. Meta-design *extends boundaries* by supporting users as active contributors who can transcend the functionality and content of existing systems. By facilitating these possibilities, *control* is distributed among all stakeholders in the design process.

This paper characterizes different design methodologies and identifies the unique challenges and opportunities for meta-design. It illustrates this approach with two examples: (a) *Web2Gether* (enriching the organizational practices and community building of assistive technology teachers), and (b) the *Memory Aiding Prompting System (MAPS)* (addressing the needs of people with cognitive disabilities and their caregivers). Assessments of our developments are used to identify some future implications and challenges for meta-design and its role in socially responsible design.

Keywords: design, design methodologies, meta-design, socio-technical environments, boundaries, control, seeding / evolutionary growth / reseeding model, Web2Gether, Memory Aiding Prompting System (MAPS), application areas for meta-design, socially responsible design.

1 Introduction

In past decades, the primary goal of most software systems has been to achieve better productivity and usability, and software design and human-computer interface (HCI) research have achieved considerable expertise for these objectives. However, we have entered a new phase of system development in exploring new application areas (including the two examples discussed in this paper) with a focus on transcending existing boundaries and redistributing control among stakeholders [National-Research-Council, 2003]. Prominent success examples of this approach include developments such as (1) open source software [Raymond & Young, 2001]; (2) collaborative developed encyclopedias such as Wikipedia [Wikipedia, 2006]; and (3)

C. Baranauskas et al. (Eds.): INTERACT 2007, LNCS 4662, Part I, pp. 193–206, 2007.
© IFIP International Federation for Information Processing 2007

digital libraries such as DLESE [Wright et al., 2002]. In these developments people are not only using software but they also are becoming involved in developing software to varying degrees [Scaffidi et al., 2005]. Existing design methodologies are insufficient to cope with the emergence of situated and unintended requirements [Suchman, 1987; Winograd & Flores, 1986]. What is needed are socio-technical environments for which the design does not end at the time of deployment and whose success hinges on continued user participation.

This paper addresses the overall theme of Interact'2007, *Socially Responsible Interaction*, by articulating *meta-design* as a new conceptual framework and by relating and contrasting it to existing design methodologies. The framework is instantiated and illustrated by a brief description of socio-technical environments in two different domains:

- enriching the organizational practices of assistive technology teachers with *Web2Gether* [dePaula, 2004]; and
- addressing the needs of new user populations, namely people with cognitive disabilities and their caregivers with the *Memory Aiding Prompting System (MAPS)* [Carmien, 2006].

2   Meta-design: A Conceptual Framework and Design Methodology for Socio-technical Environments

Meta-design [Fischer & Giaccardi, 2006; Fischer et al., 2004; Giaccardi, 2004] is an emerging conceptual framework aimed at defining and creating social and technical infrastructures in which new forms of collaborative design can take place. It extends the traditional notion of system design beyond the original development of a system by allowing users to become co-designers. Meta-design is grounded in the basic assumption that future uses and problems cannot be completely anticipated at design time, when a system is developed. Users, at use time, will discover mismatches between their needs and the support that an existing system can provide for them. These mismatches will lead to breakdowns that serve as potential sources of new insights, new knowledge, and new understanding.

2.1   Socio-technical Environments as Living Entities

Socio-technical environments [Mumford, 1987; Trist, 1981] are living entities [Terveen, 1995] that are capable of integrating computing infrastructures and participation processes supporting collaboration not only about design artifacts but also about the goals of the design activity. By allowing users to be designers, socio-technical environments offer the possibility to achieve the best fit between systems and their ever-changing context of use, problems, domains, users, and communities of users. They empower users, as owners of a problem, to engage actively and collaboratively in the continual development of systems capable of sustaining personally meaningful activities and coping with their emergent needs. Socio-technical environments evolve as a result of a flexible and collaborative development process, which in turn modifies the terms of participation itself in the production of software.

The rationale for socio-technical environments as living entities *expanding boundaries and redistributing control in design* comes from many sources, including the following prescriptive objectives and empirical observations:

- *"The experience of having participated in a problem makes a difference to those who are affected by the solution. People are more likely to like a solution if they have been involved in its generation; even though it might not make sense otherwise"* [Rittel, 1984].
- *"I believe passionately in the idea that people should design buildings for themselves. In other words, not only that they should be involved in the buildings that are for them but that they should actually help design them"* [Alexander, 1984].
- *"We have only scratched the surface of what would be possible if end users could freely program their own applications. As has been shown time and again, no matter how much designers and programmers try to anticipate and provide for what users will need, the effort always falls short because it is impossible to know in advance what may be needed. End users should have the ability to create customizations, extensions, and applications"* [Nardi, 1993].
- *"The hacker culture and its successes pose by example some fundamental questions about human motivation, the organization of work, the future of professionalism, and the shape of the firm"* [Raymond & Young, 2001].
- *"Users that innovate can develop exactly what they want, rather than relying on manufacturers to act as their (often very imperfect) agents"* [von Hippel, 2005].
- *"In the digital world, many of the distinctions between designers and users are becoming blurred. We are all, to some extent, designers now"* [Brown & Duguid, 2000a].
- *"The networked environment makes possible a new modality of organizing production: radically decentralized, collaborative, and nonproprietary"* [Benkler, 2006].
- *"The opportunity to generate vibrant customer ecosystems where users help advance, implement, and even market new product features represents a largely untapped frontier for farsighted companies to exploit"* [Tapscott & Williams, 2006].

The technological foundations to make these objectives a reality are provided by a powerful infrastructure for collaborative efforts (the Internet allows people to share their efforts) and by the increased digital fluency [National-Research-Council, 1999] of the population in general, which will make owners of problems independent of "high-tech scribes' in personally meaningful tasks [Fischer, 2002]. Emerging success models, such as open source software and Wikipedia, have provided evidence of the great potential of socio-technical environments in which users can be active contributors.

2.2 Design Time and Use Time

In all design processes two basic stages can be differentiated: design time and use time (see Figure 1). At *design time*, system developers (with or without user participation) create environments and tools for the world as imagined by them to anticipate users' needs and objectives. At *use time*, users can use the system, but because their needs, objectives, and situational contexts can only be anticipated at design time, the system often requires modification to fit the users' needs [Henderson & Kyng, 1991].

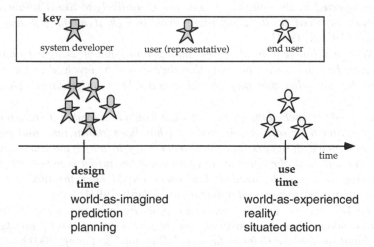

Fig. 1. Design Time and Use Time

To accommodate unexpected issues at use time, systems need to be underdesigned at design time. *Underdesign* [Brand, 1995] in this context does not mean less work and fewer demands for the design team, but it is fundamentally different from creating complete systems. The primary challenge of underdesign is to develop not solutions but environments that allow the *"owners of problems"* [Fischer, 2002] to create the solutions themselves at use time. This can be done by providing a context and a background against which situated cases, coming up during use time, can be interpreted. Underdesign is a defining activity for meta-design aimed at creating design spaces for others. It assumes that the meaning, functionality, and content of a system are not fully defined by designers and user-representatives alone at design time, but are socially constructed throughout the entire design, deployment, and use cycles of the system.

Meta-Design. By focusing equally on design and use-time activities, meta-design is different from other design methodologies such as *user-centered design* and *participatory design* . It contributes to the invention and design of cultures in which humans can express themselves and engage in personally meaningful activities. The conceptual frameworks that we have developed around meta-design explore fundamental challenges associated with design for change [Fischer & Giaccardi, 2006]:

• How can we *support skilled domain workers* who are neither novices nor naive users, but who are interested in their work and who see the computer as a device to achieve their goals?

- How can we *create co-adaptive environments*, in which users change because they learn, and in which systems change because users become co-developers and active contributors?
- How can we *provide users with opportunities, tools, and social reward structures* to extend systems to fit their needs?

Meta-design has shifted some control from designers to users and empowered users to create and contribute their own visions and objectives. Meta-design is a useful perspective for projects for which "designing the design process" is a first-class activity. This means that creating the technical and social conditions for broad participation in design activities is as important as creating the artifact itself [Wright et al., 2002].

Participatory Design for Meta-Design. Meta-design creates new demands for participatory design processes at design time by requiring: (1) the creation of systems that do not consist of a set of predetermined possibilities and functions but are designed for evolution that is being carried out by their users; and (2) a shift of focus from designing a complete system to designing a seed and mechanism for evolutionary growth and reseeding by providing content and a context for transcending the initial content.

The goal of making systems modifiable and evolvable by users does not imply transferring the responsibility of good system design to the user. Users (often being domain experts who see software development as a means to an end) will design tools and create contents of a different quality than professional software designers (for whom software is both a means and an end). Domain experts are not concerned with the tool per se, but in doing their work. However, if the tool created by the developers does not satisfy their needs or tastes, they should be able to adapt the system without always requiring the assistance of the developers. This leads to a new distribution of control for socio-technical environments.

Who Are Meta-Designers and What Do They Do? Meta-designers use their own creativity to create socio-technical environments in which other people can be creative. They must create the social conditions for broad participation in design activities which is as important as creating the artifact itself. They must encourage and facilitate the objective to develop maximum participation by activating as much knowledge as possible. The main activity of meta-designers shifts from determining the meaning, functionality, and content of a system to encouraging and supporting users to engage in these activities. Meta-designers must be willing to share control of how systems will be used, which content will be contained, and which functionality will be supported.

A Process Model in Support of Meta-Design: Seeding, Evolutionary Growth, Reseeding. The *seeding, evolutionary growth, and reseeding (SER) model* [Fischer & Ostwald, 2002] is an emerging descriptive and prescriptive model for creating software systems that best fit an emerging and evolving context. In the past, large and complex software systems were built as complete artifacts through the large efforts of a small number of people. Instead of attempting to build complete systems, the SER model advocates building *seeds* that can evolve over time through the small contributions of a large number of people. It postulates that systems that evolve over a sustained time span must continually alternate between periods of planned activity and unplanned evolution, and periods of deliberate (re)structuring and enhancement. A seed is something that has the potential to change and grow. In socio-technical environments, seeds need to be designed and created for the technical as well as the social component of the environment.

3 Examples of Socio-technical Environments Framed by Meta-design

This section illustrates with two specific examples (Web2Gether and MAPS) how meta-design expands boundaries and redistributes control in design.

3.1 Web2Gether: Supporting a Community of Assistive Technology Teachers

Web2Gether [dePaula, 2004] is a socio-technical environment embedded in the larger research project of understanding and providing social and technical means to support the use of technologies in special education [Carmien et al., 2005]. Our research activities first identified the *lack of social support* as one of the major barriers to the adequate use of technologies in this environment. This led to a shift in our approach from a simple technical solution toward a socio-technical approach that offered means for participants to reach each other, to create and develop social networks, and to share their experiences. Web2Gether transcends an access model of technology and supports a meta-design approach in which participants can act as active contributors. It allows users to share stories and personal experiences regarding unique cases for which they came up with effective solutions to address specific needs [dePaula & Fischer, 2005].

The success of meta-design approaches hinges on the participation of the users, requiring a deep understanding of the dynamic and transformative process of appropriation. In Web2Gether, the social and technical context were constantly negotiated and shaped by the various social groups participating at design, deployment, and use times. Figure 2 illustrates the complex environment in which Web2Gether operated as a socio-technical environment, including (1) *technical components* (in the lowest layer, labeled "Design Arena"); (2) *work environments* (with different stakeholders); and (3) the *influences of institutional and national concerns, rules, and regulations*. At any point of time, a change in any of these layers would require that the system be modified. Most of these changes will be experienced by the users (the community of assistive technology teachers), who need the means and knowledge to adapt and evolve the system accordingly. Our experience with Web2Gether demonstrates that the common assumption that technology's meaning, functionality, and content was set by the designers is misleading: the system was shaped by the consequences of a process of negotiation among designers, users, and other institutions.

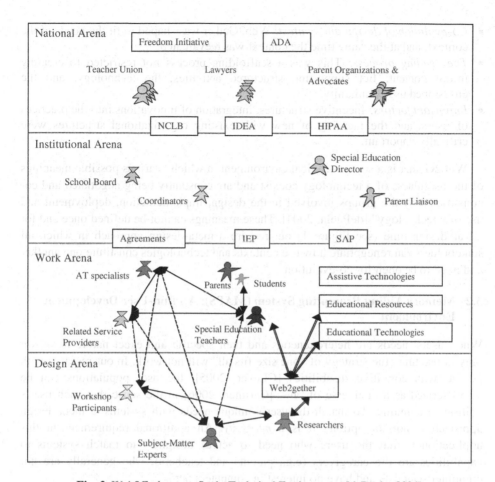

Fig. 2. Web2Gether as a Socio-Technical Environment [dePaula, 2004]

(The abbreviations used in this diagram represent the following concepts: (1) *ADA*: Americans with Disabilities Act; (2) *NCLB*: No Child Left Behind Act; *(3) IDEA*: Individuals With Disabilities Education Act; *(4) HIPAA*: Health Insurance Portability and Accountability Act; *(5) IEP*: Individualized Education Plan; *(6) SAP:* Student Disability Services; and *(7) AT*: Assistive Technologies)

Web2Gether was originally designed with a rudimentary understanding of a meta-design framework. It has substantially expanded our evolving framework about meta-design in the following ways [dePaula & Fischer, 2005]:

- *Participatory design:* Web2Gether was socially constructed by different social groups who participated throughout this research.
- *Design through cycles of closure and opening:* Web2Gether went through various stages at which its concept was defined followed by changes due to new interactions between the context and social groups.

- *Co-evolution of design and context:* Web2Gether was shaped to fit the needs of the context, and at the same time the context was reevaluated.
- *The seeding process:* This was a scaffolding process not restricted to creating initial content, but supporting structured activities, the technology, and the envisioned use community.
- *Important factors:* Incentive structures, integration of innovations into the practices of users, and the merging of new with existing organizational structures were critically important.

Web2Gether is a socio-technical environment in which "various possible meanings of the usefulness of a technology coexist and are constantly being negotiated and co-constructed by the groups involved in the design, implementation, deployment, and use of a technology" [dePaula, 2004]. These meanings cannot be defined once and for all at design time (see Figure 1) but require a meta-design approach in which all stakeholders can renegotiate how use contexts and technologies constitute one another and need to be open for co-evolution.

3.2 Memory Aiding Prompting System (MAPS): An End-User Development Environment

When users' needs are heterogeneous and their specific and exact nature is known only at use time, the strategy of "one size fits all" will not work. In our research with people with cognitive disabilities [CLever, 2005], the user populations can be characterized as a "universe of one" [Carmien, 2006] in the sense that each user's abilities are unique. To match the user's unique needs with systems, a meta-design approach is not an option—it is a *necessity.* An additional requirement in this application is that the users who need to act as designers to match systems to capabilities are the caregivers (e.g., parents and teachers), who generally are not computer scientists and have no interest in computers per se.

The specific problem addressed by MAPS [Carmien, 2006; Carmien et al., 2005] is how to create external scripts for a variety of tasks (including how to use public transportation systems, shopping lists, and recipes for cooking). The MAPS approach focuses on finding new ways to support distributed intelligence by complementing internal scripts (which people have in their head and which may be severely limited for people with cognitive disabilities) with external scripts supporting specific users in specific tasks.

An essential component of MAPS is an *end-user development environment* [Lieberman et al., 2006] supporting the creation of external scripts. Scripts consist of memory prompts with task-specific visual and auditory stimuli and feedback. In MAPS, scripts are organized as finite state sequences with state changes triggered by each unique user's actions or external events in the user's environment. One key design parameter in a scripting sequence is the granularity and specificity of a particular prompt and feedback sequence.

Fig. 3. An End-User Development Environment for Creating External Scripts

The scripts needed to effectively support users are specific for particular tasks, creating the requirement that the people who know about these tasks (i.e.: the local caregivers rather than technologists far removed from the action) must be able to develop scripts. In general, caregivers have no specific professional technology training, nor are they interested in becoming computer programmers. This creates the need for design environments with extensive end-user support to allow caregivers to create, store, and share scripts. Figure 3 shows the prototype of a *caregiver configuration environment* (embedded in MAPS) for creating complex, location-aware, multi-modal prompting sequences to support people with cognitive disabilities in using public transportation. The environment allows caregivers to assemble sound and pictures by using a filmstrip-like scripting metaphor.

4 Assessment and Implications

The goal of making systems modifiable and evolvable by users does not imply transferring the responsibility of good system design to the user. Socio-technical environments redistribute control in design by sharing it between developers and users.

Expanding Boundaries. The research described in this paper has expanded a number of different boundaries. It facilitated the collaboration of stakeholders with differing background knowledge, including software engineers, HCI designers, caregivers, and people with cognitive disabilities. It broke down the sharp distinction between designers and users, and allowed users to become co-designers. It eliminated the limitations associated with closed systems by designing socio-technical environments as living entities. It allowed all stakeholders to contribute and make their voices heard. The process was supported by the seeding, evolutionary growth, and reseeding (SER) model. It explored HCI issues by exploring and addressing the unique challenges associated with *universal usability and design-for-all* [Newell & Gregor, 1997]. Meta-design plays a significant role in several stages of design, including initial concept development, system configuration, integration with the use context, and specifically supporting design-in-use.

Redistributing Control. In meta-design, developers must accept a role in which they create mechanisms allowing users to act as designers and modify systems, thereby providing them with new levels of personal control. One of the major findings in our research activities was that users do not always accept and exercise these opportunities. This control is desired by users only in the case of *personally meaningful problems* [Fischer, 2002]. One of the pitfalls of a "do-it-yourself" society is that it can put a big burden on users (e.g., companies offloading work to customers) who may lack the experience, support, daily exposure, and interest in accomplishing these tasks. The trade-offs associated with introducing new divisions of labor [Levy & Murnane, 2004] have to be carefully evaluated.

Our experiences gathered in the context of the design, development, and assessment of the two systems described in the previous sections indicate that meta-design methodologies do not work when users are brought into the process late, thereby denying them ownership, nor when users are "misused" to fix problems and to address weaknesses of systems that the developers did not fix themselves. It *does* work when users are part of the participatory design effort in establishing a meta-design framework, including support for intrinsic and extrinsic motivation, user toolkits for reducing the effort to make contributions, and the seeding of use communities in which individuals can share their contributions [Dawe, 2007].

Contributions to Socially Responsible Design. Meta-design and socio-technical environments designed as living entities contribute to *socially responsible design* [CPSR, 2007] in the following dimensions:

- *Improving the quality of life* [Carmien et al., 2005; Newell & Gregor, 1997]: The two socio-technical environments (Web2Gether and MAPS) briefly described in this paper as part of our CLever project are developments that make an attempt to improve the quality of life for people with cognitive disabilities.
- *Democratizing innovation* [von Hippel, 2005]: meta-design allows owners of problems to engage in activities as a process of creating new possibilities and new artifacts, eliminating the constraint that users are restricted to what is given to them.

- *Making all voices heard* [Fischer & Giaccardi, 2006]: Complex design problems seldom fall within the boundaries of one specific domain; they require the participation and contributions of different stakeholders with various backgrounds.
- *Changing professional practice* [Illich, 1973]: Meta-design contributes to the creation of convivial tools which *"give each person who uses them the greatest opportunity to enrich the environment with the fruits of his or her vision."*
- *Revolutionizing the creation of systems* [Raymond & Young, 2001; Wikipedia, 2006]: Open source software systems and collaborative content creation harness the possibilities of Web 2.0 architectures [O'Reilly, 2006], which allow that social intelligence becomes alive. Rather than relying on major contributions by a small number of people, Web 2.0 architectures derive their value from a large number of people making small contributions.
- *Establishing new paradigms in learning and teaching* [dePaula et al., 2001]: The impact of meta-design on teaching and learning challenges one of the most impoverished paradigms of education in which "a single, all-knowing teacher tells or shows presumably unknowing learners something they presumably know nothing about" [Bruner, 1996]. Courses-as-seeds [dePaula et al., 2001] is an educational model that explores meta-design in the context of university courses by creating a culture of informed participation [Brown & Duguid, 2000b] by supporting community-based learning theories [Rogoff et al., 1998] with innovative collaborative technologies.

5 Conclusion

Meta-design expands boundaries and redistributes control in design by inventing, designing, and supporting a culture in which all stakeholders in socio-technical environments can express themselves and engage in personally meaningful activities. Meta-design requires a new mindset of all participants. Specifically, developers must give up some control at design time and users must be willing to act as active contributors and not just passive consumers at use time. Meta-design raises many issues and research problems of fundamental importance, including new design methodologies; new understandings of cognition, collaboration, and motivation; and the design of new media and new technologies.

Acknowledgements. The author thanks the members of the Center for LifeLong Learning & Design at the University of Colorado, who have made major contributions to ideas described in this paper. The PhD research of Stefan Carmien, Rogerio dePaula, and Melissa Dawe has specifically influenced our research about *socially responsible interaction.*

The research was supported by grants from (1) the National Science Foundation, (a) REC-0106976 "Social Creativity and Meta-Design in Lifelong Learning Communities", (b) IIS-0613638 "A Meta-Design Framework for Participative Software Systems", (c) IIS- 0709304 "A New Generation Wiki for Supporting a

Research Community in Creativity and IT"; (2) SRA Key Technology Laboratory, Inc., Tokyo, Japan; and (3) the Coleman Institute, Boulder, CO.

References

1. Alexander, C.: The State of the Art in Design Methods. In: Cross, N. (ed.) Developments in Design Methodology, pp. 309–316. John Wiley & Sons, New York (1984)
2. Benkler, Y.: The Wealth of Networks: How Social Production Transforms Markets and Freedom. Yale University Press, New Haven (2006)
3. Brand, S.: How Buildings Learn: What Happens After They're Built. Penguin Books, New York (1995)
4. Brown, J.S., Duguid, P.: Re-education. In: Brown, J.S., Duguid, P. (eds.) The Social Life of Information, pp. 207–241. Harvard Business School Press, Boston, MA (2000a)
5. Brown, J.S., Duguid, P.: The Social Life of Information. Harvard Business School Press, Boston, MA (2000b)
6. Bruner, J.: The Culture of Education. Harvard University Press, Cambridge, MA (1996)
7. Carmien, S.: Socio-Technical Environments Supporting Distributed Cognition for Persons with Cognitive Disabilities, Ph.D. Dissertation, University of Colorado at Boulder (2006), Available at: http://l3d.cs.colorado.edu/~carmien/
8. Carmien, S., Dawe, M., Fischer, G., Gorman, A., Kintsch, A., Sullivan, J.F.: Socio-Technical Environments Supporting People with Cognitive Disabilities Using Public Transportation. Transactions on Human-Computer Interaction (ToCHI) 12(2), 233–262 (2005)
9. CLever: Cognitive Levers – Helping People Help Themselves, Available (2005)
10. CPSR: Computer Professionals for Social Responsibility (2007), Available at http://www.cpsr.org/
11. Dawe, M.: Reflective Design-In-Use: Co-Designing an Assistive Remote Communication System with Individuals with Cognitive Disabilities and their Families, Ph.D. Dissertation, University of Colorado at Boulder (2007), Available at http://l3d.cs.colorado.edu/~meliss/diss/
12. de Paula, R.: The Construction of Usefulness: How Users and Context Create Meaning with a Social Networking System, Ph.D. Dissertation, University of Colorado at Boulder (2004)
13. de Paula, R., Fischer, G.: Knowledge Management: Why Learning from the Past is not Enough! In: Davis, J., Subrahmanian, E., Westerberg, A. (eds.) Knowledge Management: Organizational and Technological Dimensions, pp. 21–54. Physica Verlag, Heidelberg (2005)
14. de Paula, R., Fischer, G., Ostwald, J.: Courses as Seeds: Expectations and Realities. In: Dillenbourg, P., Eurelings, A., Hakkarainen, K. (eds.) Proceedings of The European Conference on Computer-Supported Collaborative Learning, Maastricht, Netherlands, pp. 494–501 (2001)
15. Fischer, G.: Beyond 'Couch Potatoes': From Consumers to Designers and Active Contributors, in FirstMonday (Peer-Reviewed Journal on the Internet) (2002), Available at http://firstmonday.org/issues/issue7_12/fischer/
16. Fischer, G., Giaccardi, E.: Meta-Design: A Framework for the Future of End User Development. In: Lieberman, H., Paternò, F., Wulf, V. (eds.) End User Development: Empowering People to Flexibly Employ Advanced Information and Communication Technology, pp. 427–457. Kluwer Academic Publishers, Dordrecht, The Netherlands (2006)

17. Fischer, G., Giaccardi, E., Ye, Y., Sutcliffe, A.G., Mehandjiev, N.: Meta-Design: A Manifesto for End-User Development. Communication of the ACM 47(9), 33–37 (2004)
18. Fischer, G., Ostwald, J.: Seeding, Evolutionary Growth, and Reseeding: Enriching Participatory Design with Informed Participation, pp. 135–143. Malmö University, Sweden (2002)
19. Giaccardi, E.: Principles of Metadesign: Processes and Levels of Co-Creation in the New Design Space; Ph.D. Dissertation, CAiiA-STAR, School of Computing, Plymouth, UK (2004)
20. Henderson, A., Kyng, M.: There's No Place Like Home: Continuing Design in Use. In: Greenbaum, J., Kyng, M. (eds.) Design at Work: Cooperative Design of Computer Systems, pp. 219–240. Lawrence Erlbaum Associates, Inc, Hillsdale, NJ (1991)
21. Illich, I.: Tools for Conviviality. Harper and Row, New York (1973)
22. Levy, F., Murnane, R.J.: The New Division of Labor: How Computers are Creating the Next Job Market. Princeton University Press, Princeton (2004)
23. Lieberman, H., Paterno, F., Wulf, V. (eds.): End User Development - Empowering people to flexibly employ advanced information and communication technology. Kluwer Publishers, Dordrecht, The Netherlands (2006)
24. Mumford, E.: Sociotechnical Systems Design: Evolving Theory and Practice. In: Bjerknes, G., Ehn, P., Kyng, M. (eds.) Computers and Democracy, Avebury, Aldershot, UK, pp. 59–76 (1987)
25. Nardi, B.A.: A Small Matter of Programming. The MIT Press, Cambridge, MA (1993)
26. National-Research-Council: Being Fluent with Information Technology, National Academy Press, Washington, DC (1999)
27. National-Research-Council: Beyond Productivity: Information Technology, Innovation, and Creativity, National Academy Press, Washington, DC (2003)
28. Newell, A.F., Gregor, P.: Human Computer Interfaces for People with Disabilities. In: Helander, M.G., Landauer, T.K., Prabhu, P.V. (eds.) Handbook of Human-Computer Interaction, vol. 1, pp. 813–824. Elsevier Science B.V, Amsterdam (1997)
29. O'Reilly, T.: What Is Web 2.0 - Design Patterns and Business Models for the Next Generation of Software (2006), Available at http://www.oreillynet.com/pub/a/oreilly/tim/news/2005/09/30/what-is-web-20.html
30. Raymond, E.S., Young, B.: The Cathedral and the Bazaar: Musings on Linux and Open Source by an Accidental Revolutionary. O'Reilly & Associates, Sebastopol, CA (2001)
31. Rittel, H.: Second-Generation Design Methods. In: Cross, N. (ed.) Developments in Design Methodology, pp. 317–327. John Wiley & Sons, New York (1984)
32. Rogoff, B., Matsuov, E., White, C.: Models of Teaching and Learning: Participation in a Community of Learners. In: Olsen, D.R., Torrance, N. (eds.) The Handbook of Education and Human Development: New Models of Learning, Teaching and Schooling, pp. 388–414. Blackwell, Oxford (1998)
33. Scaffidi, C., Shaw, M., Myers, B.: Estimating the Numbers of End Users and End User Programmers. In: VL/HCC'05. Proceedings of 2005 IEEE Symposium on Visual Languages and Human-Centric Computing, Dallas, Texas, September, pp. 207–214 (2005)
34. Suchman, L.: Plans and Situated Actions: The Problem of Human-Machine Communication. Cambridge University Press, Cambridge, England (1987)
35. Tapscott, D., Williams, A.D.: Wikinomics: How Mass Collaboration Changes Everything, Portofolio, Penguin Group, New York, NY (2006)
36. Terveen, L.G.: An Overview of Human-Computer Collaboration. Knowledge-Based Systems Journal, Special Issue on Human-Computer Collaboration 8(2-3), 67–81 (1995)

37. Trist, E.L.: The Sociotechnical Perspective: The Evolution of Sociotechnical Systems as a Conceptual Framework and as an Action Research Program. In: VanDeVen, A.H., Joyce, W.F. (eds.) Perspectives on Organization Design and Behavior, pp. 19–75. Wiley, New York, NY (1981)
38. von Hippel, E.: Democratizing Innovation. MIT Press, Cambridge, MA (2005)
39. Wikipedia: The Free Encyclopedia (2006), Available at http://wikipedia.org/
40. Winograd, T., Flores, F.: Understanding Computers and Cognition: A New Foundation for Design. Ablex Publishing Corporation, Norwood, NJ (1986)
41. Wright, M., Marlino, M., Sumner, T.: Meta-Design of a Community Digital Library, D-Lib Magazine, vol. 8(5), Available (2002), at http://www.dlib.org/dlib/may02/wright/05wright.html

Improving Users' Comprehension of Changes with Animation and Sound: An Empirical Assessment

Céline Schlienger[1], Stéphane Conversy[2,3], Stéphane Chatty[1,2], Magali Anquetil[1], and Christophe Mertz [1]

[1] IntuiLab
Les Triades A - Rue Galilée – BP 77242, 31672 Labège Cedex
{celine, chatty, anquetil, mertz}@intuilab.com
[2] ENAC – Ecole Nationale de l'Aviation Civile – [3] DSNA/DTI-R&D
7, avenue Edouard Belin, 31055 Toulouse
stephane.conversy@enac.fr

Abstract. Animation or sound is often used in user interfaces as an attempt to improve users' perception and comprehension of evolving situations and support them in decision-making. However, empirical data establishing their real effectiveness on the comprehension of changes are still lacking. We have carried out an experiment using four combinations of visual and auditory feedback in a split attention task. The results not only confirm that such feedback improves the perception of changes, but they also demonstrate that animation and sound used alone or combined bring major improvements on the comprehension of a changing situation. Based on these results, we propose design guidelines about the most efficient combinations to be used in user interfaces.

Keywords: Empirical evaluation, animation, sound, multimodal feedback, comprehension of changes, dual task.

1 Introduction

Animation or sound are often suggested for improving feedback on users' actions, for notifying changes, or for improving awareness of more complex but although frequent situations where users need to split their attention between multiple information sources. User Interface designers often have assumptions about the effectiveness of animation or sound as feedback to monitor an evolving situation (see [1] and [18] for examples). In this work, we address the question of the real effectiveness of animation, of sound and of the combination of both modalities in situations where changes occur. We propose ways to use each modality in such situations, and provide experimental evaluations of their benefits, be they used alone or combined.

In order to demonstrate the efficiency of sound and animation, we used the Situation Awareness framework proposed by Endsley [8]. Situation Awareness (SA) is defined by Ensley as "knowing what is going on around you", so that one can react appropriately to situations. Endsley identifies three increasing levels of situation awareness: (1) the perception of changes in the environment, (2) the comprehension

C. Baranauskas et al. (Eds.): INTERACT 2007, LNCS 4662, Part I, pp. 207–220, 2007.

of their meanings, and (3) the projection of their status in the near future [8]. Our study concerns the two first levels, with a particular focus on the second one: if empirical data on the effectiveness of animation or sound on the perception of changes do exist, empirical data establishing their effectiveness at helping users to *understand changes* are still lacking.

After reviewing previous work on the use of animation and sound in user interfaces, we explain our use of the modalities and our experimental model. We then describe the experiment and analyze its quantitative results. Finally, we discuss the interpretation and consequences of these results.

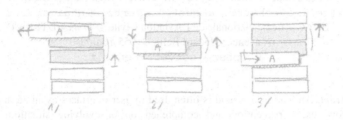

Fig. 1. Storyboard of the animation: changing element (A) moves in parallel with in-between elements (colored in grey)

2 Related Work

This section presents empirical studies or major uses of animation or sound in user interfaces, as well as work on their combination with other modalities. We classify them according to the two first levels of Situation Awareness: perception and comprehension.

2.1 Enhancing Perception

The first level of situation awareness is the perception of changes. Motion is particularly suited to attract the user's attention, because it is a pre-attentive visual feature: its detection happens at the early stages of visual perception [22,25]. Athènes *et al.* found that motion has a statistically significant positive impact on the time the user requires to detect alarms [1]. Bartram *et al.* experimentally established that motions in peripheral vision are particularly effective at grabbing attention, especially compared to other animated graphical attributes, such as shape or color [2].

Sound brings information regardless of the user's focus of attention. Thus, a large body of works showed that the audio channel is a very appropriate modality for notification of changes (see [17,24] for examples). Combined with graphics, sound is also supposed to support users in direct manipulation interaction by enhancing the perception of their actions [6,13,20].

2.2 Enhancing Comprehension

The second level of situation awareness is the comprehension of the meaning of changes, i.e. the "integration of multiple pieces of information and the user's determination of their relevance on his/her goals" [8].

Sound has been shown to help users monitor background processes [7]. For example, in the Sonic Finder [9], the sound of pouring water accompanies a graphical progress bar during long processes *i.e.* copying a large amount of files. The use of the audio channel enables a user to engage in another activity while monitoring the progression of the background process. Though not formally assessed, the Arkola simulation illustrates how sound conveys information about the ongoing activity of remote participants, so as to help the user to understand the evolution of a collaborative task [10].

Animation has been experimentally shown to be effective at replaying missed changes [4] and to support the comprehension of textual information displayed in the periphery [14]. Many other works hint at the effectiveness of animation as feedback, but real effectiveness has not been experimentally established yet. Feedback with animation is supposed to help users understand the consequence of their actions and the cause of a change [5,15,21]. Animation as feedback might also be effective at supporting collaborative work, when co-workers must be aware of what is happening on neighbors' screen [15]. Animation is also used to support users in keeping track of the relationships between changing graphical elements in complex visualizations [12,18], but no experimental study proves its effectiveness. Our work aims at assessing the benefits of using animation and sound for this particular use: supporting changes comprehension.

3 The Experiment

In this work, we study the impact of animation and sound, used alone or combined, on the perception and the comprehension of situations where changes occur. We chose to study situations where the user shares attention between distant sources from which he/she has to gather up-to-date information to perform a task, such as monitoring incoming mail while editing a spreadsheet. Such situations are good candidates for improvement with animation feedback and sound feedback. First, changes can occur outside the user's focus of attention and can be missed if the interface makes use of static graphics only. The notification effect of animation and sound may improve the user's perception of the changes. Second, sound and animation can be used to extract the relevant data of the change and they may help identifying their value.

Our study relies on a simulation of an Air Traffic Control task. Controllers in an airport tower manage aircraft, busses and other vehicles moving on the ground. They schedule concurrent access on runways and taxiways. They split their attention between actual traffic observed through the window and the traffic previsions displayed on monitoring screens; they then give orders to drivers and pilots on the radio. We designed an interface that shows in real-time the planned schedule of mobile objects at a particular location on the ground, say a crossroad between a runway and a taxiway. To simulate situations where a user splits attention between distant sources, the experiment followed a dual task paradigm: while performing a demanding main task designed to focus attention, subjects must keep track of changes occurring in the list displayed in their peripheral vision (see Fig. 2).

3.1 Experimental Model

All changes in a computing environment consist of data variations. As observed by Bertin, visual representations are mappings of that data to graphical dimensions, such as color, shape, or position [3]. When a piece of data changes, its visual representation changes as well. When the change is smooth, a user can catch it: an animation is a *smooth* change of a visual dimension, be it position, color, or shape.

We chose a list of ranked items as the object to monitor in the experiment. A list is a good candidate to model changing situations with animation: as rank is coded with position, a change in rank leads to a change of position, which can be reinforced by a smooth motion from the origin to the destination. Furthermore, a number of user interfaces use dynamic, ordered lists to display information: names of participants in a chat session, drivers' rank in racing car video games, or CPU consumption of processes in some utilities.

When a change occurs, the evaluation of invariant parameters associated with the changing item is essential to understand the new situation. Thus, the list is composed of elements of different types that do not change, but that a user has to recognize when a change of position occurs. Types are coded with a graphical icon and with a sound, as sound is often used to convey type through a metaphor [9].

We measure a user's situation awareness at the first two levels of situation awareness by quantifying *perception* as a user's ability to detect changes occurring in the list, and *comprehension* as a user's ability to correctly identify static and dynamic parameters of the list. The parameters are: the type of the object involved in the change, the rank in the list of the object before the change and the rank in the list of the object after the change.

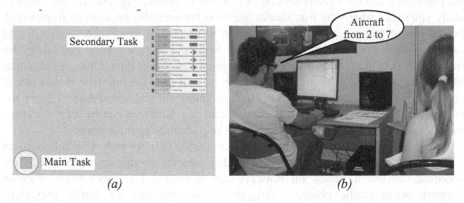

(a)   *(b)*

Fig. 2. *(a)* The experiment interface. *(b)* The experimenter (on the right) records on a dedicated interface the subjects (on the left) answers.

3.2 List Design

The list contains nine rectangular elements: three aircraft, three busses and three vehicles (Fig. 3). Each element includes four graphical attributes: a unique identifier in a colored zone, the status of the mobile object, an icon, and a time of transit on the crossroad. The identifier, the status and the icon are specific to the object type (aircraft, bus or vehicle). The list is sorted vertically according to the reference time. Users can read the rank of an item with a static digit from 1 to 9 located on the left of the item (Fig. 2a). When the estimated time of transit of an element changes (for example, because a flight is delayed), its new position is computed and the list is updated. In the simulation, elements never disappear from the list, nor do they appear: the time of transit is never reached, and no new mobile object is scheduled.

3.3 Tasks and Setting

Main task. The main task is a perceptive identification task. A point appears at random positions in the set (top, bottom, left, right) inside a static square. The pace of appearance is randomly chosen, with an average of 1.1 changes per second. Subjects are asked to identify the position of the point and to press the matching key of the keyboard (up, down, left or right). If an error occurs, a circle displayed around the square is colored in red. Subjects were asked to focus their attention on this main task with the no-error objective.

Secondary task. The secondary task consists of perception and comprehension of the changes occurring in the list. When perceiving a change, the subject was asked to say the type of the moving element, its origin position and its destination position. Should he/she not be able to evaluate all three parameters, the subject would enumerate those recognized or say, at least, that something has moved. The experimenter used a dedicated interface to record subjects' answers (see Fig. 2b). Changes occurred at random time, with an average period of 10 second between two changes.

Setting. The square of the main task is displayed at the bottom left of a 19'' screen, 25 cm away from the list displayed at the top right (see Fig. 2a). The user sits 80 cm away from the screen. There is a 17 degrees vision angle between the two zones, guaranteeing peripheral vision conditions.

3.4 Experimental Conditions

We tested the following four combinations of visual and auditory feedback (Fig. 3).

No animation – no sound. This is the control condition. When the rank of an item changes, the graphical scene is instantaneously swapped for an updated one.

No animation – sound. Before the graphical scene swaps, a sound specific to the object type is played. The sounds we designed are metaphorical, and code the object type (aircraft, bus, and vehicle). They are played through two speakers, but they are not spatialized. The type of sound is the only auditory variable.

Animation – no sound. The element smoothly moves from its origin position to its destination position. The animation involves two motions occurring in parallel as illustrated in Fig. 1:

a) a motion of the element concerned by the change in three steps:

- move to the left of the list by 20% of the element width, during 300 ms,

- move down or up to destination ordinate during a time computed as: 400ms + abs(destination position – origin position)*100 ms,

- move to the right to destination position during 300 ms.

b) a motion of the set of elements between origin and destination position: the origin position left blank is smoothly filled by the elements to empty the destination position.

Animation – sound. Before the element moves in the list, the sound specific to the type is played. Then, the element smoothly moves from its original position to its destination position (Fig. 1). The sounds used in this condition are the same as those used in the no animation – sound condition.

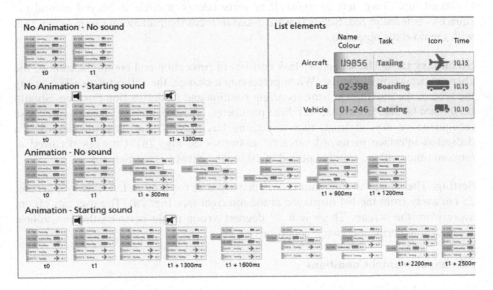

Fig. 3. Experimental conditions and composition of the list elements

3.5 Experiment Design

To get reference performances, the main task was first evaluated without the secondary task. This condition enables to evaluate the degradation of the main task performances by the introduction of the secondary task with each feedback. Then, all subjects performed main and secondary tasks under all conditions. The conditions were passed randomly to avoid order and learning effects. For each condition, three changes per object type occurred randomly in the list (to avoid order effect too); thus, there were 3 changes involving aircraft, 3 involving busses and 3 involving vehicles.

Each condition began with a learning phase during which the user performed the secondary task only. In particular, this phase allowed the user to become familiar with the animation and sound. The learning phase stopped when the user was able to perform the task with no errors (except in *no animation – no sound* condition, where it is very difficult to get the correct answer even with attention focused on the list).

All subjects were given a post-experiment questionnaire aimed at collecting their opinion about the impact of animation and sound on their situation awareness.

24 subjects volunteered for the experiment (8 females, 16 males). For results to be generic, we chose subjects in different activity domains (HCI research, healthcare, commerce, administration, air traffic control, art, culture, education, computer science) and from various ages (from 24 to 45 with an average age of 32).

3.6 Hypotheses

From the literature, we know that animation or sound is efficient at grabbing the user's attention in peripheral vision. What we tested in this experiment is whether animation and/or sound are able improve the *comprehension* of the changes. Hence, the following hypotheses were formulated:

- Animation and/or sound improve change detection. *(H1)*
- Animation improves object type identification. *(H2)*
- Sound improves object type identification. *(H3)*
- Animation improves origin position identification. *(H4)*
- Animation and sound improves origin position identification. *(H5)*
- Animation improves destination position identification. *(H6)*

4 Results

The normality of the gathered data was tested using the Shapiro-Wilk's test. The result shows that the distribution of the data is skewed, so we performed non-parametric tests. For matched samples, the appropriated tests are: 1) the Friedman test that enables to compare all conditions and identify if there are significant results within the data, and 2) if the Friedman test is significant, the Wilcoxon pair-wise test that enables to compare two conditions.

4.1 Main Task

The number of errors in the main task is significantly higher when the secondary task is introduced ($p<0.001$, Friedman). This result was anticipated, as main and secondary tasks are parallel tasks that require split attention. With the secondary task, pair-wise tests show that the number of errors in the main task is not significantly different between the conditions, except between the *no animation - no sound* and the *animation - starting sound* conditions. Hence, for all but one pair, we can attribute the significant improvement on the secondary task reported in the next sections to the difference of feedback, as expected.

Concerning the *no animation - no sound* and *animation - sound* conditions, pair-wise tests show a slight but significant ($p=0.04744$) decrease in performance in the main task (1.5% more errors for *animation-sound* condition). Users might have split slightly differently their attention resources between main and secondary task in these two conditions, precluding any firm conclusion about the effect of feedback in the secondary task. However, the large increase of performance in the secondary task (an average of 75% fewer errors for *animation-sound* condition) hints at a significant contribution of feedback. Further testing is needed to evaluate the real effect of feedback between these two particular conditions.

4.2 Detection

There is a significant effect of the feedback on list change detection ($p<0.001$, Friedman): while 20% of changes were missed with no feedback, no change was missed with animation and/or sound. Pair-wise tests show a significant difference ($p<0.001$) of no animation – no sound condition (80% of detections) in comparison to the other conditions (100% of detections). This result confirms hypothesis H1: animation and/or sound improve list changes detection.

4.3 Object Type Identification

We wanted to evaluate the subject's comprehension of the situation once he/she has detected a change. Thus, the percentages of identification of the object type, and those of the origin and the destination position presented in the following sections, are calculated on the basis of detected objects.

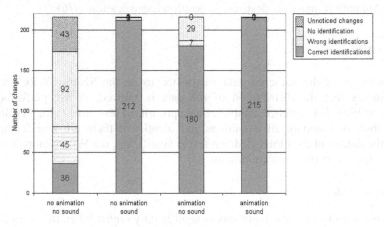

Fig. 4. Results for object type identification

There is a significant effect of the feedback on the object type identification ($p<0.001$, Friedman). Fig. 4 shows a very high number of correct identifications with animation and almost no errors with sound.

Pair-wise tests show there is a significant difference between no animation – no sound and animation – no sound with respectively 21% and 83% of correct answers ($p<0.001$). This result confirms hypothesis H2: animation improves object type identification.

The two conditions with sound provide more than 98% of correct answers with no significant difference between them. There is a significant difference between:

- *no animation – no sound* and *no animation – sound* (p<0.001),
- *animation – no sound* and *animation – sound* (p<0.001)

These results confirm hypothesis *H3*: sound improves object type identification.

4.4 Origin Position Identification

There is a significant effect of the feedback on the identification of the origin position of the object in the list (p<0.001, Friedman). Fig. 5 shows a high number of correct identifications with animation and an even higher when animation is combined with sound.

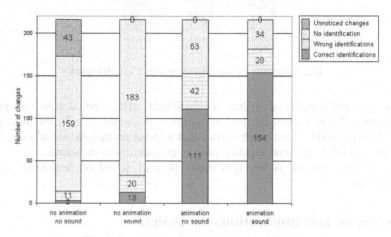

Fig. 5. Results for origin position identification

Pair-wise tests show significant difference between *no animation – no sound* and *animation – no sound* with respectively 1.5% and 51% of correct answers (p<0.001). This result confirms hypothesis *H4*: animation improves origin position identification in comparison to no animation.

With no animation, there is no significant effect of sound on origin position identification. With animation, there is a significant effect of sound on origin position identification (p<0.05). This result confirms hypothesis *H5*: animation and sound improves origin position identification in comparison to animation.

4.5 Destination Position Identification

There is a significant effect of the feedback on the identification of the destination position (p<0.001, Friedman). Fig. 6 shows an increase of correct identifications with animation and/or sound; the number of correct identifications is very high with animation, and even higher when animation is combined with sound.

Pair-wise tests show there is a significant difference between *no animation – no sound* and *animation – no sound* with respectively 7.5% and 78% of correct answers (p<0.001). This result confirms hypothesis *H6* in that animation improves destination position identification in comparison to no animation.

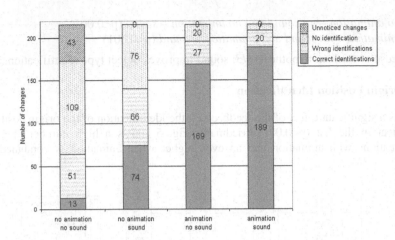

Fig. 6. Results for destination position identification

With no animation, sound has a significant effect on destination position identification (Correct answers: *no animation – no sound*: 7.5%; *no animation – sound*: 34%; p<0.001). This result shows that without animation, sound significantly improves destination position identification in comparison to no sound.

With animation, there is no significant effect of sound on destination position identification.

5   Discussion and Implications for Design

The results of the experiment show that animation and sound, used alone and combined, have effective benefits on awareness of situations where changes occur. Animation and sound improve the perception (first level of situation awareness) of changes and the comprehension (second level) of the evolving situation as the user correctly identifies data relevant to the change. In this section, we translate our results into practical design guidelines dedicated to user interface designers so that they can efficiently use animation and sound to improve users' awareness of a changing situation.

5.1   Notify Changes with Animation and/or Sound

Animation and/or sound can be used very efficiently to notify changes occurring on graphic data displayed in peripheral vision. Alone and combined, they enable to perceive all changes, bringing major improvements on the first level of situation awareness. Our results on animation used alone corroborate the results on motion that Bartram provided [2], when she found that less than 1% of changes were missed in peripheral vision. Usually, sound is used to notify changes that happen outside of the user's vision. Our experiment shows that sound also has a real positive impact as an aid for the detection of changes occurring on visual objects that are displayed in peripheral vision.

The combination of animation and sound is at least as efficient as each modality used alone to notify changes. Since the use of animation and sound alone yields a 100% detection rate, we were not able to say if their combination improves performance. In additon, this gives potential solutions to change-blindness [19]. Actually, the combination offers a major advantage: the redundancy of visual and auditory information. If one modality is overloaded or degraded, the other persists and can ensure detection.

5.2 Maximize the Identification of Essential Static Data with Sound

When a change occurs, identifying static data might be essential for the user to understand the new situation. Various graphical dimensions are offered to user interface designers to code such data: texts, colors, icons, etc. Our experiment shows that motion significantly improves the identification of data coded with graphics (the object type) when the object position changes (21% vs. 83%). Most subjects commented: "with animation, it is easier [than without] to catch the object concerned by the change, and then to look at the icon to identify the object type". However, some of them had difficulties to recognize it while the object moves and their attention is monopolized by the main task.

Auditory feedback outclasses visual feedback with more than 98% of recognition of the object type. This result provides confirmation of the assumption on redundancy made by Gaver in the SonicFinder [9], where both the icon and the sound encoded the "file" or "directory" type. In contrast to animation, the identification of the data coded by sound is not weakened when the graphical object moves.

Thus, when a change occurs, if a data displayed with graphics is essential to capture, animation can be efficiently used to improve the identification of its value. But user interface designers should prefer sound if they want to optimize identification and provide the best improvements on the second level of SA.

5.3 Improve the Evaluation of Dynamic Data with Motion

Values of a dynamic data can be coded by positions of a graphical object. When a change occurs on the data, the position of the object changes. Our experiment shows that the identification of the origin and destination positions of the object can be very efficiently improved with motion, improving thus the evaluation of the data.

The good results of positions identification can be explained by the notification effect of animation: the user look at the object when it smoothly moves from origin to destination position, but not only. As shown in Fig. 1, the animation is composed of two motions: one motion for the element whose rank changed, and one for the set of elements that glide between the origin and destination positions. As the empty space left by the changing element is progressively filled, the user has the whole duration of the animation to catch the old position before it completely disappears. In the same way, the empty space left by the set of in-between elements progressively appears, and enables the user to see in advance the destination of the changing element, before it reaches it. This design can be contrasted to one of a speed gauge, in which a user can perceive a motion, but not the starting nor the ending points.

This result is a clear improvement over Bartram's findings on benefits of animation [2]: the experiment not only shows that users are able to detect and identify changing items, but also that they can evaluate parameters of the change thanks to the animation. As such, it is an assessment of the assumption that animation may help users understand what is happening, as assumed in [18].

5.4 Optimize the Comprehension of a Changing Situation by Combining Animation and Sound

The experimental data enabled us to rank the tested combinations of visual feedback and auditory feedback. Table 1 presents a synthetic view of the results. Each combination gets a score according to users' results. They are evaluated from 1 (best) to 4 (worst). If there is no significant difference between two results, they get the same score. They are then ordered according to these marks. It is interesting to note that subjects, who were asked to rank the feedback by preference order after the experiment, provided the same results. They were not disturbed by any of those, found them useful and understood the benefits they provide.

Table 1. Ranking of visual and auditory feedback

	Object attribute	Origin position	Destination position
1. Animation – Sound	1	1	1
2. Animation – No sound	3	2	1
3. No animation – Sound	1	3	3
4. No animation – No sound	4	4	4

Table 1 shows that the combination of animation and sound provides the best comprehension of the changing situation: it provides the bests results in the identification of the essential static data and in the evaluation of the changing parameter. The improvement provided by the addition of sound to animation can be first explained by the notification effect of the sound: it notifies a change about to happen; the user focuses his/her attention on the list just before it changes and sees the animation. In addition, combining auditory and visual feedback offers the opportunity to specialize attention channels [23]. Auditory feedback can be used to identify the object type while visual feedback can be used to recognize the positions. This strategy was reported by subjects themselves and confirmed by the experimenter who noticed that subjects give the object type before the animation begins. Further studies should be conducted to evaluate each effect: notification effect and attention channels specialization.

6   Conclusion

In this study, we addressed the problem of the comprehension of changes when the attention of a user is split between different information sources. We have conducted an experiment that tested combinations of graphical, animated and auditory feedback to improve detection and evaluation of changes occurring in a list displayed in peripheral vision. We found that the use of animation and sound enables users to notice all changes, in conformance with previously available results. In addition, we found that sound can reinforce invariant data coded with graphics such as the type of an element. We also found that motion helps in identifying the old and new values of changing positions, and that a sequential combination of sound and animation is the most efficient feedback for conveying information to users. These results lead us to conclude that the use of animation and sound, alone and combined, improves users' situation awareness, for the perception and comprehension levels.

Stakeholders of interactive systems projects are often concerned with the fact that few works show that rich interfaces are actually more effective than classic ones, and question the extra expense needed for their design. Our results show statistically significant advantages when using animation and sound feedback in user interfaces. The extra effort can therefore improve efficiency and safety of operation.

Acknowledgments. This work results from the ANIMS project, funded by the Eurocontrol Experimental Center via the CARE-INO initiative (Co-operative Actions of R&D in EUROCONTROL – Innovation), and conducted in collaboration with Intactile Design.

References

1. Athènes, S., Chatty, S., Bustico, A.: Human factors in ATC alarms and notifications design: experimental evaluation. In: Proc. ATM'2000 R&D seminar (2000)
2. Bartram, L., Ware, C., Calvert, T.: Moving icons: Detection and distraction. In: Proc. Interact'01,IFIP. IOS Press, Amsterdam (2001)
3. Bertin, J.: Sémiologie graphique. Les diagrammes – Les réseaux – Les plans, « Les Réimpressions », 4ème éd (1ère éd.: 1967), Editions de l'EHESS (2005)
4. Bezerianos, A., Dragicevic, P., Balakrishnan, R.: Mnemonic Rendering: An Image-Based Approach for Exposing Hidden Changes in Dynamic Displays. In: Proc. UIST2006 (2006) (to appear)
5. Chang, B.-W., Ungar, D.: Animation: From Cartoon to User Interface. In: Proc. UIST'93, pp. 45–55 (1993)
6. Cockburn, A., Brewster, S.A.: Multimodal feedback for the acquisition of small targets. Ergonomics 48(9), 1129–1150 (2005)
7. Crease, M.G., Brewster, S.A.: Making Progress With Sounds - The Design and Evaluation Of An Audio Progress Bar. In: Proc. ICAD'98 (1998)
8. Endsley, M.R.: Toward a theory of situation awareness. Human Factors 37(1), 32–64 (1995)
9. Gaver, W.: The SonicFinder: an interface that uses auditory icons. Human Computer Interaction 4(1), 67–94 (1989)
10. Gaver, W.W., Smith, R.B., O'Shea, T.: Effective sounds in complex systems: the ARKOLA simulation. In: Proc. CHI '91, pp. 85–90. ACM Press, New York (1991)
11. Gonzalez, C.: Does animation in user interfaces improve decision making? In: Proc. CHI '96, pp. 27–34. ACM Press, New York (1996)
12. Igarashi, T., Mackinlay, J.D., Chang, B.-W., Zellweger, P.T.: Fluid Visualization of Spreadsheet Structures. In: Proc. Visual Languages'99, pp. 118–125 (1999)

13. Jacko, J.A., Scott, I.U., Sainfort, F., Barnard, L., Edwards, P.J., Emery, V.K., Kongnakorn, T., Moloney, K.P., Zorich, B.S.: Older adults and visual impairment: what do exposure times and accuracy tell us about performance gains associated with multimodal feedback? In: Proc. CHI '03, pp. 33–40. ACM Press, New York (2003)
14. McCrickard, D.S.: Maintaining Information awareness with Irwin. In: Proc. ACM CSCW, pp. 314–323. ACM Press, New York (2002)
15. Mertz, C., Chatty, S., Vinot, J.-L.: Pushing the limits of ATC user interface design beyond S&M interaction: the DigiStrips Experience. In: Proc. ATM'2000 R&D seminar (2000)
16. Mynatt, E.D., Back, M., Want, R., Baer, M., Ellis, J.B.: Designing audio aura. In: Proc. CHI'98, pp. 566–573. ACM Press/Addison-Wesley (1998)
17. Patterson, R.D., Edworthy, J., Shailer, M.J., et al.: Alarm sounds for medical equipment in intensive care areas and operating theatres, Report No. AC598. Institute of Sound and Vibration Research, Southampton, UK (1986)
18. Robertson, G.G., Mackinlay, J.D., Card, S.K.: Cone Trees: animated 3D visualizations of hierarchical information. In: Proc. CHI '91, pp. 189–194. ACM Press, New York (1991)
19. Rensink, R.A., O'Regan, J.K., Clark, J.J.: To see or not to see: the need for attention to perceive changes in scenes. Psychological Science 8(8), 368–373 (1997)
20. Vitense, H.S., Jacko, J.A., Emery, V.K.: Multimodal feedback: An assessment of performance and mental workload. Ergonomics 46(1-3), 58–87 (2003)
21. Ware, C., Neufeld, E., Bartram, L.: Visualizing Causal Relations. In: Proc. IEEE InfoViz'99, pp. 39–42. IEEE Computer Society Press, Los Alamitos (1999)
22. Ware, C.: Information visualization: perception for design. Morgan Kaufmann, San Francisco (2000)
23. Wickens, C.D.: Engineering psychology and human performance, Columbus, Merrill, CE (1984)
24. Woods, D.D., O'Brien, J., Hanes, L.F.: Human Factors challenges in process control, the case of nuclear power plants. In: Salvendy, G. (ed.) Handbook of human factors/Ergnomics (1987)
25. Woods, D.D: The alarm problem and directed attention in dynamic fault management. Ergonomics (38), 2371–2393 (1995)

Designing a Free Style, Indirect, and Interactive Storytelling Application for People with Aphasia

Elke Daemen[1], Pavan Dadlani[1], Jia Du[1], Ying Li[1], Pinar Erik-Paker[1],
Jean-Bernard Martens[2], and Boris de Ruyter[3]

[1] User System Interaction
[2] Industrial Design
Technische Universiteit Eindhoven, P.O. Box 513,
5600 MB Eindhoven, The Netherlands
[3] Philips Research, Eindhoven, The Netherlands
{E.M.L.Daemen, P.M.Dadlani, J.Du, Y.Li, P.ErikPaker}@tm.tue.nl,
J.B.O.S.Martens@tue.nl, Boris.De.Ruyter@Philips.com

Abstract. In this paper, we describe the iterative design and evaluation of a storytelling application for individuals with expressive aphasia. Our user studies show that besides basic requirements for medical care and training, there is an unmet need of aphasics to share their daily experiences and activities, anecdotes and feelings with their significant others. Thus, the goal of the proposed design is to enhance aphasics' quality of life by providing a platform for them to create and share their stories. More specifically, the goal is to enable them to play a more active role in social exchanges by providing them with a multimodal interface for storytelling that has the following functionalities: taking photos, making drawings and annotations, and recording sounds. In the end of this paper, we also summarize important design guidelines that surfaced during the course of this project and that are potentially relevant for other designers and researchers working with aphasics.

Keywords: Personal medical devices, aphasia, storytelling, multi-modal interfaces, user-centered design, iterative design, assistive technology, alternative and augmented communication, handheld devices.

1 Introduction

Aphasia is a communication disorder that is caused by brain injury or disease. Mostly it is caused as a result of a stroke that injures the language component of the brain [9]. Anyone can acquire aphasia, but most people who get affected are in their middle to late years. It is estimated that approximately 80,000 individuals acquire aphasia each year and about one million people in the United States currently have aphasia [10].

Depending on the area of the brain that is damaged, someone with aphasia can have impairments in speaking writing, reading or comprehending language. Expressive aphasia, also called Broca's aphasia, affects the production of language. Language is reduced to disjointed words, and sentence construction is poor. In extreme cases, aphasics may only produce a single word [10]. Receptive aphasia, also

C. Baranauskas et al. (Eds.): INTERACT 2007, LNCS 4662, Part I, pp. 221–234, 2007.

called Wernicke's aphasia, affects the receiving of language. For the aphasic, it seems that everyone is speaking in a foreign language she or he cannot understand and everything they read is gibberish [10]. In some cases, both the receptive and expressive language centers are impaired, which is called Global Aphasia. In this case, the individual has difficulty in producing and comprehending language.

Although the literature clearly defines different types of aphasia, in practicality aphasics are never completely of one type. Every aphasic has a unique speech language problem, so signs of impairment show up in a variety of ways in producing or understanding speech, reading or writing. In addition, aphasics vary in their physical and other cognitive abilities. For instance, many aphasics also have some degree of paralysis on their right-hand side.

The research documented in this paper investigates the needs of individuals with aphasia in different aspects of their daily life. This research motivated the design of a tool that supports aphasics in the creation and sharing of daily life stories. The research was conducted through an iterative process of designing and evaluating with both health-care specialists and aphasics.

2 Related Work

2.1 Technology and Tools for People with Aphasia

Gesturing, mimicking, pointing, drawing, and writing, are often used during aphasia therapy, while low technology aids are quite popular amongst aphasics. For instance communication books with written words, photos or icons [11] are commonly used because most aphasics prefer image-based information. Books are also cheap and can easily be carried around. The main disadvantages are their fixed vocabulary and the time taken to find what is needed.

Augmentative and Alternative Communication (AAC) devices are the major form of technology to support aphasics, and a lot of research and design has been done in this area. GPRS (General Packet Radio Service) systems, cameras and PDAs are all existing technologies that can be used for this purpose. Developments up to now have focused predominantly on devices to assist in direct communicative exchanges [8].

One of the most popular AAC devices is TouchSpeak [5]. It is a portable communication aid consisting of a PDA with specifically developed software. It supports multi-modality (i.e., images, sounds and text) by providing interfaces to a digital keyboard, a camera, a drawing pad, etc. To fulfill the requirements of different aphasics, speech therapists work together with an aphasic person to build a personal vocabulary and to select function modules. The flexible nature of the device is an especially strong feature, since vocabulary and functions can be adapted to the aphasics' needs. However, the software is installed on a PDA with limited screen size, which leads to a requirement for precise and accurate interactions. This obviously implies a limitation for the many aphasics who are physically impaired. In addition, the interface requires aphasics to browse into categories and layers, which is quite challenging for language-impaired people [1]. There are other devices that provide sentences to support simple conversations, such as ScriptTalker [5]. This device provides standard phrases of every-day situations, and it aims at aiding people with total loss of speech. It takes a lot of time and heavy cognitive efforts to construct new sentences, however.

Another popular tool is Lingraphica [5]. It is desktop software which aphasics can use to browse items within a virtually represented environment. The tool offers visual cues during the searching process. For example, if users want to drink milk, they will be presented with a home environment, they must open the door of the kitchen and a fridge will be there as a cue to help users find the milk. Once again, the need to browse into categories can pose a big challenge for the targeted users.

2.2 Working with Aphasics

Designing for people with aphasia is obviously non-trivial, since communicating with them is very difficult. Therefore, it is essential to involve expertise from several areas other than HCI. Several prior projects and research suggest that including psychologists, audiologists, speech therapists, social workers, or family members can help the design team to better identify the real needs of aphasics [2, 6]. This is because these health-care workers and family members interact with aphasics on a daily basis, and are therefore able to better understand their abilities and problems within daily activities.

Participatory design methods have been applied in many aphasia research and design projects. Methods involving speech therapists as proxies in brainstorming sessions and interviews, and getting feedback of design concepts have been adopted, such as within the design of the ESI Planner [2], a daily planner for people with aphasia.

3 User Study and Requirements Analysis

3.1 Contextual Interviews and Field Observations

Given that it is a challenge to communicate with individuals with aphasia, we used alternative ways to communicate with them through their primary caregivers, speech pathologists, clinical linguists, and social workers who assist aphasics and their families. During face-to-face interviews with aphasics, they were able to interpret and validate questions, and express attitude and emotional responses towards our design concepts. The goal was to identify which aspects of their life are not well-supported through current tools and to understand their life needs in more depth than can be deduced from literature.

During the design process, we established a good working relation with a local Aphasia Union and we were invited to join meetings that took place every two weeks where more than 20 aphasics and their partners met and spend time together sharing stories, playing games, etc. We observed how aphasics communicate with their partners and with each other in a casual and relaxed context. We noticed that they use a lot of gestures to support what they want to express. Each of them comes to these meetings with a photo album that contains new photos of themselves, their family or friends. They use their photo albums to initiate a talk with caregivers and other aphasics. Moreover, they use tags with emotions and add them to different photos to help express their feelings. We found this very interesting and inspiring, since it reveals the important role of using pictures and emotion symbols in the daily

224 E. Daemen et al.

communication of aphasics. Figure 1 shows an example of drawings used by an expressive aphasic trying to tell us what his earlier profession was. The drawing shows two swimming pools since he was a director of a swimming pool and the numbers represent the people who used to work with him. It is interesting to notice that some aphasics use letters to add to their drawings but mostly only the first letter of a word. For instance, they drew a box of milk and wrote the letter 'M' beside it.

He wrote down numbers of employees who used to work for him.

The letter "M" and a box are used to represent milk

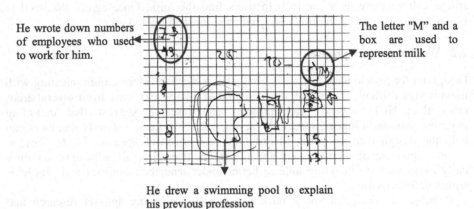

He drew a swimming pool to explain his previous profession

Fig. 1. An example of drawings made by an expressive aphasic trying to communicate what his earlier profession was

3.2 Findings

The study helped derive and prove the following needs of individuals with aphasia:

Like others, aphasic individuals want to be listened to and understood. Aphasics become nervous and get frustrated if others cannot understand what they are trying to express. This forces them to take a passive role in social interaction, which in turn increases the likelihood of developing stress and depression.

The proposed technology should not appear to be for disabled people. Although supporting devices are widely used by aphasic individuals, such as pictogram books, most aphasics would rather leave the device at home when they go to a social event. Ironically, many of them want to be social but choose not to communicate since their aiding device will emphasize their disability.

Like others, aphasics want to express their ideas, comments, anecdotes, and feelings about what occurred to them in their daily life. Although they have lost the ability to speak, there is a great need for them to communicate more about their emotions and daily activities with their significant others than only receiving daily care and help from the latter.

Aphasics require easy access and simplicity in their communication aids. Many aphasics fail to use some of the currently available technologies because these technologies do not adequately consider their capabilities. For example, the hierarchy structure used by TouchSpeak is confusing to many aphasic individuals because they find hierarchies difficult to understand.

Aphasics need the ability to communicate at a distance instantaneously. Many aphasics stay at home alone. Their primary caregivers worry about this and usually try to arrange someone (neighbors, family, or friends) to be with them. Many aphasics get afraid of being alone since they may not be able to handle unexpected or emergency situations.

In addition to physical constraints, attention should be paid to psychological problems. It is of much interest to aphasic individuals to find ways to help relieve their stress and to become more connected to the world around them.

3.3 New Insights

Based on the above findings, there are two opportunities for supporting individuals with aphasia. The first one is a specific need to support synchronous distance-based communication to help aphasics deal with emergency and the second one is to enhance their quality of life by changing their passive position in their current daily communication. We decided to take the latter insight as the starting point for our design.

Current supporting tools, such as pictogram books or TouchSpeak, are mostly used for direct communication. For example, aphasics normally would request help and daycare like medication or getting food from their significant others. Aphasics would also use these tools to support their outdoor daily activities (e.g. shopping, meeting people, or making appointments). However, many of these devices make their disability apparent in a social situation. Hence, in direct communication aphasics tend to behave passively. They start to communicate only when they have to (e.g. getting food, drink, or medications).

However, when aphasics communicate in an indirect way, such as through writing e-mail, they have a more positive attitude. Like most people, they have time to prepare what messages they want to deliver asynchronously to others. Consequently, we want to focus on supporting indirect communication by means of a storytelling application which allows creating and sharing stories of daily life activities in a free personal style for people with expressive aphasia. The reason why we choose storytelling as a solution is because a large amount of people's conversation consists of sharing stories [3] related to anecdotes and events, and their attitudes towards them [4]. In addition, aphasics can make stories about their daily life, their hobbies, job, family, friends, etc., and they can share them with others.

Such a storytelling application has the potential of (1) changing the passive position in communication of individuals with aphasia, for example by initiating a conversation with family at the dinner table, (2) being able to share their feelings and attitude towards a particular topic or activity they have come across in their daily life, (3) capturing things they want to share with others, making the communication self-entertaining for them, and (4) relieving the stress and anxiety that aphasia brought to their lives.

4 Iterative Design

4.1 Design Methods

The user study helped us to clearly understand the diversity between aphasic individuals. Designing for all aphasic people is not possible, so a persona was created based on our user study. This helped us focus on a specific instance of expressive aphasia and guided our initial design. We conducted brainstorming sessions, which led us to four concepts of creating and sharing stories. These concepts emphasized different features relevant in the creation and sharing of stories. In order to present these concepts to experts and potential users, low fidelity prototypes were made and put into a storyboard with real use context.

4.2 Initial Conceptual Interface Design of the Storytelling Application

To achieve our goal to help aphasics tell a daily story and be able to share it, four concepts were developed for initial user evaluation. In each of the concepts, users are able to retrieve, create and view stories made by them. Each concept is identified by different features of creating and retrieving stories, icons, color schemes and graphical layouts (Figures 2 and 3).

Fig. 2. Concept 1 (*left*) with a storyline and Concept 2 (*right*) where sharing stories is done manually with arrows

Fig. 3. Concept 3 (*left*) shows creating a clip with three components made of pictures, annotations and emotions, and Concept 4 (*right*) shows making a story as a one-page photo collage with annotations

4.3 First Iteration: Testing Concepts with Speech Pathologists

The first evaluation was carried out with four speech pathologists to validate the general concept of storytelling and get initial feedback of the conceptual interface designs described in 4.2. All experts agreed that the concept of storytelling is an unmet need for this population, and they envisioned the benefits of having such a tool for them.

The feedback provided us with valuable insights for further concept refining. First, in terms of physical capabilities of many aphasics, due to an impairment of the right-hand side of their body, taking pictures with one hand is difficult for them. Often, their right-hand side vision is also affected. Thus, interface elements should be placed in the center or towards the left-hand side of the interface.

Second, in order to properly match available cognitive abilities, the interface should be as simple as possible and only support the basic features that are needed to create and share a story. The visual design should not be cluttered or too colorful, and interface elements should be obvious and easy to interpret. The navigation should be simple and the number of steps required to make a story should be kept to a strict minimum.

Third, about the features used in different concepts, sound recording was preferred over video recording. Besides, annotations would not be made to videos. Many aphasics have problems with the concept of time in terms of numbers and calendars. The people library was thought to be a practical feature for making stories, whereas the pictogram library could be too overwhelming.

Changes were made based on the feedback from speech specialists. Concept 4 (Figure 3) was dropped since it was considered too complicate, with too many colors, different photo orientations, and many collage templates. Features of the other three concepts were adjusted and integrated according to the feedback.

4.4 Second Iteration: Testing Concepts with Aphasics

Low fidelity prototypes that demonstrated all interaction steps for making and viewing a story were made in MS PowerPoint for the refined design concepts. These prototypes were evaluated with three aphasics and their partners from the Aphasia Union and the feedback is summarized below.

First, simplicity was considered to be important for both the graphical design and the interaction design. Amongst others, this implied that the number of steps needed for creating a story has to be kept to a strict minimum. Second, in terms of features, the storyline at the bottom of the screen of the first concept in Figure 2 seemed important when creating a story that contained several pictures. Users didn't find the keyboard necessary for making a story. They found adding sound to pictures a feature they might use, although it may be difficult for them to understand it properly. Taking pictures and adding annotations was an attractive feature to them, but being able to take pictures themselves could again prove to be a physical challenge.

4.5 Third Iteration: Testing Interface Elements

A list of different metaphors was created to represent each interface element. We asked four aphasics with their partners to choose the icons that were most clear to represent the intended function, such as drawing, emotions, taking pictures, etc. This helped finalize the concept prior to implementation. The participants liked those icons that were not abstract but more realistic. They preferred the 3D icons because they look more like real objects than the 2D icons.

4.6 Fourth Iteration: Final Concept Prototyping

A final concept was created using the feedback from speech specialists and aphasics. Users are provided with four input modalities for creating a story: taking pictures, drawing and annotating, adding emotions, and recording sound. Figure 4 shows the final interfaces of the application.

The first interface will show all the stories in chronological order with the latest being on top. An old story can be retrieved from this interface and a new story can be created by tapping on the blank one. The second interface is for editing stories. After taking a picture, users can add annotations, emotions, or sound to it. When their editing is finished they will save it (check button) as a clip of their story, which will appear in the storyline at the bottom. Users can navigate through the storyline manually and edit or delete (with the trash button) any clip of their story. The third interface is for playing stories, which can be by means of a slide show in the sequence of the storyline.

Fig. 4. The final concept has an initial screen to retrieve stories or to start creating a new story (*left*), while creating or editing storyline clips is done by means of an interface that offers four input modalities: pictures, annotation, emotions, and sounds (*middle*). Finally an interface is made for showing and browsing the story created by a user (*right*).

We presented users a slideshow of different ways they can tell a story to someone. The basic method is to show the story directly to others, but we took a step further and showed other ways, such as connecting it to the TV to show family members and friends, or sending a story via e-mail. When spouses are at work, they worry about leaving them at home without knowing how they are doing. Sending stories via e-mail could tackle this problem. These are opportunities of expanding the storytelling concept, and the feedback was positive.

4.7 High Fidelity Prototype

The storytelling application was developed in Macromedia Director and prototyped on the Motion Computing LS800 8.4" Tablet PC. An external webcam was fixed to support picture taking (Figure 5).

Fig. 5. The storytelling application in a Tablet PC with a webcam attached to it

5 Evaluation of the Storytelling Concept

Our next step was to conduct an evaluation of the storytelling prototype. The objective of this phase was to validate our concept of storytelling for aphasics with target users, and to decide whether or not the proposed tool could potentially influence their lifestyle. We wanted to meet our initial requirements such that individuals with aphasia can (1) construct, record, and share their life stories and anecdotes with family and friends, (2) prepare their story with not too much cognitive effort, (3) carry and operate the prototype within their physical capabilities, and (4) express their feelings and thoughts on subjects of interest.

5.1 Participants

A pilot experiment was done with an elderly person to validate the testing protocol and make changes to the procedure. Five aphasic individuals (4 males and 1 female) and their primary caregivers (their spouse in one case and speech therapists in the others) participated in this evaluation.

We selected participants with different levels of expressive aphasia. Two had a severe type of expressive aphasia. They could say 'yes' and 'no' to answer questions and could say their own names. Two other participants had medium level of aphasia. One of them could use several words and write some. He also could use drawings on a notebook to make clear what he meant. Another participant could use many words but changed some as he spoke. He could write a little and could read some words. Three of them were totally right side paralyzed and were in a wheelchair. The other two patients have problems using their right arm.

5.2 Methodology

Procedure. Observations, interviews, and questionnaires were adopted as main methods for testing [12]. The sessions took place at the participants' home or in a local rehabilitation center. Each session took approximately 60 minutes. Participants, together with their spouses or speech therapists were explained the storytelling prototype by means of a video prototype. It showed them a scenario of when and how the prototype can be used. The video demonstrated the complete process using all the features and playing back the story to a significant other. Participants were then given the opportunity to explore with the prototype and clarify any doubts.

We asked participants to create a short story about anything they would like to by taking pictures and using the storytelling features, and later sharing this story with their spouse or speech therapist. Since it is not possible to get their feedback directly, observations were made of facial expressions and physical signs of confusion or enjoyment, which could be used to identify their attitude and opinion about using the prototype. After the test, participants were asked to rate a set of 36 statements in terms of agreement in the form of five smileys ('very sad' to 'very happy', to represent 'strongly disagree' to 'strongly agree'). These predefined rating scales are already being used with aphasics for other purposes in rehabilitation centers. Since the goal is to make the communication between aphasics and significant others more interactive, the opinion of caregivers is essential and interviews were made with them at the end of the session.

Measures. Qualitative measures were used for evaluation. Our main purpose was to evaluate the acceptance of the storytelling concept and of the features in the prototype. In addition to this, physical use of the prototype, ease of use and graphical design were also tested.

5.3 Results

Storytelling. In general they liked the concept of storytelling. Participants indicated that our design is useful for them to tell stories to their significant others. They thought the system was easy to learn and use. They would use the system regularly to make and tell stories to their family or friends, and in fact they believed our system is better than their current ways of communication. They indicated that they would use the system more for recording daily activities. Although the storytelling application is to support indirect communication, they found it useful and would use it to communicate directly as well.

The partners and speech therapists also indicated that storytelling is a good concept and would help aphasics and their partners tell their daily activities. It would enhance their quality of life together because when the partner comes back from a long day of work, they can sit together and share stories of the day. The therapists also indicated that the designed interface is very simple and could be understood and used by a lot of people with expressive aphasia.

Features. The impression about the features was different for each aphasic user, but this is due to their different types of expressive aphasia. We asked participants to rank the four features in order of importance using cards with the icons and names of each. After this, we gave them cards of additional features such as a pictogram library, a people library, a movie maker, a keyboard, etc. They were asked to indicate which additional feature they wanted and how important they considered them to be in comparison to the current features. They all ranked the four current features as most important, but they wanted some additional ones and this differed based on the level of expressive aphasia they had. This does demonstrate that features should be customizable for individual needs.

The first user indicated that she liked the emotions feature the most. This is because she currently finds it hard to express her feelings and the smileys helped her express how she felt. She indicated that the drawing feature is her second choice and drawing could also help her express her thoughts. When she was creating the story she made a picture of one of the observers and drew a house next to him. Later, when she was telling the story to her spouse, she indicated that the observer was visiting her house. The sound feature was the least appealing to her, since according to her it would not add much to the stories she would make. In addition to the current features, she wanted a pictogram library where she could select icons to add to her story.

The second user indicated that adding sounds to pictures was the most important feature for him. This is because he has a medium level of aphasia, and most of the times he needs to hear the first part of a word to instruct him to say it, so for him sound is very important for communication. In addition, the drawing tool was the second most important feature. He could make drawings of what he wanted to say when he wouldn't be able to find the words he needed. This participant liked the emotions feature the least because he already can express his feelings very well. He wanted the keyboard as an additional feature so he could make annotations in advance to help him tell the story.

The third participant, who had a light form of expressive aphasia, also liked the sound the most because it could help him retrieve words. Similarly to the second participant, he liked the drawing feature because it could also help him express his thoughts when he could not find the proper words. This participant did not want any additional features and found the current ones enough to create stories. The last two participants ranked taking pictures the highest and valued the importance of it when creating stories. One of them preferred sound over emotions and drawing because he could utter some words and sound could help him utter the right word, whereas the other participant preferred drawing over emotions and sound, because he could only utter 'yes' and 'no'. The latter preferred having a keyboard as an additional feature since his reading capability was not completely lost.

Prototype. Our main focus was to evaluate the storytelling concept rather than the physical product. However, based on the observations and feedback, it is essential that such a device be designed specifically for aphasics rather than using an off-the-shelf platform like our tablet. All patients indicated that the screen of the Tablet PC was big enough and although they indicated that the pen was easy to use, they all required a fair amount of training to use it properly. The storytelling device should consider the ergonomic factors of such individuals. The device was not easy to hold because all participants have an impaired right-arm and three of them use a wheelchair, so being able to hold the device with one hand and write with the other (left) was difficult for all the five participants.

6   Implications

Having gone through the user-centered design process for designing a storytelling application for people with aphasia, we feel we can also contribute some worthwhile insights that might have implications for related work. Several recommendations have been derived and divided into three broad categories: working, designing, and evaluating with individuals with aphasia.

6.1 Working with Individuals with Aphasia

Proxies are indeed important to be involved in the participatory design. We followed similar methods used by previous research to interact with aphasics by means of proxies [2]. Involving proxies to not only help communicate, but also to gather aphasics' needs and obtain their feedback about the designed product is valuable for designing for aphasics. In addition, social workers who understand many of the difficulties that aphasics and their families go through can provide key information about their real needs.

Use closed questions. Many aphasics can answer yes and no, so well designed closed questions are important for getting direct feedback.

6.2 Designing for Individuals with Aphasia

Start designing for a Persona. There is a wide variety of aphasics. Not all expressive aphasics have the same problems, and it is impossible to design for all of them. It is important to create a persona of a specific aphasic, make an initial design, and then iteratively adapt the design for a larger user group.

Simplicity is essential in interactive technologies for aphasics. The interface must be simple in all interactive dimensions. Designing abstract elements for aphasics should be avoided. The number of steps required to do a particular task should be strictly kept to a minimum. Metaphors used for icons should be as representative as possible of the intended meaning. The interface should not be too colorful or too cluttered, since this distract them and they can loose their focus of attention. Semantic categorizing should be avoided [1] and interface elements should be kept as visible and accessible as possible.

Structure and layout of the interface. Interface elements and navigation tools, should be big enough to be identified. Due to impairments on the right-hand side of their body, their right-hand side vision may be affected. For those who have this problem, anything placed on their right-hand side will not be identified as being present until it is pointed out to them. It is suggested to place interface elements either in the center or at the left-side of the interface.

Use of accessible and portable technology. The designed product should consider the ergonomic factors for those aphasics with physical disabilities on the right-hand side of their body. Aphasics should be able to use the product with one hand (typically with their left hand), hence, it should not be heavy or bulky.

When using touch screens, it is important to get the calibration and sensitivity right. Users may end up tapping on the wrong interface element leading to undesired results. From previous research, users preferred interacting with fingers and being able to concentrate on pointing only, rather than gripping (e.g. a stylus) and pointing [7]. In addition, tapping interaction has shown to be problematic for those with motoric impairments as it provides no support for targeting [8].

6.3 Evaluating with Individuals with Aphasia

Provide adequate time for evaluating with aphasics. The evaluation sessions took around an hour per participant and it was observed that half-way through, users would tend to loose confidence and become impatient. They may loose track of the goal of the session. Evaluation sessions should be broken up into shorter ones. In addition, experimenters should constantly confirm if participants are on track as they move on with the session, since aphasics may just say 'yes' to everything when they don't really mean it.

Provide detailed guided training prior to evaluating the product. Often, in evaluation methodologies, participants are given some time to explore by themselves the product after being instructed on how to use it and prior to the testing session. When evaluating with aphasics, however, a self-exploratory phase is not possible. Instead, the experimenter has to explore together with the participant, guiding them through step-by-step each interface element, and often having to repeat several times.

Add context to demonstrations. To help aphasic users understand how the product works, scenario based context should be added to low fidelity or video prototypes. On the other hand, high fidelity prototypes should look as real as possible, since aphasics may not understand the limitations of a prototype. For example, one of the users did not like the camera function very much since the picture quality processed by the software was not very good.

Use symbol-based rating scales. Rehabilitation centers use defined rating scales in terms of smileys which work very well with individuals with aphasia.

7 Conclusions and Future Work

We have presented a description of the process we followed for designing an interactive system that can support storytelling for people with aphasia. We initially made field observations and interviews to identify their needs. We further explored the concept of creating and sharing stories with significant others and iterated through low fidelity prototypes and evaluated the final concept in a working prototype. From our user study we learned that storytelling is an unmet need of individuals with aphasia that current technologies do not support and our final concept will help them (1) change their current passive position in a social environment, (2) express their ideas, thoughts, and feelings about a chosen subject of interest, and (3) support their communication with significant others.

We believe that an additional longitudinal field test is required where the prototype is kept with potential users for a period of time without any experimenters around, and have the device as part of their daily life. This can demonstrate its actual value in real life settings even after the novelty effect wears off. At the end of the trial time we will collect the same information and assess the feedback. In addition, we made an initial exploration of different ways for aphasics to show their story and we can conclude that there is an opportunity to have users share their stories in different modalities and support distance-based indirect communication.

Acknowledgments. Rehabilitation Centers in Blixembosch, Rotterdam, and Ghent, the Emilius School, the Eindhoven Aphasia Union, and Marleen Tournel for all their support. We would like to extend our gratitude to all the aphasics and their spouses for their valuable time and feedback. Many thanks to Ankun Liu for all his help with our prototype.

References

1. Ahlsén, E., et al.: Virtual reality as a commnunication aid for persons with aphasia. In: Proceedings Disability, Virtual Reality & Associated Technologies, Sweden, pp. 229–235 (1998)
2. Boyd-Graber, et al.: Participatory Design with Proxies: Developing a Desktop-PDA System to Support People with Aphasia. In: Proceedings CHI 2006, pp. 152–160. ACM Press, New York (2006)
3. Dunbar, R.: Grooming, gossip, and the evolution of language, Mackays of Chatham, Chatham, Kent, UK (1996)
4. Emler, N.: Gossip, reputation and social adaptation. In: Goodman, R.F., Ben-Ze'ev, A. (eds.) Good Gossip, pp. 117–138. Kansas University Press, Lawrence, KS (1994)
5. Kitzing, P., et al.: Communication aids for people with aphasia. Proceedings Logopedics Phoniatrics Vocology 30, 41–46 (2005)
6. McGrenere, et al.: Insights from the Aphasia Project: Designing Technology For and With People who have Aphasia. In: Proceedings CUU 2003, pp. 112–118. ACM Press, New York (2003)
7. Moffatt, K.: Designing Technology For and With Special Populations: An Exploration of Participatory Design with People with Aphasia. University of British Columbia (2001)
8. Moffatt, K.: The Participatory Design of a Sound and Image Enhanced Daily Planner for People with Aphasia. In: Proceedings CHI 2004, pp. 408–414. ACM Press, New York (2004)
9. The American Heart Association: Aphasia (December 2006), Available at http://www.americanheart.org/presenter.jhtml?identifier=4485
10. The National Institute on Deafness and Other Communication Disorders: Aphasia (December 2006), Available at: http://www.nidcd.nih.gov/health/voice/aphasia.htm
11. Van de Sandt, et al.: High-tech AAC and aphasia: Widening horizons? Aphasiology, pp. 453-469 (2000)
12. Nielsen, J.: Usability Engineering. Academic Press, Boston, USA (1993)

Supporting the Planning and Organization of Multiple Activities in the Workplace

Victor M. González[1], Leonardo Galicia[2], and Jesús Favela[2]

[1] Manchester Business School, University of Manchester, United Kingdom
[2] CICESE Research Center, México
vmgonz@manchester.ac.uk, {lgalicia, favela}@cicese.mx

Abstract. Many studies have shown how knowledge workers face challenges while multi-tasking among several projects and initiatives at the workplace. Researchers and consultants of personal productivity have identified practical strategies and processes that people use to face, plan and manage their activities. Our work is based on the analysis of those processes and strategies involved in personal activity management (PAM), emphasizing the planning aspects of it, with the goal of designing appropriate supportive information technology.

Keywords: Personal Activity Management, Planning Activities, Personal Productivity, Knowledge Workers, Information Technology.

1 Introduction

Many studies have been conducted in the last forty years to understand how knowledge workers divide their time and efforts among several projects and initiatives at the workplace [2,3,5]. Some of these studies have shown that activities performed by information workers are varied, fragmented, and brief, which forces them to focus on each activity for a short period of time [5]. This reality makes information workers to engage in explicit efforts to keep control over their commitments, and use strategies to organize, prioritize and focus on what they have and want to do [3,5]. We define this type of effort as personal activity management (PAM), a kind of meta-work that expands beyond those necessary efforts related directly to accomplish the purpose of a specific activity and focuses on the orchestration of the complete set of activities that the person has committed to do. Results of previous studies show that to a minor or greater extent all knowledge workers engage in PAM efforts on a regular basis [2,3,5].

Defining adequate technological support for PAM is an important and relevant challenge because an efficient management of activities often results on better personal and group productivity [2]. Unfortunately, studies coincide on pointing out how current technologies fail to address the challenges imposed by PAM [3,5]. Because PAM have been commonly associated to efforts toward the management of time, documents, contacts, messages and the physical space [3, 6], this has resulted on technological solutions that just partially address the issues around it. Some

C. Baranauskas et al. (Eds.): INTERACT 2007, LNCS 4662, Part I, pp. 235–238, 2007.

technological solutions are designed to pay attention to the communication channels that give origin to activities [3], others are centered in the management of resources to facilitate the fast retrieval of work context when users switch from one activity to another [6], and others aim at creating a more natural integration between PIM (Personal Information Management) tools and resources. Few available technologies focus on what we argue is the central and fundamental challenge of PAM: offering support for planning and organizing activities. This paper presents our work in progress aiming at developing an application to support PAM on that particular aspect.

2 Planning Activities

We can understand PAM as encompassing processes and strategies for planning activities in the short, medium and long-term, allowing users to be more proactive and less reactive when dealing with job commitments. With proper PAM, information workers get a perspective about the current status of each one of their activities, and with this perspective they can focus intelligently on those activities that demand their immediate attention.

We based our understanding of PAM on previous work and analyses in order to identify some of the essential characteristics of the type of support required [1,2,4,5]. Two of them [1,4] can be characterized as empirical methodologies offering advice on personal productivity, with emphasis on time-management and activity planning. The other two [2,5] emerged from ethnographic-based studies and describe the strategies and processes used by informants to manage their activities.

Gonzalez and Mark [5] proposed the *overview process*, a set of strategies to achieve a constant focalization of those activities to be done. They argue that people constantly make efforts to gain an overview of their activities, gaining knowledge about their scope and purposes, their temporal constraints, degree of development, and the next actions to conduct in each one. They also argue that with this overview (which is represented on physical or digital artifacts) people can maintain a state of preparedness; they can make better judgments with respect to their priorities and can move in and out of their activities as circumstances change or opportunities arise.

The work of Barry and his colleagues [2] shows different strategies used by managers to keep personal agendas. Their study shows how they implement their agenda and highlights the satisfaction and feeling of control they gain through this process. The *agendazing process* also highlights how managers have the fundamental function of simultaneously handling short and long term goals. Their findings provide evidence regarding the relevance of prospective and retrospective analyses

Covey's methodology [4] offers advices on how to achieve a better PAM, including better ways to plan activities. Covey's methodology is based on seven principles (habits), where the first three are focused on PAM. Covey emphasizes the importance of being proactive and clear in terms of the goals that the individual aims to achieve. In the third habit (*put first things first*), Covey offers specific processes to deal with organization and planning activities, focusing on short and medium-term activities offering a priority's framework to deal with them.

Finally, David Allen suggests a methodology named Getting Things Done (GTD) which is based on the creation of lists of tasks [1]. GTD invite people to write down all they want to do in a trusted system that will act as external reminder system as well as additional support to ensure that we will get the right reminders at the right moment. Allen suggests that materializing commitments helps to clarify what is necessary to be achieved and what are the specific actions required to achieve it. Allen's methodology also provides a framework to process and organize work at two distinct levels: personal projects and the tasks (actions) to achieve them. He makes particular emphasis on defining the next-action required for each project.

3   A Consolidated Model for PAM

Our analysis of previous work aims at integrating their main ideas and recommendations and producing a consolidated model for PAM that can be used as the foundation to design supportive technology. The model consists of five processes:

Gestation: This process is conducted to identify the efforts that people carry out to make a representation or materialization of activities, actions or job commitments that need to be done. Gestation helps to clarify what is to be achieved and what are the specific actions needed to achieve it.

Classification: This process involves efforts to provide meaning to all the representations made during the gestation process. This meaning can be implicitly or explicitly indicated by people (e.g. scheduled, to do now, delegate, etc.)

Redefinition: Activities are dynamic and evolve over time. This means that activities are likely to require new actions, discard or postpone others. Through this process people maintain their activities updated according to the circumstances.

Focalization: Every day, people can just focus on a sub-set of the entire universe of activities for which they have committed time. This subset is usually defined in advance (e.g. at the beginning of the day), and determined by personal preference or temporal constraints (e.g. scheduled meetings).

Revision: This process is used by people to get a general or partial perspective of their accomplishments to make better judgments with respect to their priorities and respond intelligently to circumstances. This process involves short, medium and long term perspectives as well as retrospective and prospective analyses.

4   Technological Approach

At this point our work is focusing on the development of a system to support the consolidated model for PAM defined in the previous section. Figure 1 shows the interface used to support the process of focalization (currently in Spanish). Our solution is a desktop application which can be synchronized with a Personal Digital Assistant (PDA) and PIM applications (e.g. MS Outlook), as well as producing paper-based reports with lists of activities. Through a floating tool bar, the user can access any of the main processes of PAM. We conceive each of the processes as interrelated but not necessarily interdependent. Consequently, the application is structured so that

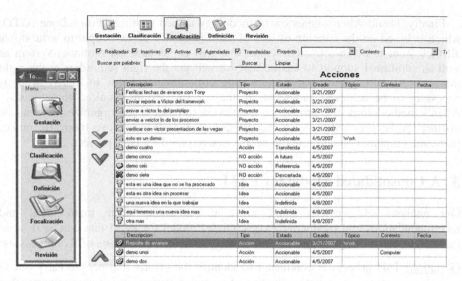

Fig. 1. PAM tool: Focalization process

people can use any of theses processes in the order and with the level of detail that they wish, avoiding with this the imposition of a particular strategy.

5   Future Work

We assume a relationship of mutual dependence between the characteristics of the technology and the practices around its usage. We plan to study the sustained use of our system by knowledge workers for at least two months. Before installing the system, we will provide general training on effective PAM using the tool. Through the analysis of how people use and adapt our tool we aim at contributing to the understanding of multiple activity management in the workplace.

References

1. Allen, D.: Getting Things Done: The Art of Stress-Free Productivity. Penguin Putnam, New York (2001)
2. Barry, D., Durnell, C., Carroll, S.: Navigating the garbage can: How agendas help managers cope with job realities. The Academy of Management Executive 11(2), 26–42 (1997)
3. Belloti, V., Ducheneaut, N., Howard, M., Smith, I.: Taking email to task: the design and evaluation of a task management centered email tool. In: Proc. CHI 2003, pp. 345–352. ACM Press, New York (2003)
4. Covey, S.: Seven Habits Of Highly Effective People. Simon & Schuster (Edit.) (1990)
5. González, V., Mark, G.: Managing currents of work: Multi-tasking among multiple collaborations. In: Proc. ECSCW 2005, pp. 143–162. Springer, Heidelberg (2005)
6. Kaptelinin, V.: UMEA: Translating Interaction Histories into Project Context. In: Proc. CHI 2003, pp. 353–360. ACM Press, New York (2003)

Creators, Composers and Consumers:
Experiences of Designing a Digital Library

Ann Blandford[1], Jeremy Gow[1], George Buchanan[2], Clare Warwick[3],
and Jon Rimmer[3]

[1] UCL Interaction Centre, UCL, 31-32 Alfred Place, London WC1E 7DP, U.K
A.Blandford@ucl.ac.uk
http://www.uclic.ucl.ac.uk/annb/
[2] Department of Computer Science, Swansea University
[3] School of Library, Archive & Information Studies, UCL, London

Abstract. Many systems form 'chains' whereby developers use one system (or 'tool') to create another system, for use by other people. Little work within Human–Computer Interaction (HCI) has considered how usability considerations propagate through such chains and yet in many situations the usability of systems is determined by design decisions made at one or more steps removed from the immediate developers of the system in question. In this paper, we relate our experiences of developing digital library components and collections to this notion of "design chains". This case study illustrates the necessity of looking beyond the immediate users to try to anticipate the needs of stakeholders elsewhere in the design chain.

Keywords: digital libraries; system development; design chains.

1 Introduction

It is widely recognised that there are many stakeholder groups in any design project. Approaches such as Soft Systems Methodology [5] encourage explicit consideration of these different stakeholder groups in design. However, when it comes to considering usability, the focus narrows immediately to the end users of the system under consideration. Blandford et al. [2] present a framework for considering 'chains' of developers and users of products, which they term 'creators' (commonly referred to as designers or toolsmiths), 'composers' (users of the tool who compose artefacts for other users) and 'consumers' (end users of artefacts). In this paper, we use those concepts to frame our experience of developing and testing digital library components for creating collections to be used by Humanities scholars.

The idea of 'design chains' is widely used in supply chain management (e.g. [7]), but the core concern there is typically with ensuring that components from different suppliers can be integrated seamlessly into a product. In contrast, Blandford et al. consider how concepts are propagated through chains of system development, as decisions made by the creator constrain or influence the behaviour of the composer.

C. Baranauskas et al. (Eds.): INTERACT 2007, LNCS 4662, Part I, pp. 239–242, 2007.

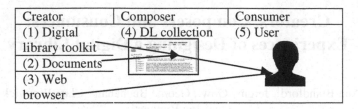

Creator	Composer	Consumer
(1) Digital library toolkit	(4) DL collection	(5) User
(2) Documents		
(3) Web browser		

Fig. 1. Creators, composers and consumers for a Digital Library interaction

Chains are not always linear: the end user's experience of web browsing will depend on both the design of a site and the environment in which pages are viewed. As well as joining, chains may also stretch further in both directions.

A digital library system is an example of a tool within a development chain: developers work with software development environments to create a layer of tools, such as Greenstone [8], with which librarians can create collections of documents to be made available to end users. Reflecting on their work as the creators of Greenstone, Witten et al. [9] note that *"The ease of acquiring and installing a software project has a direct impact on the users it attracts, and consequently—in the open source world—on the extent and nature of contributions that users make to the project"*. Here, it is clear that the users of concern are the users of the toolkit.

However, in a study [3] evaluating Greenstone, another developer suggested that the creators of the toolkit were not recognising their potential role in making it easy for composers (who typically have little HCI expertise) to construct usable digital libraries for consumers: *"[There is a] difficulty with the way Greenstone is perceived by different parties. [The developers] see Greenstone very much as a toolset which other folks should 'finish off' to make a good collection. Their conception is that it would be very hard to take Greenstone to a level where a librarian could make a few choices [with a] GUI and have a reasonable (not to say actively excellent) interface for the library."*

The user's experience depends on the design of both the web browser (which we do not consider further) and the DL collection (items (3) and (4) in Figure 1); the design of the collection, in turn, depends on the design of the DL toolkit (item 1) and that of the data (item 2), i.e. the set of documents. The creators' design decisions influence the work of the composer, and hence the experience of the consumer. This can happen directly or because of interference between the decisions of multiple creators.

2   Case Study: Developing a Humanities Digital Library

Many Humanities documents are being digitised in order to make them more accessible to scholars and enthusiasts (e.g. [6]). To investigate alternative interfaces and interaction styles for a Humanities digital library, we created collections that were accessible via the Greenstone DL interface. The designs were informed by empirical studies of the use of existing digital resources (e.g. [1]); they are now being evaluated to develop a richer understanding of Humanities users' requirements and behaviours.

To be suitable for studies with Humanities scholars, collections had to resemble real-world resources and not 'toy' ones. Hence we used large document collections containing both large and complex documents, such as the text of Early Modern bibles. The document creators had encoded these in a variety of bespoke SGML formats. Meanwhile, the toolkit creators had designed a modular plug-in architecture specifically to handle such non-standard formats, and so we wrote our own import code to map each SGML document to a corresponding Greenstone document. This preserved information about sections, which was needed for navigation given the size and complexity of some of the texts.

While implementing a basic collection was relatively straightforward, our work as composers was dictated by the decisions of the document and toolkit creators, as we attempted to shape their products into a form we judged acceptable for the consumers. The document creators had clearly aimed to faithfully encode the source documents in SGML, but some of the markup was not suitable for presentation to the consumer. For example, many section titles were excessively long or uninformative. As composers, we had to extend our import code to cope with unsatisfactory cases – in effect taking on the role of document creators.

Some of the most problematic aspects of composing the collections were due to interference between the two creators' decisions about what constituted a document section. Firstly, the SGML documents were divided into 'sections' ranging from the very large (e.g. 'book') to the very small ('verse', 'sentence'), with a great deal in between. In contrast, Greenstone sections are units of text which the reader can choose to browse individually. As composers, we had to decide which SGML tags would make sensible units of browsing – an easy task for extreme cases, but more difficult for others, particularly if poorly documented.

A second interference issue was that the SGML 'sections' could contain *mixed content*, i.e. plain 'unsectioned' text interleaved with subsections. Greenstone's presentation of documents assumes that a section may contain only *introductory text* and subsections, so all higher-level sections are placed before any subsections, putting material out of order relative to the narrative flow of the document. We had to force the documents to conform to Greenstone's view of sections by introducing special 'wrapper' sections around the problematic text.

The consumers can also negatively experience the creators' decisions in ways that the composer can do little about. For example, even between documents in the same collection, the date metadata sometimes reflected the creation date of the work, sometimes the date of the particular edition: so medieval poetry could be dated anywhere between the Middle Ages and the 20th Century.

The decisions of the toolkit creators had most impact when it came to customizing the interface. Their HTML macro language made changes to individual page components very easy, but the large-scale page redesign we required was more difficult. For instance, the 'table of contents' navigation menu was displayed above the document text, which for some large documents meant the consumer would repeatedly have to scroll down past a huge menu before viewing the section text – a particular problem for users in an earlier study [4]. To overcome this we were forced to take on the role of toolkit creator and edit the source code.

Despite our efforts as composers, consumer issues still arise where we have attempted to overcome interference between the creators. For example, some sections are inappropriate for browsing alone, being either too small or large, or not comprehensible in isolation, while other sections have inappropriate or missing titles; this impacts on the consumer's navigation of the document. Also, the 'wrapper' sections we introduced to overcome Greenstone's problems with mixed content can sometimes result in oversized and incomprehensible navigation menus.

3 Discussion

As composers, our aim was to produce a set of collections for Humanities users. The collections had to look and behave as 'realistic' resources and meet a basic standard of usability. With Greenstone the role of the composer is often played by librarians [9], with a wide variety of technical skills, so the toolkit creators have ensured that very little configuration is required to build a working collection from a set of digitized text documents. However, there are standardization issues that emerge from different creators having different tacit assumptions, e.g. over the role of a 'section' in navigating and analyzing text; this issue mirrors the compatibility concern in traditional 'design chains' from supply chain management. In addition, toolkit creators' decisions have a direct impact on the experience of consumers as they navigate the interface. As composers, we frequently had to switch into the creator's role to facilitate the development of a reliable and usable Humanities digital library for the end users. Thinking in terms of design chains has helped to clarify the responsibilities of some important stakeholder groups in the development of systems that involve the use of tools over datasets to create interactive experiences.

References

1. Bates, M.J.: The Getty End-User Online Searching Project in the Humanities: Report No. 6: Overview and Conclusions. College & Research Libraries 57, 514–523 (1995)
2. Blandford, A., Green, T. R. G., Connell, I., Rose, T.: Knowledge Representation Environments: an Investigation of the CASSMs between Creators, Composers and Consumers (2007) (to appear Proc. Engineering Interactive Systems)
3. Blandford, A., Keith, S., Butterworth, R., Fields, B., Furniss, D.: Disrupting Digital Library Development with Scenario Informed Design. Interacting with Computers 19, 70–82 (2007)
4. Blandford, A., Stelmaszewska, H., Bryan-Kinns, N.: Use of multiple digital libraries: a case study. In: Proc. JCDL 2001, pp. 179–188. ACM Press, New York (2001)
5. Checkland, P.B.: Systems Theory, Systems Practice. John Wiley, Chichester (1981)
6. Jefcoate, G.: Digitization for access: the digitization of rare books at the British Library. In: Proc. Kyoto Int. Conf. on Digital Libraries, pp. 103–109 (2000)
7. Twigg, D.: Managing product development within a design chain. International Journal of Operations and Production Management 18(5), 508–524 (1998)
8. Witten, I.H., Bainbridge, D., Boddie, S.J.: Greenstone: open-source digital library software with end-user collection building. Online Information Review 25(5), 288–298 (2001)
9. Witten, I.H., Bainbridge, D.: A retrospective look at Greenstone: Lessons from the first decade (to appear in Proc. JCDL 2007) (in press)

A Common Sense-Based On-Line Assistant for Training Employees

Junia Coutinho Anacleto[1], Muriel de Souza Godoi[1],
Aparecido Fabiano Pinatti de Carvalho[1], and Henry Lieberman[2]

[1] Advanced Interaction Laboratory - LIA
UFSCar - Rod. Washigton Luis KM 235 - São Carlos - SP - Brazil
{junia, alessandro_carlos, muriel_godoi,
fabiano,vania}@dc.ufscar.br
[2] MIT Media Laboratory
20 Ames St., 384A - Cambridge - MA - 02139
lieber@media.mit.edu

Abstract. We present a prototype of an on-line assistant to support a training course about workspace safety issues. The application uses a common sense reasoning engine and the Brazilian Open Mind common sense knowledge base, to make inferences about concepts that might be unfamiliar to the students. We explore the use of metaphors and analogies to explain topics, enhancing learning by using similarities to help students associate related topics. We believe that common sense can be used to take into account cultural considerations while helping learners to build analogies. A survey of students showed that they considered analogies useful in the learning process, that the system was helpful in understanding new concepts, and that it helped connect the information searched for with common sense knowledge.

Keywords: Distance learning, common sense, on-line assistant, training, education, cognitive strategies, metaphors and analogies.

1 Introduction

This article discusses the automatic use of common sense knowledge to support a Distance Learning (DL) course in a company with more than five hundred thousand employees that must be continually trained about workspace safety issues in order to prevent accidents.

We are developing an on-line assistant application that uses a common sense reasoning engine and the common sense knowledge base of the Brazilian Open Mind Common Sense (OMCS-Br) Project [5], to make inferences about concepts that employees are looking for.

We define "common sense" as the knowledge that most people agree with in a certain community at a certain period of time [1, 2].

Considering time and space constraints that people face in their daily work life, computer-based DL can be a solution to meet the current demand for continuing education [25] Nevertheless, the physical distance between teachers (here, the

C. Baranauskas et al. (Eds.): INTERACT 2007, LNCS 4662, Part I, pp. 243–254, 2007.

company's trainers) and students (the company's employees), distance learning reduces the opportunities for teachers to know about particular students' difficulties and to intervene in the learning process [8] in time to correct misconceptions or supply missing knowledge. In particular, the clarity of the material presented by the computer is crucial, since it has to be capable of helping students clarify any questions or doubts that appear during their studies [8].

Another way of enhancing DL is to use common sense knowledge to plan learning actions. Common sense is being used in the learning process in order to achieve pedagogical goals [3, 4, 9].

It is often possible to find metaphors and analogies in common sense knowledge bases [15] and, according to Liebman [16] and Neris et al. [18,19], these elements can be used as a stimulus to activate the use of cognitive strategies by the learner.

Cognitive strategies are defined by Gagné as skills, internally organized, which learners use to guide their processes of attention, learning, memory and thinking. The elements used to stimulate such strategies are called cognitive operators [14].

Our on-line assistant looks for metaphors and analogies in common sense knowledge base, and uses those elements as important components of the explanation process. It presents the concepts sought by the user in the context retrieved, along with common sense analogies, which help to understand the information presented.

This paper is organized as follows: the next section presents a discussion about how analogy supports learning. (Subsequently, we will refer to learning, teachers, and students; this generalizes the specific situation of workplace training, trainers and employees for which our prototype was aimed). The following section explains how common sense analogies can be found in a large common sense knowledge base. In the next section, the on-line assistant is presented. Then, we present some results of a user test with the system, evaluating the data presentation and the relevance of the analogies provided. Finally we present some conclusions, discussing our preliminary results and the potential for future work.

2 Analogies and the Learning Process

The use of analogies is one cognitive strategy adopted by people when they want to understand some concept, and a cognitive operator that is used to make other people understand a concept being explained. This is because it is easier to understand new information when relating it to life experiences [3,17].

Ausubel explains this phenomenon when he defines meaningful learning concepts [5]. For Ausubel, in order to have effective learning, the new piece of knowledge which is being taught should be presented to the learner so that it can be related to other pieces of knowledge which are already in their cognitive structure.

As an example, let's suppose that, in the learner's mind, the concept "fire" is related to the concepts of "danger" and "accident". Then the new concept "electric spark" is presented in the learning material. If "electric spark" is close to "fire", then the associated concepts "danger" and "accident" can be used to make an analogy between "fire" and the new concept "electric spark". So it helps the learner to know that, like fire, electrical sparks are dangerous and can cause accidents.

This approach of using analogies can also be justified by Paulo Freire's theories. For Freire, for learning to be successful, teachers should be concerned with the learner's common sense, to stimulate their creativity [12]. In keeping with Freinet's theory [13], if students are familiar with cities, teacher should use elements like cars, stores, buildings, and so on. If the students are familiar with farms, concepts such as animals and plants would be more suitable to make them understand what is being explained. Furthermore, analogies can also be related to Gagné's Instructional Theory [14]. According to Gagné, learners make use of several strategies to guide their processes of attention, learning, memory and thinking. The use of these cognitive strategies is very important to fix the knowledge in learners' cognitive structure and thus to effective learning.

Although cognitive strategies are skills organized internally by the student, as presented in Gangé's Instructional Theory, Neris et al. [18,19] maintain that teachers can make use of some external elements, the cognitive operators, to stimulate their use. For instance, professors can present some analogies to students so that they can activate the same internal skill (analogies) on their own. The cognitive strategy Association can be directly related to analogies since analogy can be defined as a comparison between things which have similar features as well the strategy Metaphors and analogies. Stamm [21] mentions that activating the cognitive strategy called Analogy in the students can activate the learning surprises that professors frequently desire.

It is interesting to point out how analogies lead to connections among things a person already has in mind, i.e., cognitive structure. Making these connections means to promote meaningful learning, and this is only possible because the information presented can be related to something that the student already knows, i.e., it is contextualized to his or her background knowledge.

3 Finding Metaphors and Analogies in Open Mind Common Sense Knowledge Base

This study has been using the OMCS-Br knowledge base to automatically build the analogies presented by the online assistant. This knowledge base has been built using the collaborative approach adopted by the versions of the Open Mind Common Sense (OMCS) Project, which is based on the idea that ordinary people can contribute the common sense knowledge needed to make computers more intelligent [21].

The Brazilian version of the project has been developed since August 2005, and now it has in its knowledge base approximately 137.000 sentences, which were gotten from volunteer contributors on the project website (www.sensocomum.ufscar.br).

Lieberman et al. [15] have already demonstrated the possibility of building common sense analogies from the data stored in OMCS knowledge bases, bridging the mismatch between the specialized knowledge and technical vocabulary of experts who are providing help, and the relative naïveté of novices, who are usually not in a position to understand solutions expressed by the expert in their own terms.

SuggestDesk, the assistant which presents common sense analogies, watches the interaction between the novice and the helper, and suggests to the helper analogies that will help him/her elicit problem information from the user and explain technical solutions. Besides SuggestDesk, there was also an e-mail client in the context of the OMCS Project, What is he thinking (WIHT). WIHT watches the user's input during e-mail editing, alerting the user to possibly relevant cultural differences and analogies, regarding the eating habits domain, for concepts that evoke a similar social meaning in those cultures [11]. Another version of WIHT was developed to work on four semantic networks [1]: the OMCSNet (OMCSNet.OM), which was mined from the Open Mind corpus, and three culturally specific knowledge bases – the Brazilian (OMCSNet.BR), the Mexican (OMCSNet.MX) and North-American (OMCSNet.US) semantic networks. The OMCSNet.BR was built from data mined from the Brazilian Open Mind Common Sense database [1,2].

The intelligent agent implemented in WIHT is capable of making analogies between the networks. This is possible by comparing the set of tuples retrieved from a contextual search in the American and Mexican, and the Brazilian and American semantic networks. For instance, the contextual search in the American network would return relations such as:

```
[IsA 'soft drink' 'Coca-cola']
[PropertyOf 'Coca-cola' 'sparkling']
[UsedFor 'soft drink' 'drink']
```

At the same time, the contextual search in the Brazilian network would return relations such as:

```
[UsedFor 'drink' 'Guaraná Antártica']
[IsA 'softdrink' 'Guaraná Antártica']
[PropertyOf 'soft drink' 'sparkling']
[PropertyOf 'soft drink' 'sweet']
```

Having those sets of relations, the intelligent agent compares them. If the value of one node and the semantic relations in the tuples of one set are equal to the tuples of the other cultural set, then the differentiating concept is an analogy between the two cultures that are being considered. These processes are similar to Gentner's Structure Mapping analogy method [11,1,2].

4   On-Line Assistant with Common Sense

The online assistant uses a similar approach to that used in SuggestDesk and WIHT systems.

In this context, in order to be possible to make the intended analogies, it was necessary to build a domain-specific knowledge base, ExpertNet, using the same knowledge representation used in ConceptNet. This knowledge base was built by a Knowledge Engineer, based on information from several documents about workplace safety issues provided by the company. When the student searches for a concept, it compares the set of relations retrieved from ExpertNet to the set of relations retrieved from ConceptNet so that analogies can be made. The approach used here is similar to WIHT, but applied to a new domain.

The version of ConceptNet used in this experiment is a semantic network automatically mined from the OMCS-Br corpus, and represented as a set of binary assertions. Considering that the application is intended as a tool for distance learning, it has been designed to run over the web. Therefore, we considered such issues as bandwidth constraints, which directly affect system response time and user satisfaction. Again, because of the application's purpose, we adopted a Web service architecture. This architecture is characterized by making available the searching methods of the ConceptNet's API, implemented in Python, in a ConceptNet server that receives requests from web applications, as depicted in Figure 1. Additionally, we developed a Java module, the OMCS Client, which uses the XMLRPC protocol to connect itself to the server and access the API methods, mapped as Web services. Finally, we developed a website using JSP technology, where students perform their searches.

When students provide a search query, the web server establishes a connection to the ConceptNet server through the OMCS Client module. Then the ConceptNet server lemmatizes the expression which was sent by the OMCS Client and makes inferences about it, considering the morphological variations of the words that compose the expression. Having identified the variations, the ConceptNet's API returns all relations and analogies which contain at least one of those variations.

In order to identify the morphological variations, the system uses two techniques. The first one is the expansion technique. It is useful when students use short expressions to perform the search. In this technique, the terms related to the context are retrieved by ConceptNet's Get-Context method. Then, terms that have the lemmatized expression as a substring are also retrieved. For instance, when a student provides the expression "fire" in the search's area, which is depicted in Figure 2, the system will also search for expressions like "fire alarm", "fire place", "fire door" and so on.

The second technique is useful especially when large expressions are provided by the students to be searched. In this case phrasal structures, such as noun phrases, verbal phrases and adjective phrases are identified by the system and then the system performs a search for each structure identified. For example, when a student asks the

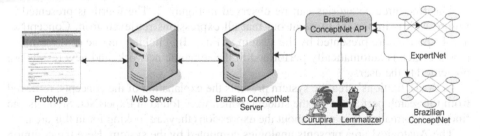

Fig. 1. The help assistant architecture

system for results related to the expression "preventing accidents in the workplace", the expression will be divided in "preventing work accidents", "work accidents", "accidents" and "accident in the workplace". This technique increases the likelihood of getting results from the search, since the terms that are searched are simpler and more likely to be found in the semantic network.

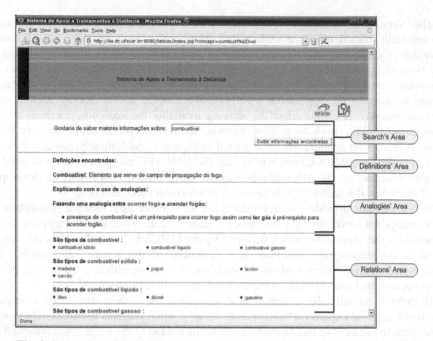

Fig. 2. Screenshot of the online assistant to distance training in work security subject

Once the system identifies the related concepts and analogies, they are presented to the student considering 4 categories in the following order:

1. Definitions;
2. Analogies;
3. Relations; and
4. Related Concepts.

The first three categories can be observed in Figure 2. The fourth is presented in Figure 4. It is important to point out that all expressions retrieved from ConceptNet and ExpertNet are presented by the system as links. By clicking on one of those links, a new search is automatically performed in the semantic network, and new results are presented to the user.

In the Definitions' area the system presents the explanation of the concepts, retrieved from the search performed by the student, which were found in ExpertNet. Students can find the information they need about the expressions they are looking for in this area.

The Analogies' area presents analogies computed by the system. Here the common sense analogies help students understand the explanations presented in the Definition area. The analogies are presented as sentences of the form, *X relation Y, as A relation B* where *relation* is the type of relation that connects those items in the ConceptNet.

An example is presented in Figure 3. We use analogies from the workplace domain to the domain of everyday life. Analogies explain specific topics with generalized examples from commonsense. In this figure, we present an example concerning the factors likely to cause workplace accidents.

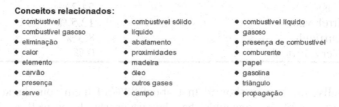

Fig. 3. An example of using analogy from common sense to explain a concept

These factors are explained by making analogies to factors that cause accidents in the home. For example:

- To expose a part of your body to dangerous machinery is like a person that leans out of a window.
- Using a machine in the workplace without proper permission is like letting a child use the stove in a kitchen.
- Adjusting or Cleaning a Machine while it is moving is like cleaning the stove with the flame on.

In the Relations' area, we show the connection among some terms of ConceptNet, related to the context retrieved. Students can use the links presented in this area to explore new concepts and enhance their learning.

Finally, we present the Related Concepts' area, shown in Figure 4. This area has some contextualized terms that can also be used by students to guide their learning process.

Conceitos relacionados:

● combustível	● combustível sólido	● combustível líquido
● combustível gasoso	● líquido	● gasoso
● eliminação	● abafamento	● presença de combustível
● calor	● proximidades	● comburente
● elemento	● madeira	● papel
● carvão	● óleo	● gasolina
● presença	● outros gases	● triângulo
● serve	● campo	● propagação

Fig. 4. Related concepts' area

We included the Related Concepts area to encourage students to be continually mindful of the context they are exploring, taking into account the importance of context for effective learning

5   Evaluating the Assisting – The Users' Opinions

To evaluate whether the developed prototype is useful to support distance training, we conducted a survey in which 24 volunteers users participated. The most part of the participants were master candidates, contacted through email, who were not previously familiar with the specific workplace safety theme in our test.

The prototype was presented to the users, and then they were instructed to interact with the system, searching for desired topics related to the workplace safety theme. After that, the users' opinions were collected using an on-line questionnaire, which can be found at http://lia.dc.ufscar.br:8080/taticas/enquete_inicio.jsp (in Portuguese).

The questionnaire was divided into two parts. The first one was about the user's profile, where 3 questions about age, educational level and gender were asked. Then, five more questions about the users' satisfaction were asked.

The questions were designed in a 5 point Likert scale, including the responses, "Very useful, useful, does not matter, somewhat useful and not useful" and the users selected the option that was closest to their opinion. We also provided a free text field in case the user wanted to express additional comments.

Before filling out the questionnaire, the users received some information about the main objective of the research and ethical aspects, including confidentiality and privacy.

The users' profile identified by the three first questions shows that 83% of the users are males between 18 and 29 years old. About 42% are master candidate, 38% are undergraduate students, and 20% are high school students.

Around 79% of the users mentioned that it was easy or very easy to use, as shown in Table 1. Some comments made in the free text field were that "the system is simple to use and intuitive", and "it seems easy to interact and find things". It is important to point out that, although very few users classified the system as difficult to use, there were also comments such as "the system should show a message to the user when the concept was not found" and "…the way that data are presented could be more concise…", which point to the necessity of improvements to the interface.

Table 1. User's opinions about the analogy utility to understand the showed concept

User opinion	Percentage
Very easy	25.0 %
Easy	54.2 %
Irrelevant	12.5 %
Difficult	8.3 %
Very difficult	0 %

Additionally, the survey showed that about 88% of them considered the system useful or very useful. We conclude that the system should be well accepted for its intended purpose, since there were no users that considered it of little or no help, as shown in Table 2.

Table 2. User's opinions about the prototype utility

User opinion	Percentage
Very useful	20.8 %
Useful	66.7 %
Irrelevant	12.5 %
Little useful	0 %
Not useful	0 %

The users were also asked about the analogies that were presented in the prototype. The first question asked about this issue was whether the user took note of the presence of analogies shown by the system. A high percentage of the users, about 88%, commented that they noticed and appreciated them.

The second question asked if the user considered the use of analogy useful to understand the concept presented. Table 3 shows that 67% of the users considered that the analogies were useful or very useful, and taking into account only the users who noticed the presence of the analogies this percentage rise to 70%. They also presented some comments like "I liked the analogies most because they help me to understand the subject that is being explained" and "the analogies were useful because gave clearer examples about the concepts' definition". Those comments just confirm what many authors have already enunciated about the use of analogies in the learning process and demonstrate the relevance of the approach adopted in this study.

Table 3. User's opinions about the analogy's utility to explain the relevant concept

User opinion	Percentage
Very useful	20.8 %
Useful	66.7 %
Little useful	12.5 %
Not useful	0 %
Analogies were not presented to me	0 %

Overall, the collected data in this survey demonstrates that most users considered the analogies useful in the learning process. Also, some observations were collected, in an optional field of the questionnaire. Following some examples are presented:

- "... the system is very interesting, especially for using analogies that facilitate the concepts' understanding from previous knowledge..."
- "... one suggestion is to drop the redundancy in some definitions..."
- "The analogies were satisfactory and coherent to the context."
- "... I had to spend some time analyzing the data before finding answers to specific questions!"

Some users criticized the fact that inclusion of the analogies sometimes causes redundancy, increasing the amount of text on the screen, possibly obscuring particular results that a user might wish to find. Comments like these should be analyzed to refine the system requirements, when systems like this are deployed for use in a real situation.

6 Conclusion and Future Works

This work presents an on-line assistant for a distance training application, using a commonsense knowledge base to make analogies between topics in the curriculum material, and everyday life. Analogies play a very important role in the learning process, because they can be used in order to help people associate new things with known things through their similarities.

Large scale common sense knowledge bases can be used to build analogies that make sense for most people, because they take into account cultural knowledge shared by most people of a specific culture [1, 2]. Explanation based on analogy has been known to help people understand new concepts [1, 2, 11, 16].

In order to verify the utility of the common sense-based approach adopted in the prototype, we conducted a survey. Respondents reported that the analogies were helpful in understanding the presented material.

Taking into account previous research [7, 16, 18, 19], we envision future work integrating the common sense engine into an instructional material editing tool, Cognitor [23], an authoring tool whose main objective is to support the teacher during the design and editing of instructional material to be delivered electronically.

The common sense engine could suggest analogies to teachers who were composing instructional material using Cognitor, so that they could be encouraged to present a suitable vocabulary, using analogies, and to present the new knowledge in a way that students can better understand.

According to Neris et al. [19], these characteristics improve the usability of the instructional material, which will be more deeply analyzed in future work.

Acknowledgments

We thank FAPESP (TIDIA-Ae FAPESP project, proc no. 05/60799-6, and Novas Fronteiras Program, proc no. 06/52412-7) and CAPES for financial support. We also thank the volunteers who have participated in the survey and all the volunteers who have been contributing their knowledge to build the Brazilian Open Mind Common Sense Knowledge base.

References

1. Anacleto, J.C., Lieberman, H., Tsutsumi, M., de Neris, V.P.A., de Carvalho, A.F.P., Espinosa, J., de Godoi, M.S., Zem-Mascarenhas, S.H.: Can Common Sense uncover cultural differences in computer applications? In: Proc. IFIP WCC2006, pp. 1–10. Springer, Heidelberg (2006)
2. Anacleto, J.C., Lieberman, H., de Carvalho, A.F.P., de Neris, V.P.A., de Godoi, M.S., Zem-Mascarenhas, S.H., Espinosa, J.: Using Common Sense to Recognize Cultural Differences. In: Sichman, J.S., Coelho, H., Rezende, S.O. (eds.) IBERAMIA 2006 and SBIA 2006. LNCS (LNAI), vol. 4140, Springer, Heidelberg (2006)
3. Anacleto, J.C., de Carvalho, A.F.P., de Neris, V.P.A., de Godoi, M.S., Zem-Mascarenhas, S.H., Talarico Neto, A., Lieberman, H.: How Can Common Sense Support Instructors with Distance Education? In: Brazilian Simposium on Informatics in Education (SBIE 2006), Brasília (2006)

4. Anacleto, J.C., de Carvalho, A.F.P., de Neris, V.P.A., de Godoi, M.S., Zem-Mascarenhas, S.H., Talarico Neto, A., Lieberman, H.: Applying Common Sense to Distance Learning: the Case of Home Care Education. In: Brazilian Symposium on Human-Computer Interaction - IHC 2006, Natal (2006)

5. Ausubel, D.P.: Significado y aprendizaje significativo. In: Psicología educativa: un punto de vista cognoscitivo, Editorial Trillas,Mexico, pp. 55–107 (1976) (in Spanish)

6. Brazilian Open Mind Common Sense Website (Visited in January 2006), http://www.sensocomum.ufscar.br

7. Beckman, P.: Strategy instruction: ERIC clearinghouse on disabilities and gifted education arlington. Disponível em: (2002)(Visited on January 2007), http://ericec.org/digests/e638.html

8. Cambridge Dictionaries Online (Visited on January 2007), Available in http://dictionary.cambridge.org/

9. de Carvalho, A.F.P.: Investigando o Uso de Senso Comum para Apoiar as Práticas de e-Learning. In: Qualificação (Mestrado em Ciência da Computação), p. 106. Universidade Federal de São Carlos, São Carlos (2006) (in Portuguese)

10. Doube, W.: Distance Teaching Workloads. In: Technical Symposium on Computer Science Education. ACM SIGCSE Proceedings, Austin, pp. 347–351. ACM Press, New York (2000)

11. Espinosa, J.H.: Reducing Complexity of Consumer Electronics Interfaces Using Commonsense Reasoning, Master Thesis. MIT Media Laboratory (2005)

12. Freire, P.: Pedagogia da autonomia: saberes necessários à prática educativa, 31th edn., São Paulo, Paz e Terra (1996) (in Portuguese)

13. Freinet, C.: Education through work: A model for child centered learning. Edwin Mellen Press, New York (1993)

14. Gagné, R.: The Conditions of Learning, 3rd edn., Holt, Rinehart & Winston (1974)

15. Lieberman, H., Kumar, A.: Providing expert advice by analogy for on-line help. In: Proc. IEEE/WIC/ACM International Conference On Intelligent Agent Technology, France (Compiègne), pp. 26–32. IEEE Computer Society, US (Washington, DC) (2005)

16. Liebman, J.: Teaching Operations Research: Lessons from Cognitive Psychology. Interfaces 28(2), 104–110 (1998)

17. Matocha, J., Camp, T., Hooper, R.: Extended analogy: an alternative lecture method. In: Proceedings of the twenty-ninth SIGCSE technical symposium on Computer science education, Atlanta, Georgia, United States, pp. 262–266.

18. de Neris, V.P.A., Anacleto, J.C.: Planejamento Estratégico para Educação Apoiada por Computador Visando a Produção de Material Instrucional para EAD Baseado em Estratégias Cognitivas(Strategic Planning for CSCL aiming at DL instructional material prodution based on Cognitive Strategies). In: XXIV Computer Brazilian Society Congress WIE Workshop on Informatics at School, 2004, Salvador. XXIV Computer Brazilian Society Congress Proceedings, vol. 1, pp. 1–11 (2004) (in Portugese)

19. de Neris, V.P.A., Talarico Neto, A., Anacleto, J.C., Zem-Mascarenhas, S.H.: Hyper Documents with Quality for Distance Learning: Cognitive Strategies to Help Teachers in the Navigational Project and Content Organization. In: Brazilian Symposium on Multimedia and Web Systems, 2005, 125th edn., Poços de Caldas, Brazil. ACM International Conference Proceeding Series, vol. 125, pp. 1–7 (2005)

20. Rosenshine, B.: The Case for Explicit, Teacher-led, Cognitive Strategy Instruction. In: Annual Meeting of the American Educational Research Association. Chicago (1997)

21. Singh, P.: The public acquisition of commonsense knowledge. In: Proc of AAAI Spring Symposium on Acquiring (and using) Linguistic (and world) Knowledge for Information Access, US (Palo Alto, CA) (2002)
22. Stamm, S.: Mixed nuts: atypical classroom techniques for computer science courses. Crossroads 10(4). ACM Press
23. Talarico Neto, A., Anacleto, J.C., de Neris, V.P.A., de Godoi, M.S.G., de Carvalho, A.F.P.: Cognitor: Um framework baseado na linguagem de Padrões Cog-Learn. In: Brazilian Simposium on Informatics in Education (SBIE 2006), Brasília (2006)
24. West, C.K., Farmer, J.A., Wolff, P.M.: Instructional Design: Implications from Cognitive Science. Massachusetts (Boston): Allyn and Bacon (1991)
25. Zhang, D., Zhao, J.L., Zhou, L., Nunamaker, J.F.: Can e-learning replace classroom learning? In: Communications of the ACM, may, vol. 47(5), pp. 75–79. ACM Press, US (New York, NY) (2004)
26. Anderson, R.E.: Social impacts of computing: Codes of professional ethics. Social Science Computing Review 2, 453–469 (1992)
27. ACM SIG Proceedings template: www.acm.org/sigs/pubs/proceed/template.html
28. Conger, S., Loch, K.D. (eds.): Ethics and computer use. Com., vol. 38(12). ACM Press, New York
29. Mackay, W.E.: Ethics, lies and videotape. In: Proceedings of CHI '95, Denver CO, pp. 138–145. ACM Press, New York (1995)
30. Schwartz, M.: Task Force on Bias-Free Language: Guidelines for Bias-Free Writing. Indiana University Press, Bloomington, IN (1995)

Proactive Assistive Technology: An Empirical Study*

Amedeo Cesta, Gabriella Cortellessa, Vittoria Giuliani, Federico Pecora,
Riccardo Rasconi, Massimiliano Scopelliti, and Lorenza Tiberio

ISTC-CNR, Institute for Cognitive Science and Technology, Italian National Research Council
I-00137 Rome, Italy
name.surname@istc.cnr.it

Abstract. This paper analyzes the problem of evaluating elderly people's perception of assistive robots and domotic environments. Specifically, we focus on aspects related to the modalities in which interaction can occur between an elder user and an assistive robotic agent. Our work benefits from the products of project ROBOCARE, namely, a domestic environment in which sensors, intelligent software components and a domestic robot provide a set of cognitive support services for the elder user. This paper analyzes a number of evaluation criteria in detail, specifically related to the robot's aspect, the way in which it communicates with the user, and the perceived usefulness of its support services. Among these criteria, the paper proposes and reports an evaluation of the Proactive interaction modality (where the system takes the initiative) and On-demand interaction (in which the user explicitly requests a service). Users evaluate the On-demand support services in personal safety scenarios as particularly useful, and less so in scenarios which are not critical. The paper also provides a discussion which can be useful for the design of future assistive agents and robotic companions.

1 Introduction

The use of intelligent technology for supporting elderly people at home has been addressed in various research projects in the last years [14,15]. In addition, recent research has been increasingly focusing on Cognitive Systems to produce aids that enhance human cognition capabilities. As an example, the project CALO [12] has as its primary goal the development of cognitive systems capable of reasoning, learning from experience, being told what to do, explaining what they are doing, and even more. These projects have highlighted a number of important issues that need to be addressed: in addition to the problem of coordinating the distributed components, the problem of providing intelligent interaction with the user is undoubtedly among the most critical. A further research area that is gaining attention concerns human-robot interaction for socially assistive applications. Again in this area the need to involve competences from several heterogeneous disciplines [7]. A key aspect of social assistive robots consists in social interaction between human users and robotic agents. For example, in [16] it is highlighted how observation and behavioral analysis of human-robot social interaction

---

* This research is partially supported by MIUR (Italian Ministry of Education, University and Research) under project ROBOCARE (A Multi-Agent System with Intelligent Fixed and Mobile Robotic Components).

in real environments is necessary in order to take into consideration all the divergent factors pertaining to the design of social robots.

This paper describes work done in the ROBOCARE project. ROBOCARE shares several of the challenges with the above mentioned projects, and has involved research groups with different background with the goal of investigating how state of the art AI techniques could be combined to create new home-service integration for elderly people [5]. As a target domain we have chosen a prototypical home environment where the presence of an intelligent assistant would be of concrete help in the daily life of an elderly person at home through the integrated performance of advanced distributed components. The most important capability of an intelligent assistant is the continuous maintenance of a high level of situation awareness. This objective is obtained through the interaction of a number of intelligent physical and/or software agents: among others, vision-based sensors, which ensure the acquisition of continuously updated data from the environment; a schedule management software agent, which analyzes the status of every activity being performed within the monitored space; a mobile robotic platform able to behave robustly and continuously in the environment. Specifically, we have chosen to incorporate the interaction functionalities on the robotic platform, henceforth called *robotic mediator*. This entity is an embodied agent whose role is to focus the attention of the user in all instances of interaction. Therefore we have concentrated most of the interaction capabilities in the robot, and, additionally, have chosen verbal communication as the main interaction modality. The ultimate goal of the overall system is to provide cognitive support both *on-demand*, by guaranteeing a real-time question-and-answer service situated to the contextual knowledge of an assisted person, and *proactively*, by providing an event-driven support again grounded on what is going on in a daily living environment.

How the different interactive functionalities are obtained is described in [4]. In this paper we focus on the complementary but very important aspect connected to the interaction between the user and the intelligent environment, namely how the robotic mediator is perceived by the elder user. We have synthesized a controlled experimental setting in which we have explored the feeling generated by some key features of the assistive environment. We analyze a broad range of features that may influence the user perception on the robot and in particular we report on the elder users' evaluation of the system's ability to provide *on-demand* interactions as well as *autonomous system initiative*.

This paper is organized as follows. In Section 2 we summarize the key features of the ROBOCARE domestic environment, emphasizing the role of the robotic mediator and its interaction capabilities. The paper then proceeds with the specific user evaluation experiment we have conducted. We outline the experimental setup, and then present the results of the evaluation. The paper ends with a detailed discussion of those results.

2   The ROBOCARE Assistive Domain

The ROBOCARE Domestic Environment (RDE) is the result of a three year project aimed at developing cognitive support technology for elderly people. Our focus on the domestic scenario stems from a series of studies of different physical environments for elderly people [5]. This choice is supported not only by the aim of improving home technology personalization, but also by recent studies, e.g., [8], that underscore the relevance of the attachment of elderly people to their home and the beneficial effects of increasing their independence at home

As mentioned, the objective of the RDE is to provide on-demand as well as proactive support in the management of an elderly person's daily activities. To this end, the RDE, sketched in Fig. 1, is composed of two fundamental subsystems. On one hand, an "intelligent observer" of the assisted person: information coming from environmental sensors[1] is used for maintaining an updated representation of what is happening in the environment. The sequence of observations

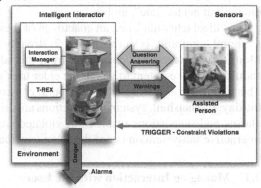

Fig. 1. Interactions in the RDE

from the artificial vision sensors allows to follow the evolution of the activities of the observed person. Based on the synthesis of these observations, the system is able to generate a report that underscores when the person's activities have been performed within "reasonable" temporal boundaries or when important anomalies or even violations on their execution have been detected. In this light, the RDE's basic functionality is an example of home *Activity Monitor* grounded on scheduling technology. Notice that, on its own, the domestic activity monitor acts as a "silent observer" and does not take initiative with respect to the elder person in any way.

On the other hand, the RDE also provides an interface with the assisted elder through an interactive subsystem. This subsystem is essentially a "proactive assistant" which closes the loop between the elder user and the intelligent environment, enabling the system to take initiatives based on Activity Monitor inference.

As a central component for the activity management we have employed an AI-based schedule management environment called T-REX – Tool for schedule Representation and EXecution [13]. T-REX

Fig. 2. Example of desired behavior specified by the care giver for the assisted person in form of a *schedule*

allows to represent a set of activities and their quantitative temporal connections (i.e., a schedule of activities that the user is expected to carry out). These temporal constraints represent the behavioral requirements to which the assisted person should adhere. To be more concrete, let us consider a behavioral pattern described by a schedule composed of 6 different activities (*breakfast, lunch, dinner,* as well as taking three different

---

[1] At the moment sensors are cameras whose observation are elaborated by artificial vision algorithms to extract useful features.

medicines). Due to medical requirements, let us also suppose that such activities must satisfy certain temporal requirements, such as "dinner should not begin before 7:30 PM, nor should it occur less than 5 hours after lunch" and "aspirin should only be taken after dinner, but not too late", and so on.

An "ideal schedule", i.e., an enactment of these activities which does not violate any temporal constraint, is shown in Fig. 2. Broadly speaking, the objective of the Activity Monitor is to recognize deviations from this ideal situation. Specifically, the system should assess the extent to which the elder user's behavior deviates from this situation. This equates to assessing which temporal constraints are progressively violated during the day. In a nutshell, system interventions are driven by constraint violations: warnings, alarms and suggestions result from violated constraints, which are processed by the interactive subsystem on board the robotic mediator.

2.1 Managing Interaction with the User

As already mentioned, interaction within ROBOCARE relies on an embodied robotic assistant as the focal point between the user and the system. Communication between the user and the robotic mediator occurs verbally. For the purposes of this study, we distinguish two form of interaction based on *who takes the initiative* to start a dialogue:

On-Demand interaction in which the user takes the initiative first. The assisted person commences interaction, for instance, by querying the system's knowledge base: "have I taken my pills?", or "can I make an appointment for tomorrow at 5 PM?".
Proactive interaction in which the intelligent environment commences interaction guided by its internal reasoning. Within ROBOCARE, constraint violations have been considered as a *trigger* for the system to take the initiative and perform some actions: issue an alarm in case of illness, or verbalize warnings and suggestions.

Our work explicitly focuses on the development of active and, at the same time, unobtrusive services to integrate within the artificial assistant. All interaction services rely on the Interaction Manager. This module essentially consists in a rule-based system that fires *situation-action* rules. In other words, it continuously assesses the situation and activates a particular submodule as an action.

The main "interaction occasions" managed in the current version of the intelligent assistant are also shown in Fig. 1. We categorize as *On-Demand* interaction the "Question/Answer" category of dialogues. This activity is triggered by a speech input from the assisted person. The generation of the answer is managed mostly internally to the manager that has information on the activities' history and/or on the current state of the environment, to answer questions like "Have I had lunch?" or "What time is it?", etc.

Instances of *Proactive* interaction are "Danger" and "Warning" scenarios. Undoubtedly, one of the important tasks for assistance is to recognize emergencies for the monitored person. The emergency trigger is fired by particular combinations of the input provided by the sensors that monitor the environment and the assisted person. As an example we can discriminate as a dangerous situation the case in which a person is "laying down on the kitchen floor" or "laying down in bed half and hour after usual wake up", rather than "laying down in bed within an expected period" which is recognized as a regular situation. The danger trigger is dealt with by a specific behavior of the multi-agent system that interrupts the usual flow of activities and undertakes an action: the robot is sent to the assisted person, a specific dialogue is attempted, and if no answer from the assisted person is obtained, an *Alarm* is immediately fired to the external world (call to a relative, to an emergency help desk, etc.).

A warning scenario is one in which constraint violations are detected by the T-REX activity monitor. Broadly speaking, the activity monitor decides the values for the variables that are used by the interaction manager to trigger a proactive dialogue with the assisted person. The content of the dialog is synthesized on the basis of the monitor's internal knowledge.

Overall the Interaction Manager in Fig. 1 is a quite simple planner that supervises the initiative of the "interactor" towards the assisted person. It is worth underscoring how the combination of this manager and the activity monitor endows the whole assistive environment with capabilities of proactive participation in a mixed-initiative interaction [6].

3 Experiments with Elder Users

The RDE's fundamental building blocks described in the previous section are the result of a multi-disciplinary research and development effort, combining robotics, artificial vision, automated scheduling and distributed constraint reasoning and psychology. Our aim in the remainder of this article is to present experiments aimed at understanding the perception of older people towards the assistance that the robot (and thus the assistive environment as a whole) is able to offer at the moment.

3.1 Previous Evaluations of Assistive Robots

A previous study [18] was aimed at drawing some preliminary desiderata and requirements for assistive robots. This evaluation analyzed laypeople's representations of domestic robots with respect to a variety of topics: the users' expectations with respect to the robot's capabilities to perform different everyday activities at home; their emotional response to a domestic robot; the image of the robot, referring to shape, size, color, cover material, speed; preferences and expectancies about the robot's personification (given name, etc.) and the modalities of human-robot communication and interaction.

Results showed that people overestimate manipulative abilities and underestimate cognitive capabilities of the robot, whose representation is somewhat unrealistic: a domestic robot is still too far away from everyday life experience of laypeople. In addition, people at different stages of their lifespan showed very divergent opinions and preferences. In particular, older people clearly indicated a preference for a small robot, hardly resembling a human being, which has to intrude as less as possible in personal and domestic life; a device which is not autonomously free to move in the domestic environment and simply responding to tasks to be performed. In fact, while its practical utility was recognized, the robot emerged as a potential source of danger and discomfort in private life, and the idea of a non-autonomous device seemed to be a way to ward off their anxiety. Another issue to be addressed has to do with the context in which the robot is expected to operate. The use of new technologies and domestic robots in the home environment is not only a matter of general human-technology interaction, but is also associated with the specific sphere of human life in which assistance is needed [8].

Elderly people showed a rather positive attitude towards a technological modification in the domestic environment, yet the inclination to use technological devices is strongly associated to the problem they have to cope with. In some situations, a technological aid seemed to be unrealistic, or unpractical, or it would have better been replaced by a more common alternative. In other ones, concerning health and personal/environmental safeness above all, it emerged as a suitable solution to cope with losses imposed by ageing.

3.2 The Present Study

The studies mentioned previously focus on users' attitudes toward a purely imaginary robotic agent, with unspecified abilities and not operating in a real domestic environment. For this reason, differences in users' reactions could have been related to both diverse knowledge and bias toward technologies.

The final prototype a-chieved by the ROBOCARE project allows us over-come this limitation. The evaluation of a tangible robot allows us to eliminate pre-conceptions and other biases. Performing the evaluation on the RDE pro-totype allows us to draw specific conclusions on the prototype itself, and also to investigate some general issues relative to the chal-lenges of assistive technol-ogy for elderly people. This analysis is in line with cur-rent recommendations for the evaluation of complex

(a) Non anthropomor-phic version of the robot.

(b) Robot showing a hu-man speaking face.

Fig. 3. The two experimental conditions of the robot

assistive technology. For instance, it is recognized in [9] that human-robot interaction is to be evaluated on socio-culturally constituted activities outside the design laboratory. In this light, the aim of our research is to analyze the potential reactions of final users to real life interactions between elderly people and an assistive robot.

The present analysis considered eight different scenarios, which were meant to be representative of daily situations in which elderly people may be involved. The situations were selected with reference to previous research on this topic [8], ranging from the most emotionally involving to less critical and emotionally neutral, with the aim of exploring elderly people's evaluations of the potential role of a domestic robot as a useful support to ageing people. Specifically, the study focuses on three main aspects.

First, we perform an evaluation of how meaningful each scenario is with respect to the respondents' every day life. This allows us to understand how useful state-of-the-art assistive technology can be in real situations. Moreover, it provides a precious indica-tion as to whether we are employing this technology to solve real needs. Scenarios were arranged in order to have evaluations of the robot in different typologies of interactive situations: we propose a main distinction between "On-demand" and "Proactive" scenarios. On-demand scenarios imply an explicit request for the robot's activity by the final user; in proactive scenarios, the robot autonomously intervenes in the domestic environment, for both an emergency and a simple suggestion. The comparison between On-demand and Proactive situations is aimed to offer a suggestion as regards the preferred level of autonomy of the assistive device.

Second, we focus on the respondents assessment of our robotic mediator. The analysis focuses on aspects related to the physical aspect of the robot, its interaction capabilities, and in general its suitability in the domestic context (e.g., size, mobility, integration with the environment).

Third, we observe user preferences with respect to robot's features evoking a human being. Although our robot is not anthropomorphic, it is possible to deploy it in two slightly different versions: one in which the robot has a 3D facial representation (whose lip movement is synchronized with the speech synthesizer), and one without a facial representation. These variants were used to toggle the variable "Similarity to human beings", which emerged as a key component in elderly people's representation of domestic robots [18].

Materials. Eight short movies (ranging from about 30 seconds to little more than one minute) were developed showing potential interaction scenarios between an elderly person and the RDE's robotic agent in a real domestic environment. The features of the robotic agent were manipulated according to two different experimental conditions: in the first condition ("Face") a robot showing a human speaking face on a notebook monitor; in the second ("No-face"), a robot with no reference to human features (see Figure 3). The eight scenarios presented everyday life situations in which the robot provides cognitive support to the elderly person, and referred to critical areas, as highlighted by previous research: (a) management of personal/environmental safety, (b) healthcare, (c) reminding events/deadlines, (d) support to activity planning, (e) suggestions. In the following, the eight scenarios are shortly described.

Scenario 1 *[Environmental safety]. The actor/actress is sitting on the sofa, watching TV. In the meantime, in the kitchen the sauce on the stove is overcooking. The sensors communicate this information to the robot. As a consequence, the robot moves toward the actor/actress and says: "The pot is burning. You should turn it off". The actor/actress immediately goes to the kitchen and turns the stove off.*

Scenario 2 *[Personal safety]. The actor/actress is sitting on the sofa, reading a magazine. Suddenly, he/she feels ill, and faints. The camera recognizes the situation and communicates this information to the robot. The robot approaches the actor/actress and says: "Are you all right?". As it gets no answer, the robot calls the actor's/actress' son at work, who calls the medical emergency. The final scene shows the son and the doctor in the living room with the actor/actress, who feels fine.*

Scenario 3 *[Finding objects]. The actor/actress is sitting on the sofa, and takes a magazine to read. Suddenly, he/she realizes that the glasses are not on the table in front of him/her. The actor/actress calls the robot and asks: "Where are my glasses?". The sensors in the rooms search for the glasses, and finally find them in the kitchen. The robot* *answers: "The glasses are on the table in the kitchen". The actor/actress goes to the kitchen and takes the glasses, then goes back to the sofa and starts reading the magazine.*

Scenario 4 *[Reminding analyses].* *The actor/actress is in the kitchen. He/she is about to have breakfast. When he/she puts the pot on the stove to warm up the milk, the robot says: "You cannot have breakfast now. You have an appointment for a medical analysis". The actor/actress answers: "You're right. I had forgotten all about it!".*

Scenario 5 *[Activity planning].* *The actor/actress is having a call in the living room. He/she is speaking to the secretary of a clinical center to have an appointment for a medical examination. The secretary proposes an appointment for the next day, with two alternatives: one in the morning, the other in the afternoon. The actor/actress asks the robot for eventual engagements in the following day. The robot answers: "You have another engagement in the morning. In the afternoon, you do not have any appointment". The actor/actress accepts the appointment in the afternoon.*

Scenario 6 *[Reminding medication].* *The actor/actress is sleeping on the sofa, and suddenly wakes up. He/she does not realize what time is it, and thus he/she asks the robot. The robot answers: "It is four o'clock". The actor/actress does not remember whether or not he/she took his/her medicine after lunch, and asks the robot. The robot answers: "Yes, you took it."*

Scenario 7 *[Suggestions].* *The actor/actress is watching TV on the sofa. It is five o'clock. The robot enters the living room and says: "You have been spending all the day at home. Why don't you go out and have a walk?". The actor/actress answers: "I really don't feel like it... I think I'll go water the plants in the garden".*

Scenario 8 *[Reminding events].* *The actor/actress is having breakfast in the kitchen. The robot reminds him/her: "Today it's your friend Giovanni's birthday. Remember to call him". The actor/actress answers: "You are right. I will do it in a while". Then he/she goes to the living room and calls Giovanni.*

Scenarios 1, 2 and 4 showed proactive situations referring to domestic healthcare and emergencies; scenarios 7 and 8 showed proactive situations implying suggestions; scenarios 3, 5 and 6 showed on-demand interactions.

Tools. A questionnaire was developed for data collection. It consisted of three sections, plus a final part for socio-demographics. The sections were arranged as follows:

Section 1. Eight fill-in papers, each of them referring to one of the eight scenarios, were presented. For each scenario, questions about the likelihood of the situation for the elderly person, the utility and acceptability of the robot were asked.

Section 2. An attitude scale, consisting of 45 Likert-type items, referring to the physical aspect of the robot, its behavior and communication modalities; the level of integration with the domestic environment; the degree of perceived intrusion/disturbance of the robot in everyday life and routines; the personal advantages and disadvantages of having such a device at home.

Table 1. Evaluation of the different types of situations. Users were asked to evaluate on a scale from 0 to 4.

Type of situation	Meaningfulness		Usefulness		Preference	
	$Mean^2$	St. dev.	$Mean^2$	St. dev.	$Mean^2$	St. dev.
Proactive (Emergency)	2.51^a	.59	2.74^a	.73	2.48^a	.87
On-demand	2.53^a	.67	2.44^b	.85	2.13^b	.97
Proactive (Suggestions)	1.99^b	.83	1.94^c	.98	1.76^c	1.13

Section 3. An emotional scale, consisting of sixteen adjectives through which respondents have to evaluate the possible presence of the robot in their home.

In the Likert-type items, the respondents had to express their level of agreement/disagreement on a scale ranging from 0 ("I totally disagree") to 4 ("I completely agree").

Participants and Procedure. Subjects recruited for this exploratory study were forty elderly people (aged 56-88; mean age = 70.3 years). Participants were 13 males and 27 females; as for their educational level, 17.9% attended primary school, 43.6% attended middle school, 25.6% attended high school, 12.9% have a degree. Most of them (82.5%) are retired. Before retirement, 22.5% were teachers, 15% were office workers. Subjects were randomly assigned to one of the two experimental conditions (Face/No-face). The movies were either projected on a notebook monitor, in a face-to-face administration, or on a larger screen, in a small-group administration. Two different sequences of presentation of scenarios were used, in order to avoid the potential influence of an order effect of episodes on results. After the vision of each scenario, participants were asked to fill the paper referring to it (Section 1 of the questionnaire). At the end of the whole presentation, subjects were asked to give general evaluations of the robot (Sections 2-3 of the questionnaire), and to fill the final part of the questionnaire, referring to socio-demographics.

3.3 Results

The results described in the following paragraphs, are obtained from a combination of quantitative (ANOVA, χ^2 and Pearson's correlation) and qualitative analyses of the user evaluation questionnaires.

On-Demand vs. Proactive Scenarios. An analysis of meaningfulness of scenarios shows that our selection was effective in identifying typical everyday situations. On the whole, both On-demand and Proactive situations involving emergency and health-care were evaluated as significantly more common than Proactive situations referring to suggestions ($F(2, 78) = 15.00, p < .001$); in Proactive situations involving emergency and healthcare the robot was evaluated as significantly more useful than in On-demand and Proactive situations referring to suggestions ($F(2, 78) = 27.84, p < .001$); finally, the preference for the robot's support was significantly higher in Proactive situations involving emergency and healthcare than in On-demand and Proactive situations referring to suggestions ($F(2, 78) = 20.83, p < .001$) (see Tab. 1).

A global picture of the robotic mediator reveals a rather positive perception. In particular, the robot emerged as a very useful device for Personal ($M = 3.10$, $sd = 1.01$) and Environmental safety ($M = 2.83$, $sd = .90$), Reminding medications ($M = 2.68$, $sd = .97$), and Finding objects ($M = 2.63$, $sd = .98$); conversely, not particularly useful in case of Suggestions ($M = 1.85$, $sd = 1.14$) (see Fig. 4).

In addition to utility, the robot was also indicated as a solution users would accept when difficulties arise, again with specific reference to Personal ($M = 2.95$, $sd = 1.06$) and Environmental safety ($M = 2.55$, $sd = 1.01$). In general, a significant correlation emerged (Pearson's r) between meaningfulness of a specific scenario, utility of and preference for the robot in that scenario (see Tab. 2).

Scores of utility were shown to be higher than scores of meaningfulness in 5 out of 8 scenarios; conversely, scores of preference were always lower, with the sole exception for the Personal safety scenario.

General Evaluation of the Robot. As to the different characteristics of the robot (see Section 2 of the questionnaire), its face-to-face interaction with people ($M = 2.60$, $sd = 1.23$) and communication modalities ($M = 2.33$, $sd = .62$) were on average positively assessed; in addition, elderly people favorably evaluate the possi-

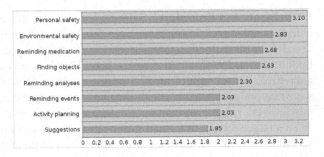

Fig. 4. Utility of the domestic robot for everyday situations

bility to interact with the robot for a training to reduce the loss in cognitive functioning ($M = 2.53$, $sd = 1.24$). The overall integration with the home environment is good ($M = 2.34$, $sd = .91$), even though a total freedom of movement is not completely appreciated ($M = 1.52$, $sd = 1.38$). Among advantages given by the robot in the domestic environment, it can make people living alone feel safer ($M = 3.23$, $sd = 1.14$), it can provide a support for cognitive functioning ($M = 3.23$, $sd = .92$) and, in general, in the organization of everyday activities ($M = 2.98$, $sd = 1.03$); on the other hand, some troubles with the management of the device (repairs, etc.) ($M = 2.95$, $sd = 1.11$) and the possible economic costs ($M = 3.25$, $sd = .84$) are expected. The robot is hardly perceived as a source of disturbance in personal life ($M = 1.43$, $sd = 1.39$) and little apprehension is expressed towards its autonomy in taking decisions ($M = 1.38$, $sd = 1.46$). Also, users seemed to worry about potentially becoming dependent on the robot in certain cognitive tasks ($M = 2.48$, $sd = 1.45$).

Finally, the emotional reaction (see Section 3 of the questionnaire) of elderly people to the robot was very good, scoring high on the positive adjectives *useful* ($M = 2.90$, $sd = 1.10$), *interesting* ($M = 2.51$, $sd = 1.30$), and *relaxing* ($M = 2.38$, $sd = 1.14$), and scoring very low on the negative adjectives *scary* ($M = .77$, $sd = 1.01$),

---

[2] The letters (a,b,c) indicate significant differences between typologies of situations.

overwhelming ($M = .97$, $sd = 1.40$), *gloomy* ($M = 1.00$, $sd = 1.36$), *dangerous* ($M = 1.05$, $sd = 1.23$), *uncontrollable* ($M = 1.10$, $sd = 1.14$).

Table 2. Pearson's r of meaningfulness, utility and preference

	Meaningfulness	Utility	Preference
Meaningfulness	1	—	—
Utility	$.854^3$	1	—
Preference	$.787^3$	$.922^3$	1

Similarity to Human Beings. As to this issue, our manipulation emerged to be effective, being the No-face version significantly preferred on the whole ($F_{(1,38)} = 6.34$, $p < .05$), specifically appearing both *less mechanical* ($F_{(1,38)} = 5.11$, $p < .05$) and less *cold* ($F_{(1,38)} = 7.25$, $p < .05$). The No-face version was also evaluated as having a significantly higher level of integration with the domestic environment ($F_{(1,38)} = 5.65$, $p < .05$) and a larger variety of advantages than the Face version, referring to *ease of use* ($F_{(1,38)} = 9.36$, $p < .01$) and a *low need for repair* ($F_{(1,38)} = 4.33$, $p < .05$) above all. In addition, elderly people seemed to be more likely to develop a psychological attachment towards the No-face version than towards the Face version ($\chi^2 = 6.11$, $df = 2$, $p < .05$).

4   Discussion and Conclusions

This study addresses some general acceptability requirements for assistive robotic agents. The general framework depicted by the On-demand vs. Proactive situations emerged to be highly meaningful in elderly people's experience, and the evaluation of proposed scenarios plainly shows their main concerns in everyday life and the potential role of a domestic robot in supporting them. Elderly people perceive a clear distinction between important and unimportant activities to be performed at home. For those activities which are perceived of greatest relevance, mainly concerning personal and environmental safety, the autonomy of the robot in the management of the home environment and in taking decisions proved to be a very useful resource. The robot is also appreciated for its capability in responding to a specific need expressed by the user, especially when referring to a cognitive difficulty associated with ageing, and involving activities related to healthcare (e.g., remembering things to do or what has been already done, with particular reference to medications and analyses).

Conversely, a robot making suggestions regarding unimportant activities is perceived as a bit irritating. A well defined relationship between likelihood of situations, perceived utility of and preference for the robot emerged. In the situation involving an emergency the preference for the robotic support is higher than the perceived likelihood of the situation itself, and the perception of utility scores highest. Conversely, with respect to activities which are not considered to be essential in everyday life, elderly people show

---

^{3} $p < .001$.

a tendency to assign a low score on likelihood of occurrence, and even lower scores on usefulness and preference.

Overall, even if emergencies are not likely to occur, their central role in elderly people's experience makes the perceived utility of and the expressed preference towards a proactive robot higher. This picture is in line with the model of successful aging put forward by [2], which stresses the role of selection and optimization of activities with increasing age, and the importance of compensation strategies to manage the loss of personal resources.

A difference emerged when comparing our results with other studies concerning evaluations of a domestic robot [17]: our study highlighted that elderly people are not afraid of the robot's autonomy, when they can actually understand what a robot can do in the domestic environment. In other words, a representation grounded on unrealistic ideas (as the ones proposed by science fiction) may negatively bias attitudes and expectations.

The overall evaluation of the robot emerged to be very positive, with reference to many specific features, ranging from interaction modalities to the degree of integration in the domestic environment. In this respect, however, the issue of safety confirmed to play a key role in elderly people's experience and, though not anxious about it, they would like the robot to move in the domestic environment only when a specific task has to be performed. The idea of the robot as a possible source of intrusion/disturbance in personal life, as depicted in previous research (see [18]) did not emerge: again, this confirms the difference between studies on mere representations and research focusing on actual interactions. The most distinctive feature of the robot was undoubtedly associated to its practical utility, as emerged from both a cognitive and an affective evaluation. The robot can help people in the management of everyday activities requiring an efficient cognitive functioning, which is likely to be defective with increasing age. In addition, the presence of such a device in the domestic environment appears to be fundamental in making elderly people feel safer, especially when they live alone. On the other hand, elderly people also showed to be aware of potential troubles with the robot, for both practical and psychological reasons. The practical difficulties are mainly expected with reference to the price they have to pay, both to acquire the assistive robot and to keep it efficient. More importantly from a psychological point of view, elderly people seem to forecast a potential loss in personal autonomy depending on the robot, which may lead them to reduce perceived competence and self-efficacy [3], key factors for a successful ageing of people [11,19,10]. In this respect, they showed to appreciate the possibility to interact with the robot not only passively relying on its capabilities, but also through an active training to enhance their cognitive functioning. Beyond the cognitive component of their attitude, also the affective one emerged to be definitely positive, being the robotic agent depicted in terms of relaxation and interest, and hardly recognized as a source of danger, fear and other negative affects.

The physical aspect of the robot emerged to be an important feature which can help support acceptability. Any allusion to human beings seemed to have an impact on the relationship between elderly people and their domestic environment. In particular, the No-face version of the robot was definitely preferred, and the physical aspect proved to affect also the evaluation of other features which are apparently unrelated. In fact, the No-face version was perceived as less artificial and psychologically distant from the user, better integrated in the home setting and easier to manage. In other words, the better the aspect, the stronger the perception of positive qualities attributed to the robot. This suggests the occurrence of a halo effect, consistently emerging in social sciences with reference to personality judgements (e.g., [1]).

Given its exploratory purposes, some shortcomings of the present study should be recognized. First of all, our preliminary results emerged from a small sample, and a stronger statistical robustness is indeed needed. In addition, our study presumably lacks external validity, in that our respondents were rather well-educated and in general in sufficiently good health conditions: the evaluation of a robotic agent which has to be a support for impairments related to ageing may be different when people are in a condition of critical need. Nonetheless, our findings can be considered an intriguing starting point to address the issue of acceptability of robotic agents in everyday life of elderly people. One concern has to do with the general role of a domestic robot in the everyday experience of elderly people. In their eyes, the robot is perceived as a practical device: they do not seem to be particularly interested in matters of aspect, shape, cover materials; and they would like it not to resemble a human being. On the other hand, interaction which involves a face-to-face relationship seemed to reduce a feeling of emotional distance from this device. In this respect, it would be interesting to evaluate in further research a possible difference in response to a domestic assistive device which cannot move about in the environment. An environmental system equipped with software, sensory and speaking services would probably be able to perform the same activities provided by the mobile device shown in this study, but acceptability might be significantly affected by such a difference. In particular, we feel the need to stress the importance of employing experimental procedures involving real users and referring to everyday domestic situations in order to get helpful guidelines for future developments in assistive home technology.

Acknowledgements

Special thanks to the colleagues of the Dept. of Computer and Systems Science (DIS) of the University of Rome "La Sapienza" for joint work on the ROBOCARE intelligent environment.

References

1. Asch, S.E.: Forming impressions of personality. Journal of Abnormal and Social Psychology (41), 258–290 (1946)
2. Baltes, P.B., Baltes, M.M.: Psychological Perspectives on Successful Aging: The Model of Selecive Optimization with Compensation, pp. 1–34. Cambridge Univ. Press, New York (1990)
3. Bandura, A.: Self-efficacy: Toward a unifying theory of behavioural change. Psychological Review 84, 191–215 (1977)
4. Cesta, A., Cortellessa, G., Pecora, F., Rasconi, R.: Supporting Interaction in the RoboCare Intelligent Assistive Environment. In: Proccedings of AAAI Spring Symposium on Interaction Challenges for Intelligent Assistants (2007)

5. Cesta, A., Pecora, F.: Integrating Intelligent Systems for Elder Care in RoboCare. In: Mann, W.C., Helal, A. (eds.) Promoting Independence for Older Persons with Disabilities, pp. 65–73. IOS Press, Amsterdam (2006)
6. Cortellessa, G., Cesta, A.: Evaluating Mixed-Initiative Systems: An Experimental Approach. In: ICAPS-06. Proceedings of the 16th International Conference on Automated Planning & Scheduling (2006)
7. Feil-Seifer, D., Mataric', M.J.: Defining socially assistive robotics. In: ICORR-05. Proc. 9th Int. Conf. on Rehabilitation Robotics, June, pp. 465–468. IEEE Press, Los Alamitos (2005)
8. Giuliani, M.V., Scopelliti, M., Fornara, F.: Elderly people at home: technological help in everyday activities. In: ROMAN 2005. IEEE International Workshop on Robot and Human Interactive Communication, pp. 365–370. IEEE Computer Society Press, Los Alamitos (2005)
9. Hutchins, E.: Cognition in the Wild. MIT Press, Cambridge (1995)
10. Lawton, M.P.: Time budgets of older people: A window on four lifestyles. Journal of Gerontology 37, 115–123 (1982)
11. McAvay, G.J., Seeman, T.E., Rodin, J.: A longitudinal study of change in domain-specific self-efficacy among older adults. Journal of Gerontology 51, 243–253 (1996)
12. Myers, K.: CALO: Building an intelligent personal assistant. In: AAAI-06. Invited Talk. The Twenty-First National Conference on Artificial Intelligence and the Eighteenth Innovative Applications of Artificial Intelligence Conference (2006)
13. Pecora, F., Rasconi, R., Cortellessa, G., Cesta, A.: User-Oriented Problem Abstractions in Scheduling, Customization and Reuse in Scheduling Software Architectures. Innovations in Systems and Software Engineering 2(1), 1–16 (2006)
14. Pineau, J., Montemerlo, M., Pollack, M., Roy, N., Thrun, S.: Towards Robotic Assistants in Nursing Homes: Challenges and Results. Robotics and Autonomous Systems 42(3–4), 271–281 (2003)
15. Pollack, M.E.: Intelligent Technology for an Aging Population:The Use of AI to Assist Elders with Cognitive Impairment. AI Magazine 26(2), 9–24 (2005)
16. Simmons, R., Sabanovic, S., Michalowski, M.P.: Robots in the wild: Observing human-robot social interaction outside the lab. In: Proceedings of the International Workshop on Advanced Motion Control, Istanbul, Turkey (March 2006)
17. Scopelliti, M., Giuliani, M.V., D'Amico, A.M., Fornara, F.: If I had a robot ... peoples' representation of domestic robots. In: Keates, S., Clarkson, P.J., Langdon, P.M., Robinson, P. (eds.) Design for a more inclusive world, pp. 257–266. Springer-Verlag, London (2004)
18. Scopelliti, M., Giuliani, M.V., Fornara, F.: Robots in a domestic setting: A psychological approach. Universal Access in the Information Society 4(2), 146–155 (2005)
19. Willis, S.L.: Everyday cognitive competence in elderly persons: Conceptual issues and empirical findings. The Gerontologist 36, 595–601 (1996)

Use and Implications of a Shared, Forecasting Calendar

Joe Tullio[1] and Elizabeth D. Mynatt[2]

[1] Motorola Labs
Schaumburg, Illinois, USA
joe.tullio@motorola.com
[2] Graphics, Visualization, and Usability Center
Georgia Institute of Technology
Atlanta, Georgia, USA
mynatt@cc.gatech.edu

Abstract. Changes in modern work environments, combined with advances in sensing and machine intelligence, have given rise to a new class of groupware applications that seeks to facilitate workplace communication through the prediction of future availability and/or location. We present the results of a four-month deployment of an experimental predictive calendar system in an academic setting. While participants appreciated several novel features of the system, most resisted adoption due to the uncertainty of its predictions, its effects on privacy and impression management, and accessibility issues. We present implications for designers who seek to incorporate forecasting components into their groupware tools using observations from the study.

Keywords: Groupware calendar system, evaluation, intelligent user interfaces, forecasting, communication, privacy.

1 Introduction

Informal communication remains a critical aspect of work. However, groupware tools that are used to facilitate and mediate informal communication are less useful when people become increasingly mobile or have more flexible schedules. In response, researchers have undertaken projects that make use of new advances in activity sensing and machine intelligence to arrive at inferences about current or future availability and/or location [4, 8, 11, 12, 15]. In most cases, they are intended to foster better informal communication in the workplace. To date, a great deal of progress has been made towards designing architectures for such systems and improving their performance through various representations and learning algorithms.

Researchers are presently in need of qualitative evaluations from real-world environments to guide the future design and deployment of predictive groupware systems. Such evaluations can provide insights beyond their feasibility, reliability, and accuracy. Important observations can be made about how forecasts of availability and presence meet objectives of facilitating both formal and informal communication while respecting privacy and social norms.

C. Baranauskas et al. (Eds.): INTERACT 2007, LNCS 4662, Part I, pp. 269–282, 2007.
© IFIP International Federation for Information Processing 2007

In this paper, we use an augmented shared calendar system called Augur as the basis such a study. By incorporating user models and machine learning techniques, Augur enhances a traditional calendar interface with predictions of attendance at future events. In addition, Augur identifies events scheduled by multiple colleagues and displays these matches in the standard calendar view.

We present the results of a field study of Augur in an academic setting, examining how participants with varying job descriptions, working relationships, and existing scheduling practices used the system over a period of four months. We found that participants appreciated the event-matching feature and used it as a means of maintaining social and workplace awareness. We also found that attendance predictions benefited a subset of working relationships within our user population.

However, we also found that the uncertainty inherent in Augur's user models, combined with non-routine periods during the study, created additional privacy and impression management tasks that may have outweighed the benefits of forecasting for some users. These issues, combined with a lack of accessibility, resulted in limited adoption of Augur as a primary calendar application. This work nonetheless provides insights for future systems by recommending lightweight design elements to support calendars as social awareness tools, to institute privacy protections for third-parties, and to include additional controls for impression management.

2 Related Work

A number of existing research systems seek to predict the current and future states of their users. These systems can manage incoming electronic notifications [9] or phone calls [11] based on sensed activity, or can forecast states of interruptibility and availability [2, 4, 5, 10, 13]. While many of these systems have been deployed, there are few published results on the qualitative effects these systems have had on the work practices of their users. The research instead focuses on system development and refinement of the core predictive models or machine learning techniques.

Fogarty et al. augmented an instant messaging client with predictions of interruptibility and deployed it to several workgroups [5]. Through quantitative analysis of use logs, the researchers examined how predictive information affected use of the client, finding that estimates were primarily used to determine presence.

The motivations underlying most systems that forecast presence and availability are to streamline informal communication, a well-studied aspect of workplace collaboration [20]. For our purposes, we used a definition that defines communicative formality as a continuum along dimensions such as preset agenda, number of participants, and advance planning [14].

Groupware calendar systems represent an important class of tools for enabling this communication. Work by Palen [16] as well as work she performed with Grudin [7, 17] examined electronic calendar use at two large companies, finding that workers often browsed their colleagues' calendars to infer where they might be and when they might return to their offices. Mynatt and Tullio observe that if two coworkers share some events on their calendars, one of them can wait until one of those shared events takes place to "ambush" the other for an informal chat [15]. When a calendar includes conflicting events or infrequently attended events, however, its value as a reliable predictor of a person's true schedule is weakened.

3 The Augur Calendar System

Augur is a web-based shared calendar system that predicts a person's attendance at their future events [19]. In addition, Augur identifies when the same event has been scheduled by multiple colleagues and displays these matched events on the user's calendar. Augur is designed to mitigate communication problems associated with poor calendar maintenance, inadequate firsthand knowledge of schedules, and low collocation by enabling a more reliable view of a colleague's calendar. By automatically synchronizing schedule data from PDAs or other desktop calendar applications, Augur does not force users to learn a new interface for creating and editing their schedules. Rather, it serves as a read-only service capable of displaying user calendars on most web browsers. Augur predicts attendance at future scheduled events by using manually-created Bayesian networks that encode the probabilistic relationships between various attributes of those events. These attributes include explicit properties such as start/end times and alarm settings as well as inferred properties such as event type (individual meeting, seminar, etc.) and building-level location. Inferred properties are classified using support-vector machines trained on labeled events. Lastly, the Bayesian models learn over time from self-reported attendance data, and attendance predictions are updated daily.

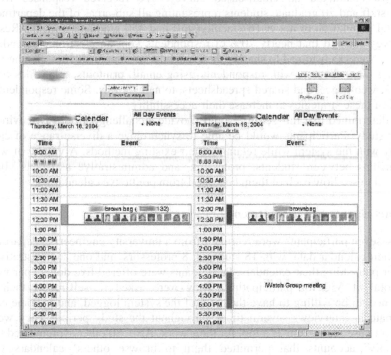

Fig. 1. The Augur calendar system. Two colleague calendars are shown side-by-side with the same event scheduled at noon. Icons within each event indicate colleagues who have also scheduled the event. Attendance predictions are shown as vertical bars next to each event, and as colored borders around colleague icons.

A screen shot of the main Augur interface is shown in Figure 1. The standard tabular calendar format is used, but additional graphical elements encode the predictive information. Color-coded vertical bars indicate attendance likelihood for a given event, while thumbnail portraits inside the event's cell indicate which of the user's colleagues also have the event scheduled. Colored borders around these portraits indicate the likelihood of attendance by those colleagues. Color codes range from bright green for a high likelihood of attendance to bright red for a very low likelihood, with yellow being neutral. Clicking on a portrait allows a user to view that colleague's schedule alongside her own schedule. Access-control lists are used to control who can view another user's calendar.

4   Method

4.1   Study Site

We deployed Augur in an academic setting that offered a familiar set of tasks and relationships but made no guarantees that existing practices were compatible with the introduction of a groupware calendar system. To gauge the extent of technology use for the purposes of scheduling and communicating among students, professors, and staff, we conducted an email-based survey. We received responses from 33 faculty/staff and 70 graduate students representing all sub-areas of the department out of a total population of about 167 faculty/staff and 450 graduate students. Results of the survey showed that nearly 70% of respondents kept an electronic calendar, and that 30% were accustomed to sharing their calendar in some fashion. Calendar sharing strategies were diverse, with respondents using email, printouts, .plan files on Unix systems, web pages, and shared spreadsheets, to name a few. Some respondents used several of these strategies to increase their accessibility.

We determined that this setting would provide a challenging but rich environment for our study. Participants would be able to synchronize a diverse range of calendar artifacts with the system while retaining their existing methods. A variety of working relationships between students, professors, and administrative assistants could be examined to see how each of them benefited from predictive calendaring.

4.2   Participants and Recruitment

Twenty-seven participants were recruited from a university engineering department to share their calendar data, with 18 students, 8 professors, and one administrative staff member publishing their calendars. Participants were offered five dollars per week up to a total of $50 for participating. They were asked to self-report their event attendance, to be willing to have their use of the system logged, and in some cases to participate in interviews several times throughout the study period. They were not required to use the system as a tool for their work. Also, 30 others volunteered to have "read-only" accounts that permitted them to browse others' calendars without contributing their own. The participants' relationships ranged from people who were physically or occupationally isolated from one other to students and advisors working closely in the same labs.

4.3 Study Structure

The study period lasted approximately four months. We structured the study to first deploy a "plain" version of Augur that did not include predictions about attendance and co-scheduled events. After six weeks, the predictive features were enabled, and participants used this full version of Augur for the remainder of the study period. The intent of this structure was threefold. First, the initial six weeks of the study allowed participants to adjust to a common calendar infrastructure. Second, it allowed comparisons to be made on use of the system before and after the introduction of predictive features. Third, the attendance information collected early in the study allowed models to be trained prior to exposing the predictive features to participants.

Both qualitative and quantitative data collection was used during the course of the study. Logging routines captured logins and event views on Augur, and also archived predictions and old calendar information. Attendance data was collected by having participants complete a web-based form that reported whether each event was attended, missed to attend another event, or simply not attended.

We selected 13 of our participants (9 students, 4 faculty) to take part in four 40-minute interviews each. They were selected based on the diversity of relationships they had with other participants and the diversity of their existing scheduling habits. They were first interviewed prior to Augur's deployment to examine initial concerns about privacy, expectations for the system, and existing coordination practices. They were interviewed again after the "plain" version of Augur was deployed to gauge how this more traditional shared calendar was used. The third and fourth interviews took place after the introduction of predictive features in Augur.

To examine the use of Augur with respect to colleague relationships, interviewed participants selected up to three colleagues with calendars on the system and described their working relationships in terms of how often the two colleagues met, the degree of formality in those meetings, how much time they spent in the same location, the degree of schedule knowledge they had of one another, and how sufficient that knowledge was for conducting work together. We documented use for a total of 28 participant relationships, revisiting them in subsequent interviews to determine what benefits, if any, were being gained from using Augur.

5 Results

Augur was deployed for one academic semester. Figure 2 shows the number of events accessed from Augur over the course of the study period. Clearly, use tapered off somewhat as the study progressed, with gaps appearing during spring break (March 8-12) and the week of final exams (April 26-30). In this section, we examine use of Augur and identify which users and relationships tended to benefit from it.

5.1 Overall Use

For work-related communication, participants generally continued to rely primarily on their existing scheduling tools, the most popular being email and office visits. For those working fairly closely, tools were typically already in place to coordinate communication. In these cases, Augur was employed on an as-needed basis when

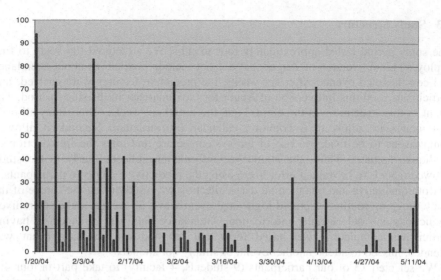

Fig. 2. Event accesses by date. Interviewed participants are shown in red.

these existing tools lacked sufficient detail. As one student stated: "I don't rely on it, but it does what I need it to do when I use it". As discussed below, however, Augur was more frequently used as a social awareness application.

By the end of the study, only two participants had adopted Augur as their primary calendar application. One, an administrator, had no other access to his superior's calendar, and the other, a student, publicized it to interested family and friends. In both of these cases, each participant had no previously existing way of sharing his calendar or browsing a desired calendar. Later, we discuss possible reasons as to why Augur was not more widely adopted.

"Calendar Surfing"
The most successfully supported and used activity on Augur was the practice of what one participant termed "calendar surfing". Almost half of the use instances (19) documented in interviews involved this activity. By embedding links to colleague calendars in its user interface, Augur lets users easily jump between, or "surf" these calendars when they share events with others. Participants most frequently mentioned using Augur in this fashion, usually stating no particular motive other than "curiosity", "out of boredom", or "for fun". Many times, however, these seemingly frivolous uses had work-related purposes behind them. When elaborating on these uses in interviews, we found that surfing behavior served several functions for indirectly sharing information between participants.

In keeping with Palen's findings, participants used Augur for information retrieval, adding events from other calendars that were not in their own schedules:

> I just had my first great moment in Augur. I found an event in your calendar, a special talk that I want to attend. I just added it to my calendar.

Participants also browsed calendars to confirm their own intuitions about a particular person's schedule. One student was surprised that a professor's calendar was the "morass" she was expecting, while another student was skeptical of the accuracy of the events on his advisor's schedule.

Lastly, participants used the calendar links embedded in Augur's UI for social purposes, either to learn more about unfamiliar coworkers or to check in on existing workplace friends.

Meeting scheduling
Augur was also used as a regular shared calendar for tasks Palen has termed "calendar work" [16]. These tasks include meeting scheduling, orienting oneself throughout the day, and reminding. The second-most popular use of Augur among interviewed participants was for meeting scheduling, with participants using the calendar to locate free/busy times. No one cited attendance predictions as a resource they used for this task, with just the presence of events being enough to cause them to look elsewhere for open times on the calendar. Instead, the main benefit of Augur was to provide scheduling information for many colleagues that had previously been nonexistent or lacking in details.

Finding another colleague
Augur's attendance prediction feature was designed to allow colleagues to more easily locate one another for informal communication. Only three participants mentioned using Augur's predictions to explicitly find someone, with a subset of participants reporting "surfing" calendars to learn more about a colleague's likely schedule. Two of these instances involved student/advisor relationships, while one involved a staff member and his superior. As an example, one student spoke of an attempt to find his advisor:

> I was trying to find out where his afternoon event was. I saw that the prediction was green (meaning likely attendance), so I didn't expect to see him in the lab then.

5.2 Use Within Relationships

Social relationships and intermittent relationships
Augur's predictions of attendance had little bearing on four primarily social relationships examined during the study. Interactions in these relationships tended to be fixed around unscheduled after-work events or a flexible lunchtime. Consequently, few uses of Augur were reported that concerned a specific pair of social colleagues. Only one instance of use, a session of calendar surfing, was reported within these relationships.

In addition, few uses were reported with to four relationships that revolved around intermittent, formal group meetings. The additional capabilities of Augur provided little benefit to them, since their working relationships are sufficiently distant that they can work purely from scheduled meetings. Thus, a system like Augur provides no benefit over a standard calendar application. The few uses that were reported were primarily out of curiosity over another colleague's schedule that had previously been a black box.

Close colleagues
Nine of the relationships we documented involve colleagues whose offices are physically collocated and who interact at least twice a week, indicating a greater

degree of interdependence. Within these relationships, however, we noticed a disparity between those colleagues who are highly *co-present* and those who are not. We recorded equal amounts of use between both of these subgroups. For those colleagues who are less co-present, Augur provided a source of knowledge that acted as a substitute for the understanding normally shared by collocated colleagues.

In one student/advisor relationship, for example, the two colleagues work in the same lab space, but due to classes, meetings, and in/out times are typically not in the lab at the same time. Meetings between the two are a mix of both formal and informal interactions. On several occasions, the student would consult Augur to find a good time in the near future to catch his advisor in the lab for an informal chat.

The closest colleagues have a number of existing artifacts available for informing one another of their schedules, including paper printouts on doors and web-based calendars. However, nearly all of these artifacts are created at the start of the term and left untouched until the next one. Thus, they lack the detail of a more fastidiously maintained personal calendar, which is more likely to contain non-recurring, special events. Since Augur shares the personal calendar of its owner, it became a last resort resource when face-to-face channels and other calendar artifacts failed.

Less close colleagues
Colleagues who meet less frequently and whose offices are not necessarily in the same location comprise a second set of working relationships that are less close than those just described. These relationships are characterized by moderate copresence and meeting frequency, and a high degree of informality. Examples include graduate students and their thesis committee members, and labmates with fairly disparate research projects. Eleven of the relationships studied fell into this category, with use of Augur reported for five of them. We found that these five relationships all exhibited insufficient schedule knowledge for coordinating unplanned meetings.

As an example, two participants included a lab manager (an administrative position) and the professor who supervises the same lab. Their working relationship requires occasional interaction. They reside in different buildings, but have a standing meeting and intermittent email communication. The professor has a number of other responsibilities which frequently delay the standing meeting. Thus, the meeting has taken on more of an informal quality, as its timing is very flexible from week to week:

> Last week was fairly typical. [The professor] missed our Friday meeting. I stopped by the office, he wasn't there. So then I went to another meeting in the same building. I came back and he was there.

The lab manager reported using Augur to determine when to make the 20-minute trip to the professor's building rather than using the oft-missed standing meeting time.

Power relationships
It is worth mentioning here that the goals of participants were somewhat different at the onset of the Augur study. With differing occupations came different power roles, whether superior/subordinate relationships or peer relationships.

It was clear that subordinates found more use for Augur than their superiors. This finding was consistent with prior reports of calendar use in industrial settings [6]. While interviewed students reported using Augur to find their advisors, thesis committee members, or instructors, interviewed professors reported participating in the system predominantly as a means to be found. Administrative assistants also welcomed the opportunity to see professors' calendars online, one of whom asked that the system continue to run after the study period had ended.

5.3 Working with Uncertainty

Image concerns

In adding predictive capabilities to Augur, we wanted to see how participants would react to shared information that was inherently uncertain and at times fallible. When participants mentioned Augur's predictions, it was often with respect to its effects on their image rather than its use in communication.

Concerns were voiced by one student even before Augur's deployment regarding control over the image presented of him to others: "I have control over my self-presentation. I can fake other meetings to control my schedule". Several other participants, both students and professors, listed control over their calendars as the primary benefit of their prior method of scheduling.

Once predictions were introduced, several participants mentioned the potentially negative effects these predictions could have on their images, echoing the concerns over manually-assigned event priorities in work by Beard et al. [1]. For instance, a student was initially disturbed when he appeared not to attend a particular event, stating that he felt like "the system was taking attendance". He was relieved, however, when he saw that a professor was predicted not to attend the same event, and said "if there are enough people that don't attend, that's ok." One professor, appearing "likely" to attend a class he was teaching, wanted to appear "very likely".

We also received several emails concerning attendance reporting. Specifically, participants were concerned about the treatment of events that were either canceled in advance or otherwise disrupted (e.g., other parties in a meeting did not show up). We determined that these worries were due to issues of image. Participants did not want to look like they were doing a poor job of attending certain scheduled events when the reasons for not attending were beyond their control. According to one professor, "with certain weekly meetings, I would always go if they were happening".

Augur tended to overstate its predictions of how many users had scheduled the same events. Models of coscheduled events that had performed well for smaller research groups [19] were inadequate for our comparatively large user population due to multiple definitions for jargon, acronyms, and initials in event descriptions. These predictions were sometimes described as "decidedly weird" or puzzling. And while users were quick to notice when a colleague was incorrectly identified as having scheduled one of their events, they did not seem to realize that they appeared on that person's schedule as well. Consequently, some users came to distrust this feature and ignore it, while others attempted to diagnose it.

Accuracy and trust

Opinions on the accuracy of attendance predictions were mixed. Some participants found the predictions reasonable, while others said that they seemed overly optimistic or were wrong for some events. One claimed that for his advisor, the predictions "made him seem too faithful" to his calendar. In expressing their degree of trust in Augur's attendance predictions, we found that participants often qualified their ratings with references to uncharacteristic or unforeseen circumstances. For instance, during the study period, one participant was injured and out of work for one week, while other participants experienced occasional sick days.

In addition to these unexpected events, participants also experienced disruptions in their schedules from periodic or long-planned events. In one case, a participant had a baby during the latter half of the study. In another example, trust in attendance predictions dropped during the final weeks of classes, when final exams and projects were on the forefront of both students' and professors' minds, with one student observing "During finals week, I'm inferring schedules more than looking at them".

Of course, one of the objectives of Augur is to infer when special events will be attended over conflicting routine schedules. However, the difficulty with these exceptional cases is that schedules were in large part not altered. Augur cannot predict attendance for events that are not present in the calendar. Predictions near the end of the study period thus decreased in value dramatically because, as one professor put it, "at the end of the semester people are skipping things left and right".

In some cases, calendar owners publicized disruptions in their schedules in advance, using "heads-up" emails before the event or mentioning them during meetings. One student complained of a professor's calendar, "If he isn't there at 10:00am then where is he?", implying that although Augur can predict when an event will not be attended, if the calendar is incomplete, it cannot offer an alternate location for that person.

Privacy and impression management
Participants reported many of the privacy management practices described by Palen [16]. For example, some users renamed appointments to obscure them. Others created appointments to block off undisturbed work time "so you don't look available when you aren't". One student was surprised at the openness of colleague calendars, saying "I looked at someone's calendar and thought 'I wouldn't share that'". Others were concerned about those mentioned in their own appointments: "I thought about third parties – does that person want their name shared?" In general, however, over half the participants interviewed increased the number of events on their calendar, often adding detail and clarity in case someone viewed their schedule.

One issue with Augur's event matching feature was that incorrect matches could more easily draw attention to event descriptions with parties who had not actually scheduled the same events. In some cases, this could give the identities of third parties involved in those events whose names were in the event descriptions. Provided they had been granted access, participants would normally need to explicitly browse the colleague's calendar to see these events.

In addition, three interviewed participants reported performing tasks specifically to manage the effects of uncertain predictions. For instance, when predictions did not meet user expectations or were decidedly wrong, some participants chose to explore Augur in an attempt to diagnose the errors. Upon noticing that a colleague was incorrectly matched to one of her events, a student reported that she proceeded to look at other calendars for similar errors, including that of the mismatched colleague.

Given that Augur presents the same calendar view to the calendar's owner as it does to any colleagues who might look at it, one participant viewed her own calendar in Augur to confirm that it was showing her events properly. In this case, she corrected typos and removed "Dr." from doctor's appointments after confirming the calendar view on Augur. Additionally, she modified her individual meetings with a professor to match his corresponding event exactly, ensuring that they would be recognized as the same event by Augur.

6 Discussion

6.1 Why Was Augur Not Adopted?

It is clear from our overview of use that in the majority of cases, participants were making more use of the shared calendar functionality of Augur than the predictive features it offered. In addition, use was infrequent and generally failed to displace the existing methods of coordination employed prior to Augur's introduction.

In terms of adoption, Augur suffered from a combination of inertia from existing methods of coordination, barriers to use in terms of accessibility, and maintenance issues with regard to privacy and impression management. While most users expressed an insufficient level of awareness to conduct work with their colleagues, Augur did not provide this information in a form that warranted its adoption over email, office visits, and existing schedule-sharing methods. Though event attendance predictions were designed to be a service supporting students, faculty, and administrative assistants alike, this additional information was not enough for busy professors who were often not in their offices or had little time to spare for navigating a web-based calendar. Judging from their recommendations, adoption may have been improved by porting Augur's interface to a mobile platform and providing one-click bookmarks to frequently browsed calendars.

In the five relationships between faculty members examined during interviews, professors indicated a strong need for improved schedule information throughout the study. Interviews revealed that professors preferred the ease of face-to-face communication over starting a browser, finding the link to Augur, and logging in. One faculty member also suggested a more portable version of Augur that could be used on a phone or PDA, thus freeing her from the need to find a PC in order to use it. While predictive information stood to improve schedule awareness that had been deemed insufficient for work, this potential benefit was outweighed by barriers to use that did not fit the needs of busy, locally mobile professors.

Augur did provide some help to close working relationships and less close relationships with a diminished ability to coordinate unplanned meetings. For close relationships, Augur's additional information occasionally offered value over existing coordination tools, while for less close colleagues, it made up for a lack of existing intuition of each others' schedules. Colleagues with more intermittent, formal working relationships tended to have less use for Augur, as did users with social, highly informal relationships that involved more impromptu coordination.

6.2 Uncertain Predictions Affect Shared Impressions

It is clear that shared predictions have the potential to cause concerns over image and privacy. In the case of Augur, participants seemed to be more interested in checking their own attendance predictions than those of their colleagues. For instance, some Augur participants found themselves double-checking their calendars to make sure events were properly matched, or diagnosing errors to determine how best to mitigate them. Even those who took no actions to manage these predictions sometimes voiced concerns with them. The benefits of creating and sharing these predictions must outweigh the costs associated with training models and maintaining a desired image. In the case of Augur, only a subset of participants, typically subordinates, seemed to benefit from these facilities, but these benefits depended largely on the participation of others, typically superiors, who received less benefit from the system.

Augur's predictive information could have benefited from more mechanisms for feedback and control, a common concern in ubicomp systems [3]. Sharing of predictions could use the same access control lists used for sharing calendar events, but providing transparency for these predictions is a critical challenge. While participants were told that their attendance information would be used to train the models used by Augur, no direct control over the models was provided. The Bayesian networks and support vector machines underlying Augur's predictions are complex systems that lack a simple, compact means of explaining their results. Mechanisms for allowing users to correct or override these models may provide this control, but users must understand the cause/effect relationships of the feedback they provide.

It is important for designers to realize that forecasting groupware systems which draw their predictions based on past behavior patterns will likely encounter exceptional cases. Conventions such as "heads-up" emails can compensate for some of the coordination problems that may occur, and designers should consider how best to support this practice such that any interested, permitted party can stay informed. Another option is to expose more of the available input to other users so that they may draw their own conclusions, as in MyVine [5].

6.3 Users Enjoy and Benefit from Calendar Surfing

One positive design element came from participants' desires to "surf" calendars, a practice that was made easier by Augur's event-matching capability and by most participants' willingness to share their calendars with all Augur users. As elements of organizational learning and socialization were reported as a result of this feature, further research could explore the potential of recommending calendar events from colleagues' schedules where access permissions allow. However, there is certainly a downside in terms of privacy. Not every workplace culture exhibits the openness of an academic research group, and familiarity with potential calendar viewers diminishes as the deployment site grows in size. In less open cultures in large institutions, additional steps may be required to aggregate forecasts among a larger group or to provide different levels of detail for different potential viewers.

7 Future Work and Conclusions

The fact that some participants expressed concern over their appearance to others through Augur demonstrates that steps should be taken to ensure that users retain control over this shared image. In recent work, we have examined how users' mental models form over the course of using forecasting groupware tools [18]. We hope to use these results to provide interface design recommendations that can enable better interfaces for conveying correct mental models. Overrides could also be incorporated into Augur, allowing users to set their own predicted attendance as needed. While this may be a less accurate picture of a true schedule in some cases, it would allow for the correct representation of exceptional cases and provide a means for one's image to better fit into a particular organizational culture. Similar mechanisms have been suggested in and [2] and [5].

In summary, the predictive capabilities of the Augur system had both positive and negative impacts on the use of what otherwise would have been a traditional groupware calendar system. Inferences about which users had scheduled the same events had the effect of encouraging exploration and organizational learning. Predictive facilities introduced new issues due to their inherent uncertainty, and suggested a need for increased transparency of Augur's reasoning. While attendance predictions provided limited benefit to certain types of working relationships, for some users they were a source of frustration when predictions misrepresented them. Designers should consider lightweight facilities to allow users to manage their appearance through the calendar system, weighing the costs of using these facilities against the benefits to be gained as presence and availability forecasting tools find their way into mainstream applications.

Acknowledgments. Thanks to the Everyday Computing Lab, Gregory Abowd, Jonathan Grudin, Mark Guzdial, and Eric Horvitz for their feedback on this work. This project was funded by NSF CAREER Award #0092971.

References

1. Beard, D., Palaniappan, M., Humm, A., Banks, D., Nair, A., Shan, Y.-P.: A Visual Calendar for Scheduling Group Meetings. In: Proc. CSCW'90, pp. 279–290. ACM Press, New York (1990)
2. Begole, J.B., Matsakis, N.E., Tang, J.C.: Lilsys: Sensing Unavailability. In: Proc. CSCW 2004, ACM Press, New York (2004)
3. Bellotti, V., Sellen, A.J.: Design for Privacy in Ubiquitous Computing Environments. In: Proc. ECSCW'93, pp. 77–92. Kluwer, Dordrecht (1993)
4. Fogarty, J., Hudson, S.E., Lai, J.: Examining the Robustness of Sensor-Based Statistical Models of Human Interruptibility. In: Proc. CHI 2004, pp. 207–214 (2004)
5. Fogarty, J., Lai, J., Christensen, J.: Presence versus Availability: The Design and Evaluation of a Context-Aware Communication Client. International Journal of Human-Computer Studies 61(3) (2003)
6. Grudin, J.: Emerging Norms: Feature Constellations Based on Activity Patterns and Incentive Differences, Microsoft Research, Redmond, WA, pp. 1–11 (2001)
7. Grudin, J., Palen, L.: Emerging Groupware Successes in Major Corporations: Studies of Adoption and Adaptation. In: Masuda, T., Tsukamoto, M., Masunaga, Y. (eds.) WWCA 1997. LNCS, vol. 1274, pp. 142–153. Springer, Heidelberg (1997)
8. Hill, R., Begole, J.B.: Activity Rhythm Detection and Modeling. In: Proc. CHI 2003, ACM Press, New York (2003)
9. Horvitz, E., Jacobs, A., Hovel, D.: Attention-Sensitive Alerting. In: Fifteenth Conference on Uncertainty and Artificial Intelligence, pp. 305–313. Morgan Kaufmann, San Francisco (1999)

10. Horvitz, E., Kadie, C.M., Paek, T., Hovel, D.: Models of Attention in Computing and Communication: From Principles to Applications. Communications of the ACM 46(3)
11. Horvitz, E., Koch, P., Kadie, C.M., Jacobs, A.: Coordinate: Probabilistic Forecasting of Presence and Availability. In: Proc. UAI 2002, pp. 224–233. AAAI Press, California, USA (2002)
12. Hudson, S.E., Fogarty, J., Atkeson, C., Avrahami, D., Forlizzi, J., Kiesler, S., Lee, J., Yang, J.: Predicting Human Interruptibility with Sensors: A Wizard of Oz Feasibility Study. In: Proc. CHI 2003, ACM Press, New York (2003)
13. Kern, N., Antifakos, S., Schiele, B., Schwaninger, A.: A Model for Human Interruptability: Experimental Evaluation and Automatic Estimation from Wearable Sensors. In: ISWC. 8th International Symposium on Wearable Computing (2004)
14. Kraut, R.E., Fish, R.S., Root, R.W., Chalfonte, B.L.: Informal Communication in Organizations: Form, Function, and Technology. In: Oscamp, S., Scacapan, S. (eds.) Human reactions to technology, Sage Publications, Beverly Hills, CA (1990)
15. Mynatt, E.D., Tullio, J.: Inferring calendar event attendance. In: Proc. IUI 2001, pp. 121–128. ACM Press, New York (2001)
16. Palen, L.: Social, Individual, and Technological Issues for Groupware Calendar Systems. In: Proc. CHI'99, pp. 17–24. ACM Press, New York (1999)
17. Palen, L., Grudin, J.: Discretionary Adoption of Group Support Software: Lessons from Calendar Applications. In: Munkvold, B.E. (ed.) Implementing Collaboration Technologies in Industry, Springer, Heidelberg (2002)
18. Tullio, J., Dey, A., Chalecki, J., Fogarty, J.: How it Works: A Field Study of Non-Technical Users Interacting with an Intelligent System. In: Proc. CHI 2007 (2007)
19. Tullio, J., Goecks, J., Mynatt, E.D., Nguyen, D.H.: Augmenting Shared Personal Calendars. In: Proc. UIST 2002, pp. 11–20. ACM Press, New York (2002)
20. Whittaker, S., Frohlich, D., Daly-Jones, O.: Informal workplace communication: what is it like and how might we support it? In: Proc. CHI'94, pp. 131–137. ACM Press, New York (1994)

Utilizing Sound Effects in Mobile User Interface Design

Hannu Korhonen, Jukka Holm, and Mikko Heikkinen

Nokia Research Center, P.O. Box 100, 33720 Tampere, Finland
{hannu.j.korhonen, jukka.a.holm, mikko.o.heikkinen}@nokia.com

Abstract. The current generation of mobile devices is capable of producing polyphonic sounds, has enough processing power for real-time signal processing, and much better sound quality than their predecessors. The importance of audio is increasing as we are moving towards multimodal user interfaces where audio is one of the major components. In this paper, we present new ways of using audio feedback more efficiently and intelligently in mobile user interfaces by utilizing real-time signal processing. To test the ideas in practice, a prototype calendar application was implemented. We arranged a one week field trial to validate the design ideas. The results indicate that sound effects are capable of passing information to the user in some extent, but they are more useful in impressing the user and making existing audio feedback sound better.

Keywords: Auditory interfaces, multi-modal interfaces, sonification, data auralization, mobile phones, calendar, non-speech audio, reverb, navigation, sound effects.

1 Introduction

Audio enhanced user interfaces have been studied for a long time. Despite this, the use of audio in UIs has not changed much and sounds have only been used for giving audio cues or simple musical tones. The current generation of mobile devices is capable of producing polyphonic sounds and has enough processing power for real-time signal processing. In addition, the devices have much better sound quality than their predecessors. Audio could be a very important element in user interfaces that can provide information for a user, give appropriate feedback on events and actions, and amuse the user.

In the 80's the main research question was how a large amount of data can be presented using audio [12]. Brown et al. demonstrated that auditory information could be used as effectively as visual information for a visual search task when speed is not a crucial issue [14]. Visual presentation of graphs was replaced with audio for data such as stock market data, economic indicators and other data [13]. Audio was also used for presenting different measurement results like infrared spectrograms and DNA sequence representations.

After the 80's, the research has extended to cover also new audio widgets, sound effects, auditory icons [3], earcons [4], as well as navigation and feedback in user interfaces. Larsson et al. have described how audio can be used in the context of

C. Baranauskas et al. (Eds.): INTERACT 2007, LNCS 4662, Part I, pp. 283–296, 2007.
© IFIP International Federation for Information Processing 2007

virtual environments [11]. However, their findings can be generalized to cover other types of audio UIs as well. According to Larsson, audio can be used to give feedback to users' actions, carry information, provide information beyond the field of view, enhance visual representation, and immerse users to the environment. In addition to the non-speech sounds, also voice can be used as an output modality. Mainly this concerns speech interfaces, in which the user can hear information given by speech.

Giving feedback to user's actions is probably the most common way of using audio in user interfaces. The user can hear clicks or opening or closing sounds when they interact with the user interface widgets. Audio can also be used to replace elements in the visual modality. As Megan [14] points it out, *"Auditory information can be used to describe certain attributes of visual displays. Not only may this combination reduce the visual workload, but it may also free screen real estate for other uses."* In addition to replacing visual information on the screen, sounds can be used to auralize events outside of the current view (see e.g. Gaver's classic Arkola paper [10]).

Audio feedback can also support the visual representation of an UI and strengthen the emotion that the UI creates. For example, if the user interface uses cold colors and metallic or sharp audio, the resulting UI can be perceived as industrial.

One way of increasing user's immersion to an application is that user interface objects produce realistic sounds. The sound can be used for providing information about the physical dimensions of an object or mimic sounds that are heard when some objects are manipulated. An example on how manipulation and physical dimension sounds can be combined is when the user copies a file to another location. Moving the file on the screen produces a dragging sound. When the copying is ready, a dropping sound is heard, but the sound depends on the size of the file. Bigger file produces a heavier sound. [3]

The traditional mobile phone UI sounds can be divided into two categories: *Alerting* and *feedback sounds*. Alerting sounds are played when there is an incoming call, the battery is running out, or there is a pre-set calendar event. Feedback sounds are played in response to some user action, and they include warning and keypad tones.

One of the major challenges with mobile phone UI sounds is the context where the devices are used, since it is more diverse than with stationary devices. According to our experience, many people find it embarrasing or disturbing, if their mobile phone makes sounds in a public place. Therefore, mobile phone users tend to turn off all sounds or at least lower the volume level. One of the reasons for this behavior is that users do not think that current sounds are useful. A good example of this is the keypad tones. If the sounds do not supply information that the user really needs, they serve no real purpose. Also, if the sounds are too distinctive or unpleasant they are usually not tolerated. These issues have to obviously be taken into account when thinking about new ways of using audio in mobile UIs.

Another major problem has been the sound quality. The older phones were only capable of producing monotonic, monophonic buzzer sounds that were not very pleasing to the ear. Fortunately, with the current generation of phones, the sound quality has become much better and the sounds can be of almost any type: monophonic or polyphonic MIDI tones, MP3 files, Wave files, speech synthesis, and so on. The phones have enough processing power to support various sound effects such as reverb, delay, or different kinds of filters.

This paper presents a study utilising UI sounds in mobile phones in new ways. The objective of the study was to provide design ideas and proposals on how audio feedback could be utilized more efficiently and intelligently in the mobile devices. Mobile devices are used in different contexts and situational impairment[1] will make the user of visual modality sometimes very difficult or even impossible. Audio modality can enhance device usability and provide an alternative output modality in order to overcome the problems and inconveniences caused by situational impairment.

2 Background

In this section, we describe some relevant background information on earcons, auditory icons, and sonification in PC and mobile phone environments. The basic theory for sound effects that were used in our study is also covered.

2.1 Earcons, Auditory Icons, and Sonification

Using non-speech sounds to convey information in a user interface has been explored quite a lot in recent years. Previous studies can be roughly divided into three categories: *Earcons, auditory icons*, and *sonification i.e. data auralization.* So far most of them have concentrated on the PC environment, but the usage of sounds in mobile devices is also being studied increasingly.

Sonification refers to translating visual or other non-auditory events into sound. In [1], it is defined as *"the use of nonspeech audio to convey information. More specifically, sonification is the transformation of data relations into perceived relations in an acoustic signal for the purposes of facilitating communication or interpretation."* In many research papers, the sonified data has been complex and high-dimensional such as stock market information [15], economic indicators, earthquake data [16], weather reports [2], or health care [19].

Auditory icons and earcons represent two different strategies for using sound to represent actions and objects within an interface. Auditory icons are based on the use of natural, everyday sounds. In [3], Gaver defines them as *"environmental sounds designed to be appropriate for the virtual environment of the interface."* They are like sound effects for the computer: *"For instance, selecting a file icon in a graphical user interface might make the sound of a notebook being tapped, with the type of file indicated by the material of the object, and the file size by the size of the struck object."* Auditory icons have an intuitive link to the object or action that they represent.

Earcons, on the other hand, rely on the use of musical sounds in presenting information to a user. According to Brewster [4], they are *"abstract, synthetic tones that can be used in structured combinations to create sound message to represent parts of an interface... Earcons are composed of motives, which are short, rhythmic*

---

[1] Situational impairment is a moment in which the user is temporarily unable to use visual modality and normal input methods. The impairment can be caused by environment context elements like bright sunlight or cold weather, or it can be caused by specific task context (e.g. driving a car) or social context (disturbance caused to other persons in the vicinity).

sequences of pitches with variable intensity, timbre and register." Earcons can be combined in various ways to produce complex audio messages, and are mostly used for supporting navigation in the menu hierarchy.

When comparing these two strategies, Gaver [3] states that "*Auditory icons are designed to be easy to understand, but this may require exacting sound design. Earcons must be learned, but they are easy to create and manipulate especially using MIDI equipment... Auditory icons tend to be judged as mapping better (more clearly, more memorably) to interface events, but earcons tend to be judged as more pleasant.*"

While the results of using earcons in the PC environment have been positive (see e.g. [4] or [5]), they have not really taken off in the mobile world. The research results have been varying depending on the study. As an example, in [6] the authors have implemented a computer-based simulation of Nokia 6110 mobile phone to evaluate the benefit of earcons. The results showed that earcons reduced the number of key presses to complete given tasks and also helped the test subjects to complete more tasks successfully.

In [7], Helle et al. have studied the effect and acceptance of a sonified menu structure in a mobile phone. The sonification design was done by using earcons, and largely based on previous studies by Leplatre and Brewster (e.g. [4], [5], and [6]) on user interface sonification in computers and mobile phones. Nokia 8210 mobile phones were used as a test platform, so the implementation had to rely on monophonic buzzer sounds, which were the only available sounds during that time. According to Helle, practically all test participants "*considered the sounds disturbing in places where others are present, especially in situations like meetings, but also in public places, trains or buses... About half of the users considered the sounds too long especially in the beginning of the main level.*" Eleven out of seventeen participants did not find them useful at all.

Luckily, during recent years the audio capabilities of mobile phones have improved greatly. New features like polyphonic sounds and sound effects give new possibilities for designing useful and informative audio feedback for mobile phones.

2.2 Reverb and Delay

Reverberation i.e. reverb is probably one of the most heavily used effects in music. It is added on separate instruments and/or the whole mix in order to create a feeling of space. As reverb is always present in our surroundings, a completely dry tone may sound unnatural.

Natural reverberation is the result of the many reflections of a sound that occur in a room or some other space. In addition to the direct sound from a loudspeaker or other sound source, we can also hear the sound waves reflecting from walls, ceiling, floor, and different obstacles in the room. The reflected sound waves arrive to listener's ears a little later than the direct sound, and are generally a little weaker in energy and high frequency content. The delay is so short that each reflection is not perceived as a copy of the original sound. Instead, we hear them as a whole i.e. as a reverb. Reverb can also be generated artificially using a dedicated or some general-purpose effect processor device.

When the reflections are sparser and can be heard as separate sounds, these sounds are generally known as the 'echo' or 'delay' effect. An artificial delay effect takes in an audio signal and plays it back after the delay time, which can range from several milliseconds to several seconds.

'Reverb time' (often referred to as RT or T60) is the amount of time it takes for the sound pressure level or intensity to decay 60 dB from its original value. The parameter is usually associated with a room size, and traditional concert halls have reverberation times of about 1.5 to 2 seconds. 'Reverb decay time' (RDT), on the other hand, indicates how long the reverb can be heard after the input sound stops. The definition of 'hearing' varies among manufacturers [8]. Reverb time and reverb decay time are sometimes mixed up in the literature.

Parthy et al. [9] propose *"an ambient communication system that modulates the reverberance applied to music with a single variable in order to communicate non-musical information to the listener."* Their test results indicate that human listeners were able to accurately detect changes in RDT from a reference value of two, five, and ten seconds when the RDT increases by more than 60% or decreases by more than 30%. Subjects were able to detect the difference between RDTs of 2.0s and 5.0s or greater, but there was a 15% error rate for RDTs of 1.0s and below.

There are also many other parameters related to reverb such as early reflections, high-frequency damping, etc. Of them, only a 'wet/dry ratio' is worth mentioning here as it is related to the implementation of our application. The wet/dry ratio refers to the level ratio of original and reverberated signal, and it is a common parameter in commercial effects processors and an audio editing software.

2.3 Time-Scale Modification

There are several ways to change the pitch and duration of a digital audio clip. One common technique is changing the sampling rate of the clip, i.e., resampling. Resampling always affects both the pitch and duration simultaneously. Lowering the sampling rate makes the pitch higher and the duration shorter. Correspondingly, raising the sampling rate lowers the pitch and lengthens the duration. The effect is analogous to a record turntable: Raising the sampling rate produces similar effects as spinning the record faster, and lowering it produces effects similar to spinning the record slower. [17]

It is also possible to change only the pitch or duration without affecting the other. Some of these techniques operate in the time domain, others in the frequency domain [18]. A common characteristic for all these techniques is that they work well only when the change in pitch or duration is relatively small.

The implementation complexity of resampling and time- or pitch-preserving algorithms varies widely. There are algorithms that implement all three types of techniques in real time. In general, the resampling techniques require less processing power than the time- or pitch-preserving techniques. However, there are exceptions to this rule. The simplest methods are most suitable to mobile environment where processing power is in short supply. Examples of suitable techniques are low-order Lagrange interpolators for resampling and synchronous overlap-add (SOLA) algorithms for time- or pitch-preserving processing [17] [18].

3 Our Approach

Enhancing visual presentation with audio can overcome problems that different contexts set for a mobile device and its use. The objective of our study was to use non-speech audio for three different purposes: data auralization, audio feedback for events, and impressing the user.

We decided to use various signal processing techniques to modify a limited set of UI sounds. As the techniques are applicable to any sound, no additional sound design is then needed and the number of UI sounds is minimized.

3.1 Sonified Calendar Application Prototype

We selected the mobile calendar application to act as a demonstrator for our design proposals. The calendar is a feature-rich application that can accommodate several design ideas. In addition, as it is a familiar application for many users and they should be able to judge whether the sonification really enhances its usability.

We copied the basic functionality of the mobile calendar to our prototype in order to maintain consistency with the normal calendar application. Users can create calendar entries and reminders, as well as browse calendar content using month, week, or day views (Fig. 1). The application notifies the user with an alarm when an important event is due in the calendar.

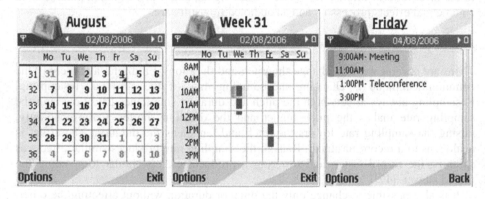

Fig. 1. Basic views in the calendar: month, week, and day views

Calendar entry types are meeting, anniversary, todo, and day note. All entries include title and alarm time. Meeting entries have starting time, duration, and location attributes, and alarm time can be adjusted relative to the meeting starting time.

3.2 Sonification and Sound Design

Many previous audio UI designs have been based on auditory icons or earcons. As there was not a clear need to imitate the sounds of real-world objects, we decided not to use auditory icons in our prototype. The main reasons for abandoning earcons were:

1. The Sonified Calendar does not include complex menu hierarchies that would benefit from the use of earcons;
2. The application was not meant for eyes-free use; and
3. There were studies (e.g. [6] and [7]) indicating that earcons do not work as well in mobile phones as in the PC environment.

Our solution was to select a limited set of simple UI sounds and apply sound effects to them.

In the month view, a short sound is played every time the user moves a cursor between the days. The sound is modified according to the content of the day. If a day has no calendar entries, the sound is played with lots of reverberation to create a feeling of an empty space. Correspondingly, if the day is full of entries, the sound is played without reverberation to create a sensation of the crammed day. There are also some degrees between these two extremes. The level of reverb is adjusted to match the 'fullness' or 'emptiness' of the day, and it decreases as the number of calendar entries increases.

Reverberated sounds were selected by ear i.e. by modifying different parameters and listening to the output. One important criterion was that the sounds could not be too long, as this could slow down the use of the calendar. Also, due to the low quality of mobile phones' loudspeakers, the sounds had to differ quite a lot from each other. The selected sounds with reverb parameters are described in Table 1.

Table 1. Mapping reverb parameters to calendar bookings

Sound	T_{60} [2]	Wet/Dry Ratio	Calendar Entries
1	0 ms	Dry Sound	7 hours or more
2	700 ms	25%	5-7 hours
3	1000 ms	50%	1-5 hours
4	1010 ms	100%	<1 hour

When the user browses from one month to another, an additional sound is played. This sound has no processing attached to it and it remains always the same.

Each calendar event type has its own sound. The events are visible in the week and day views. When the user navigates to a calendar event, a distinctive UI sound to that type of calendar event is played.

The browsing sounds have also a time-dependent adaptive behavior attached to navigation speed. When the user navigates fast in the views, the browsing sound fades out to the background so that it does not become annoying to the user. When the user navigates slower, the sound becomes more audible again. The application keeps track of time between key presses and adjusts the behavior accordingly. The adaptive fading does not affect the month change sound, which is always played with the same volume level.

Calendar notifications have an alarm sound attached to them. When a notification is triggered, the related alarm sound is also played. It is possible to react to the notification either with 'snooze' or 'dismiss'. Snooze command will postpone the

---

[2] The given T_{60} times are rough estimates that were measured manually from the waveform.

alarm for five minutes. When the user selects snooze command, a turntable stop effect is applied. The effect sounds like slowing down a vinyl on a turntable. Next time when the alarm is restored, a turntable start effect is applied and the sound restored to its original speed. Dismiss command acknowledges the alarm and a delay effect is applied to the sound. The effect will make the sound to vanish gradually.

4   Evaluation

In order to assess the usability of the concept, we arranged a qualitative evaluation.

The purpose of the evaluation was to find out how users perceived audio feedback, and whether it helped them in different tasks and mobile contexts. In addition, we wanted to know what users subjectively thought about the design after a longer period of use. The field trial method was selected because forming an opinion about the audio feedback takes longer than what is normally permitted in a laboratory test. Another reason was that arranging plausible contexts was difficult in a laboratory.

4.1   Participants

22 persons participated in a field trial. 55% of participants were young adults (25-30 years old) while the rest were older. Out of the 22 participants only two were female. We recruited participants by sending an open call for participation email to a couple of big distribution lists within our company. Participants self-registered to the study by sending an email to us. None of the participants had any prior experience with the Sonified Calendar application.

The only criterion for the participants was that they use the mobile phone calendar on a daily basis. Preferably, they should have a calendar in their PC as well, and synchronize it with the mobile phone. Participants represented this target group very well. 17 participants had a calendar in both their mobile device and PC. One participant also used a paper calendar and one participant a PDA calendar. Three participants relied only on the calendar in their mobile device. 82 % of participants synchronized data between their calendars.

It was also presumable that multiple calendar users would have several calendar entries throughout the day. 50% of our participants reported that days in their calendars are at least partially booked (Fig 2).

4.2   Apparatus

When evaluating audio feedback, the sound quality plays a critical role. Participants used their personal mobile devices during the field trial. All devices had similar sound quality. Six participants used a mobile device that has built-in stereo speakers. Three participants had a device, which is specifically designed for playing music.

4.3   Procedure

The evaluation was arranged as a field trial, which lasted for one week. We announced a "call for participation" in mailing lists and interested persons could download the application from the web site and install it to their own mobile phone. It

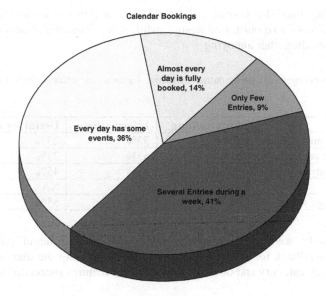

Fig. 2. Level of participants' calendar bookings

was instructed that participants would use our application instead of the original calendar application during the trial. The easiest way to do this was to replace a shortcut in the application menu to our application.

We did not give any specific tasks or situations in which the application should be used. Instead, we encouraged participants to use the application in a similar manner as they would use their current mobile calendar.

After the field trial participants were asked to fill in a web-based questionnaire, which collected subjective opinions about the introduced features.

5 Results

Our design goal was that we could introduce features that would be both entertaining and informative for the users. The results indicated that we succeeded with some features, but there is also room for improvement, especially in the sound design.

64% of the participants said that our prototype calendar was more informative than the original calendar. In addition, 50% of the participants said that the prototype was more fun than their old calendar. Finally, 68% of the participants were interested in hearing similar audio feedback in other applications as well. This is an interesting result because for the evaluation purpose we combined several design ideas into one application, but originally they were designed for various applications.

Despite the fact that participants considered the prototype calendar to be more informative, it was not easier to use. Table 2 illustrates that all features except the month change sound had more merits as an entertaining feature rather than providing information to the user. Sound effects were not really able to provide any navigation aid for the participants. On the other hand, 12 participants found the prototype to be more annoying than the normal calendar. There are two reasons for this. Some participants did not like our sound design, while others considered audio feedback in mobile devices altogether annoying.

Table 2. Percentages of participants favoring features as entertaining, informative, or navigation aid

Feature	Entertaining	Informative	Useful for navigation
Adaptive sound volume	50%	32%	23%
Day content auralization	59%	55%	23%
Calendar entry sounds	59%	41%	45%
Alarms	59%	45%	NA
Month change sound	68%	77%	55%

In this study we used non-speech audio for three different purposes: data auralization, feedback for events and actions, and impressing the user. Next we will go through each category and describe how different features succeeded in this study.

5.1 Data Auralization

For data auralization we had two ideas implemented in our prototype. The first feature was the use of reverb to illustrate the fullness of the day. This feature was used in the month view, which displays only an indicator if there are events during the day, and more detailed information is available as a tooltip after a short period.

The basic idea of reverb was perceived pretty well and half of the participants found it intuitive. However, the feature turned out to be quite difficult to hear in practice. 12 participants said that they could hear the difference between empty and full days, which have the most noticeable difference in the amount of reverb, but other two levels were more difficult to notice. 45% of the participants said that they could not really hear other levels even though there were four levels in total. For this reason the majority of participants said that feedback could not be used in navigation. Those participants who could hear the feature, considered it not to be annoying but informative (55% in favor) and fun (59% in favor). One reason for this could be that audio feedback was presented faster than the visual feedback, and the participants could at least get a rough estimate if there are any events on the day by hearing the reverberated sound.

The second data auralization feature was that each calendar event had an identifiable sound attached to it. This feature was audible in week and day views and it gave an estimation of what kinds of events the user has marked for the day. This feature was even more difficult to use than the reverb. Only half of the participants noticed that there are different sounds attached to the calendar events. Therefore, the sounds were not very intuitive or informative either. Only 41% of the participants said that these sounds have some information value. Surprisingly, these sounds were not annoying, but more like fun (59% in favor). This feature probably requires careful sound design for future iterations. Currently sounds were too similar and many participants said that the sounds were not very good.

5.2 Audio Feedback on User's Actions

In the Sonified Calendar application, there were two new features that provided audio feedback for user's actions. The first one was adaptive sound volume, which lowered the volume of the keypad tones when the participant was actively using the device, and restored the original level after a certain inactivity period. The purpose of this feature was to minimize the disturbance that continuous keypad tones would cause. The keypad tones lose their importance when the user is actively pressing keys, since usually there is also visual feedback available and the user needs to look at the display when completing a task. It can also be quite irritating for other people in the vicinity to listen to continuous click sounds when the user is, for example, typing a long text message.

Half of the participants found the adaptive sound volume feature fun. In addition, 68% of the participants did not consider it annoying if there are other people in the vicinity. This was actually the main objective of the feature. The device should be able to adapt to the context where it is used and make the usage as pleasant as possible. Participants considered that the feature did not provide much information or help in navigation. On the other hand, the purpose of this feature was not to provide any information, but to demonstrate how the device can adapt to the current interaction that the user has with the device. Overall, participants were quite satisfied with how the feature was implemented. The adaptation rate of volume level seemed to be in balance although some participants said that it could have been slightly more responsive to user's actions. Volume change speed should also be fine-tuned a bit to find the right speed. Adaptive sound volume feature was the only feature in the application in which the average user satisfaction at the end of the study was slightly higher than at the beginning, but the increase was not statistically significant.

The second feature that provided feedback on user's actions was a month change sound. This feature was the simplest audio feedback that we had in our prototype. The participants could hear a sound whenever focus moved to the next or previous month. Even though adaptive volume affected to all other sounds that were used in month, week, and day views, we wanted to keep this sound unaffected. 86% of the participants noticed the sound when they were browsing days in their calendar, and 77% of them found it intuitive and informative. Surprisingly, 68% of the participants found this feature also fun. We are not sure what made this feature fun, but it might have been the sound that we used as a sound clip. 12 participants said that they listened to the sound when they were navigating. This feature was an example of audio feedback that can enhance the usability of a user interface in a very simple manner.

5.3 Impressing the User

The most noticeable feature that was implemented intentionally to impress the user and be fun was sound effects that were attached to the calendar alarms. There were three different sound effects: turntable start, turntable stop, and fading delay.

Even though these sound effects were considered to be fun (59% in favor), they have also information value. 45% of participants considered the turntable sound effects to be informative, and for the delay effect the information value was slightly less. Sound effects confirmed the key presses in a more informative manner than simple keypad tones. Furthermore, applying the turntable start effect at the beginning of the alarm would inform the user that this alarm has been postponed earlier. Participants ranked these sound effects to be the best-loved feature in the application. The average user satisfaction was slightly lower at the end of the study compared to initial impression, but the decrease was not statistically significant.

5.4 Latency

Although real-time processing can be a bottleneck in mobile devices due to low processing power, Sonified Calendar's technical implementation seemed to be quite successful. 68% of the participants said that they did not perceive any latency in sound processing and that the application was not any slower than the original application without any audio feedback. Only three participants said that the application user interface felt slower because of audio, but this can be probably improved by optimizing the implementation. Anyway our application was a prototype and we did not have any strict requirements of minimizing the latency.

6   Discussion and Future Work

The usability evaluation of our Sonified Calendar application showed that it is possible to improve the usability of a mobile device by enhancing its visual user interface with audio feedback. Sound effects have two benefits compared to other audio methods. Many users value the possibility to personalize their mobile devices, and sound effects enable them to utilize their favorite sounds in the UI. User interface designers can still design audio feedback as they see it best. Furthermore, sound effects decrease the work load of sound designers, since they do not have to design a new sound for every situation, but can apply different sound effects depending on the case.

The evaluation showed that the selected sound effects are capable of providing information on a general level, but more detailed level may require some visual information or some other kind of audio feedback such as speech.

Another interesting aspect of the evaluation was that participants seemed to like audio feedback and they found many features amusing. This might result from the current usage pattern in which devices are usually used without any sound.

In this study, we demonstrated the benefits of sound effects in one application, but the next step would be to design appropriate audio feedback to other applications as well and to validate them at the same time. The features that we presented in the calendar application were originally developed for different applications like phone calls, photo gallery, and general navigation in the mobile user interface. However, for the evaluation purposes a collection of the features were consolidated into one application in order to make the evaluation more efficient.

Mobile devices are moving towards multimodal user interfaces, which presumable increase the utilization of audio modality. In addition, some information will be presented using haptic modality. The possibilities for combining sound effects and audio in general with haptic feedback should be studied further.

7 Conclusions

We have developed a Sonified Calendar application prototype in order to study how users perceive sound effects as audio feedback in mobile user interfaces. In order to assess the usability of the design, we arranged a field trial that allowed participants to use the application in real mobile context with their own calendar entries. The results indicated that sound effects are capable of transmitting useful information in some extent, but a more likely utilization is in impressing the user and making the mobile user interface more fun.

Acknowledgements. We would like to thank Jussi Sinkkonen, Saara Lehtola, and Jukka Kaartinen for their help in implementing the Sonified Calendar application prototype.

References

1. Kramer, G., et al.: Sonification Report: Status of the Field and Research Agenda (1997), http://www.icad.org/websiteV2.0/References/nsf.html
2. Hermann, T., Dres, J., Ritter, H.: Broadcasting Auditory Weather Reports – A Pilot Project. In: ICAD. Proceedings of International Conference on Auditory Display (2003)
3. Gaver, W.: Auditory Interfaces. In: Helander, M., Landauer, T., Prabhu, P. (eds.) Handbook of Interaction, Elsevier, Amsterdam (1997)
4. Brewster, S., Wright, P., Edwards, A.: An Evaluation of Earcons for Use in Auditory Human-Computer Interfaces. In: Proceedings of INTERCHI Conference (1993)
5. Brewster, S., Räty, V-P., Kortekangas, A.: Earcons as a Method of Providing Navigational Cues in a Menu Hierarchy. In: Proceedings of HCI Conference (1996)
6. Leplatre, G., Brewster, S.: Designing Non-Speech Sounds to Support Navigation in Mobile Phone Menus. In: ICAD. Proceedings of International Conference on Auditory Display (2000)
7. Helle, S., Leplatre, G., Marila, J., Laine, P.: Menu Sonification in a Mobile Phone – A Prototype Study. In: ICAD. Proceedings of International Conference on Auditory Display (2001)
8. Lehman, S.: Reverberation (accessed April 11th, 2007) (1996), Avalable online at: http://www.harmony-central.com/Effects/Articles/Reverb/
9. Parthy, A., Jin, C., van Schaik, A.: Reverberation for Ambient Data Communication. In: ICAD. Proceedings of International Conference on Auditory Display (2004)
10. Gaver, W., Smith, R., O'Shea, T.: Effective Sounds in Complex Systems: The Arkola Simulation. In: Proceedings of ACM Conference, ACM Press, New York (1991)
11. Larsson, P., Västfjäll, D., Kleiner, M.: Do We Really Live in a Silent World? The (Mis)use of Audio in Virtual Environments. In: Proceedings of AVR II and CONVR Conference, pp. 182–188 (2001)
12. Bly, S.: Presenting Information in Sound. In: Proceedings of Human Factors in Computer Systems, pp. 371–375 (1982)
13. Mezrich, J.J, Frysinger, S., Slivjanovski, R.: Dynamic Representation of Multivariate Time Series Data. Journal of the American Statistical Association 79(385), 34–40 (1984)

14. Brown, M., Newsome, S., Glinert, E.: An Experiment into the Use of Auditory Cues to Reduce Visual Workload. In: Proceedings of Computer-Human Interaction Conference, pp. 339–346 (1989)
15. Janata, P., Childs, E.: Marketbuzz: Sonification of Real-Time Financial Data. In: ICAD. Proceedings of International Conference on Auditory Display (2004)
16. Dombois, F.: Auditory Seismology: On Free Oscillations, Focal Mechanisms, Explosions, and Synthetic Seismograms. In: ICAD. Proceedings of International Conference on Auditory Display (2002)
17. Holm, J.: Pitch-Shifting Methods for Wavetable Synthesis. M.Sc. Thesis, Tampere University of Technology (2000)
18. Laroche, J.: Time and Pitch Scale Modification of Audio Signals. In: Kahrs, M., Brandenburg, K. (eds.) Applications of Digital Signal Processing to Audio and Acoustics, Kluwer Academic Publishers, Boston, MA (1998)
19. Davies, T.C., Burn, C.M.: Do You Hear What I Hear? Reflecting on Auditory Display in Medicine (accessed April 11th, 2007), Available online at: http://hcro.enigma.co.nz/website/ index.cfm?fuseaction=articledisplay&FeatureID=040906

Multimodal PDA Interfaces to Assist Drivers in Monitoring Their Vehicles

Giuseppe Ghiani and Fabio Paternò

ISTI-CNR, Via Moruzzi 1
56124 Pisa, Italy
{Giuseppe.Ghiani, Fabio.Paterno}@isti.cnr.it

Abstract. In this paper we present a new hardware/software solution, which allows users to easily interact with their cars' components through the OBD-II system. We propose a multimodal interface for PDAs supporting vocal and graphical commands. Our aim is to provide a safe and usable way to access the sensed engine data and vehicular status while driving. The retrieved information, which can be presented through different modalities, is used to alert the driver about some events, such as surpassing the speed limit.

Keywords: Car interfaces, mobile devices, multimodal interfaces.

1 Introduction

Vehicle driving is a daily task for most people and today's cars have a great number of high-tech devices integrated. A typical electronic assistant is the GPS navigator, which can be considered an example of assistive technology thanks to the vocal output that allows the driver to follow the route and look at the road simultaneously. Another example is the speakerphone with Bluetooth connectivity. Many car drivers use their PDAs as mobile phones and navigators because of their low weight and small size and their benefit/cost ratio. The technology has also penetrated our cars, which actually include multi-processor systems able to monitor and control the car functionalities. However, the potential benefits of such pervasive technologies are still not available for most users because of the lack of interactive solutions able to allow those with little familiarity with the technical details of car engines and computers to exploit them.

Modern vehicles are equipped with some kind of OBD (On Board Diagnosis) system to electronically read the cause of an engine failure. OBD systems were initially designed to reduce air pollution caused by road vehicles and became compulsory in California for all new cars sold since 1987. The first implementations of these systems, known as OBD-I, provided the location of a failure (which sensors or actuators were not working) and the generic cause of malfunction (typically a "circuit open" or "short circuit" problem). Since 1996 all cars sold in the United States have been required to meet the OBD-II specification [1], adopting several additional features for injection monitoring and advanced failure detection. Many other countries have since adopted these recommendations: in the European Union, EOBD (European OBD) is mandatory for all 2001 and newer vehicles, while in Japan the JOBD system is used.

C. Baranauskas et al. (Eds.): INTERACT 2007, LNCS 4662, Part I, pp. 297–309, 2007.

Most recent cars are OBD-II compliant and thus provide a standard interface to collect data from engine sensors. In fact, sensors continuously monitor the engine status and report their data to the Electronic Control Unit (ECU) that collects them. Reading and managing these parameters with a computer requires a hardware interface (usually called a scan tool) that is an intermediate layer between the car's OBD system and the computer. So far, this type of functionality has only been used for car servicing operators in order to facilitate their work.

In this paper we describe a new hardware/software solution for allowing users to easily exploit the OBD-II system services through a multimodal PDA interface. Our aim is to provide a usable way to access the sensed engine data and engine status while driving the car. Thus, for safety reasons, using the system on board should not require excessive attention from the driver. OBD-based monitoring is very practical if a handheld computer is used: PDAs with touch screens can be quickly installed on board (those equipped with GPS are often used as portable navigators). In addition, recent PDAs have enough memory capacity and computing speed to properly manage Automatic Speech Recognition (ASR) and Text To Speech (TTS) processing. Since any distraction to the driver can increase the risk of accidents, the ability for vocal input is a fundamental aspect for on-board devices: auditory information eliminates visual distraction while vocal input reduces mechanical one.

In the paper, after discussion of related work we first describe the architecture of the interactive system that we propose. We then illustrate the tasks supported and the corresponding multimodal interface designed and implemented. Lastly, we report on an early evaluation and provide indications for future work.

2 Related Work

Various works about driving support services have been presented. In [2] there is a discussion of the automotive software engineering state of practice and the newest software-driven functions, which also highlights the importance of the user interface to address the new challenges. TrafficView [3] focuses on safety and describes a PDA-based structure for inter-vehicle communication of local data between neighbouring cars (GPS coordinates and OBD gathered values). Another framework for collision avoidance is proposed in [4] where the hardware components (including a mini-PC) are integrated into the car and linked to the dashboard display. In [5] a querying model for collecting and sharing information about vehicles and roads status is described. A possible use of mobile devices and OBD systems for providing failure assistance to the driver is presented in [6]. However, none of such proposals have addressed the possibility of innovative and dynamic services to provide better support for the drivers in their daily tasks, such as indicating when the speed exceeds a given limit or the car pollution is particularly high.

Many OBD scan tools are available today. Most of them are compatible with applications that have been written for both PCs/laptops and handhelds. Some complete hardware and software solutions for PDA-based OBD monitoring already exist. [8] provides cheap scan tools and parts to build them for both PC and PDA; a freeware diagnostic application only for PC is also available for download. Software for using these kinds of scan tools with Pocket PC and Palm OS handhelds is freely available at [9]. Professional solutions for diagnostic and performance monitoring are offered in [10]. However, most scan tools are not designed to be permanently installed on the car because are promoted mainly as diagnostic devices for occasionally reading and clearing the trouble codes in case of engine failure. Several scan tools consist of an OBD cable, the interpreter circuitry and a serial cable. The most compact versions have a tiny interpreter board in the OBD connector, but do not have a switch to turn off the circuitry. Thus, when the car is not used the scan tool must be physically disconnected, and this is unpractical due to the typical position of the vehicle's OBD connector (below the driving wheel block). For this reason, we have also developed a custom wireless scan tool (see Figure 1) suitable for everyday use together with the mobile application.

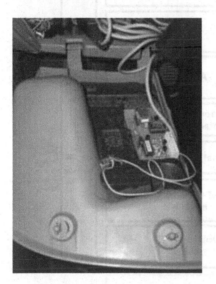 

Fig. 1. Our scan tool has been fixed to the door of the fuse box (left). The power switch is accessible from the driver's seat (right).

3 System Architecture

The system architecture includes the car's OBD and we do not make any modification on the car engine neither on the ECU. Our system is composed of the scan tool hardware and the application running on a PDA (see Figure 2).

We considered that normally a general purpose computer cannot be directly connected to a car's OBD system. The main reason is that the voltage levels on the car OBD connector differs from the RS232 ones. Thus, a direct connection may damage a serial port. Another issue is the type of OBD protocol supported by the ECU, that usually requires the bus initialization before "talking" to the car. For these reasons, we needed a scan tool peripheral to link the PDA to the OBD connector. Unfortunately, connecting a PDA to a peripheral is often difficult. An adapter cable, a special card or even an expansion device are needed to provide a PDA with the RS232 capability. Cables and adapters consume space inside the car and take time to connect whenever the driver gets on board and wants to use his PDA. For this reason, a scan tool with Bluetooth connectivity has been designed. This prototype complies with the OBD ISO9141 [14] protocol and has an integrated Bluetooth module which does not need any external power source.

The limited dimensions make this scan tool extremely unobtrusive because it can be hidden under the dashboard. The only visible component is the power switch for turning off the scan tool when it is not needed, avoiding unnecessary vehicle battery load (see Figure 1).

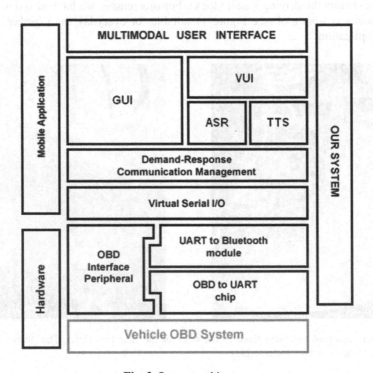

Fig. 2. System architecture

3.1   Hardware: The OBD Interface Board

The OBD Interface Board is a 100 x 50 mm circuit board. The "car side" part is the OBD to UART (Universal Asynchronous Receiver/Transmitter) interpreter, which provides a way to directly exchange ASCII bytes with the car's ECU managing the ISO9141 features [14]. Such a chip manages the OBD bus initialization and many other manners of ISO9141 features. The part communicating with the computer is a stand-alone UART to Bluetooth integrated module with Serial Port Profile (SPP). For the Bluetooth module technical details refer to [11]. It can be discovered and registered by any computer with Bluetooth capability. The computer can communicate transparently with the OBD chip through a virtual serial port. This is done by the operating system, which binds a COM port name (e.g. COM6 or COM8) to the discovered Bluetooth device; the association between port name and device is stored in the registry file, which can also be edited manually.

The designed scan tool is a very simple device: inexpensive, common components have been used to build it. Providing compatibility with non-ISO OBD-II protocols would simply require replacing the OBD interpreter with another specific version or with a multi-protocol chip. Thus, the general circuitry structure would be maintained.

3.2 Software: The Mobile Application

The OBD interpreter is quite recent and is still considered an experimental chip. No software component library is available to simplify its use. For this reason, we had to develop the communication routines following the interpreter chip specifications contained in its datasheet. Chip information and datasheet are available at [12].

The application communicates with the car in a demand-response manner. Requests are OBD "mode 1" commands. To read a parameter value, the command consists of the string "01" followed by the desired Parameter ID (PID). Parameter IDs are two-character, OBD-II compliant keywords and our application can read about 20 parameters. Note that not all of them are retrievable from every car: in the next section we will discuss how the user is informed about the PIDs supported by the vehicle. A typical PID is the "0D", which is the keyword associated to the speed sensor. Therefore, to request the current vehicle speed, the "010D" string must be sent to the scan tool. After each request, the application waits for the answer message, which contains a header and a data field. Writing and reading on the I/O stream are made through the (virtual) COM port used, specified by the user on the settings form. Since wireless connections are likely to be broken sometimes, an intermediate layer has been defined and placed between the standard serial communication library and the rest of the application, which detects the disconnection and provides the reconnection.

The graphical user interface has been designed to optimize the limited space available on the screen. Large character fonts have been used to improve readability. Input components, such as buttons, have been made wide enough to be used with a finger. The interaction is easier when the PDA pen is not required; this is true both on board if the PDA is fixed to the holder, and outboard during an engine inspection: a tiresome situation would result if the pen fell inside the engine compartment. The multimodal interface further simplifies the driver's operations: it supports vocal commands and provides vocal output so that the driver can keep his eyes on the road. ASR technology used on this application is speaker-independent and available in many languages. Moreover it is extremely tolerant of environmental noise and background speech.

4   Tasks Supported

The range of parameters that can be read from an OBD-II system depends on the vehicle's type. Every parameter is related to a sensor located on the engine compartment. Some of the sensed data are presented on the dashboard, very often by analogue instruments. However, the digital values monitoring can be useful even for the information already available on the dashboard. Reading an exact value from the PDA's display can show a bad calibration of the analogue instruments. Depending on the driver's preference a different measure unit may be used to translate the value.

Vehicle speed and air/coolant temperature can be displayed in Metric or Imperial/US units. The largest possible set of values should be readable, while the user may select just a subset of them. This is because not all drivers have the same automotive/motor skills, and each user is mainly interested in knowing parameters that s/he can understand. The next section describes the functionality currently supported.

4.1   Real Time Parameters Reading

After the OBD bus initialization, the application asks the car's ECU for the set of supported Parameter IDs (PIDs). Every PID is a keyword referring to a certain parameter that can be retrieved from the ECU. For each PID the user is provided with the flag indicating if it is supported or not by the vehicle. An unsupported PID usually means that the related sensor is not present on the car. Users may customize the parameter list depending on the sensors present in their cars and, of course, their knowledge. The upload frequency provided by the car's ECU and the scan tool is quite low. For this reason the default presentation for read values is single-parameter oriented: if just one parameter is monitored at a time its refresh rate is the highest. Another reason is that when a single parameter is presented it can be printed with the biggest font and it can be more clearly readable. Reading all the enabled parameters at the same time is also possible by the multi-scan form: the user should give a priority to every parameter. The priority affects of course the upload frequency and allows to update more often those values that changes frequently (as the engine RPM). Since the PDA screen is small, little character fonts are used to display such amount of information. Otherwise, the user can select the desired parameters from the custom list, then the parameter values are shown on a label that is updated about 2-3 times per second.

Some drivers may find it useful to correct the speedometer readout based on tyre size: this function computes a correction factor for the vehicle speed from the tyres and wheels measurements. This can be done if the user enters the original tyres size and the current tyres size for his car. When the correction is explicitly requested, the application automatically provides a vehicle speed closer to the real one. This feature may be useful when the GPS signal is not available such as into road tunnels (where speed is often controlled by police). Otherwise a simple navigator software could, provide the real car speed.

A typical OBD-retrievable parameter is the "Estimated Engine Load", computed by ECU in function of the engine status (intake air pressure, throttle position, engine RPM, etc.). As default, the user is provided with the percentage engine load value; otherwise, if the user sets the maximum Horse Power (HP) of the vehicle, the current estimated output power can be displayed.

4.2   Interesting Events Notifications (Warnings)

The driver can be alerted about some events related to the current values of the monitored parameters. When the vehicle speed is monitored, the desired speed limit can be set. The application will provide a vocal warning when the limit is exceeded. Users may also custom the warning message by entering the exact sentence that it should communicate (see Figure 3). If speech and recognition are not enabled, when the speed limit is exceeded an audio clip is played.

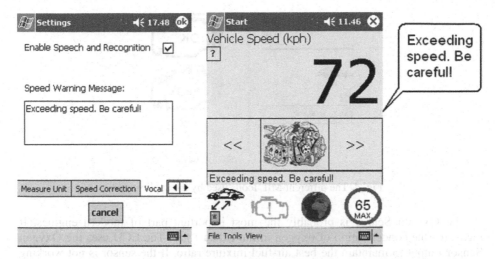

Fig. 3. Customizable speed warning message (left) and vocal notification (right)

The "head lamps reminder" informs the driver to turn on the headlights when a certain speed is reached. This function may be useful in those countries where the headlights must be always kept on in suburban areas.

Diagnostic Trouble Codes (DTCs) are error codes caused by engine malfunctions. When a malfunction is detected the ECU allocates a DTC instance on the embedded flash memory and turns on the Malfunctioning Engine Lamp (MIL) on the dashboard. If the problem is not serious the MIL indicator is soon turned off, but the DTC remains stored on the ECU. While reading the current parameter, the application periodically queries the ECU for stored DTCs. The automatic querying for DTCs provides the driver with the information about any previous failures.

Modern vehicles have a single MIL lamp that can be simply on or off. The MIL icon of this application can be in several states, supplying much more information to the user (see Figure 4). If there is no car connection the "?" caption is shown on a grey icon. When communicating with the car, if the dashboard MIL lamp is off and there are no stored DTCs, then the MIL icon caption shown is "OK". If there are serious DTCs on the ECU memory the application shows a red MIL icon. In this case, the dashboard MIL is also on, and the user should read the DTC(s) description. The orange MIL icon means that, although the vehicle MIL is off, at least one DTC is still stored in the ECU, and the user may open the DTCs form to display the previous trouble list.

4.3 Quick Efficiency Checks

Semantic analysis of monitored values may highlight an engine problem or a poorly working sensor. In the "Oxygen Test", the average and standard deviation of the Oxygen Sensor sampled data are calculated. These values allow users to estimate whether the sensor is working correctly and the engine is running well. The test result is graphically presented and a report is given in a few short sentences (Figure 5). The evaluation report is selected by following a simple decision chart (see Figure 6).

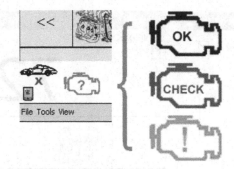

Fig. 4. The different MIL icons used by the application

The Oxygen Sensor is probably the most important part of modern engines. It measures the concentration of oxygen in the exhaust gas. The ECU uses the Oxygen Sensor output to maintain the best air-fuel mixture ratio. If the sensor is not working or its output is flawed, the engine may run badly with high fuel consumption and polluting emissions. By doing the simple oxygen test provided by our application the user can quickly check if the injection is working well and he is informed if a suspected malfunctioning exists. If so, the user can decide to bring the vehicle to a mechanic or to do a check himself. We are now considering creating other simple checks, such as the "idle RPM" and the "idle accelerator position" ones.

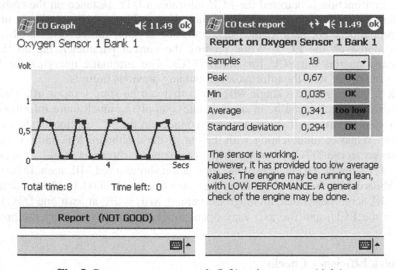

Fig. 5. Oxygen sensor test result (left) and test report (right)

4.4 Location-Aware Functions

The association between values (e.g.: speed, engine load/temperature) and vehicle terrestrial coordinates is basic to develop services based on vehicle-to-vehicle (v2v) and vehicle-to-infrastructure (v2i) data exchange [4]. We considered the location-awareness as a complementary aspect for the car status monitoring. To facilitate

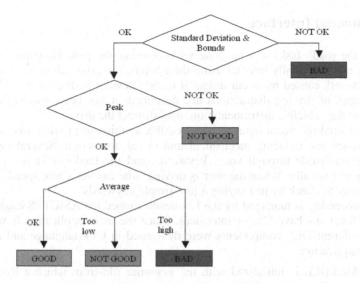

Fig. 6. Oxygen Test evaluation flow chart

future data logging enhancements, a GPS decoding routine based on National Marine Electronic Association (NMEA) protocol has been developed. Such a function connects to the GPS port and gets the downstream bytes. Coordinates values and satellites information are parsed from GGA, GSA, GSV and RMC sentences and presented on a specific form (see Figure 7).

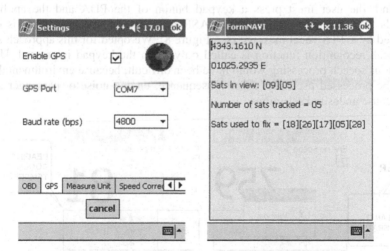

Fig. 7. GPS settings (left) and coordinates display form (right)

On the GPS settings page the user should enter the COM port of the GPS module (see Figure 7). On the combo box just the valid ports are listed. This approach allows the use of a generic GPS. The decoding function has been successfully tested on a PDA with integrated GPS and on a PDA with a CF (Compact Flash) GPS Card.

5 Multimodal Interface

Most "on the road" tasks can be done without using the pen. However, while car passengers may physically interact using their hands, the driver should not for safety reasons. The risk caused by in-car usage of mobile devices is discussed in [7], where different types of driving distractions are described: it has been proven that every device, even the vehicle's instrumentation, may distract the driver.

We considered the vocal input to be a possible solution to provide accessibility to the main functions, reducing mechanical and visual distraction. Several tasks have been made accessible through vocal keywords, and the feedback is provided both graphically and vocally. When the user is driving, s/he can set a new speed limit or a new parameter to check by just saying a few simple keywords.

Vocal processing is managed by the Loquendo Embedded ASR/TTS engines [13]. Loquendo functions have C/C++ interfaces. Since the main application is written in C#, two different DLL components were developed in C++ language and imported on the C# application:

- AsrMod.DLL is initialized with the grammar file from which a Recognition Object (RO) is created. The asrRecog( ) method listens to the user voice trying to recognize the sentence. The returned structure, basically a string, is then interpreted by the application.
- TtsMod.DLL defines the ttsRead(...) method, which accepts a string and produces a vocal audio file. The file is automatically played by the computer audio board.

The speech sessions are usually created at start up. Before saying a vocal command, the user must press a keypad button of the PDA and the application responds with an audio prompt. When ASR is successful, the new status is briefly described by a TTS vocal message (see Figure 8). We opted for this approach so that the speech recognition function is called only when the keypad is pressed. Using a continuous speech processing would have been difficult, because environmental noise would be processed uselessly. As a consequence, engine noise or passenger speech would cause undesired selections.

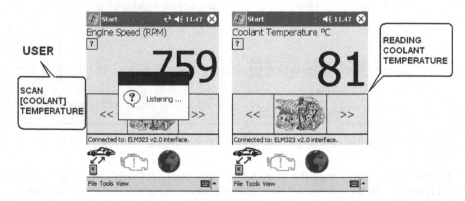

Fig. 8. After pressing the key pad, the user can say a vocal command (left) and the application provides a vocal output describing the new status (right)

The grammar containing the vocal rules is compiled "on the fly" during the ASR initialization. The grammar is recursively defined in EBNF and stored into a text file that can be easily edited without modifying the entire application. For each subsequent call the recognition function produces a string with the words (and/or numbers) provided by the user; the string is a sentence whose structure complies with the grammar rules. The grammar has been made general enough to recognize different forms of the same command. For example, to set 65 as the maximum speed limit, the user can say "Maximum speed sixty-five", or "Maximum sixty-five" or even "Sixty-five". The resulting string is processed by the application, which properly interprets the relevant words. Such flexibility is useful especially for beginner users, that are not familiar with the commands. However, excessive flexibility means a high probability of misunderstanding of the commands: the wrong command may be chosen by the ASR recognition object if too many possible choices are available. We are now evaluating the grammar structure to achieve an optimal trade off between flexibility and manageability for the speech recognition.

6 Evaluation

A preliminary user test to evaluate the interface has been performed indoors Six volunteers were involved. Users ranged in age between 24 and 33 (average 27.8). Fifteen percent were female, and 50% had previously used a PDA. Users had good experience with PC-based interfaces, but very little with vocal ones.

Users were initially asked to execute 10 tasks through traditional touch screen interaction. They had to enter the settings for the connection to the scan tool hardware, to find all the parameters retrievable by the vehicle and to disable those that they were not interested in. The configuration steps are very important for the user to realize what information would be provided and must be done at least once during the first session. Common functions were also activated through the touch screen:

- select a specific parameter (it should be enabled beforehand),
- customize the available speed limits,
- select a speed limit,
- switch to another measurement unit,
- from the graphical-selection form select a specific parameter (it should be enabled beforehand),
- cancel the speed limit.

The users were observed while trying to accomplish the tasks without any interference. The observers took note of the task completion time and any comments made by the users. At the end of the first part, users were provided with the grammar structure and some examples of vocal commands. Then, they re-executed some typical on-the-road tasks through vocal commands:

- freely select a parameter,
- request the vocal description of the new parameter,
- set a speed limit,
- select a specific parameter,
- select the next parameter available,
- cancel the speed limit.

After the session, users were requested to fill in an evaluation questionnaire. The questionnaire asked users to indicate their educational level and to evaluate the system capabilities. User were also asked to rate the parameters shown in Table 1 on a 1 to 5 scale.

Table 1. User rating for the interaction attributes

Parameters	Point score	Variance
User interface clearness	3.3	1.29
Icons intuitiveness	3.5	2.25
Customization easiness	3.3	1.75
Vocal input efficacy	4.16	0.81
Vocal feed-back efficacy	4	0.66
On-drive safety	3.3	1
Benefits	3.83	0.47

The test results highlighted that the GUI can be improved in terms of clarity. Users confirmed this, indicating that the menu structure and the icons should be more intuitive. Afterwards, we made several modifications to the GUI: menu captions and items have changed significantly and the main form icons are more intuitive.

Before starting the multimodal interaction, users received only a brief description of the vocal syntax. Nevertheless, most vocal commands were interpreted by the system surprisingly well. One reason seems to be the flexibility of the grammar, which defines different formats for the same command. Another reason is the reliability of the Recognition Object (RO) generated from the text grammar at ASR initialization time.

7 Conclusions and Future Work

We have presented a novel solution supporting a number of novel services for car drivers. Our application was developed for a typical handheld currently available in the market, the HP iPAQ hx2700. Even if the ASR and TTS functions require a lot of memory, they seem to be very efficient even while the application is communicating with the car ECU.

This aspect suggested the development of a new service: a sort of programmable scheduler for vocal notifications. The scheduler would periodically create vocal messages to describe the current value of the parameters of interest to the user. An advanced Oxygen Test may consider specifically the downstream Oxygen Sensor output. The downstream sensor is mounted after the catalytic converter on the exhaust pipe and measures the toxic substances actually emitted by the vehicle. Monitoring both the upstream and the downstream sensors output would allow estimating the actual catalytic converter efficiency. Saving the test result would provide a diagram of the catalytic converter degradation as a function of the car age. Moreover, several efficiency tests may be automatically performed by the application, which would inform the user about the test results through multimodal messages.

We are now considering improvements to our application for specific purposes. The functions that may be enhanced or created would depend on specific needs. Car rental or other companies with vehicle fleets may be interested in logging-oriented functionalities to monitor their customers' driving habits. Engine status data, together with GPS coordinates, provide information about the driver behaviour in a certain place. Logged data may be sent wirelessly to a gathering point where they would be analysed by a desktop-based specific software. In addition, several values related to the engine (such as temperature and engine load) can be considered to study the vehicles' behaviour, that is, how they react to the environment.

References

1. Society of Automotive Engineers – SAE International, http://www.sae.org
2. Boy, M.: Challenges in Automotive Software Engineering. In: Proc. ICSE 2006, pp. 33–42. ACM Press, New York (2006)
3. Nadeem, T., Dashtinezhad, S., Liao, C., Iftode, L.: TrafficView: Traffic Data Dissemination using Car-to-Car Communication. Mobile Computing And Commun ications Review 8(3), 6–19
4. Robinson, C.L., Caminiti, L., Caveney, D., Laberteaux, K.: Efficient coordination and transmission of data for cooperative vehicular safety applications. In: Proc. 3rd International workshop on Vehicular ad hoc networks, pp. 10–19. ACM Press, New York (2006)
5. Bychkovsky, V., Chen, K., Goraczko, M., Hu, H., Hull, B., Miu, A., Shih, E., Zhang, Y., Balakrishnan, H., Madden, S.: Data management in the CarTel mobile sensor computing system. In: Proc. SIGMOD 2006, pp. 730–732. ACM Press, New York (2006)
6. Houben, G., Van den Bergh, cJ., Luyten, K., Coninx, K.: Interactive Systems on the Road: Development of Vehicle User Interfaces for Failure Assistance. In: W-CarsCare. In: Proc. First Workshop on Wireless Vehicular Communications and Services for Breakdown Support and Car Maintenance, pp. 84–89 (2005), http://citeseer.ist.psu.edu/houben05interactive.html
7. Chittaro, L., De Marco, L.: Driver Distraction Caused by Mobile Devices: Studuying and Reducing Safety Risks. In: Proc. International Workshop on Mobile Technologies and Health: Benefits and Risks, Udine (June 2004)
8. http://www.scantool.net
9. Peters, D. : OBD Gauge for Pocket PC and PalmOS, http://www.qcontinuum.org/obdgauge
10. Vital Engineering Ltd website, http://www.vitalengineering.co.uk
11. Promi Esd 02 bluetooth module datasheet. Initum website support section, http://www.initium.co.kr
12. ELM323 OBD (ISO) interpreter datasheet. Datasheet section of the ELM Electronics website, http://www.elmelectronics.com
13. Loquendo Embedded Technolgy, http://www.loquendo.com
14. ISO Document Road vehicles – Diagnostic systems – Requirements for interchange of digital information

The Adaptive Hybrid Cursor: A Pressure-Based Target Selection Technique for Pen-Based User Interfaces

Xiangshi Ren[1], Jibin Yin[1], Shengdong Zhao[2], and Yang Li[3]

[1] Kochi University of Technology, Kochi 782-8502, Japan
ren.xiangshi@kochi-tech.ac.jp, 088402e@gs.kochi-tech.ac.jp
[2] University of Toronto, Toronto, Ontario, Canada
sszhao@dgp.toronto.edu
[3] University of Washington, Seattle, WA 98195-2350 USA
yangli@cs.washington.edu

Abstract. We present the Adaptive Hybrid Cursor, a novel target acquisition technique for pen-based interfaces. To assist a user in a target selection task, this technique automatically adapts the size of the cursor and/or its contexts (the target size and the selection background) based on pen pressure input. We systematically evaluated the new technique with various 2D target acquisition tasks. The experimental results indicated that the Adaptive Hybrid Cursor had better selection performance, and was particularly effective for *small-target* and *high-density* environments in which the regular cursor and the Bubble Cursor [13] failed to show significant advantages. The Adaptive Hybrid Cursor is a novel way to improve target acquisition via pressure input, and our study demonstrated its viability and potential for pen-based interfaces.

Keywords: pen-based interfaces, pressure, small target acquisition, target density.

1 Introduction

Target selection via pointing is a fundamental task in graphical user interfaces (GUIs). A large corpus of work has been proposed to improve mouse-based pointing performance by manipulating control display (CD) parameters [7, 13, 14, 17, 27] in desktop environments.

Compared with mouse-based desktop GUIs, pen-based interfaces have a number of different characteristics. First, pen-based interfaces typically use absolute pointing via a direct input device (i.e., a pen), which is very different from indirect input, such as using a mouse. Second, in addition to the 2D position (x, y) values, many pen-based devices offer additional sensory properties (such as pen pressure values) that can be useful for interaction. Third, many pen-based interfaces have limited display space and input footprint. As the amount of information displayed on the screen increases, users have to select smaller targets. This is especially obvious in mobile products, such as personal digital assistants (PDAs), pen-based mobile phones, and other mobile pen-based applications. Compared with the extensive studies carried out for

C. Baranauskas et al. (Eds.): INTERACT 2007, LNCS 4662, Part I, pp. 310–323, 2007.

mouse-based pointing, more empirical studies are needed to determine how we can improve pen-input usage and efficiency.

Although previous studies have intended to exploit novel pen-based selection techniques, such as Slide Touch [26], Drag-and-pop [5], Bubble Radar [2] and Beam Cursor [28], these techniques were mostly designed for situations where targets are sparsely distributed across a display space. When targets are smaller and densely packed, the benefit of these techniques tends to be diminished or become unavailable. To solve such problems, this paper presents the Adaptive Hybrid Cursor, a novel technique that automatically adapts the selection cursor as well as the target space based on *pen-pressure*. The experimental results indicated that the Adaptive Hybrid Cursor improved selection performance related to *high-density, small-target* environments.

Recently, an increasing amount of work has explored the use of pen pressure, which is available on pen devices (such as most Tablet PCs or Wacom tablets), as the third input dimension for interaction design [15, 18, 23, 24, 25], in addition to the 2D x-y coordinates. However, little attention has been paid to using pen pressure to improve target selection tasks. This paper, therefore, investigates the possibility of improving the performance of target acquisition tasks for pen-based environments by taking advantage of pen pressure potentials.

There are three fundamental elements in a selection task: a cursor, a target, and a selection background (including a void space). We explored how pen pressure can be employed to improve target acquisition tasks by varying these three elements. The background plays an important role in many applications but its use was often overlooked in previous work. For example, numerous functionalities have been designed to associate with the background in Windows and Mac desktops, from basic but important functions such as selecting and deselecting, to re-arranging desktop icons and also to more complex operations such as changing certain properties of applications. A background also serves as a visual storage space for future elements. Furthermore, group selection techniques (such as rectangular or lasso techniques) would be awkward to operate without being able to select an empty space. The famous quote from the ancient Chinese philosopher, Lao Tze, says, "the usefulness of the wheel, cup and house is actually based on their emptiness". Without the ability to select the background, many applications become difficult to use.

This paper makes the following contributions:

- The Adaptive Hybrid Cursor can be used to select targets that have minimal surrounding space or densely packed small targets;
- The Adaptive Hybrid Cursor improves performance by manipulating all three components of target selection: the background, the target and/or the cursor;
- The Adaptive Hybrid Cursor provides easy cancellation without having to use an extra mode-switch button;
- The Adaptive Hybrid Cursor is the first interaction technique that employs pen pressure for target selection.

In this paper, we first review the related work. Next we describe the design of our new technique. We then present the evaluation of the Adaptive Hybrid Cursor under various target acquisition conditions. We conclude with a discussion of our results and directions for future work.

2 Related Work

In this section, we discuss related work regarding both target selection techniques and pen pressure.

2.1 Previous Work on Selection Techniques

Target selection tasks can be modeled by Fitts' law [11, 19]. One common form of Fitts' law is $MT=a+b\log_2(A/W+1)$, which states that the time (MT) to acquire a target with width W and distance (or amplitude) A from the cursor can be predicted (where a and b are empirically determined constants, and the term inside the log function is called *Index of Difficulty* or *ID*). Obviously, target acquisition performance can be improved by increasing W, decreasing A, or both.

The width of a target is usually defined by the space it occupies on the screen. The *effective target width* (*EW*) may be defined as the analogous size of a target in motor space. In standard pointing, the effective target width matches the visual width. However, the effective width can be increased either for the cursor [13, 17, 27] or the target [9, 20, 29] to achieve the same effect. Most previous studies have shown the effectiveness of their proposal only for single isolated target [20, 29], while they have not been shown to work well when multiple targets are present in close proximity [9, 14, 20, 29]. The state of the art in this category is Bubble Cursor [13], a mouse-based technique that allows selection of discrete targets by using a Voronoi diagram to associate void space with nearby targets. Bubble Cursor works well even in a normal-density multiple-target environment except for the limitations mentioned in the discussion section of this paper.

There is also a large body of work that is intended to improve selection performance by decreasing A. They either bring the target much closer to the cursor such as Drag-and-pop developed by Baudisch et al. [5], and 'vacuum filtering' introduced by Bezerianos and Balakrishnan [6], or jump the cursor directly to the target, such as with the object pointing technique [14]. Overall, the performance of techniques aiming to decrease A is largely affected by the number of distracting targets between the starting position and the target. They tend to work well on large displays where targets are further away or in low density environments with few distracting targets. These techniques become less effective with high or normal density environments in regular or smaller size displays such as Tablet PCs or PDAs.

Some have tried to improve pointing and selection by dynamically adjusting the Control Display gain. The gain is increased on the approach to the target and decreased while inside the target thus increasing and decreasing the motor space at critical moments in the selection process. TractorBeam [22] is a hybrid point-touch technique that aids selection by expanding the cursor or the target, or by snapping to the target. Worden et al. [27] implemented 'Sticky Icons' by decreasing the mouse control-display gain when the cursor enters the icon. Blanch et al. [7] showed that performance could be predicted using Fitts' law, based on the resulting larger W and smaller A in the motor space. The common problems for these techniques occur when multiple small targets are presented in close proximity, as the intervening targets will slow the cursor down as it travels to its destination target.

An interesting special case here is a technique which is used on large displays to help reach targets that are beyond the arm's reach [2, 5, 6, 10, 21], e.g., RadarView [21]. However, since RadarView decreases both A and W proportionally, the ID is unchanged. The benefit of RadarView is only demonstrated on larger displays where users can operate on RadarView to save the extra movement required to reach a distant target i.e. one that is beyond arm's reach. Bubble Radar [2] combines RadarView and Bubble Cursor by first placing the objects within reach, and then applying Bubble Cursor to increase selection performance. Bubble Radar also tried to address the background selection problem of Bubble Cursor by using a button switch controlled by the non-dominant hand, however, since Bubble Radar is virtually another Bubble Cursor, its advantage is likely to diminish in a high density environment.

2.2 Related Work on Pressure

There has been less work done on pressure than on pointing-based target acquisition characteristics. Studies on pressure can be roughly divided into two categories. One category investigates the general capabilities of humans interacting with computers using pressure. For example, Herot and Weinzapfel [15] investigated the human ability of the finger to apply pressure and torque to a computer screen. Buxton [8] studied the use of touch-sensitive technologies and the possibilities for interaction they suggest. Ramos et al. [23] explored the human ability to vary pen-tip pressure as an additional channel of control information. The other category of study is where researchers build pressure enabled applications or techniques. For instance, Ramos and Balakrishnan [24] demonstrated a system called LEAN and a set of novel interaction techniques for the fluid navigation, segmentation and annotation of digital video. Ramos and Balakrishnan [25] designed Zlider widget. Li et al. [18] investigated using pressure as a possible means to delimitate the input phases in pen-based interactions. Although these works opened the door to establish pressure as a research avenue, we are unaware of any work which addressed the issue of applying pressure into discrete target acquisition. We attempt to investigate this issue in this paper.

3 Adaptive Hybrid Cursor Design

A few previous studies have shown that a reasonable manipulation of targets, cursors and context can enhance target acquisition. However, the tradeoff between the "original" state of these three elements and the "manipulation" state needs to be considered in technical design. Our approach is to employ pen-pressure which is an available parameter in some pen based devices and can be used to easily produce a continuous value or a discrete state. Pen-pressure has the potential to affect selection implementation. Based on this idea we designed the Adaptive Hybrid Cursor technique.

Adaptive Hybrid Cursor includes two states. It first determines whether it should zoom its contexts (target and background) and/or cursor according to the initial location of the cursor and the information regarding the position of targets. If the condition is not suited to the adaptive strategy, Adaptive Hybrid Cursor initiates the Zoom Cursor technique described in Section 3.1 (see Fig. 1). If the condition satisfies the adaptive strategy criteria, Adaptive Hybrid Cursor begins to zoom the targets, the cursor and background based on the pressure described in Section 3.2 (see Fig. 2).

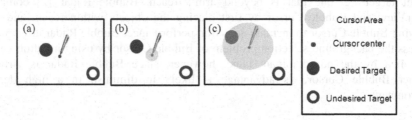

Fig. 1. The process of selecting a target with Adaptive Hybrid Cursor in State 1: the adaptive hybrid cursor employs the Zoom Cursor technique which changes the size of the cursor when targets are big in a low density environment. (a) the pen-tip lands on the screen; (b) pressure value is used to zoom the cursor. (c) pressure and location of the cursor are adjusted to make the zoomed cursor interact with the desired target. The desired target is selected by quickly lifting the pen-tip. Note that the same legend is used for Fig. 2.

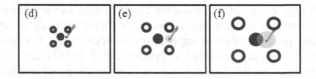

Fig. 2. The process of selecting a target with Adaptive Hybrid Cursor in State 2: Adaptive Hybrid Cursor is able to vary the size of targets, cursor and background simultaneously by pressure when approaching small targets and/or small *EW/W*. (d) the pen-tip lands on the screen; (e) using pressure value to zoom in the targets, the cursor and the background. (f) adjusting pressure and location of the cursor to make the zoomed cursor interact with the desired target. The desired target is selected by quickly lifting the pen-tip.

3.1 Zoom Cursor Technique (State 1)

One possibly fruitful direction open to the examination of pressure-enhanced target acquisition is to use pen pressure to enlarge the cursor size. Based on this intuition, we designed Zoom Cursor, a technique that allows a user to enlarge the cursor size by pressing the pen tip harder on a tablet or a touch-sensitive screen (see Fig. 1).

As determined in previous studies [3], the degree of pen pressure perceived by human users is not consistent with that sensed by digital instruments. For example, at a low spectrum of pen pressure, the sensed pressure value increases much faster than users would expect. Previous work has used a sigmoid transfer function to achieve the effects produced by pressure. In our experiments we also employed the sigmoid transfer function. The application of pressure is comprised of an initial "dead zone", slow response at low pressure levels (too sensitive for users to distinguish and control), smooth transitions at median pressure levels and quick responses at high pressure levels (users often confirm pre-selection by imposing heavy pressure on a pen-tip). We employed a piecewise linear function to approximate the pressure mapping.

If pressure causes the cursor to become too large, then more than one target might be included, and this may confuse the user. To overcome this problem, a basic principle should be specified so that when enlarging the cursor, only one target will be included at one time. Therefore, a maximum size for the cursor should be determined according to the current position of the cursor and the layout of targets. This will help to ensure that an enlarged cursor cannot include more than one target. Note that the maximum size of the cursor is dynamically changed based on the proximity of surrounding targets. We follow the algorithm used to set the radius of the cursor in Bubble Cursor. We also use a circular-shaped cursor and we allow only one target to be selected each time.

To describe the algorithm in an environment with targets $T1$, $T2$, ..., Tn we used the following definitions:

Minimum Distance i (MinDi): The length of the shortest line connecting the center of the Zoom Cursor and any point on the border of Ti.

Maximum Distance i (MaxDi): The length of the longest line connecting the center of Zoom Cursor and any point on the border of Ti.

A simplified version of the algorithm is as follows:

Calculate the Minimum Distance to each target: MinD1, MinD2,..., MinDn

Calculate the Maximum Distance to each target: MaxD1, MaxD2,..., MaxDn

Set maximum radius of Pressure Cursor = the second minimum value (MinD1, MinD2,..., MinDn, and MaxD1, MaxD2,..., MaxDn)

After a desired target is included by the enlarged cursor the target selection is achieved by the *quick release* manner [23].

3.2 Zooming Target, Cursor and Background (State 2)

Using direct pointing, the selection speed has an upper limit due to human limitations such that selecting a 10 cm wide object which is within 10 cm of the human user will take less than a second, while a target which is 10 meters away will take at least several seconds to reach. Thus Bubble Radar uses RadarView to bring the targets within arm's reach so that Bubble Cursor can be subsequently easily applied for actual target selection.

Similarly, if the targets are too small and densely packed, it becomes more difficult for the user to visually locate the target. In such cases, enlarging the workspace has the effect of simultaneously increasing A and W and thus making target acquisition easier. Based on this hypothesis, we decided to enlarge the entire workspace when the target size is smaller than 1.8 mm (about 6 pixels in our experimental setup). (Ren and Moriya's study indicated that 1.80 mm is "the smallest maximum size" [26]), or EW/W value is less than 2 where EW is *the effective width*. Here, we define EW/W as the density of targets, i.e. the amount of void space immediately surrounding a target. The result of pilot studies showed that the selection technique that zooms cursor, target and background at the same time could not show significant advantages above Bubble Cursor when the value of EW/W is more than 2. We defined an environment where the *EW/W* ratio was less than or equal to 1.5 as a high density environment, and, when the *EW/W* ratio was greater than 1.5 and less than or equal to 2, we called it a normal density environment. When the *EW/W* value was equal to or greater than 3, this was called a low density environment. High density environments are common in today's applications (e.g., a word processor or a monthly calendar viewer). Fig.2 is an illustrated walkthrough of the technique in State 2.

The maximum zoom ratio is 3 in our current design. The zoom ratio is controlled by the mapped pressure value. At the same time, Adaptive Hybrid Cursor also uses pressure and the "updated" location information of targets to zoom the cursor size according to the principles of Zoom Cursor. When the desired target was interacted by the cursor, the target selection was achieved by the *"quick release"* motion [23].

The trigger for the enlargement is pen pressure which dynamically adapts the maximum zoom size of the cursor based on the zoomed surroundings, i.e., the cursor should cover no more than one object at a time.

4   Experiment

To evaluate the performance of Adaptive Hybrid Cursor, we conducted a quantitative experiment to compare it with Bubble Cursor and with the traditional technique, the regular cursor (the regular pointing selection in graphical user interfaces) as a baseline. First, Bubble Cursor, which is the current state of the art, has been shown to be the fastest desktop pointing technique. Second, Aliakseyeu et al. [2] showed that Bubble Radar combined the benefits of Bubble Cursor in a pen-based situation. However, neither Bubble Radar nor Bubble Cursor experiments included very small targets (i.e. less than 1.6 mm). We, therefore, designed the same *EW/W* (1.33, 2, 3) ratios as for Bubble Cursor but with smaller targets (4 pixels). We wondered if Bubble Cursor offered the same advantage in smaller target situations in pen-based environments. Third, Adaptive Hybrid Cursor also employs *the effective width* of targets just as with Bubble Cursor, targets being allocated effective regions according to a Voronoi diagram.

4.1   Participants

Twelve subjects (11 male and 1 female) all with previous experience using computers were tested for the experiment. The average age was 24.9 years. All subjects used the pen in the right hand. All subjects had normal or a "corrected to normal" vision, with no color blindness.

4.2   Apparatus

The experiment was conducted on a Wacom Cintiq21UX, 43.2x32.4cm interactive LCD tablet display with a resolution of 1600 x 1200 pixels (1 pixel = 0.27 mm), using a wireless pen with a pressure sensitive isometric tip. The pen provides 1024 levels of pressure, and has a binary button on its barrel. The tablet's active area was mapped on the display's visual area in an absolute mode. The experimental software ran on a 3.2GHz P4 PC running Windows XP. The experiment software was implemented in Java 1.5.

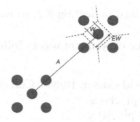

Fig. 3. Experimental setup. The solid red circle that is surrounded by four targets is the start target (as well as one of the two reciprocating goal targets), the green target is the initial goal target. The four circles around each of the start and goal targets are distracters which determined the *EW/W* ratio.

4.3 Procedure

Following the protocol [13], we also used a reciprocal pointing task in which subjects were required to select two fixed targets back and forth in succession, but, to simulate a more realistic two dimensional pointing environment, we changed the protocol into a multi-directional reciprocal pointing task which included reciprocal horizontal, vertical and diagonal movements. The targets were drawn as solid circles, and were located at various distances from each other along four directional axes. The goal target, the one intended to be selected, was colored green. When a goal target had been selected, it changed color to red which was an indication that the user now had to select the next goal target. Four red circles were placed around each goal target to control the *EW/W* ratio (Fig. 3).

Subjects were instructed to select the two goal targets alternately. They were told to emphasize both accuracy and speed. When the subject correctly selected the target, he/she heard a beep sound and the targets swapped colors, which was an indication of a new trial. At the start of the each experiment, subjects were given a warm-up block to familiarize themselves with the task and the conditions.

4.4 Design

A within-subject design was used. The independent variables were: selection techniques *ST*, amplitude *A* (288, 576, 864 pixels), width *W* (4, 6, 12, 36 pixels), *EW/W* ratios (high = 1.33, normal = 2, low density = 3), and direction *DR* (horizontal, vertical, 2 diagonals). A full crossed design resulted in 432 combinations of *ST, A, W, EW/W,* and *DR*. The order of techniques was counterbalanced using a 3 x 3 Latin-Square.

Each participant performed the entire experiment in one session of approximately 60 minutes at one sitting, including breaks corresponding to changes in selection technique. The session consisted of nine blocks of trials completed for each technique. In each block, subjects completed trial sets for each of the 144 combinations of *A, W, EW/W, DR* appearing in random order. A trial set consisted of 3 effective attempts (4 attempts in total, but the first attempt was the starting point so that it was discarded). Note we had 3 *EW/W* ratios (high = 1.33, normal = 2, low

318   X. Ren et al.

density = 3), as previously defined in Section 3.2, so we could assess the results from different density environments.

In summary, the design of the experiment was as follows:

12 subjects x
3 techniques (Adaptive Hybrid Cursor, Bubble Cursor, Regular Cursor) x
4 target widths (4, 6, 12, 36 pixels) x
3 amplitudes (288, 576, 864 pixels) x
3 *EW/W* (high = 1.33, normal = 2, low density = 3) x
4 directions (horizontal, vertical, 2 diagonals)x
3 effective attempts (4 trials total, but the first trial is discarded due to the same starting point) x
3 blocks
= 46656 total effective selection attempts

After they finished testing each technique, the subjects were asked to fill in a questionnaire which consisted of three questions regarding "selection difficulty", "fatigue", and "overall usability" on 1-to-7 scale (1=lowest preference, and 7 =highest preference). These questions were made by referring to ISO9241-9 [16]).

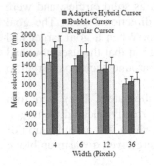 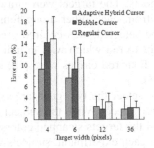 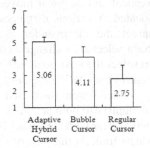

Fig. 4. Mean selection times for different sizes of targets at *EW/W* ratio=1.33

Fig. 5. Mean error rates for different sizes of targets at *EW/W* ratio=1.33

Fig. 6. Subjective ratings for the three techniques (1 = lowest preference, 7 = highest preference)

4.5   Results

An ANOVA (analysis of variance) with repeated measures was used to analyze performance in terms of selection time, error rate, and subjective preference. Post hoc analysis was performed with Tukey's Honestly Significant Difference (HSD) test.

4.5.1   Selection Time

There was a significant difference in the mean selection times among the three selection techniques, $F(2,33)=13.1$, $p<.0001$. The overall mean selection times were 1129 ms for Adaptive Hybrid Cursor, 1177 ms for Bubble Cursor and 1429 ms for Regular Cursor. Tukey HSD tests showed that both Adaptive Hybrid Cursor and Bubble Cursor were significantly faster than Regular Cursor ($p<.001$). No significant difference was found between Adaptive Hybrid Cursor and Bubble Cursor. Significant interaction was not found between selection technique and block number, $F(4,99) = 0.56$, p = .69, which indicated the learning improvement did not significantly affect the relative performance of selection techniques.

As shown in Fig. 4, at the *EW/W* ratio value of 1.33 there was a significant difference in selection time between the three selection techniques, $F(2,33)=15.1$ and 8.9 for the target sizes of 4 and 6 respectively, all p<.001. For target sizes of 4, 6 Tukey HSD tests showed Adaptive Hybrid Cursor was significantly faster than Bubble Cursor and Regular Cursor (p<.01), however, no significant difference was found between Bubble Cursor and Regular Cursor. No significant differences were found between the three selection techniques for the target sizes of 12 and 36.

At the *EW/W* ratio values of 2 and 3, both Adaptive Hybrid Cursor and Bubble Cursor were significantly faster than Regular Cursor, $F(2,33)=8.0$, 22,9, 8.8 and 19,6 for *EW/W*=2; $F(2,33)=24.2$, 14.0, 15.2 and 20.1 for *EW/W*=3, at target sizes of 4, 6, 12 and 36, all p<.01. No significant differences were found between Adaptive Hybrid Cursor and Bubble Cursor in both *EW/W* ratios.

The perspective brought by Fitts' law in terms of size and distance effects provided a useful framework for our design. However, it is questionable if it is valid to parameterize our results with a Fitts' law model. Adaptive Hybrid Cursor was more complex than a typical single pointing task in Fitts' law studies because it required the user to perform multiple steps, i.e., enlarge the curser and its contents by pressure, confirm the goal target, and select the goal target. Indeed, we obtained a rather poor fit between the Fitts' law model and the actual data collected, with r^2 value at 0.53 for Adaptive Hybrid Cursor, and 0.87, 0.97 for Bubble Cursor, Regular Cursor respectively (we defined *ID* as $\log_2(A/EW+1)$ for Adaptive Hybrid Cursor and Bubble Cursor, while for Regular Cursor $\log_2(A/W+1)$). The r^2 value for Adaptive Hybrid Cursor was much lower than the values for 0.95 or lower than those found in conventional one-step pointing tasks (e.g. [1,19]). We also looked at the data of State 1 (i.e. Zoom Cursor) described in Section 3.1. We obtained a better fit with r^2 value at 0.87 for Zoom Cursor but still lower than the values for 0.95. This was due to the fact that users had to control the size of the cursor which they do not have to do in conventional one-step pointing. The r^2 value (0.87) for Bubble Cursor was lower than the values for 0.95. This may have been due to the limitations in pen-based systems mentioned in our discussion section.

4.5.2 Error Rate

There was a significant difference in overall mean error rate between the three techniques, $F(2,33)=23.4$, p<.0001. Tukey HSD tests showed Adaptive Hybrid Cursor was better than both Bubble Cursor and Regular Cursor (p<.05). Bubble Cursor was better than Regular Cursor (p<.01). Overall error rates were 4.2% for Adaptive Hybrid Cursor, 5.4% for Bubble Cursor, and 7.3% for Regular Cursor.

As shown in Fig. 5, at the *EW/W* ratio value of 1.33, there was a significant difference between the three selection techniques for the sizes of 4 and 6, $F(2,33)=8.1$, 4.2 p<.05. For target size of 4, Tukey HSD tests showed Adaptive Hybrid Cursor was better than both Bubble Cursor than Regular Cursor (p<.05). No significant difference was found between Bubble Cursor and Regular Cursor. For a target size of 6, Tukey HSD tests showed Adaptive Hybrid Cursor was better than Regular Cursor (p<.05).

No other significant differences were found among the three techniques. There was no significant difference in error rate between the three selection techniques for the sizes of 12 and 36.

At the *EW/W* ratio value of 2, there was a significant difference between the three selection techniques for sizes 4 and 6, $F(2,33)=16.2$, 16.6 $p<.01$. For target sizes of 4 and 6, Tukey HSD tests showed both Adaptive Hybrid Cursor and Bubble Cursor were better than Regular Cursor ($p<.01$). No significant difference was found between Adaptive Hybrid Cursor and Bubble Cursor. There was no significant difference in error rate between the three selection techniques for sizes 12 and 36. The results of the *EW/W* ratio value of 3 followed trends similar to those of *EW/W*=2.

4.5.3 Subjective Preference

Fig. 6 shows the subjective ratings for the three techniques. These ratings were based on the average value of the answers given by the subjects to the three questions. Significant main effects were seen between the three selection techniques, $F(2,33)=38.4$ $p<.001$. Tukey HSD tests showed Adaptive Hybrid Cursor was better than Bubble Cursor, and Bubble Cursor was better than Regular Cursor ($p<.01$). Adaptive Hybrid Cursor was the most preferred (mean = 5.06).

5 Discussion

To improve the performance for selecting targets in a dense layout, we designed the Adaptive Hybrid Cursor (including Zoom Cursor), a novel interaction technique for pen-based systems, which enables users to adjust the size of the background, the targets and/or cursor the simultaneously. The Adaptive Hybrid Cursor dynamically adapts the permitted upper boundary of a zoomable selection cursor based on the current index of difficulty of a desired target. As shown in our Experiment, the Adaptive Hybrid Cursor showed advantages over other techniques in performance for small targets in a high density environment. The subjective preferences also showed that the Adaptive Hybrid Cursor was the most preferred technique among the three techniques tested.

Overall, the Adaptive Hybrid Cursor showed significant improvements in a pen-based selection task. It works well with a pen, and in expanding contexts. At the same time, it offers competitive selection performance without losing the background selection capability, and does not expand the context in groups of big targets, in normal and low-density environments. By contrast, many of the other mouse and pen-based interaction techniques have been shown to work well only in low density environments or on isolated targets .

Though Bubble Cursor is comparable to Adaptive Hybrid Cursor in high *EW/W* ratios or groups of larger targets in a high-density environment, it has several limitations compared to our technique, especially in pen-based environments. First, by maximizing utilization of empty screen space, Bubble Cursor trades-off the ability to select an important "target", the background. By contrast, our Adaptive Hybrid Cursor (including Zoom Cursor) allows the user to select the background (by applying lighter pressure). Second, Bubble Cursor lacks the undo function. Our technique provides "natural" cancellation by reversing the pressure value rather than using another mode-switch action like Bubble Radar [2]. Third, Bubble Cursor is not designed for pen-based environments and it does not guarantee continuous, incremental visual feedback of the selection cursor[1]. Though continuous feedback is not assured with the Adaptive Hybrid Cursor either, it can control the size of the cursor well by pen-tip pressure. Fourth, though Bubble Cursor allows denser target placement than many previous approaches, its performance advantage largely degrades when a target is closely surrounded by other objects. In theory, when the target's effective width (*EW*) approaches its actual width (*W*), little room can be used to improve the motor space. In fact, it has been shown that as the *EW/W* ratio changes from 3 to 1.33, the advantage of Bubble Cursor degrades [13]. In contrast, the Adaptive Hybrid Cursor can enlarge the targets, the background, and the cursor, according to the targets' surroundings. Fifth, neither Bubble Cursor nor Bubble Radar experiments have included very small targets. To further clarify, we also designed the same *EW/W* (1.33, 2, 3) ratios but with a smaller target (4 pixels = 1.08 mm). The experimental results showed that Bubble Cursor suffered from performance limitations in groups of small targets in high density environments.

We varied the essential parameters but we found it necessary to simplify our experimental design in some minor points. First, we set each target in each environment to the same size so that control of the target density parameters could be achieved more easily. Second, we used circular targets so that the distance between start point and destination target was constant in all four directions. Third, in Bubble Cursor's experiment, beside the circles around the target, many black-filled circles were also placed between the starting position and the final target as distracters on the mouse pathway. We omitted intermediate targets (i.e., distracter targets) for the following reasons. In indirect pointing environments, these distracters can significantly impact selection performance, since the subjects' selection pathway can't be avoided by the cursor. However, in a direct pointing pen-based environment, the user simply lifts the pen in the air to move from the starting position to the goal target where an out-of-range state is possible. This hypothesis was confirmed in pilot studies and in our Experiment. In addition, even though the distracters are placed between the start and destination targets, visual load will be similar for each of the techniques. Furthermore, the error rate for Bubble Cursor may increase because if the user selects a distracter he/she cannot perform the "undo" task with Bubble Cursor.

We explored the use of pen pressure for improving the performance of target acquisition tasks in pen-based environments. The experimental results have shown that pen pressure can be used to design more effective selection techniques for pen-based environments. The Adaptive Hybrid Cursor takes advantage of pressure information. By using pressure, the Adaptive Hybrid Cursor (particularly the Zoom Cursor aspect of the technique) achieves in-place mode switching between background and target selection and requires no additional accessories. This is different from Bubble Radar's approach [2] which uses an additional button to switch states [18].

---

[1] During the experimental process we found that continuous feedback of Bubble Cursor may not always be available on a pen device (e.g., in tracking mode) because the pen-tip often loses communication with the induction area of the tablet when lifting or landing and feedback suddenly appears or disappears as a consequence.

Our study contributes valuable empirical data for applying pressure for target selection techniques which had not been previously addressed in literature. This paper also suggests new ways to further improve target acquisition performance for small targets and high density environments. Future work includes applying a combination of strategies found in [2, 28] into the Adaptive Hybrid Cursor for large display environments and group selections.

Acknowledgments. This study has been partially supported by Exploratory Software Project of IPA (Information-technology promotion agency in Japan), and Microsoft Research Asia Mobile Computing in Education Theme. We are grateful for the work and support of all the members of the Ren Lab in Kochi University of Technology.

References

1. Accot, J., Zhai, S.: More than dotting the i's - foundations for crossing-based interfaces. In: Proc. CHI2002, pp. 73–80. ACM Press, New York (2002)
2. Aliakseyeu, D., Nacenta, M., Subramanian, S., Gutwin, C.: Bubble radar: efficient pen-based interaction. In: Proc. AVI'06, pp. 19–26. ACM Press, New York (2006)
3. Barrett, R., Olyha, J., Robert, S., Rutledge, J.: Graphical User Interface Cursor Positioning Device Having a Negative Inertia Transfer Function. Patent # 5,570,111, IBM Corp. (1996)
4. Baudisch, P., Cutrell, P., Hinckley, K., Eversole, A.: Snap-and-go: helping users align objects without the modality of traditional snapping. In: Proc. CHI2005, pp. 301–310. ACM Press, New York (2005)
5. Baudisch, P., Cutrell, E., Robbins, D., Czerwinski, M., Tandler, P., Bederson, B., Zierlinger, A.: Drag-and-pop and drag-and-pick: Techniques for accessing remote screen content on touch and pen operated systems. In: Proc. INTERACT'03, pp. 57–64 (2003)
6. Bezerianos, A., Balakrishnan, R.: The vacuum: facilitating the manipulation of distant objects. In: Proc. CHI2005, pp. 361–370. ACM Press, New York (2005)
7. Blanch, R., Guiard, Y., Beaudouin-Lafon, M.: Semantic pointing: improving target acquisition with control-display ratio adaptation. In: Proc. CHI2004, pp. 519–526. ACM Press, New York (2004)
8. Buxton, A.S.W.: Three-State Model of Graphical Input, in Human-Computer Interaction. In: Proc. INTERACT'90, pp. 449–456 (1990)
9. Cockburn, A., Brock, P.: Human on-line response to visual and motor target expansion. In: Proc. Graphics Interface 2006, pp. 81–87 (2006)
10. Collomb, M., Hascoët, M., Baudisch, P., Lee, B.: Improving drag-and-drop on wall-size displays. In: Proc. Graphics Interface 2005, pp. 8125–8132 (2005)
11. Fitts, P.M.: The information capacity of human motor system in controlling the amplitude of movement. Journal of Experimental Psychology 47, 381–391 (1954)
12. Foley, J.D., Wallace, V., Chan, P.: The Human Factors of Computer Graphics Interaction Techniques. IEEE Computer Graphics and Applications, 13–48 (1984)
13. Grossman, T., Balakrishnan, R.: The bubble cursor: enhancing target acquisition by dynamic resizing of the cursor's activation area. In: Proc. CHI2005, pp. 281–290. ACM Press, New York (2005)
14. Guiard, Y., Blanch, R., Beaudouin-Lafon, M.: Object pointing: a complement to bitmap pointing in GUIs. In: Proc. Graphics Interface 2004, pp. 9–16 (2004)

15. Herot, C.F., Weinzapfel, G.: One-point touch input of vector information for computer displays. In: Conference on Computer Graphics and Interactive Techniques, pp. 210–216. ACM Press, New York (1978)
16. ISO ISO9241-9: Ergonomic design for office work with visual display terminals (VDTs)– Part 9: Requirements for non-keyboard input devices. International Standardization Organization (2000)
17. Kabbash, P., Buxton, W.A.S.: The "prince" technique: Fitts' law and selection using area cursors. In: Proc. CHI'05, pp. 273–279. ACM Press, New York (1995)
18. Li, Y., Hinckley, K., Guan, Z., Landay, J.: Experimental analysis of mode switching techniques in pen-based user interfaces. In: Proc. CHI2005, pp. 461–470. ACM Press, New York (2005)
19. MacKenzie, I.S., Buxton, W.A.S.: Extending Fitts' law to two-dimensional tasks. In: Proc. CHI'92, pp. 219–226. ACM Press, New York (1992)
20. McGuffin, M., Balakrishnan, R.: Acquisition of expanding targets. In: Proc. CHI2002, pp. 57–64. ACM Press, New York (2002)
21. Nacenta, M.A., Aliakseyeu, D., Subramanian, S., Gutwin, C.A.: A comparison of techniques for multi-display reaching. In: Proc. CHI2005, pp. 371–380. ACM Press, New York (2005)
22. Parker, K., Mandryk, R., Nunes, M., Inkpen, K.: TractorBeam Selection Aids: Improving Target Acquisition for Pointing Input on Tabletop Displays. In: Costabile, M.F., Paternó, F. (eds.) INTERACT 2005. LNCS, vol. 3585, pp. 80–93. Springer, Heidelberg (2005)
23. Ramos, G., Boulos, M., Balakrishnan, R.: Pressure widgets. In: Proc. CHI2004, pp. 487–494. ACM Press, New York (2004)
24. Ramos, G., Balakrishnan, R.: Fluid interaction techniques for the control and annotation of digital video. In: Prof. UIST2003, pp. 105–114. ACM Press, New York (2003)
25. Ramos, G., Balakrishnan, R.: Zliding: fluid zooming and sliding for high precision parameter manipulation. In: Prof. UIST2005, pp. 143–152. ACM Press, New York (2005)
26. Ren, X., Moriya, S.: Improving selection performance on pen-based systems: A study of pen-input interaction for selection tasks. ACM ToCHI 7(3), 384–416 (2000)
27. Worden, A., Walker, N., Bharat, K., Hudson, S.: Making computers easier for older adults to use: area cursors and sticky icons. In: Proc. CHI'97, pp. 266–271. ACM Press, New York (1997)
28. Yin, J., Ren, X.: The Beam Cursor: A Pen-based Technique for Enhancing Target Acquisition. In: Proc. HCI 2006, pp. 119–134. Springer, Heidelberg (2006)
29. Zhai, S., Conversy, S., Beaudouin-Lafon, M., Guiard, Y.: Human on-line response to target expansion. In: Proc. CHI2003, pp. 177–184. ACM Press, New York (2003)
30. Zhai, S., Buxton, A.S.W., Milgram, P.: The "Silk Cursor": investigating transparency for 3D target acquisition. In: Proc. CHI'94, pp. 459–464. ACM Press, New York (1994)

ThumbSpace: Generalized One-Handed Input for Touchscreen-Based Mobile Devices

Amy K. Karlson and Benjamin B. Bederson

Human-Computer Interaction Lab, Computer Science Department
University of Maryland, College Park, MD 20742, USA
{akk, bederson}@cs.umd.edu

Abstract. In this paper, we present ThumbSpace, a software-based interaction technique that provides general one-handed thumb operation of touchscreen-based mobile devices. Our goal is to provide accurate selection of all interface objects, especially small and far targets, which are traditionally difficult to interact with using the thumb. We present the ThumbSpace design and a comparative evaluation against direct interaction for target selection. Our results show that ThumbSpace was well-received, improved accuracy for selecting targets that are out of thumb reach, and made users as effective at selecting small targets as large targets. The results further suggest user practice and design iterations hold potential to close the gap in access time between the two input methods, where ThumbSpace did not do as well as direct interaction.

Keywords: ThumbSpace, one handed mobile interaction.

1 Introduction

With the number of cell phones out-shipping more traditional computers by more than 4:1 in 2006 [17, 28], the emergence of the phone as a ubiquitous personal accessory is clear. Traditionally, cell phones have served as little more than wireless telephones, while mobile information management has been reserved for PDAs and laptops. But with rapid advances in processing power, storage capacity, and connectivity, these different device types are converging into the "smartphone": a feature-rich, Internet-enabled mini-computer. As the numbers and types of devices grow, so will opportunities to explore a wider range of interaction methods, exemplified by Apple's recent announcement of the multi-touch capacitive touchscreen iPhone [25]. Devices will remain small because mobility will remain a driving factor. Users in diverse mobile environments are bound to be visually and mentally distracted [16] and to have one or both of their hands frequently occupied. Given these trends, today's touchscreen software designs often do a poor job supporting mobility because the majority require two-handed stylus input.

Interfaces that accommodate single-handed interaction can offer a significant benefit by freeing one hand for the physical and intellectual demands of mobile tasks [20]. Surveys [14] confirm that users would generally prefer to use touchscreens with one hand when possible, but hardware and software designs of today's devices

C. Baranauskas et al. (Eds.): INTERACT 2007, LNCS 4662, Part I, pp. 324–338, 2007.

typically offer no such support. Styli are often required for touchscreen interaction because their software interfaces are composed of targets that are either too small [21] or ill-positioned to be hit reliably with the thumb. One solution is to build interfaces that explicitly accommodate thumb interaction by ensuring that all targets are thumb sized and within thumb reach [15]. Yet this "lowest common denominator" approach to interface design is unlikely to catch on. This is because small screens so severely constrain information presentation already that placing further limitations on visual expressivity can hurt the design in other ways. For example, increasing target sizes to accommodate thumbs means fewer targets can be shown per screen, and so will require more screens to present the same amount of information. This can slow down access to information, even when two hands *are* available. These observations, together with the reality that existing mobile UI toolkits include only small, stylus-oriented widget palettes, have led us to consider an alternative strategy.

We present ThumbSpace, a novel interaction technique to facilitate the thumb accessibility of rich touchscreen interfaces. ThumbSpace combats both the reach and accuracy problems that users experience when using thumbs on touchscreens. It works like an absolute-position touchpad superimposed on a portion of the standard touchscreen interface. Users can access all locations on the screen by interacting with only a sub-region of the display. Thumb reach limitations are addressed by allowing users to personalize the size and placement of ThumbSpace, thereby accommodating individual differences in hand preference, geometry, motion range, grip, and use scenario. As a result of decoupling input space and output space, ThumbSpace eliminates the dependence of target size on thumb size, and so alleviates the accuracy issues involved with directly hitting small targets with big thumbs. ThumbSpace does this without constraining the complexity of applications' interfaces; in fact, ThumbSpace is designed to be *application independent*.

Given the dynamic environments and varied tasks of mobile computing, user choice about the number of hands to use is expected to be fluid. Effective mobile interfaces will therefore maximize presentation power and interaction efficiency regardless of hand availability. With ThumbSpace, touchscreen devices can continue to take full advantage of the available display real estate for rich presentation and interaction with two hands while at the same time supporting one-handed scenarios.

In the remainder of this paper we describe the design and implementation of ThumbSpace and our evaluation of ThumbSpace versus direct thumb interaction for accessing targets of varying size, density, and location.

2 Related Work

2.1 One Handed Interaction

The physical and attentional demands of mobile device use were reported early on for fieldworkers [16, 22]. This resulted in specific design recommendations for minimal-attention and one-handed interfaces [22] which, though well suited to the directed tasks of fieldwork, do not generalize to the varied and complex personal information management tasks of average users. Since then, research in one-handed device interaction has largely focused on either the hardware or the tasks supported.

Technology-oriented efforts have investigated the potential benefits of accelerometer-augmented devices [12] and touchscreen-based gestures [7, 15] for one-handed interaction. Other research has focused on enabling one-handed support for specific tasks, including media control [23] and text entry [30]. But overall, there has been relatively little focus on thumb interaction.

Karlson et al. [14] looked more generally at human factors requirements for one-handed interaction with personal mobile devices, including situational and task preferences for hand use as well as biomechanical limitations of thumbs. They found that in addition to the common practice of one-handed phone use, there is wide interest in single-handed use of (generally larger) touchscreen-based PDAs, but that current designs do not accommodate one-handed scenarios well. Their results further suggested that users were more comfortable when interaction could be limited to a sub-region of the device surface, preferably toward the center of the device. ThumbSpace's design addresses these findings directly.

Others have studied how physical characteristics of the thumb interact with touchscreen technology. Parhi et al. [21] investigated the effect of target size on input accuracy when operating a PDA one handed with the thumb. Previously, others had determined appropriate target sizes for pen-based interaction on mobile touchscreen devices [18], and index fingers for interaction on desktop-sized displays [8, 26], but pens and index fingers are smaller than thumbs and their use scenarios differ from the mechanic constraints of holding the screen with the same hand used for interaction.

Current touchscreen interfaces consist of widgets similar in size and function to those featured on a desktop PC. While acceptable for interaction with a 1mm stylus tip, such targets are much smaller than the average thumb pad in at least one dimension, making reliable access difficult or impossible. Recently, Vogel and Baudisch [29] presented the Shift technique as an improvement over Sears and Shneiderman's offset cursor [27], both of which address issues of occlusion during finger selection of small touchscreen targets. While Shift holds great potential for one-handed selection of targets within reach of the thumb, further investigation would be necessary to understand whether pixel-level selection is effective under mobile conditions, and whether Shift works equally well for objects along the perimeter of the screen, which occur frequently in today's designs. More importantly, Shift was designed for two-handed index finger operation of mobile devices, and so does not address the limitations of thumb reach that ThumbSpace seeks to address.

2.2 Reaching Distant Objects

ThumbSpace draws its inspiration from the observation that large table-top and wall-sized displays both confront issues with out-of reach interface objects. A general problem for large display interaction is that the increase in real estate also increases the average distance between on-screen objects. Unfortunately, Fitts' Law dictates that increasing travel distance without a commensurate increase in target size will increase access time. Solutions have thus typically focused on 1) decreasing movement distance to targets and/or 2) increasing target sizes. We classify these further into indirect and direct interaction methods.

Indirect Interaction. Improving target acquisition for mouse-based interaction has often involved clever manipulation of the control-display (CD) ratio. Slowing mouse movement over interaction targets (Semantic Pointing [6]), jumping the cursor to the nearest target (Object Pointing [10]), and predicting the user's intended target (Delphian desktop [2]) are three such examples. The drawback of these techniques is that their effectiveness decreases as the number of nearby objects increases. Other approaches in smart cursor control make targets easier to hit by increasing the cursor size, such as area cursor [13] and Bubble Cursor [9].

Direct Interaction. Direct screen interaction with fingers or pens is common in tablet, mobile, and wall computing, but the absence of a remotely controlled cursor means there is 1:1 correspondence between motor and display movement, and thus no CD ratio to manipulate. Since increasing target widths has generally been achieved via CD manipulation, techniques for direct input have focused on reducing the movement distance to targets. Drag-and-pop [3] reduces an object's drag distance by drawing full-sized proxies of targets closer to the moved item. The Vacuum widget [5] allows users to select the display sector of interest before moving object proxies to within reach. Drag-and-throw and push-and-throw [11] reduce movement distance by virtually extending the reach of the finger or pen.

A final class of direct interaction techniques offers users miniaturized, nearby versions of the entire display area for manipulating distant objects. With Radar View [19], the miniature representation appears as users begin drag operations. The Bubble Radar [1] extends the Bubble Cursor to pen-based computing, using a Radar View representation and dynamic expansion of the pen's activation area. ThumbSpace uses a similar approach to the Radar View, while addressing occlusion and small displays.

3   ThumbSpace

Our goal with ThumbSpace has been to develop an interaction strategy whereby rich touchscreen interfaces can be effectively controlled with a thumb, without sacrificing the expressiveness of information presentation or the efficiency of navigation when two hands are available.

3.1   ThumbSpace Design

Karlson et al.'s investigation of thumb movement when using mobile devices with one hand [14] found that users were more comfortable interacting with some surface regions than others. Although the centers of devices were generally easy to access, and corners and edges were generally hard to access, gradations in opinion between these extremes indicated that participants were not in perfect agreement. Indeed, individual differences in hand size, thumb length, agility, and strength can all affect thumb range of motion. Furthermore, differences in use scenario will affect the freedom users have to change grip while maintaining control of the device, and so will also impact how well users can access different regions of the device surface.

Given such variations in thumb ability, hand preference, and mobile usage requirements, the first principle of ThumbSpace is to support the user's most comfortable and stable grip. Each user therefore defines his or her own ThumbSpace - a region of the touchscreen surface that is easy to reach and interact with. To configure ThumbSpace, the user is instructed to drag her thumb along a diagonal to define the upper left and lower right corners of a rectangular region (Fig. 1a). All thumb interaction then occurs within this personalized ThumbSpace, which remains fixed (but reconfigurable) across all applications.

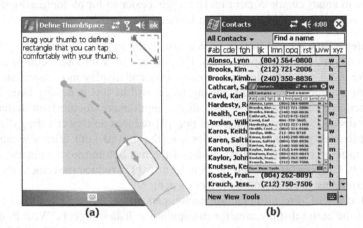

Fig. 1. (a) Defining the ThumbSpace. (b) The ThumbSpace as a traditional Radar View.

To support access to all interaction targets within the confines of the ThumbSpace, the user-defined region behaves as a type of a Radar View for the display. Traditionally, a Radar View is a miniaturized representation of a large display that serves as a within-reach proxy for out-of-reach objects; interactions upon objects within the Radar View are propagated to the associated objects in the original display, hereafter referred to as the "DisplaySpace". This approach has proven successful for accessing distant windows and icons on large displays [19], but hasn't been applied to small screen interaction, which presents novel challenges. Consider, for example, that a straightforward implementation of a Radar View for the Windows Mobile Contacts application is shown in Fig. 1b. This approach has several problems: 1) the Radar View representation occludes a large number of DisplaySpace objects; 2) the Radar View proxies are unreadable; 3) the detailed Radar View representation contributes to unacceptable visual clutter; and 4) the Radar View proxies are far too small to access reliably with the thumb.

To address problems (1-3), we avoid using a miniature representation. Instead, we offer only a whitewashed region to suggest where the user should focus her attention. Fig. 2a shows this representation of ThumbSpace, which overlays the application at all times. Even without the miniature displayed, ThumbSpace retains the spirit of the Radar View by honoring an input mapping between the ThumbSpace and the DisplaySpace. ThumbSpace is partitioned so that each object in the DisplaySpace is associated with a sub-region (*proxy*) in the ThumbSpace; tapping a proxy in ThumbSpace selects the assigned object in the DisplaySpace. If ThumbSpace were to represent a linearly scaled DisplaySpace (as in Fig. 1b), the partition of ThumbSpace into DisplaySpace proxies would be that shown in Fig. 2b. Yet the ThumbSpace partition is not required to be a scaled representation of the DisplaySpace; in section 3.4 we discuss how different partitioning strategies may improve user performance.

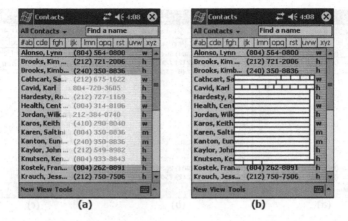

Fig. 2. (a) The actual ThumbSpace representation. (b) One possible partitioning of the ThumbSpace into proxies for DisplaySpace objects.

3.2 Using ThumbSpace

The final challenge ((4) above) in using a miniature representation as an interaction medium is that the proxies can be too small to hit reliably with a big thumb, even when users can *see* the representation. ThumbSpace introduces further uncertainty because it provides no visual cues for how its sub-regions map to DisplaySpace objects. ThumbSpace manages these uncertainties during interaction by providing dynamic visual feedback.

Object selection in ThumbSpace is performed in three phases: *aim, adjust,* and *lift.* The *aim* phase requires users to have formed a mental model of the input mapping between the ThumbSpace and DisplaySpace. Again, the simplest assumption is that the ThumbSpace represents a linear scaling of the DisplaySpace. Based on her mental model, the user makes an initial guess about the sub-region of ThumbSpace that corresponds to the intended target, and *aims* at the sub-region with her thumb (Fig. 3a). In the *aim* phase, ThumbSpace can be likened to an absolute touchpad - if the user guesses correctly, ThumbSpace provides touchdown access to objects that would otherwise be difficult (e.g., too small) or impossible (e.g., out of reach) to hit directly with her thumb.

As soon as the user's thumb touches a ThumbSpace proxy, the associated DisplaySpace object is highlighted using an object cursor, depicted as a thick orange border. The user then enters the *adjust* phase for fine-tuning the selection. During the *adjust* phase, ThumbSpace acts like a relative touchpad for controlling the object cursor. If the user rolls or drags her thumb more than 10 pixels up, down, left, or right, the object cursor animates to the closest DisplaySpace object in the direction of movement (Fig. 3b). In the *adjust* phase, ThumbSpace interaction is similar to Object Pointing [10], which ignores the whitespace between interface objects in desktop-based mouse interaction by jumping the cursor to the closest object in the direction of movement when the mouse cursor leaves an object's bounds. The *adjust* strategy

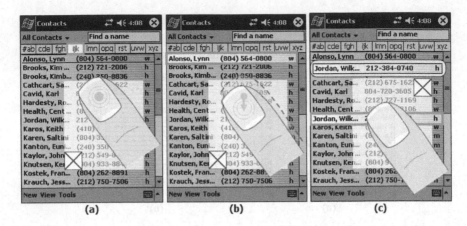

Fig. 3. Selecting objects with ThumbSpace. Assuming the user wants to select the first name in the list, she first (a) *aims* at the probable ThumbSpace proxy for 'Alonso'; (b) the initial ThumbSpace point of contact maps to 'ijk' so the user *adjusts* the intended target by dragging her thumb downward. The user confirms the selection by lifting her thumb, or cancels the selection by dragging her thumb to the X before lifting; (c) ThumbSpace occlusion correction.

differs slightly from Object Pointing because *adjust* does not take into account proxy widths and heights, only the delta of thumb movement.

Finally, the user confirms the selection by *lifting* her thumb. This manner of object selection is inspired by the lift-off strategy for touchscreen object selection developed by Potter [24], which allows users to visually confirm and adjust a selection before committing to the action. To allow users to cancel a selection, the user can drag her thumb over the red X, which appears during interaction in either the upper right or lower left corner of ThumbSpace, whichever is furthest from the first point of contact.

A ThumbSpace proxy may overlap its corresponding DisplaySpace object, or even appear below it, which may cause the thumb to occlude the DisplaySpace object. At these times, the selected item is highlighted in the original display, and an unobstructed representation appears at a fixed location above the ThumbSpace to improve the visibility of the current selection (Fig. 3c). Again, this solution can be considered an adaptation of the take-off touchscreen selection strategy [24], which avoided finger occlusion by placing the selection cursor above the user's finger. Note that, by displaying the obstructed object above ThumbSpace, and by allowing the user to specify her ThumbSpace (Fig. 1a), we support both left- and right-handed users.

A video demonstration of ThumbSpace definition and interaction can be viewed at http://www.youtube.com/user/thumbspace.

3.3 Interactions Supported

Traditional PDAs support three primary interactions: *tap* for object selection, *tap-drag-release* to drag objects and cancel selections, and *tap-and-hold* to trigger context-sensitive menus. The ThumbSpace *aim-adjuist-lift* interaction technique repurposes the traditional *tap-drag-release* for object selection. While object selection is required far more frequently than the other two in standard interfaces, failure to support them would certainly limit the utility of ThumbSpace for general-purpose use.

For widgets that support more specialized interaction than tapping, we propose a 2 step process: 1) the *aim-adjust-lift* sequence gives focus to the widget or opens an associated context-sensitive menu (leaving the red cancel box visible; and 2) any drag operation then performed in the ThumbSpace moves or scrolls the widget in sync with the thumb until the user lifts her thumb to perform the final selection, or selects the red cancel box to abort the operation. For example, selecting a combo box via *aim-adjust-lift* gives focus to the widget and opens the list of available items; dragging the thumb in ThumbSpace moves the highlight among the combo box list; lifting the thumb either selects an item in the list or cancels the selection if performed over the red cancel box. In this paper we explore the viability of object selection only, and will investigate the other interaction types in future work.

3.4 Deriving ThumbSpace Proxies

Just as manipulations of the CD ratio for mouse input has been shown to improve object selection in desktop systems under certain conditions [6, 10], our strategy for mapping ThumbSpace proxies to DisplaySpace objects also has the potential to influence system usability. An interface with a sparse object layout would suffer from a strict linear mapping between DisplaySpace and ThumbSpace because a large percentage of ThumbSpace pixels would be "dead" in that they would not be associated with any DisplaySpace object. This approach would waste scarce input space and result in unnecessarily small proxies that would be difficult to hit.

Ideally, the ThumbSpace to DisplaySpace mapping would instead optimize the size and placement of ThumbSpace proxies to achieve the following goals: (1) The ThumbSpace should be fully partitioned into proxies so that every pixel in ThumbSpace corresponds to some DisplaySpace object. Our goal is to maximize the sizes of proxies and thus improve user accuracy in the *aim* phase of object selection. (2) "Landmark" objects in DisplaySpace, such as those in the four corners and center of the display, should retain their relative positions within the ThumbSpace; ideally "landmark" proxies would be relatively larger than those for similarly sized objects, again to improve user accuracy in the *aim* phase of object selection. (3) ThumbSpace proxies should retain the same up-down and left-right positions to one another as do their corresponding DisplaySpace objects. This goal allows for efficient and intuitive targeting in the *adjust* phase of object selection.

For our initial exploration of the ThumbSpace technique, we define the mapping between ThumbSpace proxies and DisplaySpace objects by hand, and will develop generalized proxy partitions in future design iterations.

3.5 Implementation

As a real-world input system, ThumbSpace will need to cooperate with a PDA's operating system in order to capture and reinterpret thumb events for stylus-oriented interface designs. However, to first establish its viability, we have implemented ThumbSpace as a generalized input handler to custom interfaces written in C# (.NET

Compact Framework) for Windows Mobile Pocket PCs using the PocketPiccolo open source graphics toolkit [4].

4 User Study

To understand the potential of ThumbSpace in terms of usability, interaction effectiveness, and user satisfaction, we conducted a quantitative study to compare ThumbSpace to direct thumb interaction for object selection tasks.

4.1 Tasks

Because object selection via tapping is the predominant interaction type on PDAs today, we focused on basic target selection for our study. We hypothesized that users would be able to select objects faster and more accurately with one hand overall when using ThumbSpace than when using only their thumbs directly. In particular, we predicted that the relative benefits of ThumbSpace would vary by target size, distance, and overall target density as follows:

Target Size: In determining the target size conditions, we were mainly concerned with the difference in performance between selecting a target that is too small to be hit reliably with the thumb and one that is large enough to be hit. Based on previous investigations on appropriate target sizes for one-handed thumb interaction [21], we chose two sizes to study: *small* (20 pixels = 4.8 mm), and *large* (40 pixels = 9.6 mm). Since ThumbSpace decouples input and output space, we did not expect target size to impact selection accuracy, as is prevalent in direct thumb selection.

Target Distance: When operating a device with one hand, users generally find some surface areas of a device easier to access than others [14]. Using guidelines from [14], we classified targets into two distance categories: *near* (comfortable to reach) and *far* (uncomfortable to reach). Due to thumb reach constraints, we expected users would perform near tasks better than far tasks when directly tapping. Since ThumbSpace is within user reach by design, we did not expect target location to affect performance for ThumbSpace.

Target Density: Target density plays a role in ThumbSpace because it affects the size of the ThumbSpace proxies, and thus user accuracy in the *aim* phase of object selection. We chose to study 2 densities: *sparse* (proxies were 80 px^2, or 19.2 mm^2) and *dense* (proxies were 40 px^2, or 9.6 mm^2). With ThumbSpace, we expected users would be slower when hitting targets in dense conditions due to the need to perform more corrective moves in the *adjust* phase of object selection than under sparse conditions. In contrast, we did not expect density to impact direct thumb interaction.

The target configurations studied are shown in Fig. 4a. Tasks began with a message box indicating the target to select (Fig. 4b). Tapping the message box started the task timer, and if appropriate, the user's ThumbSpace would appear (Fig. 4c). Once a target was selected, a "success" or "error" sound provided accuracy feedback. The study software ran on an HP iPAQ h4155 Pocket PC measuring 4.5x2.8x0.5 inches with a 3.5 inch, 240 x 320 resolution screen, calibrated prior to the study.

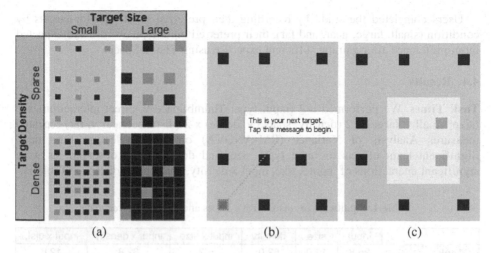

Fig. 4. (a) Target configurations for the user study. (b,c) Example study task.

4.2 Method and Measures

The study was a 2 (input type: ThumbSpace v. direct interaction) x 2 (size: small v. large) x 2 (density: sparse v. dense) x 2 (distance: near v. far) x 3 trial within subject design. For each input type, users performed the tasks in 5 blocks, for a total of 240 trials. Input type was counterbalanced across participants, and tasks were randomized within blocks. Dependent variables collected during the study included task time, error rate, user satisfaction ratings on a 7 point scale, and overall input preference.

4.3 Participants and Procedure

We recruited right-handed participants via fliers posted in our Department of Computer Science, and through flier distribution in an undergraduate HCI course for non-majors. Sixteen respondents (8 female, 8 male) participated in the study, ranging in age from 18 to 28 with an average age of 23 years of age. Participants received $10 for approximately 45 minutes of their time.

The study began with an introduction to each input type. Participants first read a description of direct thumb interaction, followed by practice with a single block of tasks. Participants then read a description of ThumbSpace, defined a personal ThumbSpace (Fig. 1a), and practiced with two blocks of tasks; the administrator demonstrated ThumbSpace for the first 5 of these tasks. After the practice phase, the study proper began: users completed 5 task blocks for one input type, followed by a usability questionnaire, then repeated the process with the second input type. After this official data collection phase, users completed a "usability" phase, which provided the opportunity to use the techniques with a real interface. With each input type, users performed 20 object selection tasks, presented as in Fig. 4b, for a Windows Mobile Start Menu and Calendar program.

Users completed the study by recording their preferred input type for targets by condition (small, large, near, and far), their preferred input type overall, and expected input preference after gaining sufficient expertise using ThumbSpace.

4.4 Results

Task Times. We performed a 2 (input type: ThumbSpace v. direct interaction) x 2 (size: small v. large) x 2 (density: sparse v. dense) x 2 (distance: near v. far) repeated measures Analysis of Variance (RM-ANOVA) on mean selection time data. Significant main effects of input type, size, and density were observed, as were significant interactions of input x size, input x density, and input x distance (Table 1).

Table 1. Significant results for Task Times and Percent Correct data

		input	size	density	input x size	input x density	input x dist.
Task Times	$F_{1,15}$	26.8	11.0	62.0	5.2	32.8	12.8
	p	<.001	.005	<.001	.04	<.001	.002
Percent Correct	$F_{1,15}$	-	18.0	5.1	69.4	5.3	9.8
	p	-	<.001	.04	<.001	.04	.007

On average, direct interaction was faster than ThumbSpace (811 ms v. 2068 ms), large targets were easier to select than small targets (1367 ms v. 1512 ms), and sparse targets were easier to select than dense targets (1312 ms v. 1566 ms). The two way interactions involving input type confirmed two of our hypotheses: (1) target size impacted user performance when using direct interaction (large = 691 ms v. small = 930 ms), but not when using ThumbSpace; and (2) target density impacted user performance more when using ThumbSpace than using direct interaction, presumably because users performed more corrective moves in the *adjust* phase of selection for dense targets than sparse targets. However, our prediction that distance would not impact access time with ThumbSpace was incorrect. In fact, users were significantly slower selecting near targets with ThumbSpace than far targets (Fig. 5a). We surmise that most users' ThumbSpaces directly overlapped the near targets, resulting in considerable thumb occlusion for during these tasks. Our study setup exacerbated the problem because targets were not visually distinct from one another, which diminished the efficacy of ThumbSpace's occlusion solution.

Percent Correct. We carried out a 2 (input type) x 2 (size) x 2 (density) x 2 (distances) RM-ANOVA on percent correct selection data. Significant main effects of target size and density were observed, as well as significant interactions of input x size, input x density, and input x distance (Table 1).

Overall, participants were more accurate selecting large targets than small targets (.95 v. .90), and more accurate selecting from among sparse targets than among dense targets (.93 v. .91). As with the time results, target size significantly influenced error rate for direct interaction (large = .87 v. small = .99) but not for ThumbSpace interaction. Target density only influenced user performance when using ThumbSpace (sparse = .94 v. dense = .90), but had no impact during direct interaction. Assuming that users perform fewer corrections in the *adjust* phase for sparse targets than for dense targets, then it is reasonable that the success rate would be higher for sparse targets. We saw a similar pattern for input x distance with error rate as selection time: with direct interaction, users were more accurate hitting near targets, whereas with ThumbSpace users were more accurate selecting far targets. In fact, users were significantly more accurate hitting far targets with ThumbSpace (.94) than with direct interaction (.92), as shown at the bottom of Fig. 5a.

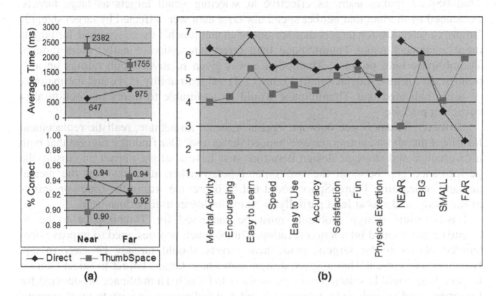

Fig. 5. (a) Average selection time and percent correct for near v. far targets by input method. Note the scale for percent correct does not start at 0. (b) User satisfaction (7 = most satisfied).

Satisfaction: User satisfaction data correlated with the performance data, with users on average preferring direct interaction ($\mu = 5.7$) to ThumbSpace ($\mu = 4.8$). Participants generally found ThumbSpace more mentally challenging than direct interaction, rated the two methods similarly in terms of task satisfaction and fun, but found ThumbSpace required less physical exertion than direct interaction. ThumbSpace received its lowest scores for accessing near targets, but was much preferred over direct interaction for selecting far targets. Only a quarter of the users stated a preference for using ThumbSpace for one-handed interaction given their comfort level at the end of the study, but 69% stated they would prefer ThumbSpace to direct interaction for general one handed device use if given sufficient practice.

5 Summary and Future Work

ThumbSpace is the result of our exploration of applying techniques from large-display interaction to small, mobile devices. We have shown that a direct application of existing techniques is not enough; issues such as occlusion, limited real estate, and users' varying biomechanics must be taken into account. ThumbSpace addresses these issues with specific, intuitive mechanisms, including a user-defined input space (Fig. 1a) and a consistent *aim-adjust-lift* interaction technique (Fig. 3).

The results from our user study indicate that applying large-display interaction techniques to mobile devices is promising and that ThumbSpace is a strong step in this direction. In particular, we are encouraged that ThumbSpace made progress toward both of our design goals: (1) "decouple target size from thumb size": ThumbSpace makes users as effective at selecting small targets as large targets, evidenced by the fact that neither speed nor error data were affected by target size; (2) "improve selection for targets that are out of thumb reach": users accessed far targets more accurately using ThumbSpace than direct interaction. Finally, users thought ThumbSpace held promise; ThumbSpace was given relatively high ratings on a 7-point scale for task satisfaction (5.1), fun (5.4) and learnability (5.4), and the majority of users indicated that ThumbSpace would be preferable to direct interaction after sufficient practice.

However, ThumbSpace does not appear to be an immediate, realistic replacement for direct thumb interaction for one-handed device use. Our findings suggest that both user practice and strategic design iterations may have a strong impact on closing the performance gap between the two input types. Further, it seems that the mental demand of learning ThumbSpace could not be overcome within the time constraints of the study, and was at least partially to blame for lower user performance.

Lastly, some design problems must be addressed for ThumbSpace to be an effective one-handed interaction solution. ThumbSpace was designed to improve one-handed access to far targets, since near targets should already be easy to tap. However, our current ThumbSpace design makes near targets harder to select than far targets. One possible solution is to allow users to launch ThumbSpace on-demand for far targets, and provide only occlusion avoidance techniques for easy to reach objects. The problems of speeding the user learning curve and reducing the mental demand of ThumbSpace requires further exploration, but offering visual cues about the proxy to object mappings, and constraining users' ThumbSpace definitions to those with the same aspect ratio as the DisplaySpace, are promising future directions.

Acknowledgments. Many thanks to Dave Levin for his helpful edit suggestions.

References

1. Aliakseyeu, D., Subramanian, S., Gutwin, C., Nacenta, M.: Bubble radar: efficient pen-based interaction. In: Proceedings of AVI '06, pp. 19–26. ACM Press, New York (2006)
2. Asano, T., Sharlin, E., Kitamura, Y., Takashima, K., Kishino, F.: Predictive interaction using the delphian desktop. In: Proceedings of UIST '05, pp. 133–141. ACM Press, New York (2005)
3. Baudisch, P., et al.: Drag-and-Pop and Drag-and-Pick: Techniques for Accessing Remote Screen Content on Touch- and Pen-operated Systems. In: Interact '03, pp. 57–64. Springer, Heidelberg (2003)
4. Bederson, B.B., Meyer, J., Good, L.: Jazz: An Extensible Zoomable User Interface Graphics Toolkit in Java. In: Proceedings of UIST '00, pp. 171–180. ACM Press, New York (2000)

5. Bezerianos, A., Balakrishnan, R.: The vacuum: facilitating the manipulation of distant objects. In: Proceedings of CHI '05, pp. 361–370. ACM Press, New York (2005)
6. Blanch, R., Guiard, Y., Beaudouin-Lafon, M.: Semantic pointing: improving target acquisition with control-display ratio adaptation. In: Proc. CHI'04, pp. 519–526. ACM Press, New York (2004)
7. Brewster, S.A., Lumsden, J., Bell, M., Hall, M., Tasker, S.: Multimodal 'Eyes-Free' interaction techniques for mobile devices. In: Proc. CHI '03, pp. 473–480. ACM Press, New York (2003)
8. Colle, H.A., Hiszem, K.J.: Standing at a kiosk: effects of key size and spacing on touch screen numeric keypad performance. Ergonomics 47(13), 1406–1423 (2004)
9. Grossman, T., Balakrishnan, R.: The bubble cursor: enhancing target acquisition by dynamic resizing of the cursor's activation area. In: Proceedings CHI '05., pp. 281–290. ACM Press, New York (2005)
10. Guiard, Y., Blanch, R., Beaudouin-Lafon, M.: Object pointing: a complement to bitmap pointing in GUIs. In: Proc. GI '04. Canadian Human-Computer Comm. Soc, pp. 9–16 (2004)
11. Hascoët, M.: Throwing models for large displays. In: British HCI Conference. British HCI Group, pp. 73–77 (2003)
12. Hinckley, K., Pierce, J., Sinclair, M., Horvitz, E.: Sensing techniques for mobile interaction. In: Proceedings of UIST '00, pp. 91–100. ACM Press, New York (2000)
13. Kabbash, P., Buxton, W.: The "Prince" technique: Fitts' Law and selection using area cursors. In: Proceedings of CHI '95, pp. 273–279. ACM Press, New York (1995)
14. Karlson, A.K., Bederson, B.B., Contreras-Vidal, J.L.: Understanding One Handed Use of Mobile Devices. In: Lumsden, J. (ed.) Handbook of Research on User Interface Design and Evaluation for Mobile Technology, Idea Group Reference (2007)
15. Karlson, A.K., Bederson, B.B., SanGiovanni, J.: AppLens and LaunchTile: two designs for one-handed thumb use on small devices. In: Proc. CHI '05, pp. 201–210. ACM Press, New York (2005)
16. Kristoffersen, S., Ljungberg, F.: "Making place" to make IT work: empirical explorations of HCI for mobile CSCW. In: Proceedings of SIGGROUP '99, pp. 276–285. ACM Press, New York (1999)
17. Milanesi, C., et al.: Market Share: Mobile Devices by Technology, Worldwide, 4Q06 and 2006, Gartner, Inc. (2007)
18. Mizobuchi, S., Mori, K., Ren, X., Yasumura, M.: An empirical study of the minimum required size and the number of targets for pen on the small display. In: Proceedings of MobileHCI '02, pp. 184–194. Springer, Heidelberg (2002)
19. Nacenta, M.A., Aliakseyeu, D., Subramanian, S., Gutwin, C.: A comparison of techniques for multi-display reaching. In: Proceedings of CHI '05, pp. 371–380. ACM Press, New York (2005)
20. Oulasvirta, A., Tamminen, S., Roto, V., Kuorelahti, J.: Interaction in 4-second bursts: the fragmented nature of attentional resources in mobile HCI. In: Proceedings of CHI '05, pp. 919–928. ACM Press, New York (2005)
21. Parhi, P., Karlson, A.K., Bederson, B.B.: Target Size Study for One-Handed Thumb Use on Small Touchscreen Devices. In: Proceedings of MobileHCI '06, pp. 203–210. ACM Press, New York (2006)
22. Pascoe, J., Ryan, N., Mores, D.: Using while moving: HCI issues in fieldwork environment. Trans. on Computer-Human Interaction 7(3), 417–437 (2000)

23. Pirhonen, P., Brewster, S.A., Holguin, C.: Gestural and audio metaphors as a means of control in mobile devices. In: Proceedings of CHI '02, pp. 291–298. ACM Press, New York (2002)
24. Potter, R.L., Weldon, L.J., Shneiderman, B.: Improving the accuracy of touch screens: an experimental evaluation of three strategies. In: Proc. CHI '88, pp. 27–32. ACM Press, New York (1988)
25. Robinson, S.: Apple iPhone: Catalyst for Capacitive Touchscreen-Only Phones to Balloon to 115 Million Units within Two Years, Strategy Analytics (2007)
26. Sears, A., Revis, D., Swatski, J., Crittenden, R., Schneiderman, B.: Investigating touchscreen typing: the effect of keyboard size on typing speed. Behaviour & Information Technology 12(1), 17–22 (1993)
27. Sears, A., Shneiderman, B.: High-precision touchscreens: design strategies and comparisons with a mouse. International Journal of Man-Machine Studies 34(4), 593–613 (1991)
28. Shao, J.: Personal Computer Quarterly Statistics Worldwide By Region: Final Database, Gartner, Inc. (2007)
29. Vogel, D., Baudisch, P.: Shift: A technique for operating pen-based interfaces using touch. In: Proceedings of CHI '07, ACM Press, New York (2007)
30. Wigdor, D., Balakrishnan, R.: TiltText: using tilt for text input to mobile phones. In: Proceedings of UIST '03, pp. 81–90. ACM Press, New York (2003)

Optimizing on Mobile Usage Cost for the Lower Income Group: Insights and Recommendations

Deepak P. and Anuradha Bhamidipaty

IBM India Research Lab, Bangalore, India
{deepak.s.p, abhamidi}@in.ibm.com

Abstract. There is an increasing trend in the penetration of mobile phones towards the lower strata (lower income) group of the society. Cost is perceived as the governing factor which determines the adoption of mobile phones in this group. This paper explores the effect of cost on the usage of mobile phones and proposes an enhanced design with features that optimize its usage cost for lower income group. These features help determine and restrict call duration, proactively alert user on usage deviations and avoid early call terminations. Preliminary evaluations of the enhanced design were decidedly positive about the effectiveness in controlling and optimizing mobile usage cost.

1 Introduction

Developing countries like India and China are increasingly noticing the unbalanced spread and reach of information industry infrastructure, which aggravates the urban-rural, rich-poor divide. Penetration of Information and Communication Technologies (ICT), mobile telephony in particular is viewed as an opportunity to bridge this gap [1]. We recognize that there are two aspects to taking Information Technology (IT) to the lower strata of the society; the availability and support of physical infrastructure and other barriers that prevents the penetration of technology. These barriers include illiteracy, socio-cultural effects, language barriers and cost. Multiple studies on penetration barriers have concluded that cost (or pre-conceived notions about it) is the largest impediment to adoption of mobile phones in developing countries ([2], [3]).

In this paper, we study the effect of *cost* on the penetration and usage of mobile phones and identify the significant cost-related pain points in mobile usage in the lower strata of the society. Using a mobile phone involves the one time cost of owing a mobile handset and the cost of maintaining it. The second factor is of more concern to the lower income group because of its recurring nature. We propose features addressing the identified pain points to be included in the *"cheap-usage"* mobile phone, and validate the importance of cost as a barrier to penetration of technology by gauging the acceptance of the proposed features among the lower-income group. We expect that the design of the proposed features provide insights into how technology has to be sensitive to the cost factor, if it hopes that the lower strata of the society would be able to leverage it.

C. Baranauskas et al. (Eds.): INTERACT 2007, LNCS 4662, Part I, pp. 339–342, 2007.
© IFIP International Federation for Information Processing 2007

2   User Study

A user study of the lower income group was conducted to get insight into their spending pattern for mobile phone. Our aim was to understand the *cost* factor and its effect on mobile usage such as their call patterns, and as to how they managed their mobile usage budgets. The survey population consisted of 30 semi-literate mobile phone users from the lower income category in and around Bangalore, a city in the state of Karnataka in India. By semi-literate, we mean that they are able to recognize English numerals, but are not very comfortable about reading and writing the language their mobile phone uses (which was English in all the 30 cases). They had an average daily income of 5-6$, were in their 20s or early 30s and were mostly from high-school dropouts who had to start earning in their teens due to poverty. Most of these people use the least expensive of the mobile phones available in the market.

2.1   Results and Inferences

It was seen that the usage patterns of most of the surveyed people were very similar and were very different from the usage patterns of the higher income groups. The results showed that people in lower income group spend as low as 3-15$ per month on mobile usage with an average of 5$. We enumerate our observations of the effect of cost on mobile usage as follows:

1. **Preference for Pre-paid Mobile Connections:** The strong conviction to keep mobile usage cost in check leads to almost all people to go in for pre-paid connections. Pre-paid connections require advance payment, and thus are effective to constrain unrestricted mobile usage.
2. **Short Call Durations:** Mobile phones are mostly used for conveying to-the-point information and hence tend to be very short. Long calls are usually scheduled and planned at regular intervals (e.g., weekly).
3. **Skewed Call Distribution:** Most of the participants reported a high skew in call distribution, with the number of contacts used on a daily basis being as low as 2-8 with an average of 4 (roughly around 5% of the size of the average contact list). Regularly contacted contacts were mostly family members and those from the inner circle of friends. This is mostly because of mobiles being perceived as devices to convey critical information only (due to the cost involved)
4. **Usage of Missed Calls to Convey Information:** With the widespread deployment of CLIP (Caller Line Identification), missed calls (which are not charged) have been used to convey pre-agreed Boolean information such as "I will give a missed call before I start home from workplace"
5. **Urge to optimize on Call Charges by controlling call durations:** Call charge is determined in terms of the number of call pulses it constitutes; each pulse has fixed duration and cost. Most participants reported that they try to check cost by trying to estimate the number of call pulses and hence the overall call duration when using the mobile phone and controlling it.

From the observations and inputs about the effects of cost on mobile usage, we identified the following as the cost related pain points of mobile usage on the lower income group

- Determining **when to end the call to optimize on call cost**
- **Managing mobile usage budget**, especially at a finer granularity than monthly (monthly being the usual frequency of mobile related payments)
- **Avoiding early call termination** and **voice breaks in call** due to erratic signal strengths and low battery charge (both these scenarios lead to repetitive and/or unfruitful calls)

In the following section, we design features for the mobile phone to address the above mentioned pain points.

3 Design of Mobile Phone for Cost-Effective Usage

Based on the findings of the user study we propose an enhanced design of the mobile phone with features that optimize the mobile usage cost for the lower income group. These features listed below focus on creating *"cheap-usage"* mobile phone that help the user reduce call duration, avoid early call termination in some cases, and provide the intelligence to keep a proactive check on cost. The features can be implemented with current technology in mobile phones.

1. *Pre-Pulse:* This feature is designed to notify the user with a beep before the current call pulse changes. For example, the phone can be configured to beep 5 seconds before the pulse switch so that the user can hang up before the pulse actually switches. This lets the user talk cost effectively. Currently some mobile phone models indicate a beep sound at the pulse change, hanging up at which time leads to wasted call charge for the additional call pulse (i.e., the beep indicates when *not* to hang up, if cost optimization is a concern). The user can configure the phone with his pulse duration and *pre-pulse* duration (i.e., the number of seconds before the pulse change that the phone should beep) as a one time activity. This feature aids cost optimized usage of mobile phones. This optimizes only the last pulse of a call, and hence the effect of this optimization would be much higher on the lower strata as they usually make very short calls.

2. *Preset Call Duration:* This feature in the mobile phone facilitates the user to preset the duration of a call before making the call, and the call gets automatically disconnected after the said duration. For example, a user can pre-determine that conveying a particular message (short one) should not take more than a minute and can pre-set it. Aligning the pre-set call duration with the call pulse duration provides the maximum talk time for a given cost. Pre-setting call duration helps control call durations and in turn optimizes the call charges.

3. *Proactive Alerts on Cost Usage:* Almost all of the survey population reported a fixed allocation of budget every month for mobile usage with very little scope of accommodating any extra usage cost. An insight into their mobile call logs showed us that their call usage pattern follows a daily pattern with some variations during holidays. The idea on providing proactive alerts is to embed intelligence into the mobile phone to be able to detect deviation from the usual call usage pattern on a daily basis, which might lead to higher cost and alert the user proactively to take check on cost usage. This prevents the user from incurring usage cost which is not aligned with their spending capacity or allocated budget.

4. Avoid Early Call Termination: This features helps avoid early call termination attributed to weak signal strength or low battery charge. If a user is attempting to make a phone call and the signal strength is weak, the mobile phone gives an alert to the user that the call may result in early termination or voice breaks, and optionally places the call details in a queue and auto connects (dials in itself) the call when the signal strength improves. The phone, optionally, alerts the user when an auto-connect is due to happen. This is critical because of erratic signal strengths due to poor mobile service infrastructure in the rural areas. Similarly, if the mobile has low battery charge and the user is about to make a long phone call (as he indicates using a pre-set call duration), an alert is signaled to the user to defer the call as it could possibly result in an early call termination.

4 Evaluation, Conclusions and Future Work

We conducted preliminary evaluation of our enhanced mobile design with 10 participants to obtain qualitative feedback on usefulness of added features and their effectiveness in controlling the mobile cost usage. The participants were drawn from the same population that was used for our user study. We explained the additional features to each of the participants and asked them to comment on what the enhancement meant to them. Interestingly, all the participants were decidedly positive about any feature in general that could help control mobile usage cost.

Of these four features, the survey population was most excited about the Pre-Pulse and Preset Call Duration features. These led to cost optimizations that they were already trying to practice manually, and hence, the automated solutions were immediately appealing to them. Incidentally, they reported an overrun of planned call duration around 20% of the time. Almost half of the survey population were unable to grasp the feature on proactive alerts well, and had concerns about whether an automated alert system was possible at all. They were receptive to the idea of tracking day-to-day mobile usage, but felt that alerts on remaining balance on a daily basis was itself very informative. All the participants found the idea on avoiding early call termination very exciting, especially because they live in areas of very erratic signal strengths. The proposed design can be achieved with current technology and would help the people in the lower strata of the society realize direct improvement over what is being offered today. We are currently working on optimizing cost on other usages of the mobile phone such as messaging and ring tones.

References

1. Sinha, C.: Effect of Mobile Telephony on Empowering Rural Communities in Developing Countries. In: Conference on Digital Divide and Global Development (November 2006)
2. Jhunjhunwala, A.: Can Telecom and IT be for the Disadvantaged?, http://www.tenet.res.in/Papers/Tel-IT/TelecomAndIT.html
3. Blixt, P.: Mobile Telephony in Rural India. Adapting the mobile telephone to the conditions of the unprivileged rural India, Master's Thesis, Royal Inst. of Tech., Sweden (2005)

Button Keyboard: A Very Small Keyboard with Universal Usability for Wearable Computing

Hyunjung Kim, Minjung Sohn, Seoktae Kim, Jinhee Pak, and Woohun Lee

Korea Advanced Institute of Science and Technology, Daejeon, Korea
{rroseoscar,sohnminjung,seoktaekim,Jenny808,woohun.lee}@kaist.ac.kr

Abstract. This paper presents the Button Keyboard, a very small wearable keyboard with universal usability. The Button Keyboard has high wearability and social acceptance due to its remarkably small size. As it is roughly button sized (33mm×33mm), it can be worn on the body without any discomfort. In addition, it adapts a mobile QWERTY layout to improve text entry for general users without special training. After an evaluation of the text input performance, it was found that the keyboard provides sufficient text input speed and learnability in spite of its small size. Furthermore, a touch-sensitive keypad divides input states by recognizing finger motions. Therefore, the system can provide visual or auditory *feed-forwards* to users. Thus, users can confirm the key before they execute. This previewable feature makes the keyboard a highly usable example of a wearable computer, in that it reduces the focus of attention and frequency of error. Moreover, it has the potential to assist the disabled by providing effective and appropriate ranges of feed-forwards.

Keywords: Wearable computing, Text entry, Keyboard.

1 Introduction

The absence of proper text input devices prevents the expansion of wearable computing. Current user interface devices for wearable computers are often considered to be obtrusive and appear unusual. Therefore, the use of wearable computing devices is limited to only researchers and a few early adopters. To ensure universal use, keyboards in the wearable computing environment should have high wearability and social acceptance. The operation of the keyboard should also be easy for all users to learn without special training. A sufficient input speed and a low error rate are important factors for text entry as well.

Many concepts and prototypes of wearable keyboards have been proposed and commercialized. However, wearable keyboards that consider universal usability have not been well researched. To make wearable computing devices usable by all, the size of the keyboard should be carefully considered [1]. It should be minimized to allow high social acceptance and wearability while providing high learnability and sufficient text input performance.

C. Baranauskas et al. (Eds.): INTERACT 2007, LNCS 4662, Part I, pp. 343–346, 2007.
© IFIP International Federation for Information Processing 2007

2   Reducing the Size of Wearable Keyboard

Keyboard size is a crucial factor in deciding the wearability and social acceptance. Wearability and social acceptance are higher with a smaller keyboard. However, the extent that the size can be reduced is limited, as the performance of a keyboard depends on the physical size of the operating part of the human body. Keyboards with key pitches under certain size result in lower text input performance and higher fatigue level compared to common keyboards [2]. Therefore, it is important to estimate the optimum point between text input performance and wearability.

A One-key Keyboard was suggested as a new minimized keyboard in our previous research by the authors [1]. This keyboard has only one key, which has the same mechanism of a desktop keyboard and provides tactile feedback. This was a significant reduction in size compared to earlier keyboards. With the One-key Keyboard, key selection is conducted using a touch screen on the top of the keyboard that detects the position of a finger. A QWERTY layout was selected to improve performance and learnability. To determine the size of the keyboard, wearability and social acceptance were tested using six different-sized keyboard models following a QWERTY layout. The results of the study showed that wearability and social acceptance were evaluated positively when a keyboard is smaller than 90mm×45mm which is the size of a business card. The One-key Keyboard was 70mm×35mm in size with 7mm key pitches. In a performance test, the participants achieved 18.9WPM (SD: 2.0) with a 6.7% (SD: 2.7%) error rate. Considering the very small size of the One-key Keyboard, the text input performance was extraordinary, as no additional instrument, such as a stylus, was used.

3   Concept of Button Keyboard

Button Keyboard is an extension of the One-key Keyboard. Although the One-key Keyboard showed good performance and usability, it was limited in that it was a wrist-worn keyboard. Users should carry the keyboard everywhere at all times, which prove to be a burden. Therefore, the focus was on minimizing the keyboard size to roughly button-size (33mm×33mm), which would allow it to be attached to clothes (see Fig. 1, left). This was thought to make the wearable keyboard more usable for everyday use. A mobile QWERTY layout [3] was adapted to provide high learnability (see Fig. 1, right).

Similar to PreSense [4], the Button Keyboard senses finger motions on the keypad by using a touch sensor array. This makes it possible to divide input states into key selecting, touching and pressing states. Therefore, the system can provide visual or auditory *feed-forwards* to users before pressing the key. Furthermore, this provides independent character selection thus avoiding entry segmentation problem. Finger motions on the keypad without pressing buttons can also be recognized as commands. The user can input a space key, a back space key and the enter key with finger gestures (see Fig. 2, left).

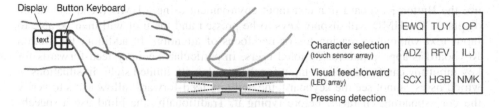

Fig. 1. Concept of Button Keyboard (left: usage, center: structure, right: key layout)

Fig. 2. Implementation and evaluation of Button Keyboard (left: finger gesture as commands, center: prototype, right: text entry speed of Button Keyboard)

4 Evaluation of Button Keyboard

In order to test the performance of the Button Keyboard, a text entry performance test was conducted. Ten college students (6 women, and 4 men; average age: 23.9) participated in the text-entry performance test of the Button Keyboard. The task was to enter short phrases of text taken from the Mackenzie et al. (2003) phrase set [5]. The subjects took part in twenty sessions lasting 10 minutes each.

On the 20th session, the entry speed was 14.7 WPM (SD: 1.70), and one of the participants achieved up to 17.0 WPM (see Fig. 4). The average error rate was 6.0% (SD: 0.66%). In a comparison with results from other mobile phone keypads (15.5 WPM, 5.0% error rate on the 20th session) [6] and considering that the participants are not native English speakers, the performance of the Button Keyboard is shown to be satisfactory. In addition, the participants used only one hand to input the text, which differs from how mobile phone keypads are used.

5 Discussion and Conclusion

The results of this study strongly suggest that the Button Keyboard provides sufficient text input performance in spite of its small size. It satisfies the requirements of high wearability, social acceptance, learnability and sufficient text input performance. Hence, the Button Keyboard is expected to be extremely useful in a wearable computing environment. In particular, the previewable feature of the Button Keyboard enables it to be used in various situations. For instance, it may be easier to use the Button Keyboard in a text input environment using a HMD (head - mounted display). The HMD will display keys to be pressed and the user will then be able to input text without increasing his or her focus of attention. In addition, the Button Keyboard is appropriate for disabled users. In particular, auditory feed-forwards for key inputting can facilitate text input for the people with limited sight. In situations in which users cannot see the keyboard, the auditory feed-forwards allow users to verify the corresponding character before typing it. Traditionally, the blind use a speech-enabled typewriter. However, this device does not offer preview information; instead, it gives feedback only after typing. The utilization of finger gestures can also make key inputting, menu structure navigation and pointing much easier.

The next steps in this ongoing research include a field study. One of the limitations of this study is that all tests were performed in a lab environment. To ensure universal use of the Button Keyboard, it is necessary to test its usability with various types of users, including the different-abled users.

Acknowledgments. This work was supported in part by MIC & IITA through the IT Leading R&D Support Project and the BK21 program.

References

1. Kim, S., Sohn, M., Pak, J., Lee, W.: One-key Keyboard: A Very Small QWERTY keyboard Supporting Text Entry for Wearable Computing. In: Proceedings of OZCHI 2006, pp. 305–308 (2006)
2. Otsuka, I., et al.: Input Performance of One-Handed Keyboard. In: Proceedings of 7th Symposium on Human Interface, pp. 5–8 (1991)
3. Hwang, S., Lee, G.: Qwerty-like 3x4 keypad layouts for mobile phone. In: extended abstracts of the ACM conference on human factors in computing systems, pp. 1479–1482. ACM Press, New York (2005)
4. Rekimoto, J., Schewsig, C.: PreSense: Bi-directional Touch and Pressure Sensing Interactions with Tactile Feedback. In: CHI 2006 extended abstracts on Human factors in computing systems, pp. 1253–1258 (2005)
5. MacKenzie, I.S., Soukoreff, R.W.: Phrase sets for evaluating text entry techniques. In: extended abstracts of the ACM conference on human factors in computing systems, pp. 754–755. ACM Press, New York (2003)
6. Hwang, S., Lee, G.: Qwerty-like 3x4 keypad layouts for mobile phone. In: extended abstracts of the ACM conference on human factors in computing systems, pp. 1479–1482. ACM Press, New York (2005)

Electronic Communication: Themes from a Case Study of the Deaf Community

Valerie Henderson-Summet[1], Rebecca E. Grinter[1],
Jennie Carroll[2], and Thad Starner[1]

[1] Georgia Institute of Technology, GVU Center, Atlanta, GA, USA
{vlh, beki, thad}@cc.gatech.edu
[2] University of Sydney, Business Information Systems, NSW, Australia
j.carroll@econ.usyd.edu.au

Abstract. We present a qualitative, exploratory study to examine the
space of electronic communication (*e.g.* instant messaging, short message
service, email) by Deaf teenagers in the greater Atlanta metro area. We
discuss differences and similarities between deaf and hearing teen's usage
of electronic communication mediums. Five common themes: **Identity,
Connection, Control, Tension,** and **Convenience** were identified
from the analysis of the data collected. These themes allow us to explore
electronic communication from the "use-centric" view of teenagers who
are indifferent to the underlying technology supporting this communication.

1 Introduction

In 1982 Barbara Wagreich, a deaf–blind computer professional wrote an article
about the possibilities of a new technology, email, and how it might prove beneficial for people with disabilities, particularly the deaf [23]. Her study, conducted
from 1978–1981 with deaf participants, their friends, and their families, showed
that email was not only a formal medium for business meetings and communications, but also an informal tool for maintaining and furthering friendships.
Twenty-four years later email is still used in this fashion but is complemented
by the technologies of Instant Messaging (IM) and Short Message Service (SMS)
or text messaging. These technologies have been widely adopted by the hearing
population [16, 12], in particular by teenagers [19, 8, 7]. However, it is unclear
how these new methods of communication are being used by the Deaf community[1] who are often reported to be early adopters of technologies [18, 10, 1], and
there is very little formalized work studying the use by the Deaf community.

---

[1] The word "deaf" can have several meanings. Medical deafness focuses on the severity
and cause of a hearing loss and is denoted with a lowercase 'd,' "deaf." The cultural
definition of Deaf, with an uppercase 'D', is a voluntary classification and refers to
the community formed by individuals whose primary method of communication is
ASL. All the participants of this study were deaf, and most identified themselves as
Deaf which is how I refer to them collectively in this paper.

C. Baranauskas et al. (Eds.): INTERACT 2007, LNCS 4662, Part I, pp. 347–360, 2007.
© IFIP International Federation for Information Processing 2007

This work begins to fill this void with an exploratory study to understand the uniqueness of Deaf teenagers' electronic communication and to suggest further research directions.

We begin with related work on teenage communication patterns, and then discuss our study, the participants, and the data obtained. This includes an in-depth look at a variety of technologies the teens used. We also discuss the technology infrastructure in the United States and how it affects the communication choices Deaf teens make. We then describe the five themes that were identified through our analysis of the data collected from the multi-method study.

2   Related Work

In their work on SMS, Barkhuus and Vallgårda found that SMS was used to communicate mainly among friends and significant others, but IM was used for a wider range of conversational partners [2]. Grinter and Eldgridge found that teens adopted mobile messaging for a variety of reasons, prominently, to coordinate conversations via another medium [7,8]. In a market report on mobile technologies, Blinkoff and Barranca found three central themes which users wanted: manage relationships, experience the unexpected, and avoid mobile stress [5]. In a study on teenage communication preferences, Schiano et al. found that home phones were the most common communication medium [19]. Much of this work points to electronic communication from mobile devices (usually SMS) as being a transition medium which is used to coordinate voice communications via mobile or "landline" phones. This usage pattern points to a reliance on the voice telephony capabilities which many deaf individuals do not use, and this situation presents a significant difference between hearing and deaf teenagers.

While it might seem that work surveying the use of electronic communication methods among hearing teenagers [7,8,19] would be sufficient to understand Deaf teens' communication, there are distinct linguistic differences between hearing and Deaf teens which warrant further exploration. For many people who are born deaf in the United States, their native language is American Sign Language (ASL). [2] Unlike English, ASL does not have a written form. It is languages' written form which enables electronic communication such as SMS, IM, email, etc. to exist. Deaf reliance on a medium which requires the use of a foreign language seems improbable. However, Bakken [1] found that Deaf teens in Norway relied on SMS messaging for building social networks, maintaining those networks, and for keeping abreast of trends and gossip. However, Bakken's work may not generalize to the United States population due to the differences between Europe and the US in SMS use and mobile device adoption.

It is also worthwhile to understand some of the linguistic issues which can arise from being born deaf in the United States. Linguists have identified the existence of a "critical period" for language development – a period during which a child

---

[2] ASL, the dominate sign language of North America, is a spatial, gesture based language which uses different hand, face, and body gestures to communicate. ASL's grammar is different from English. For a more complete discussion of ASL, see [22].

must be exposed to and immersed in any language, including ASL [15, 17] to further linguistic development. The slower linguistic development of deaf children has been attributed to incomplete language models and lack of daily interaction using a language [21] unless their parents are also deaf and can sign to them from birth. These issues contribute to the fact that the average 17–18 year old deaf student reads at a 9-10 year old level [11].

Given the different characteristics of hearing and Deaf teenagers, we designed a research study to investigate the different ways in which electronic communication technologies were used in the Deaf community. Having introduced work on communication by teenagers, we now to turn to a description of study methods, participants, and methodological issues.

3   Study Design and Methodology

We recruited twelve participants with the cooperation of the Atlanta Area School for the Deaf (AASD). This is a public school for students who are deaf, and its enrollment area covers the majority of North Georgia, including the Atlanta metro area. On average, the students lived almost 30 miles from AASD. The maximum distance between students was almost 100 miles. This distance often precluded the teenagers from associating with their social community when not attending school. The students had a strong community at school; however, these students often cannot communicate easily with the hearing teens in their neighborhood or local hang-out spots. Because of this, they often feel isolated.

The twelve participants ranged in age from 14–17 with an average age of 16. There were six females and six males, although one male student left the study after the first activity. Several of the students had some residual hearing, but not enough to make a school with auditory instruction feasible. Four students had enough residual hearing as to have some speech and to use oral communication with some degree of success.

The study had three phases designed to survey different aspects of the role of electronic communication in Deaf teenager's lives. The three phases were a social mapping activity, a diary study, and discussion groups, and these are described in more detail below.

Social Mapping Activity: The social mapping activity was designed to elicit the teenagers' social networks and give us an idea who they communicated with, whether those people were hearing or deaf, and the main techniques for communicating with those people.

Based upon the work of Smith, et.al [20], the teens were given a large sheet of paper and pencils. They were first asked to list everyone with whom they felt it was important to communicate. The definition of "important" was left to the participants, but we asked them to consider if they would be upset or unhappy if they could not communicate with a person. Second, the students were asked to label each person on their list as "hearing" or "deaf." After that, they were asked to go through their list and write down how they would communicate with that person in two different situations: face–to–face and remotely. They were asked

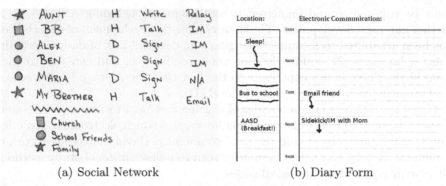

(a) Social Network   (b) Diary Form

Fig. 1. Examples of a Social Network and Diary Study Form

to write N/A or "Nothing" if they did not communicate with a contact. Lastly, the students were asked to group and categorize their contacts in any way they felt appropriate. Figure 1a shows an example of a social network similar to those generated by the students, with the contacts and their characteristics listed in the top half of the figure and the categories listed on the bottom.

Diary Study: The diary study phase involved students recording when and where they used electronic communication. Based on the work of Grinter and Eldridge [8,7], it was designed to give a clear picture of the teenagers' lives on a daily basis and how electronic communication fit into it.

This form contained space to record one day's activities per page. Each hour was subdivided into 4 15-minute blocks, and the students were asked to record the location and nature of their communication. Figure 1b gives an example of the form the students used. The students were given a booklet containing 7 forms, one for each day for a week.

Discussion Groups: After the social mapping activity and week-long diary activity, the students were interviewed. The interviews were conducted in two groups based on the student's class sections. Thus, they were with people they already knew and with whom they were comfortable talking. The interview questions were largely determined using data from the social maps and weekly diaries. We also allowed the students to highlight other topics they felt relevant.

After collecting this data we coded it according to several different schemes. We first coded the interview data by device used and looked for patterns and themes that were specific to a particular technology. We then recoded the data by more general categories such as "Who, what, when, where, why?" and looked for themes which emerged regardless of the device or technology used. We then used data from the social maps and journals to help validate or reject our emerging themes. The preliminary findings were reviewed by external researchers for further validation.

4 Results

Originally, our study set out to examine the overall space of electronic communication use. However, it soon became clear that the majority of the teens used some kind of mobile device and the data naturally reflected that fact.

In this section, we discuss the preferred methods of communication used by the teens. We then discuss communication infrastructure in the United States and how this affects the teens' choices. In Section 5, we then present five central themes of communication that we extracted from our data and present the teens' communication within the framework of those themes.

Electronic communication preferences: As email was to Wagreich in 1982, the mobile platform has become to Deaf teens today. It levels the playing field by lowering the barrier of participation and allows them to maintain their friendships in ways that are convenient and simple. When students needed to communicate with someone they knew to be nearby, they would usually seek them out in person. However, when unsure of a person's location or when the person was far away, the students usually turned to a lightweight electronic method of communication rather than the more traditional method of relay or TTY.[3] The teens we interviewed overwhelmingly favored establishing electronic means of communication after meeting new people. Most expressed a preference for exchanging email addresses or IM screen names. One student noted that many hearing people asked for an email address or a phone number for text messaging. Since he could never remember his phone number, he simply gave them his email address instead.

Devices and Infrastructures: Mobile text messaging has been increasing in popularity in the United States, but has never achieved the widespread acceptance seen in Europe or parts of Asia [12]. Few teenagers pay for their own phone usage or use "pay as you go" plans. Text messages are not included in standard mobile service plans, and providers in the US often charge both the sender and the receiver of text messages and voice calls. Additionally, most providers provide "free night and weekend" plans which allow free voice calls after 9pm on weekdays and all day on weekends. This leads many hearing teens to wait until free calling periods and not use text messaging.

The most prized mobile device among the Deaf teenagers was clearly the T-Mobile Sidekick.[4] Many of the teens already owned this device, and some

---

[3] TTYs (also called teletypewriters or TDDs) have been an accepted way for deaf individuals to communicate. If each person has a TTY, they can type messages back and forth using TTYs connected to standard telephone lines. To communicate with someone who does not own a TTY requires a third party relay operator.

[4] The Sidekick is a device marketed in the US by the service provider T–Mobile. It is designed as an out–of–the–box Internet platform with a mini-QWERTY keyboard. It includes software for web browsing, instant messaging, email, address book, and SMS. T–Mobile also offers unlimited, data-only service for this device, making it attractive to deaf students who do not need the voice capabilities.

expressed a desire to upgrade, and those that did not have one expressed a desire to own one. However, none of them paid for it themselves. The Sidekick has become so ingrained in the teens' lives that it has a unique sign in ASL which mimics the screen popping up on the device. Only one student with verbal abilities used a mobile phone for voice telephony.

Some of the students in our study did not have a mobile device, but did have a family computer. Several students with mobile devices commented that they disliked computers. Two specific complaints were that "you're stuck in one place" and that computers had "a lot of things going on." Interestingly, one student noted that a legacy technology kept him tied to the computer. He had an old screen name through a service which did not work on his mobile device. He used his old screen name on the computer and his new one on his mobile device. The use of the computer for communication was drastically different from the use of mobile devices. Students reported only occasional, not constant communication via IM or email from a computer. Like Schiano's findings [19], the teens did not mode switch to email once they were online and chatting via IM. When they did use email, they responded to emails as soon as they received them, but complained that email was much slower than IM and "it takes a whole day to get it maybe."

5   Themes of Communication

We coded the interview portions of the study using open or inductive coding [14]. Combining this data with analysis of the social maps and diary studies, five clear themes emerged. To the teenagers, communication is: **Identity**, **Connection**, **Control**, **Tension**, and **Convenient**. These themes are pervasive in the teens' communication. They are useful to designers because they emphasize the importance of the central purpose rather than the technological specifics of devices, communication methods, protocols, and other issues that often influence design decisions.

5.1   Communication Is Identity

The teenagers viewed their electronic communication as a vital piece of their identity. They also manipulated and managed the identity they created online. In certain circumstances the teens used their communication to rebel by communicating in times or places when it was forbidden. In some cases, while unable to detect the noise it made the teens were aware that they needed to mute their device to avoid detection. The vibrate setting was the de facto alert mechanism for most teens, but they were aware that even that could occasionally be detected. When asked why they went to such lengths to avoid detection, one student summed up her feelings as, "I don't want everyone looking at me." The style of communication allowed her to preserve her privacy. They were aware of how the communication affected others around them and might reflect on them in public.

Students had no qualms about IMing someone not co-present even while physically with someone else. The teens didn't consider it rude if someone they were with also messaged other people. Their diaries often showed that they were collocated with members of their social circle (at dinner with family, for example), but IMing with friends via the mobile device. However, the teens felt that messaging should be conducted during breaks or lulls in the conversation. Being kept waiting to chat face-to-face by someone messaging was "wasting my time." Messaging while collocated was seen as something to fill time when their conversational partner was distracted by talking or driving. One participant noted, "You know sometimes, like with hearing people, they'll be talking to someone, and I feel left out. So I IM my sweetheart." Her communication usage allowed her to feel included even when she was with people who excluded her.

Somewhat surprisingly, given their difficulty with written English, most students expressed only minor worries about grammar or spelling mistakes. These mistakes were considered inconsequential for the most part, particularly among friends. One student said, "If I don't know how to spell it, I just make it up" while another noted, "Sometimes, if I get the grammar wrong or whatever, I'll just send [the message] anyway." One participant said he would generally ask his mother for help, but several others relied on the Sidekick, noting that it had built in spell check and grammar help, for example adding an apostrophe to a student's spelling of "Ive" instead of "I've."

5.2 Communication Is Connection

All the students considered communication with hearing friends and relatives to be an important component of their lives. Some students saw a mobile device as a means to enable that connection. The method of communication was less important than the ability to convey meaning and establish connections. In the words of one student, "The important thing is that people understand what I'm saying."

Like Barkhuus and Nardi [2, 16], we found that the primary recipients of IMs were the Deaf teens' friends, and they valued this ability to communicate very highly. They mostly reported messaging people who were not co-present, as they preferred to communicate directly with collocated people. One notable exception was a student who told us she used her Sidekick with a hearing person, passing the device back and forth. "When I can't hear [people], but they don't know how to sign, it's the only way we can actually get the point across." Her electronic communication allowed her to easily establish a connection with people she would not have been able to otherwise.

The students also reported IMing from the Sidekick to maintain connections with groups of their friends in large, multi-user sessions. Some of the students clearly enjoyed the large conversations with "lots of chatting going on." However some students were indifferent or clearly blasé about group conversations. Several students said it depended on what was going on. Another student noted that it could be "kinda annoying." Yet another characterized group IM conversations as "Blah, blah, blah."

One student described using away messages as a social activity, maintaining a large buddy list and reading away messages because she was curious what people were doing. Grinter et al. and Nardi found a similar use of IM for awareness in their studies of IM [9,16]. While not a turn-taking form of communication, the student was still maintaining connections with her peers and awareness of their activities.

The data from the social maps also demonstrates how dependent the teens have become on staying in touch via electronic methods. When analyzing this data, we found it interesting to examine the difference in how the teenagers communicated with their hearing and deaf friends, both in face-to-face communication and when not collocated. Figure 2 shows a graph of the data obtained from the teenagers' social maps. The top node shows the total of 419 contacts the teens listed in their maps. These were broken into three main categories based on the students' contacts' hearing ability: Hearing Contacts, Deaf Contacts, and Hard of Hearing or Unknown. Each of these categories were further split into methods of communication: Face-to-Face and Remote. The methods of communication were then listed in order of preference. For example, Figure 2 shows that 201 of the 419 contacts were deaf. For 190 of those 201 contacts, ASL was the preferred method for face-to-face communication, and for 124 of 201 contacts, IM was the preferred method of remote communication.

While this data should not be generalized due to the limited number of participants, several interesting things can be seen from this chart. An interesting trend is the differences in remote communication methods between the students' deaf contacts and hearing contacts. IM is the preferred communication method between the Deaf teenagers and other deaf people, used for 124 of 201 contacts. However, there is no clear preference for their hearing contacts who are not collocated, with the Deaf teens having no remote contact with 31% (68 out of 214) of hearing contacts and email being the preferred method of only 32% (64 out of 214).

The category of friends which the students do not maintain face–to–face relationships with (*i.e.* the "None" classification under the four face–to–face communication paths in Figure 2) also bears closer examination. There were 39 contacts that the students listed that they did not have any face–to–face communication with regardless of hearing status. However, the students communicated with 36 out of those 39 people remotely via the electronic methods of email and IM. (Of the other 3 people, 2 listed no communication either face-to-face or remotely and were obvious aberrant data points; the other wrote letters.) Before electronic communication existed and was widely available, remote communication with a person you had not met face–to–face would have taken the form of written letters (*i.e.* "pen-pals"). However, the teens today are using email and IM to do the same thing but with faster and more synchronous communication.

5.3   Communication Is Control

The teens' usage of communication also showed how they used it to feel more in control of their lives. An "easy" way to communicate clearly made the teens feel safer which appeared to be a key component of feeling in control.

The students controlled their contacts in a variety of ways, including blocking and multiple screen names. Blocking is a standard feature of most IM clients and allows users to block messages from other users. One student noted she usually only blocked advertisements and spam. Another volunteered that he never blocked anyone. Several would immediately block someone they didn't know, but one student would try to talk with people before blocking them, explaining, "Maybe it's a new friend. I wouldn't mind trying to talk to them." However, that student went on to state she would block them if she did not feel comfortable with them. Students would also block people who simply annoyed them either through the content of messages or the volume of messages sent. They would block friends if they were having a fight or disagreement. Although some students reported that acquaintances they blocked were quite upset, they still utilized the feature. One student noted that she would unblock acquaintances after some time to see if they still bothered her.

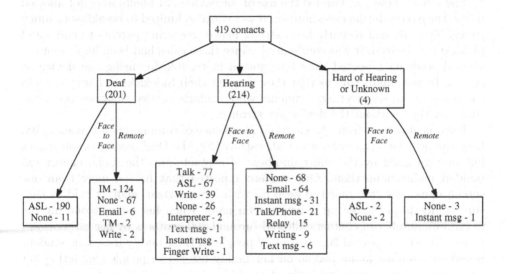

Fig. 2. Results for Social Networking Study

While not a specific medium of communication, away messages filled an important aspect in the teenager's communication spectrum, just as Baron found in her work on college students use of away messages [4]. The teens used a variety of away messages to control the flow of communication and indicate availability. Many students left a time estimating when they would return in their away messages before going out or being involved in other activities. They went to great lengths to maintain an accurate away message, including minute by minute updates. "When I get up in the morning, I immediately have to change [my away message] to my 'Hi, I'm at school now' message. I don't want people to think I'm sleeping then!" The away message removed the obligation of an immediate response.

5.4   Communication Is Tension

The communication usage also raised tension in the teens' lives. While they loved the positive aspects it provided, it also added negative artifacts to their lives.

Unlike other studies of hearing teenagers [13], very few of the students reported that their parents used the device as a tool to enforce discipline. Most students reported that their parents put few or no restrictions on the use of the device at home, including use during mealtimes or curfews. Six students reported that their parents didn't restrict their use at all, while another 2 reported some restrictions such as not using the device after a certain time on school nights or putting it away at mealtimes. One student pointed out, "Mom is fine because she knows, like, I'm Deaf and I want to communicate with people. And she knows it's OK. It's not wasting our time." One teen's parents would not allow him to have one due to the expense and possibility of losing it but used the device as incentive, hinting he might get one if he kept his grades up.

The school, however, banned the use of the devices. Students were not allowed to use the device during class hours and were instead limited to breakfast or lunch times. The rule had recently been strengthened, requiring parents to come and pick up the device if it was confiscated. Since these rules had been implemented, several students reported they had gotten in trouble for using the device at school. In fact, many told us that they now left their Sidekicks at home to avoid the temptation. However, the students who regularly carried their devices noted that any time without the device felt strange.

Tension also arose from the ease and prevalence of communication availability. Like the hearing teens in Smith et al.'s study [20], the Deaf teenagers sometimes felt overwhelmed by the sheer numbers of contacts and the social energy expended maintaining them. One student reported that having more than one screen name was "too much to keep up with." In contrast, another told us that she would simply make up a new screen name when her current one hit the maximum number of contacts allowed (around 200 contacts by her estimation.) Other students reported 20, 89, and 72 people on their buddy lists. One student noted that having many people on her buddy list led to people contacting her constantly which "gets kinda silly at times."

5.5   Communication Is Convenient

The students viewed their communication as highly convenient. It was clear that the device preferences and communication modes arose due to the convenience it afforded the users. The freedom of a personal platform was greatly valued and this freedom was exercised in a variety of ways.

The students used communication via mobile devices heavily. Most students who had a device reported using it daily with a majority of the use occurring during the free time after school or on the weekends. In their daily diaries, students reported several hour-long blocks of IM without interruptions. When questioned, the students assured us that was correct and that they were constantly chatting. One student observed, "I [chat] a lot. Even in my sleep I do it." One student admitted he chatted with his friends all day, saying his practice was, "kinda lazy, I guess."

In addition to just chatting, IM was viewed as an optimal, convenient way to schedule things with friends. This mirrored findings by Nardi et al. and Grinter and Palen [16, 9] that the immediacy of IM was useful for coordination and scheduling. Scheduling things was of great importance to the teens given their lack of transportation and distance from friends. The teens could refine their plans on-the-fly, but plans were usually made in advance due to the logistics of meeting. Only if a friend was offline was email employed to schedule things. Even then, email was usually used to establish a time when both would be available to IM and finalize the details.

The students choice of electronic communication medium also reflected the teens' desire for convenience. For example, most students preferred IM and saw text messaging as a backup communication medium (to be used only as a last resort). Text messaging was something to be used only if the other person lacked some vital functionality. The students might use text messaging if someone didn't have IM or email, if a friend wasn't online, or if a friend wasn't in a position to check email. Cost was not a deciding factor, unlike Grinter's study [7] which found that teenagers made a determination based on cost 27% of the time. This can be explained by the fact that none of the teenagers in our study paid for their own costs and the unlimited data plan that many of them had. One participant identified text messaging as a feature central to mobile phones and said that she used text messaging because most other people had a cell phone thus increasing the number of people with whom she could communicate. Another posited that he might use text messaging only in an emergency situation.

6 Discussion

In this paper we have presented a detailed report about the adoption and use of a variety of communications technologies among Deaf teenagers. We have answered questions about who they communicate with, what they use to communicate, and where and when they communicate. In answering these questions, we have raised many more, but two points bear further discussion here: first, the teens' *use-centric* view of mobile computing, and secondly the *social acceptability* of their chosen device and the tension arising from that choice.

The students' use and understanding of electronic communication was very "use-centric." While not understanding the specifics of the communication mode, they were still able to use the methods. For example, very few students could articulate the differences between text messaging and instant messaging. Instead, they characterized them based on the reply or response time. When asked what text messaging was, many of them responded from a use-centric perspective. Text messaging is "pretty fast" and "you're kinda talking." "...You kinda write a long thing out and then you send it and then you wait a minute and it comes back." This use-centric perspective extended beyond just the differences between text-messaging and instant messaging. When asked about a specific method of communication, the students responded first with the characteristics of its usage or with a list of whom they could contact by a specific method. However, while they may not have understood the underlying elements of the device, they had no trouble using the device in a variety of different ways. During the course of the study, the teens cited using the Sidekick for voice telephony, email, IM, Internet search, relay, and grammar/spelling checks.

Our study highlights that how technologists classify and distinguish technologies is different from mainstream, public use. Technologies that are drastically different can be unproblematic in use for end–users. This clarity in usage models is key for usability. In our study, the teens viewed the device as something to be used for communication, and seemed to inherently knew what service to use and when to use that particular service.

As discussed earlier, the teens drew from a wide geographical area which often limited their contact with each other. The Sidekick may have succeeded in this community because it is something which helps reduce this distance in a socially acceptable way. This device, unlike relay or a TTY, is practical to the entire population, not just the deaf or those trying to communicate with them. The Sidekick is accepted by both hearing and Deaf teens, and allows the Deaf teens to be similar to their hearing peers and establish a communication link using that similarity.

However, this similarity comes with a price. In some venues educators and linguists have expressed reservations about instant and text messaging. They have highlighted how the English used in computer–mediated communication differs from that used in more normative language [3, 6]. This is a particularly interesting issue given that our population may have problems with their second language of English, especially with structure and grammar. While the students reported using some acronyms and abbreviations, they were more concerned with whether or not the recipients could understand them. However the teens admitted that others sometimes used acronyms or slang that they didn't understand, with one participant hypothesizing, "Sometimes, they make stuff up." It is worth noting that many slang terms popular in text and instant messaging are phonetically based (e.g. "c u l8r") which would present inherent problems to the Deaf teens. By using informal language, the teens are practicing written English, something their teachers usually encourage.

7   Conclusions

While this paper cannot conclusively answer many questions about the design of mobile devices or electronic communication tools for the Deaf community, it can point the way to other avenues worthy of further exploration. Given the second language problems that many Deaf individuals encounter, should we be designing English-based (or other written language-based) interfaces? Should more designers explore ASL-based (or other visual language-based) interfaces for greater accessibility? Or, alternatively, do the good features afforded by visual language-based interfaces outweigh the usage problems for Deaf individuals?

In terms of more general accessibility, what other applications should we as ICT designers and practitioners introduce to help children who are born deaf overcome the language barriers they face?

This paper has begun to explore some of the communication preferences and platforms in the Deaf community. We have presented an exploratory study which starts to chart the space of electronic communication use by Deaf teens in the North Georgia and Atlanta areas.

We have used qualitative methods such as social mapping, diary studies, and interviews in order to spend time with the teens and learn about them, their needs, and their communication choices. We looked for communication similarities and differences with hearing teenagers and have found both. The five communication themes of **Identity, Connection, Control, Tension, and Convenience** help inform our design of "use–centric" technologies. We have found similarities in the motivation and reasons that teenagers' desire and want mobile communication technology. But we have also found differences, particularly in how different communication technologies are distinguished from one another.

This paper and the related work are the first steps toward understanding how to design accessible technology for Deaf teenagers. The challenge will be to design technology which simultaneously provides similarities to the mainstream in desirable ways and yet supports cultural differences.

Acknowledgments. Special thanks to Mary Anne Mullins and Harley Hamilton at AASD as well as the teenagers who participated. This work is funded by the NSF (Grants #0093291, #0511900, #0611519, and a Graduate Fellowship) and the US Dept. of Education (Grant #H133E010804). The opinions and conclusions of this publication do not necessarily reflect those of the NSF or the US DoEd.

References

1. Bakken, F.: The Inside Text, chapter, SMS Use Among Deaf Teens and Young Adults in Norway, pp. 161–174. Kluwer Academic Publishers, Boston, MA (2004)
2. Barkhuus, L., Vallgårarda, A.: Saying it all in 160 characters: Four classes of SMS conversations. Technical Report TR-45, IT University of Copenhagen, Cophenhagen, Denmark (April 2004)
3. Baron, N.S.: Instant messaging and the future of language. Communications of the ACM 48(7), 29–31 (2005)
4. Baron, N.S., Squires, L., Tench, S., Thompson, M.: Tethered or mobile? Use of away messages in instant messaging by american college students. In: Front Stage – Back Stage: Mobile Communication and the Renegotiation of hte Social Sphere, Grimstead, Norway, June 2003, Springer, Heidelberg (2003)
5. Blinkoff, R., Barranca, M.: Mobile lifestyles. Receiver Magazine 6, Vodafone Group (2002)
6. Crystal, D.: Language and the Internet. Cambridge University Press, Cambridge (2001)
7. Grinter, R., Eldridge, M.: y do tngrs luv 2 txt msg? In: Proc. of the Seventh ECSCW, pp. 219–238 (2001)

8. Grinter, R., Eldridge, M.: Wan2tlk?: everyday text messaging. In: Proc. of CHI, April 2003, pp. 441–448. ACM Press, New York (2003)
9. Grinter, R.E., Palen, L.: Instant messaging and teen life. In: Proceedings of CSCW '02, New Orleans, LA, November 2002, pp. 21–30 (2002)
10. Harkins, J., Bakke, M.: Oxford Handbook of Deaf Studies, Language, and Education. In: ch. Technologies for Communication: Status and Trends, pp. 407–419. Oxford University Press, Oxford (2003)
11. Holt, J., Traxler, C., Allen, T.: Interpreting the scores: A user's guide to the 9th edition stanford achievement test for educators of deaf and hard-of-hearing students. Gallaudet Research Institute Technical Report 97-1, Gallaudet University, Washington, DC (1997)
12. Lenhart, A., Madden, M., Hitlin, P.: Teens and technology. Technical report, Pew Internet and American Life Project, Washington, DC (July 2005)
13. Ling, R.: We release them little by little: Maturation and gender identity as seen in the use of mobile telephony. Personal Ubiquitous Comput. 5(2), 123–136 (2001)
14. Lofland, J., Lofland, L.H.: Analyzing Social Settings: A Guide to Qualitative Observation and Analysis. Wadsworth Publishing (1995)
15. Mayberry, R.: The critical period for language acquisition and the deaf child's language comprehension: A psycholinguistic approach. Bulletin d'Audiophonologie: Annales Scientifiques de L'Universite de Franche-Comte 15, 349–358 (1998)
16. Nardi, B., Whittaker, S., Bradner, E.: Interaction and outeraction: Instant messaging in action. In: Proceedings of CSCW'00, Philadelphia, PA, pp. 79–88 (2000)
17. Newport, E.: Maturational constraints on language learning. Cognitive Science 14(1), 11–28 (1990)
18. Power, M.R., Power, D.: Everyone here speaks TXT: Deaf people using SMS in Australia and the rest of the world. Journal of Deaf Studies and Deaf Education 9(3), 333–343 (2004)
19. Schiano, D.J., Chen, C.P., Isaacs, E., Ginsberg, J., Gretarsdottir, U., Huddleston, M.: Teen use of messaging media. In: CHI '02. Extended abstracts on Human factors in computing systems, pp. 594–595. ACM Press, New York (2002)
20. Smith, H., Rodgers, Y., Brady, M.: Managing one's social network: Does age make a difference? In: Proceedings of INTERACT '03, pp. 551–558 (2003)
21. Spencer, P., Lederberg, A.: Communication and Language: Discoveries from Atypical Development. In: Different Modes, Different Models: Communication and Language of Young Deaf Children and their Mothers, pp. 203–230. Harvard University Press, Cambridge (1997)
22. Valli, C., Lucas, C.: Linguistics of American Sign Language. Gallaudet University Press, Washington DC (1992)
23. Wagreich, B.: Electronic mail for the hearing impaired and its potential for other disabilities. IEEE Transactions on Communications COM-30(1), 58–65 (1982)

Accessibility and Interactive TV: Design Recommendations for the Brazilian Scenario

Lara Schibelsky G. Piccolo[1,2], Amanda Meincke Melo[2],
and Maria Cecília Calani Baranauskas[2]

[1] Fundação CPqD – Centro de Pesquisa e Desenvolvimento em Telecomunicações
Rod. Campinas Mogi-Mirim, km 118,5, CEP 13086-902, Campinas, SP, Brasil
lpiccolo@cpqd.com.br
[2] Instituto de Computação (IC) – Universidade Estadual de Campinas (Unicamp)
Caixa Postal 6176, CEP 13083-970, Campinas, SP, Brasil
{amanda, cecília}@ic.unicamp.br

Abstract. TV can be regarded as the most far-reaching media in Brazil. Its presence is noticed in 90% of Brazilian homes and it is the main source of information for a major part of the population. The moment of definition and consolidation of the digital TV technology provides us with a unique opportunity for analyzing and discussing this media accessibility. Making sure that TV contents and devices are flexible enough so that people are able to perceive, understand and interact with them is a main asset for its use and an essential requirement for the democratization of information via TV broadcasting. This paper analyzes interactive digital TV accessibility in informal, formal, and technical levels, considering the Brazilian context. In addition, it presents recommendations to design accessible interfaces by referring to the W3C guidelines 2.0 for Web accessibility and specific recommendations for iDTV.

Keywords: Accessibility, Interactive digital TV, User Interfaces for All.

1 Introduction

TV can be regarded as the most far-reaching media in Brazil as it is present in 90% of Brazilian homes, where it plays the role of the major information source for the majority of the population [14]. Making sure that TV contents and devices are flexible enough so that people are able to perceive, understand and interact with them is a main asset for its use and an essential requirement for any process towards the democratization of information via TV broadcasting.

Interactive TV can be defined as an artifact for the dialogue between TV viewers and TV channel producers, a program or service [11]. Therefore it represents a communication media that goes beyond the one-way mass media communication, allowing the TV viewer to change the passive attitude of simply "watching" TV to make choices and have a more direct influence upon the television system.

The digitalization of the TV signal between the broadcasting station and its final users leads to datacasting — the use of a small portion of the signal to broadcast data,

C. Baranauskas et al. (Eds.): INTERACT 2007, LNCS 4662, Part I, pp. 361–374, 2007.

in addition to the audio-visual content [22]. Therefore, a software layer may enable certain facilities such as interface customization, multiple streams of audio and video, and applications with manifold types of interactivity on a wide range of services. Regarding the user interface, these features may imply, for instance, in a more frequent use of text on-screen, page-browsing systems, the use of menus in association (or not) with remote control buttons, and special user requirements related to new ways of interacting with a device still unknown for many people.

Within this scenario, the accessibility resources provided by the analog TV can no longer be sufficient to assure that a significant number of users are able to fully enjoy this new media. Therefore, the moment of definition and consolidation of this technology, which is currently experienced in the Brazilian context, is a unique opportunity for discussing TV accessibility and implementing solutions which consider the population's needs within its widest extension.

Although directly related to people with disabilities, accessibility does not refer exclusively to this group of users. It is necessary to understand the relation between accessibility and usability, i.e., with the quality in use of computer resources and, consequently, with both digital and social inclusion [3][4][19]. The Digital TV for All report [16] presents a comparative analysis of exclusion in both analog and digital TVs. The report shows that 2.7% of the population over 16 years presented problems when switching channels on analog TV. This number raises to 7.1% when considering digital TV. For the population above 75, this number increased from 9% in the analog TV to 24.7% in digital TV. The most significant difficulties were found in the use of Electronic Programming Guide (EPG) for switching channels. Users with visual, motor, or cognitive disabilities were the most affected. Exclusion is even worst when the use of interactive services, such as the Digital Teletext, is required.

These and other experiences as well as foreign laws and conventions can subsidize the creation of an accessibility concept for the Brazilian interactive TV. Nevertheless, an analysis which defines the Brazilian context and its particularities is essential. This paper presents an analysis of the interactive digital TV (iDTV), guided by the following questions related to accessibility: How to ensure that an interactive TV application is accessible? As the interactive TV is a convergent media, holding features that have been inherited from both - the current analog TV as well as from the Web environment, is it possible to extend the analog TV accessibility norms with Web accessibility guidelines so that they are applicable to interactive TV? How?

This paper brings into discussion iDTV accessibility in informal, formal, and technical levels, considering the Brazilian context, and presents recommendations to make the interactive digital TV an accessible media. The resulting recommendations draw upon the W3C Web accessibility guidelines and on some specific iDTV recommendations. It is organized as follows: Section 2 situates the accessibility and Universal Design concepts in the Brazilian TV context. Section 3 presents a preliminary analysis of the iDTV subsidies, norms and possibilities. Based on this analysis, Section 4 synthesizes the iDTV accessibility recommendations.

2 Accessibility, Universal Design and Television

The term accessibility is commonly associated with the commitment to improve the quality of life to the elderly as well as to people with disability (e.g. perceptual, cognitive, motor, multiple impairment), as they generally feel a direct impact from obstacles in different environments, products, and services [2][19][23]. Nevertheless, accessibility considered as the possibility of reaching certain physical spaces, information, products and services, is concerned with quality of life for every human being.

For a more inclusive society, able to acknowledge the differences among people, it is even more important that proposals for the accessibility of people with specific needs be connected to the promotion of the quality of life for everyone [8][19][23][31]. Thus, people with different abilities, whether resulting from aging and disability or not, will benefit from accessible products and services, which do not discriminate them.

Accessibility is directly related to usability and, furthermore, to quality in use of computer systems [3][4][19]. Access and use of Information and Communication Technology (ICT) has received different names within the Human-Computer Interaction field: Universal Accessibility, Universal Usability, Inclusive Design, User Interfaces for All [13][23][30][31]. This approach to design does not imply the development of a unique solution for everyone [31]. It implies the proposal of flexible solutions involving a wide understanding of the role that these systems are supposed to play in the society, the acknowledgment of diversity of contexts and situations in which technology is employed, besides the participation of users in design and evaluation activities [19].

Federal Brazilian laws in effect [2] define *accessibility* as the possibility for persons with disability to access and use any physical means, communication media, products and services. TV programs are formally considered as accessible as long as they follow the Standard NBR 15290:2005 [2] established by the Brazilian Association of Technical Standards (ABNT). Along with other regulations in effect [5][20], this norm is based on the provisioning of *assistive services* by TV manufacturers and broadcasters: closed caption, audio description, dubbing and sign language window (in Brazil, the Brazilian Sign Language - LIBRAS).

Although the current regulations demand the provisioning of these services, unofficial discussion lists point out that users, mainly those with disabilities, who count on such resources as the only way to access information on TV, question the amount and quality of information made available.

3   Interactive Digital TV Accessibility: A Preliminary Analysis

Organizational Semiotics (OS) [17] has guided our research about iDTV and its artifacts have been used as analytical tool [27]. Through OS, every technical system is within the core of a socio-organizational context and surrounded by the formal and informal layers of the society or the social organization. Thus, the technical systems are under the influence of both formal and informal levels and, at the same time, they have an impact on them. The relations among the informal, formal, and technical levels of the information system are explained through the metaphor known as the "organizational onion". Figure 1 presents one of the OS artifacts, the semiotic onion, which gives an accessibility overview involving the informal, formal, and technical levels of access to information in the Brazilian iDTV.

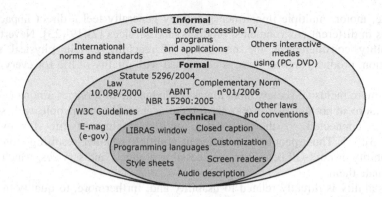

Fig. 1. Interactive Digital TV Accessibility represented by a semiotic onion

3.1 Informal Level – Subsidies

This level comprises information which does not formally fall upon the accessibility issue in the Brazilian iDTV, though they are able to support a solution proposal:

- The content production and delivery guidelines and recommendations, as well as the principles of iDTV interface development, which are used around the world.
- Existing international norms and standards, which may be a source of reference for the Brazilian proposal.
- The experience of Brazilian users with other interactive artifacts, such as DVD, computers, cellular phone, and even with the interactivity available on pay TV.

In several European countries, and other nations where the use of digital TV interactivity is consolidated, some ways of dealing with accessibility issues have been established. Nevertheless, formal norms do not exist and there are few recommendations to approach accessibility beyond audio-visual features.

In Portugal, when the digital terrestrial TV was expected to start operations in 2001, an initiative to create guidelines for subsidizing specific accessibility regulations was launched. Among other things, the guidelines suggested that digital TV receivers should be compatible with technology to support citizens with special needs. Such technology included adapted remote control, special keyboard and mouse, screen readers, voice synthesizers, and Braille terminals [7]. As the digital terrestrial TV operation was delayed in the country, this discussion was postponed.

The United Kingdom concentrates the major efforts regarding guidelines for accessible user interface designs on iDTV. The Royal National Institute of Blind (RNIB) defined a set of user interface requirements for digital TV receivers regarding presentation, browsing, and remote control. Although these requirements have been set for persons with visual disabilities, they include universal usability and accessibility principles [29]. RNIB is also one of the organizations responsible for

Tiresias [33], a font specifically created to increase readability in digital TV text. It has also provided a set of recommendations for iDTV accessible user interface design, including colors, texts, and even tips regarding tests with users [32]. The Consumer Expert Group in the UK has gathered this and other recommendations – including World Web Consortium (W3C) guidelines – in a report aimed at helping the government to ensure that the digital TV equipment is also appropriate for the elderly and physically impaired people [9].

The similarity between the currently available actions related to interactive TV and Internet services (e.g.: browsing and data input) as well as the convergence between the two media [28] can lead to the appropriation of Web accessibility knowledge that has already been acquired, even though adjustments may be necessary. Since 1999, the W3C Web Content Accessibility Guidelines 1.0 [34] has been a reference for the development of accessible websites. Currently, the 2.0 version of the guidelines has a multimedia approach involving new technologies, which surpass the scope of the Web [35]. In addition to the recommendations concerned with content accessibility, a few others have been defined for the *user agents* (e.g., Web browsers and assistive technologies), which also comprise the TV receivers that, among other things, are responsible for content presentation and browsing. The new set of guidelines was grouped under four principles considered essential to access and use of the Web by anyone: the content must be perceivable; interface components in the content must be operable; content and controls must be understandable; content must be robust enough to work with current and future user agents, including assistive technologies.

3.2 Formal Level – Norms

The Brazilian current regulations concern the formal level of information on iDTV. The use of accessibility resources and technical artifacts on analog TV broadcasting is regulated by a hierarchical set of laws and norms as represented by Figure 2.

Law 10.098, December 19 2000 – It establishes, among other issues, general guidelines and basic criteria to promote media accessibility to persons with disability or mobility impairment. The law focuses on TV broadcasting services accessibility for persons with hearing disabilities [6].

Decree-law 5.296 2 December 2004 – It covers the use of closed captioning, LIBRAS (Brazilian Sign Language) window and audio description features in analog TV programming and enforces the use of these artifacts on digital TV as well. It establishes the creation of supplementary standards to regulate the use of these artifacts [5].

Supplementary Standard 01/2006 – Accessibility in image and sound broadcasting and TV re-broadcasting for persons with disabilities. The law was enacted on June 28, 2006, after 64 days of public consultation. It defines accessibility resources, terms, goals and non-compliance penalties. It refers to ABNT Standard described below [20].

ABNT NBR 15290:2005 Technical Standard – Accessibility in TV Broadcasting. It establishes guidelines for the production and delivery of analogical and digital TV to persons with disabilities, including closed captioning, audio descriptions and LIBRAS window. Effective from November 30, 2005 [2].

Fig. 2. Brazilian current regulations on TV accessibility

Regulations [5][20] govern the transition from analog to digital terrestrial broadcasting, except for cable and satellite TV services, which in some cases are already digital and interactive in Brazil. For this reason, an initiative [21] has been launched to request changes to Decree-law 5.296/04 so that the guidelines can be extended to payable TV.

TV interactivity is mentioned in Supplementary Standard 01/2006 [20]: "*allowing the addition of sentences in Portuguese, so that persons with visual and intellectual disabilities can select the desired menu options and interactive features in an independent way*". We understand that those interactive features are related to the applications transmitted or embedded in the receiver. In addition, new technical possibilities are taken into consideration in this Standard "*to allow the optional use of the LIBRAS window in all TV programming*".

The year 2017 is the deadline for making the daily programming fully accessible, when it is expected that digital TV will be present in the majority of homes in Brazil. ABNT NBR 15290:2005 Technical Standard [2] provides guidelines for producing and delivering accessible content that apply to all TV broadcasters and producers, including cable, satellite, IP and digital broadcasting TV. An analysis of this regulation indicates that the digital technology potential has not been fully explored in regard to accessibility and some possibilities have not been taken into consideration, such as using multiple audio streams for a single video; sharing the broadcast channel to deliver simultaneously different audio-visual content; using different closed captioning presentations, among others. As occurs with international standards, aspects related to the design of interactive applications interfaces are not addressed in the Brazilian standard, such as options to allow changing color, font type, text size and positioning.

Focusing on the production and delivery of assistive services, both Brazilian and international laws and standards are addressed to persons with disabilities. However, the iDTV accessibility concept should go further, benefiting much more people.

3.3   Technical Level – Possibilities

Accessible iDTV applications depend on receiver features. In addition, existing analog TV customization solutions and services can be extended to iDTV.

W3C guidelines for Web accessibility are based on consolidated and standardized technologies, such as HyperText Markup Language (HTML) and Cascade Style Sheet (CSS), helping developers adequately encode and separate a page structure from its presentation [18]. To accomplish accessible iDTV applications, the receiver has to be prepared for it: both hardware and software must comply with specific standards and assistive technologies. If declarative language is supported – a markup language (HTML, for example), that uses a presentation engine – an interactive application implementation can be similar to the development of a Web page, making it easier to comply with W3C recommendations and helping developers to work at a higher level of abstraction. However, if the receiver contains an execution engine (procedural middleware), using JAVA language for example, the implementation of accessible applications is also possible, but developers will need to take extra care and implement for each new application some accessibility resources already included in the presentation engine. In this case, it is important to standarize a set of Application

Programming Interfaces (APIs) for the procedural middleware, optimizing the developers work and enabling the interoperability among multiple receiver models or among different TV platforms [10].

Digital TV opens up a whole range of new possibilities in terms of implementation and improvement of existing analog TV assistive services offered:

- **Closed caption:** Digital TV enables new functions to subtitling such as the option to change font style, color and size, the use of transparence or change the color of the subtitle background, the use of icons or small graphics in the text [10].
- **Audio description:** Multiple audio streams can be used for a single video, making it possible the combination of audio description and original sound or dubbing. Some receivers can send audio description to a headphone and the original sound to the conventional TV audio output. Taking into account the multimedia nature of iDTV, the audio description concept could be extended, so that non-textual output could be produced for the remaining textual or graphic elements through the use of assistive techonologies.
- **LIBRAS window:** In analog TV transmission, the LIBRAS window occupies part of the screen. In many cases, however, the window is not large enough to allow the user to read all body language signs and cues required by the sign language. It is necessary to investigate ways of implementing optional LIBRAS window and to realize a feasibility analysis of automation of sign language generation with human figures and avatars.

TV personalization – the method that captures the user's profiles, in order to use them to search or to show a specific data [1][15] – could be used to meet the needs of different users or user groups or receivers, for example, storing preferences as text size, color combination, warnings, etc in a Smart Card [12]. Although it is a trend around the world, implementing TV personalization would generate extra costs on the receiver. For this reason and considering the user experiences in this moment of transition, it is still important to consider TV as a collective medium to propose an accessibility solution to Brazil.

4 Recommendations for Accessible Services Through iDTV

An accessible iDTV solution should not be limited to assistive services. It should be taken into consideration the TV content, the artifacts used for the interaction with the user, such as a receiver and a remote control, and last, but not least, the user's expectations and experiences related to the use of interactive artifacts. Based on this fact and considering the Universal Design proposal — to promote the design of widely usable and accessible products and environments and the development of solutions that support assistive technologies — this section offers a summary of the main factors to be considered in the iDTV context and suggests recommendations for the interaction design, which involve both technical and social factors resulting from the previous analysis.

4.1   The Triad: User, Remote Control and Receiver

Surveys conducted with visually impaired persons in the United Kingdom showed which particular functions they would like to have implemented on TV: the option to change text size and combination of colors; the possibility of adding extra time to review information and removing available functions, to name a few [12]. In order to propose the development of services and artifacts suitable for all users, it is essential to know and identify the needs of the population as a whole, including persons with disabilities. Interviews, ethnographic methods, usability evaluation, semiotic analysis and even inclusive design methodologies [19] can be applied.

In Brazil, where a large section of the population has a low level of education and digital literacy and has never had access to interactive services on TV, it is absolutely necessary to find ways to identify the **user** experience with other artifacts, to understand how this experience can be reflected in the use of iDTV and also to know the population's expectations in regard to this media.

Although the **remote control** is the main device to interact with iDTV, many users restrict its use to the channel search by going up and down and by using the number buttons [11]. The high level of complexity and inconsistency in user interfaces are some of the common problems of remote control [24]. Some researchers point out the importance of establishing a standard or a convention for the use of the remote control buttons so that the user could associate the functionality with the button position [9][12][16].

To achieve an accessible iDTV, the content should be delivered to the user under the Universal Design perspective and the **receiver** should be prepared to use the technical artifacts. Although Brazil has chosen the ISDB Japanese standard for terrestrial transmission, the receiver middleware has not been defined yet. Whatever technical and market solution is adopted, it is essential to consider and establish standard accessibility requirements. Nevertheless, support to assistive technologies, personalization and other functions can incur additional manufacturing costs on the receivers.

4.2   Recommendations for iDTV Interface Design

Brazil, as well as other countries, presents gaps on formal, informal and technical levels in establishing criteria to design accessible iDTV interfaces and to provide receiver compatibility with assistive technologies.

Recommendations for iDTV interface design presented in Table 1 take as reference W3C Web Content Accessibility Guidelines 2.0 [35], as well as other specific iDTV accessibility recommendations [29][32][9], including comments regarding the Brazilian context. Besides highlighting the need to be compatible with assistive technologies, W3C guidelines also include part of iDTV recommendations, excepted by some iDTV specificities.

Table 1 was organized under the four principles defined by W3C guidelines. Specific recommendations for iDTV are primarily based on RNIB [29] followed by Tiresias [32] and The Consumer Expert Group [9]. Frequently, there are similarities between references, because they use the same research basis. Each iDTV specific recommendation was classified according to W3C 2.0 Guidelines or considered as being supplementary. Some comments are presented as a contextualized analysis of both guidelines and its relation to the Brazilian formal level on iDTV and Nielsen's Heuristics [25]. From the Ten Usability Heuristics, seven were identified showing the association between accessibility and usability. Results of the analysis and assistive services found in the Brazilian norms are summarized in the Analysis column.

Although remote control is a key-element for TV interactivity design, such device was not included due to limitation and scope of this paper. The resulting recommendations do not intend to be exhaustive regarding usability and accessibility issues; they intend to support design decisions.

Table 1. Recommendations to provide an acessible iDTV

References Guidelines	Analysis	Recommendations
Principle 1 W3C: Content must be perceivable		
1.1) Provide text alternatives for all non-text content [35]. 1.11) Avoid icons, or offer a text alternative[29].	Text alternatives are used by assistive technologies such as screen readers or Braille printers.	1. Provide text alternatives for all non-text content (icons, stable images, animations).
1.2) Provide synchronized alternatives for multimedia [35] (captions, audio descriptions and extended – added by pausing the video, full multimedia text alternative including any interaction). 5.3) Keep feature settings between services [29].	ABNT Standard [2] provides guidelines for generating closed captions, audio description and LIBRAS window, as per [20] requirements. Full multimedia text alternative is included in previous recommendation.	2. Do not change any assistive service settings while switching channels (or moving from one application to another).
1.3) Ensure that information and structure can be separated from presentation [35]. 1.3.2) Any information that is conveyed by color is also visually evident without colour. 1.2) Provide user option to change the size of displayed text [29]. 1.5) Never solely on colour to convey information [29].	Ensure compatibility among user agents (receivers), enabling different content presentations and information integrity. Font size should be also a presentation attribute, although W3C does not clearly state it.	3. The conveyed information must be clear, regardless of screen size, format, disposition and orientation.
		4. Provide user option to change the size of displayed text.
1.4) Make it easy to distinguish foreground information from its background [35]. 1.1) Provide user option to change the display to high contrast and inverted text [29]. 1.4) Avoid text over textured	The user agent may change color and contrast, relating Recommendations 5 with 3 and 4. Serif fonts are illegible on TV.	5. Provide user option to change contrast or text colours.
		6. Avoid text over textured background.
		7. Avoid color inversion when highlighting an interface element (e.g., when focus is applied).
		8. Use TV-suitable fonts. Tiresias is recommended.

Table 1. (*continued*)

References Guidelines	Analysis	Recommendations
background [29]. 1.9) To highlight an option, favour markers over inversion [29]. 1.3) Use a clear font [29]. Text size should be a minimum of 24 points [32].		9. Text size should be a minimum of 24 pts.
1.8) Apply readability guidelines [29].	For RNIB, readability is related to the presentation itself, whereas for W3C it refers to text intelligibility. ABNT defines presentation guidelines for closed captions design.	10. Favour lower case text over upper case (mixed is ideal); avoid italic, oblique and condensed text; favour left-align; follow ISO7001 arrows specification; ensure words have a clear space around them; use Arabic numerals rather than Roman.
Use of Colors on TV [32].	Screen color may strongly vary from computer to TV. The application designer must perform this check. Avoid visual tracking.	11. Avoid combinations of red and green; avoid pure red or white colours; use colours with a maximum of 85% saturation; provide generous inter-line spacing.
Principle 2: Interface components in the content must be operable.		
2.1) Make all functionality operable via a keyboard interface [35].	Remote control is the interaction device. Interacting with downloaded applications must be possible through any remote control.	12. Allow interaction through remote control main buttons.
2.2) Allow users to control time limits on their reading or interaction [35].	Users facing interaction problems may find no access to specific features due to timeout.	13. User may disable or extend an interaction timeout.
2.3) Allow users to avoid content that could cause seizures due to photosensitivity [35]. 1.7) Avoid flashing [29]. 1.10) Avoid, or provide an option to disable, brief display messages [29].	W3C refers to size, frequency and brightness boundaries for dynamic images usage. Such boundaries must be evaluated for iDTV.	14. Avoid flashing objects.
2.4) Provide mechanisms to help users find content, orient themselves within it, and navigate through it [35]. 2.1) Provide numerical navigation to all functions and links [29]. 2.2) Provide the option of audible feedback of navigation [29].	RNIB 2.1, 2.2 and 2.3 recommendations are mainly aimed at visually impaired persons. A standard interaction model prevents the user to undergo a learning process each time a new application is launched [12].	15. Provide numerical navigation to all functions and links. 16. Provide the option of audible feedback of navigation. 17. Provide spoken feedback on navigation (optional).

Table 1. (*continued*)

References Guidelines	Analysis	Recommendations
2.3) Provide spoken feedback [29].		
2.5) Help users avoid mistakes and make it easy to correct mistakes that do occur [35].	Related to Nielsen's heuristics: 3 - User control and freedom; 5 - Error prevention; 9 - Help users recognize, diagnose, and recover from errors [25].	18. Provide an exit option for each application feature.
		19. Support undo and redo.
		20. Prompt user before running an operation.
		21. Present clear error messages and troubleshooting.
1.6) Ensure that 'please wait' messages are obvious [29].	Heuristic 1 [25]: Visibility of system status.	22. Display status messages while system is running.
Principle 3: Content and controls must be understandable		
3.1) Make text content readable and understandable 3.1.5) When text requires reading ability more advanced than the lower secondary education level, supplemental content is available that does not require reading ability more advanced than the lower secondary education leve. [35].	Unlike W3C 3.1.5 recommendation, all the text must be intelligible to target audience, so it should not require additional information. Heuristic 2 - considers the user language: Match between system and the real world [25].	23. All texts in the application must be target audience-oriented, i.e., an application designed for a low-literacy audience must present texts accordingly.
3.2) Make the placement and functionality of content predictable. 3.2.4) Components that have the same functionality are identified consistently[35]. 1.7) Avoid scrolling text[29].	Scrolling text bar is an unknown TV artifact. Most users may find it difficult to encounter a specific interface component.	24. Place interface components to help users move through predictable paths.
		25. Avoid scrolling text.
5.1) Ensure consistency [29].	All interactive artifacts must be consistent, enabling the user to associate the browsing mechanism with the remote control. Multifunctional buttons: consistency and standardization when associating functions with the remote control buttons. Heuristics 4 - Consistency and standards [25].	26. All symbols and text should be consistent on the remote control, on-screen information, user manual and speech output.
		27. If case of using multifunctional buttons, be consistent when associating functions.
Offer the user possibilities to tailor functionality and interface [16].	The same as Heuristics 8 - Flexibility and efficiency of use [25].	28. Offer the user the possibility to tailor functionality and interface.
Principle 4: Content should be robust enough to work with current and future user agents (including assistive technologies)		
4.1) Support compatibility with current and future user agents (including assistive	Compatibility with assistives techonologies. According to [20], the announcement in	29. Ensure that user agents can accurately interpret parsable content, using standard controls

Table 1. (*continued*)

References Guidelines	Analysis	Recommendations
technologies) [35].	Portuguese of menus and other interactive features is required. The announcement might be played by assistive technologies.	from accessible technologies. 30. Make menus and other interactive text features compatible with assistive technologies.
4.2) Ensure that content is accessible or provide an accessible alternative.	Compliance with other guidelines. W3C describes 3 implementation success levels. All content must have at least level 1 implemented. A set of minimum requirements must be defined to iDTV.	-

This wider set of recommendations is beyond design issues. Most part of recommendations should be understood as receiver requirements for the iDTV Brazilian solution, in order to support accessible contents and applications execution. Moreover, according to W3C presentation and content separation practice, such recommendations can also optimize compatibility of iDTV contents with other devices, such as mobile terminals and the Web.

5 Conclusions

Unlike analog TV, an accessible iDTV solution should not be restricted to assistive services. It should consider the TV content, the artifacts used for the interaction, such as a receiver and a remote control and the user's expectations and experiences related to the use of interactive artifacts.

Technically, the content should be delivered to the user under the Universal Design perspective and the receiver should be prepared to use the artifacts. At present, when iDTV technology is being defined in Brazil, there is a unique opportunity for the accessibility of this media to be discussed and implemented according to the population's needs within its widest extension.

This paper presented and discussed the results obtained from an iDTV analysis regarding the iDTV informal level subsidies, the formal level presented according to the norms in effect, and the level of possibilities derived from technical issues. Moreover, based upon the W3C guidelines and the specific recommendations for iDTV, it has synthesized a set of recommendations for iDTV accessibility within the Brazilian scenario.

In continuity of this work, we intend to validate the set of recommendations in iDTV applications for e-Gov, within an inclusive design scenario. As design standards start to be considered, inclusive practices would be helpful in verifying the recommendations more effectively – before their consolidation takes place.

Acknowledgments. The authors thank FUNTTEL and CNPq (476381/2004-5) for funding.

References

1. Ardissono, L., Kobsa, A., Maybury, M.: Personalized Digital Television. In: Targeting programs to individual users, p. 331. Kluwer Academic Publishers, Boston, MA (2004)
2. Associação Brasileira de Normas Técnicas - ABNT: NBR 15290: Acessibilidade em Comunicação na Televisão, IV. Rio de Janeiro (2005), http://www.mj.gov.br/sedh/ct/corde/dpdh/corde/ABNT/NBR15290.pdf
3. Bergman, E., Johnson, E.: Towards Accessible Human-Computer Interaction. In: Nielsen, J. (ed.) Advances in Human-Computer Interaction, Ablex Publishing, Norwood (1995)
4. Bevan, N.: Quality in Use for All. In: Stephanidis, C. (ed.) User Interfaces for All: Concepts, Methods, and Tools, Lawrence Erlbaum, Mahwah (2001)
5. Brasil: Decreto Lei No 5.296, de 02 de Dezembro de 2004 (2004), https://www.planalto.gov.br/ccivil/_ato2004-2006/2004/decreto/d5296.htm
6. Brasil: Lei No 10.098, de 19 de Dezembro de 2000 (2000) (Accessed 30 September 2006), https://www.planalto.gov.br/ccivil/leis/l10098.htm
7. Centro de Engenharia de Reabilitação em Tecnologias de Informação e Comunicação - CERTIC: GUIA Lança Proposta para Necessidades Especiais (2001) (Accessed 17 December 2006), http://www.acessibilidade.net/historia/putma.php
8. Connell, B.R., Jones, M., Mace, R., et al.: About UD: Universal Design Principles. Version 2.0. Raleigh: The Center for Universal Design (1997), http://www.design.ncsu.edu/cud/about_ud/udprinciples.htm
9. Consumer Expert Group: Digital TV Equipment: Vulnerable Consumer Requirements 8-10 (2006), http://www.digitaltelevision.gov.uk/pdf_documents/publications/digtv_equipment-march06.pdf
10. European Committee for Electrotechnical Standardization - CENELEC: Standardisation Requirements for Access to Digital TV and Interactive Services by Disabled People (2003), http://www.cenelec.org/NR/rdonlyres/C4C6543B-8134-472D-BF06-009AEBA6A5B1/0/interimreportTVforAll.pdf
11. Gawlinski, M.: Interactive Television Production, p. 288. Focal Press, Oxford (2003)
12. Gill, J.M., Perera, S.A.: Accessible Universal Design of Interactive Digital Television. In: 1st European Interactive Television Conference, Brighton, pp. 83–89 (2003)
13. Hull, L.: Accessibility: It's not just for disabilities any more. Interactions 11(2), 36–41 (2004)
14. Instituto Brasileiro de Geografia e Estatística: Pesquisa Nacional por Amostra de Domicílios - Síntese de Indicadores. Tables 7.1.1b and 7.2 (2003), http://www.ibge.gov.br/home/estatistica/populacao/trabalhoerendimento/pnad2003/
15. Kastidou, K.G., Cohen, R.: An Approach for delivering personalizes ads in interactive TV customized to both users and advertisers. In: Proceedings of the Fourth European Conference on Interactive Television, Athens, pp. 121–129 (2006)
16. Klein, A.J., et al.: Digital Television for All - A Report on Usability and Accessible Design (2003), http://www.digitaltelevision.gov.uk/publications/pub_dtv_for_all.html
17. Liu, K.: Semiotics in Information Systems Engineering. Cambridge University Press, Cambridge (2000)
18. Melo, A.M., Baranauskas, M.C.C.: Design e Avaliação de Tecnologia Acessível. In: Barcellos, M.P., Loureiro, A.A (eds.) A Universalidade da Computação: um Agente de Inovação e Desenvolvimento. XXIV Jornadas de Atualização em Informática, pp. 1500–1544. SBC, Porto Alegre (2005)

19. Melo, A.M., Baranauskas, M.C.C.: Design Inclusivo de Sistemas de Informação na Web. In: Teixeira, C.A.C., et al. (eds.) Tópicos em Sistemas Interativos e Colaborativos. VII Simpósio Sobre Fatores Humanos em Sistemas Computacionais, pp. 167–212. SBC, Natal (2006)
20. Ministério das Comunicações: Norma Complementar No 01/2006. Diário Oficial da União No 122, quarta-feira, 28 de junho de 2006. Acessibilidade da Pessoa com Deficiência á Programação de Rádio e TV (2006), http://www2.portoalegre.rs.gov.br/seacis/default.php?reg=16&p_secao=24
21. Ministério Público Federal: Ata do Grupo de Trabalho Inclusão de Pessoas com Deficiência. Reunião com Agência Nacional de Telecomunicações, Ministério das Comunicações e Coordenadoria Nacional para a Integração da Pessoa Portadora de Deficiência (2006), http://pfdc.pgr.mpf.gov.br/grupos-de-trabalho/folder.2006-01-30.7327540164/ata-reuniao-anatel-e-ministerio-das-comunicacoes.pdf
22. Montez, C., Becker, V: TV Digital Interativa: Conceitos, Desafios e Perspectivas para o Brasil, 2ed. Ed. da UFSC, Florianópolis, p. 200 (2005)
23. Nicolle, C., Abascal, J. (eds.): Inclusive Design Guidelines for HCI, p. 285. Taylor & Francis, Abington (2001)
24. Nielsen, Jakob: Remote Control Anarchy (2004), http://www.useit.com/alertbox/20040607.html
25. Nielsen, Jakob: Ten Usability Heuristics (2005), http://www.useit.com/papers/heuristic/heuristic_list.html
26. Office of Communication - OFCON: Guidelines on the Provision of Television Access Services (2006), http://www.ofcom.org.uk/tv/ifi/guidance/tv_access_serv/guidelines/
27. Piccolo, L.S.G., Baranauskas, M.C.C.: Desafios de Design para TV Digital Interativa. In: Teixeira, C.A.C, et al. (eds.) Tópicos em Sistemas Interativos e Colaborativos. VII Simpósio Sobre Fatores Humanos em Sistemas Computacionais, pp. 1–10. SBC, Natal (2006)
28. Roibás, A.C., Sala, R.: Main HCI Issues for the Design of Interfaces for Ubiquitous Interactive Multimedia Broadcast. In: Interactions Magazine, March-April, pp. 51–53. ACM Press, New York (2004)
29. Royal National Institute of Blind - RNIB: Guidelines for designers of digital TV user interfaces (2005), http://www.rnib.org.uk/xpedio/groups/public/documents/publicwebsite/public_userinterfaces.doc
30. Shneiderman, B.: Universal Usability. Communications of the ACM 43(5), 85–91 (2000)
31. Stephanidis, C.: User Interfaces for All: New Perspectives into Human-Computer Interactions. In: Stephanidis, C. (ed.) User Interfaces for All: Concepts, Methods, and Tools, pp. 3–17. Lawrence Erlbaum, New Jersey (2001)
32. Tiresias: Guidelines. Television (2007), http://www.tiresias.org/guidelines/television.htm
33. Tiresias: Tiresias Screenfont - Television Subtitling (2000), http://www.tiresias.org/fonts/screenfont.htm
34. W3C: Web Content Accessibility Guidelines 1.0 (1999), http://www.w3.org/TR/WAI-WEBCONTENT/
35. W3C: Web Content Accessibility Guidelines 2.0 (2006), http://www.w3.org/TR/WCAG20/
36. Zimmerman, J., et al.: Interface Design for MyInfo: a Personal News Demonstrator Combining Web and TV Content. In: INTERACT'2003, pp. 41–48 (2003)

Guidelines for Designing Mobility and Orientation Software for Blind Children

Jaime Sánchez and Miguel Elías

University of Chile
Blanco Encalada 2120, Santiago, Chile
{jsanchez, melias}@dcc.uchile.cl

Abstract. We present a study about the use of current electronic travel aids to help blind people navigate through familiar and unfamiliar environments. We also discuss the main strengths and weaknesses of electronic travel aids and propose guidelines to design and use them adequately. We provide a proposal to develop and use traveling aids. As a result, this can be a first step towards defining major aspects to develop travel aids oriented to assist mobility and orientation of blind people.

Keywords: Mobility and Orientation, User-centered software development, Blind users, Electronic travel aids, Virtual environments.

1 Introduction

Software design for users with special needs entails strict requirements and user involvement. We cannot test software for people with visual disabilities by just blindfolding ourselves and other sighted users and try to mimic their interaction with the interfaces. A sighted user can not simulate the behavior of a blind user because their cognition and mental models are not alike [17]. Thus their feelings and tastes when interacting with digital devices are not really predicted. Therefore, when developing software interfaces for people with visual disabilities, additional efforts from designers and programmers are required. They have to understand the way blind users mental models work by continuously testing them throughout the development process.

Currently, in spite of diverse efforts [3], [7], [8], [9], [10] made to provide blind people with aids to support their navigation through indoor or outdoor environments, research on how and why to do this is scarce. Some existing aids are very sophisticated and use top of the line technology [9], [20], but not necessarily are targeting the blind user's needs and interests. Some of them are additional burden for the visually impaired. As a result, there is a clear shortage of usability studies on these issues and a lack of studies concerning the real impact of these aids on mobility and orientation performance of blind users.

This research presents traditional mobility aids and the skills involved when navigating. We introduce Electronic Travel Aids (ETAs) and discuss the main troubles with current designs. As a result of this analysis, we present guidelines for

C. Baranauskas et al. (Eds.): INTERACT 2007, LNCS 4662, Part I, pp. 375–388, 2007.
© IFIP International Federation for Information Processing 2007

developing software for people with visual disabilities with special emphasis on supporting Mobility and Orientation (M&O) skills by illustrating and classifying the main aspects involved and discussing the concretion of these guidelines in software design for blind people.

Electronic Travel Aids are assistant devices designed to support blind users during navigation through indoor and outdoor environments. They span from talking compasses to complex devices that make use of magnetometers and inertial sensors such as accelerometers and gyroscopes. ETAs comprise that employ sound beacons, ultrasonic pulse-echo sonar systems, infra-red detectors, among others [3], [7], [9], [10], [15], [20].

Many efforts have been made to complement or even replace the most employed and successful traveling aid so far: the white cane, to support blind people when traveling and avoiding obstacles by using the available technology (like GPS, RFID and WI-FI). ETAs usually have been developed by targeting on specific problems, but generally they provide an obstacle-avoiding system, location and orientation information, and optimal routes calculations during navigation [14].

The main drawback of existing ETAs is that current developments are not user-centered. This implies a series of usability and interaction issues, failing when providing solution to travel issues faced by blind people when traveling, and even creating new problems to them.

One of the main problems of current devices is the way information is presented to users. They do not present relevant information in a way users can actually be oriented and sometimes overwhelm users with a huge amount of information. For instance, some ETAs show a potential cognitive overload by presenting more than 7 ± 2 concepts on each interface, which is recommended for short-term memory processing issues and retention capacity [16]. This may be a consequence of a general understanding that, due to its difficultness and dangerousness for blind people to move around without perceiving well their surroundings, travel aids should provide a sufficient amount of information about the environment to create a mental representation of the location. This caused that many early developed ETAs pursued to present as much information about the environment as possible. This turned out to be an excessive, confusing and unnecessary amount of information which only confused blind users [12].

Leonard [6] made an experiment with blind people about interaction with information concluding that what is necessary and useful in a traveling aid is to present just small amounts of information, from which blind people can improve their navigational performance. These pieces of data about the environment should be presented in such a way that does not interfere with the information already being gathered by the blind individuals. This means that the amount of information presented should be short enough to create a mental map of the environment, without causing cognitive overload. Also, it should not occlude the information that blind people use as primary clues for mobility and orientation.

Literature shows that efforts in ETAs research aimed mainly at obstacle detection and avoidance, but as Loomis et al. [11] indicate, these devices have failed in contributing to the accomplishment of a more efficient navigation. The main reason is that providing a way of improving the navigation of blind people depends on information that is beyond the reach of these devices. Many studies fall short in determining what are real needs of blind people when navigating through familiar and unfamiliar environment. In some cases researchers have not been able to detect a need for a specific kind of information [20].

One of the most important issues of current ETAs is the lack of usability evaluations to validate the design of the interfaces being used by blind people. For instance, some devices utilize a set of headphones affecting the hearing perception of blind individuals and upon which they base most of their navigation. Other devices require that users utilize both hands to operate them, thus impeding blind individuals to use a cane or self-protection techniques.

Some devices are simply not designed for blind people and require so much learning and training (like reduced Braille and QWERTY keyboards), that they become an additional obstacle to blind users. Furthermore, there are some proposals of using big and heavy robots to guide blind people who ultimately present an additional barrier for them when taking the stairs or walking through narrow hallways. As Vogel [21] states, "...traditional navigation aids for the blind can be inconvenient to port, can be customized only with difficulty and manually, and usually cannot indicate the user's location...", p.2. In addition, formal evaluations of the impact of using one particular device for mobility and orientation of blind individuals are not frequent. This means that the real value of a particular ETA to improve the quality of life of a blind person is neither quantified nor determined.

Many ETAs research consist of highly customized devices that aim to solve a particular navigation problem. Usually they focus on the technology involved rather than in the real problems of blind people when traveling through an unfamiliar environment. One common agreement in this field is that there is no standard solution for the indoor navigation problem [7]. This leads to several unsolved problems, raising the cost of customized devices, thus making it more a barrier than a solution. Unfortunately, this widens the gap between blind people and technology. People with visual disabilities do not feel that the marginal mobility improvement provided by ETAs is worth the high price of these devices.

As a consequence, we propose to consider a more practical approach, centered on the needs and problems of blind individuals when navigating through unfamiliar environments and considering low-cost technology already tested successfully with people with visual disabilities, such as PDAs [18].

The literature proposes some elements to be considered when developing traveling aids for blind people. Loomis & Golledge [10] state that the most significant needs of visually impaired people when navigating can be summarized in: accessing to information, accessibility to the environment, and independence when navigating.

Accessing to information with their remaining senses can be achieved by devices that have multimedia features, such as audio and haptic interfaces. These devices should focus on providing information that users can not obtain by their own means. Alternative displays such as Braille labels or tactile maps can also be used when presenting information.

Accessibility means not only that blind individuals can enter and move around inside a particular environment, but also implies they will be able to recognize landmarks, understand the layout of its components and navigate safely.

Independence when navigating implies that we should focus ETAs as M&O aids to help blind users to be more independent human beings. This can be considered from different points of view. First, there is no need for providing a traveling aid that can be an additional trouble for the blind individual. Therefore, it should make navigation easier, not demanding. This is the reason why we think that complex systems, such as robots or laptop-based devices, are not the right way to go, since their size and weight are a burden to users. Second, we feel that most devices should have a bounded life cycle. This means that the technology involved should support the acquisition and development of M&O abilities, not replace the human processes involved. The goal is to enhance an independent navigation of blind individuals through the usage of mobile. The role that an electronic aid can play in navigation should decrease as the individual develop more M&O skills and strategies. Third, a person with visual disabilities should not depend on other people (sighted or blind) to navigate a surrounding environment.

According to the Colorado Department of Education [4], blind students can benefit from understanding the physical environment, orienting to different school and community environments, traveling in school and in the community and finding opportunities for unrestricted, independent movement and play. This means that blind students should be able to learn, understand, and mentally represent the environment. They should be capable of comprehending the main elements in a particular type of indoor environment such as a school, a shopping mall or a public building, and their uses and functions. They should also be able to navigating them, travel to and from common and crowded places (like the cafeteria), and experiment new environments widening their M&O skills and knowledge. In a preliminary approach [8], people with visual disabilities envisioned M&O aids that augment their perception of the environment, announced points of interest located out of the reach of users and helped them to navigate through those points, and filtered objects according to a certain classification.

Cox & Dykes [5] stated that some of the relevant skills to be developed by blind children inside the school environment are related to knowing landmarks, such as classrooms organization, common sectors (libraries, cafeteria), and knowing the location of entrances, exits and main offices. Hub et al. [7] mentioned that, according to some surveys carried out with blind individuals; these people have several problems with stairs, irregularities of the ground, and doors localization. This is stressed with their inability to realize the purpose of some rooms and buildings.

2 Methodology

We conducted several interviews in Santiago, Chile, with M&O specialists, blind children and youngsters, to gather their opinions and feelings about the issues and difficulties that blind children face on a daily basis when navigating indoor environments. We asked them questions that allowed to understand how blind children travel to and from the school, how they move inside it, what problems they face when navigating in their schools and in other indoor environments, and what opinion they have about including blind children to traditional schools.

Scenario. Six interviews were conducted in Santiago, Chile, from March to October, 2006. The interviews took place in several locations, involving two types of schools: traditional (those designed for sighted children) and special (differentiated or segregated as they are commonly named). One interview was made at the Center for Computing and Communication for the Construction of Knowledge of the University of Chile.

Sample. The participants were very diverse, five blind youngsters (ages between 20 and 32 years old) and seven blind children (ages between 8 and 14 years old). Five children attended a special school and the other two attended traditional schools. Three M&O specialists also participated; one of them is currently the teacher of M&O courses at the Metropolitan University of Educational Sciences. The other two specialists are in charge of the M&O courses taught in a segregated school for the blind. Additional participants were two special education teachers, experts on vision disorders, three teachers and three educational psychologists from two traditional schools that integrate blind students.

Instruments. Diverse open interviews were applied for students, teachers and parents. All of them were unstructured interviews based on a previously established guideline with varying number of questions. The answers and comments made during interviews were recorded and saved in audio files. The interviewers also took written observational notes during the meetings.

Procedure. We conducted a first interview in March of 2006, at the Center for Computing and Communication for the Construction of Knowledge of the University of Chile. The participants were five blind adolescents, two special education teachers (experts on vision disorders), and three computer science engineers. The focus of that interview was on the problems that blind youngsters had when facing familiar and unfamiliar environments, and how they travel from one location to another, what kind of public transportation they currently use, what strategies they have when facing different problems, etc.

In June of 2006 the teacher of the M&O courses at the Metropolitan University for Education Sciences was interviewed. She explained what the M&O courses are, and how they teach them to in-service special teachers that will later work with blind people. During the same month two teachers from the School for the Blind "Santa Lucía", were also interviewed. They were in charge of the M&O courses taught in that school. They provided information about the problems they face every day with blind children as their students, what landmarks they use as reference points, what strategies are used by children when they face problems, and what kind of information they think would be useful to deliver by an electronic travel aid. Later, another school, the private school "The Maisonnette", was contacted. They have integrated a blind girl into their school. We interviewed two of her teachers, along with the curriculum coordinator. The focus of the interviews was on problems faced by the blind girl when moving through the school, what pedagogical changes they had to do in their classes, and the impact of incorporating a blind child as student. We also had the opportunity of observing the blind child in one class and her navigation through the school's yard during breaks.

In July of 2006 we interviewed three educational psychologists of the "Lastarria" high school, a public institution that has integrated three blind children. After that we also met and interview one blind student. The focus of the interview was the same as in the other interviews previously described. In September of 2006 we interviewed five blind children (four of them with loss of vision) that attend the "Santa Lucía" School for the Blind. We asked them about the problems they face when navigating and what landmarks they use to orient themselves.

We finally made an in-depth interview on October of 2006 with the blind girl from "The Maisonnette" School, in her house. We talked with her mother, who mentioned the problems faced when her daughter navigates indoor environments and the efforts made to integrate her in a school for sighted children. Later, we talked to her, a 9 years old child who told us about how she moves inside her school, what problems she faces (such as route planning and getting lost), and how a guiding digital device should look like. All the information we gathered from these interviews were analyzed and summarized in the following section.

M&O specialists were asked about the type of information they think should be useful to provide to blind children during their navigation through the school environment. They mentioned that the most important information was the environment corners, middle points, and the location of every day visited places, such as bathrooms and exits. They mentioned that is also important to provide to blind people contextualized information of the surroundings (cardinal location of sidewalks, public transportation). The main difficulties of blind people when navigating through indoor environments pointed out by specialists were the detection of obstacles beyond the scope of their primary mobility aids (canes or even their own body). Lintels, beams, chandeliers and arches are examples of these obstacles.

When we asked blind youngsters about their problems when navigating indoor environments, they agreed that they frequently collide with obstacles not detected by their primary mobility aids. Some examples of these obstacles are stairs and entrances with low-height steps (so the cane passes right over them). When inquired about problems in their navigation within the school, blind children said that they were mainly concerned about colliding with a wall or other people, and the chance of changing the landmarks currently used to other unknown places, revealing that sometimes they use temporal information for navigation.

Blind people want to know where they are and what objects are close to them, but they do not want other people to tell them about everything. When augmenting their reality by means of artificially enhancing their perception we should opt to provide them information which cannot perceived autonomously. Once the blind person knows where he or she is, the next step is helping him or her to plan a route, providing the necessary information so he or she can make an informed decision on what legs to follow. This is obtained not only by providing information of landmarks and paths in advance, but also by providing additional information such as the cost of each path (in terms of their lengths and hazards).

According to Baldwin [2], teaching routes should have a concrete purpose to make learners able to travel to places of their interest. This is complemented with a goal-orientated strategy. After the student is able to travel a certain route it is suggested to revert it and increase the number of landmarks. It is also recommended to start with straight routes on which rotations can be included incrementally.

We should not make the decision for them when presenting ways of getting to a place. Sometimes people (blind or sighted) may choose a path that does not appear to be "optimal", but that may have hidden benefits that influence their decisions. They can actually figure out shortcuts and navigate them, but sometimes their decisions rely on factors beyond saving time. They may prefer to use a less cognitive demanding route, less crowded, with more easily detectable landmarks, and less environmental noise (distracting sounds, absence of reference cues). At times they even do not care about which route to take, even though the route chosen may be not the best route. As a blind Chilean student stated, she knows that the hallways of her school form a loop, so it does not matter which way to go, since she will always arrive safely. Blind students should develop the ability to choose between different navigational alternatives and make informed decisions.

Blind children have a restricted perception capacity as a consequence of their lack of interaction with the environment, provoked by their fear to explore and parents and teachers overprotection. They also have a weak body image and difficulties to understand spatial concepts [1]. These abilities should be developed early, altogether with motor coordination and pre-cane skills.

The lessons learned after our interviews suggest that computer systems should be designed to reduce the anxiety and stress that arise in blind navigators when dealing with unknown environments. A game-oriented approach can contribute to this objective, especially when having children as end-users. Blind children should be exposed to situations where they have to solve problems perceiving information and thinking individually at their own pace, and as a group working collaboratively in teams. This is why we suggest avoiding the development of a software solution that solves every single navigation problem; rather it should be an aid that allows them to solve problems by their own, encouraging the development and use of M&O skills and abilities.

Finally, we should also consider the children's learning curve. We should start by using familiar elements with simple lessons before starting more complex and challenging schemes. We should keep in mind that the earlier a blind child starts an M&O program, the sooner he or she would become independent and able to navigate independently. In cases when the child does not have the appropriate neuromuscular development to use of a mobility aid such as the cane, an ETA can be an appropriate aid.

Landmarks. When teaching routes to blind children (and blind individuals in general), the use of landmarks is essential. They are references within an environment that allow blind individuals locating elements in their precise position (doors and stairs) and approximate position (smell or sound). Information provided by a landmark allows finding a way and through the memorization of references, to easily rebuild a route when a landmark appears in the path. A customization feature should be provided when using landmarks. Each individual utilize different sets and combinations of textures, smells and sounds to orient themselves. What is useful for one person could not be useful to others, even not recognizable by most blind users.

The interviews with blind children evidenced different positions concerning landmarks for mobility and orientation purposes. While some of them stated that they use landmarks (such as water fountains, light variations and smells) on a daily basis, others said that they did not use landmarks while navigating (at least consciously). We believe that the latter group is not aware of the real importance of understanding and utilizing landmarks for navigational purposes. The literature stated that landmark information combined with an audio interface can enhance the mental mapping of the blind user [12]. Therefore, we should focus our efforts in developing travel aids that support training and utilization of landmarks, since this would be most beneficial for blind children navigation.

3   Guidelines for Developing Software for Context Navigation

The development of software for people with visual disabilities can be a great challenge for designers, since it implies a multidisciplinary approach. Many issues mentioned can be overcome by following a series of guidelines designed from an integration of recommendations suggested by researchers and our own formal observations previously described, that should be considered when developing software for blind people, especially for navigation of blind children. We also present some specific guidelines for developing mobility and orientation software to train individuals in their navigation of familiar and unfamiliar virtual environments and during online guidance and support when navigating real environments.

Model. In the context of M&O software we would expect to be scalable, flexible, and adaptable. One approach is to use validated models in similar contexts in the past and adjust them to current needs. Then, we want to ensure that children will actually use that aid. This can be achieved by designing software appealing and encouraging, thus motivating its use. Games and playful activities could fit well this need. Besides how attractive or entertaining is the software it has to be usable. Therefore, usability evaluations should be mandatory. Sánchez & Baloian [19] mentioned that when developing software for blind users, one of the most important guideline is that the software should be based on a model, game-oriented and consider formative ans summative usability evaluations.

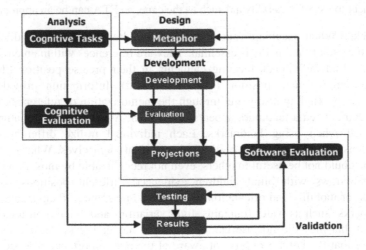

Fig. 1. Model of software for blind children (from Sánchez, J. & Baloian [19])

A suitable model and methodology that can be adapted to M&O development is proposed by [19], used for designing and developing audio-based games for blind children. In this model (see Figure 1), a combination of incremental and evolutionary development is proposed considering the stages of analysis, design, development, and validation, by making particular considerations when developing educational software for blind children. We think that this model is pertinent for developing M&O software for blind users, since it considers a prototyping approach that allows lowering the associated risk of failing to map the user's mental model, and can be adjusted to potential unrevealed requirements at a low cost.

The model proposed should also be adapted and instantiated to reflect new interactions and features arising from the use of software in mobile devices for M&O purposes. When passing from a desktop to a mobile application, the main adjustment is related to acknowledge the role played by the environment: it is dynamic and evolutionary, and triggers the user's actions.

Game orientation. By considering children as end-users the software should be game-oriented to let them to learn in a playfully way. By combining learning and entertainment (edutainment) we can provide a dynamic and appealing experience, thus enhancing a more effective learning. Gaming is an interesting way of achieving a higher commitment of learners with the learning process due to the emotional involvement of the player during the game. Games are a good and attractive way of practicing higher order skills such as problem solving. The model suggested is game-oriented emphasizing cognitive tasks embedded in the software through a game metaphor interface.

Evaluation. The proposed model considers the use of formative and summative end-users usability evaluations. This is fundamental to gather data about the users' acceptance and how well the software meets their mental models. By considering methods such as heuristic evaluations and cognitive walkthroughs, hidden requirements are highlighted to improve the user's interaction. Virtanen & Koskinen [20] stated that the evaluation of a device should not be made in terms of the information provided; rather the focus should center on the real benefits produced. Children should practice with the applications in real environments and contexts, thus assuring safe and natural activities.

Interfaces. User interfaces should be intuitive and suitable. The best possible interaction models to select type, quantity and ways of presenting information should be used [21]. Users should have modes of customizing the presentation of information according to their needs and interests. When having people with visual disabilities as users, particularly those who have loss of vision, interfaces should be designed in ways to fully exploit the remaining visual channel to perceive information. When the interface includes text (in menus and labels), sans serif fonts should be considered, since the resolution of computer screens is lower than paper. This makes screen reading easier and less exhausting. A clear interlining spacing and highly contrasting colors (such as blue/yellow or black/white combinations) should be also considered.

Iconic photographic images should be preferred. It is most likely that people with visual disabilities are not able to appreciate small details of an image (such as facial features of a character). Instead, simple and clear icons should be used. Icons must have good contrast with the background color and should be related with audio clues to let users comprehend their functionalities. Audio cues must be included so users can construct a mental model of the virtual environment, and thus improving the interaction.

Interaction. Different ways of navigating the virtual environment should be provided. This encourages users to explore several traveling strategies and the construction of knowledge about routes, locations and timings. Ultimately, this contributes to the construction of the mental representation of the virtual environment. Furthermore, exploring different navigational strategies and approaches in a controlled and safe virtual environment can be the first step to encourage blind individuals to do the same in real environments.

Users should be make decisions and take actions. They should be allowed to interact freely and directly with every element in the virtual environment. Even tough sometimes some type of guidance is necessary; users should be free to decide whether or not to accept the suggestions made. Each user's action should have an immediate and clear feedback, so he or she can realize permanently what has been done and what are the consequences of their actions, thus supporting cognitive interaction.

Audio cues. Audio is an essential channel to convey information to blind users. Good quality and easily identified audio should be used. Non spoken sounds are easier to listen than verbal audio cues [12], they do not distract users from navigation and can be easily ignored. Iconic sounds (sometimes called *earcons*) are appropriate to convey information, whether it is general, specific or quantitative. *Earcons* are also non-disruptive to users [21]. Although spoken sounds may be appealing and useful they can not be modified after recording. However, the use of *earcons* does not exclude the use of verbalized forms of audio. If spoken sounds are used to provide more complete description of landmarks, for instance, they can be more useful if we use cardinal coordinates in our descriptions, providing lengths by using step counting and M&O concepts (turns, quarter-turns).

Artificial sounds should not occlude natural sounds coming from the environment intake. One way to accomplish this is considering the "cocktail party effect" when providing audio cues in the presence of environmental sounds. This means that we can exploit the human ability of listening to several sound sources at the same time, without getting confused. This also implies users can pick one sound in particular, as humans do when several people are talking and find a conversation nearby to be of their interest.

Sound pinned to landmarks should be representative of the point of reference in such away that users can identify them through sound. For instance, if a water fountain is used as a landmark, a running water sound effect could be a good reference.

Monophonic and stereo sounds as primary navigational senses should be avoided since using them may block environmental sounds.

Content & information. Information has to be available anytime time and users should be able to listen important messages whenever they need to do so. Sometimes the interaction can be asynchronous. If a user listen environmental audio cues such as messages coming from a speaker in the subway station, or if he or she talks to a friend, the information provided by the navigational aid can be missed. Outdoor designs should consider the asynchronous features of interaction and provide ways of repeating important messages in any moment.

Instructions should be clear and simple [21], since users have to remind them during interaction with the navigational software. This pursues to present information processed by users without distracting them from navigation.

The information provided by a navigational device should to be contextualized information. Not every piece of information available is useful for navigational purposes. Only a small subset of information should be presented to users according to their needs during navigation. ETAs should provide the orientation and position of users, their targets and landmarks to avoid cognitive overhead.

Every user is different to the other and sometimes a piece of information that is essential and relevant for one user can be completely incidental for another. Therefore, some degree of customization has to be considered. ETAs should be able to adapt to users, selecting adequately the hints provided to fit the needs and experience of the current user. Customization should be made by users through adapting the related software and provided as intelligent agents that learn and plan present and future users´ needs.

Representation of the environment. Some elements should be repeated iteratively throughout different environments. For instance, most indoor environments are fairly rectangular or squared-shaped. Many of them have four walls, a floor and a ceiling, and at least one entrance/exit. One example of this type of environments is a classroom. Almost every classroom has a chalkboard, chairs, tables, and so on, therefore when students understand the layout and composition of one classroom, their knowledge can be generalized to the rest of classrooms. The same concept can be extended to other environments such as a mall, the zoo and the library. This idea can be complemented with the work done by Kàpic [8] who stated that to represent an environment and routes we should utilize a rectangular approach. Routes should be composed of straight segments that intersect each other in a 90-degrees angle and their lengths should be of not longer than ten meters (approximate 33 feet). If the right angle approach is not enough for a particular environment, then we can use clock navigation for directions.

The location and orientation of users should be known anytime anywhere. A way of detecting a missed path should be also provided.

Devices & Infrastructure. Devices utilized should be small enough to be carried comfortably (in a palm hand or in the pocket). This means that the devices used should meet three main requirements. First, the device should not interfere with the primary mobility navigation aid used by a blind user, such as canes and guide dogs. Second, as many blind individuals declare, any M&O aid should not highlight the blind user as a person with disabilities. This is one of the reasons why many blind children do not like using the white cane, since although this mobility aid has many advantages it socially shows them as blind users. The interfaces and size of the devices should also be suitable and comfortable enough for blind users.

Devices utilized in M&O contexts should have low battery consumption, so they can provide uninterrupted services for reasonable timeframes. Software designed for these devices should provide ways to alert users when battery is low loading. Many of these devices manage databases and I/O features (microphones, speakers or earphones). This implies that there is a minimal processing power required for these devices. According to Kàpic [8], devices should have a monitoring system embedded that provides information about the remaining battery and processing capabilities.

Users should be able to receive and utilize location-dependent services not only from static repositories, but also from other users, designing the infrastructure in a scalable way to preserve users´ privacy. The cost of the solution (considering devices and infrastructure) should be low and imply few changes in the current environment to make it replicable. One way of achieving this is using devices meant for other purposes, instead of building new ones from scratch. One option is the use of PDAs, which are increasingly being used in schools for educational purposes, thus lowering entrance barriers. PDAs comprise the required battery and processing capabilities, multimedia features, portability, and their cost is reasonable (compared to laptops). Cell phones also meet these requirements with the additional advantage of being worldwide massively distributed.

4 Discussion

Many efforts have been made to complement or even replace the white cane as an aid tool for blind people. ETAs developers should not focus on this "replacement" intent since it is very unlikely to redesign such a device that is cheap, portable and useful as the white cane. We should make efforts to complement this navigation aid rather than to replace it trying to change the primary navigation aids. This implies a device that can detect and inform users about obstacles and hazards beyond the reach of primary mobility aid (cane, guide dogs), and provide information about the environment to help blind people to develop a more accurate mental model of the surroundings.

Sometimes the problem is not the use of an aid but its misuse. Some specialists said that some blind individuals walk very fast and do not utilize the cane properly (they describe only a tight sweep, for instance), due to an excess of confidence or just because of trying to keep the pace of sighted people, missing some obstacles and thumping on them.

There is no such a product that can solve every single problem of every blind individual. This is not a pessimistic but a rather realistic affirmation. ETAs developers should not expect to solve all M&O problems for every blind person. Instead, we believe that research studies should encourage and promote the development and utilization of M&O skills in blind people to achieve an independent, safe and efficient navigation, promoting problem-solving features of navigational aids.

It is essential to develop a deeper understanding about blind users' interest, needs and way of knowing. As Psathas [13] stated, people navigate mechanically so many behaviors and tasks are made unconsciously, being unable to verbalize current practices and issues involved during navigation.

The cost of ETAs should not be a barrier for a blind individual. Developers should consider low-cost technology fully tested with people with visual disabilities, such as PDAs, devices that can be used for many purposes (like educational software, collaborative work) besides to M&O. Schools everywhere are starting to insert this kind of technologies into curriculum. Considering also the high social penetration of cell phones, it is most likely that in the short-term, most students will have a mobile device with the required capabilities to use them as ETAs. Therefore, the idea is to re-use existing devices and infrastructure for M&O purposes, ending up with a system that is cheap, available to blind people, that provides the information needed for navigation, allows them to understand the environment without the aid of a sighted person, has low impact on the existing infrastructure, and thus making feasible to implement it everywhere.

There is a clear need for guidelines when developing navigational software for blind users, especially for children. This is why we provide guidelines for developers that should be seen as the starting point to draw from their own experiences. For instance, we suggest that highly contrasting colors should be used, but if you use only three or four colors, children with residual vision will get bored of the interface. This is why we suggest trying new combinations of colors, images and media, starting from experience. But any design experience should be evaluated formally with real end-users, during a significant timeframe, using usability methods, and considering that it is very unlikely to come up with an interface that works for every user and suits every single need. This should be considered as a challenge to design interfaces that meet the interaction model of most blind users.

Interfaces for long-term interaction should consider that certain types of blindness are degenerative so designers should incorporate some evolutionary features to adjust itself to the loss of vision.

ETAs should not be an additional burden to blind people when navigating. This implies that blind users should be able to navigate autonomously, without the assistance of a sighted individual. The devices are portable and easy-to-use when walking through narrow hallways or taking the stairs. In addition, we should aim at letting users to diminish their dependency on the involved technologies as they develop, use and improve M&O skills for navigation.

Emerson Foulke once said that we know more about what is involved in getting a man to the moon than about what is involved in getting a blind person to cross the street. As analyzed and discussed in this report, ETAs are far from being a final solution for navigational problems of blind people, but they are a very good starting point to help blind children to develop, use and rehearse mobility and orientation skills for a better social inclusion.

Acknowledgements. This report was funded by the Chilean National Fund of Science and Technology, Fondecyt, Project 1060797.

References

1. Arnaiz, P., Martínez, R.: Educación Infantil y Deficiencia Visual. Editorial CCS. pp. 66-97 (1998)
2. Baldwin, D.: Teaching Orientation and Mobility to Blind Children (e-Book), Chapter 3: Navigating without vision. Retrieved (October 2, 2006), from www.wayfinding.net/play.htm

3. Cheung, S., de Ridder, S., Fishman, K., Francle, L., Patterson, J.: A Personal Indoor Navigation System (PINS) for people who are blind. Retrieved (November 28, 2006), from vision.psych.umn.edu/~gellab/5051/prev_projects/pgs1.pdf
4. Colorado Department of Education. Orientation and Mobility as a Related Service. Retrieved (November 28, 2006), from: http://www.cde.state.co.us/cdesped/download/pdf/OM_Related_Service.pdf
5. Cox, P., Dykes, M.: Effective Classroom Adaptations for Students with Visual Impairments. Teaching Exceptional Children 33(6), 68–74 (2001)
6. Heyes, T.: Electronic Travel Aids – Why Bother? Retrieved (August 21, 2006), from: web.aanet.com.au/tonyheyes/pa/quest.html
7. Hub, A., Diepstraten, J., Ertl, T.: Design and Development of an Indoor Navigation and Object Identification System for the Blind. In: Proceedings of the ACM ASSETS 2004, Atlanta, Georgia, USA, October 18-20, pp. 147–152. ACM Press, New York (2004)
8. Kàpic, T.: Indoor Navigation for Visually Impaired (Retrieved July 18, 2006) (2003) from www.mics.ch/SumIntU03/TKapic.pdf
9. Kulyukin, V., Gharpure, C., Nicholson, J., Pavithran, S.: RFID in robot-assisted indoor navigation for the visually impaired. In: Proceedings of IEEE/RSJ IROS 2004 Conference, September - October 2004, vol. 2, pp. 1979–1984. Sendai Kyodo Printing, Sendai, Japan (2004)
10. Loomis, J., Golledge, R.: GPS-Based Navigation Systems for the Visually Impaired. In: Barfield, W., Caudell, T. (eds.) Fundamentals of Wearable Computer and Augmented Reality, pp. 429–446. Lawrence Erlbaum Associates, Mahwah, NJ (2001)
11. Loomis, J., Klatzky, R., Golledge, R.: Navigating without vision: Basic and Applied Research. Optometry and Vision Science 78(5), 282–289 (2001)
12. Millar, D.: Spatial Audio Interface: Providing Landmark Information to Help the Blind Navigate Outdoors (Retrieved April 4, 2006) (2002), from www.cs.unc.edu/~vogel/IP/IP/info/dorianm_fall2002.pdf
13. Psathas, G.: Mobility, Orientation and Navigation: Conceptual and Theoretical Considerations. New Outlook for the Blind 9, 385–391 (1976)
14. Ran, L., Helal, A., Moore, S.: Drishti: An Integrated Indoor/Outdoor Blind Navigation System and Service. In: Proceedings of the 2nd IEEE Pervasive Computing Conference, Orlando, Florida, pp. 23–30. IEEE Computer Society Press, Los Alamitos (2004)
15. Ross, D., Lightman, A., Henderson, V.: Cyber Crumbs: An Indoor Orientation and Wayfinding Infrastructure. In: 28th Annual RESNA Conference Proceedings (Retrieved July 7, 2006) from, www.cc.gatech.edu/~vlh/pubs/resna05.pdf
16. Sánchez, J.: Visible Learning, Invisible Technology. Dolmen Ediciones, Santiago (2001)
17. Sánchez, J., Sáenz, M.: 3D sound interactive environments for blind children problem solving skills. Behaviour & Information Technology 25(4), 367–378 (2006)
18. Sánchez, J., Aguayo, F.: Mobile Messenger for the Blind. In: Stephanidis, C., Pieper, M. (eds.) EP 2007. LNCS, vol. 4397, pp. 369–385. Springer, Heidelberg (2007)
19. Sánchez, J., Baloian, N.: Modeling 3D interactive environments for learners with visual disabilities. In: Miesenberger, K., Klaus, J., Zagler, W., Karshmer, A.I. (eds.) ICCHP 2006. LNCS, vol. 4061, pp. 1326–1333. Springer, Heidelberg (2006)
20. Virtanen, A., Koskinen, S.: NOPPA: Navigation and Guidance System for the Blind. (Retrieved June 30, 2006), from virtual.vtt.fi/noppa/noppa%20eng_long.pdf
21. Vogel, S.: A PDA-Based Navigation System for the Blind. M.S. Integrative Paper (Retrieved April 6, 2006) (2003), from http://www.cs.unc.edu/~vogel/IP/IP/IP_versions/IPfinal_SuzanneVogel_Spring2003.pdf

SymAB: Symbol-Based Address Book for the Semi-literate Mobile User

Anuradha Bhamidipaty and Deepak P.

IBM India Research Lab, Bangalore, India
{abhamidi, deepak.s.p}@in.ibm.com

Abstract. Developing countries like India are observing an increasing trend in the penetration of mobile phones towards the base of the pyramid (lower strata of the society). This segment comprises of users who are novice and semi-literate and are interested in the basic usage of the mobile phone. This paper explores one of the basic features, the *address book* for its usability and presents an enhanced *symbol-based design* to cater for the semi-literate user. The enhancement uses symbols to replace current text based storage and retrieval and also includes a call distribution based address book access to align with the skewed nature of the user's requirements. The results of a preliminary evaluation of the prototype are encouraging regarding the value perceived through the design.

1 Introduction

Developing countries like India and China have seen a vast growth in the mobile user base with increasing mobile penetration to the lower (lower income) strata of the society. In countries like India where the majority of the population live in rural areas, increasing penetration of mobile devices into the lower strata of the society is critical to insulating the rural population from the vagaries of the highly inefficient and information-asymmetric markets, marked in particular by the tremendous uncertainty and risk of doing business. Mobile devices have started to benefit the poorest of the poor – a study confirming that increased stability of markets is among the effects of the usage of mobile devices [1], [2].

Mobile devices such as mobile phones as existing today assume a reasonable amount of literacy. Although different features provided with the modern mobile devices require different levels of literacy and familiarity with technology, the basic usage of the mobile phone, which is of being able to make and receive calls, requires the ability to understand numerals. The other features that are considered as *"basic"* features include the *address book* and the *short messaging system* (SMS). The former enables the user to *call by name* and display calls from known users by showing up their name, whereas the latter allows the user to send and receive *text messages*. Both these features require knowledge of the alphabet; the ability to read and type alphabet. This need is quite intuitive in the short messaging system, text being the most common and uniform mode of information exchange among multiple people. On the other hand, the *address book* is a personal and local entity, which enables storage and

C. Baranauskas et al. (Eds.): INTERACT 2007, LNCS 4662, Part I, pp. 389–392, 2007.
© IFIP International Federation for Information Processing 2007

retrieval by the user of the mobile device on the device itself. The design of the address book as a text based storage and retrieval interface causes a barrier to it's usage in the growing class of *semi-literate mobile users;* the class of users who can manage to understand numerals, but cannot read or write alphabets.

Further, people in the said category often have a small set of contacts who are contacted very frequently, whereas a large majority of their contacts are used rarely. The uniform search interface, which roughly requires uniform number of clicks to reach to any contact in the address book, is intuitively unsuitable for the highly skewed access requirements, arising out of the skewed call distribution of the semi-literate mobile user. In this paper, we investigate the usability of the current text based storage and retrieval system that common address books utilize among the class of *semi-literate mobile users*, and evaluate the effectiveness of an enhanced design for the address book, the *SymAB*. We also show that a call distribution based *address book* access mechanism aligns well with the access requirements of the *semi-literate mobile user.*

1.1 Text Usage and the Semi-literate Mobile User

A survey was conducted among the semi-literate mobile users from the low-income group in the urban area of Bangalore with 20 participants, with ages ranging from 20 to 35 engaged in a variety of manual trades such as cleaners, plumbers, drivers etc. The *largely textual interfaces* of the mobile devices affected the usage patterns for the semi-literate. Firstly, there is a psychological barrier to the usage of mobile phones as the semi-literate perceives it to be a high-end device, partly because of the textual content involved. Secondly, the semi-literate who realizes the value-add that mobile devices can cause to his work/life and chooses to use it, tends to use it minimally. We refer to *minimal usage* as the usage of a very small subset of the features available in the device.

Further investigations revealed that the literacy barrier leads to effects including things such as:

- Maintaining address books of essential contacts on sheets of paper, which are looked up when a call needs to be made.
- Seeking the assistance of a literate person to update the address book.
- Taking help from a literate person to store essential numbers into the address book and to learn a sequence of keystrokes to call commonly used numbers such as home, spouse, employer etc.

From our observations, we find that address books are indispensable for mobile usage since every user maintains it, either using the address book on the mobile or using one of the above methods. These scenarios motivate the need to explore the usability of alternate interfaces for illiterate users.

The usage pattern of mobile devices is usually much skewed for the semi-literate. They typically have a small set of contacts that they use frequently (including the employer, family and the inner ring of friends), whereas the rest of the contacts are used very rarely. Although this is true for the most mobile users, regardless of their income and literacy, we argue that the need to address this issue is more critical for the semi-literate due to two factors – (1) Accessing the address book is hard for the semi-literate making usability a critical requirement, and (2) the frequently used contacts is a much smaller set in the case of the semi-literate mobile user as compared to the more general categories.

2 *SymAB* Design

To address the issues highlighted in the survey, we propose an enhanced design of the address book, the *SymAB* which is a symbol-based interface. Symbols have been shown to be very highly preferred over textual interfaces, by the communities that we address [2].

The design composes of two parts, an enhanced mobile keypad with provision of symbols either in addition or as replacement to alphabet and a symbol based retrieval mechanism of the stored entries. A keypad button is associated with a symbol, clicking a button once will enter the symbol and subsequent clicks will bring up the other alphanumeric characters associated with it. We studied the requirements of a sample of semi-literate mobile users in Bangalore and arrived at a small set of symbols to be embedded in the 12-key mobile keypads, the trade-off being to include as much of the symbols in the set suggested by most people, at the same time trying to leave as many slots open so as to allow room for customizability i.e., these slots would be filled with generic symbols allowing users to assign their own meanings to them. The icons chosen were those of a *home, family, money, man, mobile, woman, elder-man and elder-woman*. The rest of the four icons were optionally populated from the following geometric shapes – *square, circle, rectangle, rhombus, triangle* and *pentagon*. A contact can be associated with variable length strings, each element in the string being a symbol, numeric or an alphabet. As is obvious, strings that are purely composed of symbols are assumed to be unordered, i.e., $\Box\triangle$ is assumed to be the same as $\Box\triangle$.

The second part is the symbol-based search functionality for the address book, which is based on a prefix-search, i.e., searching all matches for a prefix entered, is

Fig. 1. The design of the keypad (on the left) and the symbol-based search of the address book (on the right) of *SymAB* application

replaced by a subset-search in the *SymAB* interface wherein all contacts represented by supersets of the entered set of symbols is displayed. Figure 1 demonstrates the retrieval of all entries that contain the **home** symbol. Thus the icons on the keypad are used to limit the search for an entry.

In addition to the above, *SymAB* is further augmented by a call distribution based access which can be accessed by pressing "#". *SymAB* maintains an internal list of contacts sorted in the decreasing order of frequency of calling, k key-presses of the # key leading to the kth frequently contacted contact in the address book. This feature is aligned with the skewed call distribution of a typical user in semi-literate category thus helping the user quickly locate the most frequent contact.

3 Evaluation and Future Work

We conducted a preliminary evaluation of *SymAB* with 10 participants to obtain qualitative feedback on the value perceived by the enhanced design. All participants belonged to the semi-literate category, with ages ranging from 19 to 28 years. We educated the participants on the use of the *SymAB* interface and asked them to simulate the storage of a minimum of 3 contacts and randomly retrieve them. We also asked them questions to get an idea of the skew in their call distribution, and as to how much the frequency based retrieval would be able to help them.

All the users reported the enhanced value they perceived from the design thus making the address book feature simpler, easy-to-use and more comfortable to play around with. They not only utilized the pre-defined set of icons but created combinations of symbols for storing entries. Some of them suggested additional icons to be included, that of a *friend*, *rose* and *vehicle*. The participants also expressed that using *SymAB* their near and dear ones like elderly parents, relatives staying away from them who are semi-literate and not working would now be able contact them for any emergency/need without assistance thus making them independent. One participant indicated that since *SymAB* gives co-existence of both icon and text-based storage/retrieval mechanisms, it is multi-purpose serving the needs of both the educated and semi-literate in a family. Most of the participants reported a high skew in call distribution, with the number of contacts used on a daily basis being as low as 2-8 with an average of 4. All of them found frequency based retrieval as a useful feature, and many opined that it is easier to educate the elderly to retrieve based on such an interface than any other retrieval mechanism.

We are currently exploring the usability of other features of the mobile phone for the semi-literate class and investigating the effectiveness of alternate interfaces.

References

1. Abraham, Reuben: Mobile Phones and Economic Development: Evidence from the fishing industry. In: India, International Conference on ICT for (ICTD) (May 2006)
2. Waverman, L., Meschi, M., Fuss, M.: The impact of telecoms on economic growth in developing countries, http://web.si.umich.edu/tprc/papers/2005/450/L%20Waverman-%20Telecoms%20Growth%20in%20Dev.%20Countries.pdf
3. Medhi, I., Sagar, A., Toyama, K.: Text-free User Interfaces for Illiterate and Semi-Literate Users. In: International Conference on ICT for Development (ICTD) (May 2006)

Accessibility of Assistive Software Installation Interfaces

Lucia Filgueiras[1], Edson Sales[1], Lucy Gruenwald[2], Ana Maria Barbosa[2],
and Renato Facis[3]

[1] Escola Politecnica da Universidade de Sao Paulo, Sao Paulo, Brazil
[2] Rede Saci, Sao Paulo, Brazil
[3] LabIHC, Prodesp, Sao Paulo, Brazil
{lucia.filgueiras,edson.sales}@poli.usp.br, lucygru@ciblis.net,
ana@saci.org.br, rfacis@sp.gov.br

Abstract. Software installation is a one-time task; yet, it should work well. Regarding assistive technologies, users with disabilities will often require help in installation tasks. Five assistive software products were evaluated in order to identify barriers faced by visually impaired users performing the installation task and none of them, for different reasons, allowed full completion of installation task. Some recommendations are devised from the experience.

Keywords: Assistive technology, accessibility, installation software, usability.

1 Introduction

Assistive technology is fundamental for allowing people with disabilities to use computers in their daily life. Several studies have been devoted to assistive technologies and a few of them were focused on the usability of assistive software [1]. Traditionally, the largest part of the development effort – and nowadays, also of the usability effort – has been assigned to the core application functionalities. Online help, user documentation, installation and uninstallation interfaces were always seen as secondary in this development. This is not different with assistive technologies.

This paper reports the findings of usability evaluations performed on five assistive software tools, and focuses on the user experience with the installation interface. Section 2 presents issues about installation interfaces. Section 3 presents the evaluated assistive software products. Section 4 reviews the method and results obtained.

2 Installation Interface Usability

Installation interfaces peculiarities have motivated little research to the moment [2], [3]. Installation and uninstallation software is considered part of user documentation, according to IEEE Std 1063 [4].. Seffah and Metzker regretted that "developers with any HCI background, unfortunately by ignorance, are asked to develop software artifacts that we know have a direct impact on usability including help systems, training plans and resources, user documentation, technical support as well as installation and configuration procedures." [5]

C. Baranauskas et al. (Eds.): INTERACT 2007, LNCS 4662, Part I, pp. 393–396, 2007.
© IFIP International Federation for Information Processing 2007

Installation procedures are often performed with the help of wizards, so that most of the necessary configuration tasks are hidden from the user in the typical process. When installation cannot follow the typical path, it tends to be a very complex activity that may require lots of work [6].

Rhodes [7] developed a case study of the installation interface of widely used commercial software. He summarized his painful experience in the following learned lessons: (1) Installation can take a lot of time; (2) Users are often forced to reboot their machines many times; (3) Users are often given very little control over the installation process; (4) Users are not given good information about the installation process; (5) Users are forced to buy software that is painful to install.

Consequences of bad installation software are the same ones of all other kinds of unusable software: user dissatisfaction, high costs due to user time and errors, high support cost and even total rejection. Lack of usability in installation interfaces has one additional major consequence that is the fact that poorly installed software will result in problems in regular use. Regarding ATs, this can be very disturbing, because this technology is a precondition to provide access to all other computer features.

3 Installing Assistive Technologies

Some disabilities require the person employ some form of assistive technology (AT) in order to make use of a computer. W3C accessibility rules and other for instance, presume the user is navigating with the aid of an AT. This is also the case of Leporini and Paternò work on [8].

This paper is focused on AT implemented as software products which can be installed on a computer in order to assist users with disabilities in the general use of a computer. There are several commercial alternatives of AT, and as a software product they must be submitted to usability evaluation.

AT usability is very important because a user with disability interacts with two different systems – the AT and the system being used. Both interaction languages must be taken into account when evaluating the disabled user´s experience.

Even though AT development has cared for users´ needs, some developers have not considered the scenario of getting started with the product. Whatever their reason is, total accessibility requires that the user can perform autonomously all desired tasks. Particularly, if the user with disability cannot perform the very first interaction step, for him or her all effort in accessibility will have been wasted.

Five AT products available in Brazil have been evaluated, regarding usability and accessibility of installation procedures. All products are available to the user, either for free or commercially sold. They were designed as assistance to visual impaired and blind users; however, they are known to have broader application, for instance, by elder people and by users with cognitive impairment. Some of their characteristics are summarized in the following items:

- AT1 is an operational system shell with a voice synthesizer and browser for internet access. It was developed by a Brazilian university team and is free.
- AT2 is a screen reader that enables access to Windows® applications. AT2 can be obtained freely for personal use but companies are required to pay.

- AT3 is also a screen reader for Windows ® applications. This product has been localized for Brazilian Portuguese and its license is sold.
- AT4 is a Web application to help people with low vision. It has a voice synthesizer and other resources to improve legibility of screen text.
- AT5 is another solution for people with low vision with some resources to facilitate the visualization and reading of Internet pages.

4 Evaluation Method and Results

All AT installation procedures were evaluated in usability experiments, with five visually impaired users. Three of them were blind; two had low vision. All were daily users of the internet and three of them worked in computer-related professions. All but one had experimented at least one AT before. Computer illiterate users were excluded from the user population because the installation task is too complex for a beginner and would place an unnecessary burden on these users.

Users were given a narrative that explained the experiment scenario: they had received a publication which gave directions on how to obtain AT products and they intended to try the ones they were not acquainted with. In order to do so, they would have to obtain, install and test them. Scenario had all information needed in order to obtain the tool. They could choose their favorite AT to drive the use and were given time to customize it to start the process, if they needed it. Observers would consider the task completed when the user initiated the obtained AT.

As the objective of this paper is to present barriers found in AT installation interfaces, only qualitative findings are presented in this section, regardless of which AT caused the issue.

None of the five AT were successfully installed by any of the selected users. The following paragraphs summarize the relevant barriers to installation.

1. Absence of voice synthesizers in the installation interface. Four of the five tested assistive technologies offer a voice synthesizer. However, some ATs do not employ this resource in the installation interface. Without the auditory feedback, blind users get uncertain if the process has succeeded.
2. Two ATs seldom coexist. In our experiments, users installed ATs with the help of their favorite one, which resulted in configuration conflicts and error messages. In some cases two AT voices spoke at the same time, none of them being understood.
3. Inaccessible essential information. One of the ATs had complete user documentation in Braille; however, the software key was in a small printed label inside the package. The Braille documentation did not inform about the label as part of the package.
4. Transition from installation to product use. Generally, installation finishes by leaving a shortcut for the application. Some ATs, besides doing that, also activate the application and move the focus to its window, leaving the user unaware of the change.
5. Inaccessible instructions. Four of the five AT had on-line user instructions on installation. Only one of them had a Braille manual. This obliged the user to use another AT to access the manuals and to ask for human help.

6. Inconsistent information. User documentation referred to signs and symbols that were different from the ones actually used in the application.

Our experiments confirmed Rhodes learnt lessons for installation software and taught us some more specific ones about AT:

- AT installation interfaces must address the user they are intended for. If able-bodied assistance or special training is required to install the software, this should be stated clearly in the user documentation, again in an accessible manner.
- Users must be in control during all installation process and after it. If their actions are required, such as rebooting the computer, answering to error messages or activating the installed application, they must be aware of what they have to do, the reasons why and the consequences of not doing.
- AT installation interfaces should deal with the fact that the user may be using another similar product and avoid all kinds of conflicts.
- Software installation is considered a risky endeavor. Loss of situational awareness due to unanticipated and unannounced automatic actions should be avoided.

5 Conclusion

Assistive technologies are essential for digital inclusion of thousands of people with some form of disability. Users with disabilities are compelled to use awkward technology because they are in need of it and have few alternatives.

However, AT like any software product must be developed and evaluated considering a broad scope of the user experience with the tool – from installation to support. For some users with disabilities, having to ask for help is very frustrating.

References

1. Suttcliffe, A., Fickas, S., Sohlberg, M., Ehlhardt, L.: Investigating the usability of assistive user interfaces. Interacting with Computers 15 (2003)
2. Yeats, D.: Revising documentation deliverables based on usability evaluation findings: a case study. In: Proceedings of ACM SIGDOC'04, pp. 17–18. ACM Press, New York (2004)
3. Nichols, D.M., Twidale, M.B.: The usability of open source software. First Monday, vol. 8, n.1 (2003), http://firstmonday.org/issues/issue8_1/nichols/index.html
4. The Institute of Electrical and Electronics Engineers, IEEE Standard for Software User Documentation, IEEE Std 1063 (2001)
5. Seffah, A., Metzker, E.: The obstacles and myths of usability and software engineering. Communications of the ACM 47(12), 71–76 (2004)
6. Crawford, V., Pitts, A., Radcliffe, R., Seifert, L.A.: Solution documentation. In: Proceedings of ACM SIGDOC'04, pp. 72–74. ACM Press, New York (2004)
7. Rhodes, J.R.: Installing Norton Antivirus 2002: a usability case study. WebWord Newsletter (2002), http://www.webword.com
8. Leporini, B., Paternò, F.: Increasing usability when interacting through screen readers. Universal Access in the Information Society. Springer, Heidelberg (2004)

Model-Driven Adaptation for Plastic User Interfaces

Jean-Sébastien Sottet[1], Vincent Ganneau[1, 2], Gaëlle Calvary[1],
Joëlle Coutaz[1], Alexandre Demeure[1], Jean-Marie Favre[1], and Rachel Demumieux[2]

[1] Université Joseph Fourier, Laboratoire LIG, BP 53, 38041 Grenoble Cedex 9, France
{Jean-Sebastien.Sottet, Vincent.Ganneau, Gaelle.Calvary,
Joelle.Coutaz, Alexandre.Demeure, Jean-Marie.Favre}@imag.fr
[2] France Télécom R&D, 2 avenue Pierre Marzin, 22307 Lannion Cedex France
{Vincent.Ganneau, Rachel.Demumieux}@orange-ftgroup.com

Abstract. User Interface (UI) plasticity denotes UI adaptation to the context of use (user, platform, physical and social environments) while preserving usability. In this article, we focus on the use of Model-Driven Engineering and demonstrate how the intrinsic flexibility of this approach can be exploited by designers for UI prototyping as well as by end-users in real settings. For doing so, the models developed at design-time, which convey high-level design decisions, are still available at run-time. As a result, an interactive system is not limited to a set of linked pieces of code, but is a graph of models that evolves, expresses and maintains multiple perspectives on the system from top-level tasks to the final UI. A simplified version of a Home Heating Control System is used to illustrate our approach and technical implementation.

Keywords: User interface plasticity, user interface adaptation, context aware systems, Model-Driven Engineering.

1 Introduction

User Interface (UI) *plasticity* denotes the capacity for user interfaces to adapt to the context of use while preserving usability [34]. The *context of use* is a structured information space whose finality is to inform the adaptation process. It includes a model of the user who is intended to use (or is actually using) the system, the social and physical environments where the interaction is supposed to take place (or is actually taking place), and the platform to be used (or is being used). The latter covers the set of computing, sensing, communication, and interaction resources that bind together the physical environment with the digital world. *Usability* expresses the *useworthiness* of the system: the value that this system has in the real world [6].

From the software perspective, UI plasticity goes far beyond UI portability and UI translation. Software adaptation has been addressed using many approaches over the years, including Machine Learning [22], Model-Driven Engineering (MDE) [5, 11, 18, 20, 23, 25, 31, 32], and Component-oriented services [29]. Our approach to the problem of UI plasticity is based on the following observations. First, every paradigm

C. Baranauskas et al. (Eds.): INTERACT 2007, LNCS 4662, Part I, pp. 397–410, 2007.
© IFIP International Federation for Information Processing 2007

has its own merits targeted at specific requirements. Thus, in an ever-changing world, one single approach is doomed to failure. Second, software tools and mechanisms tend to make a dichotomy between the development stage and the run-time phase making it difficult to articulate run-time adaptation based on semantically rich design-time descriptions.

Our approach to UI plasticity is to bring together Model-Driven Engineering (MDE) and Service Oriented Approach (SOA) within a unified framework that covers the development stage of interactive systems as well as the run-time phase. Our intention is to demonstrate how the intrinsic flexibility of this approach can be usefully exploited for UI prototyping by designers as well as by end-users (if appropriately encapsulated). In this article, we focus on the MDE aspects of our solution space. The principles are presented in Section 3, followed in Section 4 by the description of an early implementation, that combines MDE and SOA. To illustrate the discussion, we use a simplified version of a Home Heating Control System (HHCS). This running case study is depicted in Section 2.

2   HHCS: A Simplified Home Heating Control System

HHCS (Home Heating Control System) enables users to control the temperature of the home using different interaction resources. A typical task consists in checking and setting room temperature. As illustrated in Fig. 1, the graphical rendering of the user interface for this task depends on the screen size (as in 1-b and 1-d), on the set of screens that can be used simultaneously (e.g., 1-a versus 1-e), as well as on the set of usability properties that the designers have considered as central. Switching between these UIs is performed at run-time under human control (i.e. by the end-user in the real setting and/or the designer while prototyping the UI).

The five UIs of Fig. 1 are functionally equivalent: they support the same set of tasks (i.e. to access a set of rooms and, if needed, to set the room temperature between 15°C and 18°C). Some UIs are centralized on a single screen but simultaneously mapped onto different displays whose size differs (Fig. 1 a-b-c-d). Conversely, in Fig. 1-e, the UI is distributed over two displays: the UI that corresponds to the task "Select room" is mapped onto the PDA, whereas the PC is used to set the temperature.

In addition, these UIs do not satisfy the same set of usability properties. In particular, prompting (cf. Bastien-Scapin's framework [3]), prevention against errors, and minimal actions, are not equally supported. In Fig. 1-a, the range of values of the room temperature is not observable. As a result, prompting is not fully supported. Prevention against errors is improved in Fig. 1-c by using a menu list while Fig. 1-b improves minimal actions by eliminating the articulatory task for selecting a room.

In the rest of the article, we present the underlying technology and its principles that enable end-users and/or designers to control the final UI (FUI).

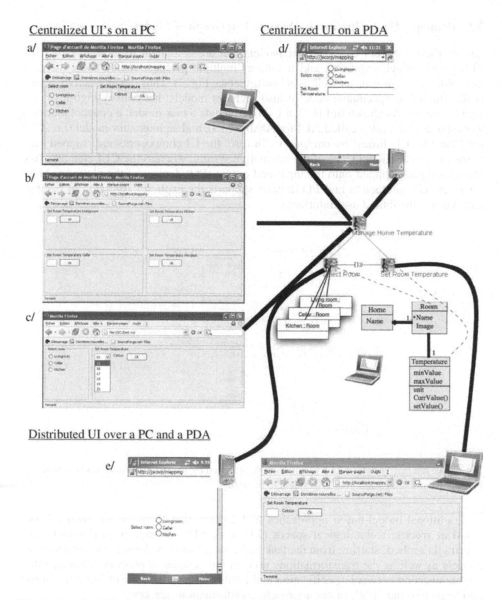

Fig. 1. Five final UIs for HHCS resulting from different mappings (depicted as black lines) between the platforms available (PC and PDA) and high-level models (e.g., task and concepts).

3 Principles

Early work in the automatic generation of UIs as well as more recent work in UI adaptation [5, 11, 18, 20, 23, 25, 31, 32] adheres only partially to the MDE principles. Our approach differs from previous work according to the following five principles.

3.1   Principle #1: An Interactive System Is a Graph of Models

An interactive system is a graph of models that are compliant to meta-models [32]. This graph, which expresses and maintains multiple perspectives on the system, is available at design-time as well as at run-time (see Fig. 2). Thus, an interactive system is not limited to executable code: it also includes models that convey high-level design decisions. As shown in Fig. 2, a UI may include a task model, a concept model, a workspace model (also called AUI for Abstract UI), and an interactor model (i.e., CUI for Concrete UI) linked by *mappings*[1]. In turn, the UI components are mapped onto items of the Functional Core of the interactive system, whereas the CUI elements (the interactors) are mapped onto the input and output (I/O) devices of the platform. Mapping between interactors and I/O devices supports the explicit expression of centralized versus distributed user interfaces.

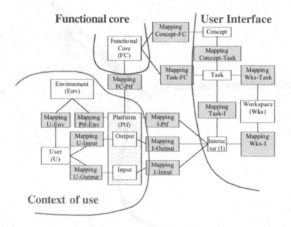

Fig. 2. An interactive system is a graph of models related by mappings. White boxes denote the models whereas lines and grey boxes denote mappings.

Traditional model-based approaches to UI generation focus on the final UI, targeted at specific technological spaces [13] (e.g., XUL, Swing, etc.). Forward engineering is applied, starting from the task and concept models, loosing the intermediate models as well as the transformations used in the generation process. Consequently, "the connection between specification and final result can be quite difficult to control and to understand" [19]. In our approach, transformations are key.

3.2   Principle #2: Transformations Are Models

In the context of MDE, a transformation is the production of a set of target models from a set of source models, according to a transformation definition. In turn, a transformation definition is a set of transformation rules that together describe how source

---

[1] In mathematics, a mapping is "a rule of correspondence established between tow sets that associates each member of the first set with a single member of the second" [The American Heritage Dictionary of the English Language, 1970, p. 797].

models are transformed into target models. In particular, our transformation rules make explicit the usability properties they satisfy (cf. Principle #3).

By promoting transformations as models, transformations can also be transformed, and frequent transformations (such as transforming sub-tasks into pull-down menus) can serve as patterns in a library. As a result, we alleviate the development and maintenance cost (by the way of a library of re-usable transformations), we support rapid prototyping based on the comparative evaluation[2] of UIs produced with different transformations, we improve run-time flexibility (since transformations, which are available at run-time, can be transformed). For example, the UIs of HHCS differ from the application of different transformations. Examples will be presented in more detail in Section 4.1.

3.3 Principle #3: The Choice of Usability Frameworks Is Left Opened

A large number of usability frameworks have been proposed to better understand and measure the usability of interactive systems. These include: Shackel [28], Dix et al. [10], Nielsen [21], Preece [26], Schneiderman [30], Constantine and Lockwood [7], Van Welie et al. [35], as well as Seffah et al. [27] who propose QUIM, a unifying roadmap to reconcile existing frameworks. More specific frameworks are proposed for web engineering (Montero et al. [17]), or for specific domains (for instance, military applications). Closely related to UI plasticity, Lopez-Jacquero et al. propose a refinement of Bastien-Scapin's framework, as a usability guide for UI adaptation [15].

Because moving to an unfamiliar set of tools would impose a high threshold on HCI and software designers, we promote an open approach that consists in choosing the appropriate usability framework for eliciting the properties that *must*, *should* or *may* be satisfied by transformations [33]. For HHCS, we have used Bastien-Scapin's framework. The transformation of a usability framework into a digital model is performed according to Principle #4.

3.4 Principle #4: Humans Are Kept in the Loop

HCI design methods produce a large body of contemplative models (i.e. models that cannot be processed by a machine) such as storyboards, and mock-ups. These models are useful reference material during the design process. On the other hand, because they are contemplative, they can only be transformed manually into productive models (i.e. models that can be processed by a machine). Manual transformation supports creative inspiration, but is prone to wrong interpretation and to loss of key information. To address this problem, we accept to support a mix of *automated*, *semi-automated*, and *manually* performed transformations. Semi-automated and manual transformations may be performed by designers and/or end-users. For example, given our current level of knowledge, the transformation of a "value-centered model" [6] into a "usability model" such as that of [3], can only be performed manually by designers. Semi-automation allows designers (or end-users) to adjust the models that result from transformations. For example, a designer may decide to map a subset of an AUI onto UI services developed with the latest post-WIMP toolkit. By doing so, we avoid the "low-cost, fast food" UIs as produced with automatic generation.

---

[2] As discussed in [16], comparative evaluations are more productive than absolute evaluations.

3.5 Principle #5: Close and Open Adaptiveness Are Complementary

Designers cannot envision all of the contexts of use in which the future interactive system will be executed. To alleviate this problem, we suggest a mix of open and close adaptiveness. A system is *close-adaptive* when adaptation is self-contained. It supports the "innate" adjustments planned at the design stage as well as new adjustments produced by its own internal learning mechanisms. The system is *open-adaptive "if new adaptation plans can be introduced during run-time"* [24].

By analogy, an interactive system is *close-adaptive* for the contexts of use that fall within its *domain of plasticity* [4], that is, for the contexts of use for which this system can adapt on its own. By design, an interactive system has an innate domain of plasticity. If it is able to learn adjustments for additional contexts of use, then the domain of plasticity extends dynamically, but this extension relies only on the internal computing capabilities of the system. An external infrastructure must be provided to support open-adaptiveness [2]. Fig. 3 shows the functional decomposition of the run-time infrastructure that we propose for open model-driven adaptation.

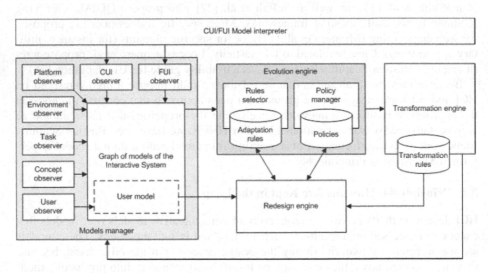

Fig. 3. Run-time infrastructure for open model-driven adaptation

Our run-time infrastructure for open model-driven adaptation includes five core functions: the Models manager, the Evolution engine, the Transformation engine, the Redesign engine and the CUI/FUI Model interpreter. For each running interactive system, the *Models manager* maintains the graph of models shown in Fig. 2. Observers monitor state changes in which they are interested and update the graph accordingly. Typically, a platform observer is interested in the arrival/departure of interaction resources; an FUI observer monitors the actions performed by the end-user on the FUI, etc. When some change occurs, the Models manager sends the appropriate notification to the Evolution engine or to the Redesign engine (if the change comes from the user model). The *Evolution engine* identifies the appropriate transformations to adapt the UI to the current change according to the current adaptation policy. These transformations are specified in the action part of adaptation rules. Typically, an adaptation rule obeys the Event-Condition-Action paradigm where the Event part denotes the trigger, and where the Action part makes reference to transformations or to other adaptation rules. Examples of adaptation rules will be discussed in Section 4.3. Policies serve at favoring such and such adaptation rules based on such and such (usability) criteria. The transformations selected by the evolution engine are then transmitted to the *Transformation engine* whose role is to apply the transformations to the graph of models. The graph of models is updated accordingly while the CUI/FUI interpreter (e.g., a Web browser) uses the new CUI to produce the new adapted final UI (FUI).

The role of the *Redesign engine* is to dynamically modify the adaptation rules and to set the current policy based on the information gathered from, or inferred by, the *User model*. Typical attributes maintained in the User model include user preferences, interests and goals, as well as interaction history (i.e. tasks in progress, completed tasks, errors, etc.) [12]. For example, the end-user using the UI shown in Fig. 1-a may keep entering wrong values when specifying a room temperature. From the information provided by the CUI/FUI observers, the User model may infer the need for error management so that the new resulting FUI be that of Fig. 1-c. The Redesign engine then searches for the transformations in the *Transformations Data Base* that promote the error management property. If a transformation is found, the Redesign engine may create new adaptation rules, and/or suppress adaptation rules from the current set, and/or modifies existing ones. Note that, according to Principle #2, these modifications are performed by the way of transformations.

Having presented the principles of our approach to UI plasticity, we now show how they have been implemented and applied to HHCS.

4   From Principles to HHCS in Action

Our hypothesis is that designers produce all or a subset of the models mentioned in Fig. 2. For HHCS, we have adopted a top-down approach starting from the task model and the domain-dependent concepts using well-defined meta-models[3]. These models are represented in a simplified manner in Fig. 2. The AUI, CUI and FUI of HHCS have been produced with transformations. Examples of transformation are presented in Section 4.1. At run-time, changes in the context of use may require the user interface of HHCS to adapt. The context of use for HHCS is discussed in Section 4.2, and examples of adaptation rules are provided in Section 4.3. In Section 4.4 we show how Principle #4 (humans are kept in the loop) is implemented with a meta-UI.

The run-time infrastructure for open model-driven adaptation is implemented as a set of OSGi services where a service encapsulates one of the core functions shown in Fig. 3. More specifically, the Models manager is implemented in Java. We draw upon the Eclipse Modeling Framework (EMF), which automatically generates the methods (the API) that make it possible for the observers and the Transformation engine to modify the graph of models. The Evolution Engine and the Redesign engine are implemented in Java as well. The Transformation engine is an ATL interpreter [1].

---

[3] Describing these meta-models would require more space than available in this paper. See [33] for more details.

4.1 Transformations Illustrated with HHCS

Transformations, which are interpreted by the Transformation engine, are expressed in ATL [1]. QVT and XSLT are other options. The following rule (called *rule TaskChoiceToGroupBox*) shows how a task of type "Choose 1 item among n" (*tsk.taskType.name='Choice 1/n'*) is transformed into a group box using XUL as the meta-model for the expression of AUIs (*XULMetaModel!GroupBox*). This rule applies to a task (*tsk : MMEcosystem!Task*) provided that the task type is 'Choice 1/n' and that there is at least one platform mapped onto the task (see the constraint *tsk.taskPlatforms->select(e|e.active=true)->size() >= 1*).

If the conditions are satisfied, then the transformation generates the corresponding XUL group (*XULMetaModel!GroupBox*) whose label is derived from the task name (*capt : XULMetaModel!Caption(label <- tsk.name)*) and whose content is derived from the concepts manipulated by the task. For each concept instance (*e in tsk.manipulatedConcepts*), the **do** block generates a radio button (see *vbx.radiobuttons <- thisModule.radioBuild(z)*) with the appropriate label (i.e., the name of the task – see *XULMetaModel!RadioGroup(id <- 'radio_'+ tsk.name)*). By doing so, the rule satisfies the guidance – prompting criterion defined in Bastien-Scapin's framework.

In ATL, transformations are grouped into modules. We use the header of ATL modules to map each usability criteria with the names of the transformations that satisfy that criteria.

```
rule TaskChoiceToGroupBox {

from tsk : MMEcosystem!Task (tsk.taskType.name='Choice 1/n' and
tsk.taskPlatforms->select( e | e.active=true)->size() >= 1 )


to gp_box : XULMetaModel!GroupBox (id <- 'group'+        tsk.name,flex <- 1,
xullnteractors <- Sequence {capt,vbx}),

      capt : XULMetaModel!Caption(label <- tsk.name),

vbx : XULMetaModel!RadioGroup(id <- 'radio_'+ tsk.name)

      do {
                for (e in tsk.manipulatedConcepts)
                for (z in e.conceptInstances)
      vbx.radiobuttons <- thisModule.radioBuild(z);
      }}
```

We have developed a library of transformations that can transform tasks and concept models into CUIs expressed in HTML or in XUL. As mentioned in the Principles section, transformations have also been defined to create and modify adaptation rules, which, in turn, are triggered on the occurrence of context changes.

4.2 Context of Use in HHCS

We model the context of use using the ontology proposed in [8]. In short, a contextual information space is modeled as a directed graph where a node denotes a context and an edge a condition to move between two contexts. A context is defined over a set E of *entities*, a set Ro of *roles* (i.e. functions) that these entities may satisfy, and a set Rel of *relations* between the entities. Entities, roles and relations are modeled as expressions of *observables* that are captured and inferred by the system. The condition to move between two contexts is one of the following: E is replaced with a different set, Ro has changed, or Rel has changed.

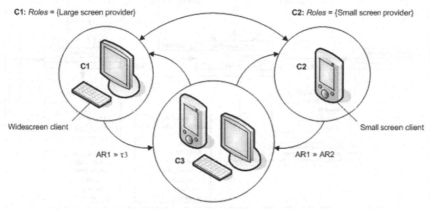

C1: *Roles* = {Large screen provider}   **C2**: *Roles* = {Small screen provider}

C1

C2

Widescreen client   Small screen client

AR1 » τ3   C3   AR1 » AR2

C3: *Roles* = {Small screen provider, Large screen provider}

Fig. 4. Context switching in HHCS. Nodes denote the Roles and Entities that define a context. Arrows denote transitions between contexts decorated with the corresponding adaptation rules.

Fig. 4 shows the three contexts of use considered to be relevant for HHCS: E is the set of platforms available to the end-user, Ro the set of roles that these platforms can play (i.e. "Large screen provider" and "Small screen provider"), and where Rel is empty. C1 refers to the case where the user can access HHCS through a large screen whereas C2 enables the user to control room temperature with the small display of a PDA. In C3, a PDA and a large screen are simultaneously available. As discussed above, the arrival/departure of a platform is detected by the platform observer: the platform model is modified accordingly in the Models manager, and a "platform modification" event is sent to the Evolution engine. Events serve as triggers for the adaptation rules interpreted by the Evolution Engine.

4.3 Adaptation Rules

Adaptation Rules (AR) comply with the meta-model shown in Fig. 5. This meta-model re-uses the classical *Event-Condition-Action* structure, with additional Pre- and Post-conditions:

- The *Event* and conditions (*Condition*, Pre- and Post-conditions) make reference to the models maintained in the Models manager; they are possibly empty.
- The *Action* references either the model transformation or the adaptation rule (AR) to be applied. The action may satisfy (or may not satisfy) a set of properties (for instance, the Bastien-Scapin's criteria).

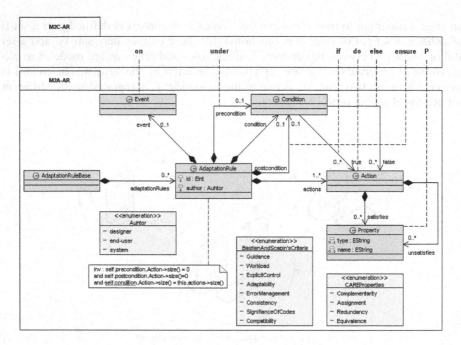

Fig. 5. Our meta-model for adaptation rules

The following adaptation rules have been defined to support the changes in the context of use depicted in Fig. 4:

AR1 {	**under** left task is "Select 1 among *n*"
	and right task is "Specify a value"
	on platform connection
	if largeScreen **do** AR2
	else do τ3}
AR2 {	**if** *numberOfConcepts n* ≠ 4 **do** τ1
	else do τ2}
AR3 {	**under** left task is "Select 1 among *n*"
	and right task is "Specify a value"
	and largeScreen
	on *numberOfConcepts n* change
	do AR2}

AR1 is triggered on the connection of a new platform and applies to tasks, like task "Set home temperature" of Fig. 1, whose first sibling consists in choosing 1 item among n, and the second sibling consists in specifying a value. AR1 invokes Transformation τ3 when the role "Large screen provider" is not satisfied. It invokes AR2 otherwise. AR2 calls for Transformation τ2 when the number of concepts referenced in the task is four, leading to the generation of the final UI shown in Fig. 1-b. This transformation, which avoids articulatory tasks, supports the "minimal action" criteria.

AR3 is triggered by the event "numberOfConcepts n change". In HHCS, this corresponds to the case where a new thermostat is installed/removed from the home. In

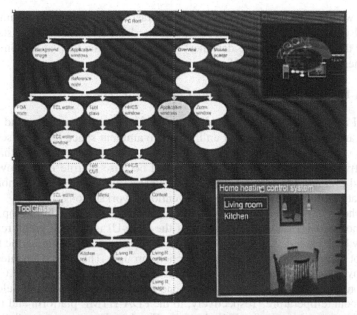

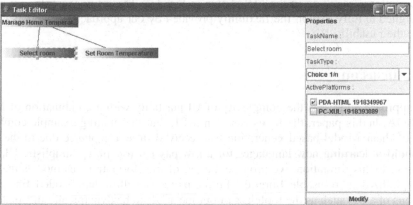

Fig. 6. Examples of meta-UIs when controlling the FUI of HHCS

HHCS, this phenomenon is detected by the concept observer. The concept model is modified accordingly, and the corresponding event is sent to the Evolution engine. AR3 is applied when the role "Large screen provider" is filled.

When several adaptation rules apply, the Policy Manager makes the final decision based on the current active policy and provides the Transformation Engine with the appropriate transformations. Interoperability between the Evolution Engine and the ATL-based Transformation Engine is ensured in the following way: Adaptation rules are produced using an EMF (Eclipse Modeling Framework) basic editor. The output of this editor is an XMI file (.ecore) that can be manipulated by EMF-based tools such as our ATL Transformation Engine.

So far, we have shown how the run-time infrastructure supports run-time adaptation based on the specifications provided by the designers. In the next section, we show how the end-user (and the designer) can be kept in the loop at run-time (Principle #4) when served by a meta-UI.

4.4 Meta-UIs to Keep Humans in the Loop at Run-Time

A meta-UI is an interactive system whose set of functions is necessary and sufficient to control and evaluate the state of an interactive ambient space [9]. This set is *meta-* because it serves as an umbrella *beyond* the domain-dependent services that support human activities in this space. It is *UI*-oriented because its role is to allow users to control and evaluate the state of the ambient interactive space. It is to ambient computing what desktops and shells are to conventional workstations.

Fig. 6 shows early versions of meta-UIs illustrated on HHCS. In the top example, the CUI model of HHCS as well as that of the meta-UI is a scene graph rendered as the display background. A subtree of the CUI is suppressed by bringing the tool-glass on the root of the subtree followed by a click through. The FUI is updated accordingly. Conversely, the user modifies the FUI with the tool-glass and the CUI is updated accordingly. In the bottom example, end-users can map the tasks "Select room" and "Set room temperature" respectively, to the PDA-HTML platform and to the PC-XUL platform, resulting in the FUI shown in Fig. 1-e. These toy examples are being redesigned to fully exploit the flexibility provided by our approach (as well as to improve their usability!).

5 Conclusion

Our approach addresses the complexity of UI plasticity with a combination of MDE and SOA. In this paper, the focus is set on MDE, but the running example combines both of them. Model-based generation has received little acceptance due to the high threshold of learning new languages for a low pay-off (obtaining simplistic UIs). In response to this limitation, we propose the use of transformations as models that can be capitalized in re-usable libraries. Furthermore, we allow hand-coded fine-tuned portions of a UI (such as the toolglass of our meta-UI) to be dynamically mapped onto high-level models provided that they comply with a component-oriented service protocol (this aspect has not been discussed in the paper). Transformations are key because they can be dynamically transformed, either automatically by a run-time infrastructure and/or by the end-users and designers through a meta-UI. Transformations can also be used to improve interoperability. In particular, we have defined transformations that translate our own meta-models into UsiXML [14] meta-models, so as to take benefit from the UsiXML arsenal of tools.

A subset of our principles has been applied to a simplified version of a Home Heating Control System. Other applications are under way for SMS and ambient computing to support conference participants in large conferences. Although this serves as our validation for this work, it also leaves several opportunities for improvements including the study of end-user development environments such as the concept of meta-UI.

Acknowledgments. This work has been partly supported by Project EMODE (ITEA-if4046), the NoE SIMILAR- FP6-507609, and France-Télécom R&D.

References

1. ATL : Atlas Transformation Language, http://www.eclipse.org/m2m/atl/
2. Balme, L., Demeure, A., Barralon, N., Coutaz, J., Calvary, G.: CAMELEON-RT: a Software Architecture Reference Model for Distributed, Migratable, and Plastic User Interfaces. In: Markopoulos, P., Eggen, B., Aarts, E., Crowley, J.L. (eds.) EUSAI 2004. LNCS, vol. 3295, pp. 291–302. Springer, Heidelberg (2004)
3. Bastien, J.M.C., Scapin, D.: Ergonomic Criteria for the Evaluation of Human-Computer. Technical report INRIA, No 156 (June 1993)
4. Calvary, G., Coutaz, J., Thevenin, D.: A Unifying Reference Framework for the Development of Plastic User Interfaces. In: Nigay, L., Little, M.R. (eds.) EHCI 2001. LNCS, vol. 2254, pp. 173–192. Springer, Heidelberg (2001)
5. Clerckx, T., Luyten, K., Coninx, K.: Generating Context-Sensitive Multiple Device Interfaces from Design. In: Proceedings of CADUI'2004, Isle of Madeira, pp. 288–301 (2004)
6. Cockton, G.: A Development Framework for Value-Centred Design. In: Extended Abstracts Proc. of CHI 2005, Portland, Oregon, USA, April 2-7, 2005, pp. 1292–1295 (2005)
7. Constantine, L.L., Lockwood, L.A.D.: Software for Use: A Practical Guide to the Models and Methods of Usage-Centred Design. Addison-Wesley, New-York (1999)
8. Coutaz, J., Crowley, J.L., Dobson, S., Garlan, D.: Context is Key. Communication of the ACM (CACM) 48(3), 49–53 (2005)
9. Coutaz, J.: Meta-User Interfaces for Ambient Spaces. In: Coninx, K., Luyten, K., Schneider, K.A. (eds.) TAMODIA 2006. LNCS, vol. 4385, pp. 1–15. Springer, Heidelberg (2007)
10. Dix, A., Finlay, J., Abowd, G., Beale, R.: Human-Computer Interaction. Prentice-Hall, New-Jersey (1993)
11. Gajos, K., Weld, D.: SUPPLE: Automatically Generating User Interfaces. In: Proceedings of the 9th international conference on Intelligent User Interfaces, pp. 93–100. ACM Press, New York (2004)
12. Johansson, P.: User Modeling in Dialog Systems. Santa Anna IT Research Institute Report SAR (2002)
13. Kurtev, I., Bézivin, J., Aksit, M.: Technological Spaces: An Initial Appraisal. In: Meersman, R., Tari, Z., et al. (eds.) CoopIS 2002, DOA 2002, and ODBASE 2002. LNCS, vol. 2519, Springer, Heidelberg (2002)
14. Limbourg, Q., Vanderdonckt, J., Michotte, B., Bouillon, L., Lopez, V.: USIXML: a Language Supporting Multi-Path Development of User Interfaces. In: Bastide, R., Palanque, P., Roth, J. (eds.) Engineering Human Computer Interaction and Interactive Systems. LNCS, vol. 3425, pp. 200–220. Springer, Heidelberg (2005)
15. Lopez-Jaquero, V., Montero, F., Molina, J.P., Gonzalez, P.: A Seamless Development Process of Adaptive User Interfaces Explicitly Based on Usability Properties. In: Bastide, R., Palanque, P., Roth, J. (eds.) Engineering Human Computer Interaction and Interactive Systems. LNCS, vol. 3425, pp. 289–291. Springer, Heidelberg (2005)
16. Molich, R., Ede, M., Kaasgaard, K., Karyukin, B.: Comparative usability evaluation. Behaviour & Information Technology 23(1), 65–74 (2004)
17. Montero, F., Vanderdonckt, J., Lozano, M.: Quality Models for Automated Evaluation of Web Sites Usability and Accessibility. In: Koch, N., Fraternali, P., Wirsing, M. (eds.) ICWE 2004. LNCS, vol. 3140, pp. 28–30. Springer, Heidelberg (2004)

18. Mori, G., Paternò, F., Santoro, C.: Design and Development of Multidevice User Interfaces through Multiple Logical Descriptions. IEEE Transactions on Software Engineering 30(8), 507–520 (2004)
19. Myers, B., Hudson, S.E., Pausch, R.: Past, Present and Future of User Interface Software Tools. Transactions on Computer-Human Interaction (TOCHI) 7(1), 3–28 (2000)
20. Nichols, J., Rothrock, B., Chau, D., Myers, B.: Huddle: Automatically Generating Interfaces for Systems of Multiple Connected Appliances. In: Proc. of UIST'2006, pp. 279–288 (2006)
21. Nielsen, J.: Heuristic evaluation. In: Nielsen, J., Mack, R.L. (eds.) Usability Inspection Methods, John Wiley & Sons, New York (1994)
22. Njike, H., Artières, T., Gallinari, P., Blanchard, J., Letellier, G.: Automatic learning of domain model for personalized hypermedia applications. In: IJCAI. International Joint Conference on Artificial Intelligence, Edinburg, Scotland, pp. 1624–1625 (2005)
23. Nóbrega, L., Nunes, J.N., Coelho, H.: Mapping ConcurTaskTrees into UML 2.0. In: Gilroy, S.W., Harrison, M.D. (eds.) Interactive Systems. LNCS, vol. 3941, pp. 237–248. Springer, Heidelberg (2006)
24. Oreizy, P., Gorlick, M., Taylor, R., Heimbigner, D., Johnson, G., Medvidovic, N., Quilici, A., Rosenblum, D., Wolf, A.: An Architecture-Based Approach to Self-Adaptive Software. IEEE Intelligent Systems 14(3), 54–62 (1999)
25. Paternò, F.: Model-Based Design and Evaluation of Interactive Applications. Springer, Heidelberg (2000)
26. Preece, J., Rogers, Y., Sharp, H., Benyon, D., Holland, S., Carey, T.: Human-Computer Interaction. Addison Wesley Publ., Wokingham, UK (1994)
27. Seffah, A., Donyaee, M., Kline, R.B.: Usability and quality in use measurement and metrics: An integrative model. Software Quality Journal (2004)
28. Shackel, B.: Usability - Context, Framework, Definition, Design and Evaluation. In: Human Factors for Informatics Usability, pp. 21–38. Cambridge University Press, Cambridge (1991)
29. Sheshagiri, M., Sadeh, N., Gandon, F.: Using Semantic Web Services for Context-Aware Mobile Applications. In: Proc. of ACM MobiSys2004 Workshop on Context Awareness, Boston, Massachusetts, USA, ACM Press, New York (2004)
30. Shneiderman, B.: Designing User Interface Strategies for effective Human-Computer Interaction, 3rd edn., p. 600. Addison-Wesley Publ, Reading (1997)
31. da Silva, P.: User Interface Declarative Models and Development Environments: A Survey. In: Proc. of DSV-IS2000, June 5-6, 2000, pp. 207–226. Springer, Limerick, Ireland (2000)
32. Schmidt, D.C.: Guest editor's introduction: Model-Driven Engineering. IEEE Computer 39(2), 25–31 (2006)
33. Sottet, J.S., Calvary, G., Coutaz, J., Favre, J.M.: A Model-Driven Engineering Approach for the Usability of Plastic User Interfaces. In: EIS'07. the proceedings of Engineering Interactive Systems 2007, March 22-24, 2007, pp. 22–24. University of Salamanca, Spain (2007)
34. Thevenin, D., Coutaz, J.: Plasticity of User Interfaces: Framework and Research Agenda. In: Proc. Interact99, Edinburgh, pp. 110–117. IFIP IOS Press Publ. (1999)
35. Van Welie, M., van der Veer, G.C., Eliëns, A.: Usability Properties in Dialog Models. In: DSV-IS'99. 6th International Eurographics Workshop on Design Specification and Verification of Interactive Systems, Braga, Portugal, 2-4 June 1999, pp. 238–253 (1999)

The Beautification Process in Model-Driven Engineering of User Interfaces

Inés Pederiva[1], Jean Vanderdonckt[1,2], Sergio España[1], Ignacio Panach[1], and Oscar Pastor[1]

[1] Universidad Politécnica de Valencia, Dep. de Sistemas Informáticos y Computación
Camino de Vera s/n, 46071 Valencia, Spain
[2] Université catholique de Louvain, Louvain School of Management,
Place des Doyens, 1 – 1348 Louvain-la-Neuve, Belgium
{ipederiva, jvanderdonckt, sergio.espana, jpanach,
opastor}@dsic.upv.es,
jean.vanderdonckt@uclouvain.be

Abstract. The beautification of a user interface resulting from model-to-model and model-to-code transformations in Model-Driven Architecture consists of performing manual changes to address user requirements which have not been supported during the transformations. These requirements may include customization, users' preferences, and compliance with corporate style guidelines. This paper introduces a beautification process into a user-interface model. This process includes a series of beautification operations based on a formal definition, as well as a constrained editor that enables designers to apply these beautification operations on a user interface. All manual changes done using these beautification operations are transformed into model-to-model transformations, thus reducing the problem of round-trip engineering. The paper also demonstrates that this process significantly reduces the number of manual changes performed on user interfaces of information systems, while preserving the quality properties induced by the transformations.

Keywords: Beautification operation, beautification process, human-computer interaction model, round-trip engineering, model-driven engineering, quality by construction, user interface description language, user interface code tweaking.

1 Introduction

The complete support of User Interfaces (UIs) requirements in Model-Driven Engineering (MDE) [4,21] is a problem that has not yet been solved. The user requirements to be addressed usually fall into two categories: requirements that are effectively supported by applying model-to-model (M2M) and model-to-code (M2C) transformations [10] and requirements that are not supported because they are not covered by these transformations. This dichotomy of requirements leads to two extremes: on the one hand, the UI that has been automatically generated by these transformations is assumed to be usable by the end user or it is simply taken for granted because of resource limitations, or on the other hand the UI is subject to manual modifications in an attempt to address the remaining user requirements. These manual

C. Baranauskas et al. (Eds.): INTERACT 2007, LNCS 4662, Part I, pp. 411–425, 2007.
© IFIP International Federation for Information Processing 2007

modifications take two basic forms: the generated UI code is tweaked manually or it is imported in a UI builder to be edited by direct manipulation. These modifications are performed to agree with the user requirements and are usually referred to as *beautification operations* since they are intended to beautify the manual changes brought to automatically generated UI. The whole process is known as *UI beautification*.

Unfortunately, this task is very sensitive to mistakes [1]: understanding generated code is usually a complex activity, and what has been constructed according to the MDE approach may easily be destroyed by manual beautification. Moreover several quality features guaranteed by construction in the MDE approach could be endangered by the beautification: usability [1]; consistency between the UI and its model [3]; correctness [7], and error-free benefit [15].

In the field of computer graphics, beautification [17] is referred to as the direct manual sketching of a shape, a drawing, or an illustration in an editor and its automatic replacement by a 'beautified' symbol. This is performed all in one step in order to remove manual clutter [8]. By analogy, in computer science, we define *UI beautification* as the whole process of improving the automatically generated UI with manual modifications to address unsupported user requirements.

The consequence of this manual beautification is that all efforts are not saved and are lost if a new UI is regenerated [18]: if the UI model changes, the generated UI changes accordingly but it is no longer compliant with the manual changes done previously. To alleviate this problem, researchers in MDE introduced various solutions to the so-called *round-trip engineering* [2]: manual modifications could be saved, interpreted, abstracted and finally replaced by a 'beautified' operation to be propagated to the model that initiated the M2M and M2C transformations. These operations could then be replicated each time the whole set of transformations is reapplied.

This paper addresses the shortcomings mentioned above by introducing a framework of beautification operations that provides a constrained UI editor where these beautification operations can be applied without endangering the qualities provided by the MDE approach. One approach is to let designers be free to do what they want in any UI builder, however, the quality of the resulting UI will depend heavily on their expertise. Another approach is to develop a brand new UI builder that supports the beautification operations using round-trip engineering, but this requires too much effort. Our solution provides a balance between these two extremes: the paper presents a constrained UI editor equipped with some beautification operations that can only be applied in the context of the editor, preserving the quality features provided by the MDE. The new definition of *UI beautification* becomes: the whole process of improving the automatically generated UI with beautification operations to address unsupported user requirements while preserving the qualities provided by MDE.

The remainder of this paper is structured as follows: Section 2 reviews how the beautification process was addressed in software engineering, and in the domain of MDE of UIs. Section 3 develops the methodological context in which our solution of a constrained editor is developed and reports observations of the tweaking performed using OO-Method. Section 4 describes how our framework performs beautification operations on graphical representations of an underlying UI model in order to support round-trip engineering. A running example is provided for this purpose to demonstrate the effectiveness and the efficiency of this solution. Section 5 reports the experience gained by using this method and its corresponding constrained UI editor. This section also identifies directions for future work resulting from this experience.

2 State of the Art

The beautification of automatically generated computer-based systems and its corollary, the round-trip engineering problem [2], are concluded to go far beyond a simple combination of forward and reverse engineering [20]. Many different techniques have been proposed to address this problem. Some of these are design patterns, framework-specific modeling languages [2], model reconciliation [20], etc. Although these techniques are generally applicable in the discipline of software engineering, they do not exploit the full potential of UI models, which are usually visual in nature: all UIs incorporate visual aspects that should be dealt with in case of beautification.

In Human-Computer Interaction (HCI), MECANO [19] was the first project to recognize the need for beautification support in the generation process: the methodological guidelines recommended that designers propagate their manual modifications into elements and relationships in the underlying model for reuse. Clerckx et al. enumerate an extensive list of similar rules that can be manually applied to the model after a transformation has been performed. Their DynaMo-AID design process is divided into several steps providing rules for propagating changes across models that are involved in different levels. MOBI-D [18] and TEALLACH [6] enable a designer to start a project from any model (task, domain, UI), thus propagating the consequences to the other models by linking and derivation. These mechanisms are similar, but not intended to really support UI beautification. WISDOM [14] also recommends keeping the models consistent with each other when a mode has been updated. In da Silva's survey of model-based tools and techniques [4], none of them provides any explicit support for UI beautification. This shortcoming is also observed in major commercial software that automatically generates UI, such as Genova [5], JaxFront [9], and OlivaNova [15]. In the following sections, we formally define beautification operations so that, in theory, they could work in any of the above environments. To be practical, the beautification process is illustrated in the context of a specific MDA-based method: the OO-Method [16].

3 Model-Driven Engineering of User Interfaces in the OO-Method

OO-Method [16] is a software development method that is MDA-compliant, i.e., it involves models of the future interactive system at different levels of abstraction (CIM, PIM, PSM [10]– Fig. 1) and provides an explicit transformation mechanism between them. The method is initiated by specifying the system functional requirements and develops the final interactive system through consecutive transformations. This method is supported by a software suite [15] that edits the various models involved and applies subsequent transformations until the final code is generated for different computing platforms: ASP, .Net, .JSP, Java, and C#.

The requirements elicitation in OO-Method [16] gathers all the user requirements in the *Requirements Model* by specifying the system's functionality in the *Mission Statement* and the *Function Refinement Tree*. The *Use Cases* detail each function and when this model is complete, system specifications are output independently of the implementation or the technological space (*Computation Independent Model* - CIM).

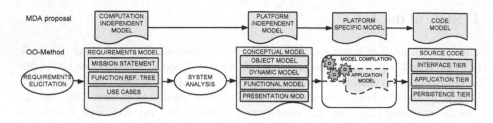

Fig. 1. Correspondences between the MDA proposal and the OO-Method

The *Conceptual Model*, equivalent to the MDA's *Platform-Independent Model or-PIM*, specifies four complementary system views. The *Object Model* specifies the static properties of the interactive application by defining the classes and their relationships. The *Dynamic Model* controls the application objects by defining their life cycle and their interactions. The *Functional Model* describes the semantics of object's state changes. Finally the *Presentation Model* (PM) models the UI.

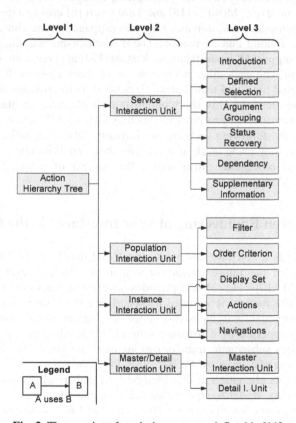

Fig. 2. The user interface design patterns defined in [11]

Fig. 2 presents the Just-UI [11] decomposition. The *Interaction Units* (IUs) represent the main interactive operations that can be performed on the domain objects:

1. The *Instance IU* shows a single object at a time, that is, one instance of a class.
2. The *Population IU* shows a group of similar objects.
3. The *Master/Detail IU* shows a hierarchical view of relationships between objects.
4. The *Service IU* modifies objects, their attributes and their relationships.

The next level of decomposition of the PM consists of restricting and specifying the behavior of each IU in the PM into an elementary pattern. For example, if a *Population IU* is being specified, then five elementary patterns could be attached to it [11]:

a) A *Filter Pattern* filters any set of objects to display only the objects needed.
b) The *Order Criteria* specifies the order in which the objects are shown.
c) The *Display Set* restricts which attributes of the objects are going to be presented.
d) The *Navigation Pattern* specifies the navigation between the objects.
e) The *Action Pattern* specifies functions that can be triggered for the object shown.

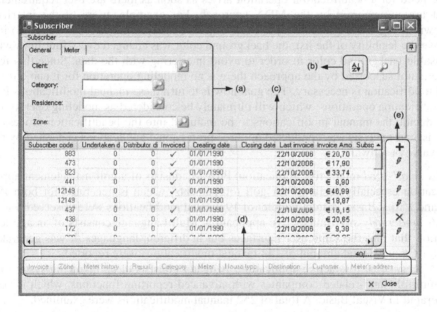

Fig. 3. Our running example as generated: a Population IU with a Filter pattern (a), an Order Criteria (b), a Display Set (c), a Navigation pattern (d), and an Action pattern (e)

The *Conceptual Model*, once achieved, is submitted to model compilation (M2C transformation). For any target computing platform, the *Source Code* is automatically generated and structured according to a three tier's architecture: the *Interface Tier*, the *Application Tier*, and the *Persistence Tier*. A fully functional application can be generated, which is not limited to database or UI (for more details, see [15,16]).

To illustrate the beautification process, a Population IU was selected. It was extracted from a real-world application delivered to Aguas del Bullent S.A.

(http://www.aguasdelbullent.com/index_en.html), a drinking water supply service company located in Oliva, Alicante (Spain). This application was chosen for several reasons: it has been entirely produced according to the OO-Method and generated by the OlivaNova without any manual modification; it represents a medium-sized interactive application of moderate complexity; it is a genuine application which is used today; and it has received the Microsoft certification of quality. Fig. 3 reproduces a Population pattern for displaying the water meters of customers located in a certain region. This Population pattern is decomposed into the five elementary patterns described above. The following section shows how this automatically generated UI is subjected to beautification operations.

4   The Beautification Process

4.1   Purpose of Beautification Operations

The need for a beautification operation arises as soon as there are user requirements that are unsupported by the MDA approach. For example, users of the interface shown in Fig. 3 complain that the list of objects displayed may become long. To improve the legibility of the list, the background color was changed every four lines with a usable background color in order to avoid interfering with the data. Since this feature is not supported by the approach there is no modeling operation for it and a manual modification is necessary. The goal now is to turn these manual modifications into beautification operations, which will ultimately be considered as modeling operations. To decide the manual modifications to be included into the beautification process, a **statistical analysis** was conducted on three professional applications generated by the OlivaNova software:

1. A *small-sized* interactive application: ProAM consists of a golf management application especially designed for golf tournaments, which is generated for both JSP and Visual Basic. A total number of 19 manual modifications were observed.
2. A *moderately-sized* interactive application: MultiLanguage consists of an application that runs the same user interfaces but in different languages. It was generated for C# and a total amount of 144 manual modifications were reported.
3. A *large-sized* interactive application: Alligator consists of an invoicing system for multiple inter-related companies with advanced reporting functions, which is generated in Visual Basic. A total of 252 manual modifications were examined.

From the total of 415 manual modifications those made by the developers were extracted (171 out of 252 were considered in the large-sized application) and classified into two sets: those relevant to the *Presentation Model* (103 out of 171) and those not relevant to it (58 out of 171) but relevant to the other models involved in the OO-Method (Fig. 1). This study shows the most frequent modifications and their level of importance in terms of the impact on the generated code. Therefore, a manual modification is considered a beautification operation because: the operation was observed in most applications; the operation occurred with a significant frequency; the operation was realistic in terms of future implementation support; and the operation was of at least moderate importance.

4.2 Classification of Beautification Operations

In order to classify a manual operation and, therefore, a subsequent beautification operation, Nielsen's linguistic model of interaction [13] was selected for these reasons: it decomposes a human-computer interaction in terms of seven inter-related, but independent, levels with a communication protocol between them; it has already been successfully used to classify usability guidelines according to their level of importance; and it allows identification criteria to univocally locate each modification to one and only one level. Table 1 decomposes a simple goal (i.e., delete a paragraph in a letter) into subsequent units of interaction for each level. The same is done here with a user's goal attached to the Population Interaction Unit Pattern shown in Fig. 3:

- **Level 1 (Goal):** expresses a user's mental goal, such as "search for a particular customer having a water meter in a specific region".
- **Level 2 (Pragmatic):** translates this mental goal into a task to be carried out in the system according to the system concepts, such as "search for a subscriber having at least one water meter in zone x" (Fig. 3).
- **Level 3 (Semantic):** translates the real-world objects into system objects and functions, such as "search for a subscriber with a code region filled in" (Fig. 3).
- **Level 4 (Syntactic):** structures the semantic into an ordered sequence of operations in time and space, such as "select a zone code from the list and launch a query".
- **Level 5 (Lexical):** decomposes each operation into the smallest possible pieces of information, such as "a zone code".
- **Level 6 (Alphabetic):** specifies the unit of information (e.g., a lexeme, a metric) for each information item, such as "an integer for representing the zone code".
- **Level 7 (Physical):** specifies the physically-coded information in terms of light, sound, color, etc., such as "display the integer in black on white for input".

Table 1. Definition of the seven levels of Nielsen's linguistic model of interaction [13]

Level	Title	Units	Definition	Example	World
1	Goal	Concepts of real world	Mentalization of a goal, a wish in the user's head	Delete a paragraph from my letter	Conceptual
2	Pragmatic	Concepts of system	Translation of a goal into system concepts	Delete 6 lines of the current paragraph in the edited text	Conceptual
3	Semantic	Detailed functions	Real world objects translated into system objects manipulated by functions	Delete a certain amount of lines	Conceptual
4	Syntactic	System sentences	Time & space sequencing of information units	DELETE 6	Perceptual
5	Lexical	Information units	Smallest elements transporting significant information: word, figure, screen coordinates, icon	[DELETE] command, [6] number	Perceptual
6	Alphabetic	Lexems	Primitive symbols: letter, numbers, columns, lines, dots, phonems, ...	D, E, L, E, T, E, 6	Physical
7	Physical	Physically coded information	Light, sound, physical moving	Pressing [CTRL]+[D] followed by [6]	Physical

4.3 Definition of a Beautification Operation

According to Table 1, any beautification operation can be classified into one and only one level. If any ambiguity persists after an initial classification, it means that the beautification operation should be decomposed into smaller operations. In order to show a significant set of operations, five beautification operations belonging to five different levels will be executed for our running example (Fig. 3) as follows:

1. **Level 7 (Physical):** *Specify (rowHighlightingType)* specifies that for every n number of lines in a table, the background color of this line should be set to a color that is different from the foreground color to ensure contrast. For instance, in Fig. 3, one in every four lines of the "Subscriber table" should be highlighted. This operation belongs to the Physical Level because it affects the physical appearance.

2. **Level 6 (Alphabetical):** *Convert (inputMetricUnit, outputMetricUnit)* converts data expressed according to one metric unit into another one. For instance, in Fig. 3, the currency of a price displayed in the column "Invoice amount" should be converted from the Euro (€) currency into the United States Dollar (U\$D) currency. This operation belongs to the Alphabetical Level because it only changes the numerical value of prices with another symbol to support internationalization.

3. **Level 5 (Lexical):** *Specify (buttonPresentationType)* specifies whether a push button should be presented with one label only (l), with an icon only (i) or with both (i+l), according to the usability guideline. For instance, in Fig. 3, a push button of the navigation pattern (e) could be presented with an icon and label together. This operation belongs to the Lexical Level because textual and/or graphical information is presented for the same object.

4. **Level 4 (Syntactical):** *Substitute (widgetType)* replaces a widget of a given type by a widget of another type by transferring its properties from the initial one to the substituted one. For instance, in Fig. 3, the edit box attached to "Category" may be substituted by a drop-down combo box because the amount of categories remains fixed. This operation belongs to the Syntactical Level because it changes the sequence of actions that the user has to do in order to select a category.

5. **Level 3 (Semantic):** *Specify (conditionalDisplay)* changes the value of a widget property depending on whether a semantic condition is satisfied or not. For instance, in Fig. 3, the "Invoiced" flag should be changed to another symbol depending on whether the invoice has been issued or not. This operation belongs to the Semantic Level because the presentation only changes according to a semantic change of the object (that is, the values of its attributes).

These five examples show that a beautification operation is executed depending on the widget types involved, the interaction unit concerned, and the elementary patterns present. Therefore, a *beautification operation* is now formally defined as a *State-Pair Action* (SAP) $B = \langle s, a \rangle$ where

s = a state of a IU where the beautification operation could be applied.
a = an action to be performed on the state s when it is found.

A SAP consists of a representation of the *Interaction Units* (IUs) contents prior to executing the action (the *state*) and a description of this action at an appropriate level of abstraction (the *action*). Consequently, these five examples of beautification operations could be formally expressed as follows:

B_1 = ⟨ *table in: DisplaySet, Specify (rowHighlightingType)* ⟩

B_2 = ⟨ *cell in:table in: DisplaySet, Convert (inputMetricUnit, outputMetricUnit)* ⟩

B_3 = ⟨ *button in:Navigation in: PopulationIU, Specify (buttonPresentationType)* ⟩

B_4 = ⟨ *inputText in:, Substitute (widgetType)* ⟩

B_5 = ⟨ *cell in:, Specify (conditionalDisplay)* ⟩

If the same beautification operation is applied on different widgets considered in different contexts, the beautification operation is repeated with the same action. Depending on the scope of the action and depending on what needs to be beautified, the action could be applied on a particular widget, on a particular widget in a container, or to a series of widgets.

Now that a beautification operation has been properly defined, the next section describes the beautification process and then decomposes this process into three steps.

4.4 The Steps of the Beautification Process

Thanks to the concept of beautification, OO-Method methodology can be improved through beautification (Fig. 4). This process is decomposed into three steps which are detailed in the following subsections.

Step 1: Derivation of a Concrete User Interface Model from the Presentation Model. Since the Presentation Model contains an abstract definition of the future UI in terms of IUs and attached elementary patterns, it is considered to be the best candidate to apply a M2M transformation in order to derive a Concrete User Interface Model from it. This model needs to fulfill at least two requirements:

1. In order to apply any beautification operation, it is necessary to know which widget must be replaced depending on the context.
2. In order to manipulate a working model, an internal UI representation that is subject to the beautification operations must be maintained.

The Concrete User Interface (CUI) model of the USer Interface eXtensible markup Language (UsiXML – http://www.usixml.org) has been selected because it satisfies these two requirements and allows us to provide the following definitions:

- A *Concrete User Interface* (CUI) consists of an abstraction of a final UI independently of the particular widgets used in a particular computing platform, thus resulting in a characterization of a UI in terms of *Concrete Interaction Objects* (CIOs). In this paper only graphical CIOs will be considered.
- Let C be the set of all graphical CIOs to be considered here.
- A *graphical CIO*, or a CIO for short here, is formally defined as a couple $c = \langle t, A \rangle$
  - where t = type of the CIO A = *decorator* iff c is non-interactive, *graphicalIndividualComponent* iff c is interactive and $\exists / c' \in C$ such that $c' \subset c$, *graphicalContainer* iff c is interactive and $\exists c' \in C$ such that $c' \subset c$, respectively.
  - where A is a set of triple (a_i, t_i, v_i): $A = \{ (a_i, t_i, v_i) \}$, of cardinality $|A| = n$ where
    i. a_i (i=1,...,n) = ith attribute of c

ii.t_i (i=1,...,n) = data type of the ith attribute of c : $t_i \in$ {boolean, time, date, integer, string}

iii.v_i (i=1,...,n) = value of the ith attribute of c = *null* if a_i is empty

- Therefore C = {decorators, graphicalIndividualComponent, graphicalContainer}
- UsiXML includes several CIOs for these different types, such as: a separator (decorator), inputText, outputText, radioButton, checkBox, listBox (graphicalIndividualComponent), dialogBox, window, and tabbedDialogBox (containers).
- A CIO is said to be *totally instantiated* when all its attributes a_i have been assigned to a value v_i: c is totally instantiated $\Leftrightarrow \forall$ i=1,...,n: $v_i \neq$ null.
- A CIO is said to be *partially instantiated* when some attributes a_i have been assigned to a value v_i: c is partially instantiated $\Leftrightarrow \exists$ i=1,...,n: $v_i \neq$ null.
- A CIO is said to be *uninstantiated* when all attributes a_i have not been assigned to any value v_i: c is uninstantiated $\Leftrightarrow \forall$ i=1,...,n: $v_i =$ null.

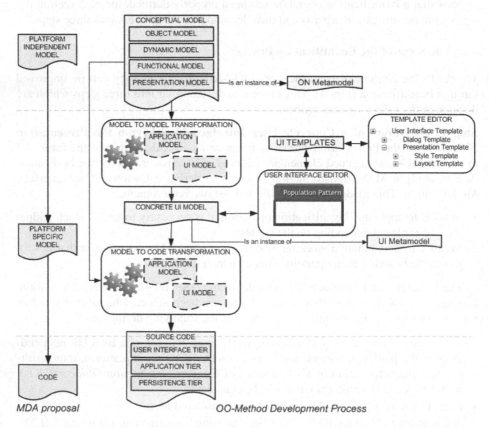

Fig. 4. Update of the OO-Method as defined in Fig. 1 with support for beautification

Once a Presentation Model is created for a UI, a corresponding CUI model is therefore derived as a tree of structured and partially instantiated CIOs whose root is a graphicalContainer. Each IU and each pattern contained in the Presentation Model is transformed into a CUI. This is a straightforward transformation.

Step 2: Execution of the beautification operations. Once a CUI Model has been derived, it can be submitted to beautification operations, applying model-to-model transformations. For this purpose, the CUI Model is opened in the constrained GUI editor. Each partially instantiated CIO belonging to the CUI Model is then subject to beautification operations. The GUI constrained editor detects potential SAPs to be applied by examining the states defined in each SAP and matching them to the CIOs of the GUI Model. If a CIO is subject to a particular SAP, the constrained GUI editor allows the designer to apply the corresponding beautification operation through a contextual menu (Fig. 5): when the cursor moves over a CIO subject to beautification (a), a contextual menu appears (b) which could be pulled down (c) so as to select the desired operation and to apply it instantly (d).

Fig. 5. Sequence of user actions to trigger a beautification operation

When it receives a new SAP as input, the constrained GUI editor finds the collection C of action steps in the model that are consistent with this input. An action step is consistent with a SAP if the step is a generalization (abstraction) of the action in the SAP. For each consistent step, for example s, it checks whether the model can be modified to contain a direct path from C.to s.

The constrained GUI editor is a program that captures the model defined in the Presentation Model and with the information given in the ON Metamodel, gives a preview of the designed interface. In order to protect the quality and good design defined in the Presentation Model, this editor is constrained by *parameters*. These parameters define which values can be defined and modified for each component in the interface. For instance, no CIO may be deleted and no new widget can be defined. Each parameter is described by: (1) The name of the parameter; (2) the data type and the values of the parameters; (3) the widgets where this parameter may be applied.

Parameters go beyond simple CIOs since they gather high-level values that are consequently applied to one or many CIOs to complete their instantiation. When the designer modifies those parameters, a preview of what will be generated by OlivaNova is produced. We call it a *Generation Preview* as it provides a UI preview before its final code is generated. A prototype of the constrained GUI editor has been implemented in Java 1.5 with 15 beautification operations using this mechanism.

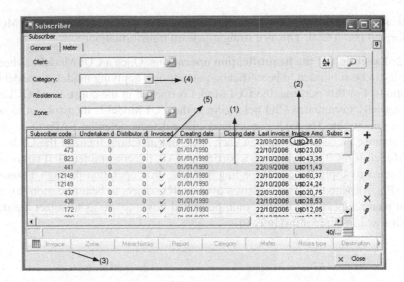

Fig. 6. The running example of Fig. 3. after applying the five beautification operations: (1) Specify(rowHighlightingType), (2) Convert (inputMetricUnit, outputMetricUnit), (3) Specify (buttonPresentationType), (4) Substitute (widgetType), (5) Specify (conditionalDisplay)

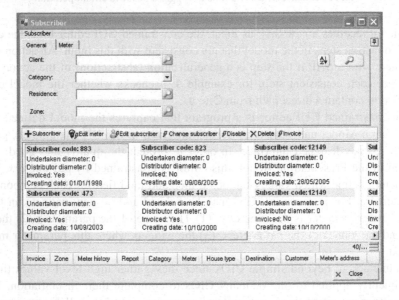

Fig. 7. The running example of Fig. 3 after applying other beautification operations

Step 3: Generation of the final user interface. Once all the beautification operations have been applied by the designer, the CUI Model is completed and sent to the model compiler so as to perform the model-to-code transformation. This transformation transforms all the models defined in the process of designing the system. With the modifications described previously, the resulting UI is shown in Fig. 6. Fig. 7 reproduces a UI resulting from other beautification operations also applied on the UI of Fig. 3.

4.5 The Parameters, the Templates and the User Interface Model

The parameters should be gathered in a UI template which is organized into a hierarchy of templates. A presentation template is decomposed into style and layout templates. A style template is decomposed into color scheme template and font template. As stated previously, the constrained GUI editor exploits these parameters. Each parameter represents an interface concept and is initially defined on a default value. Two examples are presented here:

- *flowAlignment* (type=string, status=public, inherited=no, allowed values=optional): specifies how elements should flow in a flowBox: left, middle, right.
- *labelVerticalAlignment* (type=string, status=public, inherited=no, allowed values=mandatory): specifies how identification labels and it corresponding CIO are aligned vertically.

As each interface concept is conceptualized in a parameter, with the template support, the designer can recurrently apply the same configuration to many projects or can have institutionalized styles for different customers.

5 Conclusions and Future Work

This paper has examined in detail the process of UI beautification, by analogy with the concept of "beautification" in the field of computer graphics. In the context of Model-Driven Engineering, it consists in modifying a software artifact so as to address those users' requirements which the given method could not satisfy by means of model-to-model and model-to-code transformations. When applied at the level of the automatically generated application, it supports round trip engineering in order to keep the models consistent with the tweaked code.

By restricting the scope of UI beautification to those operations which preserve usability, an intermediate approach was adopted between the two extreme and commonly taken positions (resign to the generated interface and unrestricted tweak the UI). The approach adopted consists of shifting the beautification process to a more abstract level, and this issue was tackled following several steps:

1. Identifying the most frequently demanded UI modifications.
2. Defining a Concrete User Interface (CUI) model that allows refining UI appearance and behavior.
3. Defining operations over the elements of the CUI model as a SAP performed on partially instantiated CIO, guaranteeing the fulfillment of the user's needs (step 1).
4. Constructing a Constrained GUI Editor that allows editing the CUI model via the previously defined beautification operations.

The paper defines the process formally and presents a methodological approach to deal with the unsupported requirements of the Model-Driven Engineering. An example is provided along the paper to illustrate the approach. The first experience gained with this process and tool has been satisfactory and rewarding. Although the prototyped Constrained GUI Editor supports a limited functionality, it significantly reduces not only the tweaking operations on the final generated code but also the designer's effort to cover the unsupported requirements. As future work, a more extended constrained GUI Editor will be developed and an empirical validation of the proposed modifications in OO-Method will be analyzed. This analysis will involve two aspects: the improvements on the whole production process after the adoption of the new tool and the benefits of its use in terms of final user satisfaction and UI usability.

Acknowledgements. This work has been developed with the support of MEC under the project   DESTINO TIN2004-03534 and co-financed by FEDER. We also acknowledge the support of the SIMILAR European network of excellence on multimodal interfaces (FP6-IST1-2003-507609 - www.similar.cc). The authors would like to also thank Emilio Iborra, Ismael Torres, José Maria Cubel, and Quentin Limbourg for their valuable input in this work.

References

1. Abrahão, S., Iborra, E., Vanderdonckt, J.: Usability Evaluation of User Interfaces Generated with a Model-Driven Architecture Tool. Chapter 2. In: Law, E., Hvannberg, E., Cockton, G. (eds.) Maturing Usability: Quality in Software, Interaction and Value. HCI Series, Springer, Berlin (2007)
2. Antkiewicz, M.: Round-Trip Engineering of Framework-Based Software using Framework-Specific Modeling Languages. In: Proc. of ASE'2006 (2006)
3. Clerckx, T., Luyten, K., Coninx, K.: The Mapping Problem Back and Forth: Customizing Dynamic Models while preserving Consistency. In: Proc. of TAMODIA'2004, Prague, November 15-16, 2004. ACM Int. Series, vol. 86, pp. 33–42. ACM Press, New York (2004)
4. da Silva, P.P.: User Interface Declarative Models and Development Environments: A Survey. In: Palanque, P., Paternó, F. (eds.) DSV-IS 2000. LNCS, vol. 1946, pp. 207–226. Springer, Heidelberg (2001)
5. Genova V8.0, Esito AS, Lysaker (2006), http://www.genera.no/default.htm
6. Griffiths, T., Barclay, P.J., Paton, N.W., McKirdy, J., Kennedy, J.B., Gray, P.D., Cooper, R., Goble, C.A., da Silva, P.P.: Teallach: a Model-Based User Interface Development Environment for Object Databases. Interacting with Computers 14(1), 31–68 (2001)
7. Hall, A., Chapman, R.: Correctness by Construction: Developing a Commercial Secure System. IEEE Software 19(1), 18–25 (2002)
8. Igarashi, T., Matsuoka, S., Kawachiya, S., Tanaka, H.: Interactive Beautification: a Technique for Rapid Geometric Design. In: UIST'97. Proc. of the 10th Annual ACM Symposium on User Interface Software and Technology, pp. 105–114. ACM Press, New York (1997)
9. JaxFront, XCentric Technology & Consulting GmbH, Zurich (2006), http://www.jaxfront.org/pages/
10. Model-Driven Architecture Guide, Version 1.0.1, Object Management Group (December 2006), http://www.omg.org/docs/omg/03-06-01.pdf
11. Molina, P.J., Meliá, S., Pastor, O.: Just-ui: A User Interface Specification Model. In: CADUI'2002. Proc. of 4th Int. Conf. on Computer-Aided Design of User Interfaces, Valenciennes, May 2002, pp. 63–74. Kluwer Academic Press, Dordrecht (2002)

12. Myers, B., Hudson, S.E., Pausch, R.: Past, Present, and Future of User Interface Software Tools. ACM Trans. Computer-Human Interaction 7(1), 3–28 (2000)
13. Nielsen, J.: A Virtual Protocol Model for Computer-Human Interaction. International Journal of Man-Machine Studies 24(3), 301–312 (1986)
14. Nunes, N.J., Falcao e Cunha, J.: Wisdom - A UML-Based Architecture for Interactive Systems. In: Palanque, P., Paternó, F. (eds.) DSV-IS 2000. LNCS, vol. 1946, pp. 191–205. Springer, Heidelberg (2001)
15. OlivaNova Software, Care Technologies, Denia (December 2006), http://www.care-t.com
16. Pastor, O., Gómez, J., Insfrán, E., Pelechano, V.: The OO-Method Approach for Information Systems Modeling: from Object-oriented Conceptual Modeling to Automated Programming. Information Systems 26(7), 507–534 (2001)
17. Pavlidis, T., Van Wyk, C.J.V.: An Automatic Beautifier for Drawings and Illustrations. Computer Graphics 19(3), 225–234 (1985)
18. Puerta, A.R.: A Model-Based Interface Development Environment. IEEE Software 14(4), 40–47 (1997)
19. Puerta, A.R., Eriksson, H., Gennari, J.H., Musen, M.A.: Beyond Data Models for Automated User Interface Generation. In: Proc. of HCI'94, Glasgow, September 1994, pp. 353–366. Cambridge University Press, New York (2004)
20. Sendall, S., Küster, J.: Taming Model Round-Trip Engineering. In: MDSD'2004. Proc. of Workshop 'Best Practices for Model-Driven Software Development', Vancouver (October 2004)
21. Vanderdonckt, J.: A MDA-Compliant Environment for Developing User Interfaces of Information Systems. In: Pastor, Ó., Falcão e Cunha, J. (eds.) CAiSE 2005. LNCS, vol. 3520, pp. 16–31. Springer, Heidelberg (2005)

Consistency Priorities for Multi-device Design

Rodrigo de Oliveira and Heloísa Vieira da Rocha

Campinas State University, Institute of Computing, Campinas SP 13081-970, Brazil
oliveira@ic.unicamp.br, heloisa@ic.unicamp.br

Abstract. We propose consistency priorities to support multi-device interface design minimizing the user's cognitive effort while performing the same task on different interfaces. The methodology is being evaluated through a framework that generates Pocket PC interfaces from desktop web pages. Initial results point to the acceptance of the approach.

1 Introduction

Mobile devices introduced a great challenge for Human Computer Interaction: to develop multi-device interfaces for today's applications. Some have tried device oriented designs with linear transformations, creating mobile interfaces from scratch, like Avantgo (www.avantgo.com) and Usable Net (www.usablenet. com); others looked for dynamic and automatic adaptations, but still focusing on the device [1,3,8]. These and other related approaches were well received, but the generated interfaces are different from the original in some aspects that complicate interaction with more than one device to perform the same task, especially when refinding and/or comparing information [7,9]. Many works addressed consistency and continuity problems focusing on user interface generation [4,5] and task migration [11], but their guidelines are generally not sufficiently concrete for an automatic interface framework. A recent proposal [10] solves the multi-device design problem by passing the control of every appliance to a handheld interface generated automatically. Despite the valued ideas, many device specific interaction types important to each context of use can be lost on the process, besides the need to carry a mobile device to control everything.

We propose consistency priorities for multi-device interface design that aims to improve usability and the user's experience when performing similar tasks on different devices. Some prototypes were implemented for automatic desktop web page adaptation to handhelds, such as Pocket PCs and smartphones. Initial evaluations point to the acceptance of this approach. Formal user evaluations will be conducted to check these first impressions.

2 Consistency Priorities Proposal

Pyla et al. [11] argue that consistency needs to be better defined if it is to be the overriding factor in the design of multiple user interfaces. In fact, there isn't a consensus about what consistency really is and how it can be applied [10].

C. Baranauskas et al. (Eds.): INTERACT 2007, LNCS 4662, Part I, pp. 426–429, 2007.

We think about consistency on the user's side. Individuals mentally draw conclusions about objects or events on the basis of previous observations of similar objects or events. These internal constructions that can be manipulated enabling predictions are called mental model [2]. Figure 1 sketches the user's mental model update cycle while executing tasks.

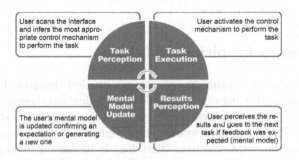

Fig. 1. User's mental model update cycle. Task perception and execution are the key processes to build a consistent mental model for decision making.

In order to help users form an accurate and useful mental model of a system while interacting with any of its interfaces, we suggest applying consistency on multi-device contexts using the following priorities:

1. *Task Perception* - the same control mechanisms to execute a task and their disposal on the interface. If these requirements cannot be followed with good usability on devices with different control attributes (e.g. size, weight, material, etc.) and properties (e.g. fluidity, flexibility, opacity, etc.), perception should be mapped to each device's interaction type maintaining usability.
2. *Task Execution* - the same actions flow to execute a task. If the control mechanisms available on a given interface had to be adapted for the others by the task perception priority, the actions flow should be maintained on a logical perspective. Although this may repass bad design decisions and lose opportunity to improve usability on each interface independently, user's decision making is supported under a consistent multi-device context, providing ease of learning/remembering and safety of use. Next priority improves efficiency.
3. *Task Personalization* - the ability to change task perception and execution according to the users' preferences. The goal is to achieve the best design for any user which is the configuration that user expects. This can be related to the *personally consistent design* concept [10], but with an active position for the user. As a result, efficiency and ease of expert use is provided to avoid the downsides of consistency [6].

It's important to understand the correct application of these consistency priorities as they can be easily misunderstood. For example, if an individual wants to check an account balance through an ATM machine, a tablet PC and a telephone, there is no possibility to perceive and perform the task in the same way. If the mentioned devices are important to the end user, adaptation to the contrasting interaction types is a price they are willing to pay. In fact, that's part of the *task personalization* priority. So the focus is to provide the same task perception and execution under a logical perspective, be it through words typed, written or said. This is in accordance with Nichols' work [10] about benefitting from user's experience, but opens space for the rich interaction types of the actual appliances in a consistent way.

3   Towards an Empirical Validation

On this section, we are going to take an application designed for multi-device access and improve it using our proposal. The application chosen is the Summary Thumbnail [7], a prototype designed to automatically adapt desktop web pages for handhelds. Here's how it works: the original web page is shrunken to fit horizontally on the smaller screen, text font is increased to improve legibility and letters are cropped from right to left until sentences fit on the available space. Complete texts can be read by accessing the *detailed view* through a click on the page, which moves to the original desktop interface with full scrolling.

After applying the consistency priorities to Summary Thumbnail, we identified two improvements: a better summarization process to avoid producing links with the same label (task perception) and a smoother transition between thumbnail and detailed views (task execution). On the first prototype generation, we used focus-plus-context to provide a faster detailed view over the thumbnail. Full texts and normal sized images are presented inside a *hint* window whenever users point to the corresponding object on the page. They can even confirm the full text to stay on page and this information is stored for future accesses (task personalization). As the hint detailed view loses format attributes useful on iconic systems, we are developing the next prototype generation with the Direct Migration [9] (no transformation applied to the page) inside the hint window with a lower opacity value to improve context view.

Currently, the automatic interface adaptation doesn't require additional Internet traffic and takes less than two seconds to adapt a web page using the browser script interpreter. The hardware used was the HP iPAQ Pocket PC h2400 running Windows Mobile 2003 but could be any other with a CSS, DHTML and JavaScript compatible browser. Recently, the first generation prototype was informally tested on a few institutions with much better impressions than the awarded commercial solution by Opera (www.opera.com/products/mobile/reviews). Figure 2 compares screens generated by both approaches.

4   Conclusions

The consistency priorities proposal aims to improve usability and the user's experience when performing similar tasks on different devices. The methodology is being tested through prototypes designed to automatically adapt desktop web interfaces for handheld screens. Informal evaluations revealed better impressions

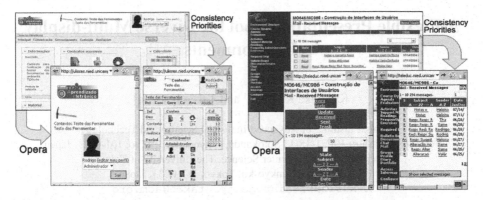

Fig. 2. Comparison between interfaces generated with the Consistency Priorities and Opera *Fit to Screen*. The first was much better evaluated on informal tests.

than a successful commercial approach. Next prototypes focus iconic interfaces and evaluations will be taken to verify the advantages of this proposal.

References

1. Berti, S., Correani, F., Mori, G., Paternò, F., Santoro, C.: Teresa: a transformation-based environment for designing and developing multi-device interfaces. In: Proc. CHI 2004 Extended Abstracts, Vienna, Austria, pp. 793–794 (April 2004)
2. Craik, K.J.W.: The nature of explanation. Cambridge University Press, Cambridge (1943)
3. Coninx, K., Luyten, K., Vandervelpen, C., Bergh, J.V.D., Creemers, B.: Dygimes: dynamically generating interfaces for mobile computing devices and embedded systems. In: Proc. MHCI 2003, Udine, Italy, pp. 256–270 (2003)
4. Denis, C., Karsenty, L.: Inter-usability of multi-device systems: A conceptual framework. In: Seffah, A., Javahery, H. (eds.) Multiple User Interfaces, pp. 373–385. John Wiley & Sons, Chichester (2003)
5. Florins, M., Trevisan, D.G., Vanderdonckt, J.: The Continuity Property in Mixed Reality and Multiplatform Systems: A Comparative Study. In: CADUI 2004, Funchal, Portugal, pp. 323–334 (2004)
6. Grudin, J.: The case against user interface consistency. CACM 32(10), 1164–1173 (1989)
7. Lam, H., Baudisch, P.: Summary thumbnails: readable overviews for small screen web browsers. In: Proceedings of CHI 2005, Portland, OR, pp. 681–690 (2005)
8. Lin, J.: Using design patterns and layers to support the early-stage design and prototyping of cross-device user interfaces. Doctoral Thesis. Berkeley, California: University of California, p. 557 (2005)
9. Mackay, B., Watters, C., Duffy, J.: Web page transformation when switching devices. In: Proc. of the Mobile HCI 2004, Glasgow, Scotland, pp. 228–239 (2004)
10. Nichols, J.: Automatically generating high-quality user interfaces for appliances. Doctoral Thesis. Pittsburg, Pennsylvania: Carnegie Mellon University, pp. 322 (2006)
11. Pyla, P., Tungare, M., Pérez-Quiñones, M.: Multiple User Interfaces: Why consistency is not everything, and seamless task migration is key. In: Proceedings of the CHI 2006 Workshop on The Many Faces of Consistency in Cross-Platform Design.

A Flexible Presentation Tool for Diverse Multi-display Environments

Kazutaka Kurihara[1] and Takeo Igarashi[2]

[1] National Institute of Advanced Industrial Science and Technology,
Akihabara Daibiru 10F, 1-18-13 Sotokanda, Chiyoda-ku, Tokyo, 101-0021, Japan
[2] Department of Computer Science, The University of Tokyo,
7-3-1 Hongo, Bunkyo-ku, Tokyo, 113-0033, Japan
k-kurihara@aist.go.jp, takeo@acm.org

Abstract. Display environments for presentations are becoming diverse, and it is common to have multiple displays in the same room. We present a system to edit and give presentations using multiple displays. The main idea is to separate the content from the views. The author prepares presentation visuals (text and images) on an infinitely zoomable canvas, and then specifies what is shown in each display by dragging a rectangular display proxy onto the canvas. The presenter can change what is shown in each display by manipulating these display proxies. We describe an example that showed that the system can handle various presentation scenarios using multiple displays.

1 Introduction

Presentation environments are becoming increasingly diverse, and it is not uncommon for presentation rooms to have multiple displays. In theory, a presenter could use a huge number of displays simultaneously, including the personal laptops in the audience. However, current presentation tools are not designed to take advantage of such a situation. Most standard presentation tools are designed primarily for single-display presentations, but do support additional control views that are automatically created for the presenter.

Chiu et al. [1] and Zhang et al. [4] proposed "slide-based" multi-display presentation systems. The user can paste slides onto a multi-track timeline that corresponds to these displays, or show the slides on multiple displays successively in an order predefined by a special script language. These methods are effective for users whose presentation environments do not frequently change and who carefully prepare the presentation; for example, in a business where presentations are given in a fixed meeting room, often following a prepared script with little deviation.

One drawback of this approach is that it is somewhat difficult to "adjust" a presentation to different multi-display configurations. The user must align the displays using the script language, or rewrite individual slides. If multiple displays are used to show a large image, the user must divide the image into sub-views for each display. In addition, this approach, due to its fixed structure, is not flexible enough to support on-the-fly improvisation, such as showing a global overview or adding

C. Baranauskas et al. (Eds.): INTERACT 2007, LNCS 4662, Part I, pp. 430–433, 2007.

discussion side notes. These online improvisations are particularly important in an educational environment, because interaction is essential for learning.

We propose a new presentation system that makes it easier to create and show presentations using multiple displays. The main idea is to separate the content from the views in order to adapt flexibly to a diverse array of display settings.

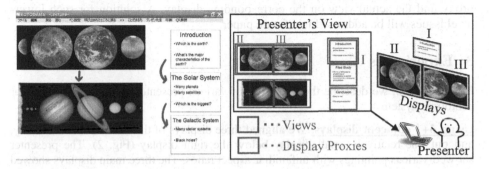

Fig. 1. System overview. (Left) Snapshot of multi-display presentation material on the editing canvas. Note that some information is presented in unfamiliar aspect ratios. (Right) Display proxy objects and view objects.

2   System Description

The system is based on the metaphor of an infinitely zoomable canvas [2, 3]. The user can freely navigate the canvas by panning and zooming, and can place presentation visuals (text and images) anywhere on the canvas (Fig. 1, left). To show visuals on a display, the user simply associates a view with a display proxy (Fig. 1 right, red), by placing the proxy object on top of the view. After the presentation visuals are prepared, the user can define a sequence of views to define the basic flow of visuals to the audience, navigated by simple button operations. To do so, the user simply presses the "capture" button to create and register a rectangular view object (Fig. 1 right, blue) that encloses the current content in the display proxy.

Importantly, the editing of visuals is separated from the presentation views. This is very important when a presenter must give the same presentation in various display settings. In traditional slide-based presentation tools (including Chiu et al. and Zhang et al.), visuals are tightly coupled with views, so it is very difficult to show the same material in different display settings. To adapt such presentations to a new setting may require making new slides from scratch. However, using our method, the user needs only to change the views; the presentation visuals remain unchanged.

The capability of continuous view control on the infinite canvas is also helpful for improvising using multiple displays. Display proxies on the canvas allow the user to quickly specify what to show in each display. When the presenter wants to discuss a topic in further detail, he can slightly zoom out or pan to a vacant space in the working display without affecting other displays, and can also quickly show a global overview by zooming out. The lasso grouping function to view proxy objects helps the user to move multiple view proxies synchronously.

Defining views on a canvas is not a new concept [2, 3]; our contribution is using them to control multiple displays and proposing methods to coordinate them. We assume that the system knows which displays are available, how to establish connections with them, and how to synchronize the presentation visuals in a display proxy and the actual view on the corresponding display. A solution for such lower-level issues will be addressed in a future paper.

3   Experiences

In this section, we describe the operation of various presentation scenarios using our prototype system.

Using 3+1 adjacent displays. We aligned three displays of the same size horizontally, and put one relatively small display below the right display (Fig. 2). The presenter showed various paintings with unfamiliar aspect ratios. The three main displays showed the paintings, while the relatively small one displayed some comments on the paintings.

Showing successive slides at a time. We tested a scenario where a presenter with a presentation designed for a single-display environment wants to show it using multiple displays (Fig. 3). We assumed that the presenter prepared a slide-based presentation in advance by arranging the slides horizontally. However, as it turned out that he could use three displays, he decided to show the previous, current, and next slides simultaneously to facilitate learning.

Fig. 2. Using 3+1 adjacent displays. (Left) Presentation material on the editing canvas. (Right) Snapshot of the environment.

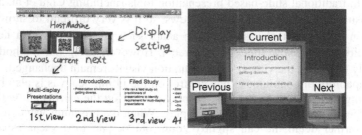

Fig. 3. Showing three successive slides simultaneously. (Left) Presentation material on the editing canvas. (Right) Snapshot of the environment.

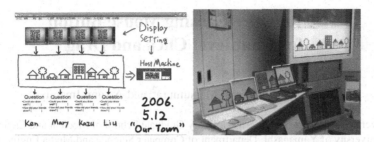

Fig. 4. Collaborative painting. (Left) Presentation material on the editing canvas. (Right) Snapshot of the environment.

Collaborative painting. We assumed that the presenter wanted students to work on a collaborative painting (Fig. 4). Each student (the audience) could work on a portion of the painting on an individual computer, while the main display in the room showed the overview of the whole painting. After the project was complete, the presenter distributed questionnaires to each student.

4 Conclusion and Future Work

We presented a prototype presentation tool that separates content from views to flexibly adapt to diverse display settings. It seamlessly extends user-working styles in ordinary single-display presentations to multi-display environments. We also described various presentation scenarios using our prototype system, which demonstrated its versatility and effectiveness.

We are planning to run a formal user study to evaluate and improve our system. Another direction of future work is to establish a method for editing presentations for non-rectangular displays by developing interfaces that allow non-rectangular view objects, enabling presentations for even more diverse display environments.

Acknowledgments. This research was partially supported by Microsoft Institute for Academic Research Collaboration (IJARC) Core2 Project and grant from MSRA Mobile Computing in Education Theme program.

References

1. Chiu, et al.: Manipulating and Annotating Slides in a Multi-Display Environment. In: INTERACT'03, pp. 583–590 (2003)
2. Good, et al.: CounterPoint: Creating Jazzy Interactive Presentations. HCIL Tech Report #2001-03, University of Maryland (2001)
3. Perlin, et al.: An Alternative Approach to the Computer Interface. In: SIGGRAPH'93, pp. 57–64 (1993)
4. Zhang, et al.: A Presentation Authoring Tool for Media Devices Distributed Environment. In: ICME'04 (2004)

A Pressure-Sensing Mouse Button
for Multilevel Click and Drag

Masaki Omata[1], Kenji Matsumura[2], and Atsumi Imamiya[1]

[1] University of Yamanashi, Interdisciplinary Graduate School of Medical and Engineering
[2] University of Yamanashi, Department of Computer Science and Media Engineering,
Takeda 4-3-11, 400-8511 Kofu, Japan
{omata, kng, imamiya}@hci.media.yamanashi.ac.jp

Abstract. This paper proposes a pressure-sensing mouse button that can better express the user's intention. When users use it for click or drag, the users can specify continuous parameters of the mouse operation by adjusting intensity of the button press between from lightly to strongly. For evaluating it, we conducted experiments to validate optimal number of pressure levels and to compare the mouse with conventional input methods. Subjects required significantly more time with eight pressure levels than with fewer levels. We also found that the mouse was not faster than conventional mice in terms of task performance time because users were not adept at adjusting force of the mouse button. We, therefore, suggest that an effective operation for the pressure-sensing mouse button is to change an insignificant effective parameter associated with fundamental determination of a mouse operation.

Keywords: Mouse button, pressure-sensing button, multilevel button press, pressure.

1 Introduction

The mouse, along with the keyboard, is the most popular computer input device. A mouse is typically used for pointing an object, selecting objects and deciding an operation in a GUI. When the user moves the mouse, a corresponding pointing cursor moves on the screen. When the user clicks a mouse button, the object on a screen being pointed to is selected.

With a conventional mouse, users can continuously adjust the position of the pointing cursor or of a scroll box by adjusting the distance the mouse is moved or by the rotation of a scroll wheel. However, with the conventional mouse button, the user can only choose the alternative of "selected" and "not selected." Whether the user clicks the mouse button lightly or heavily, there is no difference in the results.

With a mouse button that permits multilevel clicks through varying intensity of pressure, the user is able to specify a continuous parameter of an operation. Just as a pianist can express his or her intention through how hard he/she strikes the keys, we propose that multilevel clicks can better reflect the intentions of a computer user.

There have been previous studies examining multilevel mouse clicks and multilevel intensities of stylus pressure. Zeleznik et al. developed the "pop through"

C. Baranauskas et al. (Eds.): INTERACT 2007, LNCS 4662, Part I, pp. 434–446, 2007.

mouse button [1]. This button allows a user to click at two levels to control a property with a single button. Ramos et al. proposed GUIs that reflect pressure of a stylus to the state of windows, icons, menus and pointers (WIMP) [2]. Mizobuchi et al. suggested using stylus pressure in a handheld device to control a WIMP interface [3].

However, Zeleznik et al.'s pop-through button does not provide enough levels to reflect details in a user's intentions, while pressure-sensing styluses cannot be applied to most desktop computers. We, therefore, propose the "multilevel force-sensing-button mouse" that distinguishes an intensity of pressure of a mouse button and reflects user's intention to results of an operation. This paper describes experiments on human characteristics with a pressure-sensing button, compares its usability with other devices, and introduces the prototypes of applications.

2   Related Work

In this section, we introduce some related studies about multilevel input methods.

Ramos et al. suggested implications for the design of pressure-sensitive widgets [2]. They conducted an experiment investigating human characteristics in the use stylus pressure to perform discrete target acquisition tasks with different selection techniques. The results indicate that the quick release selection technique was preferable overall, and that dividing pressure space into six levels is optimal.

Ramos et al. also suggested the "Zliding" for fluid integrated manipulation of scale (zooming) via pressure input while parameter manipulation within that scale is achieved via x-y cursor movement (sliding) [4]. By using this system, users can use the pressure modality to fluidly and explicitly zoom or adjust the granularity of the parameter space, while sliding or dragging the input device.

Mizobuchi et al. suggested a potential space saving technique that can be used for selecting menus, text/number input, changing windows, zooming/panning, etc. in pen-based handheld devices [3]. They examined speed and accuracy of force input with a pen on a pressure-sensitive screen mounted on a handheld device. They reported that force for controlling a GUI are likely in the range 0 to 3 N, and the number of levels within that range should be between five and seven.

Rekimoto et al. suggested the "PreSenseII" that recognizes position, touch and pressure of a user's finger [5]. This device acts as a normal touchpad, but also senses pressure for additional control. As the example applications of the device, they introduced map navigation that allows a user to scroll a map and to zoom in/out with sliding a finger and pressing the touchpad and a long item list that allows a user to control scrolling with pressing predefined area.

Blaskó et al. developed the "Pressure-Sensitive Strips" that allows one-handed direct control of a large number of parameters by detecting contact pressure differences of user's fingers [6].

While these studies used a stylus or a touchpad to input pressure, our study uses a mouse button, which is a more popular input device. We examine the human characteristics of a pressure-sensing button because we cannot use the previous results for a stylus. However, to design experiments for the pressure-sensing mouse button, we refer to the existing data on the human characteristics of controllable range of a stylus.

Zeleznik et al. developed a pop-through mouse buttons that achieve double-action effect by converting the standard mouse buttons to pop through tactile pushbuttons

[1]. The system allows two levels of clicks, pressing lightly and pressing firmly. For example, pressing the button lightly could bring up a short menu, while pressing harder brings up a longer menu.

Forlines et al. presented a model for multilevel input devices based on a "glimpse state" [7]. By adding a glimpse state to a three-state pressure sensitive input device, user is able to preview the effects of their editing without committing to them. They suggested that the glimpse state has the added benefits that the negative effects of inconsistencies in the undo feature within an application are reduced.

Both of these studies proposed two levels of click operation with a mouse button. We propose that multilevel operations (over three states) can pick up more detail of a user's intentions. By pressing lightly or heavily, we suggest that the multilevel operations (click and drag) allow a user to input a value of properties, urgency, and his or her emotion. On the matter of emotion, Swindells et al. introduced that user interactions with tactile haptic feedback combine to strongly influence the user's emotional disposition and attitude [8]. On the matter of biometrics, Ikehara has developed a Pressure Mouse that can identify the user by the way he or she clicks it [9]. The mouse incorporates some electronic sensors to register hand pressure, speed and number of clicks exerted on the mouse's buttons.

Qi et al. mounted eight pressure sensors on a computer mouse to collect mouse pressure signals from users [10]. They suggested that the pressure mouse was used to classify two regions of each user's behavior: mouse pressure where the form-filling process is proceeding smoothly, and mouse pressure following a usability bug. This approach is based on the hypothesis that subjects apply more pressure to the mouse after encountering frustrating events. They suggested that user frustration could be measured by sensing the pressure applied to the mouse body. Our pressure-sensing mouse button, in contrast, reflects the user's intention to user's operation directly and concretely by sensing intensity of pressure while the user clicks the mouse button or drags the mouse to operate an application.

3   Pressure-Sensing Mouse Button

Fig. 1-(a) shows the prototype pressure-sensing mouse button that we developed. We mounted a commercially available pressure sensor (CUI IESP-12, Phidgets [11]; Fig. 1-(b)) on the left mouse button. It senses forces from 0 to 3 kg and generates a corresponding value from 0 to 1000. Data from the pressure sensor are sent to the computer via USB. To make the sensor more comfortable, we covered it with a cap that we made out of clay to fit the index finger. For the human perception experiment, we used the sensor without the ergonomic cap because it was necessary to analyze human perception for the sensor itself. However, in the comparison with other devices we used the ergonomic cap to make the comparisons more fair.

Fig. 2 shows the use of the pressure-sensing mouse button. It can be used for pointing, clicking the right mouse button, and dragging it by pressing the right button, as with a conventional mouse. On the other hand, a user clicks the pressure-sensing button on the left for clicking it and dragging it. As the user presses the pressure-sensing button, the underlying left button is pressed simultaneously, so the user can operate the left mouse button as easily as a normal mouse button.

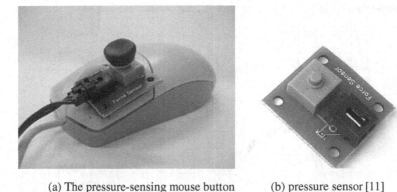

(a) The pressure-sensing mouse button   (b) pressure sensor [11]

Fig. 1. The pressure-sensing mouse button (a) and pressure sensor (b) [11]

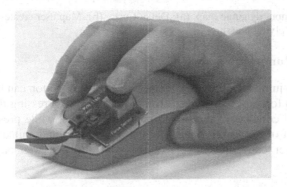

Fig. 2. Use of the pressure-sensing mouse button

4 Prototypes of Applications: Pressure-Input Dynamic Map and Pressure-Jump Web Browser

In this section, we suggest two applications using the pressure-sensing mouse button.

4.1 Pressure-Input Dynamic Map

The pressure-input dynamic map is a dynamic map controlled by the user's pressure input. The level of graphical and text detail increase with increasing pressure applied. For example, if a user wants to know information along the route to a station, the user follows the route with the pointing cursor by moving the mouse. To get greater detail about the area around the cursor, the user presses more heavily. Finally, the original map, which reflects the user's intentions, is created while the user follows the way on a map by dragging the pressure-sensing button.

Fig. 3 illustrates the system. The cells on the map are the minimum changeable areas. First, the system displays a default map, as in Fig. 3-(a). As the user drags the cursor up the street on the right while applying pressure, more detail about the route is revealed (Fig. 3-(a)). Finally, the user can get the original map to know the details of the main street.

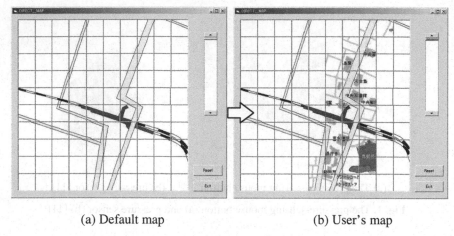

(a) Default map   (b) User's map

Fig. 3. Pressure-input dynamic map. (a): Default map. (b): Map user creates by dragging along the route while applying pressure.

4.2 Pressure-Jump Web Browser

With a pressure-jump web browser, the pressure-sensing button can be used to control the amount of information displayed from a link (Fig. 4). Pressing the button heavily displays the full contents of the linked page (Fig. 4-(b)), while pressing lightly only displays the text of the linked page, eliminating pictures and animations (Fig. 4-(c)). Therefore, a user can adjust levels of the contents of a web page in his or her intentions.

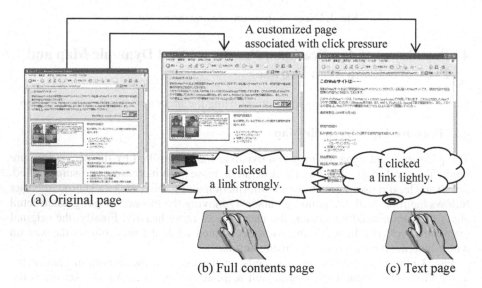

Fig. 4. A web browser using the pressure-sensing mouse button

The prototype in Fig. 4 is a mock-up. The prototype displays only pre-created pages that we created for each level preliminarily. We plan to develop the application as a plug-in for a popular web browser.

5   Human Characteristics of the Pressure-Sensing Mouse Button

We conducted an experiment to validate the human operating characteristics of our pressure-sensing mouse button. We validated two characteristics:

- The optimal number of pressure levels
- The pressure determination method decision

5.1   Optimal Number of Pressure Levels

In this experiment, we validated the optimal number of pressure levels for inputting the user's intentions. The experimental factors were the number of partitions of pressure and preconditions. Based on Ramos et al.'s finding that the optimal number of pressure levels for stylus input is six, we compared four, six and eight pressure levels. We compared two conditions: "as fast as possible" and "as accurate as possible." The dependent variables were task performance time and number of errors.

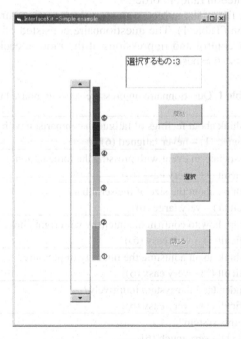

Fig. 5. Software to select a part of pressure partitions with the pressure-sensing mouse button

The experimental task is to select a part of pressure partitions and determine it by pressing the left button, adjusting the intensity of pressure of it, and clicking right mouse button. Subjects were presented with a target pressure level and asked to achieve it with the pressure-sensing button. Fig. 5 shows the software the subjects used to perform the task. A scroll bar labeled by both number and color is used to display the target levels, while the height of the scroll box reflects the pressure intensity applied to the button. Fig. 5 shows the case of six pressure levels; the lowest range is the play of pressure. On the right side of the screen, the upper and lower buttons start and finish, respectively, one block of trials, and the middle button is the home position for the pointing cursor.

The subject first depresses the pressure-sensing button and then clicks the middle button on the window. Next, a target level is presented in the text box and the subject adjusts the intensity of pressure to keep the scroll box in the target range. Finally, the user presses the right mouse button to confirm the intensity. For example, on Fig. 4, the target range number is "3" in the text box, so the subject should adjust pressure as the medium intensity.

The task performance time was measured as the time from clicking the home position button to clicking the right mouse button at the end of the task. An error is defined as when the range confirmed with the right mouse button is different from the target range.

Each subject performed all trials in all conditions: two preconditions, and three partition levels. There were 14 trials for each condition, so that each subject performed 84 trials (2 x 3 x 14). All subjects were given the same set of target levels, but they were presented in random order.

After completing the trials, subjects answered a questionnaire about the pressure-sensing mouse button (Table 1). The questionnaire consisted of eight questions about fatigue, difficulty of control and impressions of the mouse, each rated on a six-point Likert scale (1 = worst, 6 = best).

Table 1. Questionnaire on pressure-sensing mouse button

1.	What do you think about feelings of fatigue in comparison with a usual mouse? (very fatigued (1) – never fatigued (6))
2.	How is it to associate an event with pressing the force button? (very difficult (1) – very easy (6))
3.	What do you think about the size of the scrollbar? (very small (1) – very large (6))
4.	How is it to learn how to confirm the intensity with right click? (very difficult(1) – very easy (6))
5.	What do you think about adjusting the intensity of pressure? (very difficult (1) – very easy (6))
6.	How is it to understand the system intuitively? (very difficult (1) – very easy (6))
7.	Do you prefer this system? (not at all (1) – very much (6))
8.	Are you interested in this system? (not at all (1) – very much (6))

Twelve subjects (eight men and four women) in their twenties and thirties participated in this experiment. All were right handed and they typically used a computer between two to eight hours a day. The subjects practiced to use the pressure-sensing mouse button adequately before they performed an experimental task. Fig. 6 shows the average of task performance times of all subjects for each number of levels. Fig. 7 shows the average of error rate of all tasks for each number of levels. The solid line in the figures represents the results for the precondition "as fast as possible," and the dotted line represents the results for the precondition "as accurate as possible."

The results indicate that the subjects performed the task significantly faster in the precondition "as fast as possible" than in the precondition "as accurate as possible" (ANOVA: F (1, 11) =59.88, p<.01). Moreover, the subjects required significantly more time with eight levels than with six or four levels (multiple comparisons among the partition levels: p<.01).

The results indicate that the subjects performed the task significantly more accurately in the precondition "as accurate as possible" than in the precondition "as fast as possible" (ANOVA: F (1, 11) =53.95, p<.01). However, there was no significant difference among the partition levels.

Fig. 8 shows a boxplot of the results of the questionnaire. In this figure, "+" corresponds to the median, the end-points of whiskers correspond to the maximum and minimum values, and the edges of the box correspond to the first and third quartiles. Most of subjects thought that the pressure-sensing mouse button was "easy to imagine the event," "easy to learn," "likable," and "interesting."

5.2 Comparison of Pressure Determination Methods

We redesigned and improved the determination method in the above experiment. In the new method, the subject maintains the intensity of pressure for 1 s. The method allows users to adjust and confirm pressure using only the left mouse button. One

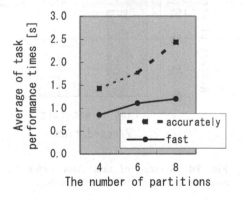
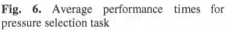

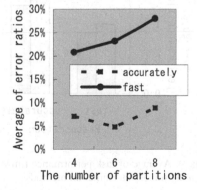

Fig. 6. Average performance times for pressure selection task

Fig. 7. Average error ratios for pressure selection task with the force-sensing mouse button

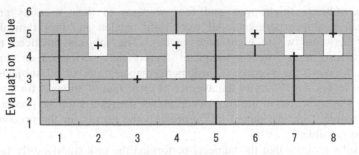

Fig. 8. Boxplot of questionnaire results

second was chosen after we contemplated it. In this experiment, we compared the determination method in the above experiment with the hold-for-1-s method by analyzing task performance time and error rate.

The task in this experiment was similar to the task in Section 5.1. The experimental factors were the precondition and the determination method, which was the main purpose. The precondition factors were similar to Section 5.1: "as fast as possible" and "as accurate as possible." There were two determination methods: maintaining the intensity of the pressure-sensing mouse button for 1 s, and clicking the right mouse button while maintaining the intensity of the pressure-sensing button. Based on the results in Section 5.1, the number of pressure levels was fixed at seven. The seven levels included six selective ranges and a play range. Each subject performed 18 trials for each condition, so that the total number of trials for each subject was 72 (2 x 2 x 18).

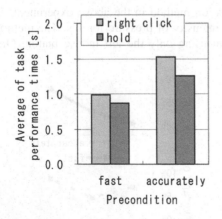

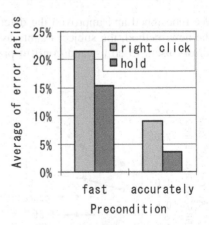

Fig. 9. Average of task performance times for comparison of determination methods

Fig. 10. Average of task error ratios for comparison of determination methods

Eight subjects, each of whom had participated in the previous experiment, participated in this experiment. Fig. 9 shows the average task performance time for each precondition, and Fig. 10 shows the average error rate for each determination method. According to ANOVA of the task performance times, there is a significant difference between preconditions (F (1, 7) =95.37, p<.01) and between intensity determination methods (F (1, 7) =10.58, p<.05). ANOVA of the error rate results showed that there is a significant difference between preconditions (F (1, 7) =15.34, p<.01), but not between intensity determination methods. The hold-for-1-s method resulted in a significantly shorter task performance time (ANOVA: F (1, 7) =10.58, p<.05), despite the requirement to maintain it for 1 s. Moreover, using just the left mouse button better matches traditional click and drag operations, so the improved mouse adds the level of pressure input to current applications.

6 Comparison with Conventional Input Methods

Our next experiment compared the pressure-sensing mouse button with conventional input methods: moving the mouse and using a scroll wheel (Fig. 11).

The task of this experiment was to select a menu item using each of the input methods. Fig. 12 shows a menu bar from the experiment. The "START" part at the top of the menu is home position. The cross-hatched item is the current position of the subject's pointing cursor and the black item—whose position is random—is the target that the subject must place the cursor onto and keep it there for 0.5 s.

For the mouse movement input, the subject clicks the right mouse button to bring up the menu and moves the pointing cursor by moving the mouse. For the scroll wheel input, the subject clicks the scroll wheel to bring up the menu and moves the pointing cursor by rolling the wheel. For the pressure-sensing button input, the subject presses the pressure-sensing button to bring up the menu and moves the pointing cursor by adjusting the intensity of the pressure; to select the target, the subject must maintain this intensity for 0.5 s.

Fig. 11. A scroll wheel mouse (Dell Inc.) for the comparison experiment

Fig. 12. Popup menu for the experimental task. The cross-hatched area is a cursor following the movement of the mouse. The black area is the target to which the curse is to be moved.

The experimental factors are input methods and the number of partitions. For each input method, six different menu lengths were tested: five items, six items, seven items, eight items, nine items and 10 items. For each menu length, subjects performed 20 trials, so that each subject performed a total of 360 trials (3 x 6 x 20). The dependent variable was task performance time.

Five subjects, all of whom participated in the human characteristics experiment in Section 5, participated in this experiment. Fig. 13 shows the average task performance time for each condition. ANOVA and multiple comparisons indicated that, for each menu length, the fastest input method was mouse movement and the slowest input method was the pressure-sensing button (F (2, 8) =18.8, p<.01). There was also a significant difference between five and nine menu items (F (5, 20) =6.11, p<.01).

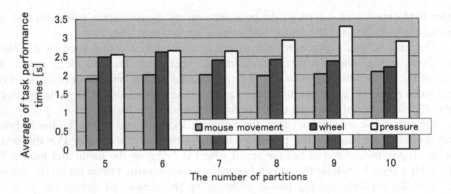

Fig. 13. Menu selection times for three input methods

One factor that made the pressure-sensing mouse slower than the other methods was the difficulty subjects had maintaining a constant pressure for the 0.5 s necessary to select a menu item. We observed that some subjects re-adjusted their intensity of pressure although they had already reached the correct intensity to hit the target.

7 Conclusions

The pressure-sensing mouse button expands the possibilities for a mouse button. The degree of freedom of a conventional button is one (pressed or not pressed), while in the pressure-sensing button there are multiple degrees of freedom, from pressing lightly to pressing heavily.

Our experiments showed that the pressure-sensing mouse button is inferior to conventional mice in task performance time. This is because subjects did not become as proficient in the pressure-sensing button as they were in the other devices. However, the scroll wheel was also once an unfamiliar device, but most users effectively use it today. We expect that the pressure-sensing mouse button will also be used efficiently with time, because subjects rated it as intuitive and easy to understand.

There are several advantages of the pressure-sensing mouse button over the other input methods studied. It is easy for a user to control in several resolutions of intensity, such as five levels, six levels, and seven levels, because the maximum and minimum intensities are constant. It is easy for a user to return the input value to zero simply by removing the finger from the button. Moreover, the pressure-sensing button is suitable for inputting intentions of a user; pressing the button heavily corresponds to an intention to perform an operation quickly, in more detail or more emphatically.

However, there are disadvantages of the pressure-sensing mouse button over the other input methods studied. It is more difficult to select a level. It is particularly difficult for a user to maintain the intended pressure. Moreover, it is difficult to maintain pressure in the minimum range or in the maximum range.

We suggest that an effective application for the pressure-sensing mouse button is to change insignificant effective parameters associated with fundamental determination. For example, in clicking a "yes" or "no" button, the user can indicate the strength of his or her opinion with the force of the click. The user may even apply this intention pressure unconsciously. However, the user's choice of "yes" or "no" does not change.

We are planning to improve the hardware of the pressure-sensing mouse button by placing the pressure sensor under the mouse button. After that, we plan to explore useful applications for the mouse. An example of applications, pressing the pressure-sensing button below the threshold for jumping to the linked page could present just a thumbnail of the page, with the size of the thumbnail corresponding to the level of pressure. As another example, the level of pressure could be used to set the priority for file downloads: pressing heavily would download the file as soon as possible, while clicking lightly would reduce the allocated bandwidth, preserving it for other uses.

Acknowledgments. We thank the members of the HCI group at the University of Yamanashi for their support of the research. This study was supported in part by the Grants-in-Aid for Scientific Research of the Japan Society for the Promotion of Science and by the RIEC of Tohoku University awarded to A. Imamiya.

References

1. Zeleznik, R., Miller, T., Forsberg, A.: Pop through mouse button interactions. In: Proceedings of the 14th annual ACM symposium on UIST 2001, Orlando, Florida, pp. 195–196. ACM Press, New York (2001)
2. Ramos, G., Boulos, M., Balakrishnan, R.: Pressure Widgets. In: Proceedings of the SIGCHI conference on Human factors in computing systems, Vienna, Austria, pp. 487–494. ACM Press, New York, USA (2004)
3. Mizobuchi, S., Terasaki, S., Keski-Jaskari, T., Nousiinen, J., Ryynanen, M., Silfverberg, M.: Making an Impression: Force-Controlled Pen Input for Handheld Devices. In: CHI 2005 extended abstracts on Human factors in computing systems, Portland, OR, USA, pp. 1661–1664. ACM Press, New York, USA (2005)
4. Ramos, G., Balakrishnan, R.: Zliding: Fluid zooming and sliding for high precision parameter manipulation. In: Proceedings of the 18th annual ACM symposium on UIST 2005, Seattle, WA, USA, pp. 143–152. ACM Press, New York, USA (2005)

5. Rekimoto, J., Schewsig, C.: PreSenseII: Bi-directional Touch and Pressure Sensing Interactions with Tactile Feedback. In: CHI 2006. extended abstracts on Human factors in computing systems, Montréal, Québec, Canada, pp. 1253–1258. ACM Press, New York, USA (2006)

6. Blaskó, G., Feiner, S.: Single-Handed Interaction Techniques for Multiple Pressure-Sensitive Strips. In: CHI 2004 extended abstracts on Human factors in computing systems, Vienna, Austria, pp. 1461–1464. ACM Press, New York, USA (2004)

7. Forlines, C., Shen, C., Buxton, B.: Glimpse: a novel input model for multi-level devices. In: CHI 2005 extended abstracts on Human factors in computing systems, Portland, OR, USA, pp. 1375–1378. ACM Press, New York, USA (2005)

8. Swindells, C., MacLean, K.E., Booth, K.S., Meitner, M.: A Case-Study of Affect Measurement Tools for Physical User Interface Design. In: Proceedings of the 2006 conference on Graphics Interface, Quebec, Canada, pp. 243–250. Canadian Information Processing Society, Toronto, Canada (2006)

9. Malamalama Online Archive, Vol. 28, No. 1 (January 2003), http://www.hawaii.edu/malamalama/archive/index.html, The magazine of the University of Hawai'i System, pp. 9-10 , the last access date: (April 5, 2007) (2003)

10. Qi, Y., Reynolds, C., Picard, R.W.: The Bayes Point Machine for Computer-User Frustration Detection via PressureMouse. In: Proceedings of the 2001 workshop on Perceptive User Interfaces, Orlando, Florida, pp. 1–5. ACM Press, New York, USA (2001)

11. Phidgets, Canada (the last access date: April 5, 2007), http://www.phidgets.com/

DeskJockey: Exploiting Passive Surfaces to Display Peripheral Information

Ryder Ziola, Melanie Kellar, and Kori Inkpen

Dalhousie University, Faculty of Computer Science
Halifax, NS, Canada
{ziola, melanie, inkpen}@cs.dal.ca

Abstract. This paper describes DeskJockey, a system to provide users with additional display space by projecting information on passive physical surfaces in the environment. The current DeskJockey prototype utilizes a projected desk and allows information to be moved easily between active and passive displays using a world-in-miniature interaction metaphor. A four-week, in-situ field study was conducted to compare usage of DeskJockey with typical multiple monitor use. The results revealed potential for utilizing passive physical surfaces in this manner and demonstrated that this type of display space has distinctive affordances and benefits which enhance traditional display space.

Keywords: Augmented desk, multiple monitors, peripheral information, display space management, user interaction.

1 Introduction

Traditional single-user, single-monitor workstations are often enhanced by adding more displays, increasing the available screen real estate. Studies of the use of multiple monitors have revealed that additional displays are often treated as a discrete place to view output, rather than being used to enlarge the user's active working area [6, 7]. Additionally, secondary monitors are often used to monitor information in the periphery, providing "instant access to a resource in a known location in peripheral vision" [6]. Given that continuity of screen space is not essential when monitoring peripheral information, the opportunity to make these dedicated locations resident on a different medium is appealing.

Currently, the division between the physical desk and the computer monitor is defined by digital or physical content; a physical clock sits on our physical desk, while virtual clocks are often placed on our computer monitor. In this paper, we examine augmented surfaces for individual users to extend their workspace onto passive physical surfaces in the environment. Our work blurs the boundary between physical and virtual, allowing active and passive media to coexist. The aim is not to turn the desk into an active display; a myriad of properties (resolution, orientation, interaction strategies) currently make it a poor substitute for a monitor for many tasks. Instead, we can capitalize on the passive nature of traditional desks to display passive digital information – information primarily used for reference, to provide context, or

C. Baranauskas et al. (Eds.): INTERACT 2007, LNCS 4662, Part I, pp. 447–460, 2007.
© IFIP International Federation for Information Processing 2007

to monitor something peripheral or unconnected to the central task The challenge therefore is to design a desk which can house real paper next to digital calendar information, digital sticky notes next to the (physical) telephone, while keeping users subtly informed about their world. While explicitly not attempting to augment reality, this system would at least allow the virtual to bump up against the physical more casually.

The overall goal of this research is to increase users' available display space by utilizing physical surfaces in the environment to casually display peripheral information (See Figure 1). This offloads the need to display peripheral information on the primary monitor(s). A secondary goal of our research was to determine whether a straightforward implementation of an augmented surface, where most of the interaction occurred on the desktop monitor, would provide benefits for individual users. While Rekimoto & Saitoh's *Augmented Surfaces* [11], provided a spatially continuous workspace to move digital information among various devices in a collaborative environment (including tables and walls), their architecture was inherently complex. Instead we are examining a more straightforward implementation based on off-the-shelf components, where most of the interaction occurs on the desktop monitor. Finally, we were interested in observing how people make use of the augmented surface, including what types of objects they put on the surface, how persistent these objects were, and how often people interacted with the objects.

Fig. 1. The DeskJockey System where digital information can be placed on a physical desk, amongst other physical artifacts that reside in this space

Paper Overview. This paper explores the design of augmented surfaces for individual users to extend their workspace onto passive physical surfaces in the environment. We describe the development of DeskJockey, a system which utilizes a projected display to place peripheral information on a physical desk (Figure 1). In this system, digital information can easily be "dropped" onto the desk for peripheral monitoring, or can be brought back into focus on the users' primary display when additional interaction or information is required. We report on a 4-week field study that observed usage of DeskJockey, compared to a multi-monitor setup, to identify how people would utilize such a system during real day-to-day activities.

2 Related Work

2.1 Augmented Desks

The idea of displaying digital information on a desk is not new. Much work has been done on enhanced desk systems, including the DigitalDesk [14], InteractiveDesk [1] and metaDESK [12]. These approaches were primarily aimed at either augmenting the physical desk with digital information [14], or interacting with virtual objects using physical artifacts [1, 12] Our approach is different in that we are not attempting to merge virtual and physical representations, instead we are taking advantage of the available space to place various types of digital information into the physical environment and enrich our periphery.

Rekimoto and Saitoh [11] introduced the notion of augmented surfaces in which tables and walls could be used to provide an extended desktop for portable computers. The motivation for this work was to support co-located collaboration and enable information to move freely between surfaces in the environment (hyperdragging). However, users are required to interact using the cursor on a tabletop display. This can be awkward, particularly if the table is cluttered. While similar to the ideas presented in this paper, Rekimoto and Saitoh's augmented surfaces are intended to be manifestations of an extended desktop which supports active interaction. Rather than creating a new workspace to replace or compete with the main monitor as the primary locus of interaction, we intend to supplement it with a physically large area used strictly for secondary output where users interact with the peripheral information from the main monitor.

2.2 Peripheral and Ambient Information

Information can be considered peripheral if it is not necessary for the current task, but may be of interest to the user nonetheless. Information monitoring tasks form a large subset of peripheral activities and centre on the problem of notification: how to minimise distraction while informing the user of potentially important or interesting changes in the system's state. This category includes tasks such as being notified of incoming e-mails, being aware of an upcoming meeting, or seeing which friends are logged into their instant messaging application. As we are interested in providing support for peripheral information monitoring, the mechanisms necessary for performing it should be examined.

Investigations into the requirements for a successful peripheral interface focus on the goal of notifying the user of a change in the information being monitored without allowing it to hinder the current task. Maglio & Campbell [9] performed three studies to compare various methods of peripherally presenting text, including a number of variations on a scrolling ticker, fading text, and visual and accompanying auditory feedback. It was found that continuous motion, in the form of a scrolling ticker, was both detrimental to performance of the primary task and unreliable at notifying users of the peripheral information. Discrete motion, active only when new information is presented, was found to be most effective. Exploring this idea further, Bartram et al. [2] studied the ability of Moticons — icons with simple motion — to notify users of changes. They reported that motion is detected better than changes in colour or shape, especially in the periphery of the user's vision, and is well suited to notification.

A subset of peripheral information, ambient information, can be identified by its intended subtlety. It is meant to implicitly communicate information not necessarily relevant to the task at hand through environmental cues and is not intended as a means of explicit notification. The ambientROOM [8] aims to create an environment that interfaces with digital information, attempting to engage the human ability to process background information. For example, the current activity-level of a loved-one is displayed as ripples projected on the ceiling of the room and the volume of a background soundtrack of nature sounds can roughly signal quantities (such as incoming e-mail). These fully-fledged ambient environments require dedicated physical objects or displays and naturally come with high infrastructure requirements.

As we are interested in supporting ambient uses, the design requirements for ambient information prove useful. Mankoff et al. [10] developed heuristics for the evaluation of ambient displays that help to inform us of the affordances a system must offer to be compatible with ambient use. In particular, two of their heuristics stand out as being specifically relevant to the design of a system capable of supporting ambient uses, rather than the design of the ambient application itself:

- *perpipherality of display:* it can be easily monitored while being unobtrusive.
- *easy transition to more in-depth information:* it is necessary to be able to easily engage the system, converting the interaction from passive to active.

A system intended for use in part as an ambient display should accommodate these properties. Unlike previous work that used dedicated displays or specifically designed embodied devices [16], DeskJockey can place ambient information on available physical surfaces. This provides unobtrusive monitoring and facilitates interactions as users shift from passive to active.

3   Augmented Surfaces for Individual Workspaces

We have designed a system that allows peripheral and ambient information to be dispersed throughout the environment by projecting virtual objects onto physical surfaces. This idea can be utilized on any workspace surface, making the tabletop or a nearby wall a potential repository for digital information (see Figure 2). Additionally, a completely clear space is not necessary (and is not practical), as the system can project arbitrary shapes and sizes on whatever space is available on the physical surface. Additionally, if a top-projected system is used, the system can display objects *on top of* physical objects in the environment. For example, if a user's desk was cluttered with piles of paper, they could turn the top paper over or place a blank sheet on the top. The system could then project onto the stack, thereby utilizing that space. When projecting on a wall, this problem is less likely to be encountered.

By default, a projected display surface is passive. While vision tracking can be used to provide various augmented reality features such as object tracking, occlusion detection, and active linking, previous research has shown that manipulating objects

Fig. 2. Any physical surface in the environment can be utilized to display peripheral information

on extended surfaces is challenging [13]. In particular, it is difficult to detect discrete events with small–scale hand movements, particularly because users frequently make movements like this in the course of their work [13]. Wilson [15] noted that computer vision techniques are often "unnecessarily complex and inferior" when emulating a single Windows cursor on a table.

Our aim was to provide lightweight access to digital objects on peripheral display spaces and to enable users to easily place, retrieve, and interact with objects. Additionally, many monitoring tasks serve as a gateway into an active task; as a result it was necessary to accommodate a passive surface as the starting point for an active task. We chose to initially investigate a system whereby most interactions with virtual objects on the passive surface would take place using the desktop computer, using standard GUI interactions.

Two types of interaction are required to support passive projected displays. First, a navigation mechanism is needed to traverse, move, and place objects on the display. Second, techniques are needed to perform detailed interaction with the objects themselves (i.e., editing a post-it note).

We identified several methods of navigating virtual objects on the projected display, employing varying degrees of abstraction with respect to interaction with the projected display. Depending on the interaction model used, detailed interaction with objects on the projected display can either occur in-place (i.e., on the projected surface itself), or on the primary monitor. Interaction in-place is intuitive; however, traditional desktop environments are better suited for standard types of interaction.

The first technique identified, *direct traversal*, simply treats the projected surface as an extension of the workstation's primary display (See Figure 3a). With this technique, the mouse travels between the primary display and the projected display, similar to a traditional multi-monitor configuration as well as Rekimoto and Saitoh's *hyperdragging* technique [11]. The second technique, *cursor jump*, allows the cursor to jump between displays by pressing a mouse button or key-combination (see Figure 3b), similar to Benko and Feiner's multi-monitor mouse [3]. The third technique, *bring here*, involves having all of the objects on the projected display zoom to the primary display for interaction (see Figure 3c), similar to the Mac OS X's Exposé

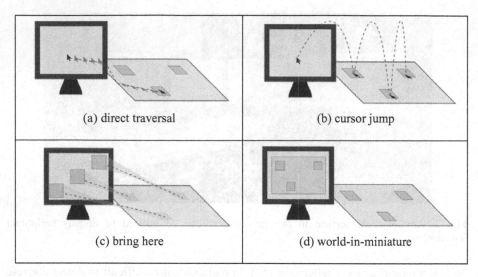

Fig. 3. Proposed interaction models to navigate and interact with virtual objects on the physical surface

feature [5]. The fourth technique, *world-in-miniature*, involves interacting with a representation of the projected display on the primary monitor (see Figure 3d).

4 DeskJockey

We designed and implemented DeskJockey, a prototype augmented surface system to further explore system design issues, and to investigate how people would utilize augmented surfaces as part of their regular, day-to-day work environment.

4.1 Physical Setup

The standard physical set-up of our DeskJockey prototype includes a workstation with a single 19" monitor (1280 x 960 resolution), a 100cm x 150cm desk serving as the extended workspace, and a projector, projecting an image to the right of the keyboard. The projected display is given a black background so that virtual objects on the desk appeared cropped, with nothing being projected on the unused parts of the desk. In order to facilitate the placement of virtual objects with respect to real objects, a simple webcam (640 x 480 resolution) is mounted overhead to provide a background to the system, comprised of real-time video of the desk. This setup could also incorporate a multi-monitor setup if desired.

4.2 WiM Interaction Model

We chose to utilize the World-in-Miniature (WiM) interaction model for DeskJockey because it provides quick access to the table and its contents, it takes advantage of the rich interaction capabilities of the desktop, and it does not interfere with interactions on the primary display. Real-time video of the desk (obtained from the overhead camera) was used as the background for the WiM. The low resolution image obtained from the camera was sufficient for distinguishing physical artifacts on the table; however, details on the virtual objects were hard to discern. We therefore chose to draw the icons representing the virtual images over top of the video of the table. This required that the icons be aligned perfectly with the video beneath them. There are too many factors — camera, projector, and table orientation — to achieve the precision necessary purely through mechanical alignment. To compensate for these effects, a perspective transform was applied to the incoming video (See Figure 4).

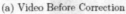

(a) Video Before Correction   (b) Video After Correction

Fig. 4. A perspective transformation is applied to the incoming video from the web cam to help align overlaid images

DeskJockey's WiM is activated by moving the cursor to a hotspot that extends across the bottom of the primary display (**Figure 5**). The bottom of the display provides a natural mapping in that moving down off the monitor moves the cursor down onto the desk. When the cursor is moved off the bottom of the screen, a transition to view the WiM is triggered. To minimize accidental triggering, the transition does not occur if the cursor is moving slower than a specified threshold.

Animated feedback is provided to signify that the user is transitioning to the WiM. The WiM view is mapped to a surface that lies perpendicular to the bottom of the primary monitor's current contents. The screen simulates a 90° rotation effect, moving the primary monitor's current contents up and off the screen (i.e., imagine a rotating cube), replacing it with a miniature view of the objects on the desk. Conversely, once viewing the WiM, moving up off the top of the screen triggers the reverse transition and the primary monitor returns to its normal view.

Fig. 5. The visual transition to the world-in-miniature

4.3 Navigating the WiM

Once the WiM has been activated, the user is presented with a representational view of the desk as shown in Figure 6. The view is centered on the projected area of the desk, in the same orientation as the projector. One consequence of working with a WiM rather than the objects themselves is the loss of context provided by the real desk. Without a mechanism for directly seeing how the extended workspace corresponds to the real desk, orientation is difficult to understand and avoiding collisions with physical artifacts on the desk becomes difficult. Real-time video of the desk provides the background for the WiM which enables the user to easily place virtual objects with respect to real objects on the desk.

Fig. 6. The WiM offers a real-time view of the desk to facilitate placement and interaction with virtual objects

Any window in the workspace can be added to the desk by dragging it to the WiM. This is achieved by dragging the window down to the hotspot on the bottom of the screen. Similarly, any virtual object can be removed from the desk and returned to the primary display by dragging it up off of the WiM. Each virtual object on the desk is represented as an icon in the WiM. In an attempt to make the metaphor as robust as possible, icons are shown as a screenshot of the object they represent, scaled to correct proportions. The icons can be dragged around the world-in-miniature to move the virtual object on the desk. When the cursor moves over an icon, it glows yellow, along with the object on the desk, to help reinforce the correspondence between the icons and the objects they represent.

4.4 Interacting with Virtual Objects on the Desk

Although the main purpose of the system is for passive information monitoring, interaction with items on the desk is nonetheless a requirement. Interaction with virtual objects in DeskJockey takes place on the primary monitor and is activated by clicking on the object in the WiM. This moves the object from the desk to the foreground of the primary monitor for interaction (see Figure 7). To return to the WiM, the user clicks anywhere off of the object or presses escape.

Fig. 7. Objects on the table are brought to the primary display for manipulation

The state transition diagram in Figure 8 illustrates the actions to transition to/from normal desktop interaction, to the WiM, to object manipulation.

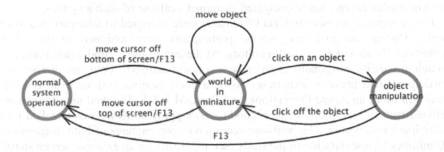

Fig. 8. State transition diagram illustrating progression from normal operation, to the WiM, to interaction

4.5 Sample Applications

Although the DeskJockey prototype can display any window on the projected surface, some applications are better suited to being placed on a passive display than others. We have selected, modified, or developed several applications to illustrate specific uses (Figure 9 provides a screen shot of some of these applications).

- *Stickies*. A program for placing Post-It style notes on your desktop.
- *Pics*. A program to display an image or PDF without a border or titlebar, at an arbitrary size
- *Clutter*. An open-source program for displaying cover art for the .mp3 currently playing and making casual piles of covers that can be selected to play the album [4]. This allows cover art for the current song to sit on the desk and digital albums to be scattered on the desk much like their physical counterparts.

- *Widget Viewer*. A generic wrapper to display a Mac OS X Dashboard widget as a window that can be placed on the desk such as a calendar widget, a weather widget, and a widget that represents new emails as flowers in a vase. Many of these small programs are designed to monitor information or status.
- *Sky*. A daylight monitor was created as an example of the ambient information potential of DeskJockey. *Sky* loads an image from a local outdoor webcam, calculates the average colour of the sky and displays a large block of that colour with the texture of the sky from the camera. During the day, it roughly communicates if the sky is blue or grey and becomes dark as the sun sets.

5   DeskJockey Field Study

Although many additional features could be added to DeskJockey to increase the novelty of the system, we first wanted to examine the potential of augmented surfaces for everyday use. A field study was undertaken to explore how DeskJockey would be used in a natural environment and how DeskJockey differed from a more traditional dual monitor environment. We were also interested in gathering feedback on the WiM interface. Although augmented surfaces have been proposed by others in past work, to our knowledge no one has investigated sustained, real-use of such a system.

Five computer science students (1 female) were recruited to take part in a 4-week study. During the first two weeks, participants were assigned to one of two conditions: DeskJockey or dual monitors. At the end of the second week, participants switched conditions (condition order was counterbalanced). Four out of five of the participants had previous experience using a multi-monitor system. Both conditions were run using an Apple PowerBook or a PowerMac G5. The dual monitor condition utilized two 19" monitors. In both conditions, logging software was installed on the participant's computer. This software recorded screen captures of both displays every 30 minutes for the duration of the study (see Figure 10 for an example screen shot).

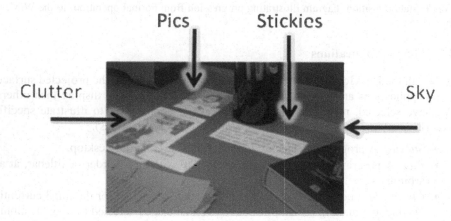

Fig. 9. Some of the supplemental applications developed for DeskJockey

Upon completion of the study, participants took part in a 30 minute interview where they were asked to describe their experiences with both display conditions. A researcher selected a small number of screen shots to be used during the interview. Using the screen shots as a guide, participants were asked to describe the tasks being performed and the applications being used in both displays (primary and projected).

5.1 Results

DeskJockey Observations. Throughout the course of the study, we observed a number of applications being placed within the projected display space (Figure 10 shows an example screen shot from the study). Weather widgets were the most commonly reported applications (by all 5 participants), followed by clocks (4/5), a digital light-fixture application that displayed coloured spotlights (4/5), pictures (3/5), and calendars (3/5). Two participants indicated that they displayed their instant messenger list while others displayed their iTunes player or a transit information widget. One interesting usage was the placement of a participant's del.icio.us cloud on the projected display. This participant remarked that due to the size of the tag cloud it was not feasible to place it on a toolbar or desktop but that DeskJockey provided a "handy off to the side" reference. Although this list is not comprehensive, it clearly indicates that all participants used DeskJockey as part of their daily activities, and provides an indication of the types of applications that participants felt were appropriate for the passive display surface.

All participants expressed overall enthusiasm for DeskJockey, and 4 of the 5 participants reported that it was useful for their daily activities. Participants cited the primary strength of DeskJockey as the ability to use peripheral display space that could not be used otherwise. While many of the applications placed in DeskJockey were also viewed within the dual monitor condition, the DeskJockey environment

Fig. 10. Example screen shot from the DeskJockey user study showing various applications that were placed on the projected display

allowed participants to keep these applications open continually throughout the day, without having to overlap windows. One participant reported that he enjoyed the ability to project onto multiple surfaces. His monitor resided on a raised surface onto which he projected his clock and calendar application while the remaining applications were projected on the desk itself. Another participant reported that he liked using DeskJockey for information that he did not want to be a distraction.

The main weakness reported for DeskJockey was the current implementation of the WiM. While the WiM was found to be useful, participants reported they often inadvertently activated the WiM when overshooting the Dock (which was located on the bottom of their screen). Three participants stated they would rather drag applications onto the desk through the right side of the monitor while one reported that he would have preferred a hotkey to toggle to the WiM. Other frustrations related to the prototype nature of DeskJockey including not being able to easily rotate applications (a limitation of the current prototype), problems manipulating objects in the WiM, and web browser windows occasionally disappearing within the DeskJockey environment.

Dual-Monitor Observations. Consistent with previous research, we observed that all participants partitioned their work across the two screens. The primary monitor typically contained an active application and the secondary monitor displayed information that was being monitored (e.g., email and instant messenger) and reference information (e.g., documents, web sites). The biggest strength of the dual monitor setup (in comparison to a single monitor setup) reported by participants was the added screen real estate.

DeskJockey versus Dual Monitor. Participants were asked to describe how they used DeskJockey in comparison with the dual monitor environment. All participants stated they placed peripheral applications that required little interaction in the DeskJockey environment. Many of these applications, such as weather, calendars, and webcam views, were not continually displayed during the dual monitor condition but were instead launched as needed. The secondary display was viewed as an extension of the active workspace where screen real estate is too valuable to "waste" on such applications. One participant stated that that "the second monitor is a place to extend my workspace, while DeskJockey is a place to put peripheral information, [such as] pictures".

6   Conclusion and Future Work

In this paper we presented a prototype system called DeskJockey, which capitalizes upon the large size and relatively static layout of a desk to provide additional peripheral display space. DeskJockey uses readily available equipment and requires little infrastructure. DeskJockey's world-in-miniature technique addresses unique interface problems that arise from secondary displays that show content but do not support interaction directly. Our prototype implementation demonstrated that it is feasible to enhance an environment without adding to the active workspace area.

The main contribution of this work is an investigation of augmented surfaces to extend individuals' virtual workspace onto passive surfaces in the environment.

Virtual objects – such as calendars, to-do lists, reminder notes, or incoming emails – can be projected alongside physical objects on the desk or walls. This approach represents a novel way of seeing a projected table as an extension to a traditional workstation, rather than a primary locus of interaction.

Another key contribution is the results from the 4-week in-situ, field study which demonstrate benefits of displaying peripheral information on physical surfaces in the environment. Our participants appreciated the ability to exploit available surfaces that would otherwise be wasted. DeskJockey was found to be fundamentally different than a second monitor; participants displayed different types of information, for longer periods of time, without sacrificing valuable screen real estate. The results also indicated that DeskJockey has strong potential for supporting information monitoring activities, which are becoming an important web and desktop activity.

While the generalizability of our results are limited given the small sample size, we felt that it was important to: (1) evaluate whether or not this type of system would be used for real-world activities, and (2) better understand the types of tasks it would be used to support. Now that we have a better understanding of how the system will likely be used, we can further refine the prototype so that it can be deployed more widely in the future. Additionally, further in-situ evaluations are necessary to determine how usage of the DeskJockey space would evolve over time.

Our current implementation chose a WiM approach, forcing all interaction to take place on the primary monitor. While this approach had merit, participants had difficulty with the interaction used to activate/deactivate the WiM. As such, they expressed frustration and would have preferred more flexibility in the types of interactions (e.g., direct interaction or the ability to use hotkeys). Further examination is needed, particularly when compared to the other interaction models proposed. As we better understand usage of this type of environment, we will be able to explore new interaction techniques for DeskJockey.

Acknowledgements

We would like to thanks the Canadian Natural Sciences and Engineering Research Council and NECTAR for funding this work. Additional thanks go to members of the EDGE Lab for their assistance and to the participants in our field study.

References

1. Arai, T., Machii, K., Kuzunuki, S., Shojima, H.: Interactivedesk: a computer-augmented desk which responds to operations on real objects. In: Proceedings of CHI '95, pp. 141–142 (1995)
2. Bartram, L., Ware, C., Calvert, T.: Moticons: detection, distraction and task. Int. J. Hum.-Comput. Stud. 58(5), 515–545 (2003)
3. Benko, H., Feiner, S.: Multi-monitor mouse. In: Proceedings of CHI '05, pp. 1208–1211 (2005)
4. Clutter, http://http://www.sprote.com/clutter/
5. Exposé, http://www.apple.com/macosx/features/expose/

6. Grudin, J.: Partitioning digital worlds: focal and peripheral awareness in multiple monitor use. In: Proceedings of CHI '01, pp. 458–465 (2001)
7. Hutchings, D.R., Smith, G., Meyers, B., Czerwinski, M., Robertson, G.: Display space usage and window management operation comparisons between single monitor and multiple monitor users. In: Proceedings of AVI '04, pp. 32–29 (2004)
8. Ishii, H., et al.: ambientROOM: Integrating ambient media with architectural space. In: Proceedings of CHI '98, pp. 173–174 (1998)
9. Maglio, P., Campbell, C.S.: Tradeoffs in displaying peripheral information. In: Proceedings of CHI '00, pp. 241–248 (2000)
10. Mankoff, J., et al.: Heuristic evaluation of ambient displays. In: Proceedings of CHI '03, pp. 169–76 (2003)
11. Rekimoto, J., Saitoh, M.: Augmented surfaces: A spatially continuous workspace for hybrid computing environments. In: Proceedings of CHI'99, pp. 378–385 (1999)
12. Ullmer, B., Ishii, H.: The metadesk: Models and prototypes for tangible user interfaces. In: Proceedings of UIST '97, pp. 223–232 (1997)
13. Voida, S., Podlasec, M., Kjeldsen, R., Pinhanez, C.: A study on the manipulation of 2D objects in a projector/camera-based augmented reality environment. In: Proceedings of CHI 2005, pp. 610–611 (2005)
14. Wellner, P.: Interacting with paper on the DigitalDesk. Communications of the ACM 36(7), 87–96 (1993)
15. Wilson, A.: PlayAnywhere: A compact interactive tabletop projection-vision system. In: Proceedings of UIST 2005, pp. 83–92 (2005)
16. Wisneski, C., et al.: Ambient Displays: Turning Architectural Spaces into an Interface between People and Digital Information. In: Streitz, N.A., Konomi, S., Burkhardt, H.-J. (eds.) CoBuild 1998. LNCS, vol. 1370, pp. 22–32. Springer, Heidelberg (1998)

Drag-and-Guess: Drag-and-Drop with Prediction

Takeshi Nishida[1] and Takeo Igarashi[1,2]

[1] Department of Computer Science, The University of Tokyo
tnishida@ui.is.s.u-tokyo.ac.jp
[2] JST Presto
takeo@acm.org

Abstract. Drag-and-guess is an extension of drag-and-drop that uses predictions which is based on application specific knowledge. As the user begins to drag an object, the system predicts the drop target and presents the result to the user. When the target is hidden in a closed folder or beneath other windows, the system makes it temporarily visible. This frees users from manual preparation such as expanding a folder tree or uncovering the target location. The user can accept the prediction by throwing the object, which then flies to the target. Or, if the prediction is unsatisfactory, the user can ignore it and perform the operation as usual. We built three prototype applications (email client, spreadsheet and overlapping windows) to show that DnG is useful in many applications. Results of the user study show that the proposed technique can improve task performance when the task is difficult to complete manually and reasonable prediction algorithm is available.

1 Introduction

Graphical user interfaces (GUI) have made much of the work using computers easy and intuitive. However, making an operation graphical does not necessarily improve performance. This is the situation with repetitive drag-and-drop operations (DnD). The user must make the source and target location visible by opening a folder or bringing the window to the foreground. Then the user must carefully move the mouse cursor back and forth for each object. This requires a substantial amount of labor especially when the user repeatedly performs DnD.

Some of these operations can be automated with user-defined macros or automatic systems. However, these approaches introduce several problems. First, defining macros or rules by hand is difficult and inflexible; it is nearly impossible for novice users. To make things worse, few macros or rules are reusable in other similar situations. Second, we cannot rely on completely automatic intelligent systems because they sometimes make serious mistakes (e.g. filing e-mail messages to incorrect folders). Because it is impossible to have a perfect prediction system, techniques that tolerate prediction errors are required.

In this paper, we propose an extension of traditional DnD, drag-and-guess (DnG), that uses predictions based on application specific knowledge. As the user starts dragging an object, the system predicts the drop target and responds

C. Baranauskas et al. (Eds.): INTERACT 2007, LNCS 4662, Part I, pp. 461–474, 2007.
© IFIP International Federation for Information Processing 2007

by showing the result of the prediction to the user. When the target is not visible (e.g. hidden in nested hierarchical folders or outside of the visible area on the screen), the system automatically makes the target location visible. If the prediction is correct, the user can accept it by throwing the object (releasing the mouse button while dragging the object) and it will automatically fly to the target. If the prediction is not satisfactory, the user can ignore it and perform the operation as usual.

DnG can be helpful in various situations. For example, when the user is distributing e-mails in an inbox to nested folders, the system can predict appropriate target folder by its content and open it. When the user is editing a spreadsheet table, the system can predict the target cell based on the regularity observed in previous DnDs. When the user is opening a document with an application program using DnD, the system can find a possible drop target based on the document file type and the usage frequency of applications.

In the following sections, we review the related work, and present the DnG interaction design and its pros and cons. We then discuss the generality of the proposed technique in three prototype applications. We attempt to cover the issues that may arise when DnG is applied to various applications. We also describe the user study that we performed to examine the usability of DnG. Finally, we describe the details of the implementation.

2   Related Work

Many extensions to traditional DnD operations have been proposed. Pick-and-drop [1] and Hyperdragging [2] are designed for multiple display environments. Pick-and-drop allows the user to pick an object by tapping on a display and then to drop it on another display. Hyperdragging allows the user to DnD an object across physically separate but semantically connected displays. Drag-and-pop [3] is also designed for physically separate displays and very large displays. As the user starts dragging an object, proxies of possible drop targets appear around the object.

Many techniques have been proposed to improve object selection. Area cursor [4] and bubble cursor [5] increase the size of the cursor, while sticky icons [4] and semantic pointing [6] dynamically adjust the control display gain to make it easier to catch the target. Delphian Desktop [7] predicts the target using the linear relationship between the peak velocity and the target distance. The cursor jumps to the predicted location when the system detects the peak velocity. This greatly reduces the movement time in long-distance tasks, but adds extra time to short-distance tasks.

One shortcoming of these techniques is that the benefits decrease when the potential targets are densely located. In addition, considerable effort is required to make the target visible in advance. DnG overcomes these problems by using information about the application and the grabbed object.

Fold-and-drop [8] allows the user to leaf through overlapping windows during the DnD operation. Windows are folded like a paper in response to the crossing-based gestures. Although this reduces manual preparation, considerable effort is still required to find the desired window from the stack of windows.

Predictions are used in various systems. Eager [9] predicts the next editing operation on a hypercard and Dynamic Macro [10] predicts the next text editing operation on Emacs. Jul [11] used destination prediction to constrain the movement to simplify navigation in a three-dimensional environment. Dulberg et al. [12] used predictions to reduce the precision needed for selecting or activating a small control from a group of candidates.

MailCat [13] predicts a target folder for an incoming e-mail message and displays the prediction result as buttons. The system achieves excellent classification performance by providing the top three suggestions instead of filing messages automatically. SmallBrowse [14] facilitates Web-browsing in small-screen computers by predicting the hyperlinks that the user would follow and inserting those predicted hyperlinks at the top and bottom of the Web page. These systems resemble our approach in that they tolerate prediction errors. They show predicted results in an unobtrusive way instead of performing the tasks automatically. We have generalized and extended the ideas presented in these systems in our interaction technique.

3 Interaction Design

DnD is an interaction technique for transferring or copying objects using a pointing device. The user grabs an object by pressing a mouse button, drags the object to the target location, and then drops the object into that location by releasing the button. DnG enhances this standard DnD by predicting the target and automating the preparation and execution processes (e.g. making the target location visible and dragging the cursor to that location).

Figure 1 shows the basic behavior of DnG. As in DnD, DnG begins when the user grabs an object, and the system presents the result of its prediction. The system shows a line connecting the starting location of the operation and the predicted target. If the target is not visible, the system makes it visible to the user. For example, when the target is hidden in a contracted path within a tree, the system automatically expands the path to the target.

The user then decides whether to accept the prediction result on the screen. If the user wants to accept it, he or she simply throws the object (releases the mouse button while the cursor is moving) and the object flies to the predicted destination. This process is presented through an animation. If the prediction is not satisfactory and the user wants to drop the object somewhere else, he or she can continue the DnD operation ignoring the DnG system. Releasing the mouse button while the cursor is stationary will drop the object to the cursor location. The automatically expanded target location returns to its original status when the operation is completed.

If the prediction is not satisfactory, the user can also ask the system to show other candidates. To show the next likely candidate, the user performs a clockwise rotation gesture; to show the previous candidate, he or she performs a

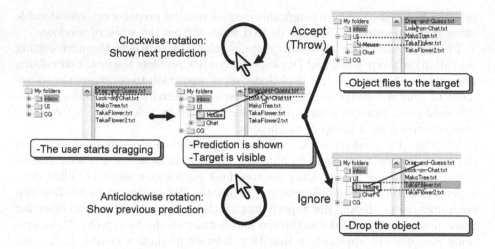

Fig. 1. Basic behavior of drag-and-guess

anticlockwise rotation. The system cancels the temporary expansion of the previous candidate and makes the next candidate visible. The user can leaf through the prediction results using these circular gestures until he or she finds a satisfactory candidate. The user is always free to ignore the list and perform the operation manually as we have described above.

The system does not, however, always show the prediction. Predictions are shown only when the task is difficult to perform manually, and the system is confident in its prediction. We discuss this topic in detail later in the implementation section.

4 Benefits and Drawbacks

4.1 Benefits

DnG improves DnD in many ways. First, it saves the user from tedious pointing tasks. When the prediction is correct, the user only has to press the mouse button on the object, confirm the target, and throw the object. This is much faster than carefully moving the cursor to the target location, especially when the target is far away or very small.

Second, DnG is helpful for finding the desired target in densely packed targets. Such targets are likely to be difficult to distinguish from each other, because they are often visually similar. For example, all targets appear almost identical when filing documents or editing spreadsheets. Our technique accentuates the differences between these targets by using semantic information and presenting it to the user.

Third, DnG saves the user from the tedious tasks of manually making the target location visible before the start of dragging, such as to expand many folders in a folder tree, rearranging windows to make the source and target visible, and scrolling in a window.

DnG has several advantages compared to other possible interaction techniques using predictions. First, unlike other techniques, it does not introduce additional widgets or consume any additional screen space. Interactions such as showing the prediction results as buttons [13] require additional space, but DnG shows only temporary visual feedback.

Second, the target is shown in its original context, which makes it easier for the user to understand where the predicted target is located. For example, showing a prediction result by using the destination folder name on a button [13] cannot distinguish multiple folders that have the same name but are at different locations in a tree. In addition, spatial memory obtained through long-term use of the application would improve task performance as seen in [15].

Third, DnG supports a smooth transition to DnD when the prediction fails. This is very important because prediction can frequently fail.

Finally, DnG is designed to be a common front-end interface for predictions. This allows the user to enjoy the benefits of predictions without having to learn specialized interfaces for each application. A user familiar with the DnG interface in one application could easily use it in other applications.

4.2 Drawbacks

DnG can cause additional overhead compared to plain DnD because the visual feedback showing the prediction inevitably attracts the user's attention. The user needs to see the prediction result and decide whether to accept it. If the prediction is correct, this extra effort is rewarded and the total execution time becomes shorter than manual execution. However, when the prediction is incorrect, it becomes an overhead added to standard DnD.

Our experience show that the overhead is relatively small and overall performance is improved given reasonable prediction accuracy. We also observed that users tend to accept these additional overheads as a necessary cost. Nonetheless, this overhead is an issue and one must carefully consider the trade-off when introducing prediction into a system.

5   Prototype Applications

The proposed interaction design is applicable to a wide range of domains. At the same time, however, it raises new issues and challenges for each application related to the visualization techniques to reveal hidden targets and the algorithms to make predictions. In this section, we introduce prototype implementations of three application systems that use DnG and discuss specific issues related to individual applications. We also briefly discuss lessons learned from informal testing using the prototypes.

5.1   Document Filing

Managing personal information is one of the most popular uses of DnD. For example, most e-mail reader applications allow users to organize their messages into user-defined folders, and for many people, distributing new messages in an inbox to appropriate folders using repetitive DnD is a daily routine [16]. Struggling with other personal information, such as bookmarks and photographs, presents a similar situation.

DnG can make this tedious task much more efficient. It reduces the time for making decision on where to file by opening the path to the folder in a folder tree, and carefully moving the object from the source to the target.

We implemented a prototype system mimicking an e-mail reader (Fig. 1). The system fills the "inbox" folder with a set of text files and provides a DnG interface when moving a text file to a user-defined folder. Predictions are made by considering the semantic distance between the grabbed text and the texts that are already filed to desired folders. Such predictions are unreliable until a sufficient number of files has been placed. However, DnG is still acceptable in this case because the user can simply ignore the initial error-prone predictions until they become reliable. It is also possible to suppress predictions until system becomes confident.

Hidden folders can be revealed by expanding ancestor folders. In addition, the space-filling strategy and animated transitions used in Expand-Ahead [17] would be beneficial to the user.

DnG in this application can be seen as an attempt to address several problems associated with automatic classification. Automatic systems require a major amount of prior labor to set explicit rules for automatic distribution. It is also difficult to recover when fully automatic classifiers have failed; every day, for example, innocent messages are labeled as SPAM and it is a laborious work to rescue them. DnG address these issues by taking semiautomatic approach, where the user confirms the process interactively. This semiautomatic approach is especially effective for mid-size problems where only imperfect classification algorithms are available.

One can apply existing algorithms used in automatic classifiers for prediction. They examine the contents of the incoming message and find a folder that contains the most similar messages [13].

We observed that DnG benefits the user not only when the prediction exactly pinpoints the target, but also when the desired target is in a nearby location by revealing the target. This is likely to be a common situation if the messages are filed to semantic hierarchies.

5.2   Spreadsheets

DnD is repeatedly used to rearrange or reformat existing data. When editing a spreadsheet, for example, a user will make summary tables collecting values from various locations, sometimes in multiple worksheets. The user also rearranges the cells for partitioning purposes [18]. We often face similar spatial arrangement problems while working with presentation slides, interior design, and so on.

We implemented a prototype spreadsheet application using DnG (Fig. 2(a)). In the current implementation, the system predicts a target cell when moving a value by observing regularity in the operation sequence, for example, moving to

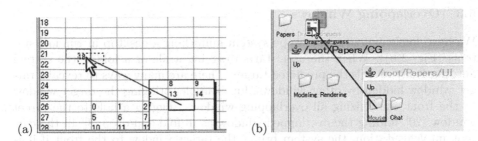

Fig. 2. Drag-and-guess applied to (a) spreadsheets and (b) overlapping windows

the cell next to the previous target cell, moving to cells with regular intervals, and so on. We employed similar rules as those used in [10].

The predicted targets are often out of view because spreadsheets tend to be very large. In such cases, the system shows a thumbnail of the target at the nearest edge of the window. Thumbnails include the context around the target so the user can easily recognize the situation. Thumbnails are also droppable; the user can manually drop onto the target cell or onto a cell around the target. This would be helpful when the prediction is not precisely correct but is near the intended target.

DnG here can be seen as a simplified version of programming by example or demonstration (PBE, PBD) techniques [9,19]. These systems observe the user's repetitive operations and try to construct a complete program by extracting rules. One problem with these traditional programming approaches is that it requires certain overhead to create and execute a program. The user typically needs to explicitly start a programming session and an execution session. A more serious problem is that these approaches fail when irregular instance appears during execution. DnG addresses these issues by presenting one prediction at a time and requires the user's confirmation instead of letting the system perform the task automatically.

DnG can coexist with PBE/PBD systems, serving as a general interface that interacts with the program being developed. It can support the user at an early stage, before he or she has performed sufficient number of examples for the PBE/PBD system to construct a complete program. Showing predictions to the user offers a guide to the inner state of the PBE/PBD system and acceptance of a prediction (throwing) works as a confirmation. After confirming that the system appropriately learned the desired rule with a sequence of successful DnG operations, the user can let the system do the remaining task automatically [9]. It is our future work to implement such PBE / PBD features and test its usability.

We observed that the users perform the tasks in comfort, mainly because it was quite clear for them when the predictions are likely to be correct. For example, when the user is constructing a two-dimensional table, the user can assume that the system makes a correct prediction while staying in the same row. In contrast, the user can anticipate that the prediction might be wrong when moving to the next row.

5.3 Overlapping Windows

We have implemented a prototype system mimicking a desktop in window systems (Fig. 2(b)). When the user starts dragging a file or a folder, the system automatically reveals the predicted target. There are many ways to reveal a target window hidden by other windows, for example, bringing the target window to the front, minimizing all overlapping windows, digging a hole to the target window [20], folding the overlapped window as in fold-and-drop [8]. In the current implementation, the system brings the target window to the front if it is hidden and restores the target window if it is minimized.

We have not yet implemented realistic prediction algorithm in this application partly because there are many possibilities in this case and it is difficult to design a general method. This is even more difficult because each target window can run different application. We discuss this inter-application DnD in the implementation section. The simplest method of using most recently used drop target as prediction result might work best for most cases (it would be better to show predictions after the user drop objects in the same window for a couple of times).

We observed that revealing the target attracts much larger attention of the user compared to other applications. This is because the system redraws a larger area to reveal the target. We suggest using a conservative way for revealing the target. Moreover, if the worst happens, the correct target might be hidden by the system. Interactions to cancel the effect would be beneficial in these cases.

6   User Study

We conducted a user study to examine the usability of DnG. In this study, we adopted two tasks, message filing and data rearrangement, which are typically done by DnD. All of the participants carried out both tasks with DnG and without DnG (= DnD).

Our hypothesis was that participants would perform faster with DnG if the system shows a prediction only when the task is difficult to do manually and the system is confident in its prediction.

Note that we evaluated the interaction techniques and not the prediction algorithms. It is our future work to evaluate the performance of our approach using real predictions. In addition, in this study, we did not address the issues that arise from showing multiple predictions to make the control of test conditions simple; subjects did not leaf through multiple candidates.

6.1   Design

Task 1. The first task was to file objects into their appropriate folders (Fig. 3). The folders were hierarchically organized three deep. Each folder contained two folders named "a" and "b," and the eight leaf folders were used as the target folders. The files used in the study were named randomly by the system, using

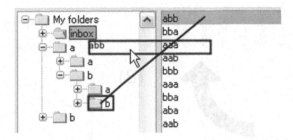

Fig. 3. Snapshot of the application used in Task 1

two letters "a" and "b." These file names served as instruction on where to file the object; a file name "aba" had to be filed to folder "a-b-a."

We used random numbers to simulate a situation in which some imperfect prediction algorithms are available and that the system only shows prediction when it is rather confident of that prediction (the system does not show prediction when it is likely to be wrong). In this experiment, the system shows predictions at the rate of 50%. If the prediction was shown, its accuracy was 80%. These numbers are chosen as a plausible setting considering available filtering algorithms [13]. All operations were treated as difficult to perform manually.

In this study, subjects were not allowed to expand the folder before performing DnD or DnG. Instead, they had to hold still on the folder for 500 ms while dragging to expand it. In addition, the folders that expanded during the operation were collapsed after each operation.

Subjects were instructed to perform the task as quickly and as accurately as possible, but were not required to redo the operation when objects were filed to incorrect folders. The subjects performed 20 filings under each condition. The order of the condition was balanced, with half of the subjects performing the tasks with DnG first, and half with DnD first.

The system recorded the time interval from when the participant started dragging an object to when the object was filed in the appropriate folder. The system also recorded the drag trajectories and the errors that occurred during the task.

Task 2. The second task was to rearrange a one-dimensional table with 32 cells into a transposed two-dimensional (8 4) table (Fig. 4 (left)). The window size was fixed so that the whole table did not fit in the view (Fig. 4 (right)). The participants had to scroll the view, either by using the scrollbar, or by dragging the object near the edge of the window. Prediction was done by observing the regularity in the operation sequence as described in the prototype applications section.

Under both conditions, subjects could undo the operations using a keyboard shortcut (Ctrl-Z). This was especially important under the "with DnG" condition because the algorithm used in the study learned from mistakes.

The subjects performed the task four times under each condition (with and without DnG), alternating between the two conditions. The order of the interface

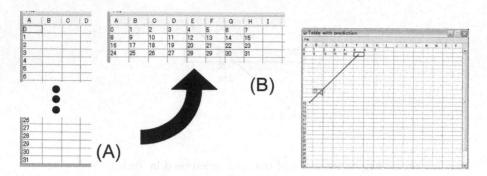

Fig. 4. Task 2. (left) Rearranging a one-dimensional table (A) to a two-dimensional table (B). (right) Snapshot of the application.

was balanced: half of the participants first performed the tasks with DnG, and vice versa.

The system recorded the interval from the time when the participant pressed the start button located outside the window, to the time when the desired table was completed. The system also recorded the drag trajectories during the task.

6.2 Procedure

Ten male subjects were recruited for this experiment. They were all right-handed and frequent mouse users ranging in age between 23 and 28 years old. The study took place in our laboratory, one participant at a time. Before the experiments, the participants were briefed on the purpose of the study and the method of operating the applications. The participants were allowed to practice the technique until they felt confident in operating the applications. The tasks followed the training. Finally, the subjects filled out a questionnaire. The study was run using a standard PC with MS-Windows XP and a 17h monitor (resolution 1280×1024) equipped with an optical mouse.

6.3 Results

Task 1. Figure 5 shows the average operation time and the average drag distance required to file one object. The error bar indicates standard deviation. According to paired t-test, subjects could file the objects significantly faster ($p < 0.05$) with significantly shorter drag distance ($p < 0.05$) using DnG. Error rate during the study was considerably low for the both conditions (2% with DnG vs. 3% with DnD).

Task 2. Figure 6 shows the average time and the average drag distance required to complete the rearrangement task. The error bar indicates standard deviation. According to paired t-test, subjects could finish the task significantly faster ($p < 0.05$) with significantly shorter drag distance ($p < 0.05$) using DnG.

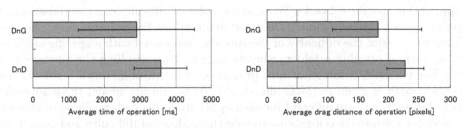

Fig. 5. Average operation time (left) and drag distance (right) of the first task

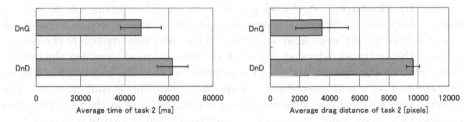

Fig. 6. Average operation time (left) and drag distance (right) of the second task

Questionnaire and Feedback from Participants. At the end of the study, participants answered a short questionnaire. Eight participants answered that they file messages manually (like task 1) with their regular e-mail readers, and six of them wanted to use DnG if the prediction accuracy is comparable to the study. Five participants answered that they perform rearrangements in spreadsheets (like task 2) with their regular applications, and all of them wanted to use DnG in those applications. Four participants felt difficulty in throwing the objects and suggested improvements. Three suggested combinations with mouse or keyboard buttons, and one suggested visual feedbacks showing what is going to happen before releasing the mouse button.

7   Implementation

7.1   Architecture

Our current implementation of DnG is written in Java. The common part is implemented as an application independent component to minimize the programming costs for the application developers. When adding the DnG feature to an existing application, they can focus on the application specific prediction algorithms and visualizations.

Filtering the Prediction List. Predictions are filtered from the prediction list if the user can manually drop the object on the target with ease. The system judges that the task is difficult when the expected operation time is longer than a predefined threshold. The expected operation time can be given as a summation of the time required for two-dimensional pointing and that required for application-specific subtasks. We used the index of difficulty of a two-dimensional pointing task [21] to estimate the effort required for the pointing task. We also have to consider the difficulty of the subtasks associated with a specific application, such as opening a folder, rearranging windows, scrolling the view, and so on. For example, a model of user performance in traveling down a tree to the desired path is given by McGuffin et al [17]. We do not model these subtasks here because they are different for each application. Instead, we chose to provide a way for software developers to encode the additional difficulty and pass it on to the system.

Detecting Gestures. A throwing gesture is used to distinguish between a normal drop and prediction acceptance when the mouse button is released. A mouse release would be treated as "throw" if the drag velocity before the release is faster than a threshold value. Rotation gestures are used to switch the prediction shown by the system. We used the exterior angle of the cursor trajectory so that the motion is not constrained to a specific circle. This is similar to [22]. The system detects a clockwise rotation when the summation of angle history reaches 2π, and vice versa. Summation will be reset to 0 when a gesture is detected.

7.2   Implementation Issues

Implementation Cost. The prediction algorithms need not be perfect; developers may choose the second-best algorithms considering the implementation cost and the computation time. This is much easier than adding completely automatic features to the application.

Computation Time. It is not necessary that prediction algorithms run at the moment when the DnG controller makes a request. If the prediction takes time, developers should choose to run the prediction in a background thread, and then return the precomputed result when requested. The current implementation does not include such multi-threading features. It has to be implemented by the software developers.

Inter-Application Predictions. Prediction algorithms for inter-application DnDs would be combinations of the approaches discussed in the application section: content-based classification, learning from operation sequence, and other heuristics. For example, we often classify documents using hierarchical folders and arrange document layout on the desktop.

In addition, many heuristics can be incorporated into the system. For example, when the user is dragging a text fragment, the most likely targets are the search boxes and the text-component which just lost the input focus. Similarly, the system should put a higher priority on folders that have just been opened, or folders in a plugged-in USB thumb drive. A simple rule, like "the user tends to repeat DnD to the same folder" might work also.

Inter-application predictions can be treated with inner-application predictions, by putting the prediction list together and presenting it to the user as a whole. Alternatively, predictions can be treated separately by extending the system to present inner-application candidates when the cursor stays inside the window and inter-application candidates after the cursor exits the window. It is our future work to implement and test such inter-application DnG methods.

8 Conclusion

We have proposed an extension of traditional drag-and-drop using predictions, called drag-and-guess (DnG). DnG enables the user to interact with various application specific prediction algorithms through a common gestural interface. We introduced three prototype applications to show the generality of the proposed method and discussed various issues specific to individual applications. We also described the user study that we performed to examine the usability of DnG. Finally, we described the details of the implementation. We believe that DnG can be a common front-end for predictions and encourage the use of predictions in many applications.

To make DnG more practical, we need to address several issues. First, we have to observe the daily usage of DnD and find more application fields that are suitable for DnG. Next, we need to develop algorithms and interactions specific to each application. Evaluating DnG under such algorithms and interactions is also another important issue; algorithms have to be precisely controlled if they are to be used in formal evaluations.

References

1. Rekimoto, J.: Pick-and-drop: a direct manipulation technique for multiple computer environments. In: Proc. UIST 97, pp. 31–39. ACM Press, New York (1997)
2. Rekimoto, J., Saitoh, M.: Augmented surfaces: a spatially continuous work space for hybrid computing environments. In: Proc. CHI 99, pp. 378–385. ACM Press, New York (1999)
3. Baudisch, P., Cutrell, E., Robbins, D., Czerwinski, M., Tandler, P., Bederson, B., Zierlinger, A.: Drag-and-pop and drag-and-pick: techniques for accessing remote screen content on touch- and pen-operated systems. In: Proc. INTERACT 2003, pp. 57–64 (2003)
4. Worden, A., Walker, N., Bharat, K., Hudson, S.: Making computers easier for older adults to use: area cursors and sticky icons. In: Proc. CHI 97, pp. 266–271. ACM Press, New York (1997)
5. Grossman, T., Balakrishnan, R.: The bubble cursor: enhancing target acquisition by dynamic resizing of the cursor's activation area. In: Proc. CHI 05, pp. 281–290. ACM Press, New York (2005)
6. Blanch, R., Guiard, Y., Beaudouin-Lafon, M.: Semantic pointing: improving target acquisition with control-display ratio adaptation. In: Proc. CHI 04, pp. 519–526. ACM Press, New York (2004)
7. Asano, T., Sharlin, E., Kitamura, Y., Takashima, K., Kishino, F.: Predictive interaction using the delphian desktop. In: Proc. UIST 05, pp. 133–141. ACM Press, New York (2005)

8. Dragicevic, P.: Combining crossing-based and paper-based interaction paradigms for dragging and dropping between overlapping windows. In: Proc. UIST 04, pp. 193–196. ACM Press, New York (2004)
9. Cypher, A.: Eager: programming repetitive tasks by example. In: Proc. CHI 91, pp. 33–39. ACM Press, New York (1991)
10. Masui, T., Nakayama, K.: Repeat and predict: two keys to efficient text editing. In: Proc. CHI 94, pp. 118–130. ACM Press, New York (1994)
11. Jul, S.: Predictive targeted movement in electronic spaces. In: CHI 02 Extended Abstracts, pp. 626–627. ACM Press, New York (2002)
12. Dulberg, M.S., Amant, R.S., Zettlemoyer, L.S.: An imprecise mouse gesture for the fast activation of controls. In: Proc. Interact 1999, pp. 375–382 (1999)
13. Segal, R., Kephart, J.: Mailcat: an intelligent assistant for organizing e-mail. In: Proc. AGENTS 99, pp. 276–282 (1999)
14. Sugiura, A.: A web browsing interface for small-screen computers. In: CHI 99 Extended Abstracts, pp. 216–217. ACM Press, New York (1999)
15. Robertson, G., Czerwinski, M., Larson, K., Robbins, D., Thiel, D., van Dantzich, M: Data mountain: using spatial memory for document management. In: Proc. UIST 98, pp. 153–162. ACM Press, New York (1998)
16. Whittaker, S., Sidner, C.: Email overload: exploring personal information management of email. In: Proc. CHI 96, pp. 276–283. ACM Press, New York (1996)
17. McGuffin, M., Davison, G., Balakrishnan, R.: Expand-ahead: a space-filling strategy for browsing trees. In: Proc. INFOVIS 04, pp. 119–126 (2004)
18. Hendry, D.: Display-based problems in spreadsheets: a critical incident and a design remedy. In: Proc. Visual Languages 95, pp. 284–290 (1995)
19. Maulsby, D., Witten, I., Kittlitz, K.: Metamouse: specifying graphical procedures by example. In: Proc. SIGGRAPH 89, pp. 127–136. ACM Press, New York (1989)
20. Ishak, E.W., Feiner, S.K.: Interacting with hidden content using content-aware free-space transparency. In: Proc. UIST 04, pp. 189–192. ACM Press, New York (2004)
21. Accot, J., Zhai, S.: Refining fitts' law models for bivariate pointing. In: Proc. CHI 03, pp. 193–200. ACM Press, New York (2003)
22. Moscovich, T., Hughes, J.F.: Navigating documents with the virtual scroll ring. In: Proc. UIST 04, pp. 57–60. ACM Press, New York (2004)

Wave Menus: Improving the Novice Mode of Hierarchical Marking Menus

Gilles Bailly[1,2], Eric Lecolinet[2], and Laurence Nigay[1]

[1] LIG University of Grenoble 1, Grenoble, France
[2] GET/ENST – CNRS UMR 5141, Paris, France
{gilles.bailly, laurence.nigay}@imag.fr, {gilles.bailly,
eric.lecolinet}@enst.fr

Abstract. We present Wave menus, a variant of multi-stroke marking menus designed for improving the novice mode of marking while preserving their efficiency in the expert mode of marking. Focusing on the novice mode, a criteria-based analysis of existing marking menus motivates the design of Wave menus. Moreover a user experiment is presented that compares four hierarchical marking menus in novice mode. Results show that Wave and compound-stroke menus are significantly faster and more accurate than multi-stroke menus in novice mode, while it has been shown that in expert mode the multi-stroke menus and therefore the Wave menus outperform the compound-stroke menus. Wave menus also require significantly less screen space than compound-stroke menus. As a conclusion, Wave menus offer the best performance for both novice and expert modes in comparison with existing multi-level marking menus, while requiring less screen space than compound-stroke menus.

Keywords: Marking menus, Wave menus, novice mode.

1 Introduction

In recent studies, much attention has been devoted to marking menus [7, 8] and their extensions [15, 16]. Marking menus are a combination of pop-up radial menus and gesture recognition. They provide two interaction modes: novice and expert modes. On the one hand, if a user presses and waits a fraction of a second, radial menus pop up and items can be selected in a manner similar to common linear menus: this is the novice mode. On the other hand, the user can select an item without waiting for the menus to pop-up, by drawing a mark that leaves an ink trail corresponding to a selection path through the hierarchical menus: this is the expert mode. The key property of marking menus is that they support a seamless transition from novice to expert mode [6]. In that sense, marking menus can be seen as pseudo-gestural interaction techniques since they make it possible to learn gesture interaction from a menu system. Several user studies have revealed their efficiency over linear and pie menus [1]. Alternate designs have also been proposed to improve their efficiency when menus contain a large number of items [15, 16].

C. Baranauskas et al. (Eds.): INTERACT 2007, LNCS 4662, Part I, pp. 475–488, 2007.

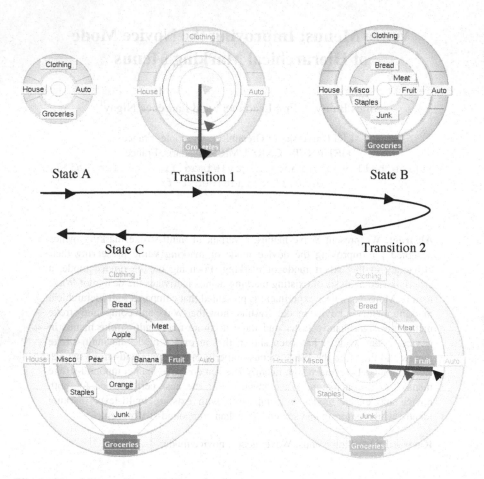

Fig. 1. WaveMenus. (State A) The menu appears centered around the cursor. By drawing a stroke towards a desired item (Transition 1), the first level menu is enlarged to leave room for the submenu (State B). With a second stroke (Transition 2), the third level appears at the center and the first and second levels are enlarged (State C).

However, most of the recent studies were driven by the efficiency of the expert mode. The key point of this article is that the efficiency of the novice mode of marking menus is crucial for user acceptance of the menuing technique. Indeed:

- *The novice mode is the first interaction mode* with the menu and *an unavoidable step* before expert mode. The users must be able to learn how to use the most used commands in expert mode. The underlying principle of marking menus is that the users will learn the expert mode implicitly by activating these commands repeatedly in novice mode. This feature obviously highlights the crucial role of the novice mode: if the user interaction in novice mode is not efficient or too cumbersome (in terms of speed and accuracy), the users may reject marking menus immediately.

- The *novice mode never disappears*. Many menu items are seldom used by users. For instance, a study showed that 90% of Microsoft Office commands are rarely used [5]. This implies that many commands will be activated in novice mode, even by expert users that are familiar with the application. Besides, users with limited physical and/or cognitive skills (including handicapped and aged users) may never use the expert mode: this is an important consideration when designing applications to ensure widespread user adoption.
- *The novice and expert modes co-exist*. As pointed out in [7], transition from novice to expert mode is not one way. Switching back and forth between novice and expert modes is an important feature of marking menus. For example after a long lay-off period, the expert users return to the novice mode to refresh their memory of the layout of the menu.

In this paper, we focus on the improvement of the novice mode of marking menus by presenting a new hierarchical marking menu technique, called **Wave Menu** (Fig. 1), that combines the advantages of two previous marking menu techniques (compound-stroke [8] and multi-stroke [15]):

- In *novice mode*, Wave menus provide better performance than multi-stroke menus and similar performance to compound-stroke menus.
- In *expert mode*, Wave menus preserve the efficiency of multi-stroke menus that have been shown to outperform the compound-stroke menus.

The first section presents previous work and criteria for characterizing marking menus. These criteria are then used as the basis for the design of our two variants of the Wave Menu. We finally present the results of a controlled experiment that compares the novice mode of our two variants of the Wave menu with that of existing marking menus while highlighting the difficult and nearly unexplored problem of experimentally evaluating the novice mode of a menu.

2   Criteria for Characterizing Marking Menus

For the sake of clarity, we first briefly describe the existing hierarchical marking menus before presenting criteria for characterizing marking menus and especially their novice mode.

2.1   Marking Menus Compared

Compound-Stroke Menus (CS menus) [8], are based on *spatial composition*: users make a compound mark that results from the combination of the elementary strokes needed to activate items in the menu hierarchy in novice mode. The gesture is performed continuously without releasing the mouse button. An important feature is that these menus are scale invariant in expert mode, so that the user does not have to look at the screen to check the location of the mouse release. As for traditional menu systems, the novice mode provides *previsualization*: users can browse submenus by dragging the mouse on their parent items or by tapping on them.

Multi-Stroke Menus (MS menus) [15], a variant of CS menus is based on *temporal composition:* the elementary strokes are drawn in quick succession, and each stroke (which is inflexion free) is completed when the user releases the mouse. A delay is needed to determine if a stroke belongs to the previous sequence, or if it initiates a new interaction sequence. In contrast to CS menus, the marks can overlap.

Zone and Polygon Menus [16], two variants of MS menus, consider both the relative position and orientation of elementary strokes. These menus improve MS menus by extending the breadth of menu to 16 items (CS and MS being limited to breadth-8) while preserving efficiency.

2.2 Criteria

The presented criteria are inspired by previous work on marking menus [6, 15, 16]. However, while most previous studies mostly focused on expert mode, we here put a special emphasis on the novice mode. The first two criteria presented correspond to system design constraints: the screen space that is required by the menuing technique and its supported number of items. The following criteria then cover the three aspects of usability [14]: Efficiency, Learnability and Satisfaction.

Screen space. The screen space required for displaying hierarchical marking menus in novice mode is a major limitation. This problem is critical for handheld devices as well as for contextual "pop-up" menus. Indeed, circular menus are at least twice as large as linear menus because items are laid out on both sides around the center point. Items must also be centered around the cursor that made them appear. These contrast with linear menus which can either appear on the left or the right side of the mouse press, depending on the space to the screen borders remaining. A 3-level CS menu hence requires more horizontal space than 10 linear menus to display its leftmost and rightmost branches (Fig. 2). This makes CS menus bad candidates for small screens or for being used as contextual menus, even on large screens: if the selected object is too close to the screen border, the menu will be partially hidden or it will not be centered around the mouse cursor, thus making user interaction cumbersome.

Other designs, such as MS menus and their variants (i.e. Zone and Polygon menus) still require more space than linear menus but are much less space consuming than CS menus because their submenus are superimposed. Moreover in expert mode, MS menus also require less space than CS menus because the performed simple marks can overlap [15].

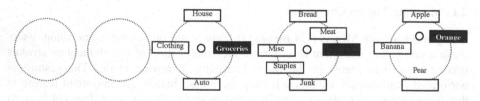

Fig. 2. Space requirements in breadth for three-depth Compound-Stroke menus

Number of items. Many applications now contain a very large number of commands (for instance, 642 commands were available in Microsoft Word 6 [5]). Traditional menu systems may have some submenus that contain a rather large number of items (typically more than 10 or 15 items) as opposed to CS and MS menus for which previous studies [6, 15] have shown a breadth equal to 8 to guarantee good performance in expert mode. Note that for multilevel CS menu, the breadth is even smaller than 8 because certain compound marks are ambiguous due to the scale invariance of the marks (for example a 3-level CS menu can allow 400 items instead of 512=8x8x8 items). The breadth limitation of CS and MS menus may imply awkward groupings of items [16] as well as an increased menu depth; two consequences that may lead to (a) a decrease in performance in expert mode (especially for CS menus, as shown in [15]) and (b) an increased decision time and possible disorientation in novice mode as the user needs to navigate in a larger number of submenus [10]. Zone and Polygon menus [15] have been introduced as a way to solve this problem by extending the menu breadth up to 16 items. However, it is important to notice that the time to select an item amongst N not only depends on the depth and breadth of the menu but also relies on various factors such as the type of menu task and the order of items. Empirical testing is thus often needed to define an optimal breadth and depth combination.

Speed and Error rate. *Speed* measures the time needed by users to activate appropriate items. *Errors* occur when the user selects an erroneous command instead of the one s/he was supposed to activate. The speed and error rate criteria are obviously related as users are more likely to make errors when they try to interact faster. The speed and the error rate also depend on the layout of the menu, especially the depth and the breadth of the menu, as explained in the previous section [4, 10] and the orientation of items in the circular submenus [8, 15]. We distinguish two cases depending on if the menu is used in expert or novice mode.

Expert mode. MS menus are more efficient than CS menus in expert mode [15]. MS menus allow for slightly faster selections and significantly reduce the error rate for large hierarchies. Their accuracy remains approximately constant (about 93%) for 2 and 3-level menus and does not decrease for diagonal directions. A possible explanation is that the spatial complexity of strokes does not vary with MS menus: users must always draw simple marks (but multiple times) while CS menus require more complex continuous compound gestures. Zone and Polygon menus are slower than MS menus for a given depth because the user must "tap" before drawing the stroke. However, as they provide a larger breadth, their depth tends to be smaller, so that the global performance of a menu system is likely to be equivalent or even better.

Novice Mode. Studies have shown that Pie menus were 15-20% faster than linear menus in novice mode [1]. Still, to the best of our knowledge, the marking menu techniques have not yet been compared in novice mode even though novice mode efficiency is a key issue for user acceptance (section 1).

The notion of "speed" is harder to define in novice mode than in expert mode. It can be viewed as the mean time needed to activate items that the user does not already know, and thus, that s/he cannot select in expert mode. Nevertheless the notion of a novice usage corresponds to different kinds of user behaviour and strategy [10]. A user can for instance search for a "concept" he has never or rarely used before. For example, the user of a new text editor will probably search the various commands for changing the text properties (such as the font size, the font style, etc.). These commands may be located in different submenus at different levels in the hierarchy. A complete novice user may explore the whole menu system to find all commands that are related to text properties. A more experienced user may approximately know where these commands are located. An even more experienced user may know the appropriate submenu but not the precise location of the command in this submenu. This last case corresponds to an *intermediate mode* [3] where the user could start her/his search in expert mode (by performing a gesture that will open the right submenu) and complete her/his action in novice mode (by selecting the appropriate item in this submenu). This intermediate mode highlights the need for supporting the switch between novice and expert mode in menu techniques (section 1). Besides, even a novice user is unlikely to perform her/his search in a completely "blind" way: s/he will probably use the semantics of the menu labels to constrain her/his search. This property makes a search task in a menu system quite different from an exploration task in an arbitrary tree where item labels may convey little or no semantic information. A search in a menu system is always *directed* by a priori user knowledge (which can be domain knowledge, knowledge from previous uses of the application or of similar applications).

As a conclusion, the time to select an item amongst N in a menu system depends on various factors, such as the menu layout as explained in the previous section. Hence, novice mode efficiency cannot be evaluated in the same straightforward way as for expert mode. As an attempt to solve this problem, we have defined a "typical novice task" to compare the relative performance of different marking menu designs. This task, which can be parameterized in order to control the complexity of the search, will be detailed in section 4.

Learning time and retention over time. *Time to learn* evaluates how fast users are able to acquire the physicals skills needed to operate the menu. This involves three different aspects: a) the time to understand how the menu works; b) the time to understand how items are organized; and c) the time needed for the transition from the novice to the expert mode.

Retention over time estimates "how well users maintain their knowledge after an hour, a day, or a week. Retention may be related to time to learn. Frequency of use also plays an important role." [14]. These criteria have only been studied for 1-level CS menus [7]: it has been found that novice users would eventually become experts using the mark-ahead feature 90% of the time. This study also highlighted that the time needed to reacquire expert mode after an idle period decreases with the amount of experience. Zone and Polygon menus may lead to significantly different results because of their more sophisticated design. This is especially true for Polygon menus where users must draw marks that do not start from a central point and that activate different items according to the direction of the mark. The time to understand how the menu works may thus be longer than for MS and CS menus. Nevertheless an informal study of these menus [6] suggests that their increased breadth (16 items instead of 8 items) may favor the learnability of the overall organization of the menu items.

Subjective satisfaction. By estimating how much users liked using various aspects of the menu system, "subjective satisfaction may be the key determinant of success" [14]. It can depend on many factors, from design to subjective efficiency. The novice mode plays an important part in the evaluation of satisfaction because it is the first mode used. If the novice mode does not satisfy the user, there is little chance that s/he will continue to use it even if the expert mode is very good.

3   Wave Menus and Inverted Wave Menus

Our rationale for designing the Wave menus is guided by the above criteria. Considering the speed and error rate criterion, for expert mode, MS menus and other variants based on temporal composition, outperform CS menus. We chose to improve MS menus, rather than Zone or Polygon menus because their more complex design may increase the time to learn and no experimentation has yet been done to study this important aspect. We then focus on the novice mode of MS menus and propose alternate designs for improving the novice mode while preserving the efficiency of the expert mode.

For novice mode, MS menus require less screen space than CS menus since a submenu is displayed on top of its parent menu. However this approach may imply problems for exploration of the hierarchical menu and cause user disorientation as the navigation path is not visible. This lack of contextual information although minimizing the required screen space criterion may therefore have a negative impact regarding the time to learn criterion. As people acquire display-based knowledge, the graphical display is crucial to learn the structure of the menu. The context in which each action is performed helps the user to recall the methods used (i.e. the sequence of actions). Moreover MS design does not allow previsualization. Previsualization is a common feature of linear and CS menus that allows the user to browse the submenus of a given menu by dragging the mouse over its items. Previsualization is a proactive feedback [13] that is important for exploring menu systems because it provides a means for a fast inspection of possible commands [12].

To sum up, the rationale for designing Wave menus corresponds to an alternate design of MS menus that improve their novice mode while preserving the efficiency of their expert mode. Its graphical design is geared towards requiring less space than CS menus while offering previsualization of submenu items and path visualization. As a consequence, Wave menus work exactly the same way as MS menus in expert mode. Fig. 1 shows an example of a 3-level 8-breadth menu that illustrates the new graphical design we designed for novice mode. In Fig. 1, *State A* shows the root menu, which is centered around the cursor. As for MS menus, drawing a stroke towards an item of the root menu opens the corresponding submenu. However, this submenu is not displayed on top of its parent but at the center of the menu system. In order to remain visible, its parent menu is then enlarged to surround this submenu (*State B*). The same effect occurs again if another stroke is made (*State C*). Submenus move outwards from the center, recalling the propagation of waves. The outmost menu is always the root menu while the inmost menu is always the deepest submenu in the hierarchy that is currently visible on screen (as deeper submenus may exist but may still be closed).

For backing up a level in the hierarchy, the user clicks in the center area of the inmost submenu. The inmost submenu then disappears and the menus that surround it are shrunk. For instance, clicking twice on the center of the menu system shown in Fig. 1 in *state C* would make it appear in *state B* then in *state A*. An important consequence is that the user mostly interacts with the inmost menu. The cursor remains in the center area of the layout thus reducing the time for pointing (length movement) and the focus of attention remains at the center. The fact that interaction location and focus of attention remain stable at the center is likely to improve performance.

Users can open submenus without releasing the mouse button. Menus start being expanded when the cursor crosses an item border of the inmost menu. A fast animation is then performed to make the corresponding submenu pop-up in the center of the menu system. This effect, that is related to crossing-based interaction [2, 11] simulates the idea of "pushing the menu outwards". It only requires small movements to avoid affecting performance. Symmetrically a fast animation occurs when the user clicks on the center for closing a submenu to produce a "collapsing effect". The role of these animations is to help users to understand layout changes when the menu is expanded or collapsed. We have informally observed during experimentation that "crossing" (i.e. interacting when reaching item borders) seemed to be quite "natural" for users. A possible explanation is that drawing a stroke that crosses an item's border affords the idea of stretching this object in order to make its content (i.e. its submenu) appear. Moreover, as submenus appear in the center, it makes sense to drag their parent items outwards to "make place" in the center.

Another important characteristic of Wave menus is that users can interact with *all* visible items by clicking or dragging the mouse on them. This makes it possible to explore different branches without closing menus and to previsualize submenus. Previsualization can be performed continuously by dragging the mouse over the items of any parent menu. The current path in the menu tree is always visible as the ascendants of a submenu appearing in the center are necessarily displayed (by construction of the Wave menu). Wave menus thus offer submenu previsualization and path visualization, two features of traditional menus that increase learnability as explained in section 2.

Finally, with regards to required screen space criterion, Wave menus require the same *minimum* amount of screen space as MS menus because they can be operated in the same way, by interacting only with the inmost submenu. Some operations, such as direct interaction with outer menu items require more space. But Wave menus can still be used, even if it is in degraded mode, when they are close to the screen borders. This property contrasts with CS menus. Besides, their layout also provide better screen space efficiency than CS menus because submenus do not appear on the side of their parents but are equally distributed around the same central point (**Fig. 1 & 2**).

Alternate design. A major feature of Wave menus, which may be surprising at first, is that the children of the menu tree appear in the center of the graphical representation while the parents (and the root nodes) are located on the outmost rings. Such a way of displaying (and interacting with) trees is somewhat unconventional. This layout scheme also differs from the marking and pie menus [1]. Hence, we also developed a variant called *Inverted Wave menus* (WM2) where tree nodes are displayed in the opposite order. With this variant, the root menu appears in the center of the graphical representation, its submenus appear around the root and so on.

The main drawback of this representation is that it requires more space to be usable. In contrast with the standard Wave menu, it cannot be used in "degraded mode" when the activation point is close to the screen borders. Besides, it also leads to more changes of focus as the user cannot focus on the center area most of the time, as is the case with our previous design. But we found it interesting to experiment with these dual designs and to compare them with some of the most promising marking menu techniques proposed so far.

4 Experimental Comparison of Novice Mode Efficiency

We conducted a controlled experiment to compare the efficiency of the *Multi-Stroke* (MS), *Compound-Stroke* (CS), *Wave* (WM) and *Inverted Wave* (WM2) menus in novice mode. As pointed out in section 2, novice mode usage can be seen as a kind of a search that is guided by the semantics of the labels and a priori user knowledge. The key point here is that users will generally not explore the entire menu tree but only a subpart of it, whose size depends on user experience. Moreover, they may want to find all commands that are related to a given topic in order to decide which of them is more appropriate.

As the knowledge across subjects is different, a search actually guided by semantics is likely to introduce bias in the exploration task. In order to avoid this effect, we gave the same name (e.g. *Name1*) to all the "possible" items in the root menu. This means that the subject must only open the submenus that correspond to *Name1* items. The number of *Name1* items (and their corresponding submenus) controls the difficulty of the task. This design modelizes a situation where the user needs to open several menus (the larger the number, the more of a novice he is).

Similarly, we gave the same name (e.g. *Name2*) to the items that must be found by the user in the submenus. Some submenus contains one occurrence of *Name2*, some other submenus do not contain it. Again, the number of *Name2* items is a fixed parameter of the task. *Name2* items are all terminal items: they do not open other submenus. While our design could easily be extended to 3-level menus we only considered 2-level menus to avoid too long experiments, that is to say less than 1 hour per subject for testing the four techniques.

The proposed task is thus as follows: the subject must activate **all** *Name1* items in the root menu in order to open the corresponding submenus and s/he must search for **all** *Name2* items in these submenus. A key factor is that the user must consider **all** *Name1* and *Name2* items. This makes it possible to control the difficulty of the task and thus to avoid excessive variability. A naive design would consist in asking the user to find and select the **first** *Name2* occurrence (instead of **all** *Name2* occurrences) in the set of possible submenus. This would make it difficult to control the task complexity as the number of submenus that users would have to open and scan for finding *Name2* would depend on chance. As the number of submenus explored is unpredictable it cannot be easily counterbalanced with trials. Hence, we preferred a design where the complexity is known in advance. In our experiments, the number of *Name1* items is fixed and set to 4, a value that corresponds to a user that is partially, but not completely, novice. The number of *Name2* items varies from 2 to 4 in a way that is counterbalanced among the techniques, so that complexity is the same for all the techniques. This number varies to force users to open all the 4 possible submenus (if it was fixed and inferior to 4, users could perform the task without opening all the submenus in some trials and this would cause inopportune variability; if it was always equal to 4, all submenus would contain the *Name2* item, a situation that is less realistic than the proposed model).We performed this experiment to check the following hypotheses:

- **H1:** Multi-Stroke (MS) menus are slower than Compound-Stroke (CS) menus in novice mode as they do not provide *previsualization* and *visible path availability*.
- **H2:** Wave menus and CS menus have similar performance in novice mode.
- **H3:** Wave menus have similar performance to their "Inverted" variant: the order of the hierarchy does not matter.
- **H4:** There is no significant effect on the number of errors and the number of missed items between menu techniques.

4.1 Experimental Design

Participants. Twelve volunteers participated in the experiment (5 women, 7 men) from 24 to 35 years (mean 26). They were all accustomed to using computers and to interaction techniques such as linear multilevel menus. None of them had prior experience with the tested techniques, nor knew which was the one we had designed.

Apparatus. The experiment was conducted on a laptop with a 2 GHz Pentium 4 processor, with a 17" display. All menus were implemented by using the Ubit [11] GUI Toolkit (version 5.0) with OpenGL acceleration. In contrasts with many prior studies, we did not use a pen interface but a Logitech (TM) mouse as an input device. The primary reason is that most of our users had no experience with using pen tablets. Much longer training time would have been required to avoid possible bias due to pen interaction learning. Besides, our study focuses on user acceptance of marking menus for common use, and the mouse is much more commonly used as an input device.

Task and Stimulus. As explained above, the task consists in finding and selecting the multiple occurrences of Name2 items in all Name1 submenus (i.e. submenus that correspond to Name1 items in the root menu). Name1 appears 4 times among the 8 items of the root menu so that the user must open 4 submenus that may contain Name2. The number of Name2 occurrences, which varies from 2 to 4, is counterbalanced over techniques and submenu breadths. As would be the case in a real task, Name1 and Name2 are existing words. They are respectively a continent and a city of this continent. To avoid bias due to different subject knowledge both names are displayed during the trial. The names contained in the menus are changed at the end of each trial. We only performed experiments with 2-level menus in order to keep their duration within reasonable limits (about 1 hour). Each submenu is filled with 4, 6 or 8 items where the position is counterbalanced in order not to favor a specific direction.

Procedure. The experiment was divided into 4 blocks, one per menu technique, counterbalanced across subjects using a Latin square design. For each block, we let users discover the menu technique for three minutes without giving indications. Participants were then instructed about how to use the menu for five minutes. Then, they had to execute 18 randomly-chosen trials for each block. Each trial works as follows: 1) the participant presses the mouse in the center of the screen to start the experiment; 2) the continent (Name1) and the city (Name2) appear on the screen; 3) the participant opens the menu by pressing the mouse; 4) he can then search and select the multiple occurrences of the city name in the menu hierarchy; 5) he presses the space bar when he thinks he has found all occurrences; 5) a new screen appears with a button to start the next trial. Participants were allowed to take breaks between trials. Breaks were enforced between different techniques. In summary, the experiment (excluding training) follows this design:

12 subjects x 4 techniques (MS, CS, WM, WM2) x
3 submenu breadths (4-6 or 8 items) of 6 selections   = 864 menu selections

The dependent variables are: the reaction, execution and total times, the number of errors and the number of missed items. Reaction time is measured as the interval between the appearance of the stimulus and the mouse press to open the menu. This interval represents the time needed by participants to understand stimuli before making a selection. Execution time is measured as the interval between this mouse press and when the user presses the space bar to finish the trial. The total time is obtained by adding up the reaction time and the execution time. The number of errors is the number of wrong selections. The number of missed items is the number of city name occurrences that were present in the menu but not selected by the user.

4.2 Results

The two-way analysis of variance indicates no significant effect for menu techniques on **reaction time**, thus suggesting there is no difference in mental preparation time. The **execution time** is calculated without taking into account trials with missed items. Analysis of variance reveals a significant main effect for technique on execution time ($F_{3,33}$= 47.25, p< .0001). A post hoc Tukey test with 1% alpha level shows that the Wave and CS menus are significantly faster than the MS and Inverted Wave menus. As expected, our results also reveal a significant main effect for submenu breadth ($F_{2,22}$= 68.69, p< .0001). There is also a significant submenu-breadth x technique interaction ($F_{6,66}$ = 2.75, p< .001), indicating that breadth changes affected menu

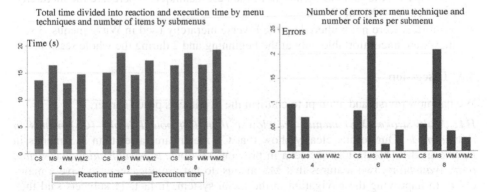

Fig. 3. Performance of the Compound–Stroke menu (CS), Multi-Stroke menu (MS), Wave menu (WM) and Inverted Wave Menu (WM2) with 4, 6 or 8 items by submenu

techniques differently. Pairwise means comparisons (Tukey test with 1%) indicate that there is no significant time difference between 6 and 8 items for the MS menu. It also indicates that the WM2 is significantly slower with 6 and 8 items. A possible explanation is that the distance between items is much larger in this design that takes longer to read all items. Finally, the analysis of **total time** (Fig. 3) shows the same significant effect as for execution time (as there is no effect for reaction time).

There is a significant effect for techniques on the **numbers of errors** ($F_{3,33}$= 13.59, p< .0001) as shown on Fig. 3. A post hoc Tukey test with 1% alpha level shows that the number of bad selections is significantly higher for MS menus than for other techniques. Wave menus produce 8 times fewer errors than the MS design. This can be explained by the fact that users have difficulty selecting the center of the menu when they want to come back one level up. The accuracy for different *submenu-breadths* is statistically significant (but the Tukey test with 5% indicates that the differences are not significant). There is also a significant submenu-breadth x technique interaction ($F_{6,66}$ = 2.75, p< 0.1). Pairwise mean comparisons (Tukey test with 1%) indicate that MS menus generate significantly more errors for 6 and 8 items. *Techniques* and *submenu-breadth* have no significant effect on the number of **missed items**.

After the experiment, we asked participants to rank-order each of the four menu techniques.

- 6 participants chose CS menus as their favorite technique and 5 of them chose Wave menus. 9 participants ranked MS menus as their least favorite technique.
- 5 participants judged CS menus as the easiest to learn, 3 chose Inverted Wave menus and 2 standard Wave menus. Conversely, 6 participants considered MS menus as the hardest technique to learn and 4 Wave menus.
- For 7 participants MS menus was the most tiring technique, for 2 participants it was the CS and Inverted Wave techniques. In contrast, 7 participants found CS as the least tiring technique, 2 chose WM and MS.
- 8 participants considered that MS menus made it hard to perceive the hierarchy and 3 found this to be the case for the Inverted Wave menus. Conversely, 7 participants said that CS menus were the best technique to perceive the hierarchy, and 2 chose WM and WM2.
- 7 subjects were not bothered by the inverse hierarchy used in Wave menus, 3 said they were uncomfortable only at the beginning and 2 during the whole session.

4.3 Discussion

We can now revisit and attempt to confirm the hypothesis posed earlier:

H1: Multi-Stroke (MS) menus are slower than Compound-Stroke (CS) menus in novice mode. Our results clearly show that CS menus are faster than MS menus in novice mode (18% faster). As seen in previous sections, *previsualization* and *visible path availability*, two features that MS menus do not provide, seem to have a major effect in improving the navigation in the menu system. In fact, 11 subjects said they felt they could easily get lost in MS menus because they were unable to remember which submenus they had already visited.

H2: Wave menus and CS menus have similar performance in novice mode. This hypothesis is confirmed by our results and can be explained in the same way as for H1: as they provide the same previsualization and visible path availability features as CS menus, they also share the same performance in novice mode.

H3: Wave menus have similar performance to their "Inverted" variant: the order of the hierarchy does not matter. Our results show that Wave menus are actually faster that their inverted variant. This may seem surprising but can be explained by a larger distance between the "most important" items. An attractive feature of the normal Wave menu is that the deepest submenu of the visible part of the hierarchy is always located in the center of the menu. This makes it possible for users to focus on this zone and to avoid multiple changes of attention, as is the case with the Inverted Wave menu. This fact was also pointed out by several users who complained about the excessive distance between the items they had to read.

Hence, it is somewhat difficult to conclude on the effect of the order of the hierarchy on performance. However, the fact that the Wave and the CS menu share similar performance tends to prove that this order does not really matter. Besides, most users (10/12) said they were not bothered by the reversed hierarchy after sufficient learning time.

H4: There are no significant effects on the number of errors and the number of missed items by menu techniques. We found no significant difference between techniques for the number of missed items. But the number of errors is surprisingly high for Multi-stroke menus, which produces 7 times more errors than other techniques. While observing participants, we noticed that many of them had difficulty clicking in the center zone of the menu to come back to the previous level, and often selected a wrong item. This problem does not occur in expert mode where users never come back to the previous level.

5 Conclusion

Motivated by a criteria-based analysis of marking menus, we have presented Wave menus, a variant of multi-stroke marking menus designed for improving their novice mode. A user experiment focusing on the novice mode showed that compound-stroke marking menus and Wave menus are significantly faster (18%) and more accurate (7 times fewer wrong selections) than multi-stroke menus. Wave menus have the same performance as the novice mode of compound-stroke marking menus and as the expert mode of multi-stroke marking menus. By always displaying the parent menus and allowing interaction on all the displayed items, Wave menus also offer previsualization and path visualization, two features that increase the browsability and the learnability of menus by supporting exploration and menu knowledge acquisition. Even though the parent menus are displayed, Wave menus require less space than compound-stroke marking menus and can be used in "degraded mode" with restricted-space conditions (proximity to screen borders). In our experiment, we used a mouse because we are focusing on user acceptance of marking menus for common use. In a future comparative study, we plan to experiment with Wave menus with a stylus, which is an adequate device for marking interaction and cross-based interaction. Finally in our experimental study we did not consider Zone and Polygon menus. Further research must be carried out to study their novice mode.

References

1. Callahan, J., Hopkins, D., Weiser, M., Shneiderman, B.: An empirical comparison of pie vs. linear menus. In: ACM CHI Conference on Human Factors in Computing Systems, pp. 95–100 (1988)
2. Guimbretière, F., Martin, A., Winograd, T.: Benefits of merging command selection and direct manipulation. ACM Trans. Comput.-Hum. Interact, 460–476 (2005)
3. Howes, A.: A model of the acquisition of menu knowledge by exploration. In: ACM CHI Conference on Human Factors in Computing System, pp. 445-451 (1994)
4. Kieger, J.I.: The depth/breadth tradeoff in the design of menu driven interfaces. International Journal of Man-Machine Studies 20, 201–213 (1984)
5. Linton, F., Joy, D., Schaefer, A.: Building user and expert models by long term observation of application usage. In: Conference on User Modeling, vol. 3. pp. 129–138 (1999)
6. Kurtenbach, G. P.: The Design and Evaluation of Marking Menus. Doctoral Thesis. UMI Order Number: UMI Order No. GAXNN-82896., University of Toronto (1993)
7. Kurtenbach, G., Buxton, W.: User learning and performance with marking menus. In: ACM CHI Conference on Human Factors in Computing Systems, pp. 258–264 (1994)
8. Kurtenbach, G., Buxton, W.: The Limits of Expert Performance using Hiearchical Marking Menus. In: ACM CHI Conference on Human Factors in Computing Systems, pp. 35–42 (1993)
9. Lecolinet, E.: A molecular architecture for creating advanced GUIs. In: ACM UIST Symposium on User interface Software and Technology, pp. 135–144 (2003)
10. Norman, K.: The Psychology of Menu selection: Designing Cognitive Control at the Human/Computer Interface. Ablex Publishing Corporation (1991)
11. Pook, S., Lecolinet, E., Vaysseix, G., Barillot, E.: Control menus: excecution and control in a single interactor. In: ACM CHI Extended Abstracts on Human Factors in Computing Systems, pp. 263–264 (2000)
12. Rekimoto, J., Ishizawa, T., Schwesig, C., Oba, H.: Presense: Interaction techniques for finger sensing input devices. In: ACM UIST Symposium on User interface Software and Technology, pp. 203–212 (2003)
13. Sellen, A., Kurtenbach, G., Buxton, W.: The prevention of mode errors through sensory feedback. Journal of Human Computer Interaction 7(2), 141–146 (1992)
14. Shneiderman, B.: Designing the User Interface: Strategies for Effective Human-Computer Interaction. Addison-Wesley Longman Publishing Co., Reading (1986)
15. Zhao, S., Agrawala, M., Hinckley, K.: Zone and polygon menus: using relative position to increase the breadth of multi-stroke marking menus. In: ACM CHI Conference on Human Factors in Computing Systems, pp. 1077–1086 (2006)
16. Zhao, S., Balakrishnan, R.: Simple vs. compound mark hierarchical marking menus. In: ACM UIST Symposium on User interface Software and Technology, pp. 33–42 (2004)

Nearly-Integral Manipulation of Rotary Widgets

Rodrigo Almeida and Pierre Cubaud

Laboratoire CEDRIC, Conservatoire National des Arts et Métiers
292, Rue Saint-Martin, 75003 Paris, France
{rodrigo.almeida,cubaud}@cnam.fr

Abstract. We present a work in progress that investigates the manipulation of virtual rotary knobs using a device with three degrees-of-freedom. We draw a brief parallel between handling real knobs in professional sound appliances and interacting with desktop rotary widgets. Then, we present an interaction technique aimed to support a natural mapping, to reduce the activation time, and to enhance the fluidity along the gestures that compose this activity.

Keywords: Interaction Techniques, Rotary Widgets, 3DOF Devices.

1 Introduction

We started this study observing the framework of activity of a sound engineer, trying to understand the specificities of rapidly controlling many rotary knobs and linear sliders. This activity is marked by concurrency and strong time constraints: when one mixes sound live, controlling two knobs at the same time, or works in audio post-production, fine-tuning multiple tracks, milliseconds matter. A mixing table has a large number of sound parameters, but for each one of them there is an associated physical control. Our goal is to make from this particular and critical scenario a more general case of study: the interaction with 'rotary widgets'. We see today a whole class of software aimed to support varied audio activities. Many of them present graphic interfaces whose elements mimic the controls of their physical analogue (Fig.1). However, such transposition raises a critical point: the impoverishing of the gestural dimension. The numerous dials and sliders of the professional sound appliances become graphic controls, but their manipulation depends on a single physical device - the mouse. The interest in this loss of expressiveness is not new[6]; between the mixing table and the mouse, there is a continuum with control surfaces and other sophisticated devices. Such solutions may however be expensive, space-consuming, application specific, and, sometimes, unable to space-multiplex the totality of parameters of the target application. The interaction technique presented in this paper tries to improve the control of multiple rotary widgets in a desktop perspective. Therefore, our point of departure is a mouse-like device that senses its orientation. We attack the problem from three different angles: reducing the activation time to manipulate each widget, providing a more coherent mapping between the device's movement and the visual feedback, and adding more fluidity to the transition of gestures that compose the overall activity.

C. Baranauskas et al. (Eds.): INTERACT 2007, LNCS 4662, Part I, pp. 489–492, 2007.

Fig. 1. Left: Screenshot of part of the interface of *Propellerhead's Reason*. Center: The *Wacom 4D Mouse* opened. Right: The 3DOF device with a hemispheric shape.

2   Rotary Widget Interaction Analysis

The handling of rotary widgets in sound software is often addressed through clicking on one of them and moving the mouse. We will analyze this interaction as a fourfold problem: phase one, one moves the cursor to pick a knob; phase two, one activates this knob, e.g., pushing mouse button down; phase three, one assigns a new value to this knob; and phase four, the knob is deactivated, e.g., mouse button up. The object of phase one is extensively studied in target acquisition research and it will not be treated here. The phase two is pragmatically decisive, for it binds the movement made to get to the widget to the one made to rotate it. In phase three, there are two common mappings in order to rotate the widget: moving the mouse vertically or making it circularly. The first relies upon the metaphor of a vertical slider, but the required movement is incompatible with the widget's visual affordance; the second requires an awkward and unusual movement. Finally, in phase four, one deactivates the knob by releasing the mouse button; at this point, the cursor may be quite far from the adjusted knob and the user must drive it to the following one. The scenario described relies upon temporal activation; our system explores instead spatial activation[2]. In such configuration, since the widget is activated and deactivated when the cursor enters and leaves its area, phases two and four need no longer explicit actions. Nonetheless, in order to make it work, the cursor must rest over the widget during its manipulation. This would be impossible using the above techniques because the same transducers that are used to drive the cursor are also used to rotate the widget. A third transducer, enabling the mouse to sense its yaw angle, frees the position transducers and also supports a natural mapping between the user's manipulation and the widget rotation. In an integral task, the manipulation is improved through the parallel control of the multiple DOFs[4]; despite selection and rotation being sequential operations, we believe that the transition from the first to the second may become more fluid if the same gesture driving the cursor to the widget starts rotating it - in a nearly-integral movement.

3   Prototyping the Spatial Activation

The orientation along the vertical axis of a mouse-like device can be sensed through different techniques: two position trackers, magnetic tracker,

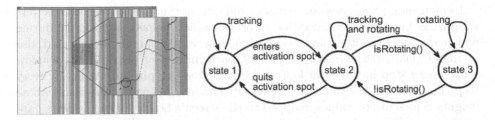

Fig. 2. Left: Screenshot of wire frame knobs interface together with input data visualization. Right: A three-state diagram of our system.

accelerometer, and computer vision[1]. We used the *Wacom 4D mouse*, a cordless device, part of the *Wacom Intuos 4* tablet set, that senses absolute orientation[1]. Its main drawbacks are its dimensions (12.5cm by 7cm) and its asymmetric shape, which constrains the ways in which one can grasp it. Its output data have however three advantages over other prototypes': steadiness, responsiveness, and precision (0.2 degree). We took the mouse's board out of its house and dressed it under a ten centimeters polystyrene hemisphere (Fig.1), making a symmetric smaller shape. We developed a simple six rotary knob graphic interface using *OpenGL*, *XInput*, and the *Linux Wacom* driver. Testing the technique indicated us that it would be difficult to conserve the cursor over the selected knob while rotating the mouse; when one rotates a movable device, it may swing and abandon its initial position. Such oscillations move the cursor, which accidentally leaves the widget's activation spot. Our approach is to detect the intentional rotation and, during it, lock the cursor on the center of the spot. Such detection must, however, take into account the following possibilities: **(1)** the cursor go through a widget, which is not the final target, and, despite its apparently linear trajectory, orientation data vary; **(2)** the user is still rotating a widget when he or she starts driving the cursor to another widget; **(3)** the most recent mouse data packet may not correctly convey the trend of the manipulation.

A three-state model (Fig.2) illustrates how we managed the above cases[3]. In *state 1*, rotating the device has no effect on the system; *state 2* is ambiguous and moving the device rotates the widget but also tracks the cursor; in *state 3*, rotation is clearly intentional, it rotates the widget while the cursor is kept locked on the center of the activated widget. There are three strong conditions to get into and to persist in *state 3*: the variations of the two position data must be below a certain threshold and the variation of the orientation data must be both continuously growing and above another threshold. *State 2* solves **(1)** and **(2)**: the cursor will not be blocked while going through a widget, neither will the concurrent movements of rotating and of leaving the widget be hindered. As to conveying a trend of the movement, we applied the filter used by Oshita in our data[5]. We set the filter's constant to a high value, e.g., 0.8, in order to strongly bias the output values by the most recent data, so that switching from *state 3* to *state 2* be enough responsive.

---

[1] We thank M. Beaudouin-Lafon for informing us about this device.

Implementing this three-state model and setting the system's thresholds were supported by a data visualization interface, which helped us to know during which moments position and orientation data varied simultaneously and also to understand such variations. In Fig.2, each column of pixels in the window represents a step in the event loop and it is pushed one pixel to the left at every step. The x, y and Yaw values are represented by red, green and blue pixels whose heights represent the values, mapped to the screen's height, of the device's data at that step. When the system is in *state 2*, the background color of the column of pixels is switched from white to light gray; dark gray when it is in *state 3*.

4   Conclusion and Future Work

We identified some aspects that could be improved in rotary widget manipulation and proposed a technique based on 3DOF devices to tackle them. The interaction afforded by our exploratory interface indicates the feasibility of such approach. The activity investigated is a special case of sequential manipulation, dubbed nearly-integral, where the first operation requires DOFs that are not those required by the second. The performance of this technique should still be evaluated in comparison with the traditional model, using a smaller better-balanced device[2], and we would like it to be tested by advanced sound edition software users as well. Finally, we would like to explore other potential nearly-integral interaction scenarios, such as picking an item in a long drop-down list, in order to test the validity and the extensibility of this approach.

References

1. Almeida, R., Cubaud, P.: Supporting 3d window manipulation with a yawing mouse. In: Proc. of NordiCHI'06, pp. 477–480. ACM Press, New York (2006)
2. Beaudouin-Lafon, M.: Instrumental interaction: an interaction model for designing post-wimp user interfaces. In: Proc. of CHI '00, pp. 446–453. ACM Press, New York (2000)
3. Buxton, W.: A three-state model of graphical input. In: Proc. of INTERACT '90, pp. 449–456. North-Holland (1990)
4. Jacob, R.J.K., Sibert, L.E.: The perceptual structure of multidimensional input device selection. In: Proc. of CHI '92, pp. 211–218. ACM Press, New York (1992)
5. Oshita, M.: Pen-to-mime: Pen-based interactive control of a human figure. Computers & Graphics 29(6), 931–945 (2005)
6. Patten, J., Recht, B., Ishii, H.: Audiopad: a tag-based interface for musical performance. In: Proc. of NIME '02, pp. 1–6, Singapore, National University of Singapore (2002)

---

[2] For example, the *3Style Mouse* (http://www.cylo.com.au)

CATKey: Customizable and Adaptable Touchscreen Keyboard with Bubble Cursor-Like Visual Feedback

Kentaro Go[1] and Yuki Endo[2]

[1] Interdisciplinary Graduate School of Medicine and Engineering, University of Yamanashi
4-3-11 Takeda, Kofu 400-8511 Japan
go@yamanashi.ac.jp
[2] Yamanashi R&D Center, HAL Laboratory, Inc.
1999-9 Ryuoshinmachi, Kai 400-0111 Japan
endo@golab.org

Abstract. This paper describes our ongoing project related to touchscreen keyboard interfaces. This customizable and adaptable touchscreen keyboard with bubble cursor-like visual feedback, CATKey, is a software keyboard for touchscreens that is designed to provide adaptable and customizable functions. We discuss its concept, prototype, and tentative evaluation.

Keywords: adaptation, bubble cursor, customization, touchscreen keyboard.

1 Introduction

Touchscreen interfaces have been attracting attention in recent years because their functionality and usability for mobile phones and information appliances have become better known. Recently, they are used as mobile phone interfaces for iPhone by Apple, KE850 by LG, and FOMA D800iDS by Mitsubishi. They are used also in public-use terminals including automated teller machines, ticket machines, and information kiosks. Touchscreen keyboards are a fundamental application for touchscreen interfaces and are used in several application areas. The key arrangement for touchscreen keyboards typically uses the standard Qwerty arrangement because users can transfer their skills and experience gained using common hardware keyboards [5]. Previous studies have shown that the text entry rate for a touchscreen keyboard is considerably slower than that for hardware Qwerty keyboard, even for expert typists [6, 7].

This paper reports our ongoing efforts at designing a Customizable and Adaptable Touchscreen Keyboard with bubble cursor-like visual feedback (CATKey). We are particularly interested in involving a wide range of user classes by improving perceived usability without decreasing the text entry rate. Many touchscreen systems are targeted at the public-use market. For that reason, users' skills and experiences are varied. Users would refuse to use them if the text entry method were to provide low perceived usability.

C. Baranauskas et al. (Eds.): INTERACT 2007, LNCS 4662, Part I, pp. 493–496, 2007.

2 Touchscreen Keyboard Design

Text entry tasks with touchscreen keyboards are cumbersome because (1) the user cannot touch, feel, or distinguish the positions of the keys displayed on the screen; and (2) it is difficult to feel the visual and tactile feedback from the keys, especially with conventional touchscreen devices[1]. However, touchscreen keyboards have practical advantages because (1) they can be designed as customizable and adaptable keyboards; and (2) they can be designed to display the visual feedback of and on the keys.

Our approach to designing touchscreen keyboards is to address the weak points using customizable and adaptable functions and effective visual feedback to improve their perceived usability.

2.1 Customizable Key Layout

Figure 1 shows an overview of our keyboard design. The left panel is the initial layout of keys. Each key has a maximum area. Consequently, the overall key area forms a Voronoi diagram. The right panel presents a key layout customized by a user, which is done in the customization mode of CATKey. The customized key area also forms a Voronoi diagram.

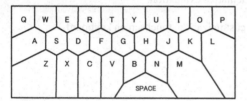

Fig. 1. Overview of CATKey: customizable and adaptable touchscreen keyboard with bubble cursor-like visual feedback. Left: the initial layout of keys. Right: a key layout customized by the user.

2.2 Adaptable Keys

We designed an adaptable function similar to [3]. In the adaptive mode of CATKey, the key centroid is moved to the centroid of recorded keystroke points in each key (Fig. 2). The keystroke coordinates are recorded for the period of the pre-specified number of keystrokes.

Fig. 2. The key adaptation mechanism of CATKey. Black point: the original centroid. X-mark: keystroke points. White circle: the centroid of the keystroke points and the weighted original centroid. Dotted line recalculated key area.

2.3 Visual Feedback

Figure 3 depicts the design of visual feedback in CATKey. The left panel

---

[1] Although some studies of tactile displays (tactile VDTs) have emerged [1], most touchscreen display products do not have tactile feedback.

shows an actual view of CATKey. We assigned a round key area to communicate the touched location to the user. The yellow f and j keys show the home positions of index fingers. The presence of the line and color of keys can be modified using the parameter-setting dialogue. The right panel shows the bubble cursor-like visual feedback [2]. The bubble-shape cursor in red adjusts dynamically to the closest key and provides the sensation of an offset cursor [8].

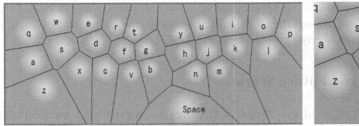 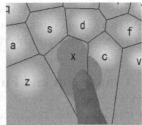

Fig. 3. Design of visual feedback in CATKey. Left: the overview of CATKey with lines and color circles. Right: bubble cursor-like visual feedback.

3 Evaluation

We evaluated the usability of CATKey based on the ISO 9241-4 [4]. We measured the entry speed and error rate using a hardware Qwerty keyboard, a software Qwerty keyboard, and CATKey, and assessed the comfort; finally, we conducted a debriefing interview.

Ten college students (two female and eight male) participated in the evaluation. They all use a hardware Qwerty keyboard regularly, but seldom use a touchscreen keyboard for their daily activities.

A CAD Center NEXTRAX 15 touchscreen computer is used. It has a 15-inch TFT monitor with 1024 × 768-pixel resolution. CATKey is implemented using C# of Microsoft Corporation's Visual Studio.Net 2003. Figure 4 shows a user typing with NEXTRAX 15, which has 20 degree mounting angle. For hardware keyboards, Dell Computer Corporation's standard keyboard was used. The sentences were chosen randomly from among pangrams such as "a quick brown

Fig. 4. Experimental setting (NEXTRAX 15)

fox jumps over the lazy dog," "how quickly daft jumping zebras vex," and "pack my box with five dozen liquor jugs."

Each experimental session included ten sentences for the typing task. The participant performed two practice sessions, then completed four sessions for measurement. The presentation order of keyboard type was counterbalanced.

Results indicate that the respective mean entry speeds of the hardware Qwerty keyboard, software Qwerty keyboard, and CATKey are 33.5, 23.8, and 22.8 wpm. A significant difference exists among the keyboards ($F(2, 18) = 7.5$, $p<0.05$); but no significant difference is apparent between the levels of the software Qwerty keyboard and CATKey. Similarly, the mean error rate of the hardware Qwerty keyboard, software Qwerty keyboard, and CATKey are respectively 3.4, 5.9, and 6.8%. A significant difference exists among the keyboards ($F(2, 18) = 6.3$ ($p<0.05$)); but no significant difference was found between the levels of software Qwerty keyboard and CATKey. In addition, no significant difference exists on the assessment of comfort between the software Qwerty keyboard and CATKey.

4   Conclusion and Future Work

In this paper, we described the design of CATKey: a customizable and adaptable touchscreen keyboard with the bubble cursor-like visual feedback. Early evaluation showed that the mean entry speed and mean input error rate of CATKey have no statistical difference from that of a standard software Qwerty keyboard. During the debriefing interview, however, the participants expressed their preference for the design and usability of CATKey. We will further investigate the usability of CATKey and explore various key arrangements such as the Metropolis keyboard [9].

References

1. Benali-Khoudja, M., Hafez, M., Alexandre, J.M., Kheddar, A.: Tactile Interfaces: A State-of-the-art Survey. In: Proc. ISR, pp. 721–726 (2004)
2. Grossman, T., Balakrishnan, R.: The Bubble Cursor: Enhancing target acquisition by dynamic resizing of the cursor's activation area. In: Proc. CHI 2005, pp. 281–290 (2005)
3. Himberg, J., Hakkila, J., Kangas, P., Mantyjarvi, J.: On-line personalization of a touch screen based keyboard. In: Proc. IUI 2003, pp. 77–84 (2003)
4. ISO9241-4. Ergonomic requirements for office work with visual display terminals (VDTs), Part 4: Keyboard requirements (1998)
5. MacKenzie, I.S., Zhang, S.X., Soukoreff, R.W.: Text entry using soft keyboards. BIT 18, 235–244 (1995)
6. Shneiderman, B.: Touch Screens Now Offer Compelling Uses. IEEE Software, 93–94 (March 1991)
7. Sears, A., Revis, D., Swatski, J., Crittenden, R., Shneiderman, B.: Investigating touchscreen typing: The effect of keyboard size on typing speed. BIT 12(1), 17–22 (1993)
8. Sears, A., Shneiderman, B.: High-precision touchscreens: design strategies and comparisons with a mouse. Intl. J. of Man-Machine Studies 34(4), 593–613 (1991)
9. Zhai, S., Hunter, M., Smith, B.A.: The Metropolis Keyboard: An Exploration of Quantitative Techniques for Virtual Keyboard Design. In: Proc. UIST 2000, pp. 119–128 (2000)

A Conceptual Framework for the Design and Evaluation of Affective Usability in Educational Geosimulation Systems

Elizabeth Furtado[1], Vasco Furtado[2], and Eurico Vasconcelos[3]

[1] University of Fortaleza and of State of Ceara
[2] University of Fortaleza, Mestrado em Informática aplicada
[3] Pontifica Universidade Católica do Rio de Janeiro, Departamento de Informática
Av. Washington Soares 1521, Edson Queiroz, Fortaleza, CE, Brazil
elizabet@unifor.br, vasco@unifor.br, jfilho@inf.puc-rio.br

Abstract. In this article we propose a conceptual framework for associating the concepts of usability, computer education and affective quality. We analyze the interaction student-teacher under the light of learning strategies used in educational geosimulators for defining the main emotional constructs that are involved in this process. We elaborate this initial analysis by identifying which interactive objects should be associated with the identified emotional constructs. We associate these objects with an architecture that defines the basics components of an educational geosimulation system as well as the learning strategies used in this context. We illustrate the utility of the framework with an evaluation of an education geosimulator for police training as well as an evaluation of the student's satisfaction during the interaction in different scenarios.

Keywords: Affective emotional quality, Educational System Evaluation.

1 Introduction

Intelligent Tutoring Systems (ITS) have been studied since the 1970s and an increasing variety of tools have emerged since then, leveraging diverse techniques from different areas of computer science and particularly from Artificial Intelligence. Educational agent-based simulation systems are one of these, in which intelligent agents support the interaction between the simulation model and the user [10]. One of the recent advances in these systems was the combined use of Geographical Information Systems (GIS) with multiagents for simulation of social or urban environments, which characterizes geosimulation [1]. With the computational development of GIS, bringing precision and realism to simulation [25], educational tools are also benefited with richer human-computer interaction strategies.

Despite the aforementioned advances, few studies have paid attention to the usability aspects of the educational systems that involve complex phenomena in urban centers, where the interaction with GIS is intense. These aspects must be taken into account in the systems design phase and can also be useful for evaluating the final quality of the User Interfaces (UIs). Moreover the approaches that focus on the

C. Baranauskas et al. (Eds.): INTERACT 2007, LNCS 4662, Part I, pp. 497–510, 2007.

usability of educational systems concern only the effectiveness of the user-system interaction (the number of successful task completions) and the efficiency (the time required to complete an interactive task) [16].

In this article we follow a multidisciplinary approach by proposing a conceptual framework for associating the concepts of usability, computer education and affective quality. Our work goes beyond the traditional view of usability by considering the affective dimension of the UI—a topic that has gained ground in recent HCI research. We claim that the affective aspect (such as users' feeling states and their involvement with the content) is particularly relevant in the context of educational systems, since learning depends strongly on how synergetic the relationship is between teacher and student. The framework construction is done in two steps. First, we analyze the interaction student-teacher under the light of learning strategies used in educational geosimulators for defining the main emotional constructs that are involved in this process. From this initial analysis we evolve the framework by identifying which interactive instruments should be associated with the identified emotional constructs.

We have chosen to associate the affective usability aspects with an architecture proposed in [7] that defines the basic components of an educational geosimulation system as well as the learning strategies used in this context. We then provide designers with orientation of how to take these aspects into account already in the interaction design phase of these systems. Moreover, we consider that our framework is also appropriate to evaluate the users' satisfaction that refers to the affective quality they have about the system in interaction. In the final part of the paper we present how the conceptual framework can be used to evaluate an already deployed system for training police officers. Finally, we evaluate the user's satisfaction using this system during the realization of different scenarios of a training process.

2 Affective Quality in Interactive Systems: Design and Evaluation Issues

HCI has often attracted considerable attention from academic communities by integrating these concepts into an educational system development process in order to obtain more usable systems. Traditionally, the usability of a developed system has been evaluated to assure both its effectiveness (such as the number of successful task completions) and efficiency (such as the time required to complete an interactive task). Recently, these assumptions have been revisited and broadened to embed the concepts of the affective quality theories. Affective quality is related to the user's emotional responses (such as the affect, activity and attitude of the users) in regards to the system that they are experiencing [3]. For instance, a learning system may elicit enjoyment (e.g. pleasure). Then, the users may continue using it for a long time and become emotionally absorbed (e.g. engagement by a content that matches with their objects of interest, preferences and restrictions). Finally, the users may decide that they like a specific learning task, which leads to the formation of an attitude (e.g., a summary evaluation of an experience supported by explanations).

In [19], the author investigates the role of emotions in the design and evaluation of a UI for any interactive product in three levels of the human brain mechanism: on the visceral level, the emotional reactions are associated to the nature of the UI (aesthetics and beauty); on the behavioral level, the emotional reactions are associated to the use of the UI (effectiveness, efficiency and errors). On this level, Norman situates the traditional usability notion; and on the reflective level, the emotional reactions refer to the meaning of the UI (rationalization and intellectualization of a product). Table 1 depicts the relation existing among the usability and affective quality concepts in which must be both considered when evaluating the users' satisfaction (such as their subjective perceived ease of use) of learning systems.

Table 1. HCI concepts from usability engineering and affective disciplines

USABILITY	AFFECTIVE QUALITY
Focus on interactive task design	Focus on emotional design, captology, funology
Concepts of usability: task, effectiveness, efficiency and errors	Concepts of affective quality: feeling states as pleasure in interactive experiences
Activity of users based on task execution, their preferences and restrictions	Activity of users based on free exploration, context and participation.
Attitude of the users supported by task completion and representation of interactive objects associated to the tasks	Attitude of the users supported by assistances through persuasive and user difficult strategies

The emphasis on both of these concepts entails a complete evaluation of the users' satisfaction as for: 1) their ability to learn about the system and to use it in a creative way. This ability that the users must have is the direct reflex of their comprehension of the UI, specifically, of the representations of its interactive objects [22]. A possible question to pose to the users is the following: How many of the interactive objects representations were not associated with your intention of use? and; 2) their emotional responses (feeling states, trust, engagement) with the system. Some evaluation methods have included the following questions in users' satisfaction tests: how fun was the user interface? How interesting was the content presented? How persuasive was the user interface? It is worthy mentioning that this broader notion of usability requires a user-centered design process, in which users must be analyzed by the designers in order to build better interactive objects (as widgets) and to understand the emotional effects that Interactive Systems (ISs) will have on users [4].

3 Educational Geosimulation Systems

Simulation aims to represent one phenomenon via another. In educational terms, simulation is important because it allows learning through the possibility of doing [21]. On the other hand, Social or urban environments are dynamic, non-linear, and made of a great number of interacting entities, characterizing a complex system. The use of Multiagent System to simulate social environments has become broadly used [2] [13].

Recently [8] brought together the components of what they consider relevant for the development of urban activities training by means of simulation systems and proposed the Educational Geosimulation Architecture (EGA). EGA encompasses the basics components of an educational geosimulation system serving as a basis to developers of this type of system. EGA follows a traditional architecture of an ITS in which three main models are distinguished: the student model, the teacher model and the domain model. However, some particular aspects are present in EGA. Geosimulators are used as a tool of the teacher model because the topic of study is dynamic and the practice in reality involves high risks and costs. The use of a GIS allows for the appropriate representation of the simulation environment (domain model). The multiagent simulation approach is followed because it provides an appropriate computational representation of independent entities that interrelate within the same environment. In this educational context, a multiagent simulation platform contains two types of agents: domain agents, that represent the domain model and/or student model and pedagogical agents representing the teacher model. Last but not least important, there are the user interfaces that are the communication channel between the system and the student. Figure 1 depicts the previously mentioned EGAs main components and indicates the three basic strategies of learning that it entails. The more traditional strategy is learning by instruction that is obtained from the material (information, examples, concepts) provided by the teacher. By using the simulation the student learns by doing. The assistances provided by the teacher to help the better understanding of the phenomena underlying the simulation leads to a process of learning by reflection.

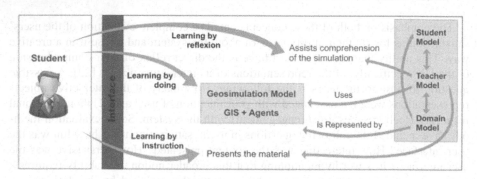

Fig. 1. Interaction among the Educational Geosimulation Architecture Components

4   Affective Usability Aspects in Educational Geosimulation Systems

We draw from this work the focus on some HCI concepts describing a multidisciplinary strategy of generating a conceptual framework from education, user interaction and affective quality theories (see Table 2). From the EGAs learning strategies, we analyzed the possible emotional responses of affect, activity and attitude that the students can have in the interaction process with the educational system. We considered, for instance, that the affect (such as feeling states) is a neurophysical state that is consciously accessible as a simple, non-reflective feeling [26]. This is the reason we associated it to the learning by instruction strategy. In scenarios of this type, the student is unconsciously accepting the instruction as being the truth (indicating a high level of trust in the teacher, or even of submission). The simulation and explanation strategies, in turn, raise emotional responses related to the behavioral (activity) and reflective (attitude) levels of a person, respectively. Then we associate affective usability design aspects that might elicit positive emotional responses from the students. For instance, an instruction-based system can be designed with sophisticated technological resources (as tangible interfaces), that positively influence users' experience on an emotional level (as having fun) when interacting with it. Note that a same system can elicit a combination of emotions. For instance, a system can be viscerally attractive through its UI and elicit reflection through the way explanation is displayed.

Table 2. Affective usability aspects in educational geosimulation systems

Learning Strategies	Emotional Responses	Affective Usability Design Aspects
Learning by instruction	*Affect* Feeling states (motivated, enthusiastic, calm) for using a system that is beautiful, attractive and with less constraining interaction; Pleasure in having fun.	Representation of interactive tasks through interactive agents; Manipulation and animation of interactive objects. Look, sound and feel dominate.
Learning by doing (simulation)	*Activity* Engagement in figuring simulations out (perceived ease of use, no feeling of risk and failure); Involvement in understanding the simulation content; Trust	Support to trials through historic of simulations; Contextual and participatory simulations
Learning by reflection (Thinking through assistances)	*Attitude* After a superficial involvement, a sense of true commitment in understanding the simulation context, that can bring to the formation of attitude.	Persuasive techniques and difficult-regulation strategies for providing adaptive, helpful, and structured assistances.

The aspects illustrated in Table 2 are admittedly incomplete: they are meant only to spawn new ways of thinking about the users' satisfaction with these systems by not only focusing on the systems' efficiency. The aspects do not address, for instance, characteristics of context in which the interaction should take place. They refer more to the way in which the interactive objects that represent the learning strategies should be perceived by the users when manipulating, creating, visualizing or controlling these objects in their learning experiences. Our goal is to provide design concerns elucidated from theoretical literature when appropriate, which can help professionals both to design and to evaluate these kind of educational systems. Specifically, we intend to show how attention paid to users' emotional responses can be used as a basis for developing and evaluating these systems in order to elicit positive responses from students. The affective usability design aspects were classified into three groups as follows.

4.1 Eliciting Emotional Responses Through the Representation of the Interactive Elements

Users expect to have not only appropriate functionality and usability, but pleasure ("benefits") in using the UI as well [12]. For this reason, many high-tech design solutions are being defined as patterns, in order to be reused in other situations. Interaction Patterns represent best design solutions for known interaction problems [23]. As the interactive agent notion is usually used in educational systems, it can be modeled as an interaction pattern and be characterized by having an interactive representation. For instance, an agent can be of the anthropomorphic agent pattern type, when realized through synthetic characters in the UI of affective systems. The description of a pattern should include the possible constraints involved in the interaction. For instance the designer should know that anthropomorphic effects can cause interaction problems when considering the fact the user can expect the system to be intelligent and cognitively potent. This expectation may lead to frustration in the user when the system can not meet these expectations [11].

In a GIS, the graphical representation presented to the user through the UI is the result of interactive objects which represent agents, users' action and/or context of study. Some aspects in the UIs of the GIS can contribute to enhance the users' satisfaction for different reasons, in particular:

- Direct Manipulation. Users need to have complete control over the system, it can be hard to accept characters in the interface that run outside their control. Users got irritated and frustrated when they could not figure it out [11]. It is important to provide users with support for free exploration when manipulating a map. The idea is to allow, for instance, the user to query the object about its features or even to control its behavior in a certain situation;
- Animation: animation through several effects (such as color changes, panning, and dynamic links) can make a UI more memorable and vivid, and more enjoyable to use, leading users to have fun. In agent-based systems, agents can be designed to navigate (virtual) spaces with movement patterns to simulating urban population as collectives of individuals with associated behaviors and traits.

We cannot forget the studies coming from other fields (such as semiotic, ergonomic, communication), related to different aspects that can bring aesthetic and beauty to the system, and consequently pleasure to the users [26]. In semiotic design; studies are about the choice of significant symbols that are an abstraction of the object of the real world and the definition of how these symbols are used during the communication of the users with the system [22]. In communicational, ergonomic and graphical design, studies are in many styles in a variety of colors in order for designers to create the artistic UI design.

4.2 Eliciting the Emotional Responses in Simulation Experiences

In a simulation process, the possible users' emotional responses can be elicited from:

- Their engagement in figuring simulations out. The design aspect refers to the support an educational system gives to trials through historic of simulations, free exploration, and treatment of errors. For instance, if the users can make trials as many times as they want, with no feeling of risk and failure, then they will have more intentions to do so. The number of times the users figured simulations out and the time spent in this process are important criteria to measure their engagement in interactive simulation experiences.

- Their involvement in understanding the simulation content (as the results, which can be boring/interesting). The design aspects refer to the simulation content's characteristics, which can be contextual. It means that the simulation takes place on a map that represents the context of the displayed content (the agents). In learning theories, it is known that users are more involved with the content when it represents objects of their own interest. For instance, if real world scale map is used, the users will be more involved in the simulation context. Such closeness with their real object makes the UI more comprehensible to the user. Another important factor of HCI to elicit pleasure of users in learning experiences is to allow them participating as active subject in the simulation process [18].

4.3 Eliciting the Emotional Responses in Assistance Experiences

Like teachers, educational systems can provide students with different modalities of assistances, such as: a) Explanation, which refers to the act or process of explaining something; b) Hint, which is a brief or indirect suggestion, a tip; and c) tutorial, this refers to instructions describing how the users can proceed at a certain moment.

Like teachers, these systems should motivate students to try out one or more assistances. Some systems' characteristics are important to encourage users in this decision moment (of looking for assistance or not) such as: trust and credibility in assistances to obtain. Several user studies show that transparency is a key factor to trusting learning systems. In [17], some explaining techniques show users the provenance of the explanations. Having decided to get help, the users start looking for interesting assistances around the screens by visiting pages, navigating among menu items, reading the main information, and so on. In this superficial involvement, persuasive interactive techniques can influence users to stay active and loyal in assistance and entail in a profound reflective process. It is expected that the understanding of the obtained assistance makes users change their attitudes.

Persuasive technologies, studied in the area of Captology, can interactively manipulate what people think and do. Examples of these technologies are the following: persuading through customization, simplifying and guided persuasion [6]. This same author gives an example that customized explanation provides users with tailored information to achieve a persuasive result. To encourage users to take action against polluting organizations, a customized graphical explanation could be given through a map when users enter their zip code. The map can enable users to view the location of pollution sources relative to where they live, work, or attend school. Tailored information is more effective than generic information in changing users' attitudes and behaviors. Hint is a kind of simplifying persuasive technique, because users know they will find brief help. Tutorial is a guided persuasion technique, and it provides opportunities to persuade users along the way. Another way to motivate students to get the assistances refers to providing them with appropriate levels of assistance regardless of students' skill. Many works refer to the difficulties in dealing with the conflicting goals of expanding system functionality (as more elaborated assistances) for expert users while simultaneously keeping the system easy to use for novice users. In [14], Larson specified difficult-regulation strategies which can be useful in computer games, such as: a) user skill selection, when the users have the power to choose what level of game play they want; and b) explicit and implicit stage progression: in implicit staging, game play becomes more difficult the longer the users play; in explicit staging, when the users complete a stage the game may stop to congratulate them, and the users start the next stage. In this educational context, explicit assistances can also be given in function of the historic of simulations.

5   Analyzing the Student's Satisfaction in Learning Experiences

In this section, we describe an educational geosimulator that follows EGA architecture and show how the framework previously define can be used to evaluate the users' satisfaction from an emotional perspective while using this system.

5.1   Case Study: The ExpertCop System

In brief, the ExpertCop system supports learning by means of simulation of phenomena that provoke crime in an urban area. Initially the student provides the system with a police resource allocation plan. Then the system simulates crime for a predefined period. The goal is to lead the students to understand the consequences of their allocation as well as understand the cause-and-effect relations. In ExpertCop, the simulations occur in a learning environment and along with graphical visualizations that aid the users' learning. The domain agents are the police team, the criminals and the targets (notable points). Criminals are the most important agents in the simulation process. Their behavior is based on a rule base which orients them to look for targets and to commit crimes (see [8] for a detailed description). The Pedagogical Agent (PA) represents the teacher model and aims at helping the users to understand the phenomena represented by the simulation.

The interaction with the domain agents is done at two moments. First, before the simulation, the user must allocate the police in the areas to be patrolled and available on the geoprocessed map. Figure 2 shows the interface for this allocation process and describes its main functionalities. Crimes are represented on the map as points—in red if the crime is committed and in green if it is not. The goal of the user is to provide a good allocation, which prevents the occurrence of crimes to the greatest extent. Second, during the simulation the movement of the police patrol routes is shown. The user can follow the simulation process in the simulation interface. At the end of the simulation process, the user accesses the system's pedagogical tools. Upon each new allocation performed, the system can comparatively evaluate the simulated moments, showing the user whether the modification brought a better effect to the crime rate or not. After the simulation, interaction is possible via queries to crimes that occurred. It is up to the PA to answer these queries.

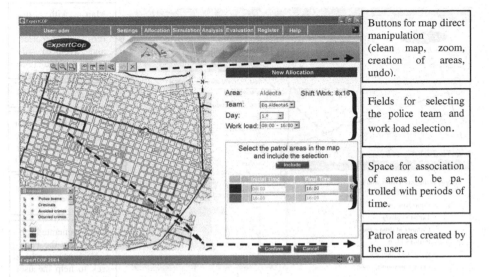

Fig. 2. ExpertCop's police allocation interface

With relation to the interaction with the PA, it is supposed that the PA elicits users' pleasure in learning experiences and a formation of attitude by providing them with different assistances. The PA uses two distinct forms to explain the events of the system, the explanation at a micro-level and at a macro-level. At a micro-level, to explain the simulation events (crimes), the system uses a tree of proofs describing the steps of reasoning of the criminal agent responsible for the event. This tree is generated from the process of the agent's decision making. The agent's evaluation of a crime is represented by a set of production rules. At a macro-level, for the explanation of the system's emerging behavior, the PA tries to identify patterns of the crimes generated in the simulation (see [7] for details of how this is done). The concepts learned by the system are displayed to the user as hints of the following type: "Did you realize that *crime*: theft, *victim*: vehicle, *week day*: Saturday, *period*: night, *local*: residential street, *neighborhood*: Aldeota Beach frequently occur together?" Having this kind of information, the user can reflect on changes in the allocation, aiming to avoid this situation. Figure 3 shows the functionalit ies for visualization.

5.2 Analyzing the Emotional Aspect of the Students Using ExpertCop

ExpertCop was used to support a course at the Ministry of Justice and the National Secretariat of Public Safety. ExpertCop was intended to help police officers reflect on the forms of treatment and analysis of information and how these influence the understanding of crime. The audience was made up of thirty professionals in the area of public safety: civil police officers, chiefs of police, and military police (which are the majority). A quantitative analysis of the effectiveness of ExpertCop in the learning process is discussed in [8]. In this paper, we will concentrate on the description of an empirical qualitative analysis of the users' satisfaction, in the light of the aforementioned concepts.

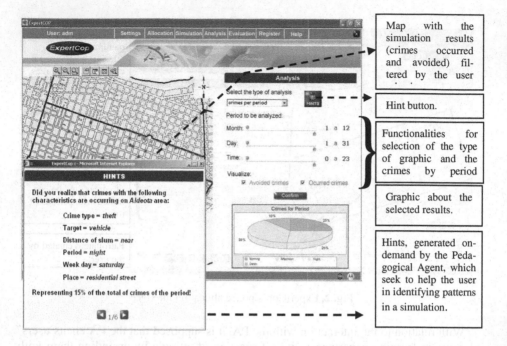

Map with the simulation results (crimes occurred and avoided) filtered by the user

Hint button.

Functionalities for selection of the type of graphic and the crimes by period

Graphic about the selected results.

Hints, generated on-demand by the Pedagogical Agent, which seek to help the user in identifying patterns in a simulation.

Fig. 3. Visualization of the Assistances

The testing session was composed by the following scenarios of the training process: familiarization, resource allocation, simulation and evaluation of simulation results. It took place from 30 to 40 minutes. Initially, students made use of the tool in an illustrative simulation to familiarize themselves with the functionalities. In the resource allocation scenario, training was carried out by a set of at least two simulations in city areas. In the first simulation, the students had to create and configure a certain number of teams (according to the size of the area), allocate them on the map, and activate the simulation. At the end of the first simulation we asked the students to identify, according to their beliefs, factors (concepts) that influenced the occurrence of the crimes. They did so by observing the map of the crimes that occurred and those that were avoided. They focused on geographical and/or visual factors that directly effect the crime rates. After collecting the students' concepts, we allowed them to use the pedagogical support of the system (hints, explanations and evaluations). After this moment, the collection of factors influencing the crimes was carried out again. In the subsequent simulation, we repeated the same area to serve as a comparison with the initial simulation already completed, and allowed them to make their allocations and use the pedagogical support of the tool according to their needs. At the end of the process we also apply a questionnaire asking about how fun the system was and how difficult to learn its use was. We participated of the testing session as experimenters. A discussion about the users' emotional responses evoked by the system is done as follows.

Arousal. The first reaction of the most part of the users (in case the students) during the initial contact with the system was of complete pleasure. Some of them asked to have a license because they wanted to use it as a tool of decision-making support. This emotional response of the users is associated to the Wow factor of the visceral level: *wow, I like it. I want it* [19]. The aesthetic aspect of the interface with interactive object and colors well chosen, and the fun aspect of the game-like structure are potential responsible for this.

Pleasure of fun vs. quality of learning. Being fun is particularly delicate in game-based ITS systems. Sometimes the system interface is so fun that it leads the user to game with the system without any intention of learning the process behind the game. It is important, then, to design the ITS to be resistant to the game factor, i.e. the user obtains good scores in the game by just guessing. Moreover, the game aspect cannot bypass the main goal which is learning from the use of the system. The difficulty of having good performance (in terms of crime rate reduction) just guessing is a particular aspect of ExpertCop and was analyzed in detail in [8]. Moreover, the sequence of the scenarios that consists of a phase of analysis of the simulation results is also an important factor because it leads the user trying to understand the simulation model.

Pleasure of using. Several graphical characteristics elicit from the users good feelings leading them to use comfortably the system. Assistances are provided in several ways, and are associated with the agents allocated on the map. One of these assistances is the possibility of visualization on map of notable points such as squares, gas stations, drugstores, schools, etc. Doing so, the user can allocate the police agents by directly drawing on the map the routes that must be followed by these agents while taking into account the hot spots to be monitored. Even the task of police allocation, that our observations and answers of the questionnaire have captured as being the most difficult to do in the system, was considered agreeable to do. Our analysis is that the direct manipulation of the agents representing the police officer in the map is the main factor that influenced this feeling.

Involvement. All the users found the results of the simulation very interesting, in particular, six users who lived in the same city represented in the GIS. They were eager to plunge into allocation then anxious to see the results. They likely took far longer than the others for performing the allocation process. These emotional responses reflected on an emotional involvement of the users with the content. We think it was provoked by the contextual identification aspect of the users with their area of work. Moreover, the simulations can be restarted as many times as the student wants. The process is friendly and a historic of simulation results can be accessed allowing the users to follow their performance.

Sense of persuasion. Users reacted most positively to the hint explanation (showing crime patterns) that made them reflect on their allocation, commenting that they understood why some crimes have not been avoided. Remember that the hints are shown to the users as a pop up window and that they can concomitantly verify their validity while visualizing the patterns in the map. The idea herein contained is to influence the users passing through the UI (in this case, through the hint button) messages that could affect the users' intentions of use (in other words, to motivate them to learn by exploring the assistances). This is a good example of how the interface, by simultaneously contemplating distinct modalities, has enhanced the way information was provided to the users and consequently persuading them.

Trust. In the first simulation users trusted in the system accuracy but not in its results. They trusted more in the system, when the explanation of the occurrence of the events was given. They could interpret the model behind the simulations. A missing point that would add credibility to the system is a summary about the origin of the information used in the simulation and makes it available in the help option in the main menu of the tool.

Formation of attitude. As for the users' attitude to the system, it is supported by explanations about the criminals' behavior for a certain scenario of preventive police that they defined. Crimes are shown on the map in terms of red dots. The user can click on these dots emulating a query of the type "why have you committed this particular crime?" Using concepts familiar to the users' discourse domain, rule-based explanation emulates the criminal's answers to the users' query. This interactivity process reinforces the users' attitude towards the system because of its contextual feature and persuasiveness.

Participation and Collaboration. During the iterative process of allocation-simulation-visualization of results, users applied some spontaneous collaborative practices (such as: users wanted to make comparisons among their simulation results and/or to comment about their allocation proposals) to identify similar strategies among themselves. They usually collaborated with the colleagues beside them and/or with a user on another computer. The possibility to accompany their evolution in the simulations by means of bar graphs helped this participation process. However, we consider that the lack of tools for collaboration is a shortcoming because would allow collaborative problem solving enriching the learning and the user involvement. In addition, a participatory simulation in which the student participates of the simulation process (reallocation police routes, for instance) would bring more realism to the system as well as more engagement of the student.

6 Related Works

There are some works that make the relation between affect and usability in several domains and in different phases of a system life-cycle. In the interaction design phase, Höök [141] suggests first understanding the users' emotional states with experiences while using the technology in the early development phases of a system when understanding their needs. In the evaluation phase, De Angeli and her colleagues [5] showed that usability and aesthetic quality criteria influence users' preferences in relation to two different interface styles (traditional menu-based and interactive animated metaphors). As we, Chorianopoulos & Spinellis [3] elaborated a conceptual framework based on Norman's affect model. This framework was used to evaluate interactive applications for Digital Television and presents a clear separation among the UI and the TV content. In this work we followed a different approach considering the system as a whole. As we can not measure a system independently, we preferred to associate these concepts by integrating them to the generic learning strategies. Moreover Zhang & Li [26] made references to several works that associate design features to affective constructs in different domains, but there was not any mention to works in the educational domain. In learning systems, the association of these concepts is still an open issue. In [20], an affective model is included in tutorial system architecture. Their idea is to identify the students' emotional status for providing adaptive assistances. Affective relations of power and identity among students have been explored in collaborative virtual learning systems, but there is no relation between these concepts and the usability in these systems [16]. Several works in games and entertainment [9] [15] use simulation with an educational propose. Game simulators have a different pedagogical strategy, because they focus on the results of the simulation emphasizing only the fun aspect of the interface. In learning systems the most important aspect is the process itself, and it should also include formation of attitude.

7 Conclusion

We identified several characteristics in the interactive learning processes that raise students' emotional responses according to the Norman's affect model. Then we proposed a conceptual framework for affective usability that should be considered in a user-centered design and/or in the evaluation of educational geosimulation systems. As a case study and with the goal to illustrate how the framework can be used, we evaluated an educational system deployed for the area of law enforcement by analyzing the users' satisfaction regarding their emotional responses in interactive learning situations. For this purpose, training courses with police officers interacting with the system were observed and three different scenarios were taken into account to discuss the results. The perceived behavior of students in ExpertCop revealed the association of their satisfaction in using the system with the HCI concepts described in our framework. We also describe the role that the interfaces played in the system to evoke positive emotional responses from the students, namely the capability to involve them with the content, the feeling of fun, arousal, etc. Such a description also contributes to designers who are going to create new software because it exemplifies how the aspects considered in the framework were used. An important point for future research consists of investigating how important the difference between traditional learning simulation and educational geosimulation is. Our feeling, in which requires validation, is that needs to be validated by comparison is that geosimulation provokes more emotions due to the proximity of reality aspect that is obtained from map using.

Acknowledgement. The first author thanks CAPES grant 2765055 for the financial support.

References

1. Benenson, I., Torrens, P.M.: Geosimulation: object-based modeling of urban phenomena. Computers, Environment and Urban Systems. Forthcoming (2004)
2. Billari, C.F., Prskawetz, A.: Agent-Based Computational Demography: Using Simulation to Improve Our Understanding of Demographic Behaviour. Phisica-Verlag, Germany (2003)
3. Chorianopoulos, K., Spinellis, D.: user Interface Evaluation of interactive TV: a media studies perspective. Univ. Access Inf Soc. 5, 209–218 (2006)
4. Cooper, Reimann: The Essentials of Interaction Design. Wiley, Chichester (2003)

5. De Angeli, A., Sutcliffe, A., Hartman, J.: Interaction, Usability and Aesthetics: What influences users' preferences? DIS (2006)
6. Fogg, B.J.: Persuasive Technology. Morgan Kaufmann, San Francisco (2003)
7. Vasconcelos, E., Furtado, V.: Educational Geosimulation. In: Brasileiro, F., Mendes, M. (eds.) Advances in Computer-Supported Learning, Idea Group (2006)
8. Furtado, V., Vasconcelos, E.: Geosimulation in education: a system for teaching police resource allocation. Intl. Journal of Artificial Intelligence in Education 17 (2007)
9. Galvão, J.R., Martins, P.G., Gomes, M.R.: Modeling Reality with Simulation Games for a Cooperative Learning. In: Winter Simulation Conference, pp. 1692–1698. Orlando, FL (2000)
10. Gibbons, A.S., Lawless, K.A., Anderson, T.A., Duffin, J.: The web and model-centered instruction. In: Khan, B.H. (ed.) Web-based training, pp. 137–146 (2001)
11. Höök, K.: User-Centred Design and Evaluation of Affective Interfaces, In: Ruttkay, Zs., Pelachaud, C. (eds.) Kluwer (2004)
12. Jordan, P.: Designing Pleasure Products. Taylor & Francis (2002)
13. Khuwaja, R., Desmarais, M., Cheng, R.: Intelligent Guide: Combining User Knowledge Assessment with pedagogical Guidance. In: Lesgold, A., Frasson, C., Gauthier, G. (eds.) ITS 1996. LNCS, vol. 1086, Springer, Heidelberg (1996)
14. Larson, J.: Out of the video arcade, into the office: where computer games can lead productivity software. Interactions ACM. vol. XIV.1 (January 2007)
15. Leemkuil, H.H., Jong, T., de Hoog, R., de Christoph, N.: KM Quest: a collaborative internet-based simulation game. Simulation & gaming 34, 89–111 (2003)
16. Mattos, F.L.: Concepção e desenvolvimento de uma abordagem pedagógica para processos colaborativos a distancia utilizando a internet. PhD. UFC (2005)
17. Mcguinness, D., Li Ding, Furtado, V., Glass, A., Zeng, H., Chang, C.: Explanation Interfaces for the Semantic Web: Issues and Models. In: Proc. of SWUI., vol. 1 (2006)
18. Miller, C.: Digital Storytelling: a creator's guide of interactive entertainment. Elsevier, Amsterdam (2004)
19. Norman, D.: Emotional Design. Basic Books (2004)
20. Perez, Y., Gamboa, R., Ibarra, O.: Modeling Affective Responses in Intelligent Tutoring Systems. In: Proc. of IEEE ICALT, IEEE Computer Society Press, Los Alamitos (2004)
21. Piaget, J.: Le comportement, moteur de l'évolution. Gallimard (ed.) Paris (1976)
22. Souza, C., Uma, S.: Abordagem Semiótica na Utilização dos Recursos Visuais em Linguagens de Interface. Isa Haro Martin (2003)
23. Sousa, K., Mendonca, H., Furtado, E.: Applying a Multi-Criteria Approach for the Selection of Usability Patterns in the Development of DTV Applications. In: IHC' 2006 (2006)
24. Stephanidis, C.: User Interfaces for All. In: Stephanidis, C. (ed.) User Interfaces for All – Concepts, Methods, and Tools, pp. 3–17. LEA, Inc., Mahwah, NJ (2001)
25. Wu, F.: Complexity and urban simulation: towards a computational laboratory. Geography Research Forum 22, 22–40 (2002)
26. Zhang, P., Li, N.: The Importance of Affective Quality. In: CACM'04 (2004)

TEMo-Chine: Tangible Emotion Machine

Omar Mubin[1], Abdullah Al Mahmud[1], and Christoph Bartneck[2]

[1] User-System Interaction Program
[2] Department of Industrial Design
Eindhoven University of Technology
P.O. Box 513, 5600 MB Eindhoven, The Netherlands
{O.Mubin, A.Al-Mahmud, C.Bartneck}@tue.nl

Abstract. We examine whether or not it is possible to determine, recognize and/or report the emotional state of a group of people through touch and/or body motion. We present the initial design of a mechanism for an asynchronous yet anonymous means of communication where the basic framework is set up by defining interaction with the system and aggregating the individual interaction components. We present the results from our initial user evaluation based on a scenario-based methodology. The results prove that users tend to exhibit similar emotional expression and interaction modalities, which could be used to determine general emotional states.

1 Introduction

In a public environment it would be interesting to have a feel of the collective emotional state of people in general, for example is the majority of the community happy or satisfied? We attempt to motivate the design of an interface that allows the general public to express themselves freely in a tangible manner.

We describe the process of the design and evaluation of an affective and interactive machine, the TEMo-chine (Tangible Emotion-machine). Our design concentrates on a unidirectional interaction mechanism by capturing physical actions of users and mapping them to emotions. Other design studies [2] are worked on a more bidirectional approach (i.e., the system responds as well based on the input) using Artificial Intelligence and various other paradigms. There have been numerous works in the area of Affective Computing (computing that relates to, arises from and influences emotions [3]) that have employed physiological measures such as blood pressure and skin conductance to measure the emotions of users [2]. However, this may be accurate but it does not allow you to explicitly express your emotions to the system [5, 6]. There has also been work in the area of gesture and facial expression recognition to capture affect. We try to motivate the design of a more tangible and yet physical interaction methodology.

There has been recent research along the lines of attaining affective feedback by using the body of the user or bodily gestures rather than verbal self-report measures [1, 4]. Our goal was to ascertain if we could actually generalize the emotional state via affective feedback from a collective group of people. We chose to investigate if physical actions could be used to interpret basic emotional state and direction (e.g., targeted object or avatar) of an emotion.

C. Baranauskas et al. (Eds.): INTERACT 2007, LNCS 4662, Part I, pp. 511–514, 2007.

2   Scenario Based Methodology

For the purposes of our evaluation and design, we employed the use of a scenario-based methodology. The idea behind TEMo-chine was to establish a design concept that could aggregate individualistic yet not personal interactions of people. We determined that one of the useful applications of such a design would be in a social context with a high degree of varying emotional state. We decided to evaluate our design idea within the workspace of a company office. An anonymous form of interaction would be desirable, to avoid any ethical and/or privacy concerns. Why we chose the scenario of an office was a relatively simple decision. Considerable emotional friction prevails in office settings and there could not be a hardly more competitive and stressful environment. The TEMO-chine was based on the paradigm that users would express their emotions with a physical action targeted towards an avatar [6].

Prototype and User Test. To physically represent our design idea we developed a simple non-working physical mock up (Fig. 1). Our TEMo-chine design consisted of two tangible iconic representations or avatars related to employees, in the context of a company office. These direction/intended targets/avatars of emotion were defined as i) Environment: Peers, Workspace and ii) Authority: Manager, Boss, Lawyers, Partners. The avatars were labeled accordingly (see Fig. 1). In the situation of a working environment, we felt these were the likely sources of emotional distress or emotional appeasement. We conducted the test with 15 participants (8 Male, 7 Female). Each user chosen for the prototype study had professional working experience in an office environment and was currently employed.

Fig. 1. The TEMo-chine prototype

Test Setup and Measurement. We predefined emotional states into two primary and basic categories: 'Happy' and 'Angry'. Our understanding was that we could easily place most levels of emotional interaction into these broad categories, it would methodologically make the experiment less convoluted, and lastly two levels of emotional categorization would suffice for an initial design. However, it is worth mentioning that future research should investigate interaction modalities for various other types of subtle emotions. To further complement the context, participants were presented with 6 scenarios randomly, 3 for each emotion type. For example a scenario was: an employee realizes that a peer is promoting him/herself at his/her expense in front of the boss.

Participants were instructed to perform one interaction of their own choice upon a preset avatar based on their prevailing emotion, once a scenario was read out. Users were observed and video recorded during their interactions with the prototype. The video coding scheme defined a set of plausible and most likely yet discernable actions for each emotion. For emotion type 'Happy' the following four possibilities were identified: a) a smooth and soft physical hand gesture, such as a pet, a caress or a rub, b) a hug, c) a kiss and d) neutral(no physical gestures carried out) or if the action was indiscernible/unrecognizable/invalid. For emotion type 'Angry' there were three options: a) a rounded fist gesture: such as a hit, bang or punch, b) an open handed (one or both hands) gesture such as a slap or flick and c) neutral (no physical gestures carried out). Therefore, for each participant we had a frequency count of which actions were performed for each emotion type.

3   Results and Discussion

After conducting the user study, we analyzed the results and came up with a frequency discretization of which user actions were usually performed for a particular hypothetical emotional situation. The resulting coded data was analyzed as a within subjects design. Pair wise comparisons of means for each interaction gesture output were carried out with other gestures within each emotion. For emotion type 'Happy' gesture A was significantly the most often adopted interaction gesture ($p = 0.019$, $p = 0.003$, $p = 0.000$). For emotion type 'Angry' gesture B was significantly the most often adopted interaction gesture ($p = 0.017$, $p = 0.000$). No significant differences were found for the other physical actions. Moreover, gender did not have an influence on the interaction modalities.

As far as the 'Happy' emotion was concerned, the mock up of the avatars might have been one reason why participants were not ready to adopt very personal interactions such as a hug or kiss. Many participants were also observed to express some reluctance at first, before actually deciding which action to carry out. On the other hand with regards to the 'Angry' emotion, participants might have been hesitant to employ a rounded fist gesture to the avatars as they seemed more animate. Generally we could expect that, humans would not care about aggressive behavior towards objects and artifacts as compared to agents which are social and/or represent some lifelikeness.

We did experience and observe some interesting interaction modalities. In one particular situation a participant exhibited a dual form of interaction, as gesture A from the 'Happy' category was subsequently followed by gesture A from the 'Angry' category. On this particular instance, the interaction was categorized under the 'Angry' gesture C category. A dual input in one interaction on the same avatar would likely be unrecognizable for a real machine, since even with limiting the input to touch a human has many intricate forms of tangible interaction which machines are unlikely to completely understand for now.

There exist various limitations of our initial design. Firstly, we feel a cultural bias might hinder accurate generalizations across large samples of population. Moreover, the user study was carried out in an unreal setting using a scenario-based methodology. Hence, the results might not pertain to all situations. There might also be a tendency amongst humans of their physical actions evolving over time. The ideal extension for this research would be to carry out an extensive experiment in a real context by placing a working prototype in the environment. Based on our design, in order to identify affect the system needs to recognize the physical action (via sensory information) and match it to an appropriate emotion.

We have presented an initial design idea of a system that can effectively sum up individual emotional interaction vectors of users into an aggregated output. This is not done by explicitly recognizing emotions but rather by interpreting physical actions and matching them to emotions. This relationship needs to be fully quantified although we believe that our initial results could be used for emotion recognition/emotion self report. Future work should also concentrate on analyzing interaction for more subtle categories of emotions, for e.g., Irritation, Sadness. Other interesting aspects to investigate include determining the exact visualization of the aggregation results to the group of people in concern and providing feedback to them, either on an individual level or on a shared medium. However, as we have suggested the next iteration would be to implement a working automated prototype and to test the system in a real environment.

Acknowledgement. The authors would like to acknowledge the contribution of Jeff Burkham, Yuan Gao, Zhihui Zhang and Kristina Höök, towards the initial phase of the study.

References

1. Katherine, I., Kia, H., Micheal, S., Jarmo, L.: The Sensual Evaluation Instrument: Developing an Affective Evaluation Tool. In: Proc. CHI 2006, pp. 1164–1172. ACM press, New York (2006)
2. Overbeeke, C.J., Vink, P., Cheung, F.K.P.: The emotion-aware office chair. In: Proceedings of the International Conference on Affective Human Factors Design, pp. 262–267 (2001)
3. Picard, R.W.: Affective Computing. MIT Press, Cambridge (1997)
4. Petra, S., Anna, S., Kristina, H.: A User-Centered Approach to Affective Interaction. LNCS. Springer, Heidelberg (2005)
5. Wensveen, S.A.G., Overbeeke, C.J., Djajadiningrat, J.P.: Push me, shove me and I show you how you feel: recognising mood from emotionally rich interaction. In: MacDonald, N. (ed.) DIS2002: Serious reflection on designing interactive systems, pp. 335–340. ACM press, New York (2002)
6. Wensveen, S.A.G., Overbeeke, C.J., Djajadiningrat, J.P.: Touch me, hit me and I know how you feel. A design approach to emotionally rich interaction. In: Proceedings of Designing Interactive Systems, DIS'00, pp. 48–53. ACM press, New York (2000)

Characterizing the Diversity in Users' Perceptions

Evangelos Karapanos and Jean-Bernard Martens

Department of Industrial Design
Eindhoven University of Technology
P.O. Box 513, 5600 MB, Eindhoven, The Netherlands
{E.Karapanos, J.B.O.S.Martens}@tue.nl

Abstract. This paper proposes a novel approach to modeling the diversity in users' perceptions, based on a mixture of qualitative and quantitative techniques: the Repertory Grid Technique and Multi-Dimensional Scaling. The proposed method can be used for identifying diverse user groups that can inspire a range of personas, or for selecting subjects for field studies and usability tests. In a case study we explored the perceptions of product creators and end users towards an innovative product in its early design stage.

Keywords: user profiling, Repertory Grid, Multi-dimensional Scaling.

1 Introduction

Understanding the diversity in users has been one of the core challenges in user-centered design. User profiling is an essential first step towards identifying the right personas for design [3], or the right subjects for field studies and usability tests [4]. Yet, current approaches to user profiling distinguish users in terms of knowledge, educational or social background, age and gender. Such information is probably overly generic and does not reflect how users differ in terms of their attitude towards a specific product under development. At the same time there is growing evidence that designers underestimate the diversity in users [4]. As a result, developed personas may lack a connection to important target users [3, 6], and subjects in user studies may not represent the wide range of actual (or potential) users of a product [4]. The need for a closer link between user profiling and product design has been repeatedly highlighted [1, 3], but as yet, novel approaches are rather scarce (e.g. [6]).

This paper describes a new method for understanding the diversity in users perceptions' and identifying homogeneous user groups, based on a mixture of qualitative and quantitative techniques. The method consists of three stages. First, users' idiosyncratic views are elicited in a structured interview approach using the *Repertory Grid Technique* (RGT) [2]. Second, a *user segmentation map* that expresses the diversity among users is derived from their dissimilarity ratings by means of *Multi-Dimensional Scaling* (MDS) [5]. Homogeneous groups of users are identified within this map by means of (hierarchical) clustering. Third, *perceptual maps* are created from the attribute, dissimilarity and preference ratings to express how homogeneous groups of subjects perceive the products being studied.

C. Baranauskas et al. (Eds.): INTERACT 2007, LNCS 4662, Part I, pp. 515–518, 2007.
© IFIP International Federation for Information Processing 2007

We have applied the new approach in a case study where we explored the perceptions of six related products by a diverse group of subjects, consisting of product creators and end users. One of the goals of the study was to identify discrepancies (i) between product creators' and end-users' perceptions, and (ii) between different individuals within a multi-disciplinary concept design team. In the following sections we describe the proposed method for user profiling, and illustrate it with concrete results from our case study.

2   Case Study

Eleven persons directly involved in the concept design phase of a new product, and eleven potential end users, participated in the case study. The end users were researchers from our department who had no prior knowledge of the product under development. The product creators were all employees of the R&D department of an international company developing document systems. They were all involved in the conception and realization of *TouchToPrint*, which is a new way of personalizing the use of a shared printer by means of fingerprint recognition. This new concept and five alternative proposals for interacting with a shared printer were presented to the participants in the form of posters. Each poster described a usage scenario of the relevant concept. First, the six products were combined in three triads. For every triad, participants were asked to "think of a property or quality that makes two of the products alike and discriminates them from the third". This resulted in a list of *attributes*, product qualities that users perceive and use while forming overall evaluations of a product. Afterwards, the subjects were asked to rate all products on their personal attributes, as well as on *preference* and *dissimilarity*. In contrast to the traditional Repertory Grid approach, we employed paired comparisons instead of semantic differentials, as this was a priori expected to deliver more stable results [5].

3   Analysis

The analysis process consists of two steps. First, a *user segmentation map* is created for identifying homogeneous groups in the participant sample. Second, a *perceptual map* is created for each homogeneous group to gain insight into how products are perceived.

To create the user segmentation map, we define the distance $D_{ij}=1-R^2_{ij}$ between participants i and j based on the correlation R_{ij} between their dissimilarity scores. Derived distances are then visualized in two or more dimensions (Fig. 1) using the MDS tool XGms [5]. Hierarchical clustering (with minimum variance) reveals two main clusters that can be further subdivided into five more or less homogeneous participant groups. Groups 3 and 4 consist entirely of end users, while groups 1, 2 and 5 consist mostly of product creators. Identification of the product creators reveals that group 1 consists mostly of technically-oriented product creators, while group 2 consists mostly of user-oriented product creators.

A perceptual space representing the products is subsequently constructed for each homogenous group, based on the dissimilarity scores from all participants within the group. We only present the results for groups 1 and 3. Both perceptual spaces can be

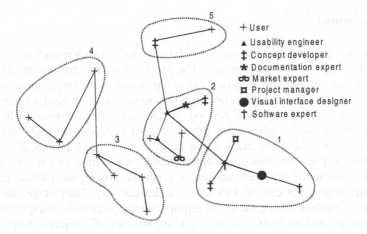

Fig. 1. User segmentation map based on correlations between dissimilarity scores

adequately visualized in two dimensions, and attribute vectors are fitted into these spaces by performing multiple regressions between the stimulus configuration (as independent variables) and the attribute scores (as the dependent variables). Only significant attributes are retained in the visualizations of Fig. 2.

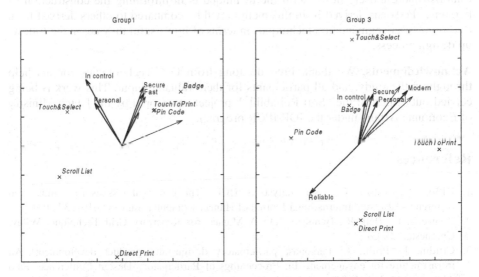

Fig. 2. Perceptual maps for groups 1 and 3. The light vectors represent individual preferences, while the other vectors represent the most significant attributes.

For individuals in group 1, *secure* and *fast* are the most important product qualities influencing their preference judgment, while participants in group 3 value *modern*, *personal* and *secure* products. Subjects within group 3 have negative concerns regarding the reliability of new products, such as Touch&Select, TouchToPrint and Badge, despite the fact that they prefer them. Such concerns are not reported by the subjects in group 1.

4 Conclusion

This paper has presented a new experimental approach to understanding the diversity in product perceptions between people. The proposed method has several advantages. First, it follows a pragmatic approach to user modeling by distinguishing users based on how they perceive and appreciate products rather than on abstract demographic and psychographic information. Second, it also accounts for users' idiosyncratic views in contrast to other approaches [6] where a priori defined attributes are imposed in the evaluation. Third, the method can be used in different phases of the product development, for instance using concept sketches, as was done in our case study, but also for benchmarking between competitor products. Fourth, the method consists of two distinct stages that can be handled in a flexible way. Only stage one, i.e., the elicitation of attributes using the RGT, requires a more experienced experimenter and is therefore practically restricted to a limited number of subjects. Stage two that consists of rating the collected attributes, as well as preferences and dissimilarities, can easily be automated and conducted with a large number of subjects.

In the future, we want to compare the proposed method of user profiling with alternative methods based on market analysis or logging of actual product use. More specifically, within an existing project we are interested in a better understanding of the relationship between user profiles and customer complaints. We also want to establish more closely how useful the technique is in informing the construction of personas. Personas derived from this method will be compared to others derived from traditional user segmentation techniques in terms of how useful they are in the follow-up design process.

Acknowledgments. We thank Fred de Jong from Océ Technologies for his help throughout the study, and all participants for their valuable input. This work is being carried out as part of the "Soft Reliability" project, sponsored by the Dutch Ministry of Economic Affairs under the IOP-IPCR program.

References

1. Dillon, A., Watson, C.: User analysis in HCI - The historical lessons from individual differences research. International Journal of Human-Computer Studies , 619–637 (1996)
2. Fransella, F., Bell, R., Bannister, D.: A Manual for Repertory Grid Technique. Wiley, Chichester (2003)
3. Grudin, J., Pruitt, J.: Personas, participatory design and product development: An infrastructure for engagement. In: Proceedings of Participatory Design Conference, Palo Alto, pp. 144–161 (2002)
4. Kujala, S., Kauppinen, M.: Identifying and selecting users for user-centered design. In: Proceedings of the third Nordic conference on Human-computer interaction, ACM Press, Tampere, Finland (2004)
5. Martens, J.-B.: Image technology design: A perceptual approach. Kluwer Academic Publisher, Boston (2003)
6. Sinha, R.: Persona development for information-rich domains. In: CHI '03 extended abstracts on Human factors in computing systems, ACM Press, Florida, USA (2003)

Stay on the Ball! An Interaction Pattern Approach to the Engineering of Motivation

Kirstin Kohler[1], Sabine Niebuhr[1], and Marc Hassenzahl[2]

[1] Fraunhofer IESE, Fraunhofer-Platz 1, 67663 Kaiserslautern, Germany
{kohler, niebuhr}@iese.fraunhofer.de
[2] University of Koblenz-Landau, Fortstr. 7, 76829 Landau, Germany
hassenzahl@uni-landau.de

Abstract. This paper introduces an interaction pattern approach to "engineer" motivation. Its goal is to provide concrete ideas (in the form of patterns) on how to design software that motivates its users to stay on a task. The paper presents an example of a motivating pattern, the Task Status Display (TSD), and its empirical validation. Preliminary results support its motivational effect, thereby lending support to the general notion of building motivation into interactive products for the workplace.

1 Introduction

Traditional usability engineering (UE) approaches (e.g., [1]) take a predominantly task-oriented perspective on designing interactive systems. They assume given behavioral goals (do-goals, e.g., "make a telephone call") and attempt to design systems in a way to optimally support goal accomplishment. However, we argue that this approach misses out on at least one important aspect of human behavior namely *motivation*.

There is an implicit assumption of UE that in the work context, goals (i.e., tasks) are provided externally and are relatively fixed. And indeed, a production line worker does not have much choice other than to perform the given task or to quit her job. However, there are other work domains where situations are less clear cut. In many work contexts, such as office work, individuals will be given relatively abstract goals; how to actually pursue them is often their choice. In addition, people often have more than one pending task, which allows for subtle shifts in priorities. Thus, whenever individuals have the autonomy to procrastinate or even fully abandon boring tasks, motivation will become extremely important.

Game design and e-learning design can be interesting sources of motivational principles in design. Both spend much effort on making their products as appealing as possible, predominantly because people will use them on a voluntary basis. Especially games are very good at motivating repetitive behavior, which would be considered as boring in a work context.

Nevertheless, it is a long way from broad principles to concrete design solutions. To bridge this gap, we use interaction patterns. Patterns describe approved solutions to recurring design problems in a structured way. By that, they store and provide

C. Baranauskas et al. (Eds.): INTERACT 2007, LNCS 4662, Part I, pp. 519–522, 2007.

design knowledge. The use of pattern has become increasingly common since their transfer from architecture to software and usability engineering (e.g.[2,3]). However, currently there are no patterns describing solutions to motivational or other hedonic aspects.

2 An Example: The Task Status Display

Tidwell [4] suggested a pattern called "Status Display". Her intention was to keep the user informed about what happens during interaction. We drew upon this general idea to develop the "Task Status Display" (TSD). TSD visualizes the current goal, shows the extent to which it has already been accomplished, which further steps have to be taken and how big these steps are (for more details see [5]). TSD visualizes the goal and goal progress. Its motivating effect is assumed to emerge from (1) helping users to stay focused on their goal, or even by providing an alternative, more interesting "substitute" goal, and from (2) providing feedback to adjust performance [6]. Note that although superficially similar, TSD is not comparable to a progress bar. A progress bar rather provides feedback about the system's state ("Don't worry, I'm working") than the user's state in the sense of goal accomplishment.

Fig. 1. Address database interface with TSD

A TSD can be implemented in different ways [5]. In order to explore the potential motivating effect, we set up a simple address database with TSD as a decreasing amount of address cards (see fig 1). The system's main purpose is to enter a fixed number of addresses into a database. With every address added, a card disappears from the row; for every ten addresses, one card stack disappears and the row is filled with new cards.

3 Does It Work?

We prepared two versions of the address entry mask; one version with TSD, the other without. Fourteen individuals (4 female, median age = 26, min = 20, max = 35) were randomly assigned to either the version with TSD ("with pattern", N=6) or without ("without pattern", N=7). All participants were asked to enter 40 addresses provided as scanned business cards. They were further told that they had a limit of 75 minutes to accomplish the task. The session was either ended by reaching the limit of 75 minutes or by having entered all addresses. In addition, they were encouraged to take breaks whenever they felt like doing so. To let the break appear a little more tempting, the desktop gave easy access to a number of games (e.g., Pacman, Sudoku) and current news (both provided by Google).

We were interested in two aspects, namely the impact of the pattern on *system perceptions and evaluations* (i.e., subjective) and on *task persistence* (i.e., objective). System perceptions and evaluations were measured with the AttrakDiff2-Questionnaire [7]. It distinguishes between perceived pragmatic quality (PQ), hedonic quality, and appeal (APPEAL). PQ is the perceived ability of a product to support the efficient and successful accomplishment of "do-goals", such as to "enter an address". In contrast, hedonic quality is the perceived ability of a product to support so-called "be-goals", such as "be something special", "be cool". Specifically, we focused on hedonic quality stimulation (HQS), a measure of the system's perceived novelty, uniqueness, and excitation. APPEAL is the general evaluation of the system as either good or bad. In general, each aspect was measured by seven single bipolar items, averaged to a single scale value (see Tab. 1 for measures of internal consistency). Example items are "confusing–structured" (PQ), "dull–captivating" (HQS), and "bad–good" (APPEAL). The participants were asked to fill in the questionnaire at the end of the session. *Task persistence* was operationalized simply by the number of breaks taken during address entry. A break was defined as switching from the address entry mask to one of the offered games or news.

In general, we expected participants to perceive the employed pattern as primarily stimulating (HQS) and not so much as adding to its pragmatic quality (i.e., usability). Nevertheless, an effect of the pattern on task persistence should become apparent, with less breaks in the "with pattern"-condition. Specifically, stimulation was expected to be linked directly (and inversely) to task persistence.

Table 1 shows the means and standard deviation of all measures for the "with pattern" and "without pattern" conditions.

Table 1. Means (standard deviation) for all measures, separately for the with-pattern and without-pattern conditions

Measure	Condition/System with pattern (N=6)	without pattern (N=7)	Mann-Whitney
System perception and evaluation			
HQS (α=.91)	3.48 (.88)	2.25 (.27)	U=5.5*
PQ (α=.72)[1]	6.03 (.89)	5.83 (.65)	U=17
APPEAL (α=.86)	4.76 (.33)	3.57 (.79)	U=4.5*
Task persistence and performance			
Number of breaks	0.00 (.00)	1.14 (1.22)	U=9*
Numbers of addresses	36 (5)	39 (4)	U=14
Duration (minutes)	67 (12)	63 (13)	U=16

Notes: *) p < .05; [1]) two items were discarded

As expected, there was a significant difference in HQS, with a higher stimulation if the pattern was apparent. PQ, however, did not differ between conditions. In general, HQS and PQ did not correlate, Spearman's $\rho(13) = .22$, ns. In other words, PQ and HQS were perceived as sufficiently different aspects and the pattern took effect only on the hedonic, not on the pragmatic quality perceptions.

Further, a significant difference in APPEAL emerged, pointing at the additional value derived from the pattern. Indeed, a stepwise linear regression with PQ and HQS as predictors and APPEAL as criterion showed HQS to be the single best predictor ($\beta = .82$, $p < .01$, 63% explained variance, corrected).

Concerning task persistence, a significant difference for number of breaks emerged. With the pattern, participants took no voluntary breaks, whereas without the pattern participants took one break on average. In addition, stimulation was significantly correlated with number of breaks, $\rho(13) = -.62$, $p < .05$, with less breaks the more the system was perceived as stimulating. No such correlation emerged for PQ, $\rho(13) = .20$, ns. As expected, the remaining task performance measures showed no significant differences.

4 Conclusion

All in all, the present study supports the notion that TSD has a positive effect on task persistence and, thus, a motivational effect. Although admittedly preliminary, this does at least not disconfirm our general claim, namely that motivation can be built into software used at the workplace. Obviously, patterns must be used for more complex, real-life applications, and their effects must be studied in the field, too. Nevertheless, we understand the present study as a first step to explore the notion of patterns to engineer motivation and the question of whether they actually work or not.

Acknowledgments. This work is supported by the German Federal Ministry of Education and Research (BMBF) within the project FUN (Grant: 01 IS E06 A). For more information see the project website http://www.fun-of-use.de

References

1. Constantine, L., Lockwood, L.: Software for Use: A Practical Guide to the Essential Models and Methods of Usage-Centered Design. Addison-Wesley, Reading (1999)
2. Gamma, E., Helm, R., Johnson, R., Vlissides, J.: Design Patterns – Elements of Reusable Object Oriented Software. Addison-Wesley, Reading (1995)
3. Dearden, A., Finlay, J.: Pattern Languages in HCI: A Critical Review. HCI 21, 49–102 (2006)
4. Tidwell, J.: Common ground: A Pattern Language for Human-Computer Interface Design
5. Niebuhr, S., Kohler, K., Graf, C.: Engaging Patterns: Challenges and Means shown at an Example, Engineering Interactive Systems, Salamanca, Spain (2007)
6. Latham, G.P., Lee, T.W.: Goal setting. In: Locke, E.A (ed): Generalizing from laboratory to field settings. Lexington Books, pp. 101–117 (1986)
7. Hassenzahl, M.: The interplay of beauty, goodness and usability in interactive products. Human Computer Interaction 19, 319–349 (2004)

Motivational Needs-Driven Mobile Phone Design

Judy van Biljon[1], Paula Kotzé[1], and Gary Marsden[2]

[1] School of Computing, University of South Africa, South Africa
[2] Department of Computer Science, University of Cape Town, South Africa
{vbiljja, kotzep}@unisa.ac.za, gaz@cs.uct.ac.za

Abstract. This paper provides support for the use of motivational needs in identifying mobile phone uses and related features. Drawing on motivational human and usage space research, the findings of interviews and surveys, this paper proposes the Mobile phone Usage Space Model (MUSM). MUSM distinguishes between two groups of features by identifying necessary and additional features, thus focusing the designer's activity on motivational needs-driven design, rather than feature escalation that currently appears to dominate.

Keywords: Mobile phone design, usage spaces, motivational needs.

1 Introduction

This paper addresses the issue of user needs in the context of mobile phone design. In Human-Computer Interaction (HCI) user needs are usually studied from task and context-oriented perspectives. This approach works well in designing systems where specified and structured tasks are involved. Since mobile phones are personal devices not strictly fitting the task domain, we argue that a different approach is required in designing such devices and the use options available. The feature driven approach has been widely used to design mobile phones this far [1]. Feature addition is driven by the need to increase the demand and desirability of the product, but in reality it may reduce usability, and tends to be counter-productive as many users find it difficult to cope with the information overload and the cognitive demands of mobile phone technology [2, 3]. *If adding features does not satisfy user needs, what does?* Focusing on motivational needs can provide designers with a new alternative to the current feature-driven approach. Section 2 sets theoretical foundations by highlighting feature-driven research, motivational human needs and the representation of mobile phone uses. Section 3 describes our research to investigate links between user needs and mobile phone features. Section 4 concludes.

2 Theoretical Framework

Much research on mobile phones in the HCI arena is directed at finding the set of key features around which the user interface should be optimised for each target group. Han et al. [1], for example introduced an approach to identifying both desirable *and* undesirable properties of critical design features and developed empirical models to

C. Baranauskas et al. (Eds.): INTERACT 2007, LNCS 4662, Part I, pp. 523–526, 2007.
© IFIP International Federation for Information Processing 2007

link design features to satisfaction levels. Ling and Hwang [4] considered specific features and found that only colour display and Internet browsing features improves overall satisfaction significantly. All these studies have an inherent limitation: they start with specific design elements, features or functions and then try to establish the value these features have for users. The number of features increase and it is impractical to study all the different combinations of features to produce reliable results.

An alternative perspective is to consider theories on human needs. One of the first theories on motivational needs was proposed in 1954 by Maslow, which he later expanded to a total of eight levels of human needs [5]. The needs are: physiological; safety and security; belongingness; esteem; cognitive; aesthetic; self-actualization; and self-transcendence. The Institute for Management Excellence [6] proposes an alternative set of needs namely: security; adventure; freedom; exchange; power; expansion; acceptance; community; and expression. Herzberg's motivator-hygiene theory from the field of industrial psychology [7], discriminates between factors which are referred to as *motivational* versus those called *hygiene*. Hygiene factors meet physiological, safety and social needs in the workplace, while motivational factors encourage job satisfaction and appeal to human needs of growth and self-advancement [8]. Applied to mobile phone features, motivational factors would serve as a discriminator for the prospective buyer. Hygiene factors will *have* to be present to satisfy basic requirements while features in the motivational group can be used to customise the device for specific users.   To be useful to designers, user needs have to be linked to features via uses or usage spaces. The usage space model by Marcus and Chen [9] provides a starting point for presenting mobile device uses.

3 Research Methodology and Findings

We investigated the link between motivational needs and mobile phone features using a questionnaire driven study. The questionnaire was based on a literature study and was verified in structured interviews (with 10 participants, gender balanced, age groups 20-29, 30-39, 40-49 and 50-59) from three ethnic groups (African, Asian and European). The following observations were made during the design and verification stage: participants *over* the age of 30 used less than 40% of the available features, thought of a mobile phone as a mobile version of the traditional phone, and identified relationship building and security as the highest use priorities. Participants *under* the age of 30 used between 40% and 50% of the features on their mobile phones, viewed the phone as a tool for communication, organization and entertainment but were inhibited by cost. The questionnaire was refined and tested in a pilot survey involving 39 participants, all questionnaires used are available [10].

Since past research (confirmed by our observations) indicated that age and technological development influences mobile phone use [11], we limited the age bracket and technological development level for our pilot survey and final survey to university students in computer science between the ages of 18 and 27. Using a refined version of the pilot survey questionnaire, the final survey involved 138 participants from two South African universities, 68% male and 32% female.

Two data reduction (statistical) methods were used to analyse the data collected during the final survey, namely exploratory factor analysis and optimal scaling. The aim of this analysis was to find whether features cluster together in terms of usage frequency. Exploratory factor analysis produced the following main usage clusters:

- New technology: Bluetooth, video player, MP3, e-mail, voice recorder, etc.
- Personal history: camera, photo-album, MMS, ring tones, personal notes, etc.
- Safety, security, relationships: phone book, caller identity, missed calls, SMS.
- Organisation: vibrating alert, reminders, profiles, calendar

Optimal scaling was applied to the same data to verify the clustering.   On inspection of the graphs (not included here) feature clusters were selected based on proximity. The following main groupings (usage clusters) were identified:

- Safety, security, relationships: phone book, caller identity, missed calls; SMS.
- Organisation: vibrating alert, reminders, profiles and alarm.
- Personal history: camera, MP3, personal organiser, photo-album, video capture.

This means that two data reduction methods, i.e. exploratory factor analyses and optimal scaling, produced similar groupings, namely: safety and security, relationships, organisation, personal history. Other additional usage spaces emerged from the literature study and the interviews, namely: personal information, non-personal information, m-commerce, entertainment, image and expansion. Integrating the findings from our survey with those from the interviews and literature survey, we propose the MUSM (Mobile phone Usage Spaces Model) consisting of a set of core spaces and additional spaces applicable to this user group as depicted in Fig 1:

- *Core (hygiene)*: relationships, personal information, organisation, safety, security.
- *Additional (motivational)*: entertainment, m-commerce, expansion, non-personal information, personal history, image.

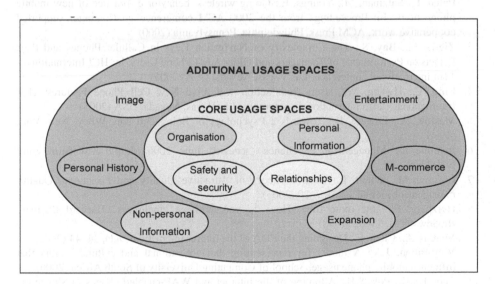

Fig. 1. Proposed usage space model with two categories of usage spaces

The usage spaces identified correspond to four of the motivational human needs identified by Maslow [5] i.e. safety and security, belongingness (relationships), cognitive (personal and non-personal information, organisation) and self-actualisation (expansion, personal-history). Dividing usage spaces into core spaces and additional spaces is supported by Herzberg's motivator-hygiene theory [8]. Furthermore, this study provides empirical support for Chen and Marcus's model [9] (that was lacking until now) and extends their model by linking usage spaces to mobile phone features.

4 Conclusion

The main contribution of our research is linking the models of Maslow [5] and Herzberg [8] to that of Marcus[9], thereby grounding mobile phone feature selection in motivational needs as opposed to a market-driven, more-is-better approach which leads to redundant features and cognitive overload. MUSM allows users to express their mobile phone usage needs in non-technical terms, while designers can use the model as a guideline to convert the expressed user needs into a set of features that fit the motivational needs of the user. Further research is needed to refine MUSM. The features associated with each usage space will have to be adapted according to new developments and the grouping of core and additional spaces could change for different target (age) groups but the structure and usage spaces identified are grounded solidly in motivational needs theories.

References

1. Han, S.H., Kim, J.K., Yun, M.H., Hong, S.W., Kim, J.H.: Identifying Mobile Phone Design Features Critical to user Satisfaction. Human Factors and Ergonomics in Manufacturing 14(1), 15–29 (2004)
2. Palen, L., Salzman, M., Youngs, E.: Going wireless: behavior & practice of new mobile phone users. In: Proceedings from the 2000 ACM conference on Computer supported cooperative work, ACM Press, Philadelphia, Pennsylvania (2000)
3. Ziefle, M., Bay, S.: The Complexity of Navigation Keys in Cellular Phones and their Effects on Performance of Teenagers and Older Adult Phone Users. In: HCI International - 11th international conference, Las Vegas, Nevada, USA (2005)
4. Ling, C., Hwang, W.: Users Satisfaction with Five New Cell Phone Features. HCI International - 11th international conference, Las Vegas, Nevada, USA (2005)
5. Maslow, A., Lowery, R.: Towards a Psychology of Being, 3rd edn. Wiley, New York (1998)
6. Institute for Management Excellence (accessed June 2006), http://www.itstime.com/jun97.htm
7. Löfgren, M., Witell, L.: Kano's Theory of Attractive Quality and Packaging. Quality management journal 12(3), 7–20 (2005)
8. Herzberg, F.: One more time: How do you motivate employees? Harvard Business Review 46(1), 53–62 (1968)
9. Marcus, A., Chen, E.: Designing the PDA of the future. Interactions 9(1), 34–44 (2002)
10. Van Biljon, J.A.: A model for representing the motivational and cultural factors that influence mobile phone usage, School of Computing.University of South Africa (2006)
11. Teo, T.S.H., Pok, S.H.: Adoption of the internet and WAP-enabled phones in Singapore. Behaviour & Information Technology 22(4), 281–289 (2003)

Mobile Application for Increasing Contextual and Emotional Work Group Awareness

Mikko Salminen[1], Kari Kallinen[1], Kliment Yanev[1], Niklas Ravaja[1],
and Timo Saari[1,2]

[1] Helsinki School of Economics, Center for Knowledge and Innovation Research,
Helsinki, Finland
[2] Temple University, Philadelphia, PA, USA
{Mikko.Salminen, Kari.Kallinen, Kliment.Yanev,
Niklas.Ravaja, Timo.Saari}@hse.fi

Abstract. This paper presents a prototype of a mobile application enhancing emotional and contextual awareness in distributed knowledge work teams. Emotional, contextual, and other types of data from users are collected both implicitly and explicitly. The benefits of such a system are hypothesized to include increased individual and group awareness, emotional awareness, location-, task- and status awareness. A novel way to visualize data on location, use context, and user's subjective emotional state on a mobile phone are also presented.

Keywords: Mobile social application, knowledge work, contextual awareness, emotional awareness.

1 Awareness in Groups

In many group work situations, awareness of others provides information that is critical for smooth and effective collaboration. Although group awareness is taken for granted in face-to-face work, it is difficult to maintain in distributed settings. Studies of distributed work have shown that much of the communication and implicit information that is available to a co-located team does not exist for remote collaborators. For example, Herbsleb and Grinter [1] found that lack of ad-hoc communication between software developers caused an increase in coordination problems and a decrease in collaboration between remote sites.

We define group emotion as the group's affective state that arises from the combination of its "bottom-up" components — affective compositional effects — and its "top-down" components — affective context [2]. That is, group emotion results from both the combinations of individual level affective factors that group members possess, as well as from group or contextual level factors that define or shape the affective experience of the group. The concept of group emotion has been shown to be reliably recognized by group members and outside raters, both on-site and through video-ratings [3], [4], [5], and has been reliably measured through a variety of statistical techniques. In our application we aim to support emotional awareness as one of the key aspects of the system.

C. Baranauskas et al. (Eds.): INTERACT 2007, LNCS 4662, Part I, pp. 527–531, 2007.

2   Technological Description of the Current Application

The system presented here consists of a mobile phone application and a server-side component. The server links into a database and performs logging and aggregation, as well as communication with the mobile application. There are aggregation rules for each measurable attribute and new aggregation rules and attributes are easy to add. The attributes are identified by name only, and the server-side application searches for a handler method for that particular attribute name. The mobile application is a J2ME MIDlet that targets MIDP 2.0 and CLDC 1.0. It facilitates text-based group communication while also showing a graphical representation of various cues about the group's status.

These attributes are gathered using a combination of self-report questions and various sensors. Sensors are either attached using Bluetooth or are local to the phone. The application does not directly distinguish between different data sources in its communication with the server, so any kind of data source can be added easily. Different phone models support different sets of sensors, and the application can adapt to this. The sensor attachment is implemented with a Bluetooth discovery for known sensor identifiers. The sensor data is periodically transmitted to a server which performs aggregation for each group. Group management is implemented on the server. Each user can belong to several groups. The aggregate values for each group and user are sent to the phone and represented there graphically in a way that depends on the screen size and device capabilities.

The application is a data collection and visualization system implemented on top of a UI library developed to work around the limitations of MIDP2. The library allows for rapid user interface and interaction model development on the limited MIDP2 platform. The application provides a set of predefined visualizations with variable parameters. The different group and individual attributes can easily be mapped at runtime to visualization parameters. This mapping can also be dynamically changed.

2.1   Information Input to the System

At the current stage self-report questions about subjective emotional valence and arousal and also about stress level are sent from the server to the users. The frequency of requests can be set from the server and the suitable frequency can be adjusted for different user groups. In the future at least part of these self-report questions are planned to be replaced by data from Bluetooth connected psychophysiological sensors, e.g. skin conductance and pulse from the fingers.

Other types of user input information are status message and instant messaging. Status message is a user typed short description of his or her current work stage or subjective feelings, in a way a profile that is visible to others and permanent until user changes it. Instant messaging allows informal textual communication between group members without the charges and limitations of SMS.

Nearby Bluetooth devices and ambient sound are collected and visualized to provide contextual information. Location data is derived from pre-set Bluetooth beacons; with Symbian phones cell-id can also be accessed. A hierarchical three level model is formed from the cell-id data. In the closest "orbit" are located those who are in the same cell with the user in the center (see Figure 1). The second orbit shows those in the same area and the third furthest orbit is a place for those who are not in the same area.

The Bluetooth framework is flexible enough to support essentially any sensor that can communicate over RFCOMM or L2CAP. This enables the use of the system to collect and visualize data not directly accessible from the phone, such as the psychophysiological sensor data mentioned above, as well as more complex external sensors that do processing the phone is not currently capable of (such as voice analysis). The data collection framework and visualization system treats sensor data in exactly the same way as any other attribute, so it is possible to map the attributes to any visualization parameters.

3   Visualization of Emotional and Contextual Cues

Visualizing data on mobile phone is still challenging. The screen size and the resolution are quite small and usually the screen orientation is vertical. We have selected an orbit schema for visualizing the group member's data. This way the user can, with a single glance, get information on each other group member. The user is in the center of the orbits and a "planet" represents each other group member. The proximity of other members to the user represents the similarity of emotional ratings or geographic distance.

3.1   Emotional Information – Sheet

In the Emotion-sheet self-reported emotional valence, emotional arousal, and stress level are visualized for each group member. The size of the "planet" represents the stress level with larger planet standing for larger amount of stress. Emotional valence is visualized with the color, blue is for negative valence and red for positive valence. The amount of fill in the planet shows the arousal level; low fill is for low arousal level. All these self-report data have been obtained by five-scale questionnaires. The proximity of planets representing users is calculated by forming an average for these three scales together.

3.2   Contextual Information – Sheet

In the context sheet the proximity of the planets represents geometric distance between group members, relative to the user placed in the center. The dots around planets show the number of surrounding Bluetooth devices and an anchor stands for proximity to a user's Bluetooth-enabled tabletop PC in the office or a Bluetooth sensor placed in the office room. The fill of the planet and the color of the fill represent ambient sound level and user activity. Status message and detailed information of surrounding Bluetooth devices can be seen from the individual user details (Figure 1, panels E and F). A green person figure represents proximity to a known persons Bluetooth enabled mobile phone. A black mobile phone is for other, unknown persons and a diamond represents any other Bluetooth enabled device.

With the presented visualization approach location, contextual and subjective emotional information can be effectively visualized in a mobile phone. Navigation requires a minimal number of buttons. The Bluetooth and cell-id based approach also makes it possible to access location information without an external GPS receiver, although it is possible in the forthcoming versions to include a specific map sheet for visualizing GPS-based location data. Our mobile application is targeted to lessen misunderstandings by providing for a richer interaction between distributed group members. Visibility of other's locations, context and emotions will be enhanced by our system. Enhancing visibility may also lead to more accessibility as people are more aware of the suitable moments to contact friends or co-workers.

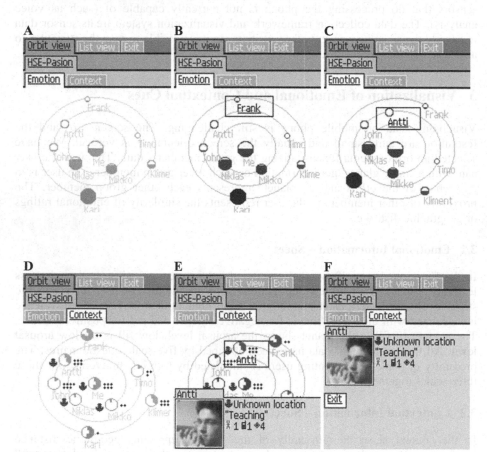

Fig. 1. Navigating in the application and cues for emotional and contextual information. Each group member is visualized as a "planet" in the orbit. First row, sheet for emotional cues: From A view to B view can be moved by zooming and from B to C by clicking previous. Second row, sheet for contextual cues: From D view to C view can be moved by zooming and from E to F by clicking Action.

We claim that increased socio-emotional awareness is relevant to distributed knowledge work teams and that it may increase efficiency and innovativeness of work. We claim that the mechanism by which this may happen is the increased communication bandwidth and contact frequency in the intimate and non-verbal communication flow within the group enabled by our prototype application. This may lead to various individual and group level beneficial effects, such as more efficient emotional regulation, mood management and general emotional awareness, linked to group trust and cohesion, for instance.

The application is at the moment in test use by a small team of knowledge workers. By the end of the year it will be used in large scale trials in four European countries with +100 users in each. In the trials it is possible to collect both qualitative (i.e. interviews, focus groups) as well as quantitative data (i.e. server log data of user performed actions, self-report questionnaires). On the server side it is possible to switch on and off certain cues in the application in order to study the effects of these cues/functions in a more controlled fashion.

Acknowledgements. The work has been conducted within the PASION (Psychologically Augmented Social Interaction Over Networks) Integrated Project, which is funded under the Presence II Initiative in the Future Emerging Technologies within the 6th Framework Program.

References

1. Herbsleb, J., Grinter, R.: Architectures, Coordination, and Distance: Conway's Law and Beyond. IEEE Software, pp. 63-70 (September/October 1999)
2. Barsade, S.G., Gibson, D.E.: Group emotion: A view from top and bottom. In: Gruenfeld, D., Mannix, B., Neale, M. (eds.) Research on Managing Groups and Teams, pp. 81–102. JAI Press, Stamford (1998)
3. Barsade, S.G.: The Ripple Effect: Emotional Contagion in Groups. In: Working Paper 98. Yale School of Management, Yale University, New Haven, CT (2000)
4. Bartel, C., Saavedra, R.: The collective construction of work group moods. Administrative Science Quarterly 45, 197–231 (2000)
5. Totterdell, P., Kellet, S., Teuchmann, K., Briner, R.B.: Evidence of mood linkage in work groups. Journal of Personality and Social Psychology 74, 1504–1515 (1998)

Employing Dynamic Transparency for 3D Occlusion Management: Design Issues and Evaluation

Niklas Elmqvist, Ulf Assarsson, and Philippas Tsigas

Department of Computer Science & Engineering,
Chalmers University of Technology, SE-412 96 Göteborg, Sweden
{elm,uffe,tsigas}@chalmers.se

Abstract. Recent developments in occlusion management for 3D environments often involve the use of dynamic transparency, or virtual "X-ray vision", to promote target discovery and access in complex 3D worlds. However, there are many different approaches to achieving this effect and their actual utility for the user has yet to be evaluated. Furthermore, the introduction of semi-transparent surfaces adds additional visual complexity that may actually have a negative impact on task performance. In this paper, we report on an empirical user study comparing dynamic transparency to standard viewpoint controls. Our implementation of the technique is an image-space algorithm built using modern programmable shaders to achieve real-time performance and visually pleasing results. Results from the user study indicate that dynamic transparency is superior for perceptual tasks in terms of both efficiency and correctness.

1 Introduction

The ability to utilize the full 3D space as a canvas for information-rich [1] visualization applications is a mixed blessing—while 3D space on the one hand supports an order of magnitude of more layout opportunities for visual elements than 2D space, visualization designers are on the other hand faced with a number of new challenges arising from the nature of 3D space which do not occur in 2D. More specifically, designers must consider the *visibility* of objects when users wish to discover relevant objects, as well as their *legibility* when the user wants to access information encoded in a particular object. For instance, whereas objects that do not intersect can never occlude each other in 2D space, this can very well happen in 3D space depending on the viewpoint and the spatial interaction between the objects.

A number of recent solutions to this problem involve the use of *dynamic transparency*, also known as virtual X-Ray [2], to make targets visible by turning intervening surfaces semi-transparency on-demand as the user moves through the 3D world (see Figure 1 for an example). However, this approach may instead introduce additional visual complexity and reduce the user's depth perception. Furthermore, the actual utility of these techniques remains unknown.

C. Baranauskas et al. (Eds.): INTERACT 2007, LNCS 4662, Part I, pp. 532–545, 2007.
© IFIP International Federation for Information Processing 2007

Fig. 1. Dynamic transparency uncovering an engine inside a jeep

In this paper, we evaluate the usefulness of dynamic transparency for solving visual tasks in both abstract and realistic environments. Note that dynamic transparency cannot be realized using the standard model for transparency, and no real-time performance algorithm exists in the literature that fulfills our requirements. Therefore, we also present an image-space algorithm for dynamic transparency that makes use of fragment shaders for the new generation of programmable graphics hardware to perform occlusion detection in the image space and with real-time rendering performance. The effect is somewhat akin to the "X-ray vision" of a superhero.

The contributions of this paper are the following: (i) a model for dynamic transparency that captures a natural way of achieving high efficiency for perceptual tasks; (ii) an efficient image-space algorithm for dynamic transparency using the new generation of programmable graphics hardware; and (iii) results from a formal user evaluation showing that dynamic transparency significantly improves both time performance and correctness for visual tasks involving discovery, access, and spatial relation of objects in 3D environments.

This paper is organized as follows: We first discuss the related work in the field and then present a model for dynamic transparency. In Section 4, we give our algorithm that realizes the requirements put down in the previous section. Section 5 and 6 present the user study and our results. We end the paper with some discussion of the results and conclusions.

2   Related Work

The general dynamic transparency approach makes heavy use of semi-transparent surfaces to reduce the impact of occlusion as well as to avoid the loss of 3D depth cues completely. In order to achieve correct results, transparent surfaces must be rendered in depth order. Everitt [3] discusses the *depth peeling* image-space algorithm for achieving this on modern graphics hardware based on the virtual pixel map concepts introduced by Mammen [4] and the dual depth buffers by Diefenbach [5]. The blueprints [6] technique uses depth peeling to outline perceptually important geometrical features of complex models using transparency and edge detection. However, depth peeling is a computationally demanding method and interactive frame rates can only be achieved for relatively low depth complexity.

Dynamic transparency is also commonly used in 3D games and virtual environments to allow users to see through occluding surfaces; Chittaro and Scagnetto [7] investigate this practice and conclude that see-through surfaces are more efficient than normal 3D navigation, although not as efficient as bird's-eye views.

Diepstraten et al. introduce view-dependent transparency [8] for use in interactive technical illustrations. While closely related to our work in regards to the general method, Diepstraten employs a fixed two-pass depth peeling step to uncover the two foremost layers of transparent surfaces, whereas our method is based on iterative back-to-front rendering and blending, and is thus not limited to a specific depth.

In another paper, Diepstraten et al. also present their work on computer-based *break-away* views [9], where interior objects are made visible through the surface of containing objects through image-space holes. While again similar to our work, Diepstraten's technique is simplified by semantic knowledge of inside and exterior objects, and the fact that the break-away view is realized by a single hole. To this end, their method is to compute the convex hull of interior objects in a preprocessing step and use it as a clipping volume. More importantly, their approach does not handle the case when several targets line up and occlude each other, a necessary requirement for dynamic visualizations with a high target density. Our method requires no off-line preprocessing and derives spatial information through sorting and rendering the scene back-to-front, smoothly blending the gradient outline of targets to the scene buffer in an iterative fashion.

Looser et al. [10] describe a 3D magic lens implementation for Augmented Reality that supports information filtering of a 3D model using the stencil buffer, allowing the user to utilize a looking glass to see through the exterior of a house and into its interior, for instance. This approach relies on the 3D model having semantically differentiated parts, whereas our method requires no such extra information. Coffin and Höllerer [11] present a similar technique with active interaction where the user is controlling a CSG volume that is dynamically subtracted from the surrounding world geometry, again using the stencil buffer. This work does not rely on any semantic target information at all and facilitates exploratory interaction like active dynamic transparency. However, the depth of the volume cutout is limited and user-controlled, and no depth cues from the world geometry are retained other than the cutout border area. With dynamic transparency, as described in this paper, we are guaranteed to always discover occluded objects regardless of depth, and some depth cues are retained using semi-transparency.

Finally, importance-driven rendering assigns importance values to individual objects in a 3D scene and renders a final image that is a composite of not only the geometrical properties of the objects, but also their relative importance. Viola et al. employ it for volume rendering [12] (IDVR) to actively reduce inter-object occlusion in the same way that we do in this work. While clearly using a more powerful interest model than our work, Viola's implementation (besides being aimed at volume rendering applications) does not provide interactive framerates, whereas our implementation makes use of modern graphics hardware to deliver real-time performance.

Dynamic transparency can also be used in 2D windowing systems (see for example [13,14,15]) instead of 3D worlds, but this is beyond the scope of this paper. Other examples of occlusion management also exist beyond the image-space approach taken in this paper, including view-space [16] and object-space [17] techniques.

3 Model for Dynamic Transparency

In this section, we present a model for the dynamic transparency approach. See [2] for a more in-depth treatment of general occlusion management.

3.1 Model

We represent the 3D world U by a Cartesian space $(x, y, z) \in \mathbb{R}^3$. Objects in the set O are volumes within U (i.e. subsets of U) represented by boundary surfaces (typically triangles). The user's viewpoint $v = (M, P)$ is represented by the view and projection matrices M and P.

An object can be flagged either as a *target*, an information-carrying entity, or a *distractor*, an object with no intrinsic information value. Importance flags can be dynamically changed. Occluded distractors pose no threat to any analysis tasks performed in the environment, whereas partially or fully occluded targets do, resulting in potentially decreased performance and correctness.

The surfaces defining an object volume have a transparency (alpha) function $\alpha(x) \in [0, 1]$. A line segment r passing through a surface at point p is *not* blocked if $\alpha(p) < 1$ and the cumulative transparency value α_r of the line segment is less than one. Passing through a surface increases the cumulative transparency of the line segment accordingly (multiplicatively or additively, depending on the transparency model).

3.2 Dynamic Transparency

The general idea behind dynamic transparency is simple: we can reduce the impact of occlusion by dynamically changing the transparency (alpha) value of individual object surfaces occluding (either partially or fully) a target object. This results in fewer fully occluded objects in the environment and thus directly affects the object discovery visual task.

The fact that the dynamic transparency mechanism operates on the transparency level of individual points of surfaces and not whole objects or even whole surfaces is vital; if whole surfaces or objects had been affected, important depth cues would have been lost. With the current approach, unoccluding parts of a surface will retain full opacity, providing important context to the transparent parts of the object. To give additional context, even occluding surface parts are not made fully transparent, but are set to a threshold alpha value α_T in order to shine through slightly in the final image. There is a tradeoff here: the use of semi-transparent occluders will make object access difficult since intervening surfaces will distort targets behind them. However, it is a necessity in order to maintain the user's context of the environment.

We define the model for dynamic transparency through a number of discrete rules governing the appearance of objects in the world:

(R1). All targets in the world U should be visible from any given viewpoint v.

The first rule is the most basic description of dynamic transparency, and stipulates that no targets should be fully occluded from any viewpoint in the world. Note that a target may still be hidden from the user if it falls outside the current view.

(R2). An occluded object is made visible by changing the transparency level of points $p \in P$ of each occluding surface s from opaque $(\alpha_s(p) = 1)$ to transparent $(\alpha_s(p) = \alpha_T)$.

The second rule describes the actual mechanics of how to make targets visible through occluding objects. The selection of the set P is not fixed; depending on the application, this could be a convex hull, circle, or ellipse that encloses the occluded object, or the occluded object's actual outline.

(R3). Surfaces can be made *impenetrable* and will never be made transparent.

The third rule provides a useful exception to the initial rule; in some cases, we may want to limit the extent of the dynamic transparency mechanism using impenetrable surfaces (and objects).

(R4). Objects are allowed to self-occlude.

The fourth and final rule provides another refinement of the previous rules; dynamic transparency is performed on object-level, even if transparency management is performed on individual surface points. This means that even if a part of a target is occluded by other parts of itself, none of its surfaces will be made transparent to show this.

4   Image-Space Dynamic Transparency

Since none of the previously presented methods fulfills our requirements, we here present a new algorithm for 3D dynamic transparency: image-space dynamic transparency.

An important observation that follows from our model of occlusion from the previous section is that occlusion can be detected in the image space by simply shooting a ray through the scene for every pixel that is rendered and checking the order it intersects objects in the scene. In modern graphics hardware, this essentially amounts to detecting whenever we are overwriting pixels in the color buffer or discarding pixels due to depth testing. In other words, programmable fragment shaders are perfectly suited for realizing dynamic transparency.

However, correct blending of transparency is order-dependent, and thus our algorithm, as well as most algorithms for transparent objects, requires the objects to be rendered in back-to-front order. This is a classical problem, since current graphics hardware cannot do the sorting for us, although suggestions for solutions exist [18]. Usually, depth sorting is performed on triangle-level. In our algorithm, for non-intersecting objects, it is sufficient to sort on object-level for normal objects that are opaque by default. For intersecting objects, sorting must be performed on a per-triangle-level. Intersecting objects are however rare and usually non-physical. As explained below, objects fully contained within other objects, like objects in a suitcase or nested Russian dolls, can be correctly treated by specifying a fixed sort order between a group of objects.

We divide the scene into groups. By default, a group contains one object. All groups are sorted with respect to their center point, which is precomputed once. The sorting metric is the signed distance to the group from the eye along the view vector. This is better than sorting by only the distance from the eye, because the former corresponds to how the z-buffer works. We use bubble sort, since frame coherency brings the resorting down to an average cost corresponding to $O(n)$.

In certain cases, like for Russian dolls, the sort order between the dolls should be from the innermost to the outermost. A fixed rendering order between the dolls is then user-defined by putting them into the same group with a predefined rendering order, for instance by the order of appearance in the group. In other words, the innermost doll should be rendered first and the outermost doll last. This results in correct transparency, since only the frontmost triangles of the dolls are visible (unlike for classic transparency). This mechanism gives the user a tool to specify which objects that should be regarded as solids and not.

Here is an overview of our algorithm:

1) The groups are rendered back-to-front.
2) All objects are blended into the frame buffer using the value in the alpha-channel of the frame buffer, which defaults to 1 (opaque), as blending factor.
3) Target objects also post-modify the values in the alpha-channel to a value < 1.

The algorithm needs to fulfill these criteria:

- Render all parts of objects (target or distractor) in front of a target object as transparent.
- Render each object as a solid, i.e. only the front-most surfaces should be visible. Thus, the objects cannot be rendered as transparent in an ordinary sense. Back-facing triangles, or more distant front-facing triangles, should not be visible through transparent frontmost triangles.

Algorithm 1. Main

Input: set of groups G.
Output: correctly rendered dynamic transparency scene.
1 BubbleSort(G), taking advantage of frame coherence.
2 **for** *all groups* $g \in G$ **do**
3   **for** *all objects* $o \in g$ **do**
4   **if** *o is a target* **then**
5   renderTargetObject()
6   **else**
7   renderDistractorObject()

- Draw a gradual transition from no transparency to a predefined transparency in an n-pixel outline region around each target object.

Algorithm 1 shows an outline of the main algorithm.

Initial requirements for rendering both targets and distractors are that (i) the alpha buffer is initiated to 1 for each pixel at the start of each frame, (ii) rendering is done back-to-front on object level, and (iii) the alpha buffer contains the desired blending factor (transparency) at each pixel. Given these preconditions, we render distractor objects in the following way:

1) Render object to the z-buffer only to mask out frontmost surfaces.
2) Blend object to the color buffer.

The first step selects the frontmost surfaces of the object. The second blends these surfaces to the frame buffer, with blending using the alpha values stored in the frame buffer. These alpha values are 1 by default and less in front of, and in an n-pixel region region around, target objects.

In contrast, target objects are rendered in the following way:

1) Render step 1 and 2 as for distractor objects.
2) Render alpha mask, i.e. multiplicatively blend an alpha mask to the alpha channel of the frame buffer.

The final step ensures that the rendered target is visible by creating a mask that essentially protects the target from being fully overdrawn by subsequently rendered objects.

Multiplying a constant alpha value to the pixels covered by the target object is easily done by simply rendering the object to the alpha-channel only and using a color with the alpha value set appropriately. Creating the alpha mask is a little trickier.

The alpha mask can be any type of shape exposing the underlying target, such as an ellipse or circle. We choose the expanded outline of the object with a transparency gradient as the alpha mask shape. To achieve this, we render to

---

Algorithm 2. RenderAlphaMask

Input: target object o, mask width n, two buffers B_1 and B_2.
Output: 128×128 alpha mask blended to the frame buffer.
1 Enable buffer B_1.
2 Render the target object o to the alpha channel only, setting the alpha values to α_T, the threshold transparency for objects in front of target objects.
3 Set buffer B_1 as texture.
4 Enable rendering to buffer B_2.
5 **for** *each layer* $\{1 \dots n\}$ *of mask* **do**
6 | Render buffer-sized quad with the fragment shader specified in Algorithm 3.
7 | Set the rendered buffer as texture and enable rendering to the other buffer. Each iteration adds one pixel-wide layer of the transition.
8 | Increase the border alpha value α_B in the shader incrementally starting from α_0 to 1.0.
9 Disable buffer and activate standard color buffer.
10 Multiplicatively blend the screen-size buffer texture to the color buffer (alpha values). Note that resolutions may differ, but linear filtering quite efficiently hides zooming artifacts.
11 Render the target region again to avoid jagginess at the border of the target object due to differences in resolution between the color and mask buffers.

Algorithm 3. FragmentShader

Input: border alpha α_B, frame buffer F, screen position P.
Output: alpha value α_P for pixel at position P.
1 **bool** IsBorderPixel $\leftarrow$ **false**;
2 **for** *each neighbor N of position P* **do**
3 | IsBorderPixel $\leftarrow$ $F(N)$.**Alpha** != 1.0 **or** IsBorderPixel;
4 IsBorderPixel $\leftarrow$ $(F(P).\mathbf{Alpha} == 1.0)$ **and** IsBorderPixel;
5 **output** IsBorderPixel ? α_B : 1.0;

---

two external off-screen buffers alternately to create a border around the target object with a smooth transition to full opacity. The resolution can be allowed to be quite low; we use a size of 128×128. See Algorithm 2 for pseudo code for the alpha mask algorithm and refer to Algorithm 3 for the fragment shader code.

4.1 Performance

Table 1 shows the performance of three example applications with and without dynamic transparency active (an abstract environment, an architectural walkthrough, and the game-like example in Figure 1). The test was performed on an Intel Pentium 4 desktop computer with 1 GB of memory running Microsoft Windows XP and equipped with an NVidia Geforce 7800 GTX graphics adapter. As can be seen from the measurements, only the GAME application is fillrate-limited (the bottleneck seems to be buffer switching). For the WALKTHROUGH

Table 1. Performance for three example applications

Application	Triangles	Resolution	Inactive (FPS)	Active (FPS)
ABSTRACT	13,000	800 × 600	87	33
		1280 × 1024	87	33
WALKTHROUGH	464,220	800 × 600	40	11
		1280 × 1024	40	11
GAME	114,629	800 × 600	300	140
		1280 × 1024	188	90

application, we are performing dynamic transparency on 50 complex objects, so 11 FPS is acceptable, if not quite interactive.

5   User Study

We hypothesize that users employing dynamic transparency for visual perception tasks in 3D environments would be more efficient as well as more correct in performing their tasks than when not having access to the technique. In order to test these hypotheses, we designed a formal user study comparing the new technique to standard 3D camera navigation techniques.

5.1   Subjects

We recruited 16 paid subjects for this study, three of which were female. The subjects were drawn primarily from our university and were screened to have at least basic computer knowledge. Subject ages ranged from 20 to 35 years of age. All subjects had normal or corrected-to-normal vision, and no participants reported color-blindness.

5.2   Equipment

The experiment was conducted on an Intel Centrino Duo laptop computer equipped with 2048 MB of memory running the Microsoft Windows XP operating system. The display was a 17-inch widescreen LCD display running at 1920 × 1200 resolution and powered by an NVidia Geforce 7800 GO graphics card.

5.3   Tasks and Scenarios

We designed the study to include two widely different scenarios, including an abstract 3D world and a virtual walkthrough in a 3D building, and four different tasks (two per environment). In this way, we aim to be able to measure not only basic target discovery, but also the more complex visual tasks of access and spatial relation.

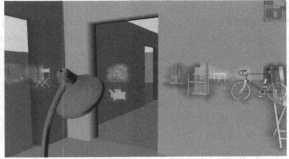

Fig. 2. The ABSTRACT and WALKTHROUGH applications with active dynamic transparency

5.4   Scenario: Abstract 3D World

The first scenario (ABSTRACT) is intended to portray an abstract 3D visualization application and consists of a cubic 3D volume of size $100 \times 100 \times 100$ filled with $n = 200$ objects of randomized position and orientation (see Figure 2 for a screenshot). The objects are simple unit 3D primitives: spheres, cones, boxes, and torii. Objects are allowed to intersect but not full enclose each other. 10% to 20% of the objects are flagged as targets and the remainder as distractors. Distractor objects are randomly assigned green and blue color component values, while targets were set to a pure red color and made visible using our dynamic transparency technique (for Task 2, distractors could be red as well). The user view is fixed at a specific distance from the center of the environment cube so that no object can fall outside of the view frustum, and can be freely orbited around the focus point to afford view from all directions.

Task 1: count the number of targets (red objects) in the environment. (Purpose: *discovery*)
Task 2: identify the pattern formed by the targets (red cones) in the environment. (Purpose: *relation*)

The pattern is one of the five capital letters C, K, R, X, and Y, rasterized in a 5×7 horizontal grid of the same scale as the environment and rotated in an arbitrary fashion around the vertical axis. The subject is informed of the range of possible letters prior to performing the task, but not the exact rasterizations.

5.5   Scenario: Virtual Walkthrough

The second scenario (WALKTHROUGH) is a little more complex in nature and designed to mimic a real 3D walkthrough visualization application more closely. Here, a one-level floor plan is randomly generated from a simple 16×16 grid, creating walls, floors and ceiling as well as ensuring that all rooms were connected with all of its adjacent neighbors through doorways. A number of $n = 50$ objects are generated and placed in the environment, and all objects are made visible through the walls using dynamic transparency. The 3D objects chosen for this scenario were more complex 3D models, including pets, vehicles, and furniture, yet were easily distinguishable from each other. The user starts each instance in the center of the environment and navigates through it looking for the target using 3D game-like controls involving the mouse and keyboard (mouse to pan the camera around the vertical axis, arrow keys to move, no strafing allowed). The view is constrained to floor level and there is no collision detection with walls or objects.

Task 3: find the unique target in the environment. (Purpose: *discovery*)
Task 4: count the number of targets in the environment. (Purpose: *discovery, relation*)

For the first task, one of the objects in the environment is unique and the user is asked to find this target. The current target is shown in the upper left corner of the screen. After finding the target, the user moves on to mark its estimated location on a 2D floorplan of the environment on a separate screen.

For the counting task, a random number of the objects in the environment are of the same type and the user is asked to count the occurrences. The current object type is again shown in the upper left corner of the screen. After having estimated that all occurrences are found, the subject enters the amount into the application.

5.6 Design

The study was designed as a repeated measures experiment for each of the four tasks, with the independent variable DYNTRANS (two levels, "true" or "false", within-subjects). The dependent variables included completion times for all tasks, and the error for the counting tasks, error distance for the search task, and correctness for the pattern task. Subjects received both the tasks and dynamic transparency in counterbalanced order to manage systematic effects of practice.

Each task set consisted of three trials per condition. Completion times and user responses to the tasks were collected and silently recorded by the application. Every task set was preceded by a training session lasting up to five minutes where the subject was instructed in the current task and was allowed to explore the scenario as well as ask questions. During the execution of the actual task set, only general questions were allowed. A full session lasted approximately 45 to 60 minutes.

6   Results

Analysis of the collected measurements indicates that both our hypotheses are correct; subjects are more efficient (i.e. use less time) and more correct when performing visual search tasks using dynamic transparency than without.

Table 2. Average completion times for all four tasks (standard deviation)

Task No.	Standard	DynTrans	Significance
1	56.26 (38.72)	40.44 (20.99)	$F(1, 15) = 7.54, p = .015$
2	22.30 (16.20)	15.80 (10.21)	$F(1, 15) = 5.28, p = .036$
3	62.78 (35.63)	23.21 (12.01)	$F(1, 15) = 22.98, p < .01$
4	140.0 (61.75)	40.80 (24.16)	$F(1, 15) = 48.61, p < .01$

6.1 Time

Overall, the average completion time with inactive dynamic transparency was 65.17 (s.d. 27.75) seconds, compared to 28.69 (s.d. 11.02) with active dynamic transparency. This was also a significant difference ($F(1, 15) = 49.54, p < .001$). Each of the individual tasks also showed significantly shorter average completion times for active dynamic transparency compared to inactive dynamic transparency down to $p < .05$. See Table 2 for a summary.

6.2 Correctness

For the counting tasks (task 1 and 4), we define correctness in terms of average relative error, i.e. the ratio between the absolute error and the total number of targets for all trials. The absolute error is the absolute difference between the sum of the targets and the sum of the subject answers for the trials. Overall, for task 1 and 4 combined, the average relative error was .100 (s.d. .141) when dynamic transparency was inactive compared to .027 (s.d. .045) when it was active. This is also a significant difference ($F(1, 15) = 6.28, p = .024$).

Task 1 in particular showed average relative error of .042 (s.d. .046) for inactive dynamic transparency and .017 (s.d. .018) for active. This too was significant ($F(1, 15) = 4.74, p = .046$). Task 4 showed .123 (s.d. .184) and .034 (s.d. .074) average relative error, respectively, not a significant difference ($F(1, 15) = 4.12, p = .061$).

For task 2, we define correctness as whether or not the subject identified the pattern as the correct one. This figure was .963 (s.d. .109) for no dynamic transparency and .963 (s.d. .150) for active. This is obviously not a significant difference.

Finally, for task 3, we define correctness as the average Euclidean distance (in world units) from the real position of the target and the point marked on the map by the subject for each trial. With dynamic transparency inactive, this average distance was 16.99 (s.d. 14.44), as opposed to 16.21 (s.d. 8.88). This difference is not significant ($F(1, 15) = .068, p = .797$), and indicates that the spatial understanding of the subjects was not negatively affected by the use of dynamic transparency.

7 Discussion

It is important to remember that occlusion is a vital depth cue that humans use to determine the spatial relation of objects in our environment. The introduction of dynamic transparency may then adversely affect this mechanism, and can actually result in "reverse occlusion", i.e. the phenomenon that distant objects all of a sudden occlude nearby objects instead.

In our approach, we address this problem by ensuring that intervening objects made transparent always retain at least some percentage of opacity in order to shine through on uncovered objects. This means that the user receives a visual indication of the existence of the transparent surfaces. Self-reported ratings from the subjects themselves seem to indicate that depth perception is still acceptable with dynamic transparency active.

Fortunately, human perception relies on many more factors besides occlusion to disambiguate depth; examples include stereopsis, motion parallax, atmospheric perspective, texture gradient, etc. Even if we weaken the occlusion cue, other depth cues will help the viewer to perceive the 3D scene correctly.

Some subjects in our study had the interesting behavior of "respecting" the world more when dynamic transparency was inactive, using the doors in the virtual walkthrough rather than going through walls, whereas they would not hesitate to pass through walls when it was active. While this is an informal observation, this behavior might indicate that the impact that dynamic transparency has on visual realism causes the world to become more ethereal and less believable to the users, thus making them ignore the implicit rules of the environment.

8 Conclusions

We have presented an evaluation of the use of dynamic transparency for managing occlusion of important target objects in 3D visualization applications. In the absence of real-time algorithms for dynamic transparency that are suitable for interactive visualization, we have further devised an image-space algorithm and implementation realizing the model. The algorithm uses the standard framebuffer as a cumulative alpha buffer, rendering the scene back-to-front and blending in alpha masks of target objects to allow for see-through surfaces. Our evaluation consisted of a comparative user study evaluating efficiency and correctness gains from using the technique as opposed to standard 3D navigation controls. Our results clearly show that dynamic transparency results in significantly more efficient object discovery. Users are also more correct with the technique than without.

Acknowledgments

The authors would like to thank Per A. Jonasson for valuable insights into superhero X-ray vision. Many thanks to members of the IIR group at Georgia Tech for their comments and feedback on the intermediate stages of this work.

References

1. Bowman, D.A., North, C., Chen, J., Polys, N.F., Pyla, P.S., Yilmaz, U.: Information-rich virtual environments: theory, tools, and research agenda. In: Proceedings of the ACM Symposium on Virtual Reality Software and Technology, pp. 81–90. ACM Press, New York (2003)

2. Elmqvist, N., Tsigas, P.: A taxonomy of 3D occlusion management techniques. In: Proceedings of the IEEE Conference on Virtual Reality, pp. 51–58. IEEE Computer Society Press, Los Alamitos (2007)
3. Everitt, C.: Interactive order-independent transparency. NVIDIA Corporation (2001), See http://developer.nvidia.com
4. Mammen, A.: Transparency and antialiasing algorithms implemented with the virtual pixel maps technique. IEEE Computer Graphics and Applications 9(4), 43–55 (1989)
5. Diefenbach, P.J.: Pipeline Rendering: Interaction and Realism through Hardware-Based Multi-Pass Rendering. Ph.D. thesis, Computer Graphics, University of Pennsylvania (1996)
6. Nienhaus, M., Döllner, J.: Blueprints: Illustrating architecture and technical parts using hardware-accelerated non-photorealistic rendering. In: Proceedings of Graphics Interface, pp. 49–56 (2004)
7. Chittaro, L., Scagnetto, I.: Is semitransparency useful for navigating virtual environments? In: Proceedings of the ACM Symposium on Virtual Reality Software and Technology, pp. 159–166. ACM Press, New York (2001)
8. Diepstraten, J., Weiskopf, D., Ertl, T.: Transparency in interactive technical illustrations. Computer Graphics Forum 21(3), 317–325 (2002)
9. Diepstraten, J., Weiskopf, D., Ertl, T.: Interactive cutaway rendering. In: Proceedings of Eurographics, pp. 523–532 (2003)
10. Looser, J., Billinghurst, M., Cockburn, A.: Through the looking glass: the use of lenses as an interface tool for augmented reality interfaces. In: Proceedings of GRAPHITE, pp. 204–211 (2004)
11. Coffin, C., Höllerer, T.: Interactive perspective cut-away views for general 3D scenes. In: Proceedings of the IEEE Symposium on 3D User Interfaces, pp. 25–28. IEEE Computer Society Press, Los Alamitos (2006)
12. Viola, I., Kanitsar, A., Gröller, E.: Importance-driven volume rendering. In: Proceedings of the IEEE Conference on Visualization, pp. 139–145. IEEE Computer Society Press, Los Alamitos (2004)
13. Gutwin, C., Dyck, J., Fedak, C.: The effects of dynamic transparency on targeting performance. In: Proceedings of Graphics Interface, pp. 105–112 (2003)
14. Baudisch, P., Gutwin, C.: Multiblending: displaying overlapping windows simultaneously without the drawbacks of alpha blending. In: Proceedings of the ACM CHI 2004 Conference on Human Factors in Computing Systems, pp. 367–374. ACM Press, New York (2004)
15. Ishak, E.W., Feiner, S.K.: Interacting with hidden content using content-aware free-space transparency. In: Proceedings of the ACM Symposium on User Interface Software and Technology, pp. 189–192. ACM Press, New York (2004)
16. Elmqvist, N., Tsigas, P.: View projection animation for occlusion reduction. In: Proceedings of the ACM Conference on Advanced Visual Interfaces, pp. 471–475. ACM Press, New York (2006)
17. Elmqvist, N., Tudoreanu, M.E.: Evaluating the effectiveness of occlusion reduction techniques for 3D virtual environments. In: Proceedings of the ACM Symposium on Virtual Reality Software and Technology, pp. 9–18. ACM Press, New York (2006)
18. Carpenter, L.: The A-buffer, an antialiased hidden surface method. Computer Graphics 18(3), 103–108 (1984)

Towards Applicable 3D User Interfaces for Everyday Working Environments

Frank Steinicke, Timo Ropinski, Gerd Bruder, and Klaus Hinrichs

Visualization and Computer Graphics (VisCG) Research Group
Institute of Computer Science, Westfälische Wilhelms-Universität Münster,
Einsteinstraße 62, 48149 Münster, Germany
{fsteini,ropinski,g_brud01,khh}@math.uni-muenster.de
http://viscg.uni-muenster.de

Abstract. Desktop environments represent a powerful user interface and have been used as the *de facto* standard human-computer interaction paradigm for over 20 years. But the rising demand of 3D applications dealing with complex datasets exceeds the capabilities of traditional interaction devices and two-dimensional displays. Such applications need more immersive and intuitive interfaces. In order to be accepted by the users, technology-driven solutions that require inconvenient instrumentation, e.g., stereo glasses or tracked gloves, should be avoided. Autostereoscopic display environments equipped with tracking systems enable humans to experience virtual 3D environments more naturally, for instance via gestures, without having to use annoying devices. However, currently these approaches are used only for specially designed or adapted applications. In this paper we introduce new 3D user interface concepts for such setups which require minimal instrumentation of the user and can be integrated easily in everyday working environments. We propose an interaction framework which supports simultaneous display of and simultaneous interaction with both monoscopic as well as stereoscopic contents. We identify the challenges for combined mouse-, keyboard- and gesture-based input paradigms in such an environment and introduce novel interaction strategies.

Keywords: HCI, autostereoscopic display environments, 3D user interfaces.

1 Introduction

In recent years 3D user interfaces (UIs) have become more and more popular and widespread due to the requirements of several application areas, where two-dimensional desktop systems lack immersive and intuitive interaction. Bi-manual interactions or six degrees of freedom (DoFs) manipulations, which do not require much effort and are easy to learn even for non-experts, have increased the user's ability to perform complex interaction tasks. Current 3D UIs are technology-driven solutions providing more immersive exploration of and interaction with complex datasets, in particular by using stereoscopic projection and tracked six

C. Baranauskas et al. (Eds.): INTERACT 2007, LNCS 4662, Part I, pp. 546–559, 2007.

DoFs input devices. Although the costs for such a setup have reached a moderate level, common and even expert users hardly use these systems – even when 3D tasks have to be accomplished [3]. One reason for this is the inconvenient instrumentation required to allow immersive interactions, i.e., the user is forced to wear stereo glasses, tracked devices, gloves etc. [12]. Furthermore the most effective ways for humans to interact with synthetic 3D environments have not finally been resolved [3,6]. Devices that enable control over multiple DoFs simultaneously still involve problems, which are often avoided by the usage of their 2D counterparts – as a matter of fact 2D interactions are performed best with 2D devices [3,9,17]. However, while in real life humans are able to move and turn objects freely in a single motion, this natural interaction is absent in two-dimensional interfaces; the user is forced to decompose 3D tasks into several 2D tasks. In addition, shortage of spatial input in typical 3D applications leads to the need to constantly switch modes. This procedure results in ineffectiveness, in particular when switching between manipulation and navigation techniques is required in a repetitive manner.

Most desktop-based 3D applications include three-dimensional content in combination with two-dimensional elements for graphical user interface (GUI) interaction. While 3D content usually benefits from stereoscopic display, 2D GUI items often do not require immersive visualization. For such a system current autostereoscopic (AS) displays can be used to view 3D data stereoscopically without wearing any devices [8]. Thus the user is able to perceive a stereoscopic image in a fixed area called *sweet spot*. When the AS display features, for instance, an optical head tracker, the user can even move in front of the display, while the tracking system can be further exploited to allow gesture-based interaction [11]. However, the separation of the stereo half images performed by an AS display (see Section 3.1) influences viewing of monoscopic content in such a way that essential elements of the GUI are distorted. Although some AS devices can display monoscopic content, simultaneous display of mono- as well as stereoscopic content is not supported. Thus, simultaneous viewing requires an additional conventional display to show the monoscopic content. But only few applications support rendering of a stereoscopic window on a different display. Nevertheless, problems arise from decoupling interaction and visualization; interactions with 2D GUI elements have to be performed on the 2D screen, whereas 3D content is displayed stereoscopically on an AS display.

In this paper we introduce new 3D user interface concepts as a solution to the lack of spatial input and intuitive interaction techniques for direct manipulation of mono- as well as stereoscopic content in desktop environments. We propose an AS display environment and present a framework which enables to display arbitrary shaped areas of the GUI either in a mono- or in a stereoscopic way. Furthermore, the framework allows interaction between both "worlds" and thus opens up new vistas for human-computer interaction (HCI). Hence, the user can interact with any 2D or 3D application via familiar mouse/keyboard devices in combination with natural gestures.

The remainder of this paper is organized as follows. Section 2 summarizes related work. In Section 3 we describe the proposed setup, while Section 4 introduces interaction strategies for such everyday working environments. Section 5 presents implementation details. The results of an experimental evaluation are discussed in Section 6. Section 7 concludes the paper and gives an overview about future work.

2   Related Work

AS Display Environments. In 2000, the Heinrich-Hertz-Institute built an AS display system consisting of a gaze tracker, a head tracker and a hand tracker [11]. The head tracker gives the user a look-around capability, while the gaze tracking activates different applications on the desktop. The hand tracker enables the user to navigate and manipulate objects in 3D space via simple gestures, where computer vision is the major technological factor influencing the type of gesture that are supported. Similar approaches support gesture-based interactions by tracking the users hand and fingers with magnetic fields [23] or optical-based solutions [2]. These approaches rather address tracking technologies than advanced 3D user interfaces. Although these systems potentially support novel forms of interaction, they are restricted to specific applications designed for these setups [2]; simultaneous display of and simultaneous interaction with both monoscopic and stereoscopic content is not considered.

Simultaneous Monoscopic and Stereoscopic Display. Although current stereo-in-a-window systems [5,22] show stereoscopic content either in one window time-sequentially or using filtering techniques, these technologies are restricted to only one rectangular window and still require glasses. Hardware-based approaches have been proposed to display monoscopic and stereoscopic content simultaneously on one AS display [13]. However, interaction concepts have not yet been developed for these displays, and these systems only exist as prototype solutions. Due to the lack of simultaneous display most interaction approaches only propose improvements for interactions either in 2D using monoscopic display or in 3D using stereoscopic display, but they do not combine both worlds. The interaction with stereoscopic content using two-dimensional strategies involves further problems, for instance, monoscopic representation of the mouse cursor disturbs stereoscopic perception and therefore precise interactions become more difficult to perform.

3D User Interfaces. In recent years, many frameworks have been proposed which extend 2D GUIs for operating systems (OSs) to so called *3D desktops*, but also existing OSs evolve to 3D and include depth information [1,16]. These approaches provide a virtual 3D space in which 2D GUI elements are replaced by three-dimensional counterparts. Hence, more space is available to display further information. Although these environments provide a fancy visualization, it has not been investigated in how far they improve the interaction process, since they force the user to perform 3D interactions where 2D interactions are intended. Due to the mentioned shortcomings of virtual reality (VR) interfaces, hybrid approaches have been proposed which combine 2D and 3D interaction using different display or interaction technologies [4,21]. For example, Benko et al. have discussed techniques to grab monoscopically displayed objects from a projection screen in order to view them stereoscopically using a head mounted display [4]. However, an instrumentation of the user is still required.

Bi-Manual Interactions. When interacting with the hands numerous factors have to be considered. With respect to the tasks, the hands need to be moved symmetrically or asymmetrically, some tasks can be performed better with the dominant, others with the non-dominant hand. Also the used input devices have a major impact on the way how bi-manual interactions are performed. For instance, the used devices can be alike (e.g., keyboard and keyboard) or different (e.g., mouse and keyboard), and they can support different DoFs or involve constraints.

These approaches are applied in everyday tasks as well as in most user interfaces. Writing on a sheet of paper, when one hand holds the pencil while the other fixes the sheet, involves asymmetrical interactions. In many computer games navigation tasks are performed by the dominant hand using the mouse, while status changes are accomplished with the non-dominant hand via keyboard shortcuts. Interaction techniques for large-screen displays or VR environments often involve symmetrical bi-manual manipulation in order to scale or rotate virtual objects.

However, the combination of traditional devices and gestures in AS display environments that run common 3D applications has not been considered until now. The aim of this paper is not to debate the validity of desktop-based interaction concepts – there is no need to throw away 40 years of 2D UI research – or the benefits of technology-driven VR approaches. The objective is to explore in how far these concepts can mutually adapt to each other in order to provide efficient interfaces that will be accepted by users as setups for their daily working environments.

3   Proposed System Setup

In this section we present the setup which we believe has the potential to be accepted by the users since natural as well as immersive interactions are supported, whereas instrumentation of the user is avoided.

3.1   Autostereoscopic Display Environment

On current AS displays users can see 3D data without wearing any instruments, for example by using lenticular rasters [8]. The lenticular screen is a molded plastic sheet that forms dozens of tiny lenses per inch. This raster operates as a beam splitter and ensures that the pixels displayed in each odd column are seen with the left eye, while the pixels displayed in each even column are seen with

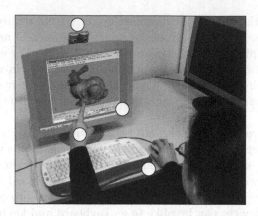

Fig. 1. 3D user interface setup includes (A) an AS display, (B) traditional mouse and keyboard, and (C) stereo-based camera setup. (D) The user applies gestures in order to perform 3D manipulations of a 3D scene. Due to the lenticular sheet the user perceives a stereoscopic image of the virtual scene displayed in 3D Studio Max.

the right eye. If the viewer positions her head in certain viewing positions, she sees a different image with each eye resulting in a stereo image. When leaving a sweet spot to a neighboring position, the stereo half images have to be swapped in order to maintain the stereoscopic effect.

The separation of the stereo half images influences viewing of monoscopic content in such a way that the most essential elements of the GUI are distorted. Therefore, we have implemented a software framework (see Section 5), which provides full control over the GUI of the OS. Thus, any region or object can be displayed either mono- or stereoscopically. Furthermore, we are able to catch the entire content of any 3D graphics application based on OpenGL or DirectX. Our framework allows to change the corresponding function calls in order to modify the visualization. The interaction performed in our setup is primarily based on mouse and keyboard (see Figure 1). However, we have extended these devices with more natural interfaces.

3.2   Stereo-Based Trackingsystem

AS displays can be equipped with eyes or head tracking systems to automatically adjust the two displayed images and the corresponding raster. Thus, the user perceives a stereo image in a larger region. Vision-based trackers enable non-intrusive, markerless computer vision based modules for HCI. When using computer vision techniques several features can be tracked, e.g., the eyes for head tracking, but it is also possible to track fingers in order to interpret simple as well as intuitive gestures in 3D. Pointing with the fingertip, for example, is an easy and natural way to select virtual objects.

As depicted in Figure 1, we use a stereo-based camera setup consisting of two USB cameras each having a resolution of 640 × 480 pixels. They are attached to the top of the AS display in order to track the position and orientation of certain objects. Due to the known arrangement of the cameras, the pose of geometric objects, e.g., user's hands, can be reconstructed by 3D reprojection. Besides pointing actions, even some simple gestures signaling *stop, start, left* and *right* can be recognized. These gesture input events can be used to perform 3D manipulations, e.g., to rotate or translate virtual objects (see Figure 1).

4   3D User Interface Concepts

In the system setup described in the previous section, traditional input devices can be combined with gesture-based paradigms. There exist similar setups for artificial environments which are restricted to applications exclusively designed for or adapted to the specific environment [11]. Hence, concepts developed for these restricted setups are not applicable in daily working environments for common applications. With the described framework we have full control over the GUI of the OS, in particular any arbitrarily shaped region can be displayed either mono- or stereoscopically, and each 3D application can be modified appropriately. The implementation concepts are explained in Section 5. In the following subsections we discuss implications and introduce several *universal* interaction techniques that are usable for any 3D application.

4.1   Universal Exploration

As mentioned in Section 3.1 our framework enables us to control any content of an application based on OpenGL or DirectX. Virtual scenes in such applications are often defined by so-called *display lists*. Using our framework enables us to hijack and modify these lists. Among other possibilities this allows us to change the viewpoint in a virtual scene. Hence several navigation concepts can be realized that are usable for any 3D application.

Head Tracking. Since binocular vision is essential for depth perception, stereoscopic projections are mainly exploited to give a better insight into complex three-dimensional datasets. Although stereoscopic displays improve depth perception, viewing static images is limited, because other important depth cues, e.g, motion parallax phenomena, cannot be observed. *Motion parallax* denotes the fact that when objects or the viewer move, objects which are farther away from the viewer seem to move more slowly than objects closer to the viewer. To reproduce this effect, head tracking and view-dependent rendering is required. This can be achieved by exploiting the described tracking system (see Section 3.2). When the position and orientation of the user's head is tracked, this pose is mapped to the virtual camera defined in the 3D scene; furthermore the position of the lenticular sheet is adapted. Thus, the user is able to explore 3D datasets (to a certain degree) only by moving the tracked head. Such view-dependent rendering can also be integrated for any 3D application based on OpenGL.

Fig. 2. Screenshot of an AS desktop overlaid with a transparent image of the user in (left) anaglyph mode and (right) vertical interlaced mode

Universal 3D Navigation and Manipulation Techniques. However, exploration only by head tracking is limited; object rotation is restricted by the tracking system, e.g. to 60°. Almost any interactive 3D application provides navigation techniques to explore virtual data from arbitrary viewpoints. Although many of these concepts are similar, e.g., mouse-based techniques to pan, zoom, rotate etc., 3D navigation as well as manipulation across different applications can become confusing due to various approaches.

The main idea to solve this shortcoming is to provide for different 3D applications the same universal paradigms to interact with a virtual scene. We use gestures to translate, scale or rotate objects or to move, fly or walk through a virtual environment. Moreover, individual strategies supported by each application can be used further on, e.g., by mouse- or keyboard-based interaction.

We have implemented these navigational concepts by using gestures based on virtual hand techniques [6]. Therefore, a one-to-one mapping in terms of translational and rotational mappings between the movements of the user's hand and the virtual scene is applied. Thus the user can start an arbitrary 3D application, activate gesture recognition and afterwards, the user can manipulate the scene by the combination of mouse, keyboard and gestures. Other concepts, such as virtual flying, walking etc. can be implemented, for instance, by virtual pointer approaches [6].

4.2   Stereoscopic Facetop Interaction

Besides depth information about the user's head and hand, we also exploit the images captured by the stereo-cameras mounted on top of the AS display (see Figure 1). Since the image planes of the cameras are coplanar and the distance between their lenses approximates the interpupillary distance of $\approx 65\,mm$, both images compose a stereoscopic image of the user. Due to the full control over the GUI, we are able to display both half images transparently into the corresponding columns of the AS display – one image into the even columns, one into the odd ones. Hence, the user sees her image superimposed on the GUI as a transparent overlay; all desktop content can still be seen, but users appear to themselves as a semi-transparent image, as if looking through a window in which they can see their own reflection. This visualization can also be used in order to enable stereo-based face-to-face collaboration which is not topic of this paper.

The technique of superimposing the user's image on top of the display has been used recently in the *Facetop* system [20]. More recently, Sony has released the Eyetoy that enables gesture interaction. In both approaches the user performs 2D interactions on the screen by 3D gestures, and visual feedback is given by displaying captured images of the user. However, besides gesturing for two-dimensional control, e.g., moving the mouse cursor by pointing, a stereo-based camera setup allows to use multiple DoF to enable 3D interaction. Furthermore, we use the stereoscopic projection of the user. This provides not only visual feedback about the position of the cursor on the screen surface, but also about its depth in order to simplify 3D interaction. A 3D representation of the mouse cursor is displayed at the tracked 3D position. A mouse click might be emulated if the position of the real finger and the visual representation of the finger stereoscopically displayed overlap in space. Alternatively, other gestures might be predefined, e.g., grab gestures. The depth information is also used when interacting with 2D GUIs. When using our framework, a corresponding depth is assigned to each window, and it is displayed stereoscopically. In addition shadows are added to all windows to further increase depth perception. When finger tracking is activated, the user can arrange windows on the desktop in depth by pushing or pulling them with a tracked finger. Figure 2 shows screenshots of two stereoscopic facetop interaction scenarios. Both users arrange windows on the desktop by pushing them with the finger.

4.3   Combined Interaction Strategies

By using the described concepts we are able to combine desktop devices with gestures. This setup is beneficial in scenarios where the user holds a virtual object in her non-dominant hand using universal exploration gestures (see Section 4.1), while the other hand can perform precise interactions via the mouse (see Figure 1). In contrast to using only common desktop devices, no context switches are required, e.g., to initiate status switches between navigation and manipulation modi. The roles of the hands may also change, i.e., the dominant hand can be used for gestures, whereas the non-dominant interacts via the keyboard.

Stereoscopic Mouse Cursor. When using the described setup we experienced some drawbacks. One shortcoming when interacting with stereoscopic representations using desktop-based interaction paradigms is the monoscopic appearance of the mouse cursor, which disturbs the stereoscopic perception. Therefore we provide two different strategies to display the mouse cursor. The first one exploits a *stereoscopic mouse cursor* which hovers over 3D objects. Thus the mouse cursor is always visible on top of the objects surface, and when moving the cursor over the surface of a three-dimensional object, the user gets an additional shape cue about the object. The alternative is to display the cursor always at

 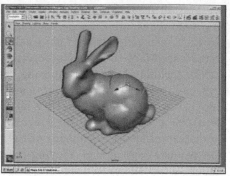

Fig. 3. Screenshots of the 3D user interface simultaneously showing monoscopic and stereoscopic content and (left) a stereoscopic mouse cursor and (right) a monoscopic interaction lens. To perceive a stereoscopic effect both images can be viewed with anaglyph glasses.

the image plane. In contrast to common desktop environments the mouse cursor gets invisible when it is obscured by another object extending out of the screen. Thus the stereoscopic impression is not disturbed by the mouse cursor, indeed the cursor is hidden during that time. Figure 3 (left) shows a stereoscopic scene in Google Earth where the mouse cursor is rendered stereoscopically on top of the building.

Monoscopic Interaction Lens. Many 2D as well as 3D applications provide interaction concepts which are best applicable in two dimensions using 2D interaction paradigms. One example are 3D widgets [7] which reduce simultaneously manipulated DoFs. Since these interaction concepts are optimized for 2D interaction devices and monoscopic viewing we propose a *monoscopic interaction lens* through which two-dimensional interactions can be performed without loosing the entire stereoscopic effect. We attach a lens to the position of the mouse cursor and project the content within such an arbitrarily shaped lens onto the image plane. Thus the user can focus on the given tasks and tools to perform 2D or 3D interactions in the same way as done on a common monoscopic display. This can be used to read text on a stereoscopic object, or to interact with 3D widgets.

5 Implementation

To provide a technical basis for the concepts described above, we explain some implementation details of our 3D user interface framework [19]. To allow simultaneous viewing monoscopic content need to be modified in order to make it perceivable on AS displays, while a stereo pair needs to be generated from the 3D content. Since these are diverse image processing operations first 2D is separated from 3D content. To achieve this separation, our technique acts as an integrated layer between 3D application and OS. By using this layer we ensure

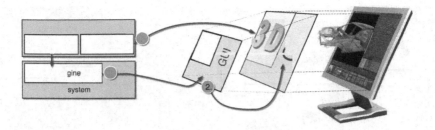

Fig. 4. Illustration of the interscopic user interface framework showing 2D and 3D content simultaneously

that the operating system takes care about rendering 2D GUI elements in a native way (see Figure 4 (step 1)).

Processing 2D Content. When viewing unadapted 2D content on AS displays the two images seen by the eyes are not correct half-images. This leads to an awkward viewing experience. To make this content perceivable we have to ensure that left and right eye see almost the same information, resulting in a flat two-dimensional image embedded in the image plane. To achieve this effect with (vertical-interlaced) AS displays the 2D content has to be scaled (see Figure 4 (step 2)) in order to ensure that the odd and even columns display almost the same information. With respect to the corresponding factor, scaling content can yield slightly different information for both half images. However, since differences in both images are marginal, the human vision system can merge the information to a final image which can be viewed comfortably. Since we achieve proper results for a resolution of 1024×768 pixels we choose this setting for a virtual desktop from which the content is scaled to the AS display's native resolution, i.e., 1600×1200 pixels. Therefore, we had to develop an appropriate display driver which allows the OS to mirror the desktop with the necessary resolution.

Generating Stereoscopic Images. Since only a few 3D applications natively support stereoscopic viewing on AS displays, in most cases we have to adapt also the 3D content in order to generate stereocopic images (see Figure 4 (step 3)). There are two techniques for making an existing 3D application stereoscopic. The first one is to trace and cache all 3D function calls and execute them twice, once for each eye. The alternative exploits image warping techniques. This technique performs a reprojection of the monoscopic image with respect to the values stored in the depth buffer. Image warping has the shortcoming that not all the scene content potentially visible from both eyes is presented in a single monoscopic image, and thus pixel filling approaches have to be applied [10]. Hence, we use the first approach, catch all 3D function calls in a display list, apply off-axis stereographic rendering, and render the content in the even and odd columns for the left respectively right eye with respect to the head position as described in Section 4.

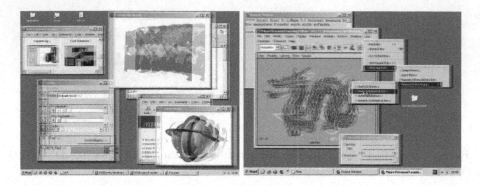

Fig. 5. Example screenshot of desktop with mono- as well as stereoscopic content shown (left) in anaglyph and (right) vertical interlaced mode

Embedding Mono- and Stereoscopic Display. To separate 2D and 3D content, we have to know which window areas are used for stereoscopic display. This can be determined either manually or automatically. When using the manual selection mechanism, the user is requested to add a 3D window or region and select it to be displayed stereoscopically with the mouse cursor. When using automatic detection, our framework seeks for 3D windows based on OpenGL and applies stereoscopic rendering.

The final embedding step of 2D and 3D content is depicted by step 3 in Figure 4. An obvious problem arises, when 2D and 3D content areas overlap each other. This may happen when either a pull-down menu or a context menu overlaps a 3D canvas. In this case the separation cannot only be based on the previous 3D window selection process. To properly render overlaying elements we apply a masking technique. This is for example important when dealing with 3D graphics applications using context menus to provide convenient access to important features. When merging 2D and 3D content the mask ensures that only those areas of the 3D window are used for stereoscopic display which are not occluded by 2D objects. Figure 5 shows two resulting screenshots in anaglyph respectively interlaced stereoscopic mode, where 3D content is shown in stereo. The windows appear at different distances to the user (see Section 4.2). The task bar and the desktop with its icons are rendered monoscopically.

6   Preliminary Experiments

In several informal tests all users have evaluated the usage of stereoscopic display for 3D applications as very helpful. In particular, two 3D modeling experts revealed stereoscopic visualization for 3D content in their 3D modeling environments, i.e., Maya and Cinema4D, as extremely beneficial. However, in order to evaluate the 3D user interface we have performed a preliminary usability study. We have used the described experimental environment (see Section 3). Furthermore, we have used a 3D mouse to enable precise 3D interaction.

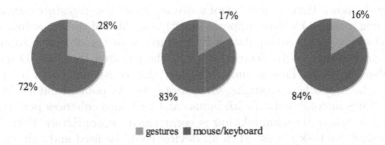

Fig. 6. Usage of gestures in comparison to traditional input devices constrained to (left) three DoFs, (middle) two DoFs and (right) one DoF

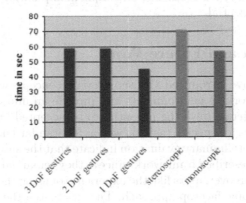

Fig. 7. Required time for the interaction task with stereoscopic display and gestures supporting three, two and one DoFs, and stereoscopic as well as monoscopic display only supporting mouse and keyboard without gesture

6.1   Experimental Tasks

We restricted the tasks to simple interactions in which four users had to delete several doors and windows from a virtual building. The building consisted of 290 triangles, where windows and doors (including 20 triangles) were uniformly separated. We have conducted three series. In the first series the user could use all provided input paradigms, i.e., mouse, keyboard, and gestures via a 3D mouse, in combination with stereoscopic visualization. In this series we have also performed subseries, where gestures were constrained to three, two and one DoFs. In the second series, only the mouse and keyboard could be used, again with stereoscopic display. In the last series, interaction was restricted to traditional devices with monoscopic visualization.

6.2   Results

We have measured the required time for the entire task and we have measured how long each input modality has been used.

Figure 6 shows that as fewer DoFs are available fewer gestures have been used. When three DoFs were supported (left), one-third of the entire interaction time was spent on 3D manipulation by gestures with the objective to arrange the virtual building. With decreasing DoFs the required time for 3D manipulation also decreases. This is due to the fact that constraint-based interaction supports the user when arranging virtual objects. As pointed out in Figure 7 using gestures in combination with mouse and keyboard enhances performance, in particular when 3D manipulation is constrained appropriately. Participants accomplished the task fastest when all devices could be used and only one DoF was supported. Monoscopic display was advantageous in comparison to stereoscopic display. This does not come unexpected since exploration of 3D objects was hardly necessary; the focus was on simple manipulation where stereoscopic display was not essential.

7   Discussion and Future Work

In this paper we have introduced 3D user interface concepts which can be embedded in everyday working environments and provide an improved working experience. These strategies have the potential to be accepted by users as new user interface paradigms for specific tasks as well as for standard desktop interactions. The results of the preliminary evaluation indicate that the subjects are highly motivated to use the described framework, since as they remarked an instrumentation is not required. Moreover, users like the experience of using the 3D interface, especially the stereoscopic facetop approach. They evaluated the stereoscopic mouse cursor as clear improvement. The usage of the monoscopic interaction lens has been revealed as very useful because the subjects prefer to interact in a way which is familiar to them from working with common desktop systems.

In the future we will integrate further functionality and visual enhancements using more stereoscopic and physics-based motion effects. Moreover, we plan to examine further interaction techniques, in particular, for domain-specific interaction tasks.

References

1. Agarawala, A., Balakrishnan, R.: Keepin' It Real: Pushing the Desktop Metaphor with Physics, Piles and the Pen. In: Proceedings of the SIGCHI conference on Human Factors in computing systems, pp. 1283–1292 (2006)
2. Alpaslan, Z.Y., Sawchuk, A.A.: Three-Dimensional Interaction with Autostereoscopic Displays. In: Woods, A.J., Merritt, J.O., Benton, S.A., Bolas, M.R. (eds.) Proceedings of SPIE, Stereoscopic Displays and Virtual Reality Systems, vol. 5291, pp. 227–236 (2004)
3. Balakrishnan, R.: A Grant of 3D. Keynote speach Symposium on 3D User Interfaces (2006)
4. Benko, H., Ishak, E.W., Feiner, S.: Cross-Dimensional Gestural Interaction Techniques for Hybrid Immersive Environments. In: Proceedings of Virtual Reality, pp. 209–216. IEEE Computer Society Press, Los Alamitos (2005)

5. Bourke, P.: Autostereoscopic Lenticular Images,
   http://local.wasp.uwa.edu.au/~pbourke
6. Bowman, D., Kruijff, E., LaViola, J., Poupyrev, I.: 3D User Interfaces: Theory and Practice. Addison-Wesley, Reading (2004)
7. Conner, D.B., Snibbe, S.C., Herndon, K.P., Robbins, D.C., Zeleznik, R.C., van Dam, A.: Three-Dimensional Widgets. In: Symposium on Interactive 3D Graphics (1992)
8. Dodgson, N.A.: Autostereoscopic 3D Displays. Computer 38(8), 31–36 (2005)
9. Hanson, A.J., Wernert, E.: Constrained 3D Navigation with 2D Controllers. In: Proceedings of Visualization '97, pp. 175–182. IEEE Computer Society Press, Los Alamitos (1997)
10. Kozankiewicz, P.: Fast Algorithm for Creating Image-based Stereo Images. In: Proceedings of WSCG, pp. 59–66 (2002)
11. Liu, J., Pastoor, S., Seifert, K., Hurtienne, J.: Three Dimensional PC toward novel Forms of Human-Computer Interaction. In: Three-Dimensional Video and Display Devices and Systems SPIE (2000)
12. Mulder, J.D., van Liere, R.: Enhancing Fish Tank VR. In: Proceedings of Virtual Reality, pp. 91–98. IEEE Computer Society Press, Los Alamitos (2000)
13. Peterka, T., Kooima, R.L., Girado, J.I., Ge, J., Sandin, D.J., Johnson, A., Leigh, J., Schulze, J., DeFanti, T.A.: Dynallax: Solid State Dynamic Parallax Barrier Autostereoscopic VR Display. In: Proceedings of the Virtual Reality, pp. 91–98. IEEE Computer Society Press, Los Alamitos (2007)
14. Philips 42-3D6C01, http://www.inition.co.uk
15. Project Looking Glass, http://www.sun.com/software
16. Robertson, G., van Dantzich, M., Robbins, D., Czerwinski, M., Hinckley, K., Risden, K., Thiel, D., Gorokhovsky, V.: The Task Gallery: A 3D Window Manager. In: Proceedings of SIGCHI Conference on Human Factors in Computing Systems, pp. 494–501 (2000)
17. Salzman, T., Stachniak, S., Stürzlinger, W.: Unconstrained vs. Constrained 3D Scene Manipulation. In: 8th IFIP International Conference on Engineering for Human-Computer Interaction, vol. 2254 (2001)
18. Smith, G., Salzman, T., Stürzlinger, W.: 3D Scene Manipulation with Constraints. In: Fisher, B., Dawson-Howe, K., O'Sullivan, C. (eds.) Virtual and Augmented Architecture, pp. 35–46 (2001)
19. Steinicke, F., Ropinski, T., Bruder, G., Hinrichs, K.: Interscopic User Interface Concepts for Fish Tank Virtual Reality Systems. In: Proceedings of the Virtual Reality, pp. 27–34 (2007)
20. Stotts, D., Smith, J.C., Gyllstrom, K.: FaceSpace: Endo- and Exo-Spatial Hypermedia. In: the Transparent Video Facetop Proceedings of the 15th ACM Conference on Hypertext and Hypermedia, pp. 48–57 (2004)
21. Szalavári, Z., Gervautz, M.: Using the Personal Interaction Panel for 3D Interaction. In: Proceedings of the Conference on Latest Results in Information Technology, p. 36 (1997)
22. Tramberend, H.: A Display Device Abstraction for Virtual Reality Applications. In: Proceedings of Afrigraph, pp. 75–80 (2001)
23. van Berkel, C.: Touchless Display Interaction. In: SID 02 DIGEST (2002)

Dwell-Based Pointing in Applications
of Human Computer Interaction

Christian Müller-Tomfelde

CSIRO ICT Centre, Cnr Pembroke & Vimiera Roads,
Marsfield NSW 2122 Australia
Christian.Mueller-Tomfelde@csiro.au

Abstract. This paper describes exploratory studies and a formal experiment that investigate a particular temporal aspect of human pointing actions. Humans can express their intentions and refer to an external entity by pointing at distant objects with their fingers or a tool. The focus of this research is on the dwell time, the time span that people remain nearly motionless during pointing at objects. We address two questions: Is there a common or natural dwell time in human pointing actions? What implications does this have for Human Computer Interaction? Especially in virtual environments, feedback about the referred object is usually provided to the user to confirm actions such as object selection. A literature review and two studies led to a formal experiment in a hand-immersive virtual environment in search for an appropriate feedback delay time for dwell-based pointing actions. The results and implications for applications for Human Computer Interaction are discussed.

Keywords: Pointing gesture, dwell time, interactive systems.

1 Introduction

Some of humans' intentions can be gained in real life situations from their actions and the context in which they are performed. An important and frequent gesture is the manual pointing action that allows humans to refer naturally and intuitively to distant objects in the environment. In a more general definition, pointing by a human at an object is understood as "how one organism manipulates the visual attention of another to some distant entity" [13]. Manual pointing can be considered as a "referential act" and therefore, represents a basic means to communicate with others beyond speech. This embodiment of communication makes use of implicit references, whereby movements of the body bind objects in the world to cognitive programs [3]. A single human can easily coordinate and execute actions and it requires little effort for another human to predict the actions and recognise the intention merely by watching the movements. Therefore, pointing represents a basic and ubiquitous device to communicate with others [14] and is often used in a communicative situation to establish a common ground over the course of the conversation [2]. Consequently, this also has implications for ways that humans interact with computers. It is important to understand what "behaviour" has to be exhibited by the computer in

C. Baranauskas et al. (Eds.): INTERACT 2007, LNCS 4662, Part I, pp. 560–573, 2007.

order to meet expectations of users, especially when a computer should operate like a dialogue partner or accept more intuitive input signals from humans. The concrete question about how long users dwell on a target to express their selections and what an appropriate delay time for a corresponding feedback is, has not been discussed in the related literature in sufficient details. It is the central subject of this paper.

The paper is structured as follows. First, we describe the motivation and review the scientific context for this research. Then two exploratory studies are presented that further provide data related to typical manual dwell actions. The information of the review and the findings of the exploratory studies lead to a qualitative experiment to test hypotheses about the subjective experience of participants performing pointing actions. The paper concludes with a discussion about the results and a recommendation for a feedback delay time for dwell-based interaction.

2 Pointing in the Context of HCI

In the typical situation of human computer interaction the user moves a physical device so that a screen cursor is placed over an element of the two-dimensional graphical user interface. With respect to the prior definition of pointing, the user's referential act raises the "attention" of the computer (as a dialogue partner) for the object located under the screen cursor. After placing the cursor on the target, the user usually clicks on a mouse button and therefore explicitly signals the intention to execute the function or the command that is associated with that interface element. This overall interaction is known as "point and click". Furthermore, an interaction technique referred to as hovering is used in situations in which a mouse-click is not applicable or available for the user, e.g., during "drag and drop" or in pen-based interfaces [10]. Nevertheless, to select a function, the user must hold the pointing device motionless for a certain period of time, to trigger a "hover event" by temporal discrimination. This provides information about the object in the focus of the attention. The "act" of hovering replaces the explicit click and allows for the selection of the target object.

In non-WIMP (Windows Icons Menus Pointing devices) based computer systems, the explicit act of clicking becomes substituted either by an event of another modality or by an event created by discriminating temporal segments. In multimodal research, information of multiple modalities becomes fused to model the content of the information at a high level of abstraction [19]. Furthermore, in virtual environment applications, the pointing gesture provides an intuitive access to distant objects using a laser pointer metaphor [5,6]. This paper concentrates on three-dimensional pointing interaction using exclusively movements of a hand or a tool.

2.1 Components of the Pointing Gesture

In order to clarify what part of the pointing gesture is addressed by this paper, we provide a detailed description of a pointing gesture. The pointing gesture is a process that consists of three major elements or sections. Firstly, persons have to position and orient their pointing tools towards the object at which they intend to point. Secondly, persons remain motionless for a certain period of time while holding the pointing device towards the target. This period of time is called the *dwell time*. It is assumed that a pointing gesture can only be recognised when the clear separation between these two periods is possible for an observer. The observer combines the information about the object the person is pointing at with the "act" of dwelling and recognises the selection of the target object. Thirdly, the person starts to move the pointing device away from the focused target. This idealistic temporal structure of a pointing gesture is less overt in real life situations. For instance, the transition between the first and second phase can happen multiple times when the person adjusts the orientation of the pointing tool. In that case, the tool does not remain motionless during the second phase. Another ambiguous situation can occur when the person aimlessly dwells in a resting position of the hand. Moreover, the definition of motionless is relative and depends on the perspective of the observer. The physical velocity of the pointing tool is a good candidate for a parameter for discrimination. The particular discrimination level of velocity has to be determined in specific applications.

The first phase of the gesture, i.e., moving toward a target can usually be described using Fitts' law [7]. In contrast, the focus of this work lies on the second phase of the pointing gesture, the period when the person holds the tool nearly motionless on the target. In some applications, feedback is provided to the user to indicate that the target has been recognised. For these situations we call the time from the beginning of the dwell period until the feedback stimulus (S) the feedback delay time (FT) (see Fig. 1). It must be smaller than the dwell time (DT). Finally, we call the time the user remains on the target after she has received a confirmation feedback stimulus about the recognition of the gesture the exit time (ET), similar to the definition in [27]. The exit time can also be considered as a simple reaction time of the user to the feedback stimulus, as described, for example, in [1].

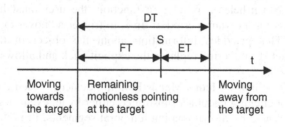

Fig. 1. The temporal structure of a human pointing gesture with confirmation feedback. The dwell time (DT) is the sum of the feedback delay time (FT) and the exit time (ET) after the feedback stimulus (S).

Touching or clicking on an object with the hand or tool can be understood as an explicit interaction, whereas pointing at objects must be considered as a more implicit interaction. It requires a method to decide whether a selection has been made or not. A particular problem that can occur during these sorts of interactions is the *Midas Touch Problem*, coined by Jacob in the context of interaction systems based on eye movement tracking [11]. This means that, for manual pointing, unwanted selections can happen without a users' intention, and, for instance, the context of the interaction has to be taken into account to further disambiguate the situation.

2.2   Pointing in HCI Applications

With the emergence of the notion of disappearing computer and intelligent environments, pointing interaction is now a popular choice. Most applications that are using pointing interactions address issues of novel forms of interaction in information enriched environments or with large computer displays. An early example of an interactive system that involves pointing in combination with other modalities, such as speech, is Richard Bolt's "Put-that-there" system from 1980 [5]. In the literature several applications can be found in which the time the user remains motionless pointing at an object is used to control an application. The research problem of detecting a pointing gesture is usually tackled using the spatial as well as the temporal information of the users' actions.

In literature we reviewed, the time the user must remain motionless to allow the system to detect an act of selection varies. The range of the dwell time begins with 300 ms [20,4], continues with 500 ms [16], 1 second [21, 28,14] and stops at values of about 2 second [18]. The adjustment of the dwell time is usually based on ad hoc experiences of the developer. Formal evaluations have been done only in applications that use eye movements to control a cursor [24,27]. Manual pointing interactions are used, for instance, to control home entertainment components, such as CD players, televisions, amplifiers etc. [28]. In this, the core interaction technique is based on pointing with a dedicated tool or wand towards the component the user wants to control. The user points at the target and holds the device motionless for a moment or presses a button to select the target. In an experimental setup, participants received an audio feedback when the pointing device was held motionless for "a brief period (less than one second)". Aspects of wall-based laser pointer interaction are examined and reported in [21]. In that study participants were asked to aim at a target with the laser pointing device. A dwell time of about one second was proposed to acquire the target. However, the selection of this dwell time was basically motivated by the accuracy constraint of the underlying technology and was not based on user preferences.

In other approaches for multimodal interaction in virtual environments, the accuracy of the pointing gesture detection increases by fusing hand and head orientation detection [18]. The authors presented work on real time tracking for 3D pointing interaction using video cameras. They stated that the average length of the pointing gesture was 1.8 s. The motionless phase revealed the highest duration variance (from 100 ms to 2.5 s). In [16] dwell-based interaction is used in combination with a force feedback device in the context of the training of motor skills. A dwell time of 500 ms is used here to discriminate gestures using a hierarchical network of sensors of activity. [14] describes another interactive application with large displays that rely only on the manual pointing gesture of the user. The author suggests a dwell time on the target of approximately one second to transform the "act" of dwelling into a "button-selected" event. However, the author did not give any further background information about this choice for the time period. In a study about interaction on tabletop computer displays with objects on the far side of a table, a dwell of the input cursor was also used to indicate a selection [20]. The dwell time there was set to 300 ms but wasn't studied further, since the authors primarily addressed issues of Fitts' law. A comparison of the performance of the selection by mouse-click and by mouse-dwelling was a subject of the study presented in [9]. The authors stated that the interaction techniques based on a mouse-click was on average about 150 ms faster than the selection by dwelling. The dwell time activation introduced more errors and was therefore less efficient. A large number of subjects also reported that the fixed dwell time of 500 ms was too short. Therefore, the authors recommended a dwell time of 750 ms for novices and proposed an adaptation of the dwell time for individual users but a formal evaluation was not reported.

2.3 Temporal Aspects of Actions

The prevailing approach in the context of temporal aspects of human actions is the hierarchical organisation of human behaviour in time scales [17,3]. The scales start at the neuron activity level where it takes about 1 millisecond to generate an electrical signal to communicate with another neuron. The scale ends at the cognitive level with period of 2-3 s [3]. The interesting interval for the work and experiment presented in this paper is assumed to be in the range of a couple of hundreds of milliseconds to about one second, since most of the previously described approaches can be found here. We now present results of related work which concentrates on the perception of the delay between an intentional action and its effect in the environment.

In [8] the authors report on an experiment that was addressing the issue of intentional binding between voluntary actions and their effects. The Participants' task was to press a key and to receive a delayed auditory feedback. They were asked to judge the onset times of their actions and the perceived feedback. The onset time of pressing the key was judged to happen later while the onset time of the feedback was judged to be earlier. At delay times between the key press and the auditory feedback of about 250 ms, the participant perceived the time gap between both events to be relatively shorter than for a delay time of about 650 ms. In other words, with a decreasing delay time between the key press action and the auditory feedback, the "perceptual attraction" or binding effect became increased. The authors argued that this phenomenon helps humans experience their own actions and provides a sense of controlling events in the outside world.

In another recent study about the action-effect relationship [23], participants were asked to which extent they felt that an effect was a consequence of their own action or of the action of the experimenter. Different temporal delays of up to 600 ms were introduced between the action and an auditory feedback. The experiment revealed that the feeling of being the author of the effect decreased with increased temporal delay. In the context of pointing and selecting of objects, it is assumed that a short or zero delay, for instance, causes a strong feeling of being author of the selection, while a longer delay suggests that the selection might be done by someone or something else.

Based on the idea of the hierarchical organisation of human behaviour suggested by Newell [17], Ballard et al. [3] argue for a time scale that defines a special level of abstraction. The level is called "Embodiment Level" because the constraints of basic physical acts influence the nature of cognitive operations at a time period of about a third of a second. It is at this level that primitives, such as movements of the eyes or taps on a key of the keyboard happen [1]. These primitives are distinguished from those of the next higher cognitive level, such as typing a word or dialing a number [3]. We assume that a pointing action is more than basic movement primitive since it includes also cognitive aspects. An appropriate temporal scale of these referential primitives is expected to be greater than the Embodiment Level (300 ms), while it should be less than the temporal scale of action of a higher cognitive level (2-3 s).

In the research area of hypertext presentation and exploration, Meyer *et al.* presented a study [15] about the relationship of system response delay and the time the user is watching a hypertext page before moving onto a new page. The experiment revealed interesting effects under the condition of different delay times between the click on a hyperlink and the appearance of the corresponding new page. The time the participants remained on the page was correlated with the time they waited for the page until a response delay of 3 s. Furthermore, the emotional workload increased above this temporal threshold. The results underpin the existence of a universal constant of segmentation for the temporal integration of successive events into perceptual units of about 2 to 3 s duration [22]. In [25], Schleidt *et al.* presented a study about the temporal integration of successive events and short term movements. Videotapes of behaviour scenes of different cultures were analysed. The result of the study supported the assumption that both the human perception and the "overt behaviour is characterised by a similar time constant". This refers also to a temporal window of 2 to 3 s, in which the "short term movement episodes" with obvious segmentations happen. The question that arises from the latter two studies is whether or not the motionless time period while pointing has a similar constant character.

In brief, the literature we studied strongly indicates a time period of about 500-1000 ms for an appropriate feedback delay time for dwell-based pointing actions. At this delay the intentional binding between action and effect still supports the users' experience of controlling the environment. The suggested time span is confined by particular time scales of human information processing and the majority of existing HCI approaches use delayed feedback below 1 s. Assuming a standard reaction time to a visual stimulus of about 300 ms (exit time, see Fig. 1) a resulting natural dwell time is expected to be about 800-1300 ms.

3 Exploratory Studies

To gain further knowledge about temporal aspects of dwelling on targets during pointing actions we conducted two exploratory studies in a similar interactive environment. We separated the process of passing on a reference from an actor to an observer into two parts. Study A was about performing a pointing action, while study B focused on the observation of such an action. The studies were done independently from each other, no direct or mediated verbal communication happened between the actor and the observer, except pointing gestures. It was assumed that the average dwell times of actors are greater than the average response times of observers or receivers. Instead of imposing a particular dwell time on the participant by providing a feedback for a selection, the actors performed simply based on of their inherent temporal organization of pointing actions. The idea of the studies was that the results would provide further indications to identify an appropriately time period for feedback for the interaction with computers.

3.1 Study A: Performing a Pointing Action

We chose a hand-immersive virtual environment for this study. The participants interacted with a stylus in a 3D scene using shutter glasses providing stereo vision. The input device reliably tracked the participants' interactions. The study was conducted with 15 unpaid participants recruited from the research organisation of the authors. Ten of the participants were male and five female. The task of the participants was to answer questions about the two most common colours of objects by pointing with a tool at the correspondingly coloured objects in the environment. For example: What are the two most common colours of flowers? As a possible answer, the participant pointed at the green object and then at the red object. Furthermore, participants answered 50 of these questions, each with a different topic and were asked to perform their tasks in a comfortable and relaxed manner. The participants were advised to perform the task so that another person would be able to understand their selections. The participants were given a verbal introduction about the environment. Written instructions about the task were handed out, and questions about the task were discussed. We observed the first few interactions then allowed the participants to finish the study alone.

3.2 Result Study A

The result of study A can be illustrated in a histogram of the detected dwell times with an interval width of 333 ms (see Fig. 2).

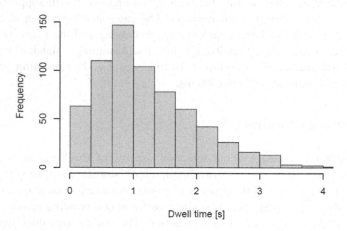

Fig. 2. Histogram of the detected dwell times of all participants in study A. The histogram is skewed to the right.

The histogram is right-skewed, because only positive dwell times can occur. The skewness of the distribution is 0.9602 and standard deviation is 0.7575. Data analysis revealed an average dwell time of 1.175 s and a median value of 0.999 s. 50 % of the data lies between 0.599 and 1.598 s. Because of the asymmetric shape of the histogram the average value is greater than the median value and the latter is more appropriate for description. The expected numbers of dwell events were 1500. Five participants touched target objects rather than pointed at them and were omitted for the analysis. The decreased number of dwell events (1000) is further reduced due to insufficiently detected dwells. Therefore, the total number of dwells contributing to this histogram is 702.

3.3 Study B: Observing a Pointing Action

Study B was done to understand how long observers need to receive the reference of a pointing action by watching the action. A standard desktop computer with a keyboard and an LCD panel was used to collect data about the reactions of the observers. Nine unpaid participants contributed to this study, 2 female and 7 male. The participants were asked to watch on the screen an animated typical trial of one participant of study A. The action was represented only by the replay of the recorded movement of the pointing tool. The task was to press the space bar of the keyboard to confirm the 100 selections that had been made by the person moving the stylus. The participants were asked to perform their tasks in a timely but comfortable and relaxed manner. The participants were given instructions about the task and questions were discussed. We observed the first few reactions then restarted the experiment and the participants finished the study alone.

3.4 Result Study B

The result of study B can be illustrated in a histogram of the detected response times with an interval width of 100 ms (see Fig. 3).

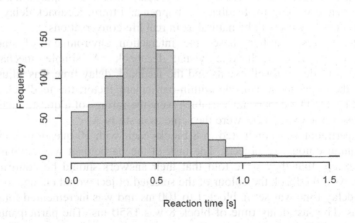

Fig. 3. Histogram of the response times of all participants observing a recorded and animated trial of one participant of study A

In the study 855 confirmations of the 9 participants had been recorded. The missing 45 confirmations are due to the fact that some selections had been overseen by participants probably because of drops in concentration or because of misinterpretations. This inaccuracy of 5 % will be ignored for the following considerations. All confirmations were set into relation to the start point of the dwelling activity, that is, when stylus started remaining nearly motionless while it was held towards the target object. 17 confirmations (2 %) revealed negative reaction times and were ignored also for further analysis. The histogram of all 838 confirmation time periods can be seen in Fig. 3, where 50 percent of the measured reaction times occurred between 0.292 s and 0.552 s. Data analysis revealed an average reaction time of 0.4325 s and the same value as median. The standard deviation is 0.215 and the skewness of the distribution is 0.5484.

The independent studies A and B showed that the median dwell time (0.999 s) is greater than the median response time (0.4325 s), although there was no feedback given to the pointing participants and the studies were independently conducted. The variances are relatively high compared to those other response time experiments because of the self-paced character of the studies without an explicit feedback stimulus to react to. Nevertheless, the studies indicated a possible existence of a natural dwell time and suggest a corresponding feedback delay time of about 0.4325 s. In the next section the latter period of time is further investigated in a formal experiment that uses an explicit and temporally controlled visual feedback.

4   Experiment with Visual Feedback

Based on the results of the literature review and the exploratory studies we formulate hypotheses. We want to test whether a variation of the delay of an explicit visual feedback for a pointing action has an effect of the perception of the interaction process. First, feedback delay time above approximately 430 ms is experienced by users to happen late. Second, for a feedback delay time above approximately 430 ms users experience waiting for feedback to happen and third, feedback delay below 430 ms is considered by users to be natural as in real life conversations.

In order to test the hypotheses the interaction environment of study A was modified to provide a discrete visual feedback. A simple mechanism was implemented to detect dwell events and the feedback delay time was adjustable. The design of the experiment had one within-participant factor, the feedback delay time (FT, see Fig. 1). The dependant variables were the ratings of a questionnaire. The 15 participants of the experiment were the same as in study A.

The experiment was conducted in 8 blocks each with 10 questions about the two most common colours of objects. The task of the participant was similar to that of study A except that they were told that their answers should be confirmed by the computer. As a feedback the colour of the selected object would change to white. The feedback delay time was set in block 1 to 100 ms and was incremented for each block by 250 ms. The last delay time of block 8 was 1850 ms. The participants were not informed about these changes but rather encouraged to act as in study A. After each of the 8 blocks the participants were asked to fill out a questionnaire with possible answers on a 7 point Likert scale. The questions were:

- Question 1: Do you have the impression that the system feedback happened in a reasonable time according to your action? Answer: confirmation occurred too fast (1), too late (7).

- Question 2: Did you have the feeling to wait for the feedback to happen? Answer: no I didn't have to wait (1), yes, I waited (7).
- Question 3: Did you have the impression that the time delay for the feedback was natural? (i.e., as in a real life communication situation) Answer: time delay is not natural (1), quite natural (7).

The questionnaire was discussed with each participant. Then the first couple of interactions were observed by the experiment supervisor while the participant finished the task alone.

4.1 Results of the Experiment

The average ratings for the three questions are shown in Fig. 4. There is a trend in the average values of the ratings under the changing condition of the feedback delay time.

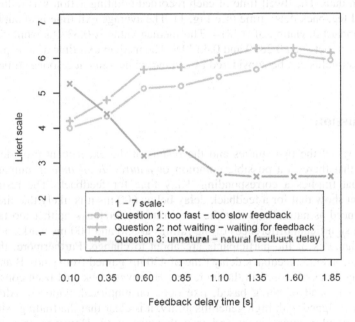

Fig. 4. Results of the questionnaire for the experiment. The ratings show a general trend and the largest changes can be reported between 350 and 600 ms.

The effects of feedback delay time on the three ratings were tested by one-way repeated measures analysis of variance (ANOVA). There was a significant main effect in the ratings of question 1, $F(7,98) = 11.289$, $p < 0.01$, question 2, $F(7,98) = 6.1828$, $p < 0.01$ and question 3, $F(7,98) = 12.667$, $p < 0.01$. The ratings for questions 1 and 2 increase, while ratings for question 3 decrease with the increasing independent variable. The largest changes of the ratings happen between 350 and 600 ms of feedback delay time (see Fig. 4).

We carried out further detailed analysis of the ratings. Several paired t-tests were calculated for the ratings of the questions. The tests revealed that the ratings of question 1 at a feedback delay time of 100 ms are not significantly different to those at 350 ms. In contrast, all other paired t-test between rating of question 1 at 100 ms and those equal and above 600 ms are significantly different. This step of significance between 350 and 600 ms is also valid for the ratings of question 3. The step in ratings of question 2 also exists but the p-values are not significant.

The results of the experiment can be summarized as followed. At a delay time of 100 ms the feedback is rated as neutral (4), i.e., the feedback is neither too fast nor too slow (Question 1). Question 2, waiting for feedback, is also judged neutral. There is a tendency to judge the system feedback as natural at the feedback delay time of 100 ms (Question 3). Towards the delay of 1850 ms the feedback was rated less natural and feedback time as too slow. On average the participant also rated that they waited for the feedback. At the step in significance between 350 and 600 ms we assume that the judgments of the participants are about to change.

As an additional outcome of the experiment the exit time is calculated from the interaction data. The dwell time of each recorded pointing action was reduced by the associated feedback delay time (see Fig. 1). The average exit time is about 0.4562 ms with a standard deviation of 0.3814. The median value is 0.3380 s while 50 % of all exit times are between 0.2890 and 0.4470 s. The median exit time as a response to the feedback stimulus can be considered as a standard movement response times of about 330 ms.

5 Discussion

The findings of the two studies and the results of the experiment provide empirical evidence that there is a possible common or *natural dwell time* in human pointing actions that implies a corresponding delay time for feedback. The results of the experiment show that for a feedback delay below 600 ms it is likely that the feedback is experienced as natural and that the users rate the feedback neither too fast nor too slow. The significant differences of the ratings at 350 and 600 ms mark an interval in which judgments of the participants are about to change. Furthermore, the interval encloses the average feedback delay time of 430 ms gained from study B and matches some delay times proposed in the literature. However, these had been constrained by technology instead of being based, like ours, on empirical evidence. Although our study was designed with high generalisability, it is clear that the findings strictly hold for the particular environment and task that was used. However, the applications reviewed in the literature resemble in many aspects the setup used in this study. We assume that our results can be even compared to those of experiments with manual 2D interaction environments with mouse and pen input devices.

In order to further link the results of the studies and the experiment we introduce the notion of an *internal stimulus*. The internal stimulus is a hypothetical event that marks the point in time when the participant's intention to act emerges. Then the motor programming stage prepares the physical action that finally becomes executed. We assume now that the process that follows the internal stimulus is equivalent to that which follows the external stimulus in the experiment with feedback. In other words, the motor programming that leads to the movement of the hand is assumed to be the same in study A and the experiment. Therefore, the time that elapses from the start of the dwell period until the participant experiences an internal stimulus to act can be deduced. We subtract the exit time of approximately 340 ms gained from the experiment from the natural dwell time of study A, 1 s. The resulting period for the internal stimulus is approx. 660 ms. The difference of about 230 ms between this derived internal stimulus time and the external stimulus time of study B is probably due to the high skewness of the data of study A. It is more likely that the natural dwell time is less than 1 s and is located in the centre of the mode at about 830 ms (see Fig. 2). Future studies have to provide more evidence.

The detection of a motionless period always requires time and will introduce a temporal delay. A feedback delay time of 350 ms to 600 ms gives detection mechanisms in dwell-based pointing applications enough time to derive the referred object from the real time interaction data and to avoid the ambiguity of short dwells. At the same time the acceptance of the feedback based on the rating is still high.

The idea of a natural dwell time is not entirely new and has been motivated by the research presented in [25, 22], which favours a universal time constant in short term human actions and by the notion of the Embodiment Level in human behaviour as proposed in [3]. Although time periods in human behaviour cannot be literally constant, we argue that the natural dwell time in pointing could indicate the existence of a particular foundational time scale for human communication. Therefore, it is important to consider the natural dwell when designing the interaction of humans with computers.

6 Conclusion

We conducted two exploratory studies and a formal experiment focusing on the dwell time of the human pointing gestures. We were focusing mainly on applications of Human Computer Interaction where no explicit and discrete actions, such as button clicks are practical or available to capture user input. Our aim was to provide empirical evidence for a possible natural dwell time during pointing to express the selection of a target object and to convey this reference to a communication partner. The findings of our studies were combined with the results of a pointing experiment with delayed visual feedback for selection. This allows us to recommend a feedback delay time for manual pointing actions of approximately 350 to 600 ms as a starting point for the development of interactive applications. We have shown that this feedback delay is experienced by users as natural and convenient and that the majority of observers of pointing actions gave feedback within a similar time span. Any further delay is counterproductive and impedes the progress of a task [26]. Therefore, it is not recommended to let technical constraints bias the choice for a feedback delay time. Instead, the user's behaviour and expectations as studied in this paper should inform the system design to achieve a high interaction quality.

Acknowledgements. The author would like to thank Carl Mistler for his valuable contribution in building the tool to play back the interaction data. Thanks also to Cara Stitzlein and Claudia Schremmer for their insight and critical review of this manuscript.

References

1. Card, S.K., Moran, T.P., Newell, A.: The Psychology of Human-Computer Interaction. Lawrence Erlbaum, Hillsdale (1983)
2. Clark, H., Wilkes-Gibbs, D.: Referring as a collaborative process. Cognition 22, 1–39 (1986)
3. Ballard, D.H., Hayhoe, M.M., Pook, P.K., Rao, R.P.N.: Deictic codes for the embodiment of cognition. Behavioral and Brain Sciences 20, 723–767 (1997)
4. Bohan, M., Chaparro, A., Scarlett, D.: The Effects of selection technique on target acquisition movements made with a mouse. In: Proceedings of the 42nd Annual Meeting of the Human Factors Society, Human Factors and Ergonomics Society, pp. 473–475 (1998)
5. Bolt, R.A.: Put-that-there: Voice and Gesture at the Graphic Interface. In: Proceedings of Computer Graphics (SIGGRAPH'80), vol. 14, pp. 262–270 (1980)
6. Bowman, D.A., Hodges, L.F.: An evaluation of techniques for grabbing and manipulating remote objects in immersive virtual environments. In: Proceedings of the Symposium on Interactive 3D Graphics, pp. 35–38 (1997)
7. Fitts, P.M.: The information capacity of the human motor system in controlling the amplitude of movement. Experimental Psychology 47, 381–391 (1997)
8. Haggard, P., Clark, S., Kalogeras, J.: Voluntary Action and Conscious Awareness. Nature Neurosciences 5, 382–385 (2002)
9. Hansen, J.P., Johansen, A.S., Hansen, D.W., Itoh, K., Mashino, S.: Command without a click: Dwell time typing by mouse and gaze selections. In: Proceeding of INTERACT 2003, pp. 121–128. IOS Press, Amsterdam (2003)
10. Hinckley, K., Jacob, R.J., Ware, C.: Input/Output Devices and Interaction Techniques. In: Tucker, A. (ed.) The Computer Science and Engineering Handbook, CRC Press, Boca Raton (2004)
11. Jacob, R.J.: What You Look at is What You Get: Eye Movement-Based Interaction Techniques. In: Proceedings CHI 1990, pp. 11–18. ACM Press, New York (1990)
12. Leavens, D.A.: Manual deixis in apes and humans. Interaction Studies 5, 387–408 (2004)
13. Kita, S., Pointing, A.: foundational building block of human communication. In: Kita, S. (ed.) Pointing: Where Language, Culture, and Cognition Meet, Lawrence Erlbaum, Mahwah (2003)
14. Malerczyk, C.: Interactive Museum Exhibit Using Pointing Gesture Recognition. In: Proceedings of the 12-th International Conference in Central Europe on Computer Graphics, Visualization and Computer Vision'2004, Short Communications, vol. II, pp. 165–171 (2004)
15. Meyer, H.A., Hänze, M., Hildebrandt, M.: Das Zusammenwirken von Systemresponsezeiten und Verweilzeiten beim Explorieren von Hypertextstrukturen: Empirische Evidenz für einen zeitlichen Integrationsmechanismus. In: Wachsmuth, I., Jung, B. (eds.) KogWis99: Proceedings der 4. Fachtagung der Gesellschaft für Kognitionswissenschaft, pp. 86–91 (1999)
16. Müller-Tomfelde, C., Paris, C.: Explicit task representation based on gesture interaction. In: Proceedings of the NICTA-HCSNet Multimodal User Interaction Workshop MMUI '05, pp. 39–45. ACM Press, New York (2006)
17. Newell, A.: Unified theories of cognition. Harvard University Press (1990)
18. Nickel, K., Stiefelhagen, R.: Pointing gesture recognition based on 3D-tracking of face, hands and head orientation. In: Proceedings of the 5th international Conference on Multimodal Interfaces ICMI '03, pp. 140–146. ACM Press, New York (2003)

19. Nigay, L., Coutaz, J.: A Design Space for Multimodal Systems Concurrent Processing and Data Fusion. In: Proceedings of the INTERCHI'93 Conference, pp. 172–178. ACM Press, New York (1993)
20. Parker, J.K., Mandryk, R., Inkpen, K.: TractorBeam: Seamless Integration of Local and Remote Pointing for Tabletop Displays. In: Proceedings of Graphics Interface, pp. 33–40 (2005)
21. Peck, C.H.: Useful parameters for the design of laser pointer interaction techniques. In: Extended Abstracts CHI, pp. 461–462. ACM Press, New York (2001)
22. Pöppel, E.: A hierarchical model of temporal perception. Trends in Cognitive Science 1, 56–61 (1997)
23. Sato, A., Yasuda, A.: Illusion of sense of self-agency: discrepancy between the predicted and actual sensory consequences of actions modulates the sense of self-agency, but not the sense of self-ownership. Cognition 94(3), 241–255 (2005)
24. Sibert, L.E., Jacob, R.J.K.: Evaluation of Eye Gaze Interaction. In: Sibert, L.E., Jacob, R.J.K. (eds.) Proceedings CHI 2000, pp. 281–288. ACM Press, New York (2000)
25. Schleidt, M., Eibl-Eibesfeldt, I., Pöppel, E.: A Universal Constant in Temporal Segmentation of Human Short-Term Behaviour. Naturwissenschaften 74, 289–290 (1987)
26. Shneiderman, B.: Response time and display rate in human performance with computers. ACM Computing Surveys 16(3), 265–285 (1984)
27. Špakov, O., Miniotas, D.: On-line adjustment of dwell time for target selection by gaze. In: Proceedings of the Third Nordic Conference on Human-Computer interaction 2004 NordiCHI '04, pp. 203–206. ACM Press, New York (2004)
28. Wilson, A., Shafer, S.: XWand: UI for intelligent spaces. In: Proceedings CHI 2003, pp. 545–552. ACM Press, New York (2003)

A Miniature, One-Handed 3D Motion Controller

Kynan Eng

Institute of Neuroinformatics
University of Zurich and ETH Zurich
Winterthurerstrasse 190, CH-8057 Zurich, Switzerland
kynan@ini.phys.ethz.ch

Abstract. Users of three-dimensional computer-aided design (CAD) and gaming applications need to manipulate virtual objects in up to six degrees of rotational and translation freedom (DOF). To date, no 3D controller provides one-handed 6DOF input with miniature size and low cost. This paper presents a prototype of the first one-handed 6DOF motion controller suitable for use in portable platforms such as laptop computers, mobile telephones and hand-held game consoles. It is based on an optical sensor combined with novel planar spring mechanics, and can be easily manufactured using low-cost materials and processes.

Keywords: 3D motion controller, optical sensor, hand-held device.

1 Introduction

With the continued increase in the number of 3D computing applications in hand-held computers and mobile telephones, there is a need for miniature one-handed input devices combining small size with many input degrees of freedom (DOF). An ideal device would provide input in 6DOF (3 translation plus 3 rotation), be operable using only the thumb and index finger of one hand, be small enough to be mounted on a device such as a mobile telephone or ultra-portable laptop, provide reasonable accuracy and be cheap to manufacture.

There is currently no available device that satisfies all of the above requirements. Well-known input devices such as optical mice [1-3], trackballs [4] and mechanical or optical joysticks [5-7] output only 2 or 3 DOF. Multi-axis input devices based on accelerometers and digital compasses are also available, but accelerometers suffer from drift and digital compasses are expensive, sensitive to interference from external magnetic fields and cannot provide translation information. Full one-handed 6DOF input is available in systems using camera-based tracking of special patterns on an index object manipulated in free air [8-10], but they have problems with uncontrolled external lighting conditions, and are unsuitable for portable applications due to the unattached index object. A range of 6DOF input devices sold as the *SpaceBall, SpacePilot* and *SpaceNavigator* [11] solves these problems by using an arrangement of springs and optical sensors inside the device's hand grip, but the volume of the sensor does not allow it to be miniaturized for ultra-mobile applications.

2 System Design

To achieve practical one-handed input, a device must track operator-initiated movements of a manipulandum in multiple DOF and return it to a zero position when

C. Baranauskas et al. (Eds.): INTERACT 2007, LNCS 4662, Part I, pp. 574–577, 2007.
© IFIP International Federation for Information Processing 2007

the operator lets go. Our device uses two key methods to achieve this functionality: visual tracking of index points on the manipulandum using standard low-cost imagers, and a specialized planar multiple spring arrangement for positioning the manipulandum. The arrangement of the components is shown in Figure 1.

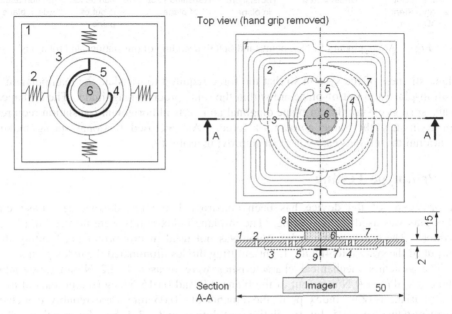

Fig. 1. (Left) Simplified view of the planar spring arrangement for the 3D controller. (Right) Overview of the design and layout of the 3D controller. The outer frame (1) holds the translational outer springs (2), which are connected to the inner frame (3) on which the torsional spring (4) is mounted. The center of the spring plate contains a mounting (5) for the grip shaft (6), which is located by means of restraining plates (7) attached to the inner frame above and below the spring plate. This arrangement allows the grip shaft to rotate but not translate relative to the inner frame, and prevents the torsional spring from bending out of the plane of the inner frame. The finger grip (8, 16-20mm diameter) is rigidly attached to the grip shaft. The index points (9) are attached to the bottom of the grip shaft. All dimensions in mm.

A standard low-cost USB webcam (Logitech, 320 x 240 pixels) facing the three-dimensional array of index points performs image acquisition (Fig. 1 and Fig. 2). Standard image processing techniques are used detect the movements of the index points. To deduce the movements of the manipulandum, simple linear rules are used which consider the relative movements of the index points (Fig. 2). The index points are 0.5 mm in diameter and are spaced 2.0 mm apart. To eliminate zero-position error noise, which is a large problem for usability of all input devices, the software adapts the zero position of the index points at different rates depending on whether above-threshold movement has been detected or not.

To improve user input precision while keeping size and manufacturing costs low, a planar multiple-spring arrangement was developed (Fig. 1). The multi-spring arrangement allows different restoring forces to be used for translation and rotation in and out of the plane, improving user ergonomics. In particular, it increases the out-of-

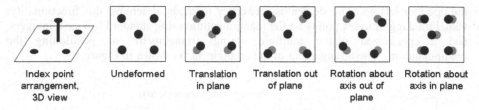

| Index point arrangement, 3D view | Undeformed | Translation in plane | Translation out of plane | Rotation about axis out of plane | Rotation about axis in plane |

Fig. 2. Arrangement of index points and 6DOF decoding of translations and rotations

plane stiffness of the system so that the force required to translate the manipulandum both in-plane and out-of-plane are within the same order of magnitude. The L-shaped outer springs ensure that in-plane diagonal and vertical/horizontal translation requires approximately the same amount of force. An enclosed torsional spring makes rotational movements easier, further improving usability.

3 Prototype Testing

A prototype of the device has been constructed and tested (Fig. 3). Laser-cut Plexiglas was used for the spring. The in-plane index points were printed on a laser printer. The out-of-plane index point was not used in this prototype, limiting the output of the system to 4DOF. Light-emitting diodes illuminated the index points.

The system's mechanical characteristics were measured: 2.2 N/mm (horizontal plane dX, dY), 1.0 N/mm (out of the plane dZ) and 0.016 N/deg (rotation about axis out of plane rotZ). Index point movements of ~0.05 mm were reliably detected, corresponding to ~4-5 bit translation resolution and ~3-4 bits for rotation. This allowed users to position and orient a virtual cube (Fig. 2) in 4DOF with a little practice. The adaptation algorithm to eliminate zero position noise worked as designed. The PC CPU load (P4 2.8 GHz) was ~20% including the graphics display.

Fig. 3. Prototype controller (left) manipulating a virtual cube on a laptop screen (right)

4 Conclusions and Outlook

While the feasibility of the miniature 3D controller's working principles has been demonstrated, further work is required to achieve a truly usable mobile 6DOF device.

A specialized low-profile webcam is needed to reduce the overall depth of the controller from >40 mm to <20 mm. In addition, the out-of-plane calibration point needs to be added – its feasibility was verified in an earlier large-scale prototype, but so far it has proved difficult to reliably assemble a miniature version by hand. Further optimization of the spring design is also needed, in conjunction with a series of usability tests on a wide range of potential users of the device. Using higher resolution imagers (e.g. 1.3 megapixels) would improve sensitivity by about 2 bits, at the cost of increasing image processing requirements. Although the CPU demands of the image processing algorithms were low compared to the computing power available on current hardware, it may also be desirable to create an embedded version of the algorithm to create a stand-alone, platform-independent device

Acknowledgments. Thanks to Wolfgang Henggeler and Rodney Douglas for their helpful advice and encouragement with the construction of the system.

References

1. Jackson, S.B., *Optical translator device*, in *US 4794384*. 1988, Xerox Corporation (Stamford, CT, USA): USA.
2. Nestler, E. and T.F. Knight, *Optical Mouse*, in *US 4799055*. 1989, Symbolics Inc. (Cambridge, MA, USA): USA.
3. Adan, M.E., et al., *Operator input device*, in *US 6,172,354, EP0572009A1, GB2272763, WO97/06506*. 2001, Microsoft Corporation: US.
4. Jackson, S.B.: Optical translator device, in US 4794384, Xerox Corporation, Stamford, CT, USA (1988)
5. Nestler, E., Knight, T.F.: Optical Mouse, in US 4799055, Symbolics Inc., Cambridge, MA, USA (1989)
6. Adan, M.E., et al.: Operator input device, in US 6, 172, 354, EP057, A1, GB2272763, WO97/06506. 2001, Microsoft Corporation, US (2009)
7. Bidiville, M., et al.: Cursor pointing device utilizing a photodetector array with target ball having randomly distributed speckles, in United States Patent and Trademarks Office, United States of America (1994)
8. Liu, S.M.: Computer joy stick having two optical generating vector signals, in JP11259228A2, JP1003150, US6597453. Primax Electronics Ltd., JP (1999)
9. Shusuke, S.: Two-dimensional direction joy stick uni optical sensor. in JP06059737A2, priority JP1992000250358, Miura Takeshi, JP (1994)
10. Yoshimi, T.: Joy stick. In: JP61276014, priority JP19850118017., Fujitsu Ltd., JP (1986)
11. Arbter, K., Landzettel, K., Hirzinger, G.: Method and Input Device for Controlling the Position of an Object to be Graphically Displayed in Virtual Reality. In: US6545663, Deutsches Zeutrum fuer Luft- und Raumfahrt e. V., Koeln (DE), USA (2003)
12. Woods, E., Mason, P., Billinghurst, M.: MagicMouse: an Inexpensive 6-Degree-of-Freedom Mouse. In: Woods, E. (ed.) Proceedings of the 1st international conference on Computer graphics and interactive techniques in Australasia and South East Asia. 2003, ACM Press, Melbourne, AU (2003)
13. ARTookit (2007), cited; Available from: http://www.hitl.washington.edu/artoolkit/
14. 3DConnexion, Arrangement for the detection for relative movements or relative position of two objects: in USPTO: US2003/0103217 A1. 2003, 3DConnexion GmbH, Seefeld (DE) USA (2003)

Use Case Evaluation (UCE): A Method for Early Usability Evaluation in Software Development

Kasper Hornbæk[1], Rune Thaarup Høegh[2], Michael Bach Pedersen[3], and Jan Stage[2]

[1] University of Copenhagen, Department of Computer Science, Universitetsparken 1,
DK-2100 Copenhagen, Denmark
[2] Aalborg University, Department of Computer Science, Fredrik Bajers Vej 7,
DK-9220 Aalborg East, Denmark
[3] ETI A/S, Bouet Moellevej 3-5, DK-9400 Nørresundby, Denmark
kash@diku.dk, runethh@cs.aau.dk, mbpedersen@gmail.com,
jans@cs.aau.dk

Abstract. It is often argued that usability problems should be identified as early as possible during software development, but many usability evaluation methods do not fit well in early development activities. We propose a method for usability evaluation of use cases, a widely used representation of design ideas produced early in software development processes. The method proceeds by systematic inspection of use cases with reference to a set of guidelines for usable design. To validate the method, four evaluators inspected a set of use cases for a health care application. The usability problems predicted by the evaluators were compared to the result of a conventional think-aloud test. About one fourth of the problems were identified by both think-aloud testing and use case inspection; about half of the predicted problems not found by think-aloud testing were assessed as providing useful input to early development. Qualitative data on the evaluators' experience using the method are also presented. On this background, we argue that use case inspection has a promising potential and discuss its limitations.

Keywords: Usability evaluation, use cases, software development.

1 Introduction

Usability evaluation has established itself as an indispensable part of the development of interactive computer applications. A broad variety of methods have been proposed to support evaluators in conducting usability evaluations; Dumas [11] and Cockton et al. [7] present overviews of recent developments. Simultaneously, practice appears to change as more development organizations begins to work focused with usability [2].

Despite these developments, most usability work takes place late in the software development process. Deferring usability work in this way ignores the general observation that faults in software, including usability problems, are much cheaper to solve early in the development cycle [2,26]. Identifying usability problems early, however, is difficult with the current software development practice because usability work is usually separated from core software development activities.

C. Baranauskas et al. (Eds.): INTERACT 2007, LNCS 4662, Part I, pp. 578–591, 2007.

Use cases have been suggested as a valuable means for integrating usability engineering directly into the software development process [10,12]. Use cases are often available early in the development of an interactive system, and are relevant both to software development and user interface design. Though scenarios have many of the same characteristics as use cases, use cases are typically considered more specific and detailed than scenarios (e.g., when described as suggested by Cockburn [5]) and form part of many mainstream development methodologies. Therefore, they form a potentially suitable basis for conducting usability evaluation on an early software development product.

In this paper, we present an evaluation method called Use Case Evaluation (UCE) tailored for usability evaluation based on use cases. Our aim is to facilitate identification of usability problems at the point in the development process where the first key use cases are described. This will also help integrating usability engineering into the development cycle. In order to evaluate the effectiveness of this method, we compare it to a baseline think-aloud test. In Section 2, we give an overview of work with early usability evaluation. Section 3 presents the UCE method. In Section 4, we describe a study designed to validate the method; Section 5 describes the results of the study. Section 6 discusses the results in a broader context and Section 7 provides the conclusion.

2 Related Work

The literature on usability evaluation discusses a variety of design products that may be evaluated early, such as prototypes [39], scenarios [14], storyboards [17], and interface specifications [24]. Among these, use cases and scenarios are two prominent approaches with several desirable characteristics. They are often available early in the development of an interactive system. They also form the cornerstone of several development methodologies, such as the Unified Software Development Process [21] or scenario-based development. In particular for use cases, several authors argue that they provide a strong connection between the fields of software development and user interface design [10,35]. Ferré et al. [12] argued that use cases offer a good starting point for integrating usability techniques into a software engineering process, with the additional benefit that they are understandable from both fields. Below we discuss in more detail the literature on use cases and scenarios.

A use case is a description of a system's behavior as it responds to requests from an actor who wants to achieve a particular goal, or, following Bittner and Spence [3], a description of a sequence of events that leads to a system doing something useful. Use cases were developed by Jacobsen [20] and are currently widely employed to capture the functional requirements of a system. They are typically expressed in ordinary language, avoiding technical jargon and description of the internal workings of a system. However, since use cases were introduced, countless variations on how to describe them have been proposed [5]. Constantine and Lockwood [10] described *essential use cases*, which are free of technology and implementation detail. An essential use case describes a complete, meaningful, and well-defined task of interest to the user. Any design decisions, especially those related to the user interface, are deferred and abstracted. *Real use cases*, as described by Larman [28], contain concrete design suggestions. Cockburn [5] has also proposed variations on how a use case should be written, including variations in degree of formality of the description, the role of illustrations, and the status of non-functional requirements.

A related stream of research focuses on scenarios. Scenarios originate from strategic management methodology and have since spread to human-computer interaction and software engineering [23]. Scenarios offer an early and systematic approach to describe users' work. Part of Carroll's [4] definition of scenarios state that it is a: "... description sufficiently detailed so that design implications can be inferred and reasoned about". Hertzum [15] has portrayed how scenarios have been used by software developers in real-world projects. He found that scenarios offered a meaningful sequence of events and activities to the developers in the initial phases of the analysis and design process, and that they assisted in preserving a real-world and recognizable feel when trying to understand how users work.

Few studies deal with usability evaluation based on scenarios or use cases. Scenario-based evaluation was investigated by Haynes et al. [14] in relation to CSCW, where it helped identify factors that impacted the system's chance of success. A number of authors propose techniques to assess the quality of use cases. Tao [37] proposed an approach based on defining a behavioural model, expressed as a state machine, which focuses on the flow of interaction between the user and the system as the user is carrying out a task. He suggests usability principles that can be used as guidance for evaluating the behavioural model. Anda and Sjøberg [1] identified typical defects in use cases and present a checklist for finding such defects. In addition, they proposed an inspection technique based on the checklist. The defects are general and deal with unclear or incorrectly expressed use cases, and not with specific usability problems. Jagielska et al. [22] also worked with assessment of use cases. They saw uses cases as expressions in natural language, and based on an analysis of a number of use cases, they suggested guidelines for writing use cases that are easier to understand. Van der Poll et al. [38] employed use case maps to check formal properties of use cases, but only assessed completeness and consistency. Thus the focus is mainly on the use case itself and not on the system it describes.

3 Use Case Evaluation

Usability evaluation with the Use Case Evaluation (UCE) method consists of three overall activities, see Fig. 1: (1) Inspection of use cases, (2) Assessment of use cases, and (3) Documentation of evaluation.

The input for inspection is a collection of *use cases* describing the use of the system under development and a brief description of the use context for the system. We recommended the fully dressed form of use case description proposed by Cockburn [5]. With fully dressed use cases, evaluators receive as much information as possible with a use case. In addition, a list of *guidelines* is required to assist the inspection. The *evaluation product* is an assessment of the usability of the system expressed as a list of usability problems. It may also include an assessment of the quality of the use cases. The evaluation product is subsequently fed back into the interaction design activity [18].

3.1 Guidelines for Inspection

UCE provides a set of usability guidelines that we suggest as being particularly apt for use case inspection, see Table 1. The guidelines were originally derived from previous research. Our aim has not been to make the guidelines non-overlapping, but merely to provide rich and varied support for identifying usability problems.

UCE is based mainly on heuristics introduced as part of Heuristic Evaluation [30,31]. These heuristics were chosen because they have shown to be applicable across a wide range of contexts, and because they are among the most extensively validated inspection guidelines. Some of these heuristics do, however, concern details of the user interface design that will typically not be specified at the time use case evaluation is likely, for instance the heuristics 'Aesthetic and minimalist design' and 'Help and documentation'. Therefore, they have been excluded from our list.

We have supplemented the heuristics with guidelines from other methods that help focus on other usability concerns, or provide better examples or more detail (see Table 1). Guideline 9 is based on a principle from Cognitive Dimensions [13], somewhat similar to an Ergonomic Criteria [13] on designing for low workload. We also used Cognitive Dimensions [13] to add guideline 10 on premature commitment. Premature commitment occurs when software requires users to do an action or supply information that they are not ready to do or supply. It is related to a principle in Cognitive Walkthrough [40]. Guideline 11 was motivated by the idea that early evaluation on use cases should help establish the utility of the proposed functionality. In particular, we wanted to allow evaluators to focus on issues like task relevance and missing functionality. It has been suggested that evaluators might be less attentive to utility issues than to issues of convenience and to surface-level interface issues [33].

3.2 Inspection of Use Cases

With UCE, the main activity is to inspect the use cases for usability problems. The aim is to identify usability problems that the evaluator is convinced one or more prospective users will experience. A *usability problem* is (cf [29])

> an aspect of the system that will hinder or delay the user in completing a task, be difficult or impossible for the user understand, or cause the user to be frustrated.

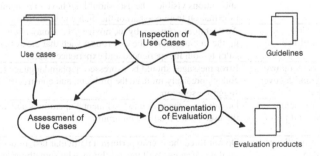

Fig. 1. Overview of Activities and Materials in Use Case Evaluation (UCE)

The inspection activity is conducted by one or more evaluators. It involves the following two steps: Brainstorm and Systematic Inspection. In the first step, Brainstorm, the evaluator goes through the use cases one by one without following any systematic procedure. The evaluator notes the usability problems that may be predicted from the use cases.

In the second step, Systematic Inspection, the evaluator employs a structured procedure for inspection of use cases. This procedure follows the one proposed in the early papers on Heuristic Evaluation [30,31]. It is supported with the guidelines presented above (see Table 1). The inspection typically lasts one to two hours. The use cases are inspected one by one. For each use case, the evaluator tries to predict the usability problems a user will experience while carrying out the use case. In doing this, the evaluator employs the guidelines. The aim is to couple the ideals of the guidelines to the use cases, trying to see similarities and cases where a guideline may be breached. As recommended for heuristic evaluation, it is fruitful to go over all use cases at least twice. The evaluator produces a list of usability problems; if more than one evaluator inspects the interface the evaluators' lists are merged into one joint list.

Table 1. Guidelines for Use Case Evaluation

No	Guideline	Explanation	Sources
1	Visibility of system status	The system should always keep users informed about what is going on, through appropriate feedback within reasonable time	[31]
2	Match between system and the real world	The system should speak the users' language, with words, phrases and concepts familiar to the user, rather than system-oriented terms. Follow real-world conventions and make information appear in a natural order.	[31]
3	User control and freedom	Users often choose system functions by mistake and will need a clearly marked "emergency exit" to leave the unwanted state without having to go through an extended dialogue. Support undo and redo.	[31]
4	Consistency and standards	Users should not have to wonder whether different words, situations, or actions mean the same thing. Follow platform conventions.	[31]
5	Error prevention	Even better than good error messages is a careful design which prevents a problem from occurring in the first place. Eliminate error-prone conditions or handle them gracefully.	[31]
6	Recognition rather than recall	Minimize the user's memory load by making objects, actions, and options visible. The user should not have to remember information from one part of the dialogue to another.	[31]
7	Flexibility and efficiency of use	Accelerators -- unseen by the novice user -- may often speed up the interaction for the expert user such that the system can cater to both inexperienced and experienced users.	[31]
8	Help users recognize, diagnose, and recover from errors	Error messages should be expressed in plain language (no codes), precisely indicate the problem, and constructively suggest a solution.	[31]
9	Avoid hard mental operations and lower workload	Do not force the user into hard mental operations and keep the user's workload at a minimum.	[13,31]
10	Avoid forcing the user to premature commitment	Do not force the user to perform a particular task or decision until it is needed. Will the user know why something must be done?	[13,40]
11	Provide functions that are of utility to the user	Consider whether the functionality described is likely to be useful to users and whether functions/data are missing.	[33]

3.3 Assessment of Use Cases

A secondary activity is to assess the quality of the use cases. In contrast to heuristic evaluation of a fully functional system, there is likely to be several cases where a use case does not give an evaluator sufficient information to decide whether or not a guideline is breached. In those cases, supplementing information may need to be provided or the evaluator may simply express why something cannot be properly analyzed. Sometimes, the use cases will not be specific enough to allow evaluation. In other cases, they will be too specific, e.g., by specifying user interaction details that can be decided later in the development process. Thus the outcome is an assessment of each use case, which emphasizes how useful the use case is for inspection. In practice, this activity is done in parallel with the primary evaluation activity.

3.4 Documentation of Evaluation

In this activity, the results are compiled into a coherent evaluation product that may be fed back into interaction design. The main content of the documentation is the list of usability problems. This list describes problems that the evaluators expect a prospective user will face when using the system. Each of these predicted usability problems should include a clear reason why it is perceived to be a problem. For example, the reason could be a reference to a guideline. As with heuristic evaluation, evaluators should describe only one problem at a time and be as specific as possible. Finally, we suggest that evaluators note ideas for improving the system or designing it differently. A supplementary evaluation product is the assessment of each use case.

4 Empirical Study

The method described above needs to be assessed with respect to its usefulness for use case evaluation. Thus we conducted an empirical study aimed at (a) comparing usability problems identified with the UCE method to a set of problems discovered with think-aloud testing and (b) understanding what problems evaluators experience in using UCE and which guidelines that are particularly useful for inspecting use cases. The rationale for (a) is to investigate if the UCE method find problems that appear in a final version of a system. The rationale for (b) is to obtain input that may be used to improve early us case inspection with the UCE method.

4.1 Evaluators

We had four evaluators use the UCE method to evaluate use cases; two of them are among the authors of this paper. We chose to use four evaluators because it conforms to the often recommended, though controversial, number of evaluators for inspection [e.g., 32], and because it seemed a realistic number of evaluators to find when bringing UCE to practical use. The evaluators were all experienced with usability work (from two to eight years of experience) and all had conducted several think-aloud tests and usability inspections. Two of the evaluators had a master degree in computer science and were working in industry, one was a PhD student working with usability evaluation, and one was associate professor in human-computer interaction.

4.2 System and Use Cases for Evaluation

The system under evaluation is a health care application (here called the HealthMonitor) that monitors elderly persons' medical conditions in their homes. For instance, it might be needed to monitor their weight, blood glucose level, or blood pressure. The HealthMonitor assists in transmitting the results through a telephone line to a central server, where they can be interpreted by medical staff. If a measurement in some way alerts the medical staff they can decide to recommend the patient to see a doctor, adjust the intake of medicine, or some other remedial action. The HealthMonitor requires connection to the telephone and interfaces with measuring devices relevant to the elderly persons' health conditions. These measuring devices might be a bathroom scale or a device for measuring blood pressure.

A set of four use cases was described for the HealthMonitor. The use cases describe situations where users of the HealthMonitor set up the hardware, use it with different measuring devices, and transfer relevant data to a central server. The use cases were written in the style of Cockburn [5] as fully dressed use cases, meaning that they were semi structured with sections on Goal in Context, Successful End Condition, Primary Actors, and a Main Success Scenario (see Fig. 2 for an example). The four use cases were an average of 472 words long and their main scenarios consisted of 6 to 19 steps. Though the use cases were not taken from the actual development activity (because no use cases had been created originally), they were validated through review by a group of master thesis students who had worked with the HealthMonitor for half a year.

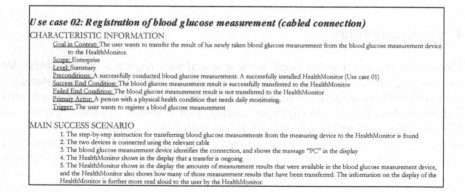

Fig. 2. Excerpt of Use Case for Connecting a Blood Glucose Device to the HealthMonitor

4.3 Procedure for Evaluation and Matching of Problems

The evaluations were conducted individually. The evaluators received descriptions of (a) the procedure to be followed, including an instruction on how to describe usability problems, (b) the UCE method, corresponding to the contents of Section 3, (c) the four use cases and an explanation of how to read them, and (d) an explanation of the HealthMonitor's general use context, target users, and basic aims.

To document the evaluation, each usability problem was to be reported by specifying its title and the place or places in the use cases that aided in predicting the problem. The evaluators also assigned a severity rating to each problem, choosing from among three ratings [29]: *cosmetic* (1), meaning that the user is delayed less than one minute or becomes slightly annoyed; *serious* (2), meaning that the problem would delay the user for several minutes or present information or options that to some extent differ from the user's expectations; and *critical* (3), meaning for instance that the user would be unable to continue or become strongly annoyed.

Previous studies [e.g., 8,19] have suggested that studying the process of evaluation may give rich information about benefits and drawbacks of inspection methods and their use. Consequently we adapted the extended reporting format proposed by Cockton et al. [9] by requiring evaluators to answer questions about the manner in which a problem was discovered, the guidelines used to predict a problem (and a comment on why a guideline was used), and if something initially considered a usability problem was excluded from the final problem report. Furthermore, we asked the evaluators to comment on difficulties in using a use case to predict a problem.

After the evaluators had completed their evaluations they met to match the problems, that is, to agree on which problems that were similar and which were unique. A total of nine hours were used on matching. After matching, each evaluator checked that the matching was correct in their view and that they agreed on how problems were treated. Below we refer to problems found by individual evaluators as *problem tokens* and matched problems as *problem types*.

4.4 Comparison to Usability Problems Found with Think-Aloud Testing

Problems predicted with UCE were compared to a set of usability problems found by think-aloud testing with the aim of discussing which problems would be useful to predict. The think-aloud test was conducted by one of the authors of this paper (who did not inspect the use cases) and five students working on a master thesis in human-computer interaction. The system was tested in five user sessions, each lasting about one hour. The sessions were based on predefined tasks that covered the same areas as the four use cases mentioned above. The sessions were recorded on video. Two of the students and the author did an Instant Data Analysis [27] immediately following each test session. This resulted in one list of usability problems. The other three students conducted a conventional video analysis with transcripts and log files to generate another list of usability problems. These two methods were used for analysis to identify as rich a problem set as possible. The resulting two lists of usability problems were merged by the evaluators through negotiation. The resulting common list included 54 usability-problem types. Below we refer to these problems as think-aloud, or TA, problems.

Similarly to John and Marks [25], we further analyzed the overlap among problems types found by the two evaluation methods. The intuition is as follows (see Table 2). For a problem found with TA but not found with UCE two possibilities exist. One is that a problem could simply not be predicted from the use case, for example because the problem concerned user interface issues decided on during implementation, difficulties with manuals and support, or performance issues (we call these problems *impossible or hard to predict*). Another possibility is that the problem was predictable but missed by UCE (*predictable but missed*). A similar analysis can be made for usability problems predicted by UCE but not found with TA. For such problems we distinguish three possibilities. First, a predicted problem may represent an actual problem or a sensible concern about usability related issues (what we call a *relevant problem*). This happens for example because a possibility for error has not been removed or because of a lack of feedback. Second, a predicted problem could have become a problem, but the actual design of the HealthMonitor has avoided the problem (a *problem avoided*). This happens for instance when feedback is given in the actual interface or when an unclear action is better explained. Thus, raising the problem as a concern early in the design process would have been valuable. Third, a predicted problem may not be an actual problem or legitimate design concern (i.e., essentially of no value as feedback or *not a problem*). An example is problems that merely speculated about a potentially difficult, but highly improbable, use situation. Each problem was rated individually by the authors on the above dimensions and disagreements were settled through discussion.

5 Results

We characterize the results of the evaluation by first discussing the problems predicted by UCE, then discussing the overlap to think-aloud testing, and finally summarizing the evaluators' experiences with using the method.

5.1 Problems Predicted

Using UCE each evaluator predicted an average of 23 problem tokens ($SD = 5.6$, ranging from 18 to 31 predictions). The average severity of the problem tokens predicted were 1.75 ($SD = 0.79$). The matching of problems allowed a set of problem types predicted by UCE to be formed, comprising 61 types. This problem set shows that evaluators have relatively limited overlap with each other: the number of unique problems (i.e., problems predicted by just one evaluator) is on average 5.25 ($SD = 3.69$). Two problem types (covering 3% of all problem tokens) were identified by all evaluators, 5 types (8%) by three evaluators, and 18 (30%) by two evaluators. Another way of illustrating this is to calculate the any-two agreement, suggested by Hertzum and Jacobsen [16] as a indicator of the evaluator effect. By that measure, the average agreement among evaluators is 18.9%. While this number is within the range of evaluator agreement found by Hertzum and Jacobsen, it suggests substantial variation among evaluators.

5.2 Overlap Between UCE and TA

The matching of problem types found by UCE and think-aloud testing allows us to calculate the overlap between methods. As shown in Table 2, we find an overlap of 24%. Thirty-nine usability problems were predicted with UCE but not found by TA; 32 usability problems were found by TA but not predicted by UCE.

Table 2 also shows that about two-thirds of the problems found by TA but missed by USE could not have been predicted. These problems concern unpredictable actions

Table 2. Problems predicted with the use case inspection (UCE) in relation to those found in think-aloud tests (TA). Percentages are relative to the total number of problem types (93).

Predicted with UCE	Found with TA	Number of problem types	Problem category	Number of problem types in category
YES	YES	22 (24%)	-	-
NO	YES	32 (34%)		
			Impossible or hard to predict	20 (21%)
			Predictable but missed	12 (13%)
YES	NO	39 (42%)		
			Relevant problem	14 (15%)
			Problems avoided in UI	9 (10%)
			Not a problem	16 (17%)

by the user and issues that arise from design solutions at a more detailed level than the use cases. A special instance of non-predictable problems concerns the direct transfer of technical terms from the use cases ("detecting a phone line") to the interface.

The problem types predicted with UCE but not found with think-aloud testing were more difficult to reason about. The bottom part of Table 2 shows that similar proportions of the problems predicted by UCE but not found with TA were seen relevant (14 problems) and not-a-problem (16 problems). Among those problems found relevant, many appear not to have been found by TA because the test setting prohibited them from occurring. Conversely, the problems that seemed irrelevant often assumed quite intricate and improbable contexts of use. This type of predictions from inspection techniques has previously been noted [7]. These analyses show that overall 45 of the 61 UCE problems (74%) would be useful to know (22 problem types found by TA, 14 problem types that seen as relevant problems, 9 problem types avoided in the user interface). If we consider just problems predicted by UCE but not found with TA, 59% appear useful.

In order to learn more about the usability problems found with UCE, all problem types were analyzed with a simple grounded theory approach [36]. The result of the analysis was five overall areas where usability problems were found. The five areas are presented in the Table 3, together with the number of problems each method identified. Table 3 indicates that there is a large overlap in the types of usability problems the two methods identifies. Looking at the specific problems, however, shows that the problems found by TA concern issues directly related to the evaluation tasks and the test setup, whereas UCE also predicts problems that are unlinked to the evaluation task and setup, such as problems related to breakdowns that were not a part of the test setup.

5.3 Evaluators' Experiences and Use of Guidelines

Evaluators used between 2.5 and 5 hours on preparing, conducting and reporting the evaluation ($M = 3.65$ hours, $SD = 1.35$). Time was mainly used for performing the actual evaluation (about two hours) and reporting the problems (about one hour).

Table 3. Usability problems categories distributed by areas ($N = 93$). Note that a problem may be related to several areas, so column sums are higher than the number of problems.

Types	Total	Found with TA	Found with UCE
Dialogue	38	25	30
External factors	4	1	3
Graphical User Interface	27	15	20
Installation of equipment	38	29	19
Procedure / task flow	38	18	26

Evaluators' comments on the process of evaluating give a couple of insights. Three evaluators commented on the role of imagination during the inspection. They suggested that evaluating use cases is demanding because they require the evaluator to be creative in filling in the many details that are not described in the use cases. Further, with HealthMonitor, imagining the physical appearance of the device was difficult. One evaluator noted that "when running through the use cases the understanding of how the devices look physically becomes an exercise in subjective imagination. This imagination may be way off the intended product".

Two evaluators commented that many predicted problems might or might not turn out to be problems when the system was implemented. One of them mentioned the feeling that "one often is describing 'maybe problems'". Another evaluator mentioned that predicted problems might turn out not to be problems after all; in the description of several of the predicted problems that evaluator listed good reasons why something might *not* be a problem after all. Also, one evaluator noted that predictions may only concern the writing of a use case, not how that use case ends up being implemented.

Two evaluators noted that it was somewhat difficult to use the guidelines during inspection. One of the evaluators noted that "I don't think I would have found fewer [problems] without them [the guidelines]".

Finally, one evaluator pointed out that it was difficult to predict problems concerning the relation among use cases, because the evaluation procedure only required use cases to be considered individually, not in concert. Problems concerning consistency between use cases, for instance, would rarely be reported. From evaluators' reports it is possible to describe which guidelines are used most frequently. The most frequently used guidelines are 1, 5 and 2; these guidelines are mentioned in 30%, 18%, and 15% of the problems that describe the guideline(s) used for discovery. These numbers corroborate the findings about problem types. Though all guidelines were used, guidelines 9, 6, and 3 were each used in 2% or fewer cases.

6 Discussion

Our study shows that the UCE method for inspection of use cases made it possible to predict a large portion of the usability problems identified in a conventional think-aloud test of the system. With UCE, the evaluators were able to find 22 usability problems out of the 54 problems found with the conventional approach, and they were able to describe a broad variety of usability problems in detail. Further, many of the predicted problems not seen with the conventional evaluation approach are assessed as being useful. These results suggest that it is feasible and of use to conduct usability inspections on use cases.

The fundamental idea of UCE, to evaluate the usability based on a design product that is available early, could have additional important benefits. First, the inspection of use cases may introduce thinking about usability early and naturally in the software development process. Second, the inspection of use cases may uncover and emphasize non-functional requirements that can be added to the use cases. Third, the inspection may improve the overall quality of the use cases. These benefits, however, remain to be empirically documented.

The idea of UCE is inherited from the group of usability evaluation methods commonly referred to as inspection or walkthrough methods. An essential limitation of for these methods is the identification of false positives. This refers to the problems that are found in an inspection but not in a think-aloud test. The opposite difficulty is the usability problems that are found with a conventional usability evaluation but not with UCE. Some of these problems can never be found. When this is taken into account, there are only 12 problem types found with the conventional method that were *not* found with UCE.

The data on the use of UCE uncovered potential improvements. They include the style of writing use cases (Cockburn, 2000), the set of guidelines we have developed for the evaluators and a step with inspection across the whole collection of use cases with the purpose of discovering inconsistencies between them.

7 Conclusion

We have presented a method called Use Case Evaluation (UCE) tailored for early usability evaluation. It is generally agreed that usability problems should be identified as early as possible in software development. This is, however, difficult to achieve with conventional usability evaluation methods. The UCE method overcomes this problem by predicting usability problems from inspection of use cases. The advantage of this approach is that use cases are often available early in the development process.

To validate the UCE method, we compare it to a conventional think-aloud test. About one fourth of all problems were found by both think-aloud testing and inspection of use cases. In addition, three-quarters of the total number of predicted problems was assessed as useful input to early development. We have also collected qualitative data on the evaluators' experience using the method, which indicate that use case inspection requires a lot of imagination.

This paper is based on an empirical study that is limited in a couple of respects. First of all, we did not assess impact of UCE evaluation in a real-life context, with use cases crafted by software developers as part of their activities. Second, the study was not a strict experiment, in that participants were not randomly assigned to either think-aloud testing or to the UCE method. Third and finally, the method needs validation with non-expert participants. Moreover, the study was partly conducted by the authors of this paper, who have also developed the method. Therefore, it is necessary with a follow-up study conducted by other researchers. The inspections were conducted by usability experts. It would also be interesting to explore to what extent less experienced evaluators could carry out the inspection. Despite these

590 K. Hornbæk et al.

limitations, our paper suggests that inspection of use cases may help introduce effective usability evaluation early in software development processes.

Acknowledgments. The research behind this paper was partly financed by the Danish Research Councils (grant number 2106-04-0022). We are grateful to Janne Jul Jensen and Christian Monrad Nielsen for serving as evaluators.

References

1. Anda, B., Sjøberg, D.I.: Towards an inspection technique for use case models. In: Proceedings of the 14th international Conference on Software Engineering and Knowledge Engineering, pp. 127–134 (2002)
2. Anderson, J., Fleek, F., Garrity, K., Drake, F.: Integrating Usability Techniques into Software Development. IEEE Software 18(1), 46–53 (2001)
3. Bittner, K., Spence, I.: Use case modeling. Addison-Wesley, Reading (2002)
4. Carroll, J.: Scenario-based design - envisioning work and technology in system development. John Wiley & Sons, Chichester (1995)
5. Cockburn, A.: Writing effective use cases. Addison-Wesley, Reading (2000)
6. Cockburn, A.: Use cases, ten years later. March/April (2002)
7. Cockton, G., Lavery, D., Woolrych, A.: Inspection-based evaluations. In: Jacko, J.A., Sears, A. (eds.) The human-computer interaction handbook, pp. 1118–1138 (2003)
8. Cockton, G., Woolrych, A., Hall, L., Hindmarch, M.: Changing Analysts' Tunes. In: Proceedings of People and Computers XVII: Designing for Society, pp. 145–162 (2003)
9. Cockton, G., Woolrych, A., Hindemarch, M.: Reconditioned merchandise: extended structured report formats in usability inspection. In: Proceedings of CHI2004, pp. 1433–1436 (2004)
10. Constantine, L., Lockwood, L.: Software for Use: A Practical Guide to the Models and Methods of Usage-Centered Design. Addison-Wesley, Reading (1999)
11. Dumas, J.S.: User-based Evaluations. In: Jacko, J.A., Sears, A. (eds.) The human-computer interaction handbook, pp. 1093–1117 (2003)
12. Ferré, X., Jurisot, N., Windl, H., Constantine, L.: Usability Basics for Software Developers. IEEE Software 18(1), 22–29 (2001)
13. Green, T.R.G.: Cognitive Dimensions of Notations. In: Proceedings of People and Computers V, pp. 443-460 (1989)
14. Haynes, S.R., Purao, S., Skattebo, A.L.: Situating evaluation in scenarios of use. In: Proceedings of CSCW 2004, pp. 92–101 (2004)
15. Hertzum, M.: Making use of scenarios: a field study of conceptual design. International Journal of Human-Computer Studies 58(2), 215–239 (2003)
16. Hertzum, M., Jacobsen, N.E.: The evaluator effect: A chilling fact about usability evaluation methods. International Journal of Human-Computer Interaction 13, 421–443 (2001)
17. Holtblatt, K., Wendell, J.B., Wood, S.: Rapid contextual design. Morgan Kaufman, San Francisco (2005)
18. Hornbæk, K., Stage, J.: The Interplay Between Usability Evaluation and User Interaction Design. International Journal of Human Computer Interaction 21(2), 117–123 (2006)
19. Hornbæk, K., Frøkjær, E.: Two psychology-based usability inspection techniques studied in a diary experiment. In: Proceedings of Nordichi 2004, pp. 1–8 (2004)

20. Jacobson, I.: Object oriented development in an industrial environment. In: Proceedings of OOPSLA '87, pp. 183–191. ACM, New York (1987)
21. Jacobson, I., Booch, G., Rumbaugh, J.: The unified software development process. Addison-Weley, Boston (1999)
22. Jagielska, D., Wenick, P., Wood, M., Bennett, S.: How Natural is Natural Language? How Well do Computer Science Students Write Use Cases? In: Proceedings of OOPSLA'06, pp. 914–923 (2006)
23. Jarke, M., Bui, X.T., Carroll, J.: Scenario management: an interdisciplinary approach. Requirements Engineering 3(3&4), 155–173 (1998)
24. John, B.E., Mashyna, M.M.: Evaluating a Multimedia Authoring Tool. Journal of the American Society of Information Science 48(9), 1004–1022 (1997)
25. John, B.E., Marks, S.J.: Tracking the effectiveness of usability evaluation methods. Behaviour & Information Technology 16(4/5), 188–202 (1997)
26. Juristo, N., Windl, H., Constantine, L.: Introducing usability. IEEE Software, 20–21 (2001)
27. Kjeldskov, J., Skov, M., Stage, J.: Instant Data Analysis. In: Proceedings of the third Nordic conference on Human-computer interaction, pp. 233–240 (2004)
28. Larman, C.: Applying uml and patterns: an introduction to object-oriented analysis and design. Prentice Hall, Upper Saddle River (1998)
29. Molich, R.: brugervenligt webdesign. Nyt Teknisk Forlag (2005)
30. Molich, R., Nielsen, J.: improving a human-computer dialogue. Communications of the ACM 33(3), 338–348 (1990)
31. Nielsen, J.: Heuristic Evaluation. In: Nielsen, J., Mack, R. (eds.) usability inspection methods, pp. 25–62. John Wiley & Sons, Chichester (1994)
32. Nielsen, J., Landauer, T.: A mathematical model of the finding of usability problems. In: Proceedings of CHI 1993, pp. 206–213 (1993)
33. Nørgaard, M., Hornbæk, K.: What Do Usability Evaluators Do in Practice? An Explorative Study of Think-Aloud Testing. In: Proceedings of DIS2006 (2006)
34. Scapin, D.L., Bastien, J.M.C.: Ergonomic Criteria for Evaluating the Ergonomic Quality of Interactive Systems. Behaviour & Information Technology 16(4/5), 220–231 (1997)
35. Seffah, A., Djouab, R., Antunes, H.: Comparing and reconciling usability-centered and use case-driven requirements engineering processes. In: Proceedings of the 2nd Australasian conference on User interface, pp. 132–139 (2001)
36. Straus, A., Corbett, J.: Basics of qualitative research. Sage, Thousand Oaks (1998)
37. Tao, Y.: Developing Usable GUI Applications with Early Usability Evaluation. In: Proceedings of Proceedings: Software Engineering - 2005 (2005)
38. van der Poll, J.A., Kotzé, P., Seffah, A., Radhakrishnan, T., Alsumait, A.: Combining UCMs and Formal Methods for Representing and Checking the Validity of Scenarios as User Requirements. In: Proceedings of SAICSIT 2003, pp. 59–68 (2003)
39. Walker, M., Takayama, L., Landay, J.A.: High-fidelity or Low Fidelity, Paper or Computer? In: Proceedings of HFES 2002, pp. 661–665 (2002)
40. Wharton, C., Rieman, J., Lewis, C., Polson, P.: The cognitive walkthrough method: a practitioner's guide. In: Nielsen, J., Mack, R.L. (eds.) Usability inspection methods, pp. 105–140. John Wiley & Sons, Chichester (1994)

Evaluating Reduced-Functionality Interfaces According to Feature Findability and Awareness

Leah Findlater and Joanna McGrenere

Department of Computer Science
University of British Columbia
Vancouver, Canada
{lkf, joanna}@cs.ubc.ca

Abstract. Many software applications continue to grow in terms of the number of features they offer. Reduced-functionality interfaces have been proposed as a solution by several researchers, but evaluations have been limited in number and scope. We argue that traditional performance measures are not sufficient for these interfaces, so we introduce and distinguish feature findability and feature awareness measures. We have conducted a controlled study that demonstrates the tradeoff between these two measures: findability in a minimal layered approach was better than in the full interface alone, but subjects were more aware of advanced features if they used the full interface from the outset. A marked layered approach was also evaluated, but provided little benefit over the other interfaces. Ours is also the first experiment comparing more than one multi-layer approach to a control interface.

1 Introduction

Feature-rich user interfaces can provide necessary features for users, yet can also be overwhelming for many, especially novices. Even experts tend to use only a subset of features and can be plagued by the array of options in the menus and toolbars [13, 14]. As a solution, reduced-functionality interfaces, such as the layered interfaces approach [17], have been proposed by several researchers, either for regular use or for an initial training period. Despite these advances, evaluations been limited in number and have focused largely on the benefits of reducing functionality. Our goals are: (1) to introduce new evaluation metrics, findability and awareness, that reveal a more comprehensive understanding of the impact of reducing functionality; and (2) to apply these metrics to compare two 2-layer interfaces to a control interface.

Several methods for reducing functionality have appeared in the research literature and in commercial applications. The layered interfaces approach, for example, gradually introduces new functionality to the user by starting with a simple interface containing a core set of features, and allowing the user to control his transition to increasingly feature-rich interface layers [17]. In contrast to many methods for personalizing menus and toolbars that block individual features (e.g., [10, 15]), layered interfaces offer a relatively coarse-grained approach; that is, relatively large sets of functionality are grouped in layers. Examples to date allow the user to

C. Baranauskas et al. (Eds.): INTERACT 2007, LNCS 4662, Part I, pp. 592–605, 2007.
© IFIP International Federation for Information Processing 2007

transition from between 2 to 8 layers, and evaluation has been mainly qualitative [7, 8, 16, 17]. A related approach to reducing functionality is the multiple interfaces approach, which offers users a "personal" interface in addition to the full interface of the application [15]. The user can easily switch between the two interfaces and specify the functions contained in his personal interface. Another earlier reduced-functionality approach is the training wheels interface, which blocks the use of advanced functionality for novice users but does not remove it from the interface [5]. In contrast to these, adaptive mechanisms can also be used to automatically reduce functionality; for example, Microsoft Office 2003 provides personal menus that contain only an automatically-generated subset of features when they are initially opened. Mixed-initiative mechanisms that combine both system and user control have also been proposed, most commonly through the use of adaptive suggestions to support the user's customization (e.g., [4]).

Evaluations of these reduced-functionality approaches have shown that they can make novice users faster, more accurate and more satisfied with the interface [5], and that such approaches can be preferred by a large proportion of intermediate and advanced users [15]. However, we argue that satisfaction and initial speed only reflect part of the impact of functionality reduction. When features are removed from the interface, the user's level of awareness of the full feature set is also affected. A severely feature-reduced interface may promote ease of accessing functions, but likely impedes awareness of those functions only available in the full application interface. A survey of 53 users of Microsoft Word 97 reflects this tension: while many of the users requested that their unused functions be "tucked away", many also indicated that it was important that they be continually able to discover new functions [14].

To address this problem, we distinguish two new evaluation measures: *findability* and *awareness*. Both of these can impact performance. Generally speaking, findability measures the speed with which users can find known functions, and awareness measures the degree to which users are conscious of the full set of available functions. While several previous evaluations have measured performance that maps to our findability measure (in some cases findability related to transferring from a simpler to a more complex interface) [2, 5, 6, 11], none have included a measure of awareness.

We have conducted an experiment to empirically validate the tradeoff between findability and awareness and to provide the first controlled comparison of more than one multi-layer interface. Our study compares two 2-layer interfaces, Minimal and Marked, to a control condition and shows that findability in the Minimal approach is significantly better than in the Control, but that subjects are more aware of features in the Control. The Marked approach provided little benefit over the other two.

2 Findability and Awareness Definitions

The distinction between findability and awareness allows for a more nuanced evaluation, which is particularly important for reduced-functionality designs, where the potential impact on awareness may be greater than in more traditional approaches.

- **Findability** is the speed with which the user can locate a function she knows exists. The set of findable functions includes those the user has already used, those the user has heard about from others or from documentation, those the user has

used in a previous version or reduced-functionality version (or layer) of the same application, and those the user has a strong basis for believing exist (e.g., Save is found in most document-centric applications).
- **Awareness** is the degree to which the user notices (through using an application) and can recall functions which do not fall into the findable function set above.

Findability is essentially the speed of accessing a specific set of functions. By contrast, the speed to complete a task as a whole is a more compound measure, impacted potentially by both findability and awareness. For example, the speed with which a user completes a task is related to the time it takes her to do the steps she is familiar with (using the set of findable functions) and those steps that she needs to "discover" how to complete. The time to complete the latter steps will be in part related to her prior awareness (of the set of aware functions). We propose specific techniques for measuring findability and awareness in our experiment, described later.

3 Study Motivation

Findability and awareness are likely impacted by many design factors and we focus on two of these in our study. The first is *change direction*. Most approaches to reducing functionality begin with a small feature set which increases over time. For example, layered interfaces [17], multiple interfaces [15], training wheels interfaces [5], incremental interfaces [3], and the MS Office adaptive menus all fit within this category. An approach that moves from less to more functionality should maximize the findability of those functions in the initial interface states, but the awareness of potentially useful advanced functionality is surely compromised. Moving in the opposite direction, from more to less functionality, should allow for improved initial awareness of the full functionality set of an application but initial findability suffers. Our study compares the effect of using a reduced-functionality design that moves from less to more functionality versus working in the full application interface. Since some related evaluations have used metrics that are similar to findability, we use these to inform the findability hypotheses of our study (given later in Section 4.7). In particular, related work has shown that: (1) novice users were faster with a training wheels version of an interface than the full interface [5], and (2) users who initially used the training wheels interface performed no differently on a follow-up similar task in the full interface than those who had used the full interface from the outset [6].

The second design factor incorporated into our reduced-functionality designs is *visibility of change*. When functionality is blocked in an interface, it can remain visually unchanged, be visually marked, or be completely removed from the visual interface. Removing the visual affordance associated with blocked functions (e.g., [15, 17]) should emphasize the findability of the remaining functions. On the other hand, the training wheels approach, which blocks functions but leaves them visually unchanged [5], should allow users to develop an awareness of the more advanced features available in the full interface. Visually marking, yet not fully hiding a widget, may offer a compromise between the two extremes. To understand whether this is the case, our study compares a design that visually marks blocked features to one that completely hides blocked features.

Previous subjective results are conflicting and highlight the importance of including both subjective and objective measures in our evaluation. For example, the original training wheels approach was shown to be both more efficient and preferred by novice users [5], but a more recent, less tightly-controlled study suggests that users may not see the value of a training wheels approach in a graphical user interface [2].

4 Experimental Design

This study compares two 2-layer interfaces to a control condition (a default full interface) based on findability and awareness. We chose Microsoft PowerPoint 2003 as our experimental application. Though not as complex as some applications (e.g., animation software), PowerPoint does not require specialized domain expertise, easing subject recruitment, and the menus and toolbars are highly programmable.

4.1 Interviews to Define Command Sets

To inform the design of the experimental conditions and tasks, we interviewed 10 frequent users of PowerPoint XP and 2003 from varying backgrounds (academic, business and medical). For each of the 361 selectable items (commands) found in the pull-down menus and on the 12 main toolbars, we asked users to specify their frequency of use (never, irregular or regular). From this, we defined a baseline interface, composed of menus and toolbars that were used by at least half of the 10 users. This included all the menus and the Standard, Formatting, Drawing, and Picture toolbars, a total of 260 commands; it did not include several context-based toolbars that are not visible by default. (Two duplicate commands were also removed: Slide Show appeared twice in the menus, and Font Color appeared twice in the toolbars.)

We then categorized the commands in our baseline interface according to two independent dimensions: (1) **basic** commands are used by at least 8/10 of our users, while the remaining are **advanced**; and (2) **generic** commands are common to the default layout of other MS Office or MS Windows applications (such as Save) while the remaining are considered **specific** to PowerPoint. These categorizations impacted our interface and task designs, and we often refer to the intersections of the sets, for example, generic-basic commands. The relative frequencies are shown in Table 1. We note that our data and categorization offer only an approximation of PowerPoint commands and their usage. This is sufficient for our experimental setup, but more accurate usage data and categorization adjustment would be needed for a deployable reduced interface for PowerPoint.

Table 1. Breakdown of baseline command set (from the menu bar and the Standard, Formatting, Drawing, and Picture toolbars)

	Basic	Advanced	Total
Specific	12 (5%)	123 (47%)	135 (52%)
Generic	32 (12%)	93 (36%)	125 (48%)
Total	44 (17%)	216 (83%)	260 (100%)

4.2 Conditions

We evaluated three conditions: two 2-layer conditions (Minimal and Marked), and a control condition (Control). In the layered conditions, subjects completed a simple task in the initial interface layer of the respective condition, then transitioned to a full interface layer for a second, more complex task. This simulated the predicted use of a layered interface, where users start in a reduced layer to complete easier tasks, then transition to more complex layers for advanced tasks [17]. In the Control condition, subjects completed both the simple and complex task in the full interface layer. Each of the three layers is described below and Figure 1 shows samples of their menus and toolbars. Context menus and keyboard shortcuts are disabled in all conditions to constrain the interaction and to focus on the persistent visual complexity that comes from the menus and toolbars. The MS Office adaptive menus are also turned off.

Full Interface Layer: The baseline interface, which contains 260 commands, as described above.

Minimal Interface Layer: Contains only the 44 basic commands (both general and specific). Since the Tools menu, Window menu, and Picture toolbar contained no basic commands they do not appear in this layer.

Marked Interface Layer: Extends Carroll and Carrithers' training wheels approach [5] by visually marking as well as blocking access to all advanced commands, leaving only the 44 basic commands accessible. Marking is achieved by fading a command's icon (if it has one) and adding a small 'x' (see Figure 1, *B* and *E*); if selected, a dialog box informs the user that "This item is unavailable for this task". Limitations in PowerPoint's API forced two secondary design decisions: (1) submenus with all blocked commands are completely removed, and their parent item is visually marked, which reduces the total command set to 210; and (2) only the icon is changed on blocked menu items (ideally the APIs would have allowed us to pilot test options for changing the background or text colour as well).

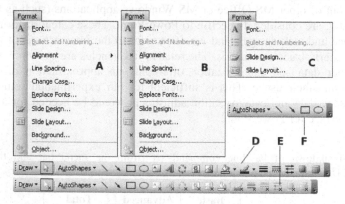

Fig. 1. Sample menus and toolbars from the three experimental conditions: *A*, *B*, and *C* show the Format menu for the full, marked and minimal layers, respectively; *D*, *E*, and *F* show the Drawing toolbar for the full, marked and minimal layers, respectively. (The marked toolbar is narrower than the full one because the drop-down arrows on some commands could not be replicated for blocked functions.)

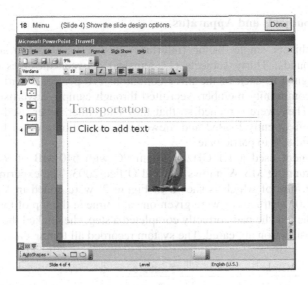

Fig. 2. Screenshot of experimental system in minimal interface layer; at the top of the screen, the current instruction specifies that a menu item is required

The Minimal and Marked conditions both reduce functionality by providing a small feature set which increases over time. Comparing Minimal to Marked also provides insight into the impact of different types of visibility of blocked functions: as discussed in Section 3, we anticipated that visually distinguishing, but not removing blocked functions could offer a compromise between findability and awareness.

4.3 Task

We designed two tasks (simple and complex), each consisting of a list of step-by-step instructions to modify a pre-existing short presentation. On each step, the user performed one interface operation: steps requiring specific-basic or specific-advanced commands were interspersed among generic-basic commands, navigation, and text entry steps to create a realistic task flow. The instruction indicated when to use a menu or toolbar, but did not specify the exact name of the command. For example, Figure 2 shows a screenshot of the experimental system with an instruction that specifies that the subject should use a menu command to show the slide design options (which maps to Slide Design command in the Format menu).

The interested reader can see the command distribution by task in Figure 3. The tasks were as follows:

- **Simple task:** This relatively short task could be completed in any of the three interface layers. It included all 12 specific-basic commands, 6 of which were repeated twice to increase task length (18 specific-basic invocations in total); 12 generic-basic commands were also included.
- **Complex task:** This longer task could only be completed in the full interface layer, and introduced advanced functionality, such as animation. It included 18 specific-advanced commands in addition to the exact same set of commands used in the simple task.

4.4 Design, Subjects and Apparatus

A between-subjects single factor (interface) design was chosen to prevent any learning confounds. Thirty subjects (17 females) between the ages of 19-55 were randomly assigned to each of the three conditions (10 per condition). Subjects were students and community members recruited through campus advertising and a local subject pool. They were screened so that they had either never used PowerPoint or had at most infrequently loaded and viewed a presentation created by others. Each subject was paid $20 to participate.

The experiment used a 1.1 GHz Pentium PC with 640 MB of RAM, 18" LCD monitor, and running MS Windows XP and Office 2003. The experimental versions of PowerPoint, one of which is shown in Figure 2, were coded in Visual Basic for Applications 6.0. Instructions were given one at a time at the top of the screen. When the subject believed she had correctly completed a step, she clicked the "Done" button and the next instruction appeared. The system recorded all timing data.

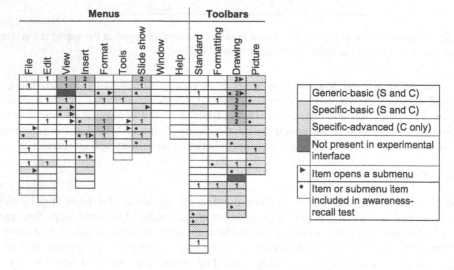

Fig. 3. Distribution of task commands in the full interface layer. Each item contains the number of times it was used in each task (S = simple, C = complex). Items that open submenus are shaded based on their submenu's most advanced item.

4.5 Procedure

The experiment fit in a two hour session. Subjects first completed a background questionnaire and were given a brief introduction to the experimental system using the initial layer of their condition (Minimal, Marked or Control). The introduction covered where the menus and toolbars were located, how to navigate to a particular slide, and, for the Marked condition, the behaviour of a marked function. Subjects then completed the simple task in their assigned interface, followed by a short questionnaire, and then a ten minute break with a distractor activity. Next, all subjects used the full interface to complete the complex task, followed by another short questionnaire. Finally, subjects were given an awareness-recall test, described below, followed by a five minute interview and discussion period to elicit additional subjective feedback.

During the tasks, subjects were told that the goal was twofold: to complete the steps in a timely manner and to familiarize themselves with the interface while doing so. They were told they could not ask for help on completing steps. If a subject had particular difficulty with a step, the system timed out after two minutes and the experimenter showed the subject how to complete the step so the task could continue. Subjects were allowed to make errors, but if an error was critical to completing subsequent steps, the experimenter corrected the situation.

4.6 Measures

Each step was measured as the time elapsed until the user clicked the "Done" button.

Findability. We differentiate 3 types of findability:
1. *Used-before findability:* Functions a user has used before in the same interface. By design, all our subjects were new to PowerPoint, which means we were not able to measure the used-before findability. (At first glance it may appear that the generic-basic steps could be used for this measure; variation in previous MS Office experience, however, would have confounded the result.)
2. *Heard-about findability*: Functions a user has heard exist (from others or documentation), but has never used. Time to complete the 18 specific-basic steps in the simple task approximates heard-about findability, because the instructions loosely simulate having heard from a colleague that such a function exists.
3. *Transfer findability:* Functions a user has used before in a previous or reduced-functionality version (or layer) of the same application. Transfer findability is measured as the time to do the 18 specific-basic steps in the complex task.

Awareness. We measured awareness using two methods:
1. *Direct awareness:* As a direct measure of awareness we administered a recall test. This was a questionnaire that listed 20 of the specific-advanced functions that were present in the full interface layer but were not used for either of the two tasks, and five distractor functions (commands that do not exist in PowerPoint, but could be believed by a novice to exist; e.g., Assign Slide Manager). Icons were also provided for those commands that had one. Half of the valid commands were menu items and half were toolbar items.

   The distribution of commands tested is shown with a '•' in Figure 3. For each item, subjects noted if they definitely remembered it. We then calculate the *corrected recognition rate*, a commonly-applied method in psychology to account for individual variation in the amount of caution a subject applies when responding to a memory test; it is simply the percentage of targets correctly remembered minus the percentage of distractors incorrectly chosen [1]. When an individual user's corrected score was negative, we assigned her a score of zero.

2. *Indirect awareness*: We used time to complete the 18 specific-advanced commands in the complex task as an indirect measure of awareness. These commands are used for the first time in the second task, which all subjects complete using the full interface layer. A difference in access time for these commands should be a result of different levels of awareness gained during the simple task.

Secondary objective measures. Our secondary objective measures included timeouts, errors, and exploration. Errors only included incorrectly completed steps not already counted in timeouts. Exploration was defined as the number of toolbar or menu items that a subject selected before selecting the target item, or in the case of incorrectly-completed steps, before clicking "Done."

Subjective measures. We report six subjective measures. After each task, all subjects ranked on a 5-point Likert scale how overwhelmed they felt by the amount of "stuff" in the menus and toolbars, and how difficult it was to navigate through them. Additionally, after completing the second task, Minimal and Marked subjects ranked on a 5-point Likert scale how easy they found it to transition from the menus and toolbars in the first task to those in the second, and whether they preferred those in the first task to those in the second. In follow-up interviews, these subjects were also asked which version they would prefer to use in the future, and whether or not they could see themselves switching between the two versions for different tasks.

4.7 Hypotheses

Our main hypotheses, based on discussion in Section 3, were as follows:

H1. *Heard-about findability:* Minimal is faster than Marked, and Marked is faster than Control.
H2. *Transfer findability:* No difference between conditions.
H3. *Direct and indirect awareness:* Control is better than Marked, and Marked is better than Minimal.

5 Results

We performed one-way ANOVAs on each dependent measure, except where noted. All pairwise comparisons were protected against Type I error using a Bonferroni adjustment. We report measures which were significant ($p < .05$) or represent a possible trend ($p < .10$). Along with statistical significance, we report partial eta-squared (η^2), a measure of effect size, which is often more informative than statistical significance in applied human-computer interaction research [12]. To interpret this value, .01 is a small effect size, .06 is medium, and .14 is large [9].

On average across all conditions, the simple task took 15.5 minutes ($SD = 6.3$) while the complex task took 26.1 minutes ($SD = 5.3$).

5.1 Findability

As expected, the conditions did impact heard-about findability significantly differently ($F(2,27) = 4.03$, $p = .029$, $\eta^2 = .230$). The means and standard deviations are shown in Figure 4(a). Pairwise comparisons showed that Minimal subjects were significantly faster on this measure than Control subjects ($p = .027$), but no other comparisons were significant.

Also as expected, no significant effect of interface was found on transfer findability ($F(2,27) = .708$, $p = .501$ $\eta^2 = .050$). The overall average to complete the specific-basic steps in the complex task was 211 seconds ($SD = 68$).

For completeness, we ran an ANOVA on the generic-basic steps in both tasks, and, not surprisingly, found no significant differences. This suggests that previous experience with MS Office dominated over interface condition.

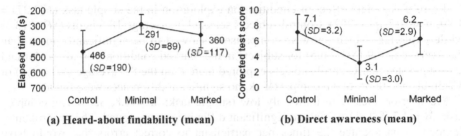

(a) Heard-about findability (mean)   (b) Direct awareness (mean)

Fig. 4. Means of findability for the simple task and direct awareness, by condition; findability is displayed using a reverse scale for time, thus higher scores are better in both graphs ($N = 30$)

5.2 Awareness

For direct awareness, there was a significant main effect of condition on corrected recognition rate ($F(2,27) = 4.81$, $p = .016$, $\eta^2 = .263$). Table 2 shows the hit rate, false alarm (distractor) rate and corrected recognition rate from the awareness-recall test. Control subjects had an average corrected recognition rate of 7.1 out of 20 items ($SD = 3.2$), which was significantly more than Minimal subjects ($p = .019$), who only remembered on average 3.1 items ($SD = 3.0$). A trend suggested that Marked subjects, scoring 6.2 ($SD = 2.9$) on average, were aware of more than Minimal subjects ($p = .090$). The trade-off between findability and direct awareness is shown graphically in Figure 4. High findability is matched with low awareness and vice versa.

Unexpectedly, no significant effect of interface condition was found on indirect awareness ($F(2,27) = .172$, $p = .843$, $\eta^2 = .013$). Across all conditions, the specific-advanced steps took on average 780 seconds ($SD = 167$).

Table 2. Average awareness scores as percentage of items answered affirmatively ($N = 30$ subjects)

	Correct targets (%)	Incorrect distractors (%)	Corrected recognition (%)
Control	.46 ($SD = .16$)	.1 ($SD = .17$)	.36 ($SD = .16$)
Minimal	.36 ($SD = .18$)	.24 ($SD = .30$)	.16 ($SD = .15$)
Marked	.43 ($SD = .19$)	.12 ($SD = .14$)	.31 ($SD = .14$)

5.3 Timeouts, Exploration, and Errors

There was a significant main effect of condition on timeouts for the simple task ($F(2,27) = 4.18$, $p = .026$, $\eta^2 = .236$). The one significant pairwise comparison was between the Minimal and Control. Minimal subjects never timed out, which was significantly less than the average 1.6 timeouts ($SD = 2.1$) for Control subjects ($p = .030$). This result suggests that our heard-about findability measures favoring Minimal are conservative, since Control subjects' scores would have been worse without timeouts than they were with timeouts. In the complex task there were more timeouts (across conditions: $M = 2.3$, $SD = 1.6$), but not surprisingly no significant effect of condition was found.

There was a main effect of condition on exploration in the simple task ($F(2,27) = 4.79$, $p = .017$, $\eta^2 = .262$). Control subjects selected on average 18.6 items ($SD = 13.3$) while exploring, which pairwise comparisons showed to be significantly more than the average of 6.9 ($SD = 6.5$) for subjects in the Marked condition ($p = .023$). A trend also suggested that Control subjects explored more than the 8.7 average ($SD = 5.4$) of Minimal ($p = .066$). In the complex task, no significant differences were found.

Mean error rates were uniformly low (simple task: $M = 1.8$, $SD = 1.6$; complex task: $M = 1.7$, $SD = 1.6$), and no significant differences were found. The experimenter stepped in on average 0.9 times per participant to correct errors that would have affected further steps ($SD = 1.3$).

5.4 Subjective Responses: Questionnaires and Interviews

Questionnaire responses showed that there was a significant main effect of condition on the degree to which subjects felt overwhelmed by how much "stuff" there was in the menus and toolbars after the first task ($F(2,27) = 4.50$, $p = .021$, $\eta^2 = .250$). Pairwise comparisons showed that Marked subjects felt more overwhelmed than Minimal subjects ($p = .020$). In terms of navigation, a trend also suggested that interface condition may have had an effect on the degree to which subjects felt it was difficult to navigate through the toolbars in the complex task ($F(2,27) = 2.54$, $p = .098$, $\eta^2 = .158$).

Using one-tailed t-tests, we evaluated the Likert-scale questions completed by only Minimal and Marked subjects. Marked subjects felt more strongly than Minimal subjects that they were easily able to transition between the menus and toolbars used in the two tasks ($t(18) = 1.89$, $p = .038$). Minimal subjects preferred their initial interface to the full interface more than Marked subjects did ($t(18) = -2.76$, $p = .007$).

During interviews, participants were asked which interface they would prefer to continue using. Minimal subjects overwhelmingly chose the minimal layer over the full layer (9 subjects, $\chi^2(1,10) = 6.4$, $p = .011$) while Marked subjects were equally strong in their preference for the full layer (9 subjects, $\chi^2(1,10) = 6.4$, $p = .011$). This replicates recent subjective findings of training wheels on a modern word processor [2]. Trends suggested that subjects who had used the minimal interface could see themselves switching between a minimal and full layer for different tasks (8 subjects, $\chi^2(1,10) = 3.6$, $p = .058$), whereas subjects who used the marked interface felt exactly the opposite about their interface (8 subjects, $\chi^2(1,10) = 3.6$, $p = .058$).

5.5 Summary

We summarize our findings in terms of our hypotheses:

H1 *Partially supported:* Minimal had significantly better heard-about findability than Control, but there were no other significant differences.
H2 *Supported:* No difference for transfer findability.
H3 *Partially supported:* In terms of direct awareness, Control was better than Minimal and a trend suggested that Marked was better than Minimal. There were no other significant differences for direct awareness, nor any for indirect awareness.

6 Discussion and Future Work

Awareness measure adds value. The comparison of the Control condition to the Minimal 2-layer condition shows that there is a measurable tradeoff between findability and awareness. Taken in isolation, the findability results replicate related work on training wheels interfaces [5], and could lead us to reach the straightforward conclusion that a minimal 2-layer interface is better than the full interface alone: it was faster in the first task and had no cost when transferring to the full interface layer for the second task. By teasing apart performance and demonstrating that improved findabilty can come at a cost of decreased awareness, we provide a richer understanding of the experience.

Two-layered minimal interface is promising. The qualitative and quantitative data together suggest that a two-layer minimal interface offers significant advantages over a default full functionality interface alone, although the findings need to be tempered by its reduced awareness. Eight out of 10 subjects indicated that they would prefer to have a minimal interface in conjunction with a full interface. Subjects had better findability in the simple task in the Minimal condition, and transfer findability in the complex task was no worse than in the Control condition. The Control condition did, however, have better direct awareness. We speculate that if users could freely switch between a minimal and full interface the impact on awareness could be smaller, but further research is required to substantiate that claim.

Two-layered marked interface is problematic. We theorized that visually marking, yet not removing, blocked functionality would offer a compromise between findability and awareness. This was not shown in our study. A trend-level result suggested the Marked condition improved direct awareness over the Minimal condition. Combining this with the means in Figure 4 suggests that the Marked condition may have a small positive effect on findability and awareness but we simply did not have sufficient power to detect this. However, the preference of 9 out of 10 subjects for the full interface over the marked one is a strong indicator that even if a 2-layer marked interface offers a small performance improvement over a full interface, it would not achieve widespread adoption. The marked interface, in its current form, is not a fruitful direction for further research. An alternative would be to try a different form of visual marking that allows users to filter out advanced items more easily, which could lessen the negative reaction. Further work would be needed to investigate this.

Measuring awareness is challenging. The two measures of awareness in our study produced inconsistent results. The direct measure, assessed by questionnaire, partially supported our hypotheses that the Minimal condition would have the least awareness, the Control the most, and the Marked condition would be in between. By contrast, the indirect measure, assessed by performance on the specific-advanced commands in the complex task, provided no support for our hypotheses. This is likely due to a lack of power for the indirect measure: the impact of awareness on the complex task could have been small relative to the overall difficulty and time needed to find specific-advanced features in the full interface. Beyond using a within-subjects design, one possibility to increase power is to use a less directed task that would encourage subjects to explore more during the simple task, thus magnifying any differences in awareness before starting the complex task. For example, leaving subjects to discover commands that will help them replicate a sample final presentation should encourage more exploration of the interface. Our challenge in achieving convergent evidence for awareness points to a need for further investigation of how it should be measured.

Need exists for a design and evaluation framework. Despite advances in research on reduced-functionality interfaces, there has never been an overall framing of the design and evaluation space. Our study focused exclusively on novice users, and explored the design factors of *change direction* and *visibility of change*. It provides a first step towards understanding how design decisions impact findability and awareness. Further work, however, is needed to identify and map out the set of major design factors that impact findability and awareness and to understand the nature of this impact. We must also strive to understand the maximum possible effect that a reduced-functionality interface can have on findability and awareness. Finally, our study protocol did not have users interacting with the mechanism to reduce features since the experimenter set the interface layer for each task. Although the goal of reduced-functionality designs is to reduce complexity, the very inclusion of a mechanism to do so adds some complexity to the interface. This impact needs to be outweighed by the beneficial effects of working within reduced functionality.

7 Conclusion

There is a strong tendency to add, rather than eliminate, features in new versions of software applications. The need for managing functionality is thus increasing, which underscores the motivation behind approaches to reducing functionality. We have introduced findability and awareness, two evaluation measures that offer a decomposition of more traditional performance measures. They allow for a more nuanced comparison of different designs. In a controlled laboratory study to evaluate layered interfaces, we have demonstrated a measurable tradeoff between findability and awareness: findability in a minimal layered interface approach is better than in the full interface alone, but subjects were more aware of advanced features if they used the full interface from the outset. Previous research on reduced-functionality designs had largely focused on the benefit of such approaches, including improved initial performance and reduced visual complexity. Our work reveals a more comprehensive understanding of the impact of reducing functionality.

Acknowledgements. We thank IBM Centers for Advanced Studies and NSERC for funding for this work, and Rebecca Hunt Newbury for helping to conduct the experimental sessions.

References

1. Baddeley, A. (1976). *The psychology of memory*. New York: Basic Books.
2. Bannert, M.: The effects of training wheels and self-learning materials in software training. Journal of Computer Assisted Learning 16(4), 336–346 (2000)
3. Brusilovsky, P., Schwarz, E.: User as student: Towards an adaptive interface for advanced web-based applications. In: Proc. of the Sixth International Conference on User Modeling, pp. 177–188 (1997)
4. Bunt, A., Conati, C., McGrenere, J.: Supporting interface customization using a mixed-initiative approach. In: Proc. Intelligent User Interfaces, pp. 92–101 (2007)
5. Carroll, J.M., Carrithers, C.: Training wheels in a user interface. Communications of the ACM 27(8), 800–806 (1984)
6. Catrambone, R., Carroll, J.M.: Learning a word processing system with training wheels and guided exploration. In: Proc. SIGCHI/GI, pp. 169–174 (1987)
7. Christiernin, G.L., Lindahl, F., Torgersson, O.: Designing a multi-layered image viewer. In: Proc. NordiCHI '04, pp. 181–184 (2004)
8. Clark, B., Matthews, J.: Deciding layers: Adaptive composition of layers in a multi-layer user interface. In: Proc. HCI International (2005)
9. Cohen, J.: Statistical power analysis for the behavioral sciences, 2nd edn. Lawrence Erlbaum Associates, Hillsdale (1988)
10. Findlater, L., McGrenere, J.: A comparison of static, adaptive and adaptable menus. In: Proc. ACM CHI 2004, pp. 89–96. ACM Press, New York (2004)
11. Franzke, M., Rieman, J.: Natural training wheels: Learning and transfer between two versions of a computer application. In: Grechenig, T., Tscheligi, M. (eds.) VCHCI 1993. LNCS, vol. 733, pp. 317–328. Springer, Heidelberg (1993)
12. Landauer, T.: Chapter 9: Behavioral research methods in human-computer interaction. In: Helander, M.G., Landauer, T.K., Pranhu, P.V. (eds.) Handbook of Human-Computer Interaction, 2nd edn., pp. 203–227. Elsevier, Amsterdam (1997)
13. Linton, F., Joy, D., Schaefer, H.-P., Charron, A.: Owl: A recommender system for organization-wide learning. Educational Technology & Society 3(1), 62–76 (2000)
14. McGrenere, J., Moore, G.: Are we all in the same "bloat"? In: Proc. of GI 2000, pp. 187–196 (2000)
15. McGrenere, J., Baecker, R., Booth, K.: An evaluation of a multiple interface design solution for bloated software. CHI Letters 4(1), 163–170 (2002)
16. Plaisant, C., Kang, H., Shneiderman, B.: Helping users get started with visual interfaces: Multi-layered interfaces, integrated initial guidance and video demonstrations. In: Proc. HCI International 2003, vol. 4, pp. 790–794 (Universal Access in HCI) (2003)
17. Shneiderman, B.: Promoting universal usability with multi-layer interface design. In: Proc. of the 2003 Conference on Universal Usability, pp. 1–8 (2003)

Playful Probing: Making Probing More Fun

Regina Bernhaupt, Astrid Weiss, Marianna Obrist, and Manfred Tscheligi

HCI & Usability Unit, ICT&S Center, University of Salzburg
firstname.lastname@sbg.ac.at

Abstract. We present a methodological variation of cultural probing called playful probing. In playful probing games are developed according to the area investigated, to enhance participants' involvement in the studies. The games are used as additional probing material and enhance participants' involvement. Based on an experimental case study with 40 households participating in a ethnographic study on new forms of media usage in the home context we show how playful probing can successful support users' engagement during the ethnographic study. We found interesting insights, for example the amount of data provided on creative cards doubled for households using the playful probing approach compared to households not using playful probing. Thus the methodological extension seems worth the effort when used in ethnographic studies within the home context.

Keywords: Ethnography, cultural probes, playful, method, computer technology usage in households, interactive TV.

1 Introduction

Today there is a steady growth of technology usage in the context of peoples' homes. To address the need for understanding technology usage in everyday life, various methods have been used. In the field of human-computer interaction ethnographic methods are used to better understand how technology is adopted and used in the home context. In the Casablanca project, for instance, Hindus et al [14] investigated how media space concepts could be incorporated into households and family life. They used ethnographically inspired field studies and in-depth interviews to evaluate early prototypes for home communication in real world settings. Taylor & Swan [26] or Crabtree & Rodden [8], among many others, used ethnographic methods and variations focusing on domestic routines and the role of technology in home life. All these ethnographically inspired studies have in common, that they involve researchers as integral part of the field study. To limit the effects of researchers taking part in the field studies, new methods (like cultural probing) are used enabling the investigation of daily life without researchers' participation.

Cultural probes were invented to provoke inspirational responses from participants [11]. This method uses a package of materials, for example post-cards, maps, photo albums or media diaries. Participants use the material to describe their everyday experiences and to answer questions in an informal way. Cultural probing turned out to be a valuable method to gather rich in depth qualitative data about the private life

C. Baranauskas et al. (Eds.): INTERACT 2007, LNCS 4662, Part I, pp. 606–619, 2007.

of the participants to inform design of technology (like computers). Meanwhile several variations of cultural probing were developed like empathy probes [19], technology probes [17] or mobile probes [15]. Moreover, Crabtree et al. [7] adopted cultural probes for the care sector in order to better inform the design of applications for this sensitive environment, and Iversen & Nielsen [18] further developed cultural probes for the use with children.

Depending on the material used for the cultural probes method, results and return rates can vary extremely. To improve cultural probing we wanted to intensify participants' involvement in the study and enable children's participation. We wanted participants to have more fun when taking part in the study. Thus we developed a new methodological approach called playful probing.

In the following we present playful probing, a methodological variation supporting active participation by using games as integral research tool. We present the concept "playful" as an advanced way to involve users in the data collection process and demonstrate the development and usage of playful probing and show in an experimental case study how this methodological variation increased users' participation, especially the involvement of children.

2 Related Work: The Concept of "Playful" and Cultural Probes

Children Research Net (CNR) [9] defines playful as "a certain feeling or emotion, the thoughts, curiosity and inquiring mind that arise when an individual is absorbed in something. The definition of 'playful spirit' also includes sympathy for others, positive attitudes, and a concern for people and things. In other words, a playful spirit encourages children's spontaneous learning". The CRN stresses that playfulness enhances children to fully use the capabilities of mind and body, and that general a person being absorbed in play is filled with excitement and 'joie de vivre' enabling mind and body to work intensively.

Using games to make experiences more enjoyable was addressed in various disciplines. Especially in the area of (e-)learning the concept of play was used. For instance Egloff [10] conducted a case study on interactive CD-ROM play-sets where correlations between gender, age and knowledge regarding edutainment were investigated.

Overall, games and gaming can be seen as an adequate methodological extension to conventional methods in order to increase children's participation in research and in the design process. However, games can also help to increase participant's motivation to take part in the study. Muller et al. [22] summarized the benefits of gaming as research technique as follows: Enhanced communication, enhanced teamwork, improved articulation of the perspectives, knowledge, and requirements, and new insights leading to important new analyses and designs. Based on this advantages Muller [21] developed several games for the practice of participatory design, like CARD, a card game for visualising work activity flows, PICITVE, a paper - and – pencil game for screen design, Icon Design Game for generating new ideas for icons, and Interface Theatre for design reviews.

A growing amount of literature has emerged discussing the involvement of children in the research process of human-computer interaction. Different methods were already used to integrate children into the design process. For instance Burov [4] used observations with videotaping to discover activity patterns in children's' play and used additionally standardised questionnaires. Candy and Edmonds [5] conducted a study concerning on the computer usage to support the learning process of children with particular basic language difficulties. The dialogues between the students and the computer were recorded and discussed afterwards. Others showed patterns of children's interactions with different system tools by capturing logging data [23], or conducted observations of children's reactions to HyperCard menus and commands and tracked their navigation patterns [24]. Wyeth [27] conducted an ethnographic study on children's play experiences in a Kindergarten. The study focused on how new playful technology for young children needs to be designed. To better address children's' needs Read [25] developed special questionnaire instruments called "funometer" and "smileometer" measuring the satisfaction rate of children.

To add a 'playful' component in a methodological approach seems to be a reasonable step to enhance participation and to increase involvement of children in research studies.

Cultural probing is a method developed in the tradition of artists and designers rather than being based on the more typical engineering approaches. Developed by Gaver et al. [11], the cultural probes approach plays an important role in the initial phase of a user-centered design process. Cultural probes are purposefully designed to inspire, reveal and capture the forces that shape an individual and his/her life, at home, at work or on the move [13]. It is a method for understanding participant's behavior and experiences in situ. Probes are mainly used to gather insights on the users' context in order to better inform the design process in an early stage [11], [19]. Cultural probing differs from traditional field and ethnographic methods, like observation and interview, as the researcher is remote from the participants. The participant is the observer him/herself.

When conducting a study using cultural probing a so called probe packages is provided to the study participants. The probe package normally consists of diaries, cameras, post cards, sometimes maps of the explored environments, and several other means to obtain as much data as possible from the participants. Participants are free to control time and means of capture. Gaver et al. [11] reported that return rates of materials can vary significantly in different settings and populations.

Apart from the traditional cultural probe approach new methodological variations have been developed, like domestic, technology or mobile probes ([17], [7], [1], [15]). Mobile probes are mainly used to explore the mobile environment in order to explore people's activities in mobile contexts, but it is not a usability evaluation method. Technology probes involve installing a technology into a real use context, watching how it is used over a period of time, and then reflecting on this use to gather information about the users and inspire ideas for new technologies [17]. Especially in the ethnographic study of Battarbee et al. [2] it was tried to address children with cultural probes. Animal stickers were used which should be assigned to the different technologies in the children's surrounding. The presumption therefore was that children imagine electronic devices as „sort of alive" and that animal metaphors can give a deeper insight on how children experience technology. However, the study revealed that the abstraction level with the stickers was quite difficult for children. Iverson et al. [18] used digital cultural probes for addressing children's everyday live. Therefore children were asked to send audio-visual material by a mobile phone to a web-page to investigate what is interesting, funny or relevant for them. The produced content could be shared by the children as well as by the researchers.

Cultural probes can inspire design by providing a range of material reflecting important aspects of the participant's context of use and potential usability factors. In the initial setting results were used to inspire the design of new technology. Other studies used the gathered material to inform design in a more structured way, for example by developing scenarios and personas based on the findings.

3 The Method: Playful Probing

Playful probing is a new variation of the cultural probing method. It uses the standard set-up of cultural probing, taking for example post-cards or post-its as probing material to gather insights on people's habits and usage. The playful probing approach differs from the traditional approach as it uses games that are specially designed for the study. In playful probing the games are designed focusing on the research area addressed within the study. The development for the game itself depends on the study set-up. Depending on the topic to be investigated, variations of existing games can be used or even new games are developed.

Within playful probing, games are used to evoke users' insights on the areas and themes explored within the study. As a major advantage we expected that users will focus on the areas explored, while using the games and gain new insights. Based on these insights other probing material is used and answered in more detail. Additionally games could help to better involve children in the ongoing study.

Using the method of playful probing is challenging Based on the area to be investigated a game has to be designed. First, the game should include the topic of research. The developed game also has to fulfil all expected characteristics of a game [20]: fun while playing the game, clear goals and rules, defined beginning and end. To facilitate the development of the games we started with existing and frequently used games.

We developed several variations of traditional card playing games. Variation one was a card playing game called "Neunerln". We extended the normal card game by additionally printing questions on the cards. The goal of the game is to get rid of all the cards as soon as possible. Cards have four kinds of symbols (colours) and numbers on them. In the beginning one card is in the middle (visible) and the first player can lay down a card either if one card has the same symbol or the same number. The player wins, if he is the first one to have no cards left. To reduce the number of negative points in the case of loosing, the player could answer a question card on the game. We used this game in an ethnographic study in May/June 2006 investigating users' experiences with interactive TV during a local field trial. Based on our first experience with playful probing, we recognized that the more professional the cards look like, the more the participants were motivated to use the game. Moreover, it became clear that changing original rules in the game made it more difficult to play. Participants neglected to use the changed rules, as they were used to play the game with the original rules and it was difficult to remember the changed rules.

A second variation was the development of a game using small cards with verbs and adjectives on them. The goal of the game was to describe objects using verbs and adjectives on the cards. We started to use technology-oriented objects. The goal of the game was to describe the object with the verbs and adjectives on the cards. We used this game in internal trials and found out, that the number of verbs and adjectives available was too large, rules were too complicated, and production costs too high to be effectively used.

When using playful probing, the adoption of an existing game without replacing the rules of the game is important. On one hand, it is the easiest and cheapest way to develop the needed material. On the other hand, it doesn't require the participant to get used to the game, thus increases the potential of usage. These insights and lessons learned from the two trials built the basis for development of a novel playful probing design which will be described in the following chapter.

4   The Experimental Case Study

Based on former experiences with playful probing and the development of variations of several games, we conducted an ethnographic study using playful probing in September 2006. Main goal was to evaluate if playful probing improves the "traditional" methodological set-up of cultural probes. The study focussed on TV and media consumption habits and the use of remote controls. Results from that study can be found in [3].

For the material we developed a basic probe package consisting of specially designed creative cards including modelling clay, post-its, and sweets which all participating households received. We called this special collection of material creative cultural probing. Usage and development of creative cultural probing is described in [3]. The methodological impact of this kind of material is still the focus of a long-term investigation and will be described elsewhere. Additionally we developed a playful probe package for selected households consisting of a game based on two frequently used games in Austria and Germany. The development and usage of the games are described in the following.

4.1   Developing the Game

To be able to profit from the moment of playfulness we combined the card-game UNO with some additional question cards following the standard rules of the game. We chose this well known card game as basis, because it is easy to play for children, but also addresses adults. We knew from experience, that the game is easy to learn, as it follows easy rules.

Each player receives seven cards. The remaining cards are placed face down to form a drawing pile. The top card of the drawing pile is turned over and acts as discard pile. The first player has to match the card in the discard pile either by number, colour or word. If the player can not use one of his cards, he has to take one card from the drawing pile. If the drawn card fits he can play, otherwise it's the next person's turn. UNO got his name from the rule that in case a player has only one card left, he has to say UNO. Failing to do so, results in taking again two cards from the pile. The goal of the game is to get rid of all the cards as fast as possible. The first one without any cards is the winner. The other ones have to count (negative) points, based on the remaining cards in their hands (see Figure 1).

Fig. 1. The playful probing package (left) and a family playing the game developed for the study (right). All photos used with permission of the participants.

We rebuilt the cards and extended the gaming rules by using concepts from a game called "Activity". As we learned in previous studies, that changing the rules might be too difficult for people to follow, we simply added some features according to the rules. We introduced a new card showing a question mark. If the "question mark" card was used, the following player had to draw a card from an additional card pile and had to fulfil the given task. To relate the game to the research area, we used so called "activity" tasks. We included various kinds of activity tasks to address different skills and to make the game more diversified. Examples for the tasks are for instance: "Think of a technology and describe it with the words: unaffordable, open, vitamin-packed, simple, and professional. Let the others guess". "Pantomime: Imitate the Internet and let the others guess.", "Draw a combination of a remote control and a mobile phone. Let the others guess which two devices you have drawn." If the other players could not guess the right answer it was a failure and they had to take cards from the regular drawing pile as penalty. The activity tasks were inspired by a common game in Europe called "Activity". The activity tasks consisted of 48 cards which were addressed to the three research areas we wanted to investigate. Additionally all participants were asked to write down their answers on a notepad so the data could be used as probing material.

A further variation - especially created for adults - was the usage of sand glasses with 30 seconds duration instead of the "question mark" cards. Whenever the sand glass finished, the one currently laying down a card, has to answer an activity task. This variation made the game flow quicker. Participants reported increased fun, when playing this variation among adults.

The main advantage of this game is that it is reusable for different research areas by simply changing the questions or activity tasks. We currently explore other games to be used as an additional instrument for data collection considering factors like ease of use and cheap production within a reasonable time frame.

4.2 Study Set-Up

Our ethnographic study focused on how technology is used in everyday life. We focused on new forms of media usage in the home, to explore possible new concepts of interactive TV navigation and remote control development. To thoroughly explore the different aspects of technology in the households we used creative cultural probing with the above described materials for all households and playful probing for selected households. The playful probe package consisted of the developed game (see Figure 1).

To evaluate the playful cultural probes method, 40 households were recruited. 20 households being media-entertainment oriented (means above-average equipped with and interested in entertainment technology), 20 households representative for the population of Austria (concerning media usage, household size and income). We balanced the number of household members in the two groups, choosing 14 households with three or more family members and six households with couples. 20 households were equipped with a multi-functional video camera (Mustek DV5200 or Mustek DV9300), all other households used a one way disposable camera. We had requested the participants to take a photo each time there was a symbol on the creative cultural probing card or they are on the road and in contact with technology (the importance of this was made clear to participants as it was necessary to obtain more information for the extended home concept).

All households received a package with creative cards and some modeling clay. The creative cultural probing cards are designed following a special topic for each week within the ethnographic studies, like "When I am on the move". We investigated three concepts: extended home, shared experiences and new forms of interaction techniques with a special focus on remote controls. Additionally the playful probing material was distributed counter-balanced between the two household-groups, number of household members and recording device. The study lasted three weeks, with a first introductory visit and a final in-depth interview conducted by a researcher in each participating household.

5   Results

Based on in-depth interviews at the end of the study and based on the quantitative demographic data collected by a questionnaire, we evaluated how the participants used the game in particular. To *present the gathered data* and material in a reader-friendly way, we *report the main findings in two usage scenarios*. These scenarios are based on the interviews and show a summary of typical usage scenarios of playful probing as reported by the participants.

Family Maier consists of four persons, Christina (42), her husband Mario (47) and the sisters Susi (6) and Nicole (10). Mario is working full time as a teacher in a secondary school while Christina is working half time as a secretary. Mario gives private lessons in his free time to improve his wage and allow his family a small amount of luxury.

Susi and Nicole enjoy their time in primary school. Even more than their time in school they love the free afternoons, when they leave the flat of the family and meet their friends in the shared garden. When it's raining the sisters get really nervous because they can not go into the garden so Christina tries to distract them by offering them some activity like playing a game or baking a cake. Although playing games with her mother is fun it is even better when Mario joins and the family is together.

Both parents do not watch TV very often, firstly because they don't like most of the programme and secondly because they want to give an example to their children. Therefore, Mario and Christina often try to find alternative activities for the evening, when the whole family is together. Instead of watching TV they prefer talking about the day or playing games. When the children are sleeping, Christina is doing the household, while Mario is preparing the material for the lessons for next day. That is the time of the day where the radio or the TV runs in the background.

Eva (26) and Peter (32), a young couple, are not married so far, but they life together in a small flat for two years now. Peter just finished his studies and is now working as research assistant at the university. In his spare time he loves to play on his game station or online games in the Internet. He always tries to stay informed about new technological innovations and devices, and thus he reads a lot of computer magazines. He wishes to have a better wage for buying more entertainment devices, because most of the time Eva decides that there is no money left for something new. Eva is still studying at the university. She has little leisure time because besides writing her diploma thesis she is working half time in a call centre. She is not really interested in technology and entertainment devices and wishes that Peter would spend more time in the evening with her instead sitting in front of the computer. Therefore she tries to convince Peter as often as possible to play the card game with her, as she knows that Peter really loves to put the last card on the staple in the moment the sand glass finishes. He enjoys making the game a bit more difficult for her to play, and she is happy to spend some time with him.

The usage scenarios describe the typical usage of playful probing, as reported during the final interviews from several participating households. The data (described as scenario) shows that even households without children were using the game. Reasons therefore are that the game in general is also suitable for adults and that the variation with the sand glass supports the fun experience of adults.

5.1 Influences of Playful Probing

The game stimulated families to play. One father stated: *"The game was good, as it brought all family members at one table; it mobilizes family members to play together."* (household 20, male, 42 years old)

The fact that we chose a well known game was appreciated by the participating households: *"It was funny to play, because everybody knows how to play the game, also the combination of 'Activity' and 'UNO' was nice."* (household 17, male, 25 years old)

One household did not play the card game at all, because of little leisure time, but the family father mentioned that the idea was excellent: *"I had the game, but we never played. The idea is great, [...] but we never played, it was an unfavourable time, because other things were of more interest"*(household 13, male, 40 years old).

Two more households only played a short time and later on filled in the answers on the notepad without playing. The following tables show an overview how many of the activity task cards were answered in the participating households (with the playful probing material).

Only one out of the 18 households[1], which actually played, complained about the game and stopped playing it, because the family did not like it: *„The question cards disturbed the flow of the game, we did not want to play any longer; we (our family) always played a lot [...] therefore we only played the game once, because that was not a game any longer"* (household 5, female, 46 years old).

Table 1. Answering rate of the question cards (max N=48)

Standard households with playful material (N=9):

Media-oriented households with playful material (N=9):

household 2	35
household 3	20
household 4	30
household 5	40
household 6	20
household 7	48
household 8	16
household 9	16
household 10	46

Mean 30.12 (SD 12. 73)

household 11	45
household 12	29
household 13	9
household 14	44
household 15	34
household 16	24
household 17	46
household 18	7
household 19	36

Mean 30,45 (SD 14, 73)

Table 1 Number of question cards answered by participants using playful probing showing that household interests and knowledge in the domain do not have an effect on playful probing.

5.2 Results from Cultural Probing Cards

To understand our impression from the qualitative analysis of interviews and other data, we started to investigate possible influences of the game. We do not want to analyze the material on a quantitative (statistical) level but show on a more qualitative base, how the method can help to improve the involvement of participants. We analyzed the collected material from the probe packages separately for households with and without the playful probing material. Sample 1 are households *with* the playful material (20 households, 74 participating household members), sample 2 are households *without* the playful material (again 20 households, 57 participating household members). As described before, we balanced the number of household members in the two groups, choosing 14 households with three or more family members and six households with couples for each group. We compared these samples in the amount of information given on the creative cards. As we collected all the material during the final interview we had a 100% return rate[1].

---

[1] One of the 20 households, which received the playful probing material, quit the participation of the whole study (without mentioning any reasons).

Three categories to quantitatively measure the amount of content were built on how detailed the cards were filled in: 1: under average (less then 70 % filled in), 2: average (70-80% filled in), 3: more than 80% filled in. Each of the 13 creative cards were assessed in amount, afterwards the categories were coded with -1, 0, 1.

The comparison showed that playful probing has an impact on the percentage of creative cards filled out: the summarized card values from the two household samples equalled 82 for sample 1 and 38 for sample 2. Standardised by participants results equalled a value of 1,2 for sample 1 and a value of 0,67 for sample two. For sample 1 (with the game) the value is doubled compared to sample 2 (no game).

In general it can be said that the households with the playful probing material produced about twice as much content on the creative cards compared to households without the game. We see our assumption confirmed, that the playful probing method involves the participants more into the topic, even though six of the participating households self-estimated in the final interview that the game did not influence their engagement with the topic.

5.3 Results from the Photographs

The households in the playful probing condition took 182 photos and videos for self-documentation. The households without the playful probing took 181 photos and videos. So it seems that the game neither increased, nor reduced the user motivation to take photos.

Worth to mention is the fact that all households who received a one way disposable camera took pictures, but 8 out of the 20 households who received a multi-functional video camera did not take any photos or videos. The reason therefore could be that parents are afraid that their children could damage the camera or that in general not media-entertainment oriented households are skeptical using a camera never used before. Probably it is more useful when working with children and not media-entertainment oriented households to use one way disposable cameras.

Interesting is also that according to the split design regardless of the playing condition there is no clear difference between the normal and the media-oriented households. The normal households documented more by photographing (214 photos and videos) than the media-entertainment oriented households (149 photos and videos). A reason therefore could be that the media-entertainment oriented households understand more technologies as self-evident in their every day life and consider them not worth documenting, so they only photographed "uncommon" situations.

5.4 Results from the Modelling Clay

The 40 households invented 38 devices as response to the thematic area new interaction techniques. 17 households created their innovations with modelling clay and three households even formed more than one device. Seven households from sample 1 created their invention with modelling clay and built 10 objects. On the other hand eleven households from sample 2 built thirteen figures with modelling clay. The number of inventions did not seem to be affected by using the game or not using the game.

Fig. 2. User participation and creations of ideas for interaction techniques by using modeling clay. All photos used with permission of the participants.

5.5 Results from the Post-interview

The results from post in-depth interview were clustered into answer categories and can be summarised as follows:

18 households from sample 1 played the card game and wrote their answers on the notepad. One household even played the game while they were on holidays, all other households only played at home. In general the game was judged positively by all participants except one. Seven people mentioned that the idea was funny, two described the game as pretty nice, three answered that UNO is a card game everybody knows and which is always funny to play. Two households described the question cards as funny and two other households even wished to have more question cards.

The opinion whether the game supported the examination with the topic "household and technology" differed between the 18 households: six participants answered yes, four not really and six participants also mentioned that the game showed how many useless devices they store at home (indicating that participants gathered new insights into existing habits). Only two households mentioned that no stimulation is needed to be in touch with this topic, because it is present every day.

Nevertheless, 12 households answered in the final interview that they did not develop any new ideas for devices inspired by the game. Other households mentioned that they invented the following devices because the game inspired them: a mobile phone remote control (two times invented), a remote control that can be operated from far distances even outside the house, a remote control for the fridge and a combination between a turntable and a radio.

In general the idea of the game was appreciated by the participants. They favoured the fact that they already knew the game and did not have to learn new rules. Furthermore the game supported the participants recognizing already existing habits regarding technology, so the game seems to help revealing existing domestic routines.

6   Advances and Shortcomings of Playful Probing

The main advantage of playful probing is the higher user involvement during the research process. As ethnographic studies normally last over longer periods it is important to motivate the participants to be engaged with the research topic. Playful probing presents an amusing way of self-observation, which helps participants answering the probing materials faster and more efficient. Participants even engage in the study while playing the game. Using the game described in the case study, participants answered questions on three research areas while playing the game.

Furthermore playful probing involves children into the research project. They can prove their knowledge with the question cards and integrate their own ideas. Therefore playful probing is a way to get a deeper insight in everyday life of children and their interests in technology.

Definitely playful probing is a promising way to investigate the daily routines of families with children in the context home, above all it can reveal family habits based on the relationships of the family members. When all family members are playing together discussion and topics can arise in the family which would probably never develop without the gaming situation. For households without children it will be necessary to make the game more attractive, because adults seem to quickly loose the interest of playing if the challenge is too low.

Summarized the experimental study showed that participation of households in the playful probing sample was higher compared to households not using the playful probing approach. Playful probing has no negative effect on other probing materials, like taking photos or using the modelling clay. It is thus a useful extension of cultural probing to increase participants' motivation and children's involvement. We will further explore the concept of using games in ethnographic research. We will extend the samples to larger populations (more than the 40 participating households like in the described ethnographic study) and will use playful probing in other research areas beyond media usage in the home.

7 Conclusion and Future Work

Playful probing is a reasonable method to increase participant's engagement in a study using the cultural probing approach. Children can be more actively involved into the research using cultural probes. The experimental methodologically case-study showed that the answers provided by the participants doubled when in the playful-condition compared to participants not using (having) the game. The game does not influence the number of photos or videos taken, nor does it influence the number of material used. But it helps people to focus on the investigated area. The game helps to gain new insights in a playful way (for example when answering the question: Guess how many cell phones all the people playing the game own).

Based on the experience when designing and developing the probing material we can say that playful probing is a new and innovative way to attract participants and to motivate their active participation. It also helps to include children in the research process and is a good starting point for discussion in the post in-depth interviews in order to gain more detailed user feedback on the addressed research topics. The development of the game showed, that not all kind of games might support playful probing, but the game presented in the experimental study has proven to be functional and re-usable for other research topics by simply adjusting the question and activity cards if the method of playful probing should be used.

Playful probing proofed to be a method for gathering in-depth data of participant's opinions, attitudes, and ideas in a favourable way for the participants. Based on these findings we will develop further variations of the method based on the feedback from the participants and preliminary lessons learned.

Concerning the game we will iterate the card game to extend different sets of activity cards for different age classes. So we can gain direct insight in the world of children and adults. Second we will enhance the concept by using more than one game to address participant's preferences in game selection. By developing more variations on the game we will also develop a set of guiding principles for playful probing game design.

From the methodological perspective we will explore possible influencing factors (especially the material developed for the creative cultural probing concept) on a long term scale. Currently we are working on a meta-review of four ethnographic studies using the playful probing and creative cultural probing method.

References

1. Arnold, M.: The Connected Home: probing the effects and affects of domesticated ICTs. In: Adrian, B (ed.) Artful Integration: Interweaving media, materials and practices, Proceedings of the Eighth Biennial Participatory Design Conference, PDC'04, Vol. 2 (2004)
2. Battarbee, K., Soronen, A., Mäyrä, F.: Living in a zoo: bringing user experiences with technology to life. In: Proceedings of the NordiCHI'04, pp. 373–376. ACM Press, New York (2004)
3. Bernhaupt, R., Obrist, M., Weiss, A., Beck, E., Tscheligi, M.: Trends in the Living Room, Interactive TV a shared experience. In: Cesar, P., Chorianopoulos, K., Jensen, J.F. (eds.) EuroITV 2007. LNCS, vol. 4471, Springer, Heidelberg (2007)
4. Burov, A.N.: Development of creative abilities of students on the basis of computer technology. In: First Moscow International HCI'91 Workshop, pp. 289–296 (1991)
5. Candy, L., Edmonds, E.A.: A study of the use of a computer as an aid to English teaching. International Journal of Man-Machine Studies 16(3), 333–339 (1982)
6. Crabtree, A.: Ethnography in participatory design. In: Proceedings of Participatory Design Conference (PDC'98), pp. 93–105. CPSR, Palo Alto, CA (1998)
7. Crabtree, A., Hemmings, T., Rodden, T., Cheverst, K., Clarke, K., Dewsbury, G., Hughes, J., Rouncefield, M.: Designing with care: adapting Cultural Probes to Inform Design in Sensitive Settings. In: Proceedings of OzCHI2003: New Directions in Interaction, Information Environments, Media and Technology (2003)
8. Crabtree, A., Rodden, T.: Domestic Routines and Design for the Home. CSCW: The Journal of Collaborative Computing 13(2), 191–220 (2004)
9. CNR - online
10. Egloff, T.H.: Edutainment: A Case Study of Interactive CD-ROM Playsets. In: Computers in entertainment, ACM Press, New York (2004)
11. Gaver, B., Dunne, T., Pacenti, E.: Design: Cultural Probes. Interactions 6(1), 21–29 (1999)
12. Goldin, R., Bell, N.: Ethno-Design research: Making a space for the user in the future of media devices. Workshop Position Paper for CHI 2006, April 22-27, Montreal, Canada (2004), available at: http://soc.kuleuven.be/com/mediac/chi2006workshop/files/ethno-design_research.pdf (last visited 31-01-2007)
13. Hemming, T., Crabtree, A., Rodden, T., Clarke, T., Rouncefield, M.: Probing the Probes. In: Proceedings of the Participatory Design Conference, pp. 23–25 (2002)

14. Hindus, D., Mainwaring, S.D., Leduc, N., Hagstrom, N.L., Bayley, O.: Casablanca: Designing Social Communication Devices for the Home. In: Proceedings of the CHI'01, pp. 325–332. ACM Press, New York (2001)
15. Hulkko, S., Keinonen, T., Mattelmäki, T., Virtanen, K.: Mobile Probes. In: Proceedings of NordiCHI'04, pp. 43–51 (2004)
16. Hunka, S.: The computer-aided instruction activities of the Division of Educational Research Services at the University of Alberta. International Journal of Man-Machine Studies 5(3), 329–336 (1973)
17. Hutchinson, H., Mackay, W., Westerlund, B., Bederson, B.B., Druin, A., Plaisant, C., Beaudouin-Lafon, M., Conversy, S., Evans, H., Hansen, H., Roussel, N., Eiderbäck, B., Lindquist, S., Sundblad, Y.: Technology Probes: Inspiring Design for and with Families. In: Proceedings of the CHI'03, pp. 17–24. ACM Press, New York (2003)
18. Iversen, O.S., Nielsen, C.: Using Digital Cultural Probes in Design with Children. In: Proceedings Interaction Design & Children, pp. 154–154. ACM Press, New York (2003)
19. Jääskö, V., Mattelmäki, T.: Observing and Probing. In: Proceedings of the International Conference on Designing Pleasurable Products and Interfaces DPPI'03, pp. 126–131. ACM Press, New York (2003)
20. Juul, J.: Half-Real: Video Games between Real Rules and Fictional Worlds. MIT Press, Cambridge (2006)
21. Muller, M.J.: Participatory design issue. CPSR Newsletter 12(3) (1994), http://www.cpsr.org/publications/newsletters/issues/1994/Summer1994
22. Muller, M.J.: Participatory design: the third space in HCI. In: Jacko, J.A., Sears, A. (eds.) The human-computer interaction handbook: fundamentals, evolving technologies and emerging applications, pp. 1051–1068. Lawrence Erlbaum Associates, Mahwah
23. Neal, A.S., Simons, R.M.: Playback: A method for evaluating the usability of software and its documentation. In: Proceedings of the CHI'83, pp. 78–82. ACM Press, New York (1983)
24. Nicol, A.: Interface design for hyperdata: Models, maps, and cues. In: Human Factors Society 32nd Annual Meeting, pp. 308–312 (1988)
25. Read, J., MacFarlane, S., Casey, C.: Endurability, Engagement and Expectations: Measuring Children's Fun. In: Proceedings of Interaction Design and Children, pp. 189–198 (2002)
26. Taylor, A.S., Swan, L.: Artful Systems in the Home. In: Proceedings of the Human Factors in Computing Systems Conference (CHI'05), pp. 641–650. ACM Press, Portland (2005)
27. Wyeth, P.: Ethnography in the kindergarten: examining children's play experiences. In: Proceedings CHI'06, pp. 1225–1228. ACM Press, New York (2006)

Do I Do What I Say?: Observed Versus Stated Privacy Preferences

Kay Connelly[1], Ashraf Khalil[1,2], and Yong Liu[1]

[1] Computer Science,
Indiana University, Bloomington, USA
Connelly,yonliu@cs.indiana.edu
[2] Abu Dhabi University
Abu Dhabi, United Arab Emirates
Khalil.ashraf@gmail.com

Abstract. This paper examines the use of surveys in measuring privacy concerns in ubiquitous computing environments. Two evaluation techniques are used to study the privacy concerns of sharing context information: a paper based survey and in-situ questionnaires. Results from the two techniques differ significantly, suggesting that surveys are not reliable in predicting privacy concerns regarding context-aware services. Further, the surveys are not consistently biased; for some information, people shared more in-situ than they predicted they would share in the survey, while for other types, they shared less.

1 Introduction

Ubiquitous computing applications, by definition, exist in the complex situation of our daily lives. Not only is an application's behavior dependent on the current context, but a person's reaction to an application often depends on the context as well. These unique characteristics introduce many challenges that make it difficult for surveys and polls to capture the full picture of a user's privacy concerns and preferences.

The use of surveys to study privacy concerns have been questioned by many researchers in the field of consumer market and ecommerce [1-4], where experimental studies have found a poor match between users' behaviors and their privacy preferences gathered by surveys. Bettman, Luce, and Payne attributed this discrepancy to decisions based on heuristics rather than rational consideration of all possible factors at play due to limited processing capacity (bounded rationality) [5]. Acquisti discussed different hypotheses beyond bounded rationality to explain the dichotomous privacy preferences and concerns between reported and actual behaviors [1].

Similar studies have yet to be performed in the field of ubiquitous computing and context-aware services; indeed, researchers have used surveys to report on privacy preferences in this domain [7]. In this paper, we examine the validity of using surveys as tools to study privacy in ubiquitous computing by measuring the differences in the level of privacy concerns reported by participants using traditional surveys and in-situ studies. If the techniques produce similar results, then researchers could rely on surveys because they are much cheaper to conduct than in-situ studies. However, a significant difference implies that surveys do not accurately capture participants' true privacy preferences, requiring the use of the in-situ approach.

C. Baranauskas et al. (Eds.): INTERACT 2007, LNCS 4662, Part I, pp. 620–623, 2007.

2 Experiment Design

The test application in our study is a context-aware service aimed at minimizing cell phone interruptions by providing a potential caller with cues about the current context of the receiver; thereby helping the caller make a more informed decision about whether or not to call [6].

People perceive different kinds of personal information with varying degrees of sensitivity or privacy comfort [7]. Patil and Lai attribute the difference in the rate of context disclosure to the level of privacy comfort associated with a particular type of context information [8]. For this study, we identified four types of contextual information that participant's could choose to share with a potential caller: their *location*, their current *activity*, if they were *talking*, and if they were in the *company* of others.

We used the rate of context disclosure between different social relations as a measure of privacy concerns, looking at 6 distinct categories of social relations between caller and receiver based on Olson et al. [9]: *significant other, family member, friend, colleague, boss* and *unknown*. A full description of the experimental design and detailed results from the in-situ study are presented in an earlier paper [10].

We measured participants' privacy concerns for this context-aware service using both a survey and in-situ questionnaires. We used a survey format previously used to examine privacy concerns in pervasive computing [11]. For different locations, participants were given a table where the rows listed common activities performed in that location and the columns contained the 6 social relations. Participants were asked to indicate which context information they would share in each cell of the table, giving us data points for unique combinations of location, activity and relationship to caller.

For the in-situ portion of the study, we gave participants a Palm PDA running iESP, a general purpose Experience Sampling Method (ESM) application [12]. Throughout the day, participants received inquiries from the PDA prompting them to choose what context they would like to disclose to a potential caller. Participants were asked to assume the role of the receivers of a cell phone call. The caller assumed one randomly chosen role out of the 6 social relations. In addition to inquiring about participants' willingness to disclose different types of context information, every questionnaire included a list of questions about the current location, activity, if they were in a conversation, number of surrounding people, and the social relationship to the surrounding people. These questions allowed us to compare the in-situ answers to the survey under the same environmental conditions. The study lasted for 10 days during which participants were prompted 13 times a day at random intervals.

We recruited 20 participants equally divided between genders. Participants were ages 18-51 (average 24), were mostly students and all had either a full-time or part-time job. All had owned cell phones for more than a year (4.4 years on average) and regularly used their cell phones (daily average: made 5 calls and received 4).

3 Experiment Results

There were 2422 completed in-situ questionnaires, and 2520 entries from the survey. Given that we had no control over the location and activity of the participants during the in-situ portion of the study, we extracted data points where the situations had the

same conditions for both the survey and in-situ questionnaires, i.e. the same participant, location, activity, and caller role. There were 422 of these.

Out of the 422 answer pairs, only 31% of the answers from the two studies were
identical. Each of the remaining answers contained at least one type of contextual
information (location, activity, talking, or company) that a participant disclosed in the
survey but did not disclose in-situ, or vice versa, given the same conditions. The maximum number of mismatched contexts was 4, which means that the participant incorrectly predicted what she or he would be willing to share for all four types of context.
A one-sample t-test on the average number of mismatched contexts shows that the
difference between the answers from survey and in-situ study is statically significant
(mean = 1.59, $t_{19} = 24.51$, p < 0.001). This means participants gave different answers
to the same questions depending on the type of evaluation technique.

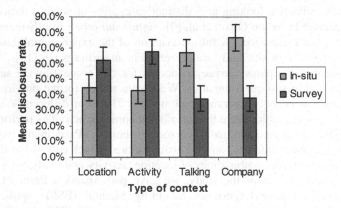

Fig. 1. Disclosure rates for four types of context using the two different evaluation techniques

Figure 1 shows the disclosure rate for each type of context information that participants revealed using both the survey and the in-situ techniques. Disclosure rate for a
particular context is the frequency at which participants released their context information relative to the total number of times they were able to release it. For each
particular type of context, we found that participants' answers to the survey questions
were significantly different from their answers in the in-situ study. Participants were
much more willing to reveal their company (M_i =76.8%, M_s =37.8%, t_{19} =5.74, p <
0.001) and talking (M_i = 67.1%, M_s =37.7%, t_{19} =4.34, p < 0.001) information in the
in-situ study than they had predicted to disclose using the survey[1]. However, they
predicted they would disclose more information in the survey than they did in the in-
situ study for activity (M_i =42.7%, M_s =67.7%, t_{19} =4.91, p < 0.001) and location (M_i
=44.6%, M_s =62.5%, t_{19} =3.05, p < 0.01). Our results suggest that, in the survey, participants tended to overestimate their privacy concerns associated with disclosing
company and talking contexts and underestimate their privacy concerns associated
with disclosing location and activity contexts.

---

[1] M_i is the mean disclosure rate in in-situ study. M_s is the mean disclosure rate in survey.

4 Conclusions

We empirically demonstrate that surveys are not able to accurately reflect participants' true privacy concerns when using context-aware services. For some contexts,
surveys overestimate user disclosure behavior, while for others, they underestimate.
The in-situ technique may not be the ideal tool for measuring privacy preferences, but
we expect it to fare better when compared to the survey tool. Our aim is to contribute
to the understanding of using surveys as tools to study privacy concerns. The discrepancy between privacy attitudes (measured by the survey technique) and privacy behavior (measured by the in-situ technique) is well-documented in the field of online
commerce and market research [1]. Our results extend such findings to the field of
context-awareness and ubiquitous computing.

Acknowledgments

This work was supported by NSF grant EIA-0202048 and a grant from the Lilly En-
dowment.

References

1. Acquisti, A., Grossklags, J.: Privacy Attitudes and Privacy Behaviour: Losses, Gains and
   Hyperbolic Discounting. The Economics of Information Security (2004)
2. Berendt, B., Günther, O., Spiekermann, S.: Privacy in E-Commerce:Stated Preferences vs.
   Actual Behavior. Communications of the ACM, 48(4) (2005)
3. Junglas, I.A., Spitzmueller, C.: A Research Model for Studying Privacy Concerns Pertaining to Location-Based Services. In: 38th Hawaii Inter. Conf. on System Sciences (2005)
4. Jensen, C., Potts, C.: Privacy Practices of Internet Users: Self-report versus Observed Behavior. International Journal of Human Computer Studies (2005)
5. Bettman, J., Luce, M.F., Payne, J.W.: Constructive Consumer Choice Processes. Journal of
   Consumer Research 25, 187–217 (1998)
6. Pedersen, E.R.: Calls.calm: Enabling Caller and Callee to Collaborate. In: CHI 2001
   (2001)
7. Goffman, E.: The Presentation of Self in Everyday Life, Garden City, NY (1959)
8. Patil, S., Lai, J.: Who Gets to Know What When: Configuring Privacy Preferences in an
   Awareness Application. In: CHI 2005 (2005)
9. Olson, J., Grudin, J., Horvitz, E.: A study of preferences for sharing and privacy. In: CHI
   05, Portland, OR, USA (2005)
10. Khalil, A., Connelly, K.: Context-aware Telephony: Privacy Preferences and Sharing Pat-
    terns. In: Computer Supported Collaborative Work (CSCW) (2006)
11. Barkhuus, L., Dey, A.: Location-Based Services for Mobile Telephony: a study of users
    privacy concerns. In: Interact 2003 (2003)
12. Consolvo, S., Walker, M.: Using the Experience Sampling Method to Evaluate Ubicomp
    Applications. Pervasive Computing Mobile and Ubiquitous Systems 2(2), 24–31 (2003)

In and Out of the Hospital: The Hidden Interface of High Fidelity Research Via RFID

Svetlena Taneva and Effie Law

Swiss Federal Institute of Technology (ETH Zürich), Zurich, Switzerland
{tanevas, lawl}@ethz.ch

Abstract. The use of RFID technology in HCI research is emerging. We identify its promising application in the healthcare sector by empowering the process of capturing, extracting and analyzing data, which help understand task patterns underlying human errors and other intriguing phenomena. RFID and video as research tools are compared to identify their strengths and weaknesses. RFID can be cost-effective and powerful, especially when combined with the hospital information system and optionally with video analysis.

1 Introduction

A major impediment to the advancement of safety science in healthcare usability is that it is very difficult to obtain precise data for the activity under consideration. Observations are incomplete and subjective. Video captures a wealth of data, but is limited to a single point of view. Doing research on medical activity is especially challenging as there is a great number of participants and technologies involved in a medical workflow, all distributed across time and space – thus, the sources of data go beyond the boundaries of an operating room, a ward, a floor, or even a hospital building. Multiple cameras can solve the problem of incompleteness, but at the extremely high cost of having to align different tapes. The implication for safety research is a compromise between scope of analysis and completeness.

Radio Frequency Identification (RFID) is being exploited in tangible computing and ubiquitous computing. Within the healthcare sector RFID is currently utilized as an operations management tool. We argue that RFID data complements video data in a way that accelerates the process of analysis by automating and systematizing most data collection, extraction and analysis. Thus, it alleviates many of the issues described and significantly reduces the total cost of analysis. Further, RFID as a research tool is a comparable alternative to video technology in settings where no recording is allowed or where adverse reactions to its use are expected.

2 RFID as a Research Tool

RFID is a real-time wireless identification technology that communicates data by radio waves. Data is encoded on a chip, called an RFID tag. Depending on the practical application, tags can store personal information such as patient's name and blood type, and can be coupled with various sensors that provide contextual data to be stored – e.g. temperature, motion, and orientation.

C. Baranauskas et al. (Eds.): INTERACT 2007, LNCS 4662, Part I, pp. 624–627, 2007.

Tags are usually attached to or integrated in physical objects such as garments, wristbands, medical devices, and blood sample containers. A tag's unique ID number is associated with a patient, staff or object record stored in the hospital's back-end information system. Data written on the tag can be read automatically, without any user intervention, by readers located throughout a hospital. This allows the automatic tracing of patients, staff, lab samples, and assets. Identification is possible with mobile readers as well (PDAs). In many instances safety is significantly improved through real-time alerting and prevention of medical error [4], and the quality of patient care is enhanced [1]. RFID is implemented in the outpatient care services as well – patient medication intake is monitored through home smart-cabinets, and bleeding is detected and treatment remotely adjusted for home hemodialysis patients.

RFID technology is implemented in many hospitals around the world to seamlessly provide information used to improve healthcare operations. We suggest that data RFID technology provides can be used to alleviate many of the problems introduced by video data analysis – RFID data is accurate, objective, time-stamp ordered, and ubiquitous – in and out of the hospital. RFID data, in combination with video, can significantly reduce the total time-cost of healthcare video research. Additionally, RFID data is an adequate replacement of video for situations where video utilization is not possible. Unlike video, there is no setup-cost associated with RFID in hospitals where it is already implemented for operational purposes.

Data collection with RFID technology is transparent to the participants in the healthcare process and therefore prevents the practical challenges of videotaping – adverse reactions and sometimes even bans on videotaping, which hinder systematic data sampling in healthcare settings [5]. A leading obstacle to the use of video is also the loss of confidentiality [6], which is easily addressed with RFID data by hiding identity information from an analyst, where required. In addition, people and asset trajectories are easily identifiable with RFID data, as well as trajectory intersections. The frequency of RFID data acquisition is an adjustable parameter.

Data extraction is a major methodological challenge of video research [6]. Data extraction has an extremely high cost with video analysis – transcription and coding are labor intensive; movement through the tape is sequential and thus it is difficult to instantly search for particular types of events; correlating multiple tapes is cumbersome. Extraction with RFID data is reduced to defining appropriate queries over a database. Sequential and predicated data reviewing is possible, and alignment is a trivial task. The raw data together with the results of queries make rich data sets for analysis. However, database knowledge is required to define the search queries.

Data Analysis with video research provides powerful qualitative analysis material. However, the wealth of qualitative information is hard to quantify and requires subjective analysis. The challenge of video empirical data is to produce generalizable theories. RFID data, on the other hand, strips some of the richness of video data in exchange for a systematic quantification of socio-technical data. Events from the Hospital Information System (HIS), such as patient state alarms, can complement RFID data for a richer analysis. Trends and outliers can be detected through automated analysis methods (visualization tools and queries) and these initial analysis outputs can guide the ethnographic video research in a more selective manner, thereby further reducing the time-cost of analysis. The massive amount of data from a HIS could conceal certain events from an analyst, while at the same time affording the

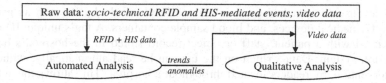

Fig. 1. The process of analysis based on RFID, other HIS data and video data, in its general form. The process is iterative (not shown). Video becomes more of a tool to help explain phenomena (trends, patterns, anomalies) identified through the automated analysis.

advantages of accelerated phenomena discovery [2]. The basic methodology we propose is shown in Fig. 1. Where video data is not available, RFID data can be used to recreate a simulation of the discrete events.

The types of data and steps of analysis that the Exploratory Sequential Data Analysis framework identifies as requirements for solid theory building [3] are mostly covered by data from a HIS with an RFID component. Such data includes all system events; and a subset of the environmental and behavioral events. HIS data is sequential and open to exploratory research. The smoothing operations that guide exploratory video analysis and encourage hypothesis generation are also applicable to RFID and other HIS data analysis (see Table 1).

Table 1. Applying the ESDA smoothing operations [3] is possible with video and RFID data

Smoothing operation	Video	RFID (and HIS)
Chunking data into coherent groups	Manual operation	one-time query definition; automated
Commenting data and chunks	Manual	Manual
Coding data	Manual operation	Automated
Connecting related data elements	Manual operation	Manual and/or automated
Compare data manipulation outcomes	Manual and/or automated	Automated
Constrain data views	Manual and/or automated	Automated
Convert data views	Manual and/or automated	Automated
Compute summary representations	Manual and/or automated	Manual and/or automated

Some questions of interest in healthcare safety science are what task patterns lead to human error; what kinds of cooperations emerge in critical situations; and how closely physicians and other staff work together. To answer such crucial questions, one can look at a variety of metrics in the RFID data. We illustrate these in Table 2. Further, one can easily adjust the grain of analysis – from one person's perspective – where all system events generated around a person are considered, to a one space perspective – where all events generated within a given physical space are considered.

The automated analysis of RFID data with appropriately defined metrics can reveal rapidly patterns and results that might otherwise be difficult to detect. It is important to look for recurrent patterns and for those situations where the patterns do not hold. Insights from RFID data analysis are powerful guides to the kinds of phenomena that we should look to explain with the more demanding task of video analysis.

Table 2. Examples of metrics that can be defined over a simple set of RFID data including information on the position and trajectories of patients, staff, and assets. Read error rates are insignificant (<10%) and therefore the data provides confident results.

Metric	Operational definition
Interaction between X and Y	The IDs for X and Y are in close proximity for a period of t-time
Participation of X in activity	Number of system events from X
Degree of cooperation of X with Y	Frequency of close proximity interactions per unit of time
Patient seen nurse	Nurse ID and patient ID in close proximity for a period of t-time
Patient care quality	Patient outcomes per illness condition compared with frequency of "patient seen nurse" and of "length of patient seen nurse" (or doctor)
Interruption	An event causes the nurse to leave the patient within 60secs of the event. The even can be: another staff comes in close proximity; the system raises an alarm; the nurse receives a page.

3 Concluding Remarks

The challenges of using video as a research tool for healthcare are high time- and labor-cost, issues of confidentiality, and negative effects on people's behavior. We proposed that in healthcare settings where RFID is implemented, using data from the HIS can relieve most of these issues. The total cost of analysis can be significantly reduced, and the data is objective, accurate, ordered, and ubiquitous. Most of the analysis can be automated to quickly reveal patterns and results. Consequently, it is possible to more selectively engage in the labor-intensive task of video analysis. However, the benefits of using RFID for analysis need to be scientifically validated.

One consideration with our proposed approach is to find an effective way to deal with the massive amounts of data from RFID and other HIS components. Before any analytical processes can begin, data acquisition intervals should be considered, and data filtering requirements appropriate to the research topic need to be established. Also, good database skills are required to define complex and correct queries. In either case, the support of technically knowledgeable individuals is necessary.

References

1. Bacheldor, B.: Memorial Health OR Unit Chooses UWB RFID. RFID J. (January 16, 2007)
2. Ritter, F.E., Larkin, J.H.: Developing Process Models as Summaries of HCI Action Sequences. Human Computer Interaction 9, 345–383 (1994)
3. Sanderson, P.M., Fisher, C.: Exploratory sequential data analysis: foundations. Human-Computer Interaction 9, 251–317 (1994)
4. Swoboda, S.M., Earsing, K., Strauss, K., Lane, S., Lipset, P.A.: Electronic monitoring and voice prompts improve hand hygiene and decrease nosocomial infections in an intermediate care unit. Crit. Care Med. 2(32), 358–363 (2004)
5. Xiao, Y.: The LOTAS Group. Understanding Coordination in a Dynamic Medical Environment: Methods and Results. In: McNeese, M., Salas, E., Endsley, M. (eds.) New Trends in Collaborative Activities. Hum. Fact. Erg. Society, pp. 242–258. California (2001)
6. Xiao, Y., Mackenzie, C.F.: Introduction to the special issue on Video-based research in high risk settings: Methodology and experience. Cogn. Tech. Work 6, 127–130 (2004)

Exploring Multiple Usability Perspectives

Tobias Uldall-Espersen

Department of computing, University of Copenhagen, Universitetsparken 1,
DK-2100 Copenhagen, Denmark
tobiasue@diku.dk

Abstract. Industrial usability work often fails to produce the expected impact on software products even though significant resources have been used on uncovering problems and suggesting improvements. So, it seems that feedback from industrial usability work lacks persuasiveness, i.e. it fails to convince the key stakeholders that actions need to be taken. This study reports from interviews with 26 stakeholders in software development projects. Our data suggests that the interviewees address usability using different perspectives and based on our observations we describe five such perspectives. Further, we discuss how applying different usability perspectives might inform the persuasiveness of usability work.

1 Introduction

One important problem when developing software is that usability work does not sufficiently inform software development even though a large number of usability issues are identified. This problem is in the literature described as lack of design-change effectiveness [4], lack of downstream utility [2], or lack of impact [1], and can partly be explained by lack of persuasive power [4] in the usability feedback. Recent studies show that a large number of usability issues are known to stakeholders prior to usability evaluations are conducted [1,3,5], and this suggests that feedback given to stakeholders are not adequate. In this paper we suggest an approach to explore and possibly increase adequacy and persuasiveness of feedback from usability work. In a resent paper [6] we argue, that usability as defined in ISO 9241-11 can be oriented towards (1) the user interface or user interests, and/or (2) the organization or other stakeholders. Here, we expand this approach by arguing that different usability perspectives are in play when developing software. Data originates from an ongoing interview study involving 26 stakeholders from six industrial software development projects in Denmark. Our observations are extracted using grounded theory (see [6]). The limited space in this paper makes it impossible to fully document our findings, but we aim at describing five frequently observed significant usability perspectives.

2 The Five Usability Perspectives

2.1 The Interaction Object Usability Perspective

Interaction object usability concerns whether users are able to successfully perform isolated interactions with user interface objects in the product. We saw how

C. Baranauskas et al. (Eds.): INTERACT 2007, LNCS 4662, Part I, pp. 628–632, 2007.

consistency was a concern using this perspective, and how standards and guidelines informed the visual design and interaction design of user interface objects. We also saw how developers were given considerable freedom regarding interaction object usability. Our data suggests that interaction object usability interplays with the applied technology (i.e. hardware, software and infrastructure), and thus that technology can inform the possibilities to produce usable software. For example we saw how a shift to wireless technology in a mobile sales support application significantly changed the usability of input fields. Online data validation was introduced reducing the amount of errors in data, but increased response time when entering data in the system. Furthermore we saw how development standards informed interaction object usability, e.g. by disallowing use of "mouse over" events on buttons, which in one case was requested by the designer.

Our data shows how interaction object usability was handled through use of a number of the traditional usability evaluation methods, such as user tests, expert evaluations, and use of guidelines or standards. Using this perspective our findings suggest that we need to take both the users and the context of use into consideration, and especially the users skills and familiarity with the technology seems important.

2.2 The Task Usability Perspective

Task usability concerns whether the users are able to complete single tasks, i.e. fulfill a (sub) goal through a combination of interactions with user interface objects. We observed how some tasks received high level of attention when implementing new software in organizations and that the level of attention dedicated to individual tasks varied considerably. Simplicity and completeness of tasks received high attentions. Simplicity means that users only need limited knowledge related to the task to complete it, and lack of simplicity was to some degree counterbalanced through user education. Completeness means that tasks should embrace and successfully complete the corresponding work process. We observed how technology informed task usability since different technologies provide different possibilities and solutions. Furthermore we observed how techniques determining task flows informed task usability and the motivation to evaluate task usability. For example we saw how a strong process oriented development approach supported developing tasks that covered the entire process, but with an ineffectively implemented design.

Evaluating task usability required knowledge about the tasks, the users, the domain, and the context of use and was often done using different variations of user testing. Also, role-plays showed to be useful when testing tasks involving interaction between humans while using the system, e.g. in sales or interview situations.

2.3 The Product Usability Perspective

Product usability concerns whether the product supports the users in reaching the coherent set of goals with efficiency, effectiveness and satisfaction. We observed how product usability was depending on whether the product provided flexibility, consistency, and completeness during usage.

Product usability seems to play a more important role in products with complex user interaction or products with an explorative nature compared with simple products. Task usability concerns having a straight way to reach a specified goal. In contrast product usability concerns interplay between different parts of the product allowing numerous roads to reach important goals. We observed how the degrees of freedom of use made it hard to predict and evaluate product usability, since it required a thorough overview of the product and its usage. Knowing the specified tasks is not sufficient and a very open approach is needed. Furthermore our data shows that field observations were neither extensively nor widely used, but occasionally used in small scale.

2.4 The Context of Use Usability Perspective

Context of use usability concerns to what extent use of the system, possibly interplaying with other systems, in the actual context of use is effective, efficient, and satisfactory. Consistency across IT-systems and/or manual systems, systems integration, and inter-human relations during use of the system were important factors that influenced context of use usability. We saw how these factors had significant influence on business performance. Further we saw how users in complex work situations worked with and combined data from various systems, also informing context of use usability.

Context of use usability was rarely addressed systematically in the cases in our study. This could be explained by the fact that context of use experts only superficially were involved in the usability work. Also, systems interplay issues need to be addressed across projects rather than within projects, which increases the complexity of usability work using this perspective. Furthermore, we saw how important context of use usability issues were known from earlier versions of systems, and how workshops with context of use experts were used to address such issues in the early phases of the projects.

2.5 The Enterprise Usability Perspective

Enterprise usability concerns to what extent goals of the enterprise are fulfilled effectively, efficiently, and satisfactorily through use of the system. This concern is not necessarily related to the users of the systems, but rather depends on whether use of the system informs or is informed by the enterprise. Enterprise usability seemed informed by three conditions: First, we saw how visions combined with IT-development projects supported stakeholders in working towards common goals rather than individual goals. Second, we saw how systems integration supported utilizing information across the enterprise and enabled support to related work processes in other departments. We also saw how failing to integrate systems could jeopardize the success of a project. Third, we saw how consistency and completeness in processes across the enterprise supported that individual completed tasks together made out a coherent environment.

In our study enterprise usability was addressed by involving key stakeholders in the initial phase, e.g. through workshops, and by maintaining their involvement throughout the process. Since enterprise usability concerns issues from all over the enterprise, it seems necessary to involve the widest range of stakeholders and filter the information afterward rather than limiting the number of involved stakeholders.

3 Discussion

In an ongoing interview study covering six software development projects, five perspectives on usability was observed. In relation to the conducted usability work in the projects, the observed perspectives had a significant practical importance. They rose from different approaches to usability among the stakeholders and revealed both conflicting and coherent interests regarding identified usability issues. Our data suggests that usability issues related to different perspective have different properties, and studying these properties will be objects for further research. We will do this by addressing the following hypotheses:

• Persuasiveness of usability issues increases if different usability perspectives point to the same solution. Persuasiveness decreases if they point to conflicting solutions.
• Different usability perspectives appeal to different stakeholders and inform business value differently.
• Different usability perspectives are relevant at different stages of the software development process.

At the time of this writing we are looking for everyday examples from industry and related research to support our observations. One example comes from the eCommerce sector where business revenue and user experience are closely tied together bringing multiple usability perspectives into play. Another example comes from development of safety critical systems where usability problems can have severe consequences for the entire enterprise. Thus, multiple perspectives on usability could help ensuring that no stakeholders suffer from lack of usability.

In the cases we have studied, the multiple perspectives of usability were not treated systematically. Even in current research and in the state-of-the-art techniques, we rarely see such perspectives addressed and the literature fails to support practitioners in working with and understanding the perspectives. Consequently, the outcome of usability work could continue to be inadequate and non-persuasive constituting a significant risk of failure when developing industrial software.

Acknowledgement

This work is part of the USE-project (Usability Evaluation & Software Design) founded by the Danish Research Agency through the NABIIT Programme Committee (Grant no. 2106-04-0022). I thank Erik Frøkjær for rewarding discussions developing the ideas to this paper.

References

1. Følstad, A.: Work-Domaine Experts As Evaluators: Usability Inspection of Domain-Specific Work-Support Systems. IJHCI 22(3), 217–245 (2007)
2. Hartson, H.R., Andre, T.S., Williges, R.C.: Criteria for Evaluation Usability Evaluation Methods. IJHCI 13, 373–410 (2001)

3. Hornbæk, K., Frøkjær, E.: Comparing Usability Problems and Redesign Proposals As Input to Practical Systems Development, pp. 391–400. ACM Press, New York (2005)
4. John, B.E., Marks, S.J.: Tracking the Effectiveness of Usability Evaluation Methods. BIT 16, 188–202 (1997)
5. Molich, R., Dumas, J.S.: Comparetive Usability Evaluation (CUE-4). BIT, 1–19 (2007)
6. Uldall-Espersen, T., Frøkjær, E.: Usability and Software Development: Roles of the Stakeholders. In: HCI International, Springer, Heidelberg (2007)

Author Index

Almeida, Rodrigo   489
Anacleto, Junia Coutinho   243
Anquetil, Magali   207
Arnautovic, Edin   136
Assarsson, Ulf   532
Atterer, Richard   74

Bailly, Gilles   475
Baranauskas, Maria Cecília Calani   361
Barbosa, Ana Maria   393
Barbosa, Clarissa Mª de A.   31
Barbosa, Clarissa Maria de A.   5
Bartneck, Christoph   511
Bederson, Benjamin B.   324
Bernhaupt, Regina   606
Bhamidipaty, Anuradha   339, 389
Biljon, Judy van   523
Blandford, Ann   239
Bouguet, A.   59
Brodersen, Christina   179
Bruder, Gerd   546
Buchanan, George   239
Bødker, Susanne   179

Calvary, Gaëlle   397
Carroll, Jennie   347
Carvalho, Aparecido Fabiano Pinatti de   243
Cesta, Amedeo   255
Chatty, Stéphane   207
Chung, Kon Shing Kenneth   19
Coldefy, F.   59
Collobert, M.   59
Connelly, Kay   620
Conversy, Stéphane   207
Cortellessa, Gabriella   255
Corvaisier, D.   59
Coutaz, Joëlle   397
Coyette, Adrien   124, 150
Cubaud, Pierre   489

Dadlani, Pavan   221
Daemen, Elke   221
Deepak, P   389
Deepak, P.   339

Demeure, Alexandre   397
Demumieux, Rachel   397
Du, Jia   221

Elías, Miguel   375
Elizabeth D. Mynatt   269
Elmqvist, Niklas   532
Endo, Yuki   493
Eng, Kynan   574
Erik-Paker, Pinar   221
España, Sergio   411

Facis, Renato   393
Falb, Jürgen   136
Favela, Jesús   235
Favre, Jean-Marie   397
Filgueiras, Lucia   393
Findlater, Leah   592
Fischer, Gerhard   193
Furtado, Elizabeth   497
Furtado, Vasco   497

Galicia, Leonardo   235
Ganneau, Vincent   397
Ghiani, Giuseppe   297
Giuliani, Vittoria   255
Go, Kentaro   493
Godoi, Muriel de Souza   243
González, Victor M.   235
Gow, Jeremy   239
Grinter, Rebecca E.   347
Gruenwald, Lucy   393
Guerin, J.   59

Hüsken, Peter   116
Hassenzahl, Marc   519
Heikkinen, Mikko   283
Henderson-Summet, Valerie   347
Hinrichs, Klaus   546
Holm, Jukka   283
Hornbæk, Kasper   578
Horvitz, Eric   120
Hossain, Liaquat   19
Høegh, Rune Thaarup   578

Igarashi, Takeo   430, 461
Imamiya, Atsumi   434
Ingold, Rolf   102
Inkpen, Kori   447

Jelinek, Helmut   136

Kaindl, Hermann   136
Kallinen, Kari   527
Karapanos, Evangelos   515
Karlson, Amy K.   324
Kellar, Melanie   447
Kellogg, Wendy   4
Khalil, Ashraf   620
Kieffer, Suzanne   150
Kim, Hyunjung   343
Kim, Seoktae   343
Klokmose, Clemens Nylandsted   179
Kohler, Kirstin   519
Korhonen, Hannu   283
Kotzé, Paula   523
Kurihara, Kazutaka   430

Lalanne, Denis   102
Law, Effie   624
Lecolinet, Eric   475
Lee, Woohun   343
Lefebvre, L.   59
Leitão, Carla Faria   5
Li, Yang   310
Li, Ying   221
Lieberman, Henry   243
Liu, Yong   620

Müller-Tomfelde, Christian   560
Mahmud, Abdullah Al   511
Mani, Senthil   165
Marsden, Gary   523
Martens, Jean-Bernard   221, 515
Matsumura, Kenji   434
McGrenere, Joanna   592
Melo, Amanda Meincke   361
Mertz, Christophe   207
Morris, Meredith Ringel   120
Mubin, Omar   511
Murshed, Shahriar Tanvir Hasan   19

Namoune, Abdallah   88
Niebuhr, Sabine   519
Nigay, Laurence   475

Nishida, Takeshi   461

Obrist, Marianna   606
Oliveira, Rodrigo de   426
Omata, Masaki   434

Pak, Jinhee   343
Pan, Yingxin   45
Panach, Ignacio   411
Pastor, Oscar   411
Paternò, Fabio   297
Pauchet, A.   59
Pecora, Federico   255
Pederiva, Inés   411
Pedersen, Michael Bach   578
Perron, L.   59
Picard, S. Louis Dit   59
Piccolo, Lara Schibelsky G.   361
Popp, Roman   136
Prates, Raquel Oliveira   31

Röck, Thomas   136
Ramachandra, Thejaswini   165
Rasconi, Riccardo   255
Ravaja, Niklas   527
Ren, Xiangshi   310
Rigamonti, Maurizio   102
Rimmer, Jon   239
Rocha, Heloísa Vieira da   426
Ropinski, Timo   546
Ruyter, Boris de   221

Sánchez, Jaime   375
Saari, Timo   527
Sales, Edson   393
Salminen, Mikko   527
Schimke, Sascha   124
Schlienger, Céline   207
Schmidt, Albrecht   74
Scopelliti, Massimiliano   255
Shneiderman, Ben   1
Sinha, Vibha   165
Sohn, Minjung   343
Sottet, Jean-Sébastien   397
Souza, Clarisse Sieckenius de   2, 5, 31
Stage, Jan   578
Starner, Thad   347
Steinicke, Frank   546
Stolze, Markus   165
Sukaviriya, Noi   165

Sutcliffe, Alistair   88

Taneva, Svetlena   624
Tiberio, Lorenza   255
Tscheligi, Manfred   606
Tsigas, Philippas   532
Tullio, Joe   269

Uldall-Espersen, Tobias   628

Vanderdonckt, Jean   124, 150, 411
Vasconcelos, Eurico   497
Vielhauer, Claus   124

Warwick, Clare   239
Weiss, Astrid   606
Wnuk, Monika   74

Yanev, Kliment   527
Yin, Jibin   310

Zhao, Chen   45
Zhao, Shengdong   310
Ziegler, Jürgen   116
Ziola, Ryder   447

Lecture Notes in Computer Science

Sublibrary 3: Information Systems and Application, incl. Internet/Web and HCI

For information about Vols. 1– 4254
please contact your bookseller or Springer

Vol. 4723: M.R. Berthold, J. Shawe-Taylor, N. Lavrač (Eds.), Advances in Intelligent Data Analysis VII. XIV, 380 pages. 2007.

Vol. 4715: J.M. Haake, S.F. Ochoa, A. Cechich (Eds.), Groupware: Design, Implementation, and Use. XIII, 355 pages. 2007.

Vol. 4663: C. Baranauskas, P. Palanque, J. Abascal, S.D.J. Barbosa (Eds.), Human-Computer Interaction – INTERACT 2007, Part II. XXXIII, 735 pages. 2007.

Vol. 4662: C. Baranauskas, P. Palanque, J. Abascal, S.D.J. Barbosa (Eds.), Human-Computer Interaction – INTERACT 2007, Part I. XXXIII, 637 pages. 2007.

Vol. 4658: T. Enokido, L. Barolli, M. Takizawa (Eds.), Network-Based Information Systems. XIII, 544 pages. 2007.

Vol. 4656: M.A. Wimmer, J. Scholl, Å. Grönlund (Eds.), Electronic Government. XIV, 450 pages. 2007.

Vol. 4655: G. Psaila, R. Wagner (Eds.), E-Commerce and Web Technologies. VII, 229 pages. 2007.

Vol. 4654: I.Y. Song, J. Eder, T.M. Nguyen (Eds.), Data Warehousing and Knowledge Discovery. XVI, 482 pages. 2007.

Vol. 4653: R. Wagner, N. Revell, G. Pernul (Eds.), Database and Expert Systems Applications. XXII, 907 pages. 2007.

Vol. 4636: G. Antoniou, U. Aßmann, C. Baroglio, S. Decker, N. Henze, P.-L. Patranjan, R. Tolksdorf (Eds.), Reasoning Web. IX, 345 pages. 2007.

Vol. 4611: J. Indulska, J. Ma, L.T. Yang, T. Ungerer, J. Cao (Eds.), Ubiquitous Intelligence and Computing. XXIII, 1257 pages. 2007.

Vol. 4607: L. Baresi, P. Fraternali, G.-J. Houben (Eds.), Web Engineering. XVI, 576 pages. 2007.

Vol. 4606: A. Pras, M. van Sinderen (Eds.), Dependable and Adaptable Networks and Services. XIV, 149 pages. 2007.

Vol. 4605: D. Papadias, D. Zhang, G. Kollios (Eds.), Advances in Spatial and Temporal Databases. X, 479 pages. 2007.

Vol. 4602: S. Barker, G.-J. Ahn (Eds.), Data and Applications Security XXI. X, 291 pages. 2007.

Vol. 4592: Z. Kedad, N. Lammari, E. Métais, F. Meziane, Y. Rezgui (Eds.), Natural Language Processing and Information Systems. XIV, 442 pages. 2007.

Vol. 4587: R. Cooper, J. Kennedy (Eds.), Data Management. XIII, 259 pages. 2007.

Vol. 4577: N. Sebe, Y. Liu, Y.-t. Zhuang, T.S. Huang (Eds.), Multimedia Content Analysis and Mining. XIII, 513 pages. 2007.

Vol. 4568: T. Ishida, S. R. Fussell, P. T. J. M. Vossen (Eds.), Intercultural Collaboration. XIII, 395 pages. 2007.

Vol. 4566: M.J. Dainoff (Ed.), Ergonomics and Health Aspects of Work with Computers. XVIII, 390 pages. 2007.

Vol. 4564: D. Schuler (Ed.), Online Communities and Social Computing. XVII, 520 pages. 2007.

Vol. 4563: R. Shumaker (Ed.), Virtual Reality. XXII, 762 pages. 2007.

Vol. 4561: V.G. Duffy (Ed.), Digital Human Modeling. XXIII, 1068 pages. 2007.

Vol. 4560: N. Aykin (Ed.), Usability and Internationalization, Part II. XVIII, 576 pages. 2007.

Vol. 4559: N. Aykin (Ed.), Usability and Internationalization, Part I. XVIII, 661 pages. 2007.

Vol. 4558: M.J. Smith, G. Salvendy (Eds.), Human Interface and the Management of Information, Part II. XXIII, 1162 pages. 2007.

Vol. 4557: M.J. Smith, G. Salvendy (Eds.), Human Interface and the Management of Information, Part I. XXII, 1030 pages. 2007.

Vol. 4541: T. Okadome, T. Yamazaki, M. Makhtari (Eds.), Pervasive Computing for Quality of Life Enhancement. IX, 248 pages. 2007.

Vol. 4537: K.C.-C. Chang, W. Wang, L. Chen, C.A. Ellis, C.-H. Hsu, A.C. Tsoi, H. Wang (Eds.), Advances in Web and Network Technologies, and Information Management. XXIII, 707 pages. 2007.

Vol. 4531: J. Indulska, K. Raymond (Eds.), Distributed Applications and Interoperable Systems. XI, 337 pages. 2007.

Vol. 4526: M. Malek, M. Reitenspieß, A. van Moorsel (Eds.), Service Availability. X, 155 pages. 2007.

Vol. 4524: M. Marchiori, J.Z. Pan, C.d.S. Marie (Eds.), Web Reasoning and Rule Systems. XI, 382 pages. 2007.

Vol. 4519: E. Franconi, M. Kifer, W. May (Eds.), The Semantic Web: Research and Applications. XVIII, 830 pages. 2007.

Vol. 4518: N. Fuhr, M. Lalmas, A. Trotman (Eds.), Comparative Evaluation of XML Information Retrieval Systems. XII, 554 pages. 2007.

Vol. 4508: M.-Y. Kao, X.-Y. Li (Eds.), Algorithmic Aspects in Information and Management. VIII, 428 pages. 2007.

Vol. 4506: D. Zeng, I. Gotham, K. Komatsu, C. Lynch, M. Thurmond, D. Madigan, B. Lober, J. Kvach, H. Chen (Eds.), Intelligence and Security Informatics: Biosurveillance. XI, 234 pages. 2007.

Vol. 4505: G. Dong, X. Lin, W. Wang, Y. Yang, J.X. Yu (Eds.), Advances in Data and Web Management. XXII, 896 pages. 2007.

Vol. 4504: J. Huang, R. Kowalczyk, Z. Maamar, D. Martin, I. Müller, S. Stoutenburg, K.P. Sycara (Eds.), Service-Oriented Computing: Agents, Semantics, and Engineering. X, 175 pages. 2007.

Vol. 4500: N.A. Streitz, A. Kameas, I. Mavrommati (Eds.), The Disappearing Computer. XVIII, 304 pages. 2007.

Vol. 4495: J. Krogstie, A. Opdahl, G. Sindre (Eds.), Advanced Information Systems Engineering. XVI, 606 pages. 2007.

Vol. 4480: A. LaMarca, M. Langheinrich, K.N. Truong (Eds.), Pervasive Computing. XIII, 369 pages. 2007.

Vol. 4471: P. Cesar, K. Chorianopoulos, J.F. Jensen (Eds.), Interactive TV: A Shared Experience. XIII, 236 pages. 2007.

Vol. 4469: K.-c. Hui, Z. Pan, R.C.-k. Chung, C.C.L. Wang, X. Jin, S. Göbel, E.C.-L. Li (Eds.), Technologies for E-Learning and Digital Entertainment. XVIII, 974 pages. 2007.

Vol. 4443: R. Kotagiri, P.R. Krishna, M. Mohania, E. Nantajeewarawat (Eds.), Advances in Databases: Concepts, Systems and Applications. XXI, 1126 pages. 2007.

Vol. 4439: W. Abramowicz (Ed.), Business Information Systems. XV, 654 pages. 2007.

Vol. 4430: C.C. Yang, D. Zeng, M. Chau, K. Chang, Q. Yang, X. Cheng, J. Wang, F.-Y. Wang, H. Chen (Eds.), Intelligence and Security Informatics. XII, 330 pages. 2007.

Vol. 4425: G. Amati, C. Carpineto, G. Romano (Eds.), Advances in Information Retrieval. XIX, 759 pages. 2007.

Vol. 4412: F. Stajano, H.J. Kim, J.-S. Chae, S.-D. Kim (Eds.), Ubiquitous Convergence Technology. XI, 302 pages. 2007.

Vol. 4402: W. Shen, J. Luo, Z. Lin, J.-P.A. Barthès, Q. Hao (Eds.), Computer Supported Cooperative Work in Design III. XV, 763 pages. 2007.

Vol. 4398: S. Marchand-Maillet, E. Bruno, A. Nürnberger, M. Detyniecki (Eds.), Adaptive Multimedia Retrieval: User, Context, and Feedback. XI, 269 pages. 2007.

Vol. 4397: C. Stephanidis, M. Pieper (Eds.), Universal Access in Ambient Intelligence Environments. XV, 467 pages. 2007.

Vol. 4380: S. Spaccapietra, P. Atzeni, F. Fages, M.-S. Hacid, M. Kifer, J. Mylopoulos, B. Pernici, P. Shvaiko, J. Trujillo, I. Zaihrayeu (Eds.), Journal on Data Semantics VIII. XV, 219 pages. 2007.

Vol. 4365: C. Bussler, M. Castellanos, U. Dayal, S. Navathe (Eds.), Business Intelligence for the Real-Time Enterprises. IX, 157 pages. 2007.

Vol. 4353: T. Schwentick, D. Suciu (Eds.), Database Theory – ICDT 2007. XI, 419 pages. 2006.

Vol. 4352: T.-J. Cham, J. Cai, C. Dorai, D. Rajan, T.-S. Chua, L.-T. Chia (Eds.), Advances in Multimedia Modeling, Part II. XVIII, 743 pages. 2006.

Vol. 4351: T.-J. Cham, J. Cai, C. Dorai, D. Rajan, T.-S. Chua, L.-T. Chia (Eds.), Advances in Multimedia Modeling, Part I. XIX, 797 pages. 2006.

Vol. 4328: D. Penkler, M. Reitenspiess, F. Tam (Eds.), Service Availability. X, 289 pages. 2006.

Vol. 4321: P. Brusilovsky, A. Kobsa, W. Nejdl (Eds.), The Adaptive Web. XII, 763 pages. 2007.

Vol. 4317: S.K. Madria, K.T. Claypool, R. Kannan, P. Uppuluri, M.M. Gore (Eds.), Distributed Computing and Internet Technology. XIX, 466 pages. 2006.

Vol. 4312: S. Sugimoto, J. Hunter, A. Rauber, A. Morishima (Eds.), Digital Libraries: Achievements, Challenges and Opportunities. XVIII, 571 pages. 2006.

Vol. 4306: Y. Avrithis, Y. Kompatsiaris, S. Staab, N.E. O'Connor (Eds.), Semantic Multimedia. XII, 241 pages. 2006.

Vol. 4302: J. Domingo-Ferrer, L. Franconi (Eds.), Privacy in Statistical Databases. XI, 383 pages. 2006.

Vol. 4299: S. Renals, S. Bengio, J.G. Fiscus (Eds.), Machine Learning for Multimodal Interaction. XII, 470 pages. 2006.

Vol. 4295: J.D. Carswell, T. Tezuka (Eds.), Web and Wireless Geographical Information Systems. XI, 269 pages. 2006.

Vol. 4286: P.G. Spirakis, M. Mavronicolas, S.C. Kontogiannis (Eds.), Internet and Network Economics. XI, 401 pages. 2006.

Vol. 4282: Z. Pan, A. Cheok, M. Haller, R.W.H. Lau, H. Saito, R. Liang (Eds.), Advances in Artificial Reality and Tele-Existence. XXIII, 1347 pages. 2006.

Vol. 4278: R. Meersman, Z. Tari, P. Herrero (Eds.), On the Move to Meaningful Internet Systems 2006: OTM 2006 Workshops, Part II. XLV, 1004 pages. 2006.

Vol. 4277: R. Meersman, Z. Tari, P. Herrero (Eds.), On the Move to Meaningful Internet Systems 2006: OTM 2006 Workshops, Part I. XLV, 1009 pages. 2006.

Vol. 4276: R. Meersman, Z. Tari (Eds.), On the Move to Meaningful Internet Systems 2006: CoopIS, DOA, GADA, and ODBASE, Part II. XXXII, 752 pages. 2006.

Vol. 4275: R. Meersman, Z. Tari (Eds.), On the Move to Meaningful Internet Systems 2006: CoopIS, DOA, GADA, and ODBASE, Part I. XXXI, 1115 pages. 2006.

Vol. 4273: I. Cruz, S. Decker, D. Allemang, C. Preist, D. Schwabe, P. Mika, M. Uschold, L. Aroyo (Eds.), The Semantic Web - ISWC 2006. XXIV, 1001 pages. 2006.

Vol. 4270: H. Zha, Z. Pan, H. Thwaites, A.C. Addison, M. Forte (Eds.), Interactive Technologies and Sociotechnical Systems. XVI, 547 pages. 2006.

Vol. 4261: Y.-t. Zhuang, S.-Q. Yang, Y. Rui, Q. He (Eds.), Advances in Multimedia Information Processing - PCM 2006. XXII, 1040 pages. 2006.

Vol. 4256: L. Feng, G. Wang, C. Zeng, R. Huang (Eds.), Web Information Systems – WISE 2006 Workshops. XIV, 320 pages. 2006.

Vol. 4255: K. Aberer, Z. Peng, E.A. Rundensteiner, Y. Zhang, X. Li (Eds.), Web Information Systems – WISE 2006. XIV, 563 pages. 2006.